0100523
237999

G000022441

THE LIBRARY
CITY COLLEGE PLYMOUTH

Sustainable Hospitality and Tourism as Motors for Development

It is now widely agreed that the climate is changing, global resources are diminishing and biodiversity is suffering. Developing countries – many of them considered by the World Tourism Organization to be 'Top Emerging Tourism Destinations' (UNWTO, 2009) – are already suffering the full frontal effect of environmental degradation. The challenge for developing countries is a triple-edged sword, how can economic prosperity be achieved without the perpetual depletion of nature's reserves, the destruction of rural habitat and the dislocation of traditional societies? Many emerging nations are looking increasingly to the tourism industry as the motor for economic development, with hospitality businesses at the forefront.

This book uses twenty-five case studies to demonstrate how it is possible to create income and stimulate regional socio-economic development by using sustainable hospitality and tourism attractions. These case studies focus on issues such as the protection of indigenous cultures as a source of touristic curiosity; the preservation of the environment and the protection of endangered species such as the plight of turtles in Sri Lanka or butterflies in Costa Rica to encourage tourism. Some cases cover government supported projects, for example, the green parks venture and regional tourism development in the Philippines, an archaeological park initiative in Honduras and the diversity of nature tourism in St. Vincent.

Sustainable Hospitality and Tourism as Motors for Development is designed to give students, academics and practitioners a guide for best practices of sustainable hospitality operations in developing countries. Based on case studies, it provides a road map of how to achieve the goals of sustainability giving benchmark examples. The book not only taps into a contemporary business subject, but aims to provide readers with a better understanding of how sustainable theories can be put into practice in hospitality and tourism industries in developing countries.

Philip Sloan Department of Hospitality Management at the International University of Applied Sciences Bad Honnef, Bonn, Germany.

Claudia Simons-Kaufman Department of Business Administration and Economics, International University of Bad Honnef, Bonn, Germany.

Willy Legrand Department of Hospitality Management at the International University of Applied Sciences Bad Honnef, Bonn, Germany.

Sustainable Hospitality and Tourism as Motors for Development

Case studies from developing regions of the world

Edited by
Philip Sloan, Claudia Simons-Kaufman
and Willy Legrand

Routledge
Taylor & Francis Group

LONDON AND NEW YORK

First published 2012
by Routledge
2 Park Square, Milton Park, Abingdon, Oxon OX14 4RN

Simultaneously published in the USA and Canada
by Routledge
711 Third Avenue, New York, NY 10017

Routledge is an imprint of the Taylor & Francis Group, an informa business

© 2012 Philip Sloan, Claudia Simons-Kaufman, Willy Legrand

The right of Philip Sloan, Claudia Simons-Kaufman, Willy Legrand to be
identified as the authors of the editorial material, and of the authors for their
individual chapters, has been asserted in accordance with sections 77 and 78
of the Copyright, Designs and Patents Act 1988.

All rights reserved. No part of this book may be reprinted or reproduced or
utilised in any form or by any electronic, mechanical, or other means, now
known or hereafter invented, including photocopying and recording, or
in any information storage or retrieval system, without permission
in writing from the publishers.

Trademark notice: Product or corporate names may be trademarks or
registered trademarks, and are used only for identification and explanation
without intent to infringe.

British Library Cataloguing in Publication Data
A catalogue record for this book is available from the British Library

Library of Congress Cataloging in Publication Data
A catalog record has been requested for this book

ISBN: 978-0-12-385196-3 (hbk)
ISBN: 978-0-12-385197-0 (ebk)

Typeset in Times New Roman
by Cenveo Publisher Services

LIBRARY AND LEARNING RESOURCES
CITY COLLEGE PLYMOUTH
CLASS NO. 338·4791 SLO
ACCESS NO. 0100523

RECEIVED

– 1 JUL 2013

MIX
Paper from
responsible sources
FSC
www.fsc.org   FSC® C004839

Printed and bound in Great Britain by the MPG Books Group

Contents

Figures and tables

Figures

Tables

Contributors

Suchandra Bardhan born and educated in India, Suchandra Bardhan is an architect with a specialization in Landscape Architecture and a doctoral degree in Engineering. Currently serving in the Department of Architecture, Jadavpur University, Kolkata, India, as a faculty member, she is also associated with several academic institutions as an external expert and resource person. With research interests in built environment and historic, urban & regional landscapes, she had been involved in academic activities for the last ten years and is currently pursuing research on buildings and the environment. Her work has been published in many national and international volumes. She also takes an active part in professional work as well as community outreach programs at the University.

Monica Borobia a Brazilian biologist with a graduate degree from Canada, Monica has worked as a marine researcher and as a programme manager for nine years in different positions and countries for the United Nations Environment Programme-UNEP. She has focused on environmental management and biodiversity conservation. Currently she is the Director of Environment for the Roteiros de Charme Hotel Association.

Gemma Cànoves is a titular professor at the Department of Geography at the Universitat Autonoma de Barcelona. She has been director of the undergraduate Geography course and the lead researcher on a number of projects, both regionally and nationally funded. She is also the coordinator for postgraduate studies at UAB's Tourism and Hotel Management School. Her main research interests are Rural Geography and Tourism, Local and Rural Development, Tourism and Environment, Tourism Planning, and Geography and Gender.

Nartsuda Chemnasiri after obtaining a BS in Agricultural Education, an MS in Agriculture and a PhD in Development communication Nartsuda is an Associate Professor in the Faculty of Agriculture and Life Sciences at Chandrakasem Rajabhat University, Bangkok, Thailand. Nartsuda is also a Quality Assurance(QA) assessor for The Commission of Higher Education, Ministry of Education and Vice president for policy and planning at Chandrakasem Rajabhat University. Research interests are in agricultural extension, agro-tourism and education, etc. Nartsud is also an ex-Vice president for policy, planning and research at Chandrakasem Rajabhat University.

Luís Garay is the director of the Labour Sciences Program at Universitat Oberta de Catalunya, where he is also a professor teaching courses on the area of Economic History and Economy of Tourism. He has also been a professor on the undergraduate Tourism course on the Tourism and Hotel Management School of the Universitat Autonoma de Barcelona. His main research interests are centred on the study of the Economic History and the socio-cultural development of the destinations and the current path from this process towards a new tourism paradigm, analyzing also the impact of information technologies and communication on the sector.

Claudia Hensel is a professor at the University of Applied Sciences in Mainz, Germany. She holds a degree in Business Administration from the University of Cologne. After her studies she worked in the role of Product Manager at an American FMCG Blue Chip Company. Within this time she spent four years in the European Headquarters in England, where she held the position of Marketing Manager as well as Market Research Executive. After returning to Germany she successfully studied on the PhD program with Prof. Dr. Günter at the Heinrich-Heine-University in Düsseldorf. Her thesis dealt with the iImpact of experience marketing on business-to-business buying becisions. At the same time she started lecturing on 'International Marketing', 'Brand Management' and 'Communication Strategy' at the University of Applied Science in Wiesbaden on various study courses. After having been a visiting professor at the University of Applied Science Darmstadt from March 2007 until June 2008 she was a professor at International University of Applied Sciences in Bad Honnef. For ten she has tutored at the Open University Milton Keynes within the Executive MBA Program Worldwide where she has been responsible for change management modules on Addis Ababa (Ethiopia), Moscow (Russia) and Bucharest (Romania). Furthermore since 2007 she has lectured at the University of Applied Science Kempten within the MBA Program, where she has also tutored in cooperation with the German-Iranian Chamber of Commerce International Marketing Courses in Teheran (Iran). She has gathered more practical experience as well as a partner in a full service marketing agency. Her research interests lie in the area of empowering underserved countries.

Corazon Catibog-Sinha is a Senior Lecturer in Tourism. She completed her BS and MS degrees from the University of the Philippines and her PhD from Oklahoma State University (USA). She has published numerous refereed articles and presented conference papers on her research in ecotourism, visitor and environmental impact studies, urban tourism, environmental monitoring, wildlife ecology, protected areas, and biodiversity conservation. She has written a book entitled 'Philippine Biodiversity: Principles and Practice' (2006, 495 pp.). Currently, she is completing another book, 'Sustainable Tourism: Concepts and

Case Studies in the Philippines - Caring for Nature, Culture, and People'. Before coming to Australia, she served as the Director of the Protected Areas and Wildlife Bureau of the Philippine Department of the Environment and Natural Resources. She was also on the Executive Committee of the Species Survival Commission of the International Union for the Conservation of Nature for ten years, serving as the focal point for the training and capacity building component (1996-2000) and the regionalization component (2000–2004). She is also a member of the World Commission for Protected Areas in Australian-New Zealand and the global Task Force of Parks and Cities.

Oliver-André Hölcke was born in Hamburg, Germany and in 2009 moved to Quito, Ecuadorto work as a journalist, photojournalist and public relations consultant for GIZ (*Deutsche Gesellschaft für Internationale Zusammenarbeit* GmbH). He has specialized in public affairs and the press, and economic development, as well as urban policies, professional photography and blogging. In 1997 he did a Master's degree in Public Affairs and Communication & Theatre Science at the Freie Universität in Berlin. He worked from 2001 to 2009 as Chief Radio Editor & Broadcast Presenter for the public radio station *Saarländischer Rundfunk* in Saarbrücken, Germany. For two years (1999–2001) he was Senior Editor for the private radio station *Landeswelle Thüringen* in Erfurt, Germany. Before that he worked from 1997 to 1999 for the private radio station *Antenne Thüringen* in Weimar, Thüringen, as editor, broadcast presenter and local correspondent.

Kurt Holle has dedicated his career to the conservation economy. A Peruvian forest engineer, he has worked as a field researcher, naturalist guide, consultant and social entrepreneur. Since co-founding Rainforest Expeditions in 1992, he has led all aspects of operations, including start-up, marketing, finance, IT & general management. Kurt is a well-respected leader in ecotourism and shares his expertise across sectors, consulting for USAid, IDB, UNDP and Conservation International projects, advising university teams including Stanford, Cornell & Harvard in the preparation of case studies on Rainforest Expeditions, and speaking at workshops for start-up small tourism entrepreneurs. In 2008, Kurt was chosen a Young Global Leader by the World Economic Forum.

Dorian Hoy was born in Cyprus and at a very early age moved to South Africa with his parents and siblings. Here he spent his early years in the Natal Midlands where he completed his schooling. Following this he went on to study at the Royal Agricultural College in the UK for three years and since then his career has mostly been in the tourism industry. He started off at the Mala Mala Game Reserve and then went across to Dubai to set up the Al Maha Desert Reserve. He then returned to South Africa after two years where he ran and guided horse safaris in the St Lucia Wetland Park. Following this Dorian spent a further four years in Abu Dhabi and Morocco working on separate wildlife projects. Dorian lives in Kasane with his wife and two young sons and has been the Regional Managing Director for the Botswana arm of Great Plains since 2008.

Ariane Janér (MSc Zoology Leiden, MBA Rotterdam) has been living in Brazil since 1988. She is building a wide experience in marketing and finance in the private sector and since 1991 has applied this to the area of ecotourism and sustainable development. She has also consulted on projects in many parts of Brazil. In 1993, she helped found EcoBrasil, the Brazilian Ecotourism Society, and has been actively involved with this NGO since 1993. She is currently (2010) on the advisory board of The International Ecotourism Society. As a consultant she looks for challenging projects that become a practical benchmark or mean for constructing a platform for change and remains involved after completing her assignment.

Thushan Kapurusinghe started his wildlife carrier in 1985 and received his academic training from the Open University of Sri Lanka and the Duke University Marine Laboratory in North Carolina, USA. He has extensive working experience in marine and coastal resource management with community participation in Sri Lanka. He is the project leader and co-founder of the Turtle Conservation Project (TCP) in Sri Lanka which has been in operation for eighteen years and employs over 100 local community members in various conservation and livelihood development projects. He has also worked as the co-coordinator of the tsunami recovery program which was implemented by the UNDP GEF SGP Sri Lanka and has extensive experience in turtle conservation, mangrove restoration, sand dune restoration, exotic fish breeding, nature tourism, etc., with community participation. Further, he worked as the Programme Development Officer (UNV) for the Disaster Management Unit of UNDP Sri Lanka. Thushan is currently undertaking his MSc in Conservation & Tourism at the Durrell Institute of Conservation and Ecology (DICE) at the University of Kent at Canterbury in the United Kingdom. His main interests are community based ecosystem conservation, the diversification of community livelihoods, protected area co-management strategies and the sustainability of community based projects.

Friedrich Kaufmann is currently working as an international consultant in the area of Private Business Development, SMEs, BMOs and Public-Private Dialogue, mostly in Africa and Latin America. He lived for ten years in Africa, namely in Mozambique, where he worked as a Professor and Dean for Economics and Director of the Consultancy Unit GEA at the Catholic University in Beira. Until 2009 he was coordinator and team leader for the German International cooperation (GIZ) in the program Sustainable Economic Development in Mozambique's Ministry of Trade and Commerce.In Germany Friedrich worked for ten years as a research team leader at the Institute for Small and Medium-sized Enterprises in Bonn. He studied at the Universities of Regensburg, Zurich, ESDE/Barcelona and Cologne. In 1985 he obtained a Degree in Business Management at the University of Cologne and in 1993 he received his PhD/Doctorate at the University of Cologne with a thesis about 'Internationalization via Cooperation – A Strategy for SMEs (Friedrich. Kaufmann@gmx.net).

Pascal Languillon is an expert in sustainable tourism development, ecotourism and eco-luxury travel. He specializes in developing communication strategies aimed at broadening and increasing the market for sustainable tourism and linking travellers to environmentally and socially responsible tourism destinations and organizations. He holds a Master's degree in Environmental Science from the University of Auckland, New Zealand, where he specialized in ecotourism. He is the director of www.voyagespourlaplanete.com, France's leading responsible travel online guide. He also recently authored several responsible travel guide-books for various editors such as Lonely Planet and the Chic Collection. His recent book *Ecochic* presents the best eco-luxury hotels in the world. Luxury ecotourism is his main research interest, and he is currently undertaking a PhD at Auckland University of Technology, exploring the influence of environmental responsibility on the buying behaviour of affluent travellers.

R. Harvey Lemelin an Associate Professor in the School of Outdoor Recreation Parks and Tourism at Lakehead University in Thunder Bay, Canada. He has been examining the human dimensions of wildife management (Inamely polar bears, black bears and cougars) for the past ten years. For the past five Years he has begun to focus his attention on human-insect interactions in leisure and tourism settings. Several publications and conference presentations have emerged from these studiesHarvey has also organized two arthropod symposi-ums in Thunder Bay (namely a dragonfly symposium in the summer of 2007 and a bee symposium in the summer of 2008). He was recently awarded a research grant from the Social Sciences and Humanities Research Council of Canada to continue and expand his research on insects and people.

Christopher C. Mayer is a specialist in natural resource communications. He is a founding partner of *Interpret the World*; a company that offers educational and communications services to parks and protected areas in Latin America and beyond. He has worked as interpretive specialist for the U.S. National Park Service's Natural Resource Information Division. He has also taught about environmental interpretation and planning and interpretive media design at Colorado State University, USA and at the Universidad del Valle, Guatemala. Chris served three-years as a Peace Corps Volunteer in Honduras working on numerous environmental education and interpretation projects. He is based in Guatemala, Central America, where he uses communications to conserve and promote nature and Maya culture.

Simon Milne was born in New Zealand and has been conducting research on issues relating to tourism and regional economic development for over 15 years. He completed his MA in Geography at Auckland University in 1985 and his thesis focused on the economic impact of tourism in the Cook Islands.

He then went to Cambridge to complete a PhD in industrial geography. His doctorate focused on the impacts of technology and new management strategies on the corporate location and labour market needs of various manufacturing firms in the UK. For much of 1988 he also worked for the United Nations Development Program as a tourism economist in the South Pacific. He joined the Department of Geography at McGill University in 1989. In 1990 he formed the multidisciplinary McGill Tourism Research Group, which he continues to co-ordinate. Simon Milne created the New Zealand Tourism Research Institute in 1999. The new millennium took him to Auckland University of Technology (AUT) in the position of Associate Dean of Research. He became in 2007 the Associate Head of School (Research), School of Hospitality and Tourism, at AUT.

Velvet Nelson has a PhD in geography from Kent State University in Kent, Ohio, USA, and is currently an Assistant Professor in the Department of Geography and Geology at Sam Houston State University in Huntsville, Texas, USA. Her research has examined both past and present patterns of tourism in the Caribbean, with a particular emphasis on the relationships between tourists and the environments of the destinations they visit. As such, she has been especially interested in the less developed islands of the Lesser Antilles, such as Grenada, Dominica, and St. Vincent. Although her primary research area is the Caribbean, she was recently awarded a Fulbright Scholar Grant in the Department of Geography at the University of Primorska in Koper, Slovenia. where she is interested in exploring the issues of Central Europe as an emerging destination region in contrast with the Caribbean as a well-developed destination region.

Fernanda Oliveira has been the Assistant Professor at the Polytechnic Institute of Leiria (Portugal) since 1997.Before that Fernanda was a tourism PhD student having gained a Master's degree in Urban and Environmental Planning; Fernanda's research interest also focused on sustainable tourim as a. researcher at the Center for Identity(ies) and Diversity (ies), IPL.

Joseph Onchwati early education was undertaken in Kenya and India. He obtained a Bachelor Degree in Hotel Management and Catering Technology from the University of Pune, India in 2003; a Post Graduate Diploma in International Hotel and Tourism Management from HTMi (Hotel and Tourism Management Institute Switzerland) in 2007; and an MBA in Hospitality Management from Queen Margaret University Edinburgh, Scotland in 2007. He was given the HTMi Excellent Student Award 2007 in recognition of his outstanding performance as a student, his professional approach to work, and his overall contribution to HTMi student life. After graduating, Joseph worked in several five-star hotels in India and Switzerland before returning to Kenya, where he was recruited by the Top Chefs Culinary Institute as a Kitchen Lecturer and Instructor. His personal interests include cooking, travelling, photography, drama, music, nature and wildlife, reading and following events in the hospitality industry, as well as interacting with people of different backgrounds. His favourite sports are football, cricket and basketball. He has travelled widely throughout the world.

Nelissa Peralta Bezerra studied Politics and Development Studies at the University of Wales, Swansea. She began graduate studies in Brazil in the Nucleo de Altos Estudos Amazonicos, at the Para Federal Universit,y with a Masters Degree in Sustainable Development. Currently a PhD student in Sociology at the Minas Gerais Federal University, her major research interests include gender relations, economics of rural populations, the social impacts of ecotourism and conservation, and common use of natural resources. She has worked for ten years with local populations to implement community-based tourism in a protected area in Brazil. She currently lives in the Brazilian Amazon and works as a researcher for the Mamiraua Institute for Sustainable Development.

Xueqin Qiu is an Associate Professor in the School of Business and Tourism Management, Yunnan University (Kunming, Yunnan, China). She specializes in ethnic culture and history, tourism aesthetics, and hotel management. She has led and participated in many provincial and national research projects and has published extensively in refereed journals. She received her PhD in Chinese Nationality History and Culture from Nationalities Research Institute, Yunnan University.

Prema Rajagopalan an Indian Sociologist, specializes in the areas of Sociology of Science & Technology, Sociology of Development, and Built Environment and Society. Her current research relates to identifying and strengthening potential areas and sectors (of which tourism is one) to make India competitive in the Knowledge Economy. She has also served as a consultant for an international NGO in the context of the Tsunami and rehabilitation in Tamil Nadu. She gained her PhD in Sociology of Science & Technology from IIT Kanpur in 1990. Her Post-Doctoral Research area is Women in Science & Technology. She was also the recipient of an India-China Bilateral Cultural Exchange Program. At present, Dr. Prema works as an Associate Professor in Sociology at theIndian Institute of Technology, Madras.

Ulf Richter received his Doctorate in Economic Sciences from the University of Lausanne for his thesis on corporate responsibility in a globalizing world. He has taught courses on business strategy, international management, international marketing, global economy, global governance and business ethics in the United States, Peru, and Côte d'Ivoire. He currently serves as Visiting Assistant Professor of Management at Portland State University. Previously, he was a visiting fellow at Harvard University. He frequently presents his work at international conferences such as the AOM Annual Meeting or the AIB Conference. He has published in the *Journal of Business Ethics* and in *Business Strategy and the Environment*, as well as a book on corporate responsibility. His research interests include the intersection of strategy and sustainability, social innovation, emerging markets, bottom-of-the-pyramid strategies, corporate responsibility, global supply chains, and global governance. He is also an active entrepreneur and has founded companies in Côte d'Ivoire, Peru, and Switzerland, and has conceptualized and coordinated several international conferences.

Sibylle Riedmiller a German-born social scientist, worked from 1973 in Latin America and Africa for UNESCO and the German Aid Agency GIZ, for over nearly 20 years, mostly managing education reform programs and conducting field studies on community development, water supply and natural resource management. In 1991, she initiated and became the main investor for Chumbe Island Coral Park Ltd. (CHICOP), a private island nature reserve in Zanzibar/ Tanzania. She has lived and worked in Tanzania since 1982.

Aivar Ruukel is Lecturer at the Estonian University of Life Sciences. He has also run a local ecotourism business in Soomaa National Park since 1996 and is an active member of the Ecotourism movement in Estonia. His research focuses on the internet use of ecotourists (aivar.ruukel@emu.ee).

Leena Mary Sebastian is a research scholar at the Department of Humanities and Social Sciences, Indian Institute of Technology, Madras, India, specializing in sustainable tourism and community based tourism. The author is the recipient of the Young Leisure Scholar Award (2008) at the First ISA Forum of Sociology, Barcelona, Spain, at the Panel on Leisure, Tourism and Environment.

Filipe Silva Assistant Professor Polytechnic Institute of Leiria (Portugal) since 2007; Filipe graduated in Hospitality and Tourism Management, was a postgraduate in Touristic Organizations Management and Business Administration, and an International Trade PhD Student. His specialization is sustainable tourism. He has also served as a researcher at the Tourism Research Group (GITUR), IPL.

Donald Sinclair is the Coordinator for Tourism, Transport, Infrastructure and Communication at the Amazon Cooperation Treaty Organization in Brasilia. He has held that position since October 2006. As Tourism Coordinator his principal responsibility is to sustain the collaboration among the eight Member Countries of the Treaty of Amazon Cooperation in order to advance a tourism agenda for the Amazon. Prior to assuming his post in Brasilia he worked for two years as the Director of the Guyana Tourism Authority and was also Programme Convener and Senior Lecturer in the Tourism Studies Unit of the University of Guyana. Donald has also lectured in ecotourism at the University of Guelph, Ontario, and at Florida Gulf Coast University. His academic training includes degrees in literature, tourism and international relations. For a number of years he has been engaged in research into a wide range of tourism issues. These include community-based tourism, sustainable tourism, eco-tourism and sports tourism. He is the author of a number of papers and jJournal articles on tourism. Most recently he co-edited with Chandana Jayawardena the *World Hospitality and Tourism Themes Journal* on the development of sustainable tourism in the Amazon, which was published by Emerald in April 2010 (don9_sinclair@yahoo.com).

Hazel Sommerville early education was undertaken in Northern Ireland. She studied at universities across the UK and has obtained BSc (Honours), MSc and PhD degrees. Hazel started her career as a lecturer in Psychology, holding posts in universities in UK and Canada. After some time as a departmental manager in the University of the West of Scotland, she moved into educational research and undertook many studies into issues of widening access to higher education in UK, developing part-time study routes in UK higher education and improving the student experience. She has worked on research projects with the Quality Assurance Agency UK, the Universities UK and the Scottish Further and Higher Education Funding Council. Since 2008 she has been Head of Research at the Hotel and Tourism Management Institute Switzerland. She is Editor of the *International Hospitality Student Journal* and has presented papers at many international conferences including EuroCHRIE 2009 and 2010 in Finland and Holland, ATLAS 2010 in Cyprus, Sustainable Tourism 2010 in UK and Sustainable Food in Tourism and Hospitality in Sweden. Hazel's personal interests include hill-walking, cycling and travelling.

Paul Strickland has a Bachelor of Business (Hospitality Management) and Master of Arts (Research) and has gained extensive knowledge and experience in the hospitality field from around the globe. Paul has successfully held positions as Restaurant Manager, IT Manager, Food and Beverage Manager, Tour Desk Manager, Sales Manager, Silver-Service & Guéridon Waiter and Master of Ceremonies to her Majesty, Queen Elizabeth II to name only a few. With a love for travel, he has worked in Australia and abroad and focuses his research towards ethnic restaurants and small businesses in Australia, wine tourism and hospitality education. Currently lecturing in Australia at La Trobe University, Paul teaches Food and Beverage Services, Accommodation Operations Management, Hospitality Enterprise Management, Wine Tourism and Marketing at the undergraduate level and Wine Tourism and Concepts in the Master of Tourism program. Having strong industry links, Paul prefers to train students in operational 5 star hotels and restaurants therefore giving students practical hospitality skills as well as academic guidance. Future research will include completing a PhD in space tourism and teaching hospitality management related subjects in other institutions around the world.

Paul Strickland has a Bachelor of Business (Hospitality Management) and Master of Arts (Research) and has gained extensive knowledge and experience in the hospitality field from around the globe. He has successfully held positions as Restaurant Manager, IT Manager, Food and Beverage Manager,

Tour Desk Manager, Sales Manager, Silver-Service & Guéridon Waiter and Master of Ceremonies for her Majesty, Queen Elizabeth II, to name only a few. With a love for travel, he has worked in Australia and abroad and focuses his research towards ethnic restaurants and small businesses in Australia, wine tourism and hospitality education. Currently lecturing in Australia at La Trobe University, Paul teaches Food and Beverage Services, Accommodation Operations Management, Hospitality Enterprise Management, Wine Tourism and Marketing at the undergraduate level and Wine Tourism and Concepts in the Master of Tourism program. Having strong industry links, he prefers to train students in operational 5-star hotels and restaurants, thus giving students practical hospitality skills as well as academic guidance. Future research will include completing a PhD in space tourism and teaching hospitality management-related subjects in other institutions around the world.

Amanda Stronza has researched ecotourism and its impacts in conservation and rural communities since the nineties. She has a doctoral degree from Stanford and is a professor at Texas A & M. She has followed the evolution of the Posada Amazonas project since its inception and has worked in community tourism in Belize, Bolivia, Botswana and Ecuador. She designed and directs the Applied Biodiversity Sciences graduate program at her university.

Raul Suhett De Morais did his undergraduate tourism course in Brazil (UFMG) and continued his academic life with a Master's degree at Universitat Autonoma de Barcelona on Geography. Currently, he is a researcher and a PhD candidate at UAB's Department of Geography. His research interests are centred on tourism and urban geography, tourist image and tourist information.

Bui Thi Tam was a senior lecturer and vice-rector of Hue College of Economics, Vietnam. She specializes in tourism and development economics. She obtained her Master of Science degree at Chiang Mai University, Thailand and Doctorate degree in Nanyang Technological University, Singapore. Her doctorate aimed at examining tourism dynamics and sustainable tourism development – the principles and implication in the Southeast Asia. She has been active on many research and development programs, professional and educational organizations, and has traveled extensively in Asia and Europe. Her research and publications address the issues of trade liberalization and poverty reduction in Vietnam, pro-poor value chain development for sustainable tourism, and responsible marketing. Dr. Bui Thi Tam is now the Dean of Faculty of Hospitality and Tourism, Hue University.

Hanna Sophia Theile was born in Guatemala-City in 1986; however, she grew up in the sedate municipal of Wenden, North-Rhine-Westphalia. After having passed her A-Levels at the Städtisches Gymnasium Olpe she continued her studies at the International University of Applied Sciences Bad Honnef., Bonn, in the field of 'International Hospitality Management'. In 2010, she submitted her Bachelor Thesis themed 'An analysis of community-based ecotourism as sustainable development tool for Guatemala' and successfully obtained her diploma. As of March 2011, she has been working for the Kempinski AG at the Schloss Reinhartshausen in Eltville, Hessen.

Karola Tippmann holds a Master's degree in Political Science, is an International Tourism Advisor, and has been working in the context of German Development Cooperation since 1993. She advised the Ministry of Tourism of Costa Rica from 1993 and 1998. Together with tour operators and hotel owners which are dedicated to the European market she created the FUTUROPA initiative as a model of public and private cooperation. From 1999 to 2006 she was the main coordinator of the FODESTUR Supra Regional Program developed by the Central American Integration System (SICA) and the German International Cooperation (GIZ). Together with seven Central American countries they developed and implemented the regional tourism brand *Central America – so small so big*. From 2006 to 2009 she advised the Argentinean government with a view to the implementation of the Federal Strategic Plan for Sustainable Tourism in the five provinces of northern Argentina. Together with partners from the public and the private sector they introduced a new concept of regional chamber in Argentina. Since March 2009 Karola has been working at ACTO. She was sent by the Integrated Experts Programme (CIM) to act as Consultant on Specific Aspects of Sustainable Tourism in the Amazon Region. Her activities currently focus on strengthening integration processes and she has published several articles on these topics (karola. tippmann@web.de).

Heli Tooman is Associate Professor of Tourism Management, and Head of the Department of Tourism Studies at Pärnu College of the University of Tartu. Her research focuses not only on sustainable tourism destination development, tourism marketing, quality in tourism and customer service, but also wellness and spa tourism. She has published several tourism textbooks, articles and tourism dictionaries. She has worked for many years as a tour guide and hotel manager (heli.tooman@ut.ee).

Sigbjorn Tveteras has a PhD in Economics from the Norwegian School of Economics and Business and is a professor at CENTRUM Católica Business School at Pontificia Universidad Católica del Perú. His main reaserch area is industrial economics where the bulk of the research has focused on issues related to seafood and tourism. He has participated in several research projects and published a number of journal articles and book chapters. Among the current research issues that he is pursuing is the effect of direct flights on tourist arrivals to Peru.

Helenio Waddington is a Brazilian lawyer and a former Director in the banking sector of Brazil. Having embraced a new career as an hotelier Helenio has long been a pioneer in bringing environmental practices to the Brazilian tourism industry, such as the use of solar energy at his property, the Hotel Rosa dos Ventos, since 1976. He is also the founder and president of the Roteiros de Charme Hotel Association.,

George N. Wallace is a professor in the Department of Human Dimensions of Natural Resources at Colorado State University. He was for many years the Director of the Center for Protected Area Management and Training (CPMAT). He has devoted his career to capacity building for protected areas (PAs) through his teaching, research, writing, training, graduate students and by personal example. In additions to the many graduates and undergraduate students taught at CSU, CPMAT has improved the capacity of hundreds, if not thousands, of protected area professionals in the Americas via training courses, technical assistance, materials development over a 25-year period. Examples include a five-week intensive field course taught in Spanish – for Latin American managers, as well as two decades of in-country PA training courses and technical assistance. Dr Wallace has helped establish PA training centers in the US, Brazil, Mexico, developing new PA courses, degree programs and cooperative studies programs. He assisted with the development and delivery of capacity-building streams for World Parks Congresses in Caracas and Durban. He is also one of the founders of the Consortium for International Protected Area Management involving the US Forest Service, the Universities of Idaho, Montana and Colorado State and other partners. His work has produced many committed PA professionals, management innovations, and a heightened awareness about the importance of landscape level conservation via the full spectrum of protected areas. The Wallaces have restored a badly degraded farm, which has since won several awards for the blend of agriculture, wetlands, wildlife habitat and education it now provides.

Greg Williams since 2002, Greg has been the director of the Cree village ecolodge in Moose Factory, Ontario, Canada. Prior to that, he was the manager ofseveral golf courses located in southern Ontario.

Li Yang is an Assistant Professor in the Department of Geography at Western Michigan University. Her research career has focused on tourism planning, marketing, cultural tourism, ethnic tourism, tourism analysis and forecasting, and applied statistics. Her research interests are interdisciplinary as she has a diverse background in tourism, planning, statistics, and economics. She has also been involved in many tourism research projects and has obtained university and governmental research grants and awards. She received her PhD in Planning from the University of Waterloo, Canada, and her MSc in Statistics from Yunnan University, Yunnan, China.

Rodrigo Zomkowski Ozório has a degree in Tourism and MSc in Environmental Management and Ecotourism from the University of Costa Rica. Hailing from the central-western region of Brazil, his professional involvement in ecotourism began in 2002 as a naturalist guide in the southern Pantanal. His interest in conservation and sustainable development issues led him to the Central Amazon in 2003. He currently conducts research on Tourism and Protected Areas issues and coordinates the community-based ecotourism program at the Mamirauá Sustainable Development Institute.

Foreword

Global tourism has, for reasons that can be best described as 'borne out of necessity', become one of the key pillars of the economies of most developing countries. In many it is even viewed as the engine of growth in the early days of development.

The upside has been investments, job creation, an increase in GDP, and even the promotion of cultural understanding. These are the key indicators that provide ammunition for the advocates of globalization to continue to call for unfettered free markets, the free flow of capital, and open access to resources, as the means to address a range of economic challenges as well as alleviating poverty.

However, the downside for the rapid and unchecked growth of the global tourism industry has brought with it various negative consequences, ranging from environmental degradation and resource stresses to various social ills including cultural erosion. These have for far too long been downplayed as if they are inevitable or not worth addressing and that they are a small price to pay for the benefits that arise, especially from creating employment. And so the debate ranges on ...

Much of this now focuses on the concepts of sustainability in tourism and the term 'eco-tourism' was coined in response. Unfortunately a great deal of the discussion of these concepts in the hospitality and tourism industry, including the media coverage, is often facile and even superficial, thus not raising a true awareness of the trade-offs or furthering an honest debate.

This therefore allows for arguments that conveniently ignore the hard questions, contradictions and inherent challenges of the world we live in, with its penchant for glossy marketing, public relations, half-truths, demands for instant solutions, the desire for short-term feelgood outcomes, and a constant quest for more via the miracle of economic growth at any cost.

It is thus extremely gratifying to see a hospitality university take the lead in introducing these critical concepts to students who are typically taught all the finest aspects of service and hospitality but not are forced to think about the implications of the thorny issues that exist within the underbelly of the industry in which they will become professionals.

The authors' case study approach is most important as it moves beyond the usual rhetoric and principles to include real locations, with real challenges and real people, as well as real lessons to be learnt and real results to be measured. The range of locations and projects include examples across the continents and provide students with an understanding not only of geography, but also of a whole set of different sustainability issues and criteria depending on the local social economic and political realities. This is critical as most sustainability challenges are not simply environmental challenges with technical solutions, they are also challenges with political objectives.

The challenge is also one of courage and implementation and a book that offers students an in-depth analysis of successful businesses employing these principles is a significant contribution to how the industry can promote these. The developing world in particular needs good examples which are rooted in an entrepreneurial spirit, indigenous knowledge, and an awareness of constraints and ethical practices. The importance of the industry taking into account the true cost of offering the goods and services that are part and parcel of the experience cannot be overstated given that the current economic models thrive on underpricing resources and externalizing the impacts.

Whilst the book has been mainly written for a student audience it should also be one that policy makers in the governments of the developing nations would use for reference in order to see what is possible if the right questions are asked and taken into account when drawing up their plans for the future.

In this regard I also hope that the proponents of tourism projects, be they developers or investors, will dip into the rich examples shown here, learn some valuable lessons, be inspired, and then incorporate them into those same plans.

Chandran Nair
Founder and CEO of the Global Institute for Tomorrow

Editors' preface

This book is aimed at undergraduates and postgraduates studying international hospitality management and international tourism management. It will also be of use to practitioners in the field of hospitality and tourism project development in the developing economies around the globe and to social science students. Although this compendium of case studies is not intended to be a companion volume to our previous book *Sustainability in the Hospitality Industry: Principles of Sustainable Operations* (Chen, Sloan & Legrand, Elsevier, 2009), it does complement the knowledge of the subject by giving many examples in the context of developing economies.

The prime motivation for producing this book is that there are no other publications that deal with the impacts of sustainable hospitality and tourism operations in developing economies. Many books exist on the international hospitality and tourism industry and much has been written generally about sustainability, but it seems that no one has attempted to combine these contemporary subjects within the context of economic development in some of the poorer countries of the world. Hopefully, this text addresses these deficiencies and provides help and inspiration for all those studying, teaching and working in this field.

We are immensely grateful to all the contributing authors for taking the time to write the chapters and for the good humour they have shown in answering our numerous emails as well as their patience over the production of this book.

Philip Sloan, Claudia Simons-Kaufmann, and Willy Legrand

Editors' biography

Claudia Simons-Kaufmann

Claudia Simons-Kaufmann is Professor at the International University of Applied Sciences in Bad Honnef, Germany. She received her Doctorate in Economic Sciences from the University of Freiburg/ Sachsen for her thesis on the economic transformation process of a less developed country, taking Mozambique as an example. She has lectured courses in 'Economics' and 'Accounting' at the University of Public Administration in Cologne and was involved in lecturing and training in the process of the Public Sector Reform (the introduction of the  *Neue Steuerungsmodell*) in the Public Administration in North-Rhine-Westphalia. From 1998 until 2001 she lectured and did research at the Universidade Católica de Mocambique, in Beira/Africa. Since then she has been doing short-term consultancies for the German Development Organization (GIZ), the German Ministry of Economic Cooperation (BMZ), the Austrian Cooperation, and the German Industry Association (BDI) in Mozambique and Ghana in the areas of Private Sector promotion and Donor coordination. At a private company in Mozambique she was working as a project manager in developing and structuring new business ideas. Her research interests lie in the area of sustainability and developing countries.

Willy Legrand

Willy Legrand is lecturing in the Department of Hospitality Management at the International University of Applied Sciences Bad Honnef, Bonn, Germany. After completing his undergraduate degree in Geography, Willy held numerous managerial positions in the hospitality industry in Canada and Germany. Willy holds a Master of Business Administration degree with a specialization in Environmental Management. In Bad Honnef he teaches a variety of courses within the Hospitality curriculum, including Principles of Sustainable Hospitality Operations and Hospitality Facility Management. As an international guest lecturer, Willy teaches undergraduate courses on sustainable management in leading hospitality management universities. With co-authors Philip Sloan and Joseph S. Chen, Willy published a leading university textbook on sustainable matters in hospitality (*Sustainability in the Hospitality Industry: Principles of Sustainable Operations*, Elsevier). His personal background includes formative years spent working in agriculture in Canada and with a family involved in organic cultivation and production in France. As a wine enthusiast and founder of the university's wine club, Willy, together with co-author Philip Sloan, created an organic vineyard, which functions as an educational tool for hospitality management students (w.legrand@iubh.de).

Philip Sloan

Philip Sloan is one of the founding members of the lecturing team that started the Department of Hospitality management at the IUBH in Bonn, Germany, in September 2000. Philip's earlier career was in the management of London hotels

before creating his own small chain of organic restaurants in England and then in Strasbourg France where he is now based. He holds a Master's degree in Environmental Management as well as an M.B.A., and has a long list of peer-reviewed scientific journal articles to his credit. In addition to teaching sustainable hospitality management studies, he is a passionate environmental entrepreneur and is currently working on various sustainable food projects in addition to running a small organic vineyard with co-writer Willy Legrand on the University campus (p.sloan@iubh.de).

An overview of the book

The focus of this book is on sustainable hospitality and tourism initiatives in developing countries and special areas (as in the Estonian case study and in the flora/fauna tourism case study) around the globe. Achieving equitable employment opportunities while also protecting the natural environment and achieving financial profit are common denominators throughout the chapters.

By the deployment of 26 case studies this book demonstrates how opportunities to create income and stimulate regional socio-economic development are made possible by using sustainable hospitality and tourism attractions. Ideally, sustainability should be the watchword in all projects of this nature. However, in reality experienced project leaders can successfully incorporate the principles of sustainability into ongoing ventures.

The road to full sustainability can be long and arduous and requires determination as well as business sense and investment. Some of the case studies show that sustainability is sometimes only possible at the beginning in small doses. It can be concluded that there is no fixed point at which sustainability begins or ends, especially in developing countries where other pressing needs exist and the business culture does not always lend itself to a more radical approach.

Thus, all case studies are unique and have their own specific experiences to draw on since they cover a multitude of different facets of sustainability. Some focus more on communication and the protection of indigenous cultures as a source of touristic curiosity like the case study from China. Others focus mainly on the preservation of the environment like the Chumbe Island Coral Park in Tanzania, the Selinda Reserve in Botswana and the Guiné-Bissau project, while the Kerala case study focuses more on the improvements in the living conditions of local people.

Education as a means to good environmental practices and social cohesion is the main goal of the Roteiros de Charme Hotel Association in Brazil and in the case study from Bhutan on hotel management education. The protection of endangered species is also covered in this publication, such as the plight of turtles in Sri Lanka or butterflies in Costa Rica. The merits of organic farming in ecotourism are developed in the case studies from Thailand and Bonito in Brazil. Cultural heritage in the form of a traditional architectural renovation in an ecotourism area is described in the Sundarbans in India.

Some cases are government supported projects like the green parks venture and regional tourism development in the Philippines, an archeological park initiative in Honduras and the diversity of nature tourism in St. Vincent. Others are more concerned with local co-operations between government and private initiatives like jungle exploration in the Amazon region.

Community based eco-tourism is seen by many as the best approach to overcoming poverty. Examples can be observed from Guatemala, the Amazon Basin, the Huaorani Ecolodge in Ecuador, or the project between private investors and local communities in the Peruvian jungle. Voluntary development work as a tourism activity with social engagement is highlighted in Ethiopia.

The Six Senses hotel case study in Vietnam and the Inkaterra case study in Peru show that there is no contradiction between preserving the environment and offering high class luxury accommodation.

How to use this book

This textbook is primarily intended to provide best practice examples of sustainable hospitality and tourism in developing economies. The first part deals with a presentation of our understanding of economics and especially of economic development. In this context, developing countries are defined and classified. Then sustainable hospitality and tourism operations are discussed. The second part presents the case studies themselves. In the lecture hall, we suggest discussing each case study by asking the following questions:

- What is the main area of sustainability in question?
- What further steps could be taken to develop the project?
- How does the case study contribute to the pursuit of the millennium development goals?
- Are there possibilities for local people to earn more money from the initiative? And would this be directly or indirectly?
- If a cultural change has taken place, can it be considered to be to the advantage or disadvantage of local people?

The following are more general questions:

- Is there an impact on eco-tourism products when local people become wealthier through tourism?
- How will the eco-tourism attraction change?
- Why is it necessary to understand the socio-economic environment in order to protect it?

The following is a set of sustainable tourism and hospitality indicators that can be checked through all case studies:

- monitoring environmental impacts
- ongoing contributions to local sustainable development
- reductions in non-renewable resource use
- local ownership
- environmental stewardship
- ongoing contributions to biodiversity

- intercultural understanding
- financial incentives for resource conservation

The following map provides a geographical overview of all cases. All cases are indicated with their respective number, color-coded according to the continent, and referenced to the country or location name in the table below.

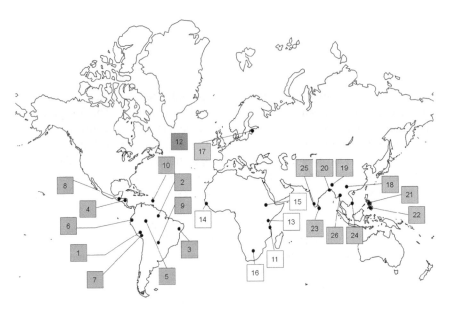

Map 1 Geographical Location of Case Studies

The table below can serve as a useful tool to cross check the content of all the case studies.

Table 1 Listing of Cases with Content Cross-Check Form

	Monitoring/research	Ongoing contributions to local sustainable development	Reductions in non-renewable resource use	Local ownership	Environmental stewardship	Ongoing contributions to biodiversity	Intercultural understanding	Financial incentives for resource conservation
1. Peru Inkaterra								
2. Amazon								
3. Brazil (Roteiros de Charme)								

4. Honduras									
5. Brazil (Amazon Basin)									
6. Ecuador									
7. Peru Amazon									
8. Guatemala									
9. Brazil (Tourism cluster)									
10. St. Vincent and the Grenadines									
11. Tanzania									
12. Global (Insects)									
13. Kenya									
14. Guiné-Bissau									
15. Ethipia									
16. Botswana									
17. Estonia									
18. China									
19. Bhutan									
20. India (Sundarbans)									
21. Philippines (Urban Green Parks)									
22. Philippines (Tourism)									
23. Sri Lanka									
24. Vietnam									
25. India (Kerala)									
26. Thailand									

1 Introduction

Scarcity of natural resources or 'Cockaigne'?

Claudia Simons-Kaufmann,
Friedrich Kaufmann, Philip Sloan
and Willy Legrand

Imagine a world where you can fulfill immediately all the needs and wants you have in any quantity without making too much effort and without paying any price. All resources are in abundance and you only need to pick them up and direct them to whatever purpose you wish.Unfortunately, the real world is no 'land of plenty'. The fundamental economic problem since mankind has existed has been that of 'scarcity'. All resources are scarce, our needs, wants and necessities are not. Therefore, we are forced to deal with our scarce resources economically. Human activities have influenced the earth's ecosystem for many thousands of years. While prior civilizations believed they inhabited a world with endless resources beyond the horizon, current generations are faced with the impacts of human activity from past generations. The limits to the natural environment are now restricting the uncontrolled use and destruction of precious resources. While every person carries an individual responsibility for the state of the planet, businesses can be cited as possible black sheep but also as providers of long-term solutions and innovations that are able to redress the negative imbalances in nature and society. In some spheres of business it almost seems as if companies have been operating as rogue entities since the Industrial Revolution, tarnishing with the same brush everything and everyone on the path towards profit accumulation. Fortunately, examples in our past do exist of entrepreneurs realizing the importance of investing in the well-being of their employees, such as the English eighteenth-century mill owner Robert Owen, who went on to become the renowned social reformer. Traditional cultures knew about conservation and were careful never to exceed the ecological limits in the regions they inhabited.

History may prove that capitalism has given humanity various forms of development, many of which are based on property ownership and the accumulation of products. This form of development is questioned by a growing number of organizations and citizens. Corporate social and environmental responsibility, aside from being fashionable subjects, are difficult topics to comprehend due to the fact that they are subject to biased interpretations, inconsistent implementation, and sometimes, dubious reporting.

With the growing awareness that the task of dealing with scarce resources is becoming more and more difficult to resolve because many non-renewable natural resources are being exhausted, action to remediate this disastrous situation only really began in the late 1970s. When the 'Club of Rome' was founded it stated in its first report that 'if present growth trends in world population, industrialization, pollution, food production and resource depletion continue unchanged, the limits to growth on this planet will be reached sometime within the next one hundred years' (Meadows et al., 1972). It can be concluded that mankind is no longer respecting the limits set by the planet as levels of consumption rise exponentially and natural resources become evermore scarce. There seems to be a preference for turning natural resources into short-term profits instead of securing them for future generations. Natural resources are regarded as so-called 'free goods', as there is no price to pay for using them.

The terms 'sustainability' or 'sustainable development' has been mostly accredited to the Brundtland Report, which was published by the UN's World Commission on Environment and Development in 1984. According to this, sustainability is defined as 'meeting the needs of present generations without compromising the ability of future generations to meet their own needs' (UNWCED, 1987). This includes the economic, social and environmental systems. Sustainability refers to the idea of conserving or better improving our economic situation, the environment and social well-being at the same time (Crane and Matten, 2007). This concept is alternatively called the 'three pillars of sustainability' or 'the triple bottom line' or 'people, planet and profit'. The environmental dimension describes impacts on flora and fauna which should be kept as minimal as possible. Renewable resources should be used in such a way that they can be renewed simultaneously. *Non-renewable resources should be used only to the extent that substitutes can be provided.* The economic dimension refers to the fact that any industry must be profitable in order to survive. People have to be able to make a living, otherwise they would not be attracted to the activity. The social dimension underlines the importance of community empowerment and the participation of everyone in the benefits of industry of goods and services that respond to the real needs of the population. This implies excellence in systems of public health, social justice, human rights, labour rights and education (Sloan et al., 2009). In sustainable development, businesses, public authorities and civil society work in partnership in order to reconcile these three fundamental constituents.

At the Earth Summit in 1992, the United Nations (UN) launched a comprehensive blueprint of actions related to environmental protection, regeneration and conservation labeled Agenda 21. Under this agenda, to engage in sustainable development requires adopting, changing or improving behaviours using the following five principles:

- The principle of precaution i.e. to prevent any risk occurring that are deemed possible
- The principle of responsibility i.e. to adopt social and environmental responsibility for all activities and decisions.

- The principle of transparency i.e. to make all relevant information available to stakeholders
- The principle of social and technological innovation i.e. to move forward technological innovation in a way that benefits humankind and the planet
- The principle of responsible citizenship i.e. to contribute to local, national and global tasks.

According to present economic theory, the existing world economy is required to grow eternally in order to meet the escalating needs of an ever increasing global population where wealth is unevenly distributed. The principles of sustainability will have to be applied increasingly if we are to avoid cataclysmic consequences. Countries that are classified as poor need to grow in order to improve the living standards of their populations and scarce resources have then to be distributed between a world population that is set to reach 9 billion by 2050 (WTO), an increase of another two billion people compared to the present day. Countries with lower standards of living, where infrastructure is on the threshold of development, have the chance to implement the principles of sustainability from the beginning. Without giving up on growth, they have the possibility to develop in a way that is sustainable for the present generation and will ultimately benefit future generations as well.

PART 1: WHAT DO WE MEAN BY DEVELOPMENT?

There is no unique or comprehensive definition of development. It means different things to different people and organizations. In conventional economic terms it means the ability of a national economy to generate and sustain an annual increase in its national gross product. Or, in other words to increase income per capita, meaning that a nation is able to expand its output at a growth rate that is faster than the growth of the population, and hence leading to increased economic well-being (Todaro, 1999).

These economic indicators are supplemented by social indicators like gains in literacy, schooling, health conditions and services, as well as the provision of housing, drinking water, irrigation and other utilities.

A more recent view considers development as a more complex process. This amounts to improving quality of life, especially in the world's poorest countries, by increasing incomes, which by itself is not enough. Development also refers to better education, higher standards of health and nutrition, less poverty, a cleaner environment, more equality and opportunities, greater individual freedom and a richer cultural life. This process is multidimensional, involving major changes in social structures, popular attitudes, and national institutions, as well as economic growth and reduction of inequality.

Todaro summarizes the term development with three essential core values:

1) **Sustenance**: the ability to meet basic needs.
   All people have basic needs without which life is not possible. These life-sustaining basic needs include food, shelter, health and protection. When any

Market in Bolivia, La Paz (*Photo*: Friedrich Kaufamnn)

of these are absent or short in supply an absolute under-development exists. In this context development equates to providing as many people as possible with the means of overcoming misery and helplessness. Economic development that includes universal employment opportunities is a minimum condition.

2)   **Self-esteem:** the ability to be a complete person.
A second, all embracing component of development is the notion of a 'good' life through self-esteem and not being abused by others. All people and societies will seek some basic form of what can be referred to as authenticity, identity, dignity, respect, honour, and recognition. The nature and form of self-esteem will vary between regions, cultures and periods in history.

3)   **Freedom from servitude**: the ability to choose.
A third universal value of development is the concept of freedom. Freedom here can be understood in the sense of emancipation from alienating material conditions and from the incertitudes of nature, ignorance, misery, institutions and dogma. Freedom involves an expanded range of choice for societies and their members.

In order to promote these values in politics and achieve more development, especially in poorer countries, science has tried to analyse and formulate theories about its origins. So far the 'great theory' that explains 'underdevelopment' and helps to overcome poverty has not been found yet. It seems that many complex factors drive development in different societies and cultures. Nevertheless it is possible to identify the main theories that were and are still used in development-making policy.

The main 'development theories'[1]

In the fifties and sixties the so-called **'modernization theory'** was dominant. The USA mainly promoted the idea that development equals growth and that growth depends largely on the stock of capital a country owns, meaning that increasing the available stock of capital in poor countries in order to follow the development patterns of industrialized western countries would trigger development.

In contrast, the **'dependency theory'** (the theory of imperialism) postulates that the capital stock of the rich countries was driven by the exploitation of the still underdeveloped countries which were characterized by an abundance of raw material, labour and agricultural production. Rich countries therefore never had a serious interest in helping these poor countries (in many cases former colonies) to become economically independent.

Another theory that is related to the dependency theory is the **'model of development through centralized governmental planning'**. Here, mainly the nationalization of the economy and bureaucratic planning were seen as the solution to overcome development gaps. The government is also considered to be the only driver for development.

While the above mentioned approaches can be considered as failures, the so-called **'neoliberal model'**, which is also known as the Washington Consensus of the Bretton Woods institutions (the World Bank and the International Monetary Fund), is still the accepted norm. This model supports the liberalization of markets, especially financial markets, limited influence of the government and an enabling business environment for investment. Here, the private sector is the main driver for development and the concept of good governance is gaining ground. Nowadays the importance of reliable public institutions like an independent justice system and an efficient administration is broadly recognized.

During the Asian crisis in the nineties the model was proved to be at least partly incorrect. Many Asian economies grew on the basis of private investment but were actively coordinated and regulated by their governments. Japan and the south-east Asian neighbouring countries especially regarded themselves as one economic area. They have developed in a 'cascading pattern', which means that the successful countries concentrate on the production of sophisticated, capital intensive goods and services while the poorer countries benefit from outsourcing and subcontracting their more labour intensive production. Together with strong government this is referred to as the **'Asian Way'**.

All these theories concentrate mainly on economic growth. The following approaches broaden this perception of development by including culture and sustainability.

'**Culture**' as an explanation of development postulates that a strong relationship exists between economic development, value systems, norms and religion. The most famous contributor to this theory is the sociologist Max Weber. Most modern economists would admit that culture is an important factor for development, but as a concept it is regarded as too complex to integrate it into a comprehensive theory. Nevertheless '**Institutional Economics**' combines economic, cultural and political factors. It considers the interaction between informal institutions (norms and values) and formal institutions (official laws and written regulations) but has not yet developed into a complete development theory.

The concept of '**Sustainable Development**' has only existed since the Brundtland Report of 1987. Already in the early twentieth century economists like Pigou and later Georgescu-Roegen (1971) had worked on the foundation of sustainable economic development. The merit of the Club of Rome Report in the seventies was the result of intensive political debate and public awareness that led to a recognition that natural resources are limited and the environment has to be respected.

Nowadays it is widely accepted that we cannot fulfil our own needs without considering the needs of future generations as well. This includes not only ecological and economical factors but also social and political aspects as the above mentioned core values of development highlight. Hence, the concept of sustainable development is not a theory which explains the status of underdevelopment but is more an approach to show how to move forward in an ecological and socially progressive fashion. It is also about more than just growth. Growth is part of development and refers just to the quantitative dimension. Sustainable development includes a qualitative dimension in addition to the quantitative i.e. environmental protection, socioeconomic change and progress.

Before examining tourism and hospitality as possible development factors in developing countries it is necessary to consider the characteristics of a developing country. The above theories are concerned with developed countries and underdeveloped countries. But what does they mean in reality?

Common characteristics of developing countries

There is no one official and generally accepted definition of developing countries. Many simplified non-scientific classifications exist such as:

- 'rich and poor' countries
- 'third world' countries
- 'northern and southern' countries
- 'industrialized and non-industrialized' countries.

All these classifications are obviously not wrong but are not always clear and sometimes too general. Therefore, we concentrate here on some topics which usually characterize most developing countries although the following characteristics are very general and not applicable in all respects to all countries.

Economic characteristics

Most developing countries can be regarded as poor. This is expressed by a low income per capita for most of the population. Typically wealth and income distribution is very unequal and normally there is no social system that balances these disparities. Value added during the production process in the country of origin is low since most of the population works in the agricultural sector (i.e. what is classed as the subsistence economy). Salaries, if they exist at all, are very low and it is not possible for most of the local people to save or invest. The small existing stock of capital is often created by foreign investors interested in the exploitation of the natural resources in the country.

Governments in many developing countries are usually highly indebted and they will depend heavily on aid money. In spite of huge official development aid (ODA) for many years, the public infrastructure and human capital are often still weak. It is not uncommon for the best educated people to migrate and live abroad. The economic structure in these countries is not very diversified. They export mainly unprocessed agricultural goods and raw material. As the value chain in the country is short it is typical that only a few formal employment opportunities exist.

Ecological characteristics

Natural resources are one of the most valuable assets for developing countries. Unfortunately they are hit hardest by problems of depletion and ecological disasters. Some are the result of local mismanagement; others like global warming will have an international dimension. According to the United Nations Environmental Programme (UNEP) 90% of global environmental destruction and degradation takes place in developing countries. The most critical items are:

- erosion
- desertification
- unplanned and uncontrolled urbanization
- water and air pollution
- de-forestation.

Political characteristics

Most developing countries are young nations; some of them have been artificially created by colonizing nations. Their political systems are still developing. Although, almost all these countries have officially introduced democratic systems, civil wars and violence are still threats. The new political institutions are not always stable and depend on single personalities. Many of these modern formal institutions like elections, laws and regulations are still not known or accepted by the population. Despite the fact that democracy has been formally introduced, political elites will sometimes enforce their power through patronage and corruption is not uncommon. Many people say that the lack of good governance is at least partly responsible for slow development in many countries.

The transformation process of the liberalization movement in the former colonies towards independent and consolidated states that count on the loyalty of citizens is not yet complete, especially in Africa.

Socio-cultural and public health characteristics

Tribes or casts will usually play an important role in the process of interaction. They can be more important than the state or anonymous institutions and together with extended families they will often form an essential link in the sociological structure of developing countries. Since markets sometimes do not work efficiently personal relations tend to dominate economic transactions.

As life expectancy is a lot lower than in industrialized countries and birth rates are significantly higher the demographic pyramid shows a high percentage of young people.

Reasons for short life expectancy are:

- insufficient health care
- bad hygiene
- a lack of public health education
- malnutrition
- insufficient drinking water
- epidemic diseases like HIV, malaria and cholera.

The high birth rates are due to specific cultural and religious circumstances. The lack of a public social network and low educational standards for women will further force them to rely on having many children. Hence, child work is not untypical in these countries and as a result children are also seen as contributors to the household income.

Definition criteria of the United Nations and the World Bank for developing countries

The supra international institutions like the United Nations (UN) or the World Bank (WB) have defined their own quantitative or qualitative characteristics of developing countries. These classifications are used by the Bretton Woods institutions to qualify countries in certain assistance and support programmes like the credit schemes of the WB. Therefore the WB uses a one-dimensional indicator of income per capita and a certain poverty line, expressed by the amount of US dollars per day an inhabitant lives on. The UN tries to apply more multi-dimensional indicators. They use the concept of less developed countries (LDC) and least developed countries (LLDC), which is composed of economical and sociological facts. The most well known UN indicator is the Human Development Index (HDI).

Additionally both organizations have a variety of specific indicators dealing with different topics and objectives. For example, every year the WB conducts a survey which gives an idea about the ease and costs of doing business in the private sector, as in the case of start-ups and international trade. This is the so-called Doing Business Ranking of countries. Many other indicators from all areas are published in the World Bank's development indicator database.

Income per capita classification by the WB

The WB distinguishes between low income countries (LIC), middle income countries (MIC) and high income countries (HIC). Countries belong to the LIC when their income per capita is below US 935 (2007), while MIC are differentiated as lower MIC (≤ US $3705) and higher MIC (≤ US $11455).

The HDI of the UN

The HDI is composed of the following:

An economic indicator of income per capita on the basis of purchasing power in
    the respective countries[2];
A health indicator (life expectancy);
An educational indicator (the rates of illiteracy and school enrollment).

The HDI is measured in absolute terms where a value of 0 indicates the lowest development and 1 is the maximum level of development. In relative terms this shows a ranking of 182 countries. Currently Norway is ranked number 1 with an indicator value of 0.938 and Zimbabwe last at 169 with 0,140.

Actual goals of international development policy

As the above description of various development theories suggests, for many decades international and bilateral development policy did not follow a comprehensive and coordinated concept concerning aid. Donors as well as recipient countries often had no common goals and results were poor. In the year 2000 the UN started an initiative, called the **Millennium Development Goals** (MDGs), which is still broadly supported by governments, defining the comprehensively specific development goals all nations have agreed upon. Adopted by world leaders, they are set to be achieved by 2015. The MDGs are both global and local, tailored by each country in order to suit specific development needs. They provide a framework for the entire international community to work together towards a common end, making sure that human development reaches everyone. They form the essential framework for cooperation for supranational (WB and IMF), international and most bilateral development aid. They also include goals to alleviate poverty, hunger, maternal and child mortality, disease, inadequate shelter, gender inequality and environmental degradation, in addition to the creation of the Global Partnership for Development. These eight time-bound goals provide concrete, numerical benchmarks for tackling extreme poverty in its many dimensions and are broken down into quantifiable targets that are measured by various indicators:

Goal 1: Eradicate extreme poverty and hunger by 2015
- Halve the proportion of people living on less than $1 a day.
- Achieve decent employment for women, men, and young people.
- Halve the proportion of people who suffer from hunger.

Goal 2: Achieve universal primary education
- By 2015, all children should complete a full course of primary schooling.

Goal 3: Promote gender equality and empower women
- Eliminate gender disparity in primary and secondary education preferably by 2005, and at all levels by 2015.

Goal 4: Reduce the child mortality rate
- Reduce by two-thirds the mortality rate of under-fives by 2015.

Goal 5: Improve maternal health
- Reduce by three quarters, the maternal mortality ratio by 2015.
- Achieve universal access to reproductive health by 2015.

Goal 6: Combat HIV/AIDS, malaria, and other diseases
- Stop the spread of HIV/AIDS by 2015.
- Achieve universal access to treatment for HIV/AIDS by 2010.
- Stop malaria and other major diseases by 2015.

Goal 7: Ensure environmental sustainability
- Integrate the principles of sustainable development into country policies and programmes; reverse the loss of environmental resources.
- Reduce biodiversity loss. Achieve a significant reduction in the rate of loss by 2010.
- Halve the proportion of people without proper access to safe drinking water and basic sanitation by 2015.
- Achieve significant improvement in the lives of at least 100 million slum-dwellers by 2020.

Goal 8: Develop a global partnership for development
- Further develop open, rule-based, predictable, non-discriminatory systems of trade and finance.
- Address the special needs of the Least Developed Countries (LDC).
- Address the special needs of landlocked developing countries and small island developing states.
- Deal comprehensively with the debt problems of developing countries by creating realistic lending facilities.

- Together with pharmaceutical companies make available necessary medication in developing countries.
- In unison with private companies ensure the deployment of new technologies, especially in the fields of information and communication.

If these goals are achieved, world poverty will be cut by a half, tens of millions of lives will be saved, and billions more people will have the opportunity to benefit from the global economy. Nevertheless, it is to be expected that most of these ambitious goals will not be fully achieved.

Presentation of the countries concerned in this book

After clarifying the term 'developing countries', the following table gives an overview of the countries which are presented in this book by showing some selective indicators which describe their development status. Although there is something critical to say about each one of them, the combination of the following indicators gives a consistent and realistic image of the development status of the individual country (see Table 1.1).

- Total population gives an idea about the demographic dimensions of the country.
- The human development index (HDI) is the composite development indicator showing the relative position amongst other countries.
- Illiteracy rate, life expectancy and GDP per capita in purchasing power parity (PPP) are the main sub-indicators which compose the HDI.
- GDP per capita in US dollars is GDP in absolute numbers divided by the number of people in the country.
- Population below 1.25 US dollars per day indicates the percentage of the population living below the poverty line, here defined as 1.25 US dollars.
- The Doing Business Ranking shows the position of a country relative to others in terms of ease and costs of doing business. Economies are ranked on their ease of doing business, from 1 to 183, with first place being the best (i.e. Singapore) and the last place being the worst (i.e. Chad). A high ranking on the ease of doing business index means the regulatory environment is conducive to the operation of business. This index averages the country's percentile rankings of ten topics, made up from a variety of indicators. The rankings are from the Doing Business 2011 report, covering the period June 2009 through May 2010.
- The corruption perception index (CPI) conducted by Transparency International shows how corruption is perceived by a panel of experts in individual countries. The index is between 0 and 10, with 10 meaning no corruption and 0 the highest level of corruption. The rank shows again the relative position of the country. Denmark is ranked 1 in 2010 with a value of 9.3 and Somalia is ranked 178 with a score of 1.1.

Table 1.1 Country comparison of development status indicators

Country	Total Population (2009 in Mio.)	HDI Rank (2010)	GDP per capita (PPP) in US$	Illiteracy Rate in % aged 15 and above	Life expectancy in years at birth	Population below US $1.25 per day in %	Doing Business Ranking (2010)	CPI Rank / Value (2010)
Africa								
Botswana	1,949	98	13.462	15,2	55,5	n.a.	52	33/ 5,8
Ethiopia	82,824	157	991	64,1	56,1	39,04	104	116/2,7
Guineé-Bissau	1,610	164	554	30,5	48,6	n.a	176	154/2,1
Kenya	39,802	128	1.622	26,4	55,6	19,72	98	154/2,1
Tanzania	43,739	148	1.426	26,8	56,9	88,52	128	116/2,7
Asia								
Bhutan	0,697	n.a.	5.532	47,2	66,8	n.a	142	36/ 5,7
China	1.331	89	7.206	5,8	73,5	15,92	79	78 3,5
India	1.155	119	3.354	31,7	64,4	41,64	134	87/ 3,3
Philippines	91,983	97	3.601	6,3	72,3	22,62	148	134/ 2,4
Sri Lanka	20,303	91	4.999	9,2	74,4	n.a.	102	91/ 3,2
Thailand	67,764	92	8.328	5,3	69,3	<2	19	78/3,5
Vietnam	87,279	113	3.097	9,7	74,9	21,45	78	116/ 2,7

South and Central America

Bolivia	9,862	95	4.502	9,3	66,3	11,86	149	110/2,8
Brazil	193,733	73	10.847	10	72,9	5,21	127	69/3,7
Colombia	45,659	79	8.959	7,3	73,4	16,01	39	78/3,5
Costa Rica	4,578	62	11.143	3,7	79,1	<2	125	41/5,3
Ecuador	13,625	77	8.170	9	75,4	4,69	130	127/2,5
Guatemala	14,026	116	4.761	24,7	70,8	11,7	101	91/3,2
Guyana	0,762	104	3.344	n.a.	67,9	n.a.	100	116/2,7
Honduras	7,465	106	3.845	16,4	72,6	18,19	131	134/2,4
Peru	29,164	63	9.016	10,4	73,7	7,69	36	78/3,5
St. Vincent and the Grenadines	0,109	n.a.	8.967	11,9	72	n.a.	75	n.a.
Suriname	0,519	94	7.856	8,9	69,4	n.a.	161	n.a.
Venezuela	28,384	75	11.820	4,8	74,2	3,53	172	164/2,0

Europe

Estonia	1,340	34	18.355	0,2	73,7	<2	17	26/6,5

Sources: World Bank, World Development Indicators, UNDP HDI, various years.

The Tourism Industry in general is one of the biggest economic sectors in the global economy. For all countries in the above table and later presented as case studies, growth in tourism and hospitality is part of the development strategy and can be one of the main development motors. Comprehensively planned and executed hospitality and tourism development can work in line with the criteria of sustainable development.

PART 2: SUSTAINABILITY IN TOURISM AND HOSPITALITY

An introduction to the tourism and hospitality in developing countries

The boom in the tourism and hospitality has given rise to millions of new jobs and increased economic prosperity in countries around the world. Although the numbers of international arrivals decreased by 4% in 2009, UNWTO forecasts an increase of between 3%-4% for 2011. In 2008 tourism and hospitality generated US $946 billion in export earnings (WTO, 2010). Consequently, there is growing potential for enterprise development and employment creation, which in turn will stimulate further investment and support the development of local services. As a result, it generates income and can forward productive intercultural understanding. It also has the potential for earning substantial foreign exchange and contributing to the balance of payments. Developing countries typically have comparative advantages in the tourism. They not only possess land, sun, sea, and adventure possibilities but also assets like wildlife, landscape and cultural experiences which are all demanded by consumers from richer and often more densely populated countries.

When describing a phenomenon such as the hospitality sector of the tourism industry it is difficult to define not only its size and activities but also its role in communities. The diversity of its products and services from luxury hotels, to casinos, to catering firms, to even hot dog stands outside sports stadiums, defies the conventional definition of an industry as being 'a set of firms all making the same product'. In the context of this book, the hospitality outlets described include an up-market, luxury class hotel in Vietnam and examples of small lodges and hotels catering almost uniquely for tourists. Naturally, the provision of hotels falls within the general context of hospitality, an aspect of human activity which has important social dimensions as well as meeting the physiological needs of shelter and comfort.

From an international perspective the notion of a hotel is understood as a culturally bound phenomenon that represents a certain set of assumptions. The types of accommodation in this book are designed to appeal primarily to Western tourists who largely wish to experience an authentic vacation where they will experience local traditional culture in an unspoilt environment. The establishments offer a particular combination of meal and drink services, staff and guests operate to given social codes where Western norms are met. This can of course be challenging for some indigenous local people who may have their own social behaviour codes that are at odds with their tourist guests' and even their own traditional interpretation of hospitality. However, it must be stated that these very differences in behaviour are often factors that attract visitors to what can be referred to as the cultural component of tourism.

The successes of tourism and hospitality products are governed by other factors in addition to the charm of the local people and their traditional way of life. Travellers are increasingly sensitive to price or the comparative economic value of their holiday. In an era of cheap package holidays it is not every tourist who will shell out their hard earned shekels to sleep in a bamboo hut with rudimentary bathroom facilities.

Tourists are also not blind to political strife and most will stay away from any area where there is any threat of terrorism. Embedded in the conscience of many eco-tourists is, of course, the price they will have to pay in terms of environmental costs i.e. the carbon footprint. While the average European tourist may way up the price differences between of a winter break in the Canaries or a week on beaches of southern Tunisia, the eco-tourist might consider a bicycle tour of the Black Forest as being more ethically sound and environmentally friendly than a jungle safari in Brazil that would include a long haul flight in a 747. Domestic tourism in Europe and North America, be it traditional or the new vogue for

A rudimentary bamboo bathroom, Mozambique (*Photo*: Ronald Meyer)

adventure holidays, has seen increases in recent years. The tendency is now for confirmed eco-travelers to still experience exotic, far-flung destinations but to inter-space their love of the original with more down key pleasures in their own regions. The business of eco-tourism and sustainable hospitality is now a complex interplay of factors and is the fruition of a wide range of actors from NGOs, governments, overseas companies and local people.

Issues of tourism and hospitality sustainability

The foundations of sustainable development were set by the United Nations World Commission on Environment and Development (WCED) who formulated the Brundtland Report 'Our Common Future' in 1987. The World Tourism Organization (UNWTO) defines sustainability in the context of tourism as a set of principles referring 'to environmental, economic and sociocultural aspects of tourism development, and a suitable balance [which] must be established between these three dimensions to guarantee long-term sustainability' (UNWTO, 2006). Inspired by the above, the authors of this book define sustainable hospitality as a set of business strategies that meet the needs of today's guests, stakeholders and hospitality operations without compromising the ability of future generations of guests, stakeholders and hospitality operations to enjoy and benefit from the same services, products and experiences. This definition embodies the first principle of sustainability, that of intergenerational equity. Emanating from the current body of knowledge on sustainable tourism and hospitality several other principles emerge.

Efficiency and resource maintenance

Hotel construction and operations have extensive direct and indirect impacts on the environment. Hotels and tourism operations use resources such as energy, water and raw materials, generate waste, and emit potentially harmful atmospheric emissions. Sustainable design seeks to minimize these impacts and lower the carbon footprint of goods and services.

Internalization of external environmental costs and the polluter pays

Both short- and long-term environmental costs, regarded as externalities, resulting from the social, cultural and environmental repercussions of tourism, should be included in the sales price of hospitality and tourism goods and services. The polluter pays principle should be adopted (i.e. those who generate pollution and waste should bear the cost of containment, avoidance or abatement).

Precaution

The precautionary principle states that if an action or policy has a suspected risk of causing harm to guests, the public at large or to the environment, in the absence of a scientific consensus that the action or policy is harmful, the burden of proof that it is not harmful falls on those taking the action. As there is much discussion as to the dangers to health of substances such as volatile organic compounds (VOC) and genetically modified foodstuffs (GM), the sustainably-minded hotelier would do well to question the use of such items.

Protection of biodiversity and animal welfare

Hospitality and tourism professionals must make every effort to protect biodiversity, either through the choice of wood for furnishings that do not cause depletion of the world's remaining primeval forests or by encouraging guests to choose dishes low in animal protein that require the destruction of vast tracts of land to produce the cereals and soya on which these animals are fed. Sustainability is not about raising cattle in feedlots, pigs in farrowing pens, or chickens in battery farms.

Shared Value

Creating Shared Value is based on the idea that corporate success and social welfare are interdependent. A business needs a healthy educated workforce, sustainable resources and adept management to compete effectively. Shared Value encourages each hospitality and tourism company to create economic and social value simultaneously by focusing on the social issues that each is uniquely capable of addressing.

As major users of the natural environment, the tourism and hospitality industries should embrace sustainable business development. Unfortunately, this is not always the case and natural resources are still squandered in an unsustainable way. For tourism to contribute towards sustainable development in poor countries the three dimensions of sustainability should be applied simultaneously. Long-term economic sustainability can only be achieved if the environment is protected. In order to achieve societal sustainability, the local population must form an integral part of the tourism development process in the fabric of local economies. Although a financial profit is essential to the futurity of tourism and hospitality operations it should in no way endanger the fine balances that exist in local communities and that could, if overturned, lead to social deprivation and in some cases to even greater poverty.

While embarking on the path to sustainable economic profit and attracting the necessary investment, the industry must not deplete or destroy the resource base on which it depends. This process involves caring for both natural and built environments in a way that will ensure their continuing viability and long-term well-being (Goelnder and Richie, 2009).

Hospitality impacts, solutions and developments

The hospitality industry is diverse in its content and form, ranging from properties owned and operated by local people to global chains. Hospitality companies can adapt themselves towards local traditions and culture or conversely disrupt

Local fishermen at work, part of the hospitality food supply chain (*Photo*: Martin Simons)

traditional living activities in a community; hotels and resorts may equitably and tangibly enhance the living conditions of local communities or create greater gaps in purchasing power by price inflation in and around tourist destinations. The industry can have significant socio-cultural, economic and environmental impacts. One of the most visual and positive impacts of the hospitality industry is financial profit.

The hospitality industry is a highly labour intensive industry that can contribute directly to local economies by employing local inhabitants, who in turn will inject money into institutions and services which are part of the local infrastructure. The development of tourism and hospitality services provides a growing source of opportunities for enterprise development and employment creation as well as stimulating investment and supporting local services, even in quite remote communities. The industry not only creates jobs in the tertiary sector, it also encourages growth in the primary and secondary sectors of industry. This is known as the multiplier effect which in its simplest form is how many times the money spent by a tourist circulates through a country's or a region's economy. In developing economies this effect can be hugely beneficial to local communities. Money spent at a hospitality destination helps to create jobs directly at source and indirectly elsewhere in the economy. The hotel, for example, has to buy food and fish from local farmers and fishermen, who may spend some of this money on fertilizer or clothes. The demand for local products also increases as tourists often buy souvenirs, which increases secondary employment.

The hospitality industry contributes revenues to government in terms of taxes and other fees such as overnight stay taxes and licence fees. These contributions provide governments and local authorities with the funds needed to manage resources, environmental conservation programmes and restoration activities. Local people as well as tourists benefit from improved transportation facilities and improved amenities. Medical care develops and as communities grow around touristic development local people experience improvements to their education and welfare. Within the larger scale of tourism, a proportion of revenues earned by cultural sites and natural parks can be re-injected into the rehabilitation of old buildings and subsequently turned into hospitality facilities. Large structures can be converted into hotels, museums and conference centres while smaller houses, cellars and warehouses can be used as guesthouses, bed-and-breakfast facilities and bars and restaurants. Former industrial sites (mills and factories, for example) and historic buildings can also serve as visitor attractions in their own right or be converted into hospitality facilities. The development of hospitality is largely responsible for the introduction of administrative and planning controls to ensure that environmental quality is maintained and visitors have a satisfactory experience. Improved environmental management, planning and control, based on analysis of the environmental resources of the area, of hospitality facilities can increase the benefits to natural areas. Examples of such controls include building restrictions and permits, mandatory environment-related criteria for infrastructure development, and the zoning of natural areas to provide extra protection for fragile ecosystems.

Hospitality facilities located in natural areas have the potential to increase the public appreciation of the environment and to spread awareness of environmental problems when it brings people into closer contact with nature and the environment. This confrontation may heighten awareness of the value of nature and lead to environmentally conscious behaviour and activities to preserve the environment. Hospitality facilities located in urban areas also have the potential to create a positive public image through an active community involvement from supporting local charities, sponsoring sporting events and purchasing directly at local markets.

Hospitality businesses, suppliers and guests consume an enormous quantity of goods and services; changing buying habits and encouraging them towards consuming those that are produced and distributed in a sustainable way, from cradle to grave, can have a huge positive impact on the environment at large.

But the tourism industry is not without risks. It can be an unstable source of income because of natural catastrophes and political turmoil that will discourage tourists from visiting exotic destinations. Also, worldwide GDP growth influences the propensity of people to travel and to spend money on tourism activities. Such activities may lead to inflation, since tourists are able and willing to pay more than local populations for goods and services and thus consumer prices will increase. Leakages will also occur, because tour operators and hotel chains are mainly foreign owned and managed. Goods and services are often sourced abroad due to a lack of required quality and quantity from local suppliers. Workers are also often brought in to operate hospitality and tourism installations where local people are not perceived to have adequate skills. In terms of local development, the multiplier effect is small and sometimes contributes little or nothing.

All of this can put pressure on fragile ecosystems and on host communities and lead to the dislocation of traditional societies and a rise in alienation among the local population. Social problems like increasing crime and corruption can occur because of increasing socio-economic inequality. Due to the ever increasing scarcity of natural resources and worsening global atmospheric pollution conflicts now well up on a permanent basis. However, a thoughtful location of properties can often result in a substantial reduction in fossil fuels consumed while journeying to and from properties, not to mention greenhouse gas emissions and air borne pollutants caused by road transport. Needless to say that the hospitality industry cannot be held responsible for all environmental impacts but responsible hospitality management will be concerned with educating customers on how to reduce their carbon footprints and providing eco-friendly transport options. Responsible hospitality managers are advised to think carefully about providing grouped transport facilities to and from airports and providing bicycles for guests once they are at their destination.

While the levels of environmental pollution produced in-situ by the hospitality industry can in no way be compared to heavy industry, it must be remembered that hotels and restaurants consume considerable amounts of non-renewable natural resources and discharge large amounts of solid, liquid and air-borne waste. Hotels are generally considered to be major energy end users and are involved in activities that have adverse environmental effects. Through their intensive direct consumption of fossil fuels for heating systems and indirectly in the form of electricity, they are responsible for high emissions of toxic chemicals such as sulphur dioxide and nitrogen oxide that have environmental implications such as acid rain and global warming. Due to its sheer size the tourism industry places a direct pressure on fragile ecosystems, causing degradation to the physical environment and harm to wildlife. The hospitality industry also disrupts and exerts considerable pressure on host communities that can lead to a dislocation of traditional societies. The introduction of luxury hotels may result in competition for the use of scarce resources, notably land and water, for which the local inhabitants are often the losers.

Tourism academics (Butler, 1980) have suggested that destinations go through a cycle of evolution: exploration, followed by progression, development and consolidation, leading to stagnation, and eventually, either rejuvenation or decline. Environmental and socio-cultural impacts will begin to occur right at the very beginning during the exploration stage, and if no planning and control measures are put in place, these will increase during evolvement and development. The full consequences becoming apparent during the consolidation stage. Environmental degradation and societal tensions are key factors in a destination's stagnation and eventual decline. The preservation of environmental and social stability is a key resource, critical for tourism and the hospitality industry which are disrupted in the decline stage. All over the world, from coastlines in Asia, the Caribbean and the Mediterranean to national parks in Africa, and to mountain resorts in North America and Europe, environmental degradation is caused by tourism and continues to cause business losses. Few would want to go to a beach where the water is polluted, or visit a countryside lined with ribbon developments or walk in parks littered with packaging and disposable waste. As visitor numbers fall, so do prices, then profits. Prices are slashed as hospitality owners and managers struggle to stay in business. Financial liquidity becomes a problem leading to little or no maintenance, repair, or waste management, and prevailing negative impacts are worsened. Shabby facilities and poor service further reduce quality and demand continues to drop; this vicious cycle is the decline stage. The development of the hospitality industry is one of the main components linked to the life-cycle of a destination and also one which accounts for the greatest impacts, positive or negative. Sustainable hospitality is one of the ingredients within a destination that can ensure that the stagnation period is reduced to a minimum, that impacts are identified, measured and managed, and that the destination passes from consolidation to continuous rejuvenation.

Recommendations for sustainability

The net result here is that all those involved in the tourism and hospitality industries, from development to operations, will have a responsibility to recognize the importance of sustainable development. In addition, those directly involved in the hospitality industry, whether as developers, owners and managers, or all other stakeholders, must equally assume their role in full towards hospitality's sustainable development.

Business and tourism development policies that address economic, social and environmental issues should be developed with an awareness of the potential these can have both for harm and for benefit. Governments and corporations need to channel the energy that results from a sector's dynamic growth in a positive direction. For the hospitality industry, accepting this responsibility is not only good citizenship it can also be seen as self interest in the viability of hospitality and tourism enterprises and activities in the long term. In summary, sustainable hospitality should consider three distinct but interrelated dimensions.

1   Make optimal use of environmental resources that constitute a key element in tourism and hospitality development, maintaining essential ecological processes while helping to conserve natural heritage and biodiversity.
2   Respect the socio-cultural authenticity of host communities, conserve the built and living cultural heritage and traditional values, and contribute to inter-cultural understanding and tolerance.
3   Ensure viable, long-term economic operations, providing socio-economic benefits to all stakeholders that are fairly distributed, including stable employment, income-earning opportunities and social services to host communities that contribute to poverty alleviation (UNWTO, 2004).

If the hospitality industry is to continue to expand and be profitable, it must develop and operate within these three dimensions.

Notes

1 The following theories are described by Thiel (1999).
2 The Purchasing Power Parity (PPP) concept considers exchange rates and price levels in different countries in order to measure the real purchasing power for the consumers. How many kilos of rice can be bought with one USD in the United States, Tanzania or Vietnam?

References

Butler, R.W. (1980). The Concept of Tourism Area Cycle of Evolution: Implications for Management of Resources. *Canadian Geographer, 24 (1)*, 5–12.

Chabal, P., & Daloz, J.P. (1999). *Africa Works: Disorder as Political Instrument*. Oxford: James Currey.

Crane, A., & Matten, D. (2007). *Business Ethics* (2nd ed.). Oxford: Oxford University Press

Georgescu-Roegen, N. (1971). *The Entropy Law and the Economic Process*. Cambridge: Harvard University Press.

Goelnder, C.R., & Richie, J.R. (2009). *Tourism: Principles, Practices, Philosophies* (11th edn). New Jersey: Wiley.

Meadows, D., Randers, J. & Behrens, W. (1972). *The Limits to Growth*. Retrieved March 10, 2010, from http://www.clubofrome.org/docs/limits.rtf

North, D.C. et al. (2009). *Violence and Social Orders*. Cambridge

Pigou, A.C. (1932). *The Economics of Welfare* (4th edn). London: Macmillan.

Shirley, M. (2008). *Institutions and Development*. Cheltenham: Edward Elgar.

Sloan, P., Legrand, W. & Chen, J. (2009). *Sustainability in the Hospitality Industry: Principles of Sustainable Operations*. Burlington: Elsevier.

Thiel, R.E. (1999). Zur Neubewertung der Entwicklungstheorie. In Thiel R.E. (ed.), *Neue Ansätze zur Entwicklungstheorie* (pp. 9–34). Bonn: DSE/IZEP.

Todaro, M. (1999). *Economic Development* (7th edn). London: Longman.

Transparency International (ongoing). Corruption Perception Index. Retrieved March 10, 2010, from http://www.doingbusiness.org/

United Nations. (n.d.). 2015 Millenium Goals. Retrieved July 16, 2010, from http://www.un.org/millenniumgoals/

United Nations World Commission on Environment and Development (1987). *Our Common Future: Report of the World Commission on Environment and Development*. Retrieved July 6, 2010, from http://www.worldinbalance.net/agreements/1987-brundtland.html

United Nations Development Report (ongoing). *Human Development Report*. Retrieved July 7, 2010, from http://hdr.undp.org/en/

UNWTO (2004). *Sustainable Development of Tourism: Conceptual Definition*. Retrieved July 7, 2010, from http://www.world-tourism.org/frameset/frame_sustainable.html

UNWTO (2006). *Sustainable Development of Tourism*. Retrieved July 7, 2010, from http://www.unwto.org/std/mission/en/mission.php

Weber, M. (1947). *The Theory of Social and Economic Organization*. New York: Free Press.

World Bank (2002). *World Development Report 2002: Building Institutions for Markets*. Washington, DC: World Bank.

World Bank (ongoing). *World Development Indicators*. Retrieved July 7, 2010, from http://data.worldbank.org/

World Bank Group (ongoing). *Doing Business: Measuring Business Regulations*. Retrieved July 6, 2010, from http://www.doingbusiness.org/

2 The case of Inkaterra

Pioneering ecotourism in Peru

Ulf Richter[*] and
Sigbjorn Tveteras[**]

Introduction

Ecotourism is a growth industry around the world. As an industry it offers tremendous opportunities for developing countries due to (i) low capital requirements, (ii) an increasing global awareness for the need to preserve our planet, and in many cases (iii) access to pristine nature. Inkaterra, based in Lima, Peru, offers ecotourism targeting wealthy tourists. It is a high-profile tourist operator in Peru that has received wide coverage in the popular press around the world (Chan, 2008; O'Riordain, 2010; *The Economist*, 2008; *The Guardian*, 2010). Each year it receives around 46,000 hotel guests and has served more than 900,000 travellers since its foundation. In 2009, the company had a turnover of around 10 million USD and over 500 employees.

Jose Koechlin founded Inkaterra in 1975 to combine the conservation of the rainforest with a sustainable business model. Koechlin's interest in conservation of the Amazonian rainforest grew from his participation in Werner Herzog's movie production *Aguirre – The Wrath of God* (1972) and later *Fitzcarraldo* (1982), both set in the Peruvian rainforest. Inkaterra started its operations in 1978 with 15 handmade cabins in the Peruvian Amazon rainforest, next to an area that later became the Tambopata National Reserve. Today, Inkaterra has turned into a large tourism complex, Inkaterra Reserva Amazonica (see Figure 2.1). In addition to its operations in the Amazonian rainforest, Inkaterra operates two other luxury hotels in Peru: the Inkaterra Machu Picchu Pueblo Hotel in the village below the Inca citadel, and Inkaterra La Casona in Cusco, the Andean capital of the Inca.

All its hotels are unique in the way they are designed and built. The rainforest operation consists of 35 luxury-style eco-friendly cabins and a canopy tree house; the Inkaterra Machu Picchu Pueblo Hotel is made up of 85 small stone and on-site handmade cement brick houses built in nouveau Andean style; and la Casona consists of 11 suites in a luxury boutique hotel (Relais & Chateau) in a restored Spanish colonial building. With its three hotels in Cusco, Machu Picchu

[*]CENTRUM Católica Pontifica Universidad Católica del Perú, urichter@pucp.edu.pe
[**]CENTRUM Católica Pontifica Universidad Católica del Perú, stveteras@pucp.edu.pe

Figure 2.1 The main building of the Inkaterra Reserva Amazonica (photo by author)

Pueblo and in the Amazonian rainforest, Inkaterra can offer its guests some of the major iconic attractions that mark Peru as a tourist destination.

In this article, we analyze the case of Inkaterra and its business model with a focus on strategies and challenges that had to be overcome. The research question we address is this: how did Inkaterra pioneer a business model for ecotourism in the Peruvian rainforest, facing a lack of human capital, an institutional void, bad national conditions, and competition from other industries?

The chapter is structured as follows. First, we provide a brief overview of the tourist industry in Peru, emphasizing the current travel and tourism boom and the underlying success factors. Second, we introduce Inkaterra, outlining the managerial, economic and cultural challenges it had to overcome to develop its model for sustainable tourism in Peru. Third, we clarify strategies and the social environmental and economic impact of its operations in Peru, mainly in the Amazon region. We then conclude with a critical overview of the future of the model of ecotourism developed by Inkaterra and its wider applicability, emphasizing the lessons learned and future threats and opportunities.

The Setting: The Tourism Industry in Peru

Tourism in Peru has experienced firm economic growth in the last two decades. From 1990 to 2000 the number of international tourist arrivals rose from 317,000 to 800,000, with an annual growth rate of 10.3%. After the turn of the century arrivals continued to increase, reaching 2.14 million in 2009 (UNWTO, 2001).

In 2009, the travel and tourism industry accounted for 361,000 jobs and 2.8% of the GDP, or 887,000 jobs and 6.8% of the GDP if investments in the tourism infrastructure are included (WTTC, 2009). While still modest compared to other Latin American countries like Brazil or Mexico, which in 2008 received 5.1 and 22.6 million arrivals respectively, the industry is projected to grow 4.3% annually from 2009 to 2018.

International visitors to Peru can be distinguished into Latin Americans or long-haul travellers. Most tourists from North America and Europe visit Peru to enjoy its nature, wildlife and the diversity of cultures (PromPerú, 2006). They are likely to have high income levels and to visit only once due to the remote location from the perspective of North Americans and Europeans (McKercher, Chan, & Lam, 2008). They also tend to stay longer and spend more money than those from South America (PromPerú, 2008). They usually opt for reasonably priced accommodation such as hotels in the range of one to three stars.

There are several explanations for the rapid growth of the Peruvian tourism industry. Firstly, the country is blessed with a huge endowment of natural and cultural resources. Peru is characterized by a rich historical heritage and a cultural diversity that can be experienced by visiting its many archeological sites, among them the famous UNESCO heritage site Machu Picchu, as well as festivals and traditional events. According to Mittermeier et al. (1997), Peru is one of seven mega diversity countries due to one of the highest biodiversities in the world. One can find 84 out of the 104 life zones of the world (using the Holdridge Scale) which are characterized by specific plants and animals. Peru has a number of protected areas covering coast, mountains and the rainforest. This is particularly important for the growing trend towards ecotourism which requires relatively intact natural areas, as these are central to the tourist experience (Christ, Hillel, Matus, & Sweeting, 2003). There are also several other ecotourism lodges in the Tambopata area including the Explorer's Inn, Corto Maltez, the Tambopata Jungle Lodge, the Tambo Lodge, the Sachavaca Inn, the Wasai Lodge, the Sandoval Lake Lodge, the Tambopata Research Center, Iñapari, Danny's Mirador, Loero Lodge, the Ecoamazonía Lodge, Posada Amazonas, Inotawa and Jungle Odyssey (Kirby, 2002). They are in a range of 30 minutes to several hours of ground transportation from Puerto Maldonado and offer diverse activities like guided walks in the rainforest, bird watching, and visits to local farms and communities.

Secondly, the end of the political turmoil and social unrest that was caused by the military revolution (1969) and the rise of the Maoist Shining Path movement in the early 1990s allowed for a rapid expansion of the tourism industry. Economic growth and political stability in Peru have allowed for improvements in the transportation networks and the tourism infrastructure, including a serious facelift of the historic downtown of the capital Lima.

Third, international marketing efforts made by Prom Peru, the national investment promotion agency, have been successful in attracting new visitors to Peru. For instance, PromPeru has started to promote new tourist destinations besides the traditional candidates such as Cusco and Arequipa. Moreover, to boost tourism the Peruvian government has issued the *Plan Estratégico Nacional de Turismo* (PENTUR), initiated by the Ministerio de Comercio Exterior y Turismo in 2004 (MINCETUR, 2008). The objectives include 1) promoting an affinity for tourism and increase security for the visitors, 2) developing a competitive and sustainable supply of tourist products, 3) promoting a sustainable demand, and 4) strengthening the institutions related to the tourism economy.

Finally, Peru has managed to become the 'gastronomical capital' of South America, fusing different gastronomical traditions into a variety of classical and new dishes (Mapstone, 2009). Today, the Peruvian cuisine has become a reason to visit the country and has also started to export it around the world.

Despite these developments, there is still a lack of investment in the tourism infrastructure according to the *Travel & Tourism Competitiveness Report 2009* (World Economic Forum, 2009). Potential investors in tourism encounter weak property rights,a lack of transparency in government policy making, long timescales to start a business, and high startup costs for new businesses.

Methodology

This chapter is based on a larger case study research project that was initiated in February 2010 with Inkaterra's founder and CEO Jose Koechlin. In April 2010, we did an initial round of interviews in Spanish with the top-level executives of Inkaterra to explore common research interests and the potential for collaborating on a joint research project. Based on our first analysis, we prepared an interview guide with open-ended questions, focusing on strategies, stakeholder interaction and Inkaterra's institutional environment. Two weeks later, we conducted a two-hour focus group with the top-level executives of Inkaterra. The interviewees received a consent form and a copy of the interview guide in advance. The focus group was audio-taped and transcribed. The authors are currently in the process of coding and analyzing the data.

Preliminary Findings

Challenges

Over time, Inkaterra encountered six main challenges: (i) a lack of markets, (ii) a lack of human capital combined with legal restrictions, (iii) cooperation with indigenous communities in the Amazon region, (iv) competing industries, (v) an institutional void, and (vi) the socio-political environment. All of these are detailed below.

- *A lack of markets*: When Inkaterra started in the 1970s, the Peruvian south rainforest was an isolated destination with little infrastructure and no tourism. Only Iquitos in the Peruvian Amazonian rainforest was occasionally visited by tourists. Inkaterra had to create a market for its offerings and build the necessary infrastructure for it, including arranging for flights to its destinations.

A scant reputation, modest marketing budgets and large distances to the principal markets in North America and Europe initially made it a challenging task to find the tourists willing to travel to the Peruvian rainforest. It also faced a lack of goods and services in the forest to operate with.

- *The lack of human capital and legal restrictions:* The Amazonian rainforest is scarcely populated. In the 1970s, the indigenous population of Madre de Dios was estimated to be around 8,000 in an area whose size corresponds to over the surface of Costa Rica. Inkaterra operates in a demanding market segment. Few local people have received any formal training or education to prepare them for the needs of Inkaterra that are characterized by discipline, routines and structure. Moreover, according to Peruvian law, official guides have to have received a formal, five year university education. Therefore, Inkaterra could not legally employ indigenous people as guides despite their expert knowledge of the local plants and wildlife.

- *Cooperation with indigenous communities*: Problems encountered included different understandings of concepts, a lack of exposure to modern technologies, and communication failures. The cultural difference between a tourism operator like Inkaterra and indigenous groups was due to the latter group's lack of exposure to the modern society. Thus, many indigenous people initially lacked an understanding of concepts that were important for the operations of Inkaterra, such as the importance of good sanitary conditions, the meaning of democracy, the respect of property rights, and their obligations.

- *Competition from other industries:* Ecotourism operators in the Amazon rainforest face competition from the extractive industry involved in logging and mining. Many of these extractive businesses are small-scale activities involving local people and immigrants to the region. They rely on the same resources as the ecotourism industry, but for very different purposes. The construction of a new paved highway stretching coast to coast from Brazil to Peru has intensified the competition for these resources, as it provides easier access to the rainforest (*The Economist*, 2008). The Peruvian Minister of Environment stated that the informal extraction of gold is turning the rainforest in Madre de Dios into a desert (El Comercio, 2009). This is a real concern also to Inkaterra as the illegal gold mining activity is moving closer to its ecological reserve in Tambopata.

- *An institutional void:* When Inkaterra started its operations there was only a weakly defined regulatory framework to support their activities in ecotourism. Early on, Inkaterra was granted a 10,000 hectares reserve for tourism and research. However, in the late 1980s it lost its natural reserve. Authorities deemed the reserve a legal anomaly since prior to 1994 there were no legal structures for giving land titles. Due to the lack of legal protection, local people spotted an economic opportunity and land encroachment became a problem (Yu, Hendrickson and Castillo, 1997). Many areas in the Amazon rainforest (like the Tambopata National Reserve) that are today well known for their rich biodiversity were not protected. The lack of functioning local institutions of public governance combined with an underdeveloped public policy represented a huge threat to Inkaterra's long-term investment in the region.

- *The socio-political environment*: throughout the second half of the twentieth century, Peru had been characterized by difficult political, economic, and social conditions. The military coup and dictatorship from 1968 to 1975 was a left-leaning revolution that led to expropriation and nationalization of industries. After military rule during the 1970s, and two unsuccessful presidencies of Belaunde and Garcia during the 1980s, the economy collapsed in and experienced a period of hyperinflation in 1988. During the same decade the Maoist guerrilla organization Shining Path emerged, resulting in an escalating violence that eventually reached the capital, Lima. In the 1990s, a centralized Fujimori government opted for shock therapy for the economy through liberalization and privatization and reduced the terrorist activities of Shining Path through a merciless military campaign.

Strategies

Inkaterra has managed to pioneer the field of sustainable tourism in the Peruvian part of the Amazon region over the last 35 years by developing a comprehensive concept that included indigenous communities into their operations. It has focused on (i) creating a new tourism destination in South Eastern Amazonian Peru, (ii) engaging and capacitating local communities, (iii) building a knowledge base on the biodiversity of the region in collaboration with the scientific community, (iv) creating an institutional environment that was favourable to ecotourism and disfavouring competing industries such as logging and mining.

- *Market creation*: In the 1970s, there was no local market for ecotourism in Peru. As a consequence, Inkaterra never targeted the domestic market and decided to bring in groups from Europe. This strategy was used by tourist developers in Spain and Portugal at the time that brought in tour operators from principal markets such as Germany to evaluate the viability of developing new tourist destinations. The first tourists from France and Germany went to the Manu area, which at that time was very difficult to reach by ground transportation, and Puerto Maldonado. In those days, Puerto Maldonado was a settlement of around 2,000 inhabitants and could be reached by DC3, DC4 and DC6 propeller aircrafts that landed on a dirt runway. Today, Puerto Maldonado has 90,000 inhabitants and a national airport with four daily flights. Today, 95% to 98% of Inkaterra guests are international travellers.
- *Capacity building*: Inkaterra focuses its capacity building projects on its personnel and local communities. Training its own personnel covers 35 areas which represent virtually all aspects of its operations (e.g. ecotourism, housekeeping, logistics, English language). Training is a necessity since local people receive little training or formal education and it is difficult to attract well-trained staff from Lima. Inkaterra also provides fringe benefits above the Peruvian average to its employees, such as accommodation, food,

round-trip air fares for those not from the area, accident insurance, recreational activities, interest free loans, and legal benefits. However, Inkaterra Reserva Amazonica mainly recruits from the urban areas in the Amazon basin like Puerto Maldonado, which are dominated by immigrants from the Pacific coast and the Andean mountains, or directly from cities that offer a university education, such as Cusco, and Machu Picchu's surrounding mountain areas for the Inkaterra Machu Picchu Pueblo Hotel.

- *Local engagement:* Direct employment benefits relatively few local families. As a result, to distribute the economic gains of ecotourism other channels must be used (Yu, Hendrickson and Castillo, 1997). Inkaterra engages with local communities through different cooperative projects, campaigns and workshops. It provides educational support, engages in health campaigns, organizes workshops in agro-forestry, beekeeping, fish farming, and the raising of wild animals, and engages in raising awareness of biodiversity and archeology. Good community relationships are perceived as crucial for the long-term viability of Inkaterra's hotels and for promoting ecological tourism in the Amazon region as against mining and lumbering.

- *Conservation:* As part of its agenda to provide authentic nature travel, Inkaterra has an explicit commitment to conservation. To fulfil this commitment Inkaterra works along three lines: 1) research on biodiversity; 2) a contribution to the development of legal frameworks relevant for conservation, such as the management of natural reserves; and 3) conservation of Inkaterra's natural reserves, the restoration of vegetation and running a rescue centre for spectacled bears (*Tremarctos ornatus*). Inkaterra today has 17,000 hectares of rainforest in the Amazon basin in Southeast Peru, including the Reserva Ecológica Inkaterra, five hectares of cloud forest in the urban area of the Machu Picchu Historical Sanctuary, twelve hectares in the Urubamba Valley, and 2,500 square metres in Cusco city. In its properties, at Inkaterra Machu Picchu Pueblo Hotel, researchers have documented 111 butterfly species, 192 bird species (including 18 hummingbird species), and 372 orchid species. In Inkaterra Reserva Amazonica researchers have described 67 amphibian species, 300 butterfly species, 419 bird species, 442 arachnid species, and 362 ant species, always with the help of local experts from the indigenous community. Inkaterra's conservation projects also contribute to the global fight against climate change. The conservation of 17,000 hectares of protected rainforest, the Reserva Ecológica Inkaterra, accounts for the storage of 3,400,000 metric tons of CO_2 emissions since 1989. Moreover, Inkaterra is working on sustainable Marlin catch and release fisheries on 38 hectares at Ernest Hemingway's legendary home Cabo Blanco in northern coastal Peru. Marine conservation is planned for the near future.

Inkaterra has also stated a dedication to preserving native cultures and has had a good relationship with the native Ese'eja-Sonene since starting up in the Tambopata area in 1975. Inkaterra tries to maintain their traditions and their guests are offered the opportunity to visit their communities and learn about the natives' way of life. The Ese'eja-Sonene have worked exclusively in activities related to food harvesting, hunting and fishing activities for their livelihood. Over time the growth of the neighbouring Puerto Maldonado has greatly influenced their customs, to the point that future generations will study and work in this city, mixing their traditional lifestyles with mining, logging and office work with traditional activities that identify them as ethnic.

- *Collaboration with the scientific community*: Inkaterra created an inventory of the Amazonian 'natural capital' represented by its flora, fauna and ecosystems in order to better understand its environment. It invited fully paid researchers from the University of Berkeley to discover the large biodiversity through a rapid assessment of the area. Inkaterra has continued its strategy of inviting researchers and maintaining collaborations with a number of universities and institutions up to the present day, amongst others the Missouri Botanical Garden, the University of Berkeley, University of Kansas, University of Leeds, California Academy of Sciences, Munich, Switzerland, the American Orchid Society and Great Britain's Orchid Society. Inkaterra has also financed and supervized research for three scientific publications on the natural riches of the Amazon rainforest and the cloud forest in the Andes. At Inkaterra properties species new to science have been discovered, of which 15 species have already been described. The careful documentation of its work on conservation that sets Inkaterra apart from many of its competitors has helped it gain credibility within the scientific community. In Inkaterra's view, the ongoing research work is indispensable for its conservation mission.
- *Nonprofit arm*: Originally a sole for profit venture, Inkaterra added a formal nonprofit organization in 2001, the Inkaterra Association. This is consistent with Inkaterra's philosophy: during its history, it has never distributed profits to its shareholders. It was formally separated for accounting purposes to comply with an IFC loan which required the hotel to follow the Hotel Uniform System of Accounts. The association has received a loan and grant from the United Nations Global Environment Facility, via the World Bank, and also grants from the National Geographic Society, resulting in the expansion of facilities and infrastructure (see Figure 2.2).
- *Institutional entrepreneurship*: Scholars generally perceive weak institutional frameworks as the biggest threat to conservation (Barrett, Brandon, Gibson, & Gjertsen, 2001). Reacting to the situation encountered in the Amazon region, Inkaterra developed legal proposals for the private sector to reserve areas for conservation and ecotourism and thereby created a new legal conservation instrument. At that time, it was allowed by the government to operate the Cusco Amazonico reserve while coordinating with the Agricultural Minister. This was the first time this had happened in Peru. However, the institution in charge, INRENA, considered this a legal anomaly that should not be repeated and eventually took it back in order to avoid creating an original precedent. After 16 years of lengthy negotiations, the

Figure 2.2 Grants financed the canopy walkway together with a tree house (Photo by author)

'Inkaterra Ecological Reserve' in Inkaterra Reserva Amazonica was created in 2004.

Discussion

Inkaterra's business model resembles the symbiotic relationship between hollow trees and fire ants in the Amazonian rainforest. The tree provides shelter and in return receives the ants' protection against competing plants and animals. A similar symbiotic relationship exists between the business and conservation side of Inkaterra. The business generates the financial resources to support the research-driven conservation work, which in return provides Inkaterra with international recognition and new knowledge about nature and the local conditions. Inkaterra then translates this knowledge into engaging educational tourism products. Its commitment to conservation sets it apart not only from conventional hotel operators, but also from many of its peers in ecotourism. It has developed three key competitive advantages (knowledge, uniqueness and authenticity) and is hungry to grow and to be replicated.

- *Knowledge:* Inkaterra's model of ecotourism is highly knowledge driven. Its focus on conservation and preservation and its close relationship with the scientific community have been instrumental in developing the model of sustainable tourism. Initially, Inkaterra's approach to conservation ran up against common thinking in the 1960s and 1970s. At the time, many thought that nature should be isolated from human activity. Jose Koechlin, however, was convinced that nature had a social function: a way of interacting with man to improve the quality of life while, at the same time, nature in itself should be kept intact. This philosophy permeates Inkaterra's explanation of geotourism on its webpage: 'And while geotourism is incompatible with loss of natural or cultural diversity, it does not seek to stop the clock and preserve a destination in amber. What it does seek to preserve is geographical diversity, the distinctiveness of a locale. Destinations that offer nothing but look-alike international franchises lose their distinctiveness and appeal. They end up at the mercy of package-resort mass tourism that seeks only the cheapest price' (Inkaterra, 2010).

- *Uniqueness:* The knowledge-intensive model of Inkaterra is difficult to imitate. Ecotourism is a blurry concept. Both time and resources are required to obtain knowledge of local fauna and flora, local culture and social conditions. The generation of this knowledge is not only based on collaborations with the scientific community but also on a close cooperation with local communities. Inkaterra's unique locations have facilitated partnership development and fundraising for research and conservation. It has only one direct competitor, Rainforest Expeditions, that can rival its deep knowledge of the Peruvian Amazonian rainforest and capacity for minimizing the ecological footprint of expensive tourism.

- *Authenticity:* Inkaterra stresses the 'authenticity' of its tourist product, referring to local origin and high quality. This includes references to its locally-trained hotel personnel and tour guides, the food served, the style and construction of its hotels, wildlife, food, arts, landscaping, furniture, in-room amenities, decor, materials, music and local culture (see Figure 2.3). Inkaterra's focus on authenticity in its eco-friendly luxury hotels in order to offer high-quality services and products in underdeveloped regions requires a long-term horizon and a training programme for the local hotel staff and tourist guides that covers all aspect of its operations.

- *Remaining challenges:* Scaling up will be a challenge for two reasons: (i) with an estimated annual turnover of 10 million USD, Inkaterra is small compared to tourism giants from developed countries such as TUI from Germany or US hotel chains such as Marriot or Hilton. These companies could move into the ecotourism niche with massive capital investments mainstreaming the industry; and (ii) it will be difficult to stay true to their conservation strategy while growing the business at an accelerated pace.

- *Future growth strategy:* Growing the market base to match an expanding hotel capacity remains a challenge today. In May 2010, Inkaterra opened a new hotel in the Machu Picchu village, El MaPi (48 rooms), targeting the upper middle-class segment. In late 2010 Inkaterra was planning to open the Hacienda Concepcion Lodge (15 rooms) in the buffer zone of the Tambopata

Figure 2.3 Furniture inside the main building of the Inkaterra Reserva Amazonica based
on local materials and crafts (Photo by author)

National Reserve. Inkaterra believes that the market for its model of luxury
tourism in the Machu Picchu area and the Amazonian jungle is saturated
for the time being; higher returns are perceived to come from tapping into
new market segments. In late 2011, Inkaterra had also planned to open the
Hacienda Urubamba in The Sacred Valley of the Inca, in the Cusco region;
all of these should start a circuit for this new segment under the brand 'by
Inkaterra', which will be augmented by Cabo Blanco and Cusco. Inkaterra
will also build high-end facilities at Urubamba and Cabo Blanco under its
brand 'Inkaterra', thus having both brands in every location so as to reduce
its unit administration cost. At each one of these locations a third segment
will complement the offering: field research stations, for students and
researchers. Inkaterra eventually aims to export its model to other countries
and consider a franchising or licensing model that allows entrepreneurs to
adopt its brand and the success strategies it has pioneered.

Conclusion

Despite its many challenges, Inkaterra has managed to pioneer the field of
sustainable tourism in the Peruvian part of the Amazon region by developing an
holistic concept to include legal private sector forest management concepts and
indigenous communities in their operations. Furthermore, they have been able to
use luxury tourism as a vehicle to promote ecotourism, which in Inkaterra's case

entails (a) research for the conservation of the biodiversity of the Amazon rain-forest, (b) protecting the rights of indigenous communities, and (c) protecting the rights of investors. Inkaterra's example illustrates the managerial and cultural challenges that need to be overcome for successful ecological tourism to happen in the Amazon region.

References

Barrett, C.B., Brandon, K., Gibson, C. & Gjertsen, H. (2001) 'Conserving tropical biodiversity amid weak institutions'. *Bioscience*, 51(6): 497–502.

Chan, M.J. 2008. *Travel: Incan Adventure*, Newsweek, Washington DC.

Christ, C., Hillel, O., Matus, S. & Sweeting, J. (2003) *Tourism and Biodiversity: Mapping Tourism's Global Footprint*. Washington/Durban: Conservation International.

El Comercio (2009) *Madre de Dios se está convirtiendo en un desierto*, El Comercio. Lima.

Inkaterra. 2010. 'Geotourism'. Accessed June 10, 2010, http://www.inkaterra.com/en/nature/Geoturism

Kirby, C. (2002) Estándares Ecoturísticos para la Reserva Nacional Tambopata, el Parque Nacional Bahuaja Sonene y sus Zonas de Amortiguamiento, Madre de Dios, Perú. WWF – Oficina del Programa de Peru. (http://www.ibcperu.org/doc/isis/5441.pdf)

Mapstone, N. (2009) *Teaching the world to love Peruvian food*, Financial Times, London.

McKercher, B., Chan, A. & Lam, C. (2008) 'The impact of distance on international tourist movements'. *Journal of Travel Research*, 47(2): 208–224.

MINCETUR (2008) PENTUR 2008-2012: Síntesis para la puesta en operación. Lima: Ministerio de Comercio Exterior y Turismo.

MINCETUR (2009) 'Perú: Llegada mensual de turistas internacionales, enero 2002 – diciembre 2009'. Accessed April 29, 2009, http://www.mincetur.gob.pe/newweb/portals/0/turismo/PERU_Lleg_Mens_Tur_inter_2002_2009.pdf

Mittermeier, R. A., Robles-Gil, P. & Mittermeier, C. G. (1997) *Megadiversity: Earth's Biologically Wealthiest Nations*. Monterey: CEMEX/Agrupación Sierra Madre.

O'Riordain, A. (2010) *Leave only your footprints*, The Independent: 5, London.

PromPerú (2006) *Perfil del Turista de Naturaleza*. Lima: PromPerú.

PromPerú (2008) *Perfil del Turista Extranjero 2007*. Lima: PromPerú.

The Economist (2008) *Rumble in the jungle: Ecotourism in Peru*, The Economist: 10 April, London.

The Guardian. (2010) *The Green Travel List*, The Guardian, 58, London.

UNWTO (2001) 'International Tourist Arrivals by Country of Destination'. Accessed April 29, 2009, http://www.photius.com/rankings/tourism_2001.pdf.

World Economic Forum (2009) Peru. In J. Blanke & T. Chiesa (Eds), *The Travel & Tourism Competitiveness Report 2009: Managing in a Time of Turbulence*. Geneva: World Economic Forum.

WTTC (2009) *Travel and Tourism Economic Impact - Peru*. London: World Travel & Tourism Council.

Yu, D. W., Hendrickson, T. & Castillo, A. (1997) *Ecotourism and conservation in the Amazonian Perú: short-term and long-term challenges, Environmental Conservation*, 24(2): 130–138.

Books by Inkaterra:

- *Cusco Amazónico: The Lives of Amphibians and Reptiles in an Amazonian Rainforest* (by William Duellman, Cornell University Press, 2005).
- *Flórula de la Reserva Ecológica Inkaterra* (published by the Missouri Botanical Garden and Inka Terra Asociación, 2006).
- *Orchids at Inkaterra Machu Picchu Pueblo Hotel* (published by Inkaterra, 2007).

3 Integrated circuits as a tool for the development of sustainable tourism in the Amazon

Karola Tippmann and *Donald Sinclair*

Introduction

Ever since the publication of Rachel Carson's *Silent Spring* (1962) awareness has grown world-wide of the threats to the global environment from both natural and man-made sources. Although some schools of thought question the degree to which the earth may be in peril, a torrent of studies and scholarly writing still appears to establish that care for the earth is not a choice but an obligation and that 'green' approaches, as expressed over a wide spectrum of human endeavours from architecture to zoo-keeping, are the best guarantee that life on earth can be sustained well beyond the 21st century. Tourism of course is widely regarded as an important tool that can sustain precious natural resources while conferring economic and other benefits upon the societies or communities involved in the practice of sustainable tourism. This chapter will examine the case of the Amazon and show how a project for the establishment of integrated tourism circuits can be used as a tool for the development of sustainable tourism in that region.

This chapter's authors view sustainable tourism to mean those forms of tourism that seek to protect, preserve and sustain natural and cultural resources even as those resources provide the base for satisfying and fulfilling visitor experiences and are a means for generating economic benefits and enhancing the overall welfare of resident communities. Sustainable tourism in the Amazon must therefore be a mechanism that assists the process of conservation of nature, strengthens the economic position of resident communities, adds value to local cultural traditions and expressions, and enhances the revenue-earning capacities of those countries that must share the Amazon.

*Tourism Consultant, Amazon Cooperation Treaty Organization, Brasilia, Brazil
**Tourism Coordinator, Amazon Cooperation Treaty Organization, Brasilia, Brazil

Case Study Main Section

Methodology

The authors relied upon the following methods for garnering information and data for this chapter:

- Primary sources as constituted by the minutes of meetings and consultations with tourism officials, representatives and stakeholders from the Member Countries of the Treaty for Amazon Cooperation.
- Secondary sources as constituted by articles appearing in journals, books and other scholarly publications.

The primary sources are official documents in the possession of the Permanent Secretariat of the Amazon Cooperation Treaty Organization, located in Brasilia, and represent reports obtained over three years of meetings, stakeholder consultations and workshops held in different countries and facilitated by tourism personnel from the Permanent Secretariat. Secondary sources include both electronic and printed matter that focuses on such principal topics as tourism, sustainable tourism, climate change and development.

The Amazon: location

Although the exact location of the Amazon region (on the continent of South America) is a matter of common knowledge (PNUMA and OTCA, 2009), there is far greater disagreement about both the definition and physical delimitation of the region. Employing strictly physical, basin-based criteria, confining the Amazon to that land-mass that actually forms the basin of the Amazon river, this emerges as a much smaller entity than if one employs ecological, biome-based criteria. There are also political criteria employed in some cases to determine its definition. Even the number of countries that comprise the Amazon region will differ depending upon the criteria employed. The application of strict hydrographic criteria (indicating the countries that actually share the Amazon basin) produces a region comprising eight countries – Bolivia, Brazil, Colombia, Ecuador, Guyana, Peru, Suriname and Venezuela. Using biome-based criteria that group expands to include Suriname and French Guiana. While Suriname is a signatory to the Amazon Cooperation Treaty and a full member of the Amazon Cooperation Treaty Organization, French Guiana is not a signatory to the Treaty of Amazon cooperation.

Tourism appeal of the Amazon

It may be an enduring irony that the Amazon, despite its vast tourism resources, receives far fewer visitors than such resources would lead one to expect. The trend has been for the bulk of visitors to head for the familiar, beaten tracks in the

Dje Mongo Forest Lodge, Suriname
Source: Photo property of Karola Tippmann

non-Amazon coastal or urban centres of those Amazon member countries. The 7 million square kilometres of the Amazon basin contain over 5.5 million square kilometres of forest, an expanse equal to half of the planet's remaining rainforests. The basin is the largest and most species-rich expanse of forest in the world and is of unequalled biodiversity – with 25 million insect species, 2000 birds and mammals, 40,000 plant species, 3000 fish, 378 reptiles and 1294 birds. The region is also rich in cultural diversity being home to a kaleidoscope of dialects, cuisines, forms of dress and worship, music and dance. It is this teeming diversity in the Amazon that is the basis of the special appeal that the region has for visitors wishing to have an authentic experience at the hands of nature.

Role of ACTO

The Amazon Cooperation Treaty Organization (ACTO) is a multi-lateral organization established by treaty with the mission of promoting the integrated and sustainable development of the Amazon. This mandate was enshrined in the Treaty of Amazon Cooperation that was signed by the 8 Member Countries in July 1978. With its Permanent Secretariat in Brasilia, the organization comprises five areas of Coordination – Education, Science and Technology; Environment; Health; Indigenous Affairs; Tourism, Transport, Infrastructure and Communication. The organization works in close collaboration with the Ministries of Foreign Affairs for the eight Member Countries (its first points of contact) and with the subject Ministries for each area of Coordination.

In July 2010 an important Regional Tourism Meeting discussed and proposed a Draft Regional Tourism Agenda 2011-2020 for the approval of the Ministers of Foreign Affairs of Member Countries who will meet in December 2010. This Regional Meeting forms part of the process of the revision of the Strategic Agenda of ACTO that is aimed at elaborating a working agenda for the organization in the short, medium and long term (2011-2020).

The Amazon and sustainable tourism

Sustainable tourism is best understood when viewed within the larger theoretical framework of sustainable development. The ground-breaking moment in terms of the articulation of a formula for sustainable development is widely believed to be the publication of the report of the World Commission on Environment and Development in *Our Common Future*. The definition of sustainable development contained in that report ('Sustainable development is development that meets the needs of the present without compromising the ability of future generations to meet their own needs': WCED, 1987) has since informed much of the thinking and planning in the area of sustainable development. Commenting upon the location of sustainable tourism within a context of sustainable development Chandana Jayawardena remarked that the concept marries together two conflicting ideas, those of development and sustainablilty (Jayawardena, 2002).

The term 'sustainable tourism' now commands enormous popularity in the tourism domain (Cater, 1995; Priestley and Edwards, 1996; Hall and Lew, 1998; Turner and Pearce, 2001; Edgell, 2006). A number of useful definitions do emerge from this fairly voluminous literature on sustainable tourism, but the articulation of the World Tourism Organization is of particular relevance to this article.

> Sustainable tourism development meets the needs of present tourist and host regions while protecting and enhancing opportunities for the future. It is envisaged as leading to management of all resources in such a way that economic, social and aesthetic needs can be fulfilled while maintaining cultural integrity, essential ecological processes, biological diversity and life support systems. (WTO, 1998)

This definition of sustainable tourism is a clear and faithful adaptation of the WCED formulation on sustainable development to the context of tourism. This adaptation, with its reference to 'cultural integrity, essential ecological processes, biological processes and life support systems', is full of resonance for the Amazon region where such issues assume paramount importance.

Key issues

Sustainable tourism in the Amazon of necessity embraces a range of developmental contexts – economic, social, cultural, political and environmental. This holistic application of the concept endows sustainable tourism with the greatest relevance and meaning for the region. The principal issues are the following:

- Legislation
- Land use
- Standards
- Planning
- Mass communication
- Monitoring
- Community tourism.

Legislation – The development and practice of sustainable tourism are unlikely to succeed in the absence of a proper legislative framework that provides the appropriate safeguards as well as incentives and sanctions to support the practice of sustainable tourism.

Land use – An effective and well-ordered land use regime is commonly regarded as an important foundation for the development of sustainable tourism. Such a regime should support constructive and sustainable land use practices while reducing or eliminating incompatible patterns of use.

Standards – Sustainable outcomes in tourism are seldom, if ever, possible without the drafting of regulations relating to standards. Once these standards are agreed and committed to by the industry then compliance mechanisms will come into play in order to ensure that the product being developed is truly one of quality and sustainability.

Planning – It is often observed that official verbal commitments to the pursuit of sustainable development are not always supported by the kind of strict planning agenda that would introduce the hard decisions needed to accelerate sustainable development. Sinclair and Jayawardena (2003) note that 'In many contexts the processes that should hasten the legislation, implementation and enforcement of sustainable development mechanisms are cumbersome, tedious and protracted.'

Mass communication - The communications media have a special contribution to make to the development of sustainable tourism. Their role in heightening awareness of best practices and in stimulating reflection upon the whole dynamic of sustainability should not be lost sight of.

Monitoring - One example of the systemic weakness associated with the introduction of sustainable tourism is the absence of provision for adequate monitoring and audits. Often environmental scrutiny is limited to an initial environmental impact assessment and there is a failure to conduct a periodic monitoring of environmental impacts that would determine contraventions and violations of environmental best practice.

Community tourism – In the Amazon region much of the tourism product either resides in or is located near rural communities. Also cultural resources, as expressed in the cuisine, dance and music, dress and traditional practices of communities in the Amazon, are often of great interest to tourists visiting the Amazon. Therefore it is to be expected that this form of tourism would be of seminal importance to any pursuit of sustainable tourism.

With due attention given to these issues the development of sustainable tourism in the Amazon emerges as an engagement with the totality of the Amazonia experience in its social, political cultural, environmental and economic dimensions. That pursuit gains added significance and assumes greater urgency when viewed in the larger context of sustainable development – an imperative for the Amazon given its precious resources in biological diversity and its impact upon both fresh water resources and the climate of the earth. Sustainable tourism, therefore, is not only a tool for economic development, cultural enhancement or environmental conservation in the Amazon, it is also a factor in a grander and more all-embracing equation of the sustainability of the Amazon itself.

Sustainable Tourism strategy of ACTO

Article XIII of the Amazon Cooperation Treaty lays out the following mandate:

> The Contracting Parties shall cooperate to increase the flow of tourists, both national and from third countries, in their respective Amazonian territories, without prejudice to national regulations for the protection of indigenous cultures and natural resources.

This formulation clearly underscores the importance that the Treaty attaches to regional mechanisms for cooperation designed to augment tourism flows into the Amazon region, whilst also recognizing the over-riding sovereignty of Member States and stressing the imperative of protecting indigenous cultures and constituent natural resources. This formulation logically leads to a path of sustainability for a regional tourism industry, in which development does not threaten natural resources or compromise the integrity of indigenous cultural forms.

Further, the Declaration of Manaus 2009 recognizes that, for Amazon Member Countries, tourism is one of a range of tools vital to the process of building *'an integral regional Amazonian cooperation vision … with a view to promoting the harmonious and sustainable development of their respective Amazonian spaces.'* The Declaration later makes a call for States to *'foster eco-tourism'* as part of this strategy.

Member Country Consultations: 2007-2009

These were in response to the mandate of the Amazon Cooperation Treaty to *'cooperate to increase the flow of tourists.'* In recognition of the importance of consensus in the elaboration of regional actions for tourism, and in deference to national tourism programmes and development plans, the Coordination in 2007 embarked upon a process of interaction and consultation with a wide cross-section of stakeholders in the Amazon Member Countries. These consultations were sustained and structured on three levels:

1) The level of the Ministers of Tourism and other high authorities.
2) The level of a Technical Committee comprising representatives from within the various Ministries of Tourism.
3) The level of public stakeholders, comprising representatives of other Ministries, private sector and community organizations, NGOs, research institutions and sections of civil society.

The following are among the principal tourism conclusions reached at these meetings and consultations:

1. Agreement on what were the principal Amazonia attractions and events in each country to be highlighted in Destination Amazonia Year 2009.
2. A commitment to the initiation of a structured, regional approach to the realization of tourism goals and objectives.
3. A recognition of the merits of tourism circuits as a tool for presenting a trans-border experience of Amazon tourism.
4. Support for the development of community-based tourism in the Amazon.
5. Concern for the image of the Amazon in the wider tourism market.

The new process of the revision of the ACTO Strategic Plan offers an excellent opportunity to marry the insights gained over three years with current national priorities in order to define and elaborate a Regional Tourism Agenda for the short, medium and long term.

Proposed Strategic Lines of Action in Tourism

Based upon discussions, insights, recommendations and conclusions gained during the three-year round (2007–2009) of visits, stakeholder meetings and consultations, the Coordination is proposing the five following Strategic Tourism Lines of Action as the substance of a Tourism Agenda for the Amazon in the short, medium and long term:

- Line 1 – Systematization of Regional Tourism Information.
- Line 2 – Establishment of trans-border integrated circuits.
- Line 3 – Development of community-based tourism.
- Line 4 – Strengthening of the tourism image of the Amazon.
- Line 5 – Creation of a Regional Tourism Financing Mechanism.

The Amazon Region

Because of its vast expanse the Amazon River as well as the whole of the Amazon Basin feeds the potential tourist's imagination: its history, culture, and reputation as the last 'adventure resort' and, in our climate change days, as the world's green lung and preservable bio system. The Amazon region, with its 6,7km long Amazon River and its widespread net of tributaries covers 40 percent of the landmass of the continent of South America. There are more than 33.5 million people depending on its water system, 21 million of whom live in cities like Manaus (Brazil) with approximately 2 million inhabitants and Iquitos (Peru) with app. 400,000 as well as in other big cities. Covering 8.187.965 km² (the Greater Amazon) the Amazon Region is 33 times as big as the United Kingdom or would cover approximately 85 percent of the United States' surface.

Even the hunt for El Dorado traversed the Amazon region. The prospectors literally struck gold but they had to use 3g quicksilver in order to gain 1g of gold and thus polluted the rivers with 24 kg quicksilver per square-kilometre, not to mention all the other chemicals used for the gold extraction process. At a later date came also the extraction of other important raw materials like bauxite, oil and precious woods, which initiated dramatic changes in both economical and social respects and would lead the world's public to cast a wary eye on the region: 420 different indigenous peoples also make up the Amazon region's huge cultural inheritance, with more than 86 languages and 650 vernaculars being spoken, and much of the knowledge about the protection of nature and how best to make use of the biological diversity in the possession of the Aguaruna, the Zagua, the Maku, the Auka and other indigenous inhabitants.

It is obvious that the Amazon basin is one of the most endangered regions on earth. Uncontrolled deforestation, oil drilling and gold-seeking each intervene in their special ways in the social and natural structure. The question is how to get a grip on these problems. Governments are willing but very often, despite their own best interests, they will soon encounter obstacles and difficult choices while all the time keeping their own best interests in mind.

Tourism as a Contribution to Sustainable Development

Tourism and the implementation of sustainable conceptions is regarded as an opportunity to put this fragile region on a solid base which could, through the valorisation of biological and cultural diversity, help to generate income. It is thought that through the development of carefully planned touristic products which involve the local people, their awareness of their surroundings can be heightened, while at the same time the tour operators would develop an interest in sustainability and thus help to improve the internal structures. Not every tourist knows that eight sovereign states form part of the Amazon Basin, each giving it its own imprint. Studies in various European countries, important countries of origin worldwide, have shown, that the complexity of the Amazonian region is not yet sufficiently marketed and that neither the cultural nor the social diversity of its bordering countries is reflected in any of the touristic products on offer. It is akin to marketing the image of a giant.

This is understandable if one takes into consideration that the Amazon region is presented as a scarcely populated, inaccessible area, rather than a colourful region full of cultural heritage, embracing different ethnic groups, traditions and culinary delicacies. The river is the region's economical lifeline and the boat is the most important means of transport which connects the cities of Manaos, Belem in Brazil, Iquitos in Peru, Leticia in Colombia and countless other places.

There is a widespread misapprehension that the Amazon River belongs exclusively to Brazil, although the latter country does have the greatest share at about 59 percent (Quelle: GEO-Amazonia: Perspectivas del Medio ambiente en la Amazonía/PNUMA). Bolivia, Ecuador, Peru and Bolivia share 27.3 percent. The two smaller countries, Guyana and Suriname, with 100 percent of their territory are also true Amazon states even if their share doesn't add up to more than 4.8 per cent. Looking at their historical development, both countries are regarded as part of the Caribbean and passports show that their inhabitants are without doubt members of the Caribbean community. They are still divided between their political-historical mapping as part of the Caribbean and their geographical location on the South American continent. The Andes states of Bolivia, Peru Ecuador and Columbia, which are at the same time Amazon states, are also members of the Comunidad Andina, where they pool their interests.

It is not easy to measure the exact volume of tourist flows to the Amazon region. Brazil gives an estimate of around 350,000 international tourist arrivals per year and the overall figure could be just under one million. German tour operators sell the Amazon region normally under the 'green lung'-aspect and as that part of their Brazil-package, where tourists can go on a river boat and, if they are lucky, watch parrots, capuchin monkeys and caimans.

Cross-Border Trails

ACTO in cooperation with the Tourism Ministries of its member states has thought about how to implement a sustainable system of cross-border trails. During a workshop with representatives from the municipal and the private sectors of all eight bordering countries, three possible trails were identified and analysed which topically connect two or three countries.

In this regard ACTO and key tourism actors from Amazon member countries have defined three integrated tourism circuits with the following titles:

1. The Amazon-Andes-Pacific Route/Peru – Brazil – Bolivia.
2. The Amazon Water Tourism Route/Bolivia – Brazil – Colombia – Ecuador – Peru.
3. The Amazon–Caribbean Tourism Trail/Guyana – Suriname – Brazil.

The Amazon-Andes-Pacific Route

The objective of this route is to capture tourist flows from Cuzco and expose them to the attractions of the Peruvian Amazon region of Madre de Dios where there exists the greatest bio-diversity in flora and fauna in the Amazon region. The trail then extends to the Federal State of Acre in Brazil, a state known for its protected areas, indigenous tourism enterprises and ecological riches, and then into Bolivia. Part of the attraction is in the contrast between the Andean highlands and cultures and the more tropical landscapes and cultural forms of the Amazon regions of Peru and Brazil.

Table 3.1 The Amazon-Andes-Pacific Route

Most important Hotspots	Ruta Chico Mendes, Comunidad de Xapurí, Machu Pichu/ Cusco, Reserva Nacional de Tambopata
Tourist Attractions	Living culture Archaeology Ecotourism, Adventure-tourism
Target Markets	Regional tourists from all three countriesUSA, UK, Germany
Main Players	National and regional tourism offices, Environmental Protection Agency, regional and national tour operators, small hotel and eco-lodge owners, NGOs, communities
Infrastructure	The road that will connect the Pacific with the Atlantic is planned to pass through this area, therefore a long-term tourism concept.

The Amazon Water Tourism Route

The objective of this route is to explore the connection between the human populations and the river system which is the most authentic in the Amazon. So far the tourism establishments range between two and five stars. ACTO has been working with Tourism authorities at the local and national levels, and in conjunction with the private sector and civil society, to elaborate an integrated concept. Bolivia, Brazil, Colombia, Ecuador and Peru are involved in this circuit.

Table 3.2 The Amazon Water Tourism Route

Most important Hotspots	Brazil: Estado do Amazonas, Manaus, Tabatinga, Peru:Loreto (Iquitos, Indiana, Pevas – Caballococua) Ecuador: Sucumbios, Orellana, Napo Cities: Tena, Coca, Lago Agrio, Roca Fuerte
Tourist Attractions	Bird-watching, eco- and nature tourism, living culture, gastronomy, archaeology
Target Markets	Regional, Europe, USA
Main Players	National and regional tourism offices, environmental protection agencies of the countries involved, local government, regional and national tour operators, small hotel and eco-lodge owners, NGOs, communities
Infrastructure	As the main traffic artery is the river, laws and regulations have to be updated and observed

The Amazon-Caribbean Tourism Trail

This trail combines Suriname, Guyana, and Brazil through the federal state of Roraima. Suriname has a strong connection to the Dutch tourism market with several flights daily from Amsterdam. Guyana and Suriname are little known as member countries of OTCA. They have an excellent offer of nature and biodiversity in their combination of the Amazon experience and Caribbean flavour. Paramaribo and Georgetown are places with a great mix of different cultures expressed in music, dance, cuisine and architecture.

Table 3.3 The Amazon-Caribbean Tourism Trail

Most important Hotspots	Georgetown, Kaieteur National Park, Iwokrama Rainforest Reserve, Rupununi, Essequibo Region In Suriname: Paramaribo/ Commewijne, Galibi, Upper Suriname River, Central Suriname nature reserve, Nickerie
Main segments	Rainforest, eco-tourism, culture-tourism, adventure-tourism, canoeing, bird-watching, sports-fishing
Target Markets	Local and InternationalEurope, Netherlands/Belgium/ France/UK/Germany; USA, Caribbean States.
Main Players	National and regional tourism offices, Environmental protection agencies of the countries involved, local government, regional and national tour operators, small hotel and eco-lodge owners, NGOs, Communities
Infrastructure	Construction of the Takutu-Bridge across the Takutu River between Guyana and Roriama, opening up new economic possibilities. Easy ferry and air links between Guyana and Suriname

Tourism Planning

It is often observed that in places where authorities and population have embarked upon tourism development they still lack ideas and knowledge concerning planning and implementation. And while Nature as the main subject is the focus, it is not sufficient to attract paying tourists to the region. That is why it is an important prerequisite to provide information as well as clearly defined quality standards. Until recently the Amazon region has not been the basis of a regional tourism plan. Even less attention has been paid to the realisation of cross border planning concepts which are mandatory if the idea is to issue an offer which envelops and connects a number of different countries. As a first step the players from the countries involved were brought together, in order to exchange information and discuss common questions. The results were pooled and formed the stock for a reference book.

Quality Improvement

The integrated circuits serve as a mechanism that territorially structures the Amazon region, creating three different integrated experiences. The political commitment of the governments involved has to be guaranteed in order to assure a quality improvement of the touristic product and thus further the ability to compete.

Diversity in tourism has to be carefully managed in order to avoid mis-steps. ACTO has received the political mandate of the countries involved to identify the obstacles to tourism development and suggest ways to overcome them. There exist differing regulations in connection with infrastructure, transport, communication, and environmental concerns, as well as health and indigenous matters. While there have been initiatives in a number of areas critical to the development of the region, a fully integrated vision has not been realized. This could be a possibility in the area of tourism if it becomes a priority to implement uniform quality standards as a first step. Thematically structured units, as e.g. the trails, would be a prerequisite, as standards not only have to be defined and implemented but also have to be regularly monitored and consolidated. Thus the demands are met to connect the Amazon region to regional and international markets.

In the case of the Amazon-Caribbean Trail all three countries held workshops involving tourism stakeholders. As the cooperation amongst the states of Suriname and Guyana and the province of Roraima is so far the most advanced, the Amazon-Caribbean Trail will serve as an example and will be looked at in more detail.

The Amazon-Caribbean Concept

Tourism authorities in the states of Suriname and Guyana have, through the ACTO initiative, seized an opportunity to engage in an initiative of cooperation in tourism that links them with the continent of South America and at the same time consolidates their own touristic visions. The countries connected via this trail are Suriname, Guyana and Brazil through the Federal State of Roraima. During a number of workshops with participants from the three countries the Amazon region with Caribbean flair was identified as the connecting link. It also showed that Guyana and Suriname especially made use of the chance to position themselves as countries with a Caribbean background based on the Southern American continent.

Model of cross-border tourism development in different steps

- States – which co-ordinate the formulation of the tourism policy.
- Entrepreneurs – who formulate and execute the strategy and work of development.
- Municipalities and Social Organizations – which coordinate actions between different countries.
- Creation of the Common Tourism Area for the development of a promotion strategy of several international destinations.
- Accord of standards for the control and organization of tourism services.

Arrowpoint Nature Resort, Guyana
Source: Photo property of Karola Tippmann

- Implementation of mechanisms of training and building awareness for tourism development, based on the best tourism practices and code of ethics from the private and public sectors.
- Consolidation of the Mixed Bilateral Council of Tourism between partner countries.

First of all the status quo had to be established. In Guyana and Suriname an inventory of the touristic infrastructure and tourist attractions was taken. These were then rated under certain criteria. The entrepreneurs who were present and who came from different parts of the country had a good and realistic idea of the situation in their own country as regards local tourist facilities. There were also representatives from the tourism ministries and representatives of the municipalities. This is what was discussed:

1. The precise configurations of the Suriname and Guyana tourism routes.
2. The rating of the attractions, accommodations and services of the route areas.
3. The principal selling points in that tourism configuration.

Thus the first design of the trail was drafted, the hotspots were fixed, and an assessment of the touristic infrastructure was given. Each country named five hotspots with an acceptable infrastructure. These were meant to form the core from which the touristic development would go forth.

For Guyana:

1. Georgetown
2. The Kaieteur National Park
3. The Iwokrama Rainforest Reserve
4. The Rupununi
5. The Essequibo Region

For Suriname:

1. Paramaribo/Commewijne
2. Galibi
3. Upper Suriname River
4. Central Suriname nature reserve
5. Nickerie

In a joint meeting amongst main stakeholders from both countries the following questions were discussed for the first time:

1. What is the main tourism product of Guyana/Suriname? (Description of the touristic situation)
2. Is there interest for Guyana/Suriname to become part of the Amazon-Caribbean Trail? (For and against)
3. What are the expected benefits?
4. Has Guyana/Suriname worked before on a combined tourism product? (History of product development)
5. What are the HOTSPOTS for Guyana/Suriname? (Some detailed information about every HOTSPOT)
6. Thinking in a commercial way, what are the indicators of packages? (Time, money, interests of clients)
7. Which stakeholders have to be involved?
8. What kind of activities happened before?
9. Are the markets decided?
10. Is there any promotion activity?
11. Are there any challenges identified?
12. What can be the role for ACTO?

The main attractions

- Nature
- History
- Culture
- Festivals

Challenges

- Language
- Visas
- Limited flights
- Infrastructure in some sites, especially in the borders
- Accommodation – some challenges with classification, qualification
- Finances – different structures and administrative systems (Suriname and Guyana act as countries, Roraima is a Federal State of Brazil)

The expected benefits

- New markets
- Savings in costs and resources
- Access to additional funds
- Strong partnerships that will survive in this globalized world.
- A lot of partnerships possible (border with France, CARICOM, etc.)

Prospects of the Amazon-Caribbean-Tourism Trail

The cooperation between the national tourism organizations of Suriname, Guyana and Brazil (through the State of Roraima, including in a further moment the State of Amazonas and the Amazon region of Venezuela) resulted in the implementation of a combined Amazon tourism product. Suriname, Guyana and the corresponding state of Brazil, agreed to merge the infrastructure and unique tourism assets into a combined product with the core-elements of the Amazon, shared by all three countries. The objective was to create an opportunity for visitors from all three partner countries to travel to and border cross each of the neighbouring nations either by land or by air transport. This was also the opportunity to launch a new concept of product development on the international market that was interested in connecting different countries and combining nature and culture elements for a special integrated circuit, called the Amazon-Caribbean Trail.

The three countries will derive benefit in having a more competitive product developed in a general context of sustainable management and quality. The route includes in Guyana the touristic highlights like the capital Georgetown, the Kaieteur National Park, the Iwokrama Rainforest Reserve, the Rupununi, and the Essequibo Region. In Suriname the route goes to the hotspots Paramaribo/ Commewijne, Galibi, the Upper Suriname River, Central Suriname nature reserve and Nickerie. The West route from Suriname runs to the district Nickerie where the border with Guyana is connected to South Drain. A drive over the Guyanese Lethem road continues through the Roraima area all the way to the city of Boa Vista in Brazil. The success of the AMCA-Trail Combined is already visible since various tour operators of all three partner countries are offering this adventurous trip with great frequency to both national and international visitors.

Guidebook/Information Manual

The second step that is now being worked on is the conception of a guidebook or manual which shall provide the most important information for the entrepreneurs involved and put everybody on the same page. Its aim is to help them see their countries in the bigger picture and plan their marketing measures based on solid data. Access to these data is in many parts of South America very limited. Some data do not exist, some are not systematically accessible. Data as such are a very abstract concept and it's not quite clear where their value should come from if these do not touch on the local or communal problems. As soon as the data are shown their relevance in the touristic context the situation is different and interest is strong. This is what makes the guidebook for the Amazon-Caribbean-trail so important and the aim is to have it finished by the end of the year.

Following a set pattern, touristically relevant information concerning the hotspots is catalogued.

This has given the Manual the following structure:

A.   Geographical situation, cities, climate, distances etc.
B.   Historical situation, important information on colonial heritage, and independence
C.   Cultural situation of the different ethnic groups, their rites and customs
D.   Socio-economic situation with reference to education, health system and economic data
E.   Political administrative situation with regarding the infrastructure as provided by the state, e.g. electricity, administration etc.
F.   Those in charge of tourism either in the official or the private domain like administrative boards, associations and other key players
G.   Means of transport on waterways, ground and in the air (*connectivity*)
H.   Touristic infrastructure like hotels, restaurants and other services with special regard to the border areas, as they are not always located in the hotspots.

Special attention is being paid to the following subjects: indigenous aspects (peoples, history of peoples and colonization, local myths and rituals, art and cuisine, valorization of cultural identity, social organization), biodiversity and the utilization of water. The manual, with its cross border, trail -relevant information, offers participants the opportunity to think within bigger structures and find a base for joint marketing.

Another important foundation on which to build this cross border trail is to find an approach to common criteria for sustainable tourism.

Companion Green Book

The third stage involves the production of a Companion Green Book, which summarizes the essential information given aboutm the hotspots in the anual and presents recommendations for 'travelling green' in the tourism circuits.

Criteria for Sustainable Tourism

The idea of the integrated trail is to introduce quality criteria to the hotspots which have a reference to real life in the circuits. The main concern is a standardisation in the field of accommodation, i.e. the eco-lodges which are important means to channel touristic development. So far, the countries in question find it difficult to agree on common criteria, but they have come up with a kind of checklist covering the following points:

Sustainable Management of Eco Lodges:
This offers a guideline for the management on how to organize and lead their company with regard to economical, social and ecological sustainability.

Sustainable Quality-Management in Eco-Lodges:
The management shall be encouraged to develop and implement sustainable quality criteria.

Security for the Tourist in Eco-Lodges:
This is meant to enable companies to establish security standards which allow the tourist peace of body and mind.

Heightened awareness in all three fields in regard to eco-lodges in the Amazon-Caribbean circuit is meant to establish comparability and in the medium term will lead to a better ability to compete. In cooperation with the national tourist administrations the standards will be analyzed, discussed and adjusted, and finally safeguarded.

Future Prospects

The Amazon region which is formed by eight sovereign states is one of the biggest and most complex eco-regions worldwide. This presents a very special challenge to the tourism experts and developers. How to preserve the charm of this region which fascinates adventurous travellers and explorers alike? And how at the same time to close the gaps in knowledge and establish uniform quality standards? ACTO, as an inter-governmental organization, has the political mandate for five key development areas amongst them the coordination of tourism development. The idea of the integrated circuits is an approach which tries to form a three-pillared structure and thus create sub-units which are thematically grouped.

The Amazon-Caribbean Trail is one of three possible ideas and involves Guyana, Surinam and Brazil adding Caribbean flair to an Amazonia base. Information about this newly formed unit has been gathered and can now be used as a basis for further political decisions. It serves as an anchor for the communities which helps them to be taken note of as part of an overall geo-destination. The entrepreneurs are given the chance to improve the quality of their services. Those politically responsible have a guideline along which to decide about infrastructural measures and how to direct their marketing resources. It is common to connect the Amazon region with sustainability. It is not enough to use this as a catch phrase but it needs suggestions how to actually implement measures which guarantee the said sustainability. Awareness can be heightened and the way for sustainability be cleared by pursuit of specific criteria. Thus the people who live in the Amazon region are given a chance to develop economical alternatives which would not isolate them further but connect them to the bigger economic developments. It is already getting easier to jump on international promotional wagons which can be seen by the fact that the Amazon Caribbean Trail is already being marketed at trade shows in Europe even if the outlay is still modest.

Lessons learnt

ACTO is the player that has the mandate to moderate regional processes. On the one hand it is of great importance that there is a neutral party involved. On the other hand it hinders the entrepreneurial dynamics because the decision making process is far more complex.

There are also language issues in the Amazon Caribbean trail, as there are three official languages: Portuguese, English and Dutch.

The financing of every single measure is highly dependent on governments and international sponsors. Although the general ACTO tourism strategy also covers plans for sustainable financing these will only take effect in the medium to long term. Necessary infrastructural measures can be identified but their implementation will be slow.

The cross border cooperation amongst the tourism organizations creates a new stronger confidence which has a positive effect on negotiations with international tour operators, airlines and others on the outside.

Although the Amazon region is vast there are people living there taking care of their small lodges, cosy restaurants and souvenir shops, people who earn their living as tourist guides and wardens. It is in cooperation with them that realistic goals have to be set which will then help to preserve the Amazon region as a habitable place for people and 'the' great eco-region on this planet.

References

Carson, R. (1962). *Silent Spring.* Boston: Houghton Mifflin.
Cater, E. (1995). "Environmental contradictions in sustainable tourism." *Geographical Journal* **161**(1): 21–28.
Edgell, D.L. and Sung Chon K. (2006). *Managing Sustainable Tourism: a Legacy for the Future.* New York: The Haworth Press.
Hall, C. M. and Lew, A.A. (Eds) (1998). *Sustainable Tourism: a Geographical Perspective.* Harlow: Longman.
Jayawardena, C. (2002). "Future challenges for tourism in the Caribbean." *Social and Economic Studies,* **51** (1): 1–23.
PNUMA and OTCA (2009) *Geo Amazonía.* Panama: PNUMA.

Priestley, G. K., Edwards, J.A., et al. (Eds) (1996). *Sustainable Tourism? European Experiences.* Wallingford: CAB International.

Sinclair, D. and Jayawardena, C. (2003). "Sustaining tourism development in the Guianas." *Hospitality,* June, p. 3.

Turner, R. K., Pearce, J.D., et al. (2001). *Mediterranean Islands and Sustainable Tourism Development: Practices, management and policies.* New York: Continuum.

World Commission on Environment and Development (1987). *Our Common Future.* Oxford: Oxford University Press.

WTO (1998) Guide for local authorities on developing sustainable tourism, www.otca.org.br/en/institucional/index.php?id=29

4 Bringing sustainability to the Brazilian hotel industry

Monica Borobia and
Helenio Waddington***

Introduction

Economic development is a never ending challenge for businesses and communities alike. As the global marketplace has become increasingly competitive, municipalities, states, and regions seek new strategies for attracting good investments, generating jobs and enhancing quality of life. Furthermore, communities everywhere are demanding improvements in local environments.

Achieving excellence in business today means that environmental performance needs to be recognized as critical to success and be integrated as part of the development of such businesses. Introducing an environmental management policy into business activities or investing into environmentally sustainable projects are increasingly becoming the norm in business practices. In adopting sustainable practices in the management of their operations many industries in the private sector can make a valuable contribution to sustainable development by reducing the negative environmental and social impacts of their activities and by optimizing favorable ones.

Such models for development open up innovative new avenues for managing businesses and conducting economic development, as well as creatively fostering dynamic and responsible growth through partnerships with various segments of local communities. Antiquated business strategies, based on isolated enterprises, are no longer responsive enough to market environmental and community requirements.

Biodiversity is a vital asset to the tourism industry. Travelers, tourism operators, investors and professionals all have an inherent interest in the conservation and sustainable use of biodiversity resources; it is, after all, one of the industry's main assets. In fact, not only can tourism directly help finance the conservation and sustainable use of biodiversity, it has also proven to be one of the most effective public awareness raising tools for environmental protection (Secretariat for the Convention on Biological Diversity, www.cbd.int).

*Roteiros de Charme Hotel Association
**Visconde de Pirajá 414, sls 921/922, Ipanema, Rio de Janeiro, RJ, Brazil 22410-002

Tourism impacts and benefits various other important economic industries. The long-term sustainability of tourism as the engine for growth depends on the industry's ability to interface and support these other sectors such as agriculture, health and public utilities. Tourism has a large and growing environmental footprint. Additional stress is being placed on already burdened ecosystems: quickly depleting fresh water supplies, increased volumes of solid waste, loss of habitats, increased pressures on public utilities, inadequate and costly energy sources, and lack of environmental awareness by local inhabitants and foreign visitors.

Tourism's footprint can be significantly reduced by cleaner production and sustainable consumption patterns. If allied with the involvement of and capacity building opportunities for local communities, particularly embodying traditional lifestyles at the destination level, tourism development can directly benefit the people and communities who become stewards and custodians of biodiversity (CBD, 2010). The involvement of local communities in tourism development and operation is a fundamental condition for the conservation and sustainable use of biodiversity.

Increased global collaboration, interdisciplinary approaches and new forms of partnerships are urgently needed to assure growth that is environmentally sustainable and a more equitable sharing of benefits derived from the industry. Environmental treaties, Action Plans and the agendas of international organizations such as the World Tourism Organization (UN-WTO), the Convention on Biological Diversity (CBD) and the United Nations Environment Programme (UNEP) have recognized the need for the development of tourism that is environmentally sound. In this context the international community, through different fora and declarations (e.g. WTTC/WTO/Earth Council – Agenda 21 for the Travel and Tourism Industry, 1996; Québec Declaration on Ecotourism, 2002; Djerba Declaration on Tourism and Climate Change, 2003; the Global Sustainable Tourism Criteria, 2008 and the Global Partnership for Sustainable Tourism – UNEP, 2010) has encouraged and has called upon hoteliers and the associated tourism trade to meet the challenges it faces to reach sustainability, particularly through voluntary action and partnerships.

It is against this background that conservation of biodiversity by the hotel industry is addressed in the present chapter with the aim of illustrating, through case studies of its member hotels, the lessons learned and experiences that can be drawn from a Brazilian context – Roteiros de Charme Hotel Association – in mobilizing and securing involvement from hoteliers in generating sustainability in their own operations and through the capacity building of local communities.

Case Study: Roteiros De Charme Hotel Association

The Roteiros de Charme Hotel Association was founded by five independent hoteliers in Brazil in 1992, immediately following UNCED (The United Nations Conference on Environment and Development - The Earth Summit), as a private, non-profit organization. As of 2010, the Association comprises 50 independent hotels, inns and ecological refuges, from Northern to Southern Brazil, which recognize the importance of environmental and social responsibility for the sustainability of their operations and future generations. The critical location of various member hotels, which are set in conservation areas and fragile ecosystems such as the Atlantic Rainforest and the Amazon, points to the importance of a continuous and sound environmental programme (Associação de Hotéis Roteiros de Charme, 2004a).

In addition to uniting their individual standards of charm, quality of service and comfort, Roteiros de Charme members are devoted to the preservation of the tourism destinations where they are established through the conservation of their natural ecosystems and environmental education of those who depend on such destinations (Associação de Hotéis Roteiros de Charme, 2004b).

All hotels of the Association seek to serve as centers to generate multipliers for social and environmental practices in the communities in which they operate. The Association's programme has sought to build human capacities and to contribute to more sustainable and viable forms of social development.

Member Hotels are admitted yearly through a selection process and on-site visits by the Board of Directors that considers various criteria such as location, design and siting, quality of services, environmental and social performance. Once admitted, they maintain their administrative, commercial and financial independence.

The main publication of the Association, the *Roteiros de Charme Passport Guide*, with information on member hotels, has been published annually since 1994 and is distributed free of charge to guests, the public and trade operators, agencies and professionals.

Partnerships are also an important component in the Association's development. Roteiros de Charme and the United Nations Environment Programme (UNEP), through its Tourism Programme at the Division of Technology, Industry and Economics (DTIE) based in Paris, have cooperated since 1999 when the Association developed and adopted its voluntary *Ethics and Environmental Code of Conduct* with the technical collaboration of UNEP. Since then, UNEP and Roteiros de Charme have signed a Memorandum of Cooperation in 2003, which has been renewed three times, with the goal of continuing collaboration on training, awareness raising, and the further implemention of its Code of Conduct.

In 2007, Roteiros de Charme was accepted as an Affiliate Member of the UN World Tourism Organization's Business Council and subsequently elected as a Vice-President of the Council for a two year term. UN-WTO and Roteiros have also cooperated in the dissemination of best practices.

The Sustainability Programme

In addition to uniting their individual standards of charm, quality of service and comfort, Roteiros de Charme members are devoted to the preservation of the tourism destinations where they are established through the conservation of their natural ecosystems and the environmental education of those who depend on such destinations (UNEP, 2003).

Implementation of the directives in the Code of Conduct by all hotels focuses on target areas related to the Environmental Code of Conduct (available through www.roteirosdecharme.com.br):

- Energy conservation
- Water conservation
- Wastewater treatment
- Preservation of local areas of high biodiversity/endemism or of cultural/ historical value
- Reduction of noise and atmospheric pollution
- Reduction of environmental impacts of new projects and constructions
- Reusing, reducing and recycling materials
- Control of chemicals and harmful substances to the environment
- Elimination of waste incineration, burning of pastures and deforestation
- Involvement of service providers and suppliers
- Information and interaction with guests

Monitoring of the voluntary Ethics and Environmental Code of Conduct is carried out independently and annually by professionals (biologists and environmental engineers) in all member hotels of Roteiros de Charme (UNEP, 2000; Associação de Hotéis Roteiros de Charme, 2005). Implementation of the directives in the Code of Conduct includes the application of best management practices, and various social and environmental actions mobilizing host communities (NGOs, local authorities, schools, businesses and others) as well as the environmental education of hotel employees and their families, which is actively pursued through seminars, talks and courses and target areas related to the Environmental Code of Conduct.

The First Environmental Evaluation is carried out within six months of entrance into the Association (a selection process of hotel candidates is made annually through a set of criteria on service, quality, environmental and social commitment). The evaluation includes a report containing findings on potential environmental impacts in light of the Code of Conduct with recommendations for the short, medium and long term. During the evaluation personnel training is carried out and meetings are held with local partners and service providers of the hotel. Subsequent Environmental Evaluations are held annually to evaluate progress and barriers.

Based on the experience accumulated, a core set of indicators, focusing on business and sustainability performance, have been developed and are available on-line for member hotels to provide a basis for a results-oriented and quantitative analysis in the implementation of the Code of Conduct.

Other internal tools used are: Environmental Checklists, Environmental bulletins, a Best Practice Electronic Forum and Intranet for Members.

Components of the Environmental Programme

- Commitment
  (Principles and Directives of the Code of Conduct)

- Planning
  (Diagnostics, Action Plan: short, medium and long-term)
- Means of Implementation
  (Responsible staff, Training, Information, Communication)
- Evaluation
  (Monitoring, Checklists, Business Performance and Sustainability Indicators)
- Analysis and Continuous Improvement
  (Feedback to Board of Directors and member hotels, Dissemination of results to partners and community)

Activities and Results

About 80% of the Association's hotels are located in fragile ecosystems such as the Atlantic Forest and the Amazon. By adopting and implementing its Code of Conduct, the Association has set an important benchmark, as a private initiative, for the conservation of biodiversity and such threatened ecosystems in Brazil. Its activities have contributed to reducing pressures and impacts, through:

- preventing pollution from untreated sewage, the depletion of fresh water supplies, and the contamination of waterways and marine environments
- reducing the generation of solid waste and inappropriate waste disposal
- preventing a loss of habitats and pressures on fauna and flora
- strengthening public awareness of biodiversity issues for guests, staff, local inhabitants, authorities and businesses
- supporting conservation projects for endangered species
- preventing inappropriate design, building and land-use
- promoting sound guest consumption patterns
- supporting protected areas and biodiversity corridors such as the creation of private reserves (RPPN-Brazilian System of Protected Areas).

Activities developed by the Association include:

- The implementation of projects and activities by individual hotels that generate social benefits and improvement in the quality of local communities, such as marine aquaculture,a reforestation programme, and horticultural projects
- Participation in local, national and international fairs, conferences and meetings with the aim of sharing experiences and mobilizing partnerships towards common goals
- Participation in local academic and scientific projects, such as the conservation of manatees and sea turtles

Innovative aspects of this initiative are:

- The Association provides technical and managerial guidance to hotels which would like to join the Association, but do not yet meet the environmental and social criteria for entrance, with a view to encouraging social engagement and environmental improvements.

- The Code of Conduct is independently monitored annually by professionals at each member hotel, aiming at evaluating impacts and progress and setting targets for improvement.
- Costs from the first independent monitoring are covered by its own members and those of subsequent years, with resources levered through partnerships established by the Association.
- High level of social involvement with active participation of hotel employees and their families and host communities in the application of the Code of Conduct.
- Financial incentives and awards of various kinds provided to employees from savings derived from environmental actions in the hotels and projects in local communities.
- Encouragement for participation of all hotels in a tourism destination in the Association's Environmental Programme, even if they are not members of Roteiros de Charme.
- Partnerships are sought with local, national and international partners who share the philosophy of environmental and social responsibility.

Our programme has sought to improve the socio-economic conditions and well-being of local communities at destinations, building human capacities and contributing to more sustainable and viable forms of social development. To this end, members of the Association will:

- Provide direct employment at all levels from local communities, and strive to provide health and social benefits to their employees beyond those simply required by law
- Give preference to local service providers and suppliers so as to generate maximum possible benefits to local economies
- Donate furniture, bed and bath linens, and food to local charities
- Share and offer the use of facilities to local communities and businesses for the storage and disposal of garbage
- Support education programmes for children and social projects such as housing improvements/renovations in local communities
- Purchase and distribute local products such as decoration items, handicrafts and local food produce

Selected Case Studies From Member Hotels

Hotel e Fazenda Rosa dos Ventos, Teresópolis, Rio de Janeiro: Protecting water as a biodiversity asset

Hotel e Fazenda Rosa dos Ventos is located in Teresópolis, Rio de Janeiro, Brazil, in a private park of one million square meters and has over 50% of its property preserved with Atlantic rainforest. Over the last 36 years, 40 hectares of land have been transformed from deforested pasture to rainforest in medium to advanced stages of recovery, which in turn have contributed to the conservation of natural water sources and native fauna.

The hotel is situated on the surroundings of two protected areas which are part of an important ecological corridor for the conservation of natural resources of the Atlantic Rainforest of Rio de Janeiro. The region also acts as a 'bread basket' for the city and state of Rio de Janeiro, with the largest production of vegetables and fruits in the state, mostly originating from small and medium sized agricultural family-based businesses. Hence the rational use of a valuable resource such as freshwater, which is used for many purposes and vital to ecosystem conservation, is a key issue and the preservation of natural water sources becomes an integral part of water conservation measures.

Rosa dos Ventos provides guests with the opportunity to savour vegetables and herbs in their restaurant from an organic garden located within the property. The same garden supplies vegetables and herbs as well for meals offered to all staff of the hotel.

As of 2008, Hotel e Fazenda Rosa dos Ventos is offering an unique attraction to its guests: naturally fluorinated mineral water from the existing natural ground water fonts within the hotel property. In the hotel, the natural mineral water is used in showers, baths and vanities of guests´ suites and apartments as well as in the restaurant, saunas, swimming-pools and in other hotel facilities and services. Through the information folder in the apartments, guests are advised of the existence of naturally fluorinated water sources and the option to consume such water in the hotel.

The water has been analysed regularly since 2002 and classified as Natural Fluorinated Mineral Water. The various natural water sources are preserved and monitored regularly by hotel staff, who have been trained to understand and value such sources for what they represent for biodiversity conservation as well as for rational human consumption and various life-maintenances uses, especially outside the hotel property. Care is taken to preserve natural rain forest vegetation and to prevent eventual disturbances to water sources (walking, movements by surrounding domestic animals etc). The goal is to maintain the sources in a pristine state and only a portion of such sources are used on a rotation basis.

In terms of environmental and social benefits, this action has contributed to the prevention of improper land-use including, potential clearing, contamination by agrochemical use associated with agro-industries, and accelerated erosion. It has also raised guests' and the communities' awareness about the value of environmental services provided by natural, forested catchments and the importance of such natural fluorinated water sources, including the health benefits. For the hotel in particular, it is an added value to offer such luxury item and to be able to contribute to the maintenance of biodiversity and ecosystem health within the threatened Atlantic rain forest.

Using Hotel e Fazenda Rosa dos Ventos as an example, the goal is now to mobilize and form partnerships with adjacent land owners towards the establishment of biological corridors contributing to the expansion of preserved rainforest areas and the conservation of biodiversity, thus enhancing the integrity and effective maintenance of existing protected areas in the region.

Ronco do Bugio Pouso e Gastronomia, Piedade, São Paulo: Helping to fight climate change by off-setting carbon emissions

Located 130 km from the city of São Paulo, Southeastern Brazil, Ronco do Bugio Pouso and Gastronomia ('The roar of the Howler Monkey Inn and Gastronomy') is set in the mountain region of Paranapiacaba, where howler monkeys can be heard in the Atlantic Rainforest. Buildings were constructed with demolition materials and the inn offers gastronomy and therapeutic spaces.

As part of their effort to promote sustainability and increase awareness towards climate change control, guest are encouraged to plant native trees within the property of the inn to off-set carbon emissions deriving from their travel and stay at Ronco do Bugio. The inn provides the calculation information to the guests (to off-set transportation, energy and fossil fuel consumption, as well as the solid waste generated) and the native trees (endemic species from Atlantic Rainforest) which are cultivated at a nursery located at the inn. Each planted tree receives a number and is registered in a data base. Guests can revisit the inn and monitor the growth of the trees they planted. In partnership with the certification scheme U-GO Green, the inn also calculated its own carbon foot print derived from its operation which is off-set by the preservation of a refor-estation area of 16 hectares (40 acres) of the Atlantic Rainforest. Since September 2007, 65 trees were planted by guests who wished to do so. Planting occurs on Sunday mornings organized by staff of the Ronco do Bugio, usually before check-out.

Using a coefficient of 0,2t CO_2/tree, 13 tons of CO_2 have been off set to date. Considering that the inn has only 13 rooms and guests stays occur primarily on weekends, with about 5% of guests during the reported period having voluntarily adhered to this initiative.

Given the innovative nature of this effort in the realm of small and medium hoteliers in Brazil, off-setting carbon emissions remains a promising tool to be consolidated in helping fight climate change.

Pousada Cravo & Canela, Canela, Rio Grande do Sul: The Promotion of Social Responsibility

The inn Pousada Cravo & Canela, in the mountain town of Canela in the Brazilian state of Rio Grande do Sul, has begun to involve its guests in its social and envi-ronmental contribution to the region. Already committed to best practices and environmental management within its property since the beginning of its opera-tions, the inn now reaches out to the community where it operates, at the same time increasing the social and environmental awareness of its guests.

An optional room/night tax of R$ 1,50 Brazilian Real (approximately 0,86 USD cents) has been added to the bills for voluntary payment by guests who so wished. The aim was to benefit three local community charity organizations: a home for the elderly, a home for underprivileged children, and a hospital.

Between January 2008 and June 2010, USD 3.247 was collected and reverted to the purchase and donation of organic food supplies to these charities. The goods are acquired directly from small local producers and include items such as jams, juices, brown sugar and fruits. The inn also collects from the three organizations the used food containers such as glass jars which are returned to the producers for re-utilization. Plastic wrappings and other packaging materials are also destined for recycling after use rather than being wasted or improperly discarded. By involving local producers, the inn contributes to the local economy as well as helping to prevent an exodus of the labour force to larger urban centres, thus maintaining a traditional regional vocation, the production of home-made family produce. It also reduces the carbon footprint which otherwise would have been incurred in longer distance transportation of goods.

This initiative demonstrates that small hoteliers can have an important role in the social development of destinations in a developing country scenario, where businesses are increasingly active in complementing or acting in partnership with governmental social programmes.

Fazenda Capoava, Itu, São Paulo: Guest communication

Located in Itu, 90km from the city of São Paulo, Fazenda Capoava is set in a historical farm mansion from the 1750s, amidst a 1.210.000 m² property of lakes and native Atlantic forest. The farm is an example of how tourism can be an important vehicle to ally rural development and environmental conservation. The rich historical background of Itu, significant in its cultural aspects from early explorers, pioneer settlers, and the colonial production of sugar cane, followed by the coffee plantation years, is a core value at Capoava and enhances guests' visiting experience. Similarly, the farm is actively engaged in the environmental preservation of the property and the sustainability of tourism in the region.

A cultural centre has been established using the old coffee storage building which includes: original coffee production machinery from the 19th century, a library, a small museum, designed by the Museum of Archeology and Ethnology of the University of São Paulo, and a video room. In this space, guests and visitors can learn about the cultural heritage of rural São Paulo, through documents, artifacts, photographs and personal statements.

A series of four booklets focusing on the history, culture, traditional culinary and environment and nature trails, were produced by Capoava as a means for informing and raising guests' awareness of the importance of local assets and promoting responsible behaviour to minimize impacts on habitats and wildlife. Interpretation signs and the identification of native trees are also made available throughout the trails on the farm. An animal center licensed by the National Environmental Agency and overseen by a team of biologists, houses native species of birds and mammals and serves as an educational and conservation site.

In-house, guests are encouraged to save water and energy through the re-use of bath linens which is communicated via signs in three languages.

The efforts of Capoava to widely communicate its initiatives to rescue cultural heritage and to maintain the environmental integrity of the farm and Itu as a destination have resulted in concrete local achievements as well as direct benefits to the farm. Two of these are highlighted: (1) the establishment in 2003 of a regional non-profit Association of businesses and institutions (PROTUR ITU) for the development of sustainable tourism, today with 50 members, whose proposals for the creation of initial stakeholders meetings were held at Capoava, and (2) the conclusion of a tripartite partnership with a national environmental NGO and the State Highway operating company, with the selection of the farm in the reforestation programme (Forests for the Future) which made it possible to plant 14,000 trees and increase the native forest cover of the farm from 14% to 21% of its total area. These and other benefits would not have been possible without the proactive communication strategy for guests and visitors of Fazenda Capoava.

Staff training: Pousada Toca da Coruja, Praia da Pipa, Rio Grande do Norte

Since its opening, Pousada Toca da Coruja has been operating with a vision to contribute to the sustainable development of Pipa Beach and its community. The entire physical structure of the inn, today with 23 accomodations, is integrated with great care for its lush gardens and vegetation.

Located away from major urban centres, Toca da Coruja has implemented for the last five years a technical tourism and personal skills capacity building programme, 'Learning at the Inn', that has focused on the youth of the local community who are pre-selected and will enter a trainee programme with the aim of being placed into the job market at the destination and surroundings. This programme not only increases the professional qualifications at Pipa Beach but also prevents their migration to larger towns, thus helping to promote social and economical development. Since its beginning, 40 young people have gone through the training programme which lasts on average three months and has had a 100% success rate for those trained, as well as being absorbed by the hotel management market and related tourism trade chain.

Among the contents of the programme are specific courses on the benefits of responsible environmental and social practices which are carried out in partnership with private and government sponsored business management institutions. One of such courses on energy efficiency generated a management plan with the adoption of several best practices and the identification of opportunities for further energy savings throughout the inn. These included the installation of lighting activated by motion sensors and timers and keycard-controlled electric switches, in addition to the use of solar power already adopted by the inn. As a result, Toca da Coruja successfully led the development of an environmental module for inclusion in all future courses by the state sponsored training and has been a pioneer in a state piloted capacity building programme, 'Better Tourism'.

As a result of staff mobilization, since 2005, an internal environmental commission has been established with a coordinator position, and assists in the monitoring of progress of environmental performances by the inn and acts as a catalyst for environmental engagement and the generation of multipliers in the municipality. One of the most recent achievements which the inn actively supported and contributed to was the designation on 14 September 2006 of the State Park of Mata da Pipa, with 299,88 ha., which as a conservation unit will focus on environmental education and low-impact tourism activities.

The strategy adopted by Toca da Coruja, of continuously promoting the education and capacity of its staff and of local youth, has generated tangible social, economical and environmental benefits: 1) reducing the costs of staff turn-over and of recruiting; 2) increasing the destination quality both in environmental terms and in the professional skills of the tourism industry; 3) increasing biodiversity maintenance with the creation of a new conservation unit which in turn will generate revenues from visitors and tourism related activities.

Waste Management: Pedra da Laguna Lodge, Armação dos Búzios, Rio de Janeiro

Armação dos Búzios is located some two hours' drive from the city of Rio de Janeiro. Búzios is known for its beautiful beaches and sea views. Sited 150m from the charming Ferradura Beach, Pedra da Laguna Lodge is perched on a coastal hill side which overlooks Ponta da Lagoinha, one of the protected geological sites of interest in Búzios as the region presents a gigantic chain of mountains with characteristics comparable to the Himalayas and registers as part of the evolutionary formation of Gondwana land.

With 25 apartments, Pedra da Laguna has adhered to the practices of waste separation and recycling since 2002, encouraged by its admission to a national non-profit private sector hotel Association which requires the commitment to a voluntary environmental code of conduct. Since then 100% of the solid waste generated by the lodge is recycled, including aluminum, glass and paper. The average monthly waste recycled (per room night) is 5 kgs during the low season, increasing to an average of 10 kgs during the austral summer months. The Lodge also treats 100% of its sewage and reuses 50% of the water from sewage treatment for watering its gardens and for other non-potable purposes.

The proceeds from recycling solid waste are shared by the lodge staff which averages about USD 100 per month. While 100 USD may seem as a token amount, it generates incentives for adhesion to other environmental practices and attitude changes towards environmental preservation, not only within the lodge's property but also in generating multipliers in the local community. The Lodge also reduces operational costs for waste disposal with such recycling practices, as it would have to spend an additional USD 150 on average per month on waste transport to the town's landfill.

Sustainable design and construction: Hotel Canto das Águas, Lençóis, Bahia

The Hotel Canto das Águas is located in the historical town of Lençóis in the heart of the Chapada Diamantina – the diamond highlands – in the state of Bahia, some 450 km from the capital city of Salvador. The area is rich in cultural and historical aspects, having been a prosperous diamond mining center, reaching its peak in the late 19th century. Today, Chapada Diamantina is recognized by its spectacular scenery of cliffs, canyons and caves, as well as for the style of its houses and architectural details, with bright colors and neogothical traces typical of the late 19th century and the beginning of the 20th century.

The hotel is situated on a property on the margins of the Lençóis River in the historical centre of the town, having been operating for over 18 years, during which period it has been extended with the aquisition of adjacent land and renovations. Today the property comprises 12.500m^2, with 22% of built area and a total of 44 apartments and suites.

The architecture of Canto dos Àguas was designed to be in harmony with the surrounding environment, especially in light of its siting by the river with a view of the Lençóis river rapids. Natural ventilation and lighting were incorporated as much as possible, and the hotel utilizes solar energy hence contributing to the conservation of energy. The newer wing, inaugurated in 1996 with two pavements and 26 apartments, is inspired by the colonial style of the houses in the historical centre. The construction of the hotel used certified wood and a mosaic of materials from demolition sites, such as beams, railway tracks, bricks and wood, as well as typical local construction techniques, all with great charm and in keeping the atmosphere of Lençóis. The entire decoration of the hotel, including the apartments and social areas, gave preference to local crafts from artisans and artists that vary from ceramics, tiles, paintings to sculptures and handicrafts from recycled paper and fabrics.

The outdoor swimming pool was designed to mimic rapids and the external stone paths and steps throughout the gardens were aimed at resembling the natural stones found throughtout the Lençóis river.

Given the importance of conservation of water resources and sources, in 2003 the hotel initiated a new landscaping project giving priority to native regional plant species throughout the entire hotel property and with the reforestation of a hilly side at the edge of the river, establishing identification signs of key endemic Brazilian trees.

Conclusion

Roteiros de Charme Hotel Association has become a benchmark for sustainable quality and environmental commitment within the tourism industry in Brazil. It is our belief that the sustainability of this initiative comes from three main elements: (1) training and education, (2) monitoring and evaluation, and (3) building partnerships.

One of the essential pillars for success and sustainability of the principles advocated by Roteiros de Charme in promoting business with social responsibility is education and capacity building. To continue informing, educating and training is a crucial objective in attaining results and development that are truly sustainable, in a developing country context such as Brazil. Experiences accumulated so far indicate that mobilizing and engaging the families of hotel staff in the environmental programme has proven to be very effective in building environmental consciousness and establishing ties with local communities.

By applying environmental management practices, and by continuously monitoring the impacts of its operations, the Association has been building a knowledge-base and a feedback mechanism which are essential for the credibility and sustainability of its work.

Equally important are the establishment and expansion of alliances for the implementation of the environmental program. Partnerships allow for strengthening of activities and projects, breaking down barriers among stakeholders, minimising the duplication of efforts and devising alternative solutions to common problems.

References

Associação de Hotéis Roteiros de Charme (2004a). Hospitalidade e Turismo Sustentável. Charme Responsável. *Revista Host. No. 1.*

Associação de Hotéis Roteiros de Charme (2004b). Turismo Sustentável no Brasil: A experiência da Associação de Hotéis Roteiros de Charme. *Revista Eco 21 No. 93*, pp 40–43.

Associação de Hotéis Roteiros de Chame (2005). Roteiros de Charme Hotel Association, Brazil. *Green Hotelier Issue 35*, April.

CBD (2010). Fact Sheet "Biodiversity and Tourism". Convention on Biological Diversity. www.cbd.int/tourism

UNEP (2000) – Roteiros de Charme Associação de Hotéis (Brazil): Combining hospitality and environmental consciousness Industry and Environment. *Tourism Focus.*

UNEP (2003). *A Practical Guide to Good Practice: Managing Environmental and Social Issues in the Accommodations Sector.* Best Practice Annex on Roteiros de Charme (in Portuguese)

UNEP (2010). Fact Sheet "The Global Partnership for Sustainable Tourism". www.unep. fr World Travel and Tourism Council, World Tourism Organization and the Earth Council (1996). *Agenda 21 for the Travel & Tourism Industry: Towards Environmentally Sustainable Development.* http://www.world-tourism.org/sustainable/IYE/quebec/anglais/declaration.html

5 Preferences regarding restoration and development at Copan Archeological Park, Honduras

Linkages between setting, visitor experiences and sustainability

Christopher C. Mayer * and
George N. Wallace **

Introduction

In western Honduras, near the Guatemalan border, archeological remnants are scattered across the wide Copan River Valley with none more spectacular than Copan Archeological Park (CAP) — a monument to the artistic zenith of the Maya civilization (see Figure 5.1). Copan, the ancient Mayan city, was a major center for trade, art, and religion in the Maya world. Today the archeological park is Honduras's second most popular tourist destination and its only profitable national park. It was declared a World Heritage Site by UNESCO in 1981 and a national monument in 1982 and the managing agency is the Honduran Institute of Anthropology and History (*Instituto Hondureño de Antropología e Historia,* or IHAH).

Throughout Mesoamerica, ruins like those at CAP have been restored with the hope of attracting more tourists. In the 20th century, for example, elaborate reconstructions of temples at *Chichen Itza* in the jungles of Mexico's Yucatan peninsula successfully attract tens of thousands of visitors to the park each year (Kelleher, 2004). In 1975, the Honduran government initiated a project, the *Proyecto Arqueológico Copán,* to enhance the tourist trade by restoring temples and palaces and also to better understand the city's ancient growth and development (Baudez, 1994; Sabloff, 1994). Overall, the restoration and promotion of the ruins at CAP as a means of attracting tourists has been successful. Barborak (2004) noted that CAP has turned *Copán Ruinas* into one of the most prosperous rural towns in all of Central America. Tourism has increased tenfold since the late

*Affiliate, Center for Protected Area Management and Training, Warner College of Natural Resources, Colorado State University
**Professor, Warner College of Natural Resources, Colorado State University

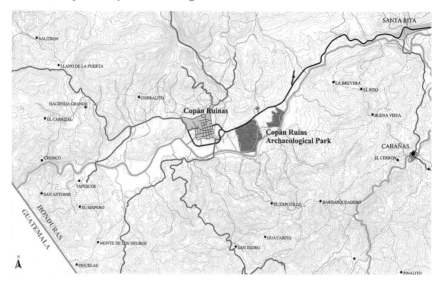

Figure 5.1 Map of the study area (Source: Instituto Hondureño de Antropología e Historia)
Source: Instituto Hondureño de Antropología e Historia

1970s, when 10,000 visitors came to CAP (Fash, 2002; *Informe Final del Año 2002*, 2002).

The town of *Copán Ruinas* is located 45-kilometers or a 2.5 hour drive south-west of San Pedro Sula, the business capital of Honduras, and one-kilometer west of the park boundary. Pine- and oak-forested mountains surround the 24 square-kilometer valley that at 600 meters above sea level provides an agreeable climate. The contemporary *Copán Ruinas* is small but bustling. The town's cobble-stoned streets are clean and safe, and its central park serves as a congenial meeting place for locals and tourists alike. Restaurants catering to the tastes of tourists and a variety of accommodations are available to meet every budget and comfort level. Unless one arrives by tour bus or private vehicle, most visits to the archeo-logical park will originate in the town of *Copán Ruinas*. The 15-minute walk from the town to the park provides time for geographic orientation and mental preparation. Visitors cross a bridge over *Cacahuatales* creek, and are immedi-ately immersed in a pastoral valley landscape. This affords an opportunity to observe traditional rural agriculture before arriving at the ruins. Although a good number of ruins have been restored within the 68-hectare archeological park, others have not. In some places, gigantic ceiba trees (*Ceiba pentandra*) grow out of immense temples, allowing visitors to witness the passage of time first hand and nature's ability to reclaim a city-state that once had over 10,000 inhabitants (Fash, 2001). The forest that surrounds the ruins filters out the sounds of moder-nity, while birds and insects provide a soothing soundscape for a visit that includes the opportunity to see whitetail deer, toucans, and giant blue morpho butterflies.

In 2002, the Wildlife Conservation Society (WCS) was contracted to direct an updated management plan for CAP. The WCS, noting that there was limited information about visitors or their experience, suggested a variety of studies and activities including an analysis of visitor preferences, characteristics, and perceptions to inform the planning process, infrastructure development and visitor management. The authors assisted with pre- and post-planning efforts over a three-year period. Their participation included: carrying out two comprehensive visitor surveys; conducting two sets of interviews with visitors to probe setting preferences; a mixed-methods survey of managers about the effects of adjacent land use on the management of CAP; multiple meetings with managers, community members and other key contacts; and the planning and development of the *Yax Ché* interpretive trail with counterparts. Throughout this process, the authors recorded much information as participant observers both in written and photographic form. The lead author lived continuously at *Copán Ruinas* for over a year. On three occasions, the study results were formally presented and discussed with stakeholders and conference attendees and follow-up sessions were held with CAP and municipal administrators to discuss the management implications. Together, these activities comprised an extensive case study from which a number of recommendations emerged and which could contribute to sustainable tourism at CAP and elsewhere.

Changes to Internal and External Settings at Copan

We saw forces at work at CAP and similar sites and wondered if they could potentially change both internal and external settings and either add or detract from the quality of the visitor experience, the cultural, historic and natural values and the interpretive potential. We wanted to know more about the right amount of restoration at a site like CAP. Was there also a value in allowing visitors to witness the collapsed structures and tree-covered mounds as well as restored temples, stele, ball courts and hieroglyphic staircases? Some archaeologists, tourists, and managers wanted to see CAP's archeological remnants developed and restored to the greatest extent possible. They reasoned that this would attract more tourists, capture more revenue, and bring the past to life. Some authors like Feilden and Jokilehto (1998) pointed out that once exposed, the elements take a toll on archeological remains and that an overemphasis on tourism can lead to unjustified reconstructions. We were interested in how different levels of restoration might affect the experience of visitors.

We were equally interested in the effect of the intensifying external development of adjacent pastoral lands and how that might affect the quality of the visitor experience. Given the importance of tourism as an income generator, economic planners and national and local decision makers often make decisions encouraging the expansion of tourism development without a full appreciation of the implications – especially for the preservation of cultural sites (World Tourism Organization, 2001). Shackley (2000) describes several potential threats to the *genius loci* or special setting attributes of a place associated with the World

Heritage designation. Among them, he lists increased visitor numbers, over-restoration, and damage to the surrounding landscape by intrusive development. The International Council on Monuments and Sites cautions that excessive or poorly-managed tourism and tourism-related development can threaten the physical nature, as well as the integrity and significant characteristics of cultural sites, and the visitors' and host communities' experience of place (ICOMOS, 1999). Pederson (2003) suggests that balanced economic development at World Heritage Sites must acknowledge the dynamic and often conflicting relationship between heritage places and tourism and the classic community tourism cycle that leads sequentially to unplanned and unrestrained growth and deleterious effects on local communities. In a study of 16 protected areas in six Mesoamerican countries that included the town of *Copán Ruinas* and CAP, Wallace et al. (2005) document a pattern of land use around protected areas where real or anticipated tourism growth causes forested or agricultural lands to be slowly replaced by poorly planned commercial and residential development.

Finally, the World Heritage List application for CAP itself pointed out that, 'the natural surroundings of the area were being threatened by the infringement of the neighboring town of *Copán Ruinas*' (UNESCO, 1980). Accordingly, we set out to see how visitors themselves perceived the relationship between the internal and external setting and their desired experience outcomes at Copan.

Linking Activities, Settings, Desired Experience Outcomes, and Benefits

This chapter builds on the behavioral approach to analyzing the visitor experience which holds that visitors to parks and protected areas are motivated to engage in activities in specific settings in order to achieve desired experience outcomes which in turn lead to personal and social benefits (Manning, 1999). Sometimes referred to as Experience-Based Setting Management (EBSM) or Benefits-Based Management (BBM), this consumer-oriented approach has for over three decades used quantitative methods to probe visitor activities, motivations and setting preferences and the links between them (Floyd & Gramann, 1997; Schreyer & Driver, 1989; Driver, 1975; Driver & Brown, 1975). This conceptual framework suggests that while managers cannot guarantee that desired experiences or benefits will be achieved, they can control the integrity of the physical, social and managerial setting attributes with careful zoning (Clark & Stankey, 1979; Brown et al., 1978) and offer a range of settings or experience opportunities making it more likely that a diversity of visitors will achieve desired outcomes and benefits from their visit.

Although the relationship between setting and desired outcomes is often intuitive, the studies that have been conducted have produced only a modest confirmation of the link between them (Manning, 1999). With a few exceptions (Mayer, 2003; Wurz, 1996; Wallace & Smith, 1996), most studies using a behavioral approach have been in North America or Australia and few, if any, have taken place at cultural or archeological sites where the range of motivations for visiting may be more specialized (Mayer, 2003), and where managers have a more specific mission and less latitude to provide for a variety of management zones or settings. Additionally, few studies that relate motivations and setting prefer-ences have compared results for national and international visitors. Finally, studies have seldom used mixed methods that pair visitor interviews with survey data. We hoped to remedy several of these shortcomings with our study design.

Case Study Methods

Research Questions

The key research questions can be summarized as follows:

1) *For the internal setting,* what are visitor preferences for differing levels of archeological restoration in the Park and do these differ among local, national and international visitors?
2) *For the external setting,* what are visitor preferences for differing land uses and levels of development on lands adjacent to the park and do these differ among local, national and international visitors?
3) *For both internal and external settings,* how might changes in internal or external settings attributes affect the visitor experience and the achievement of desired experience outcomes at CAP?

Methods

To answer these questions we used a mixture of methods including: a self-admin-istered, post-visit survey with a probability sample of visitors to CAP; two sets of in-depth interviews with a smaller sample of visitors; discussions with key contacts; and participant observation (see Table 5.1). A comprehensive visitor survey was developed in collaboration with CAP managers, Honduran and US protected area specialists from the Wildlife Conservation Society, and staff from the Center for Protected Area Management and Training at Colorado State University. The quantitative survey included items that probed visitor character-istics; preferences for the level of archeological restoration and specific manage-ment actions like tree removal; and preferences for differing land uses adjacent to CAP. The survey was pre-tested with visitors, improved, then administered in both English and Spanish visitors between June and September 2002 (n = 640) each week day between 8 a.m. and 4 p.m. for 13 weeks as they left the ruins. All visitors with the exception of tour groups had an equal opportunity to participate. Additionally, a sample of residents of the town of *Copán Ruinas* (n = 125) were given surveys to ensure that the perceptions of local people were included (McKercher & Du Cros, 2002).

Semi-structured interviews were also conducted in 2002 during the peak of visitation (May – August) with exiting visitors or small groups (n = 20) and again in July of 2003 (n = 23). The latter were more structured (Manning, 1999; Berg, 1998; Furze, De Lacy, & Birckhead, 1996) and utilized photo cues (Fairweather & Swaffield, 2002; Manning, 1999; Furze et al., 1996; Wallace &

Table 5.1   Research phases, methods used, sample sizes and type of data gathered at CAP

Phase	Method	Data gathered
1a	Quantitative survey of general visitor pop. N = 640	Trip characteristics
June-Sept. 2002	Developed using key contacts, pilot test w visitors	On-site activities
		Motivations for visit
		Preferences regarding development/ restoration:
		How natural setting affects the visit
		Preference for level of archeological restoration
		Preference adjacent land use, level of development
		Perceptions of management actions
		Demographics: age, gender, group size, education, country, religion
1b		Preferences regarding development/ restoration:
Aug. 2002	Quantitative survey of *Copanecos* N = 125	Preference for level of archeological restoration
		Preference adjacent land use, level of development
		Perceptions of management actions
		Demographics: age, gender, education, religion
2a		
May – Aug. 2002	Qualitative interviews w gen. visitor pop. N = 20	Perceptions regarding appropriate levels of internal & external restoration/ development
		Spiritual components of visit
2b		Experience outcomes, meaning & significance
July 2003	Qualitative interviews w gen. visitor pop. N = 23	Perceptions regarding appropriate levels of internal & external restoration/ development
		Perceptions of management actionsExperience outcomes, meaning & significance
Continuous	Participant observation, discussions w key contacts	Journal entries, photos of settings, shadowing of managers and guides, clarification of legal framework for recommendations

Figure 5.2 Photo cue showing the external setting of the Copan Archeological Park,
Source: Honduras, from reforestation and agriculture to residences and
businesses like modest and luxury hotels (Photos by Chris Mayer)

Trench, 1995; Whyte, 1995; Wallace, 1990) to help visitors envision a range of
both levels of restoration and differing intensities of adjacent land use (Figure 5.2).
Small groups were allowed to talk together about both their collective and individual experiences at the ruins. Interviews probed: (a) the effect provided by the
juxtaposition of restored ruins and those being reclaimed by nature as well as
other setting attributes; (b) the appropriate level of restoration at the ruins;
and (c) experience outcomes derived from internal and external settings in their
existing state (see Figure 5.3).

Participant observation was used to gather additional data. Immersion in the
community and credibility that Peace Corps service granted the lead author
allowed him to participate in planning meetings and community events and
permitted full access to the ruins, park staff, and visitors over many months.
Observations included taking photographs of setting attributes and elements of
the ruins experience as well as journal entries based on the shadowing of managers and guided tours. Key contacts were consulted to clarify the Honduran legal
framework for land use decisions and to answer questions about CAP's enabling
legislation, zoning, and restoration plans.

In addition to the descriptive statistics used for all survey items, Chi-Square,
pair-wise comparisons and a potential for conflict index (Manfredo et al. 2003)

Figure 5.3 Photo cue showing the internal setting from non-restored to totally restored ruins at the Copan Archeological Park, Honduras (Photos by Chris Mayer)

were used to look for differences in setting preferences among local, national and international visitors. Interview notes were taken and transcribed daily during the 2002 interviews, and audio recorded then transcribed during 2003. Free-form analysis (McQuarrie, 1996) was initially used to analyze responses into sub-theme categories relevant to the study objectives. Then three rounds of transcript review (open, axial, and selective coding) were used to code and improve the development and description of sub-themes pertaining to each research question (Neuman, 2000).

Study Findings

Visitor Characteristics

Visitors to Copan Archeological Park (see Table 5.2) were young (most were under 35) and better educated than the general population in their countries of origin. Excluding the sample of 125 people from *Copán Ruinas* (referred to as '*Copaneco'*), visitors came from Latin America (70%), Europe (19%) and North America (12%). Slightly more than half of the Europeans and Latin Americans were men while two thirds of the North Americans were men. The primary moti-vations for all visitors were to learn more about Mayan history and culture and to imagine what Mayan life was like.

Visitor Preferences for Internal Setting: levels of restoration and maintenance

All visitor segments showed a preference for retaining a mixture of restored ruins and those in the process of being reclaimed by nature. Europeans and North

Table 5.2 Characteristics of study participants/visitors to CAP by country of origin

	Europeans n = 112	North Americans n = 70	Latin Americans* n = 427	Copanecos** n = 125
Gender				
Females	45%	31%	47%	42%
Males	55%	69%	53%	58%
Age				
16-29	52%	53%	79%	73%
30-39	25%	14%	9%	15%
40-49	11%	16%	7%	4%
50-59	9%	14%	3%	7%
60-69	3%	3%	1%	1%
> 70			2%	1%
	M = 32	M = 34	M = 24	M = 27
Education (years)				
1 – 8	1%	4%	23%	19%
9 – 12	3%	10%	44%	45%
13 – 16	28%	38%	20%	26%
17+	68%	47%	13%	10%
	M = 18	M = 16	M = 12	M = 11

*Includes Honduran visitors both local and national
** Sample of *Copán Ruinas* residents only

Americans were similar in their strong preference for maintaining this combined setting and although the majority Latin Americans and *Copanecos* preferred the combined setting (see Table 5.3), that preference was not as strong as it was for others. Pair-wise comparisons revealed that there were no significant differences between Europeans and North Americans or between *Copanecos* and other Latin Americans.

One of the management (restoration) actions being proposed by archeologists was the cutting of trees that were growing on the un-restored ruins and in the surrounding forest to protect archeological remnants. A survey item explained that this was done to protect the ruins and then asked respondents if this would add or detract from their experience. This item served as an additional indicator of setting preference related to differing levels of restoration. The majority of respondents indicated that cutting trees would detract from their ruins experience. Figure 5.4 is a 'bubble chart', also known as the Potential for Conflict Index (Manfredo et al. 2003), and shows means and variances simultaneously with the size of each bubble denoting the degree of in-group consensus or potential for conflict (the smaller the circle, the greater the consensus of in-group opinion). Europeans, North Americans, and *Copanecos* all indicated that cutting the trees that were growing on the un-restored ruins would detract from their experience. Overall, Latin Americans were neutral and the difference with other visitors was significant ($P <. 05$), but they also had the least in-group consensus. *Copanecos*

Table 5.3 Setting attribute preferences for the level of archeological restoration within CAP

	Europeans	North Americans	Latin Americans*	Copanecos**
Restore all eventually	30%	27%	44%	44%
Maintain contrast	70%	73%	56%	56%
	n = 107	n = 70	n = 387	N = 125

*Includes Honduran visitors both local and national
** Sample of *Copán Ruinas* residents only
Pearson Chi-Square: 12.99, df = 3, Cramer's V: .14, $p < 0.01$

were strongest in their opinion that a setting with fewer trees would degrade their experience.

Interviews added rich information regarding preferences for internal setting attributes. Informants were asked to comment on the appropriate mixture of restored and un-restored ruins at CAP. Photo cues depicted different levels of restoration and the juxtaposition between restored and un-restored ruins. Several themes emerged from the analysis of responses given by visitors and these are shown here along with illustrative excerpts.

1) **Having both restored and un-restored ruins (combined setting) helps to define the essence of what ruins are and makes the passing of a civilization more apparent.** Whether due to previous experiences visiting other ruins or exposure through formal or self-study, most visitors arrive with a

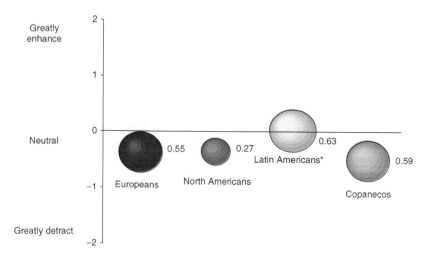

Figure 5.4 The impact of cutting trees on un-restored ruins on the visitor experience at CAP

pre-conceived notion of what Mayan ruins are. The setting they encounter either reinforces or contradicts their ideas. An *over-restored* setting is perceived to be sanitized, sterile, or inauthentic. Many informants equated advanced restoration with a loss of realism, a distortion of history, and a reduction in the affective aspects of ruins. *'It's interesting to see what it would have looked like when the Spaniards found it.'* – Terry, 27, England; *'... part of the site should reflect how nature reclaims. It's a damn good lesson actually.'* – Patrick, 25, USA; *'It just wouldn't feel like you were outside seeing ruins. It would be like you just saw a model and in restoration are we sure what it looked like?'* – Carl, 25, USA; *'Everything should not be too perfect.'* – Donald, 60, Honduras; *'It would all be sanitized* (with too much restoration).*'* – Dan, 25 England; *'Restoration up to a certain point is necessary to conserve them but at times they can make them look very superficial, so if you change them totally, it isn't the same anymore.'* – Susan, 25, Mexico. Several of those interviewed urged managers to maintain an equilibrium between what was natural and what was restored so as to avoid creating a simulacrum   a setting that has the form but not the substance of 'authentic' ruins.

2) **The combined setting provokes a broader historical context – both cultural and natural – that connects the ancient with the contemporary.** A setting that includes fully restored, partially restored and ruins being reclaimed by nature is desirable to many because it enables them to access a longer historical period and to appreciate more fully the ancient Maya civilization at Copan. One informant said, *'The image is better with the trees. When the Maya left, the jungle ate up the cities. It is very impressive to see the trees growing out of the ruins.'* – Luis, 56, Spain; *'... so that you can appreciate the art that the Maya have left for us, for me, about 80% restored is good and the rest left as you find it.'* – Roland, 21, Guatemala; *'This site gives you a good feel for the culture that without the trees* (taking over some ruins) *I wouldn't get.'* – Marcy, 25, USA; *'You bridge a couple of centuries because those trees are at least three or four hundred years old.'* – John, 59, Holland.

3) **The combined setting provokes reflection about sustainability and the human/nature relationship**. For many years, the reasons behind the collapse of the Mayan civilization were a mystery. Travel writers used this to create a romantic mystique that fueled the imaginations of visitors (Webster, 2002). In recent years, anthropologists and archaeologists have linked the collapse of the ancient Maya civilization to environmental exploitation and degradation (Diamond, 2005; Fash, 2001; Webster, 2002). Many informants drew from the setting distinct parallels between the collapse of the Maya, the use of natural resources, and the future direction of our own civilization: *'Man can do many things but nature is stronger.'* – Ben, 58, Belgium; *'It is good to see the park surrounded by forest. It raises questions in my mind like, what are we doing today, what track are we on?'* – Steve, 33,

USA; '*… they didn't live in harmony with the environment. It's the same thing we are doing in the whole world.*' – Bill, 67, Canada.

4) **The combined setting retains the enchantment/mystery of the still undiscovered and can enhance tranquility, introspection and spirituality**. The mixture of forest and ruins as well as the intangible mystery and the allure of the yet undiscovered are valued setting attributes. '*The jungle has a more spiritual ambience to it rather than only a history museum, it is fairly quiet and you can find a part you like and just absorb the atmosphere a little bit. It is tranquil.*' – Roger, 25, Great Britain; '*These places can be doorways to your own inner self. Here there is mystery, just enough magic left to draw people in.*' – Jude, 57, USA; '*It is much easier to connect with yourself here* (in the combined setting)*…a perfect place for meditation.*' – Lisa, 31, Germany; '*To see the stones displaced by the roots, I prefer that. You can philosophize much, much better.*' – Paul, 43, USA.

5) **The combined setting is more hospitable, relaxing, and enables an appreciation of nature as well as culture for many.** Many informants referred to the importance of maintaining the trees and natural vegetation for their amenity value. Instead of being perceived as damaging to the ruins, the trees, understory, lichens, and birds enhanced the value of the experience at the ruins: '*It is the trees that give the refreshing climate to this place.*' – Anna, 28, Honduras; '*Can you imagine walking at noon without the trees?*' – Maria, 25, from the town of *Copán Ruinas*; '*Nature cannot be separated. It is as important as the architecture. The sound of the birds is part of the enchantment of the place.*' – Thomas, 52, USA; '*I came to appreciate the works of the Maya, but one can relax looking at the ruins in the total silence of the forest. It is fascinating because there are no car sounds … there are only the sounds of beautiful nature.*' – Roland, 21, Guatemala.

6) **Some restoration is essential as non-restored ruins are inscrutable**. Maya structures in the form of tree-covered mounds are spread throughout CAP. To the untrained eye, these mounds can easily be mistaken for natural hillocks. Some respondents commented that un-restored remnants were less enjoyable, or that restored ruins were more comprehendible and revealed the design, artistry, craftsmanship and ingenuity of the Maya: '*Some nature is great, but I don't understand what it is … what did the Maya create?*' Nicholas, 47, Italy; '*I thought it was a little hill or something. If you want to show the world the culture of the* (ancient) *city, you have to develop the site.*' – Roberto, 20, Guatemala.

7) **Remnants must be protected**. Many visitors recognized the need to protect restored and un-restored remnants at CAP but responses varied about when it is best to clear vegetation near restored ruins or on top of un-restored ruins: '*If you have a street and a tree's roots are ruining the street, you have to do something about it.*' – Edward, 22, Costa Rica; '*If the roots of your tree are dying then your ruin is dying because after so many years, it hangs on the trees.*' – John, 59, Holland; '*When the Park removes the protection of the shade, the sun and water fall directly on the stones and causes even more damage.* – Charles, 25, *Copán Ruinas*.

Visitor Preferences for External Setting: Appropriate land uses adjacent to Copan Archeological Park

The majority of visitors indicated a strong preference for maintaining agricultural or forested lands between the park and the nearby town of *Copán Ruinas*. Respondents were given a multiple choice question where they could indicate whether they preferred to see the private land surrounding CAP: (a) kept in some mix of natural and agricultural uses; (b) returned to a natural condition like forest; (c) the town should be allowed to grow to meet the Park; or (d) used for tourism-related development such as restaurants, lodging, or retail stores. Table 5.4 indicates that all visitor types showed a strong preference for maintaining a pastoral or forested buffer around the park. Latin Americans were more likely to approve of urban expansion (10%) or tourism infrastructure (19%). *Copanecos* were nearly evenly divided in their preference for agricultural land use or reforestation (44% and 45% respectively). Europeans were the least likely to approve of either urban expansion or tourism related development (P <. 01). Overall results suggest that respondents showed a strong affinity for maintaining a natural or pastoral setting in the CAP buffer zone.

During the two sets of interviews, questions and photo cues probed visitor perceptions about appropriate land use adjacent to CAP. Their comments mirrored survey results and provided much detail regarding the dominant preference for not intensifying land uses between the park and the town or around the park. Again, interview data were analyzed for salient themes and connections between setting and desired experience outcomes. Themes were accompanied by illustrative interview excerpts.

1) **The walk from *Copán Ruinas* provides an important transitional setting that enhances the visitor experience at Copan Archeological Park**. Several interviewees described how the walk between the town and the park provided historical context, geographic orientation, and a cultural appreciation for a mixed ancient and contemporary yet traditional rural landscape. Some described the setting as one which allowed them to anticipate

Table 5.4 Visitor perceptions of appropriate land uses adjacent to CAP

Preference	Europeans	North Americans	Latin Americans*	Copanecos**
1. Agricultural	60%	48%	35%	44%
2. Reforestation	38%	45%	36%	45%
3. Town grow to meet park	1%	6%	10%	5%
4. Tourist infrastructure	1%	1%	19%	6%
	n = 111	n = 69	N = 377	n = 125

*Includes Honduran visitors to CAP
** Sample of *Copán Ruinas* residents only
Pearson Chi-Square: 62.63 Cramer's V: .18, $p < 0.01$

the ruins experience, form questions and to see the Honduran countryside more intimately than they had previously been able to do: *'... it prepares you to see the ancient civilization.'* – Paul, 43, France; *'I like to see the agriculture and the local people going about their day.'* – Sam, 27, USA; *'It was kind of fun having that buildup of getting more excited about what you are walking towards.'* – Carl, 25, USA; *'I thought it was very pleasant walking under the trees. I just got here yesterday, so I really hadn't had a chance to feel the countryside, or feel the nature except from the window of a bus.'* – Laura, 47, USA.

2)   **Copan Archeological Park is a relatively small area which needs buffering if the internal setting is to be protected and the valley as a cultural landscape associated with ancient Copan is to be recognizable.** Visitors valued the quiet, the tranquility, the night sky, and other aspects of their visit that were currently intact because the surrounding area does yet not interfere with these qualities: *'Sincerely, I am afraid that this whole area will be nothing but concrete here. We only have this area and we have to restore, recuperate and buy more of it.'* – Donald, 60, Honduras; *'We should maintain it* (adjacent lands) *intact and not permit them to fill it with electricity, cars, construction and all. They should preserve the entire area's natural history – it would have to be an area much bigger- not just the area of the pyramids* (CAP area).' – Javier, 44, Ecuador. Since ancient Copan once utilized the whole valley around CAP, visitors felt that the scope and scale of the experience would be diminished if the area was changed from pastoral to developed: *'It* (the walk) *gave me a sense of the physical scope of the entire site. If it were urbanized, I would have a harder time figuring out what is Copan versus the* (original) *Maya city.'* - Gavin, 29, USA; *'The government should buy the land around the park. It is surrounded by archeologically significant lands.'* – Maria, 25, *Copán Ruinas*. Maria went on to suggest that adjacent lands should become a mixture of other Mayan sites, reforestation and recreational areas for families.

3)   **Visitors enjoy the current size, scale and level of tourist infrastructure in *Copán Ruinas* as well as the fact that it is close but not too close to CAP.** Most of those interviewed commented on how much they enjoyed the town as part of the experience, but that it depended on its not losing its friendly small town atmosphere. Many feared that it might: *'It* (urban expansion) *would be like a circus, but they could prohibit that. I would like to come back with my children in 20 years and see it like it is now.'* – Edward, 31, Costa Rica; *'I don't think that the town growing will help us much. The people come here and they say 'Copan isn't a city, it is still a town'. It is peaceful and still beautiful, but I don't think the peace we have will last.'* – Carlos, 25, *Copán Ruinas*; *'I like how it is now because it isn't so exaggerated. Everybody likes the environment of a small town, with the customs and culture that have not been affected.'* – Susana, 25, Mexico; *'It is just that you see a lot of this* (development) *in big cities. We lose what is Honduras – the*

green, the mountains, the trees. You lose a lot because it will look like any other place.' – Emily, 20, Honduras. Other informants noted that a rural setting that protects open space demonstrates respect for the significance of the ruins. Many commented that the town was the appropriate center of tourism infrastructure if CAP is to remain more competitive with other Mayan sites.

4) **Many visitors recognize the ecological benefits of reforestation around CAP but feel that both agriculture and natural forest provide an appropriate setting next to CAP.** Reinforcing survey results, those interviewed may prefer forest but can support an external setting that promotes either forest related or traditional farming. A pastoral or agricultural countryside with low densities of people working the land was seen as natural and acceptable for many: *'To reforest is one solution but the forest reserve or the agriculture are both similar. They both appear alike to us – like nature.'*– Nicholas, 47, Italy; *'For me, reforested is close to perfect, however an environment in the middle, like agriculture, is good too. This way people can live there without destroying the natural environment totally.'* – Roberto, 20, Guatemala.

5) **Informants were reluctant to impose their values on the local community.** When it came to control over the development of adjacent lands, many informants followed the expression of their personal preferences by assigning importance to the opinions, well-being and autonomy of local residents: Dave, 21, from France preferred to see *'… the level (of development) that is good for the people.'* Although Nicholas, 47, from Italy, said that reforestation would be *'… the safest for everything,'* he added *'… it would feel like the people around here didn't have a stake in this and that it was all being preserved for visitors.'* Dan, 24, from England said *'It is important for the community or whoever controls the development to keep their eye on the needs of the community because these ruins are going to bring people regardless.'*

Discussion and Recommendations

Protected area managers, and municipal officials for that matter, must make decisions that balance 1) user preferences with 2) legal and institutional directives, 3) natural resource constraints and 4) the economic and human resources they have to work with. The visitor preferences revealed by this study indicate that restraint should be used with regard to both the level of restoration within Copan Archeological Park and the level and type of development permitted on private lands adjacent to the Park. Moreover, visitors have articulated how particular setting attributes are related to the experience outcomes they seek providing much information for those doing on-site interpretation. Principal visitor motivations of wanting to learn more about Maya history and culture and imagine what Maya life was like, turn out to be more nuanced than survey questions alone might indicate. For many, such learning incorporates reflection on why civilizations succeed or fail, on the human-nature relationship and personal introspection, for example, and a setting having restored, partially restored ruins and ruins being reclaimed by and integrated with nature makes those experiences easier to achieve.

Because of Copan's small size, visitors perceive a need to protect the internal setting by buffering the Park with appropriate adjacent land uses or by land acquisition. There was a shared apprehension that intensifying development would create steep ecological, cultural and aesthetic gradients at the Park's edge that would change the nature of the visitor experience within the Park as well. Nearly all visitors found both the location and size of tourist infrastructure in *Copán Ruinas* and the walk through the rural countryside to be important setting components that enhanced their experience. Without planning and taking action, the current trajectory of both internal and external development are likely to alter these preferred setting attributes and perhaps affect the long-term quality and economic sustainability of tourism in Copan, as has happened in many similar locations (Pedersen, 2003; Wallace et al., 2005; McKercher & Du Cros, 2002). To maintain the quality of the visitor experience, comply with IHAH and World Heritage guidelines and deal with the physical constraints of the CAP site will require a sound internal and external zoning strategy, careful visitor management and a cross-boundary collaboration between CAP and the Municipality of *Copán Ruinas* regarding land use decisions and land conservation.

Managing the Internal Setting

Both the 1984 and 2003 management plans for CAP call for zoning within and around the Park. Study results and the behavioral approach suggest that several internal zones are needed to insure diverse experience opportunities and appropriate levels of protection for Park resources (Manning, 1999). These might include: an 'intensive use' or group activity zone where the entrance, visitor center, outdoor classrooms, interpretive trail, and picnic areas are located; a 'core archeological zone' taking in the Central Ruins (Great Plaza, Acropolis, Cemetery, Ballcourt, Hieroglyphic Staircase, etc.) many of which are restored with hardened viewing areas and interpretive signage capable of accommodating larger groups; and a 'natural archeological' zone with smaller, more intimate viewing areas with shaded alcoves, benches or large rocks and native vegetation that emphasize the juxtaposition of restored and un-restored ruins and sounds of nature. The latter areas with centuries old trees, lichen and moss growing on ruins should, as Woodward (2001) suggests, reveal 'the hand of Time, and the contest between the individual and the universe.' These zones would be distinguishable not only by their physical setting attributes but also by the level of infrastructure development, the permitted group sizes, the activities available, and the type of managerial presence including the presence of CAP staff, signage, and trail design among others. There could be some mix of restored and un-restored ruins in each of the last two zones so that tour groups visiting the Central Plaza might also witness the contrast.

Interpretation for visitors should address the full-spectrum of ruins from un-restored to fully-restored. Some un-restored or partially restored ruins could be interpreted for visitors in a way that helps to overcome their inscrutability and boost interest, understanding, and appreciation. Tree covered mounds could be compared to others like them that have been restored or utilize artistic renderings depicting and interpreting what they may have looked like thus reducing the need for restoration, disturbances to the archeological record or natural surroundings and nature's propensity for self-renewal. Whenever possible, non-native or tree species not used by former Mayan residents should be removed to improve naturalness and historical accuracy. Historically significant trees such as the rubber tree (instrumental in the Maya ballgame), the ceiba (Maya *tree of life*), and cacao (the *food of the gods*) can be planted where they support the interpretive program and do not threaten archeological remnants.

Obviously, managers must also be concerned that substituting interpretation for restoration or the slowing of restoration activities does not lead to the stagnation of a research program that pursues information about the past that has value for its own sake (Lipe, 1984). New restoration projects do peak curiosity and attract new and repeat visitors and deepen the understanding of Maya culture. Fortunately, there are many sites in the Copan Valley outside of CAP that can, if IHAH and the Municipality collaborate and provide incentives to private landowners, allow such research to continue. Another option is to unearth and explore sites internal to CAP and then return them to an un-restored state that protects them from the elements.

Managing the External Setting

Visitors have confirmed that land use around CAP can have an impact on the quality of the visitor experience and the realization of desired outcomes within the park. They have described important setting attributes for both the buffer zone and the town of *Copán Ruinas*. Meanwhile, a number of subsistence activities such as firewood gathering occur in and around the Park, and commercial development projects including, an airport, hotels, private schools, quarries, communications towers, water lines and roads have been proposed or started adjacent to CAP. Some of these projects were stopped, others mitigated to some degree but the land use decision process has been reactive, confusing, and the responsibilities of overlapping jurisdictions are unclear (Wallace et al., 2005). Enabling legislation for CAP does include the designation of a buffer zone around the Park and both management plans have proposed management sub-zones within that buffer zone. Additionally, the national Law for Cultural Heritage (*Ley Para La Proteccion del Patrimonio Cultural,* 1998) gives IHAH the power to regulate development that 'alters the cultural or natural context' of archeological sites which presumably includes within buffer zones. At the same time, with the advent of decentralization in Honduras, the Municipality governing Copan has the authority to create land use plans and authorize development on private land within its jurisdiction and the national level Natural Resources and Environment

Ministry is responsible for the environmental impact statements required for developments of a certain size or for public works. Focus groups and meetings with key contacts during the case study found that it was still unclear how these overlapping jurisdictions would create and implement a collaborative land use decision process.

Recommendations for strengthening the local land use decision process

Ultimately, sustainable tourism in Copan will require an adopted sub-area land use plan and code that recognizes a buffer zone around CAP, and sets acceptable land uses and densities and performance criteria (height, bulk, setbacks, lighting, landscaping that would not compete with the grandeur of or impact the ruins) for any proposed development in that zoning district. The plan and land use code would be best adopted by both the IHAH and local government officials and become part of the Municipal master plan and referenced in the park's management/implementation plan. Moreover, there should be a joint commission, development review, and decision process for such proposals with shared responsibility and decision power by both the Municipality of *Copán Ruinas* and IHAH. A shared data base regarding land tenure, infrastructure, resource constraints and capabilities, cultural sites, sensitive natural areas as well as joint oversight and patrolling - especially along the walkway used by visitors - would serve to galvanize inter-jurisdictional collaborative efforts. Joint planning of this type is already being carried out by the Lake Yojoa Commonwealth in Honduras which has established a legal precedent for collaboration between protected area and local government officials (AMAPURLAGO, 2002).

In other countries, the use of transferable development rights has been incorporated into such sub-area plans to protect special places. As was done in another World Heritage Site, the Sian Kaan Biosphere Reserve in Mexico, the town of *Copán Ruinas* could designate a receiving area where tourist development is desirable and require the transfer the rights for such development from the buffer zone. This would be in keeping with the perceptions of visitors regarding the appropriate location for such development. At the time he co-authored CAP's first management plan, Barborak (1984) wrote 'It should be stressed that concentrated, modest, architecturally integrated tourist facilities can provide many more benefits to local communities than high-class, high-cost hotels, restaurants, and guide services.' An equally important and complementary approach for retaining the rural/pastoral setting that is important to visitors and which buffers CAP is the purchase of private land or conservation easements in the buffer zone. Land purchased in fee could either be turned over to IHAH, a conservation organization, or be leased back to original owners or conservation buyers with deed restrictions ensuring land uses that are compatible with CAP. The Copan Foundation, a strong local NGO, is a logical entity to spearhead fundraising for such conservation efforts.

Recognizing the Interpretive Potential of Setting

We saw how visitors to cultural heritage sites like CAP appeared to have motivations and desired experience outcomes that were closely tied to particular setting attributes that still exist but may be threatened. According to Lipe's comparative study of world cultural resource management, 'When one encounters a cultural resource, the vision of the past that it evokes and the affect associated with the experience is highly conditioned, if not determined, by the other knowledge about the past that the participant brings to the encounter or that he is provided on the spot' (1984, p. 4).

The interpretive potential of cultural heritage sites like CAP resides in a seamless landscape that is both within and adjacent to the site. The setting itself can be considered a form of interpretive media that can instruct, inspire, and connect visitors to cultural heritage sites such as ancient ruins to their inherent significances. Interpretive potential as we define it here is the *best possible physical, social, and cultural/historical milieu for transmitting and receiving the emotional and intellectual meanings of a place and is closely tied to the elements of setting.*

The interpretive potential of setting is not an entirely new idea. Tilden (1968) acknowledged that a well preserved monument 'speaks for itself' but does so partially in a language not understood by all visitors, thus requiring the help of interpreters to 'give life to the ideas and images of material remains' (Silberman, 2006). Others have long acknowledged that protected area visitors seek out the settings that will make the achievement of desired experience outcomes more likely (Manning, 1999). Since the 1970s, it has been suggested that to optimize visitor experience satisfaction, protected area managers should understand visitor motives, provide some diversity of management zones and pay attention to the setting integrity of each (Clark & Stankey, 1979; Brown, Driver, & McConnell, 1978).

Visitors and local residents provided considerable information about what combination of internal and adjacent land setting attributes bestowed the richest experiences and facilitated connection to the *genius loci* (spirit of place) of the park (Mayer & Wallace, 2007). We found that visitors expect, are stimulated by and glad to find non-restored ruins that provide the juxtaposition of nature and culture inherent in carved stones inextricably tangled with roots and vines. Perspectives about the passage of time, the collapse of the Mayan empire, their use of natural resources, and the future direction of our own civilization depend on visitors being able to ponder the mix of restored, partially restored, and non-restored ruins. Restoration creates interpretive potential but can also remove it. Many informants equated advanced restoration with a loss of realism, a distortion of history, and a reduction in the affective aspects of what ruins are. Restored and non-restored ruins work together as interpretive media that protect the spirit of the place and provide a wider diversity of possible interpretive messages and experience opportunities.

The walk through a traditional agricultural landscape before arriving at the ruins provides a setting that enhances each visitor's experience better than moving from an urbanized setting directly to entrance to the cultural site. The interpretive potential of the site itself or of the programs that might emanate from it may be diminished if the balance of restored and non-restored ruins is lost or if development intensifies adjacent to them. Some combination of setting attributes that optimize interpretive potential can be recognized and planned for.

CAP's external setting provides a valued transition zone between the town and the park that primes the visitor experience and is bound to the interpretive potential of the park. The buffering mix of agriculture and forest possess the 'extant' natural and cultural contexts that have existed since the time of the ancient Maya at Copan (Schlesinger, 2001). The pastoral setting holds potential for visitors to better understand local history and traditional agricultural practices including maize production and agro-forestry, the origins of which reach back to ancient Copan. It also protects a natural soundscape and night sky that were at the center of Mayan cosmology. The walk through this setting permitted one to better envision the scope and scale of the valley during the time when the ancient Maya flourished thereby providing context and extending the experience.

If valued setting attributes become threatened, then protecting interpretive potential should then become a high priority for managers and those who earn their living from tourism. We suggest that being able to inform and influence planning decisions so that they yield an optimal mixture of setting attributes is itself a seldom discussed part of the interpreter's art. This is especially true for cultural sites where both the 'original objects' (Tilden, 1977) and the emotional and intellectual connections to the inherent meaning of the resources (Brochu and Merriman, 2002) are complex and often occur within a limited spatial context. This form of interpretive planning is proactive and might be thought of as 'experience design' that is informed by visitor research. Interpreters and guides who are the voice for the resource must now use that voice with archaeologists, site managers, and local communities during the planning process and to inform the day-to-day management decisions that affect settings and their interpretive potential. Testimony from interpreters about the interpretive themes that particular settings provide and the relation of the setting to experience quality and sustainable visitation can be compelling for planners and decision makers who must make controversial decisions about land use.

Implications for the Behavioral Model

Finally, it was mentioned earlier that the Behavioral Model assumes a linkage between the settings visitors seek and the fulfillment of desired experience outcomes, and while managers cannot guarantee visitors a satisfying experience, they can control the integrity and quality of setting attributes that visitors seek out, thereby making the achievement of desired, often psychological, experiences more likely. Past, largely quantitative studies have shown a modest relationship between visitor motivations and setting (Manning, 1999) and McCool and others (1985, 1982) have suggested that some motivations or desired experience

Figure 5.5 Copan Honduras
Source: own

outcomes can be achieved in multiple settings. In one of the few studies involving international visitors, Wallace and Smith (1996) found a weak relationship between motives and setting preferences among visitors to five Costa Rican protected areas. In the Copan study however, especially in the qualitative data provided by interviews, visitors have clearly linked the satisfaction of particular outcomes – learning about Mayan history and culture, gaining a broader under-standing of human-nature relationships, social sustainability, and one's place in the world - with particular setting attributes. It may well be that cultural sites like the Copan Archeological Park, which have a more specific purpose and concom-itantly draw a visitor with a narrower range of visitor motivations or desired outcomes, are where such linkages are seen most clearly and where changes in setting attributes can have a more profound affect. Using a mixed-methods approach, which questions visitors directly about the importance of setting in a variety of sites, will continue to inform the behavioral model.

In conclusion, this case study reveals the importance of information about user preferences for both internal and external settings. Finding appropriate levels of internal and external development is essential for making tourism in sites like Copan more sustainable. These challenges exist in many protected areas and their gateway communities worldwide and will require a collaborative cross-boundary approach to achieve their solution.

References

AMAPURLAGO. (2002) *Personería Jurídica y Estatutos del Asociación de Municipios del Lago de Yojoa y su Área de Influencia.* Lago de Yojoa, Honduras.

Barborak, J. (2004) Personal interview: Reflections on 25 years of association with Copan. Fort Collins, CO.

Barborak, J., McFarland, C., & Morales, R. (1984). *Plan de Manejo y Desarrollo del Monumento Nacional Ruinas de Copán.* Turrialba, Costa Rica: UNESCO, IHAH, CATIE.

Baudez, C. F. (1994) *Maya sculpture of Copan: The iconography.* Norman: University of Oklahoma Press.

Berg, B. L. (1998) *Qualitative research methods for the social sciences* (3rd ed.). Boston: Allyn and Bacon.

Brochu, L., & Merriman, T. (2002). *Personal interpretation: connecting your audience to heritage resources.* Fort Collins, CO: InterpPress.

Brown, P. J., Driver, B. L., & McConnell, C. (1978) *The opportunity spectrum concept and behavioral information in outdoor recreation resource supply inventories: Background and application.* USDA Forest Service General Technical Report (RM-55). Fort Collins, CO.

Clark, R. N., & Stankey, G. H. (1979) *The recreation opportunity spectrum: a framework for planning, management, and research.* Portland, OR: USDA Forest Service Pacific Northwest Forest and Range Experiment Station.

Copan Archeological Park Management Plan (draft). (2003) Tegucigalpa, Honduras: Instituto Hondureño de Antropología e Historia.

Diamond, J. M. (2005) *Collapse: how societies choose to fail or succeed.* New York: Viking.

Driver, B. L. (1975) *Elements of outdoor recreation planning.* Ann Arbor: University of Michigan. School of Natural Resources.

Driver, B. L., & Brown, P. J. (1975) A socio-psychological definition of recreation demand, with implications for recreation resource planning. In *Assessing Demand for Outdoor Recreation.* (pp. 62-68). Washington, DC: National Academy of Sciences.

Fairweather, J.R., and Swaffield, S.R. (2002) Visitor's and locals' experience of Rotorua, New Zealand: an interpretive study using photographs of landscapes and Q method. *International Journal of Tourism Research* 4 (4): 283–87.

Fash, W. L. (Winter, 2002) *Tourism and the archaeology of state-facing challenges: the case of Copan, Honduras.* ReVista: Harvard Review of Latin America.

Fash, W. L. (2001) *Scribes, warriors and kings: the city of Copan and the ancient Maya* (Rev. ed.). London and New York: Thames and Hudson.

Feilden, B. M., & Jokilehto, J. (1998) *Management guidelines for world cultural heritage sites* (2nd edn). Rome: ICCROM.

Floyd, M. F., & Gramann, J. H. (1997) Experience-Based Setting Management: Implications for Market Segmentation of Hunters. *Leisure Sciences, 19*, 113–127.

Furze, B., De Lacy, T., & Birckhead, J. (1996) *Culture, conservation, and biodiversity: the social dimension of linking local level development and conservation through protected areas.* Chichester, New York: John Wiley.

ICOMOS. (1999) *International Cultural Tourism Charter, Managing Tourism At Places Of Heritage Significance*: ICOMOS.

Informe Final del Año 2002. (2002) Instituto Hondureño de Antropología e Historia. Tegucigalpa, Honduras.

Kelleher, M. (2004) Images of the Past: Historical authenticity and inauthenticity from Disney to Times Square. *CRM: The Journal of Heritage Stewardship, 1*(24), 6–19. U.S. National Park Service.

Lipe, W. D. (1984) Value and Meaning in Cultural Resources. In H. Cleere (Ed.), *Approaches to the archaeological heritage: a comparative study of world cultural resource management systems.* New York: Cambridge University Press.

Ley para la Protección del Patrimonio Cultural de la Nación. Decreto 220–97. (1997) *La Gaceta* (pp. 5–9). Tegucigalpa, Honduras.

Manfredo, M. J., Vaske, J. J., & Teel, T. L. (2003) The Potential for Conflict Index: A graphic approach to practical significance of human dimensions research. *Human Dimensions of Wildlife, 8*(3), 219–228.

Manning, R. E. (1999) *Studies in outdoor recreation: search and research for satisfaction* (2nd ed.). Corvallis, OR: Oregon State University Press.

Mayer, C. C. (2003) *Audience analysis report of findings: Copan Ruins Archeological Park.* Copán Ruinas, Honduras: Instituto Hondureño de Antropología e Historia.

Mayer, C. & Wallace G.N. (2007). Appropriate levels of restoration and development at Copan Archaeological Park: setting attributes affecting the visitor experience. *Journal of Ecotourism*, 6(2), 91–110.

McCool, S., Stankey, G., and Clark, R. (1985) Choosing recreation settings: processes, findings and research directions. *Proceedings - Symposium on Recreation Choice Behavior.* USDA Forest Service General Technical Report INT -184, 1–8.

McCool, S. and Utter, J. (1982) Recreation activity packages at water-based resources. *Leisure Sciences, 1,*

McKercher, B., & Du Cros, H. (2002) *Cultural tourism: the partnership between tourism and cultural heritage management.* New York: Haworth Hospitality Press.

McQuarrie, E. F. (1996) *The market research toolbox: a concise guide for beginners.* Thousand Oaks, CA: Sage Publications.

Neuman, W. L. (2000) *Social research methods: qualitative and quantitative approaches* (4th ed.). Boston: Allyn and Bacon.

Pedersen, A. (2003) *Managing tourism at World Heritage sites.* Paris: United Nations Environment Programme.

Sabloff, J. A. (1994) *The new archaeology and the ancient Maya.* New York: Scientific American Library.

Schlesinger, V. (2001). *Animals and plants of the ancient Maya: A guide* (1st ed.). Austin: University of Texas Press.

Schreyer, R., & Driver, B. L. (1989) The benefits of outdoor recreation participation. In *Outdoor Recreation Benchmark 1988: Proceedings of the National Outdoor Recreation Forum.* Vol. SE-52, (pp. 472–482): USDA Forest Service General Technical Report.

Shackley, M. L. (2000) *Visitor management: case studies from World Heritage sites.* Oxford; Boston: Butterworth-Heinemann.

Silberman, N. (2006). ICOMOS-Ename Charter: New principles for interpreting cultural heritage sites. *The George Wright Forum, 23*(1), 28–39.

Tilden, F. (1977). *Interpreting our heritage; principles and practices for visitor services in parks, museums, and historic places.* Chapel Hill: University of North Carolina Press. (Originally published in 1957).

Tilden, F. (1968). *The fifth essence, an invitation to share in our eternal heritage.* Washington, DC: The National Park Trust Fund Board.

UNESCO. (1980) *Convention Concerning the Protection of the World Cultural and Natural Heritage* (No. CC-80/.016.10). Paris: United Nations Educational Scientific and Cultural Organization.

Wallace, G. N. (1990) *The impacts of external development on the economic and aesthetic Values of Theodore Roosevelt National Park*. Laramie, WY: University of Wyoming, NPS Research Center.

Wallace, G.N., Barborak, J., and C.G. MacFarland (2005) Land use planning and regulation in and around protected areas: A study of best practices and capacity building needs in Mexico and Central America. *Natureza y Conservacao* (Brazilian Journal of Nature and Conservation) 3(2): 147–167.

Wallace, G. N., & Smith, M. (1996) A comparison of motivations, preferred management actions, and setting preferences among Costa Ricans, North Americans and European Visitors to five protected areas in Costa Rica. *Journal of Park and Recreation Administration, 15*(1).

Wallace, G. N., & Trench, K. (1995) *A study of rock climbers in Joshua Tree National Park: implications for the visitor experience and resource protection (VERP) management framework*: National Park Service.

Webster, D. L. (2002) *The fall of the ancient Maya: solving the mystery of the Maya collapse*. London; New York. Thames & Hudson.

Whyte, W. F. (1995) Interviewing in Field Research. In R. G. Burgess (Ed.), *Field Research: A sourcebook and field manual*. (pp. 111–122). London: George Allen & Unwin.

Woodward, C. (2001) *In ruins* (1st American ed.). New York: Pantheon Books.

World Tourism Organization (2001) *Cultural heritage and tourism development: a report on the International Conference on Cultural Tourism*, Siem Reap, Cambodia, December 2000 (No. 9284404843). Madrid, Spain: World Tourism Organization.

Wurz, J. B. (1996) *Applying a recreation opportunity spectrum framework in Galapagos National Park: Implications for managers and theorists.* Available from the Center for Protected Area Management and Training, College of Natural Resources, Fort Collins, CO: Colorado State University.

6 Mamirauá

Community based ecotourism in a sustainable development reserve in the Amazon Basin

Ariane Janér*, Nelissa Peralta Bezerra**
and Rodrigo Zomkowski Ozório***

Introduction

The Mamiraua Sustainable Development Reserve is located in the state of Amazonas in Brazil and today is part of the UNESCO World Heritage Site – Central Amazonian Complex. Ecotourism was introduced here in 1999 after a business plan showed it was feasible to build and operate a small floating ecolodge. Since then economic, environmental and social results and impacts have been measured by the Instituto de Desenvolvimento Sustentável Mamiraua.

This case study looks at the 10 years of community-based ecotourism of as a sustainable business and examines the triple bottom line of the Uakari Floating Lodge.

In order to understand the context, some key data about tourism in Brazil and the history and importance of Mamiraua are given. The ecotourism concept as laid out in the business plan is then summarized.

Next the economic, environmental and social impacts are discussed in detail. The economic dimension is also discussed from the business case point of view and uses both the detailed internal data of the IDSM, as well as external data. For evaluating environmental and social impacts only internal data are used.

The case study also reviews the main obstacles that the ISDM team encountered in successfully managing the ecotourism program.

Mamiraua Case Study

a) Brazil Country Report

Brazil is a huge and complex country. It has one of the largest economies in the world and is considered an important emerging economy together with India, China and Russia (BRIC).

*Instituto EcoBrasil, Rio de Janeiro, RJ, Brazil
**Instituto de Desenvolvimento Sustentável Mamirauá, Tefé, AM, Brazil
***Instituto de Desenvolvimento Sustentável Mamirauá, Tefé, AM, Brazil

The GDP per capita of US$ 10.000 hides the fact that there are many pockets of poverty and big income inequalities in Brazil. But the socio-economic indices are improving and the gap between rich and poor is steadily reducing.

Brazil has **six major biomes**: the Amazon Rainforest, Atlantic Rainforest, Cerrado (Savannah), Caatinga (scrub desert), Pantanal, (wetlands) and Pampas (grasslands). Of these the Amazon is the largest and most intact, but increasingly under threat. In terms of (un)sustainable development, there are tensions between the use of space and natural resources between major economic activities such as forestry, cattle ranching, agriculture, energy and mining versus conservation and tourism.

The World Economic Forum (WEF) ranks Brazil 45 out of 133 countries in terms of international tourism competitiveness. The report considers tourism infrastructure and lack of qualified labour as weak points, while pointing to its immense natural and cultural resources as strong points.

The World Travel and Tourism Council on the basis of Tourism Satellite Account analysis estimates that the tourism industry in Brazil accounts for 2.5% of GDP and jobs, while the tourism economy as a whole is about 6% of GDP.

Brazil has a **huge domestic market** and this is true for tourism as well. In 2008 Brazilians took an estimated 160 million domestic trips, whilst foreign arrivals numbered 5 million. In terms of tourism revenues the difference is much smaller, as average expenditure on domestic trips is considerably lower than that for international visits.

Table 6.1 Brazil General and Tourism Indicators

Brazil Indicators	Value	Comment
Area	8.5 million km^2	*5th largest*
Population	> 190 million	*5th largest, 84% urban*
GPD	US$ 2 trillion	*Ranking 9*
GDP/cap PPP	US$ 10.000/cap	*Ranking 75*
Human Development Index	0.81	*75 out of 182*
Number of Municipalities	5500	
Number of Cities > 1 million	14	*+/– 20% of population*
World Heritage Sites	17 (19)	*19 destinations*
National Parks	64	
Federal Protected Area	> 7%	*of total territory*
Domestic Market Trips 2008	160 million	*Estimate*
Domestic Airport Arrivals 2008	49 million	
Foreign Tourism 2008	5,1 million	*Rank 41 out of 107*
Foreign Airport Arrivals 2008	6,5 million	
Number of Tourism Destinations	1800	*A third of municipalities*
Number of Priority Destinations	65	*For international market*

Source: EcoBrasil compiled from IBGE, Ministry of Tourism, ICMBio, UNDP, World Bank

b) Description of Project Context

Geographic Area

The **Mamirauá Sustainable Development Reserve** protects 1.1 million hectares of *'várzea'* (flooded forest) at the confluence of the Japurá and Solimões rivers in the Central Amazon Basin. *'Varzeas'* are the most fertile areas of the Amazon and, because of their easy accessibility, very vulnerable to unsustainable exploitation of their natural resources. One key characteristic of the these is the water cycle. In the Mamiraua area differences in water level of 14 meters between the 'dry' and 'wet' season have been recorded.

The gateway to Mamirauá is the municipality of **Tefé.** This town which is 663 km upriver from Manaus was founded in 1686. Its economy depends on fishing, agriculture, commerce and services.

Since 1998, Mamirauá has had an adjacent sister Sustainable Development Reserve, Amanã, which protects *'terra firme'* rainforest. Since 2002 the two reserves, together with the Jaú National Park, have been part of a **World Heritage Site: the Central Amazonian Conservation Complex** (see Figure 6.1).

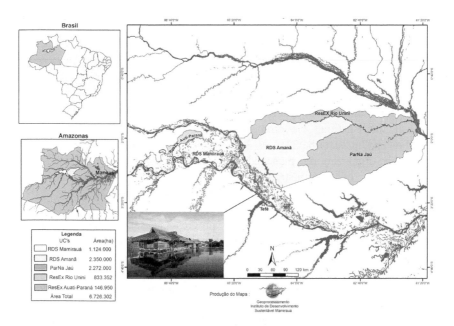

Figure 6.1 Mamirauá Sustainable Development Reserve and Central Amazon Conservation Complex.
Source: IDSM

Project History and Timeline

The Mamirauá story started with a doctoral study by Dr Marcio Ayres on the endemic White Uakari monkey (*Cacajao calvus calvus*) in 1983. Dr Ayres realized that these monkeys would not survive without protection of their habitat and Mamirauá became a protected area called Ecological Station in 1986. He also anticipated that the protected status of their habitat would not be effective without the involvement of the local community and he therefore lobbied for a new type of conservation unit: in 1996, Mamirauá became Brazil's first Sustainable Development Reserve.

Involving the community meant they needed an alternative income and to learn how to use their natural resources in a sustainable way. Sustainability planning for such an enormous area needed a sound scientific base, a long-term view, and sensible implementation. The reserve was created with a detailed **Management Plan with input from scientists and social workers.** The plan also contained key baseline data on the state of the natural environment and human development in the Reserve.

The Management Plan identified potential alternative sources of income and specified that all projects which seek to generate of income from sustainable use of natural resources required business plans and yearly reviews. **Ecotourism** was one of the alternative sources of income identified for local communities and a business plan was commissioned in 1998 and implemented between 1998 and 2001. Other sustainable economic alternatives are Fishery (including the highly prized Pirarucu fish), Forestry, Family Agriculture and Handicraft.

During its journey from PhD thesis to a major sustainable development program, the management of Mamirauá was gradually strengthened. A Civil Society was created in 1992 followed by the **Mamirauá Sustainable Development Institute (IDSM)** in 1999.

Instituto Mamirauá is financed through public and private funding, which involves the Brazilian Government (Ministry of Science and Technology), Brazilian and international Donors. Today most of the funding (70%) comes from Brazil. The organization is managed by a group of directors, who are responsible for the areas of Administration, Science & Technology and Sustainable Development. They are overseen by an Administrative Board and assisted by a Scientific Board.

The Institute pursues and monitors progress in **seven strategic macro processes**: Organization and Mobilization for Management of the Area, Information and Communication, Sustainable Use Programs, Quality of Life for Inhabitants and Users of the Area, Research on Conservation, Biodiversity and Social Development, Institutional Development and Protection of Biodiversity.

Table 6.2 below gives the timeline of the Mamiraua Reserve and the development of the ecotourism initiative.

Table 6.2 Timeline for Mamirauá Reserve and ecotourism activities

1983	Márcio Ayres starts PhD thesis in White Uakari Monkey	Visiting scientists
1986	Creation of Federal Ecological Station (ESEC) Mamiraua	Visiting scientists
1987	Project Mamiraua : start of scientific studies (biology, natural resources and population)	Visiting scientists
1990	Mamiraua becomes state conservation unit	Visiting scientists
1992	Mamiraua Civil Society founded	Visiting scientists
1993	ESEC Mamiraua declared RAMSAR site	Visiting scientists
1996	Mamiraua Sustainable Development Reserve (RDS) created. Reserve Management Plan published	Ecotourism is proposed as one of the alternative sources of income for the local community
1998	Amaná Sustainable Development Reserve (RDS) created	Ecotourism Business Plan
1999	Official visit of President Fernando Henrique Cardoso	Soft opening using existing floating lodge (used for visiting scientists)
	Creation of Mamiraua Sustainable Development Institute (IDSM)	Ecotourism Marketing Plan (detailed)
2000	RDS Mamiraua and Amanã incorporated in National Conservation Unit System (SNUC) and become part of UNESCO Central Amazon Biosphere Reserve.	Construction of first floating 2 room chalet unit.
2001	RDS Mamiraua and Amanã part of UNESCO World Heritage Site Central Amazonian Conservation Complex	Finalization of lodging with four more chalet units giving total of ten rooms
2002	José Marcio Ayres wins Rolex Award	Brazil Destination Highlight Lonely Planet Brazil
2003	Groundbreaking on terrain of HQ and Research Centre of the Mamirauá Institute in Tefé.	Best Ecotourism Destination – Conde Nast Traveler.Smithsonian Sustainable Tourism Award
2004	Mamiraua Civil Society wins UNDP Equator Prize	First Lodge Manager for the Local Community
2006		New Central Unit of Lodge finishedTefé Airport closed twice Jul – Sept and Dez- Apr 2007
2008	Inauguration of Research building of Mamirauá Institute	Feasibility Studies for Introduction of Ecotourism to adjacent Amana Reserve

Source: IDSM

Description of the Ecotourism Component

The Mamirauá Reserve management plan created a **Special Ecotourism Management Zone** of 35 square kilometers in the area of the reserve closest to the gateway city Tefé. The area offers a variety of habitats and landscapes, including the beautiful Mamirauá lake and excellent opportunities for wildlife viewing on trails previously used by scientists and on the water. There are also several scientific project bases in the area.

c) Goals of the Ecotourism Project

The goals of the project are threefold:

1. To offer quality tourism hospitality services (recreation, accommodation, food and transport)
2. To contribute to conservation and provide income to the local population
3. To be a reference for a high quality, positive environmental and social impact, community-based ecotourism product in the Brazilian Amazon

The components of the **ecotourism marketing mix** are:

Product
–   **10 room floating lodge** in the designated ecotourism area. Rooms are spacious and comfortable and have private verandas. Hot water is provided by solar heating;

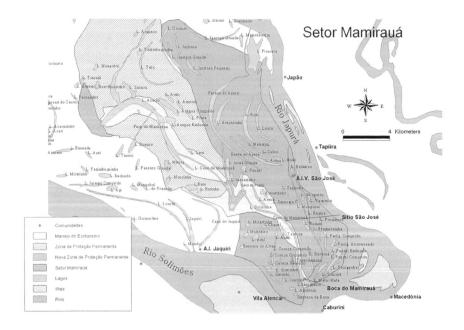

Figure 6.2 Detailed map of Mamirauá Sector
       Source: IDSM

- **two-storey floating central unit** with reception, kitchen, restaurant, meeting room, library (books/dvd), observation deck and small swimming pool;
- **excursions** by motorized canoe, paddle canoe and on foot to explore the area on trails used in research projects;
- **interaction with scientists** (talks and visits) and local community (at the lodge and in the community);
- **community based operation** overseen by Mamiraua Institute and aided by bilingual naturalist guides;
- **Food: tasty local Amazon cuisine served buffet style. Fish and other fresh supplies from the reserve itself, rest from Tefé.**

Price
- **all inclusive package** (transfer in/out from Tefé, accommodation, food, guided tours)
- **price competitive** with other products in Amazon Basin

Promotion
- product positioning: quality Amazon wildlife observation in unique area, one of the few places where you can experience the *'real Amazon'* (authenticity factor), interact with the local community and learn about *'sustainability in action'*

Figure 6.3 Clockwise from top right: researchers' house at the location of the lodge, floating chalets in 2001 (Mamiraua Image Bank), floating chalets in 2007, central unit in 2007 after refurbishment (Ariane Janér)

Figure 6.4 Clockwise from top right: food Buffet, room interior, motorized canoe in front of old central unit (Mamiraua Image Bank), sunset on the Mamiraua Deck (Peter Schoen)

– main communication channel **website** (www.uakarilodge.com.br and www.mamiraua.org.br), word-of-mouth and through partners
– presence at selected trade fairs and sustainable development events

Distribution
– direct (email, phone)
– through tour operators (national and international) and third party websites

d) Impacts

All three dimensions of sustainability are equally important for the success of the **Ecotourism Program**. The Program is a not-for-profit operation and surpluses are used to create a reserve for future investments in tourism (to safeguard future income), finance community surveillance of the area (conservation) and finance community projects.

Economic Impacts

The following positive impacts are expected from the ecotourism operation:

1) **Income from working at the lodge** (guides, cooks, chambermaids, manager)
2) **Income from selling supplies (food) or non-tourism services (maintenance, construction) to the lodge**

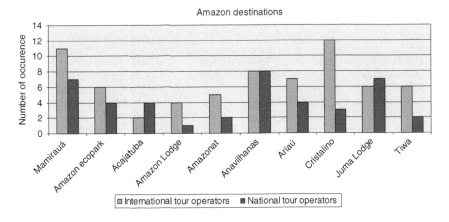

Figure 6.5 Mamiraua compared to other lodges as offered by tour operators
   Source: Coelho e Ozorio

3)   **Income from selling handicraft to tourists**
4)   **Distribution of surplus from operation of lodge between the communities in the Ecotourism area**

Apart from these direct economic impacts, the Ecotourism Program also provides training to the communities in various tourism related areas and creates a market for handicrafts, thus increasing the overall skills level in the community.

Key to providing positive economic impacts is having a **quality product** that attracts a sufficient number of long haul tourists each year. To be able to offer a quality product for a community based operation in a conservation area is a delicate balancing act and until now Mamirauá has been quite successful in doing this. This is an important differential with competing lodges. The rainforest lodges around Manaus, the main Brazilian Amazon destination, cannot offer the same authentic quality experience in terms of wildlife viewing and interaction with local communities and scientists. Many community-based lodges suffer from not being able to offer a consistent quality of operation and nor can they match the wildlife viewing opportunities.

In Brazil the main rival of the Uakari Floating Lodge at Mamirauá is the Cristalino Jungle Lodge, which is located in a different part of the Amazon. This lodge is privately owned, but its owners are committed to sustainability in operation and conservation and also work with scientists. In this case the Mamirauá differential is the community based operation. Because of the different locations and Amazon habitats, in this case Cristalino is both a competitor and a complement to Mamirauá.

Both **IDSM internal surveys** (IDSM 2001/09) plus publicly accessible reviews on sites like **TripAdvisor** confirm that the Uakari lodge delivers on its premise as a quality authentic Amazon experience.

Table 6.3 Mamiraua differential

Product Type	Examples	Mamiraua Differential
Rainforest lodge Manaus Area – Amazon Basin	Ariau Jungle Tower, the best known lodge in the Amazon Basin Anavilhanas Jungle Lodge boutique lodge	Authentic Quality of Experience, Low environmental impact, contribution to Conservation & Community
Community Lodges	Aldeia dos Lagos, a well known community based hotel	Consistent Quality of Experience Conservation
Quality Ecolodge in the Amazon	Cristalino Lodge, prizewinning lodge in the Southern Amazon	Community-based Different Habitat/species

Source: EcoBrasil

The Uakari Lodge **performance** is measured using the following **indicators**: food, activities, guides, room, information level, wildlife viewing and overall visit evaluation. Tourists can give scores between 1 (bad) and 5 (excellent). On all aspects Uakari scores between 4 and 5 consistently over the years. Figure 6.6 shows the overall visit evaluation, guides (highest score in 2009) and information level (lowest score in 2009). Information level was one of the 'weak' points of the Uakari Lodge in the beginning, due to the use of local guides, who did not speak English and the complexity of information available on Mamiraua. However this aspect has now much improved, due to better printed information and more guide training. Interestingly, the local guides are much appreciated by the visitors and their quality is closely related to the overall appreciation of the visit. All other indicators measured are between the scores for information level and guides.

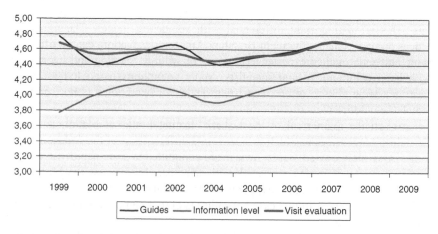

Figure 6.6 Satisfaction level of tourists with overall visit, guides and information at the Uakari Lodge (1999–2008)
Source: IDSM

Table 6.4 Reviews of Uakari/Mamiraua on TripAdvisor 2005–2010

Caption	Rating	Stars
The most remarkable trip in my life	Oct 2007	*****
The best of the Amazon	Dec 2005	*****
The Experience of a Lifetime	Sep 2006	*****
The Best	Jan 2007	*****
Once in a Lifetime Experience	Feb 2010	*****
Great	Aug 2009	*****
What an experience!	Apr 2009	*****
An enchanted experience	Aug 2006	*****
A treasure for the semi-adventurous	Jan 2009	*****
Wonderful experience!	Mar 2008	*****
Pink Dolphins and Red-Faced Monkeys	March 2010	****
Lovely lodge in the reserve	Apr 2010	****
Some reservations	Sep 2007	***
In the heart of Amazonia	May 7 2010	*

Source: Trip Advisor

Of 11 reviews on **TripAdvisor**, only one was negative, but when reading the review it sounds more like this wasn't the right kind of visitor. The full reviews are available at www.tripadvisor.co.uk/Hotel_Review-g303226-d620447.

Economic impacts are related to the revenue generated by number of tourists-nights sold, average package price (mostly in US$) and costs (in R$).

The **volume of tourists** grew quickly the first years and reached over 300 in 2001. It is now at about 600-700 per year with an average length of stay of 3,5 nights. About 70% are foreign tourists. Tourism to Mamirauá has outpaced both global international tourism and long haul tourism to Brazil. Figure 6.7 shows

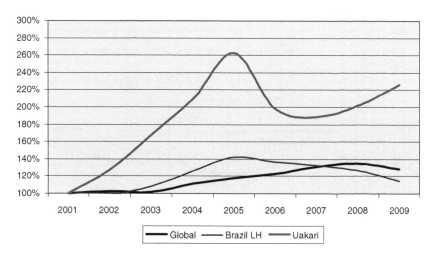

Figure 6.7 Increase of tourism to Mamiraua compared to long haul tourism to Brazil and Global International Arrivals (2001–2009)
Source: IDSM

that between 2001 and 2009, global international tourism grew 29%, long haul to
Brazil 15% and visitors to Uakari Lodge 126%. However all numbers are down
on 2005, which was the top year for long haul tourism to Brazil and when the
Real currency was relatively weak compared to US$ and Euro.

An increased number of visitors does not translate directly into more operational surplus. The Uakari Lodge must consider not only its cost base, but also
prices of competitor lodges in Manaus and of comparable experiences in other
parts of the Amazon.

Prices for a 4d/3n package have increased from between US$ 360 to US$ 550
in 2009. Visitors to Mamirauá must also be willing to invest in an extra plane
ticket and more transfer time. The main direct operating costs for Mamirauá are
salaries, supplies and fuel. Salaries are linked to evolution of Brazil's minimum
salary, which has risen faster than inflation in the past years. Fuel cost is
linked to oil price and exchange rate, both of which have seen great fluctuations.
Figure 6.8 shows that while the minimum salary increased more than 150%
between 2001 and 2009, the price in R$ and US$ has increased less than 50% in
order to remain competitive internationally.

Customer satisfaction surveys show that over 70% find the Mamirauá price
fair, despite the increase over the years (see Figure 6.9).

About a quarter of the revenue generated goes to communities for services,
supplies and share of the surplus. Due to the increase in minimum salary and the
higher number of people employed, in 2009 about 90% of the monetary community benefits (R$ 170 thousand total) generated was for services rendered as
compared to 2004, when this was around 50% (see Figure 6.10).

The fluctuation in community benefits are caused by the size of the surplus
generated by the business and confirms the importance of not creating dependence of the communities on tourism income alone.

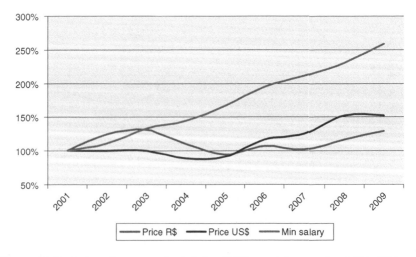

Figure 6.8 Evolution of average price in R$ and US$ vs minimum salary 2001–2009
       Source: IDSM

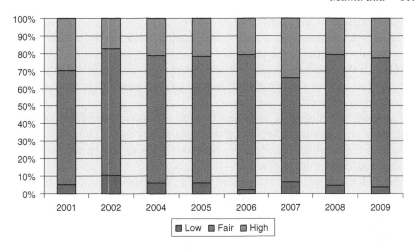

Figure 6.9 Mamirauá price perception 2001–2009 (no data for 2003).
   Source: IDSM

Environmental Impacts

The floating lodge was planned for:

– **High quality** of Amazon experience for the tourist
– **Low environmental impacts** of tourism operation
– Contributing to the **conservation** of the area and wildlife.

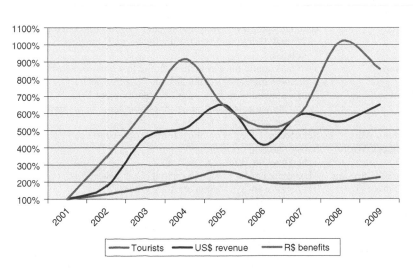

Figure 6.10 Evolution of numbers of tourists, revenue and community benefits 2001– 2009
   Source: IDSM

These objectives are interdependent. The quality of the experience depends on the quality of infrastructure and tourism operation, but also on the quality wildlife viewing opportunities at the lodge and during the excursions.

If the local community is actively collaborating in the conservation of the area and wildlife and the tourism operation has low environmental impacts, this will help to enhance the visitor experience.

The local community is rewarded through economic incentives, as satisfied customers are a key ingredient in the success of the lodge.

Part of the surplus of the tourism operation goes to community surveillance against poachers in the reserve.

The lodge was planned as a reference for sustainable operation in a fragile habitat and these are the main precautions taken with the use of resources and disposal of residues.

In order to verify that environmental objectives are met, the Ecotourism Programs monitors the following key indicators.

Water quality

Possible changes in water quality due to higher human occupation (sewage, boat movement) around the lodge area were a major concern for the Instituto Mamirauá. Effluent from the septic filter sewage system is analyzed for microbial parameters monthly. The water around the lodge is verified for physical-chemical changes.

Table 6.5 Environmental impacts and precautions to minimize them

Impact	Precautions taken to lower Impact
Energy	Solar for water heating and electricity with generator backup
Water	Bathing water is drawn from the 'lake'. Water for cooking is filtered. Drinking water is mineral water. Rainwater is also collected.
Sewage	Two tank septic filter system, with the first tank for aerobic fermentation and second tank for filtering water
Food	Partly sourced from local suppliers, partly from Tefé
	Buffet style meals and supplies bought in large packaging to reduce leftovers and waste
Organic Waste	Selected and used as compost fertilizer or fed to fish
Inorganic Waste	Partly reused/recycled
	Taken back to Tefé
Tourist (Carrying Capacity)	Maximum number of tourists on trail (4), at lodge (20) per year (1000)
	Tourists are always accompanied by guides
	Trails are varied
Logistics (Boats)	Logistics are planned so as to be as efficient as possible (in/out). Currents are strong in the area, so solar powered motors are not an option. Within the reserve 4T motors are preferred and horsepower depends on distance and group size. Paddle canoes are also used.

Source: IDSM

The results (PEREIRA 20089) are within the limits set by CONAMA (National Environmental Board) Resolution N° 357/2005 and are also adequate for 'varzea' water environment.

Chance of observing species on trails

Another concern was that tourists would have an impact on the animal communities. The density of species seen on the tourists trails is measured since 2007. Marker species chosen by the scientists were five monkey species (White Uakari – *Cacajao calvus*, Red Howler – *Alouatta senicula*, Brown Capuchin – *Cebus macrocephalus*, Black-faced Squirrel Monkey – *Saimiri vanzolinii* and Common Squirrel Monkey – *Saimiri sciureus*) and two large bird species (Wattled Curassow – *Crax globulosa* and Great Curassow – *Mitu tuberose*). This is monitored three times a year (high, low and receding waters) and compared to trails that are not visited by tourists.

The results (PEREIRA, 2009) show that there is no difference between the trails used by tourists and other trails and confirm the caution exercised in planning the ecotourism operation and the importance of respecting the carrying capacity limits set.

Social impacts

Community welfare, social organization and emancipation are very important in the Mamirauá philosophy. This includes both general programs of health, education and community empowerment which extend to all communities in Mamirauá and specific ones linked to the Ecotourism Program.

Today eight communities are directly involved with the Ecotourism Program. These communities live close to or inside the Ecotourism Management Zone within the Mamiraua Sector (the Reserve has a total of 8 Sectors). Communities are free to decide if and how they want to participate in the ecotourism program. They can work for the lodge, supply goods, sell handicraft and/or receive tourists in their communities.

Depending on the season, the members of these communities will undertake a number of activities such as fishing, family agriculture and forestry. They produce for themselves and for the market. The objective of the ecotourism program is not to substitute these traditional activities and create dependence on tourism, but to be a source of extra income for the local population. In case of a downturn in tourism, which is always a risk for a remote long haul destination, the economic effect on the community is buffered by other income.

Mamirauá has only a few fixed employees for key posts and draws from pool of temporary guides and help from the communities that live in the Ecotourism Sector.

The Uakari Lodge employs five fixed employees from the local community: two Janitors, one General Manager who is also a Supervisor of Food, Beverage and Accomodation, one Tour, Activities and Maintenance Supervisor, and one Logistics Supervisor. They are assisted three employees, who are not members of the local community: a bilingual naturalist guide and a two-person marketing and administration team in Tefé. Additionally, there is a researcher employed by the Mamirauá Institute, who is responsible for the coordination.

The pool of temporary personnel formed an association in 2000, called AAGEMAM. The association started with 27 members and now has 62.

Personnel at the lodge regularly receive training to learn new skills or enhance their capabilities.

The communities in the ecotourism area decide jointly how to distribute their share of the surplus from the lodge operation for 50% community projects and 50% area surveillance (against poachers and other illegal activities).

This system has the following advantages:

1)   Direct benefits are spread amongst a large group
2)   Avoids dependence on the ecotourism income alone
3)   Promotes self organization
4)   Transfers knowledge.

The presence of the lodge also provides new opportunities for those not directly involved in the ecotourism operation, such as selling fresh produce or making and selling handicrafts. Handicrafts are sold both at the lodge and distributed to other markets.

In 2002, the first year that there was an operational surplus, this was shared equally amongst the participating communities. In 2003, the communities proposed a better system based on a code of conduct they drew up amongst themselves and considers:

–   Participation of communities in Sector meetings
–   Active participation in sector events such as: women's encounters, religious events, preparation of the General Assembly of Inhabitants and Users of RDSM, contribution in bringing food to meetings
–   Participation in area surveillance by reporting illegal activities
–   Participation in area surveillance by collaborating with one volunteer per community, when requested by the Environmental Agents Volunteers and Sector Rangers
–   Communities cannot make use of natural resources in the fully protected area from Pagão to the Research Platform of the River Dolphin Project
–   Respect for period of no fishing (November 1st to March 31st) and minimum fish size
–   No fishing of the endangered Pirarucu
–   Good reception of ecotourists in the communities (this will be evaluated by AAGEMAN and the naturalist guide)
–   Communities cannot receive clandestine tourists
–   Involvement of communities in ecotourism activities
–   Communities must follow the guidelines of the Sector Occupation Policy

Table 6.6 How the communities of the Mamirauá Sector distributed and used the ecotourism surplus

Community	Amount Received	Approved Community Development Projects
VILA ALENCAR	R$ 2999,00	Renovation of Community Boat
BOCA DO MAMIRAUÁ	R$ 2999,00	Acquisition of Motorized Saw Acquisition of 7 meter Canoe Finish Community Center
SÍTIO SÃO JOSÉ	R$ 1500,00	Construction of Manioc Processing Unit
CABURINI	R$ 3427,10	Community Center Expansion Acquisition of Radio Communication System Installing Water Catchment System
JAQUIRI	R$ 2999,00	Acquisition of Materials for Community Bakery Construction of a Community Center
NOVA MACEDÔNIA	R$ 2571,00	Acquisition of 8 HP motor and 7 meter canoe
TAPIÍRA	R$ 1500,00	Construction of a Community Center
SETOR MAMIRAUÁ	R$12.000,00	Acquisition of a Boat for the Sector

Source: IDSM

Table 6.6 shows how seven communities decided to divide their share of the surplus of R$ 30.000 in 2003.

e) Main Obstacles

Though the Uakari Floating Lodge at Mamirauá has been a successful ecotourism initiative, it has had a few challenges to overcome and cannot be complacent. The main challenge is in the economical dimension: providing a quality product in a competitive market.

Paradoxically, economic success also brings new challenges in the social dimension as extra income changes relations within communities and families.

Economic

As a tourism enterprise Mamirauá is affected by the normal ups and downs of tourism caused by external factors such as economic confidence in their target market and exchange rates. The current exchange rate, where the R$ gained value against the weak dollar and euro, means that Brazil destination can seem expensive to international tourists.

In terms of marketing, this means that more focus should be given to the value of the Mamirauá experience. At the moment Mamirauá is still a bit timid in its promotion, as any marketing expenses mean a lower operational surplus to share with the communities.

As a small ecolodge off the main tourism routes, Mamirauá is always vulnerable to accessibility problems. The gateway airport Tefé is served by regional airlines, which tend to change their schedules. The cheapest one-way ticket from Manaus to Tefé is about US\$ 100 but can cost more than three times as much for a late booking.

Between July 2006 and April 2007, the Tefé airport was closed for several months because of the bird hazard to planes. Airport movement dropped 35% between 2005 and 2007 and visitor numbers to Mamirauá showed a similar fall, as the only alternative was to come by boat (which could take 12 hours to two days). Though the situation is now under control, this aiport problem caused a major disruption for growth of tourism to Mamirauá, after their banner year in 2005.

In terms of quality of product, it is very important for Mamirauá to train the local communities in the skills they need to give the tourists an authentic and quality experience. This includes basic things like hygiene, appearance, and safety procedures, but also communication and knowledge about the natural and cultural environment. The quality of both the local and the bi-lingual naturalist guide is very important.

As Mamirauá does not want communities and individuals to depend solely on tourism income, there is rotation amongst the people who work at the lodge. On the one hand this rotation has the advantage of keeping people 'fresh'. On the other hand, it can cause operational problems: service suppliers who have not been working for some time lose their routine and attention to detail, thus affecting the quality of service.

For now the bilingual naturalist guide does not come from the community and comes from another part of Brazil. Because of a lack of growth potential within Mamirauá, these guides usually move on after one or two years and this can cause temporary continuity problems.

Environmental

The Mamirauá Institute is very focused on any environmental impacts of introducing tourism in the Reserve. The positive environmental impacts of creating the Reserve and implementing tourism are very much in evidence. Hunting and fishing pressures have reduced and the populations of top species like the black caiman and the pirarucu have increased significantly. Communities, who participate in sustainable activities, are also very aware of how important conserving natural resources is to their economic welfare.

Social

Despite the efforts to not make communities dependent on ecotourism, there is a certain substitution of income. The rotation system, which was devised to guarantee a better distribution of economic benefits and minimize (negative) social impacts, does not always work perfectly. Some workers can become too dependent on the ecotourism income.

Another impact is that ecotourism gives women more economic independence from their husbands. Working outside the house, interacting with other social groups and often earning more than the spouse can lead to matrimonial conflicts.

Local community associations have been facing some management problems, due to less participation from members. The AAGEMAM appears to be dependent on too few good leaders. When they leave their director posts due to limited mandates, their substitutes do not show the same dedication and capacity to manage the association.

One social impact actually comes from outside the Reserve and that is 'jealousy' from the inhabitants of Tefé. They are not allowed to fish in the Reserve and at the same time see foreign visitors go there and this can lead to some malicious gossip.

Lessons Learned

Many community based tourism projects underestimate how difficult it is to have success in the tourism market and how important the quality of the operation is.

The Mamirauá ecotourism experience is a clear example of the importance of following a **Plan, Do, Check, Act (PDCA)** cycle for implementing and operating a community based tourism project.

The **Planning** phase was greatly helped by the groundwork done by scientists and social workers for the general Mamirauá Reserve Management plan. This, in turn, enabled a clear framework and focus for the business plan. The business plan then made a realistic assessment of both the market potential and operational challenges and costs of the community based venture.

The **Do** or implementation part of the cycle was done in phases and allowed both the Mamirauá Institute and the community, who had no previous experience with tourism, to learn by doing.

The general Mamirauá policy to monitor results and make yearly reviews (**Check - Act**) is also essential and enables to adjust the operation according to new opportunities and challenges.

The fact that ecotourism is only part of the Mamirauá success story also helps create a virtuous circle where free publicity on the Reserve creates interest that motivates tourists to visit the area.

Another key point is that the Mamirauá communities were already organized before the introduction of the ecotourism operation. They had also been working with the scientists and social workers for a long time and trusted them. Mobilizing the communities for ecotourism could therefore use already existing channels and methods. In turn ecotourism strengthened the community organization and this was demonstrated when decisions about the operational surplus needed to be taken.

The communities are also gaining more managerial experience and this gave Mamirauá the confidence to appoint local managers for the lodge and logistics.

However, it is clear that economic success can cause new social stresses as well and these need to be managed too. For this reason community-based tourism projects must be prepared to take a medium to long term view and also be prepared to manage both too high expectations and resolve potential conflicts.

References

Alecar, E. F; Peralta, N. (2008). Ecoturismo e mudança social na Amazônia Rural: efeitos sobre o papel da mulher e as relações de gênero. *Campos 9/1*: 109–129.

Armend, M., Pictures http://picasaweb.google.com/marcosamend/RDSMamirauAM

Ayres, M. http://www.primate-sg.org/PDF/NP11.1.ayres.seal.memoriam.pdf

Brandon, K. (1995). Etapas Básicas para incentivar a participação local. In: Lindberg, K. e Hawkins, D. *Ecoturismo um Guia para Planejamento e Gestão*, São Paulo: Editora Senac.

BRASÍLIA. (2000) Sistema Nacional das Unidades de Conservação LEI No 9.985, 18 dejulho de 2000.

Coelho, E. A. and Ozório, R.Z. (2008) *Identificação dos intermediários turísticos que comercializam o destino Pan-Amazônia: inserção de Mamirauá e subsídios para Amanã.*

Da Rin, A. (1999). *Relatório Anual do Programa de Ecoturismo da RDSM.* Tefé: Instituto de Desenvolvimento Sustentável Mamiraua.

Endo, W. (2002) *Guia de Aves do Mamiraua.* Tefé: Instituto de Desenvolvimento Sustentável Mamirauá.

Equator prize http://equatorinitiative.org/index.php?option=com_content&view=article&id=486:sociedadecivilmamirau&catid=105:equator-prize-winners-2004&Itemid=541&lang=es

Fleck, L. (2001). *Avaliação do Monitoramento de Impacto à Fauna do Programa de Ecoturismo da RDS Mamirauá.* Tefé: Instituto de Desenvolvimento Sustentável Mamiraua.

Google earth. ##http://maps.google.com/maps?f=q&source=s_q&hl=en&geocode=&q=Tef%C3%A9+-+Amazonas,+Brazil&sll=-22.903539,-43.209587&sspn=0.651485,1.0107 42&ie=UTF8&hq=&hnear=Tef%C3%A9+-+Amazonas,+Brazil&ll=-3.063039,-64.849291&spn=0.02207,0.047936&t=h&z=15

IDSM – Instituto Desenvolvimento Sustenável Mamirauá (2001 – 2009). Relatório de Gestão Anual IDSM. http://www.mamiraua.org.br/pagina.php?cod=107 [Accessed 26th of June 2010]

Jáner, A. (1998) *Estudo de Viabilidade Econômica para o Desenvolvimento do ecoturismo na RDS Mamirauá.* Tefé: Instituto de Desenvolvimento Sustentável Mamirauá.

Mamirauá, www.mamirauá.org.br (many publications cited in bibliography can be downloaded here).

MPE FUNBIO. (2002) *Polo Mamirauá: Atualização do Plano de Marketing.* Rio de Janeiro: Funbio.

Peralta, N. (2001). *Relatório Anual do Programa de Ecoturismo da RDSM.* Tefé: Instituto de Desenvolvimento Sustentável Mamiraua.

Peralta, N. (2001). *Relatório da Reunião de Avaliação das Visitas às comunidades.* Tefé: Instituto de Desenvolvimento Sustentável Mamiraua.

Peralta, N *et al.* (2008). Renda Domestica e Sazonalidade em Comunidades da RDS Mamirauá, 1995-2005. *Uakari, v5 no 1*, p 7 -19, jun.

Pereira, S.A. (2009) Monitoramento da Fauna nas Trilhas de Ecoturismo Na Reserva de Desenvolvimento Sustentável Mamirauá, Tefé, Amazonas. In : *VI Seminário Anualde Pesquisas do Instituto de Desenvolvimento Sustentável Mamirauá.* Tefé. Amazonas.

Pereira, S.A. (2009). Qualidade da Água Na Pousada Uacari, Reserva de Desenvolvimento Sustentável Mamirauá, Refé, Amazonas. In : *VI Seminário Anual de Pesquisas do Instituto de Desenvolvimento Sustentável Mamirauá.* Tefé. Amazonas.

Souza, M. (2001). *Relatório do I Encontro de Artesãs e Artesãos dos Setores Jarauá e Mamiraua.* Tefé: Instituto de Desenvolvimento Sustentável Mamiraua, 2001.

Souza, M. (2001) *Ata do Encontro do Setor Mamirauá sobre a Divisão de Lucros do Ecoturismo,* Tefé: Instituto de Desenvolvimento Sustentável Mamiraua, 2001.

Souza, M.(2001) Artesanato: alternativa econômica para as comunidades de Mamirauá. http://www.mamiraua.org.br/5-1-4.html Tefé: Instituto de Desenvolvimento Sustentável Mamiraua.

Storni, A *et al* (2007). Evaluation of the impact of fauna caused by the presence of ecotourists on the trails of the Mamirauá Sustainable Development Reserve, Amazonas, Brazil. *Tourism and Hospitality: Planning and Development 4(1)* :25–32 (abril).

TRIPADVISOR (2010). http://www.tripadvisor.com/ShowUserReviews-g303226-d312492-r58099104-Mamiraua_Sustainable_Development_Reserve-State_of_Amazonas.html [Accessed 26th of June 2010].

Uakari Lodge, http//www.uakarilodge.com.br

World Heritage Site, http://whc.unesco.org/en/list/998

7 Ecuador

Huaorani Ecolodge

*Oliver-André Hölcke**

Country report: facts, short description

Ecuador is located in western South America, bordering the Pacific Ocean at the Equator, between Colombia and Peru. Its terrain is divided into coastal plain (*costa*), inter-Andean central highlands (*sierra*), and flat to rolling eastern jungle (*oriente*). Ecuador has 14.7 Mio inhabitants, and almost two thirds of the rural population are considered poor.

The numbers of foreigners who entered Ecuador had been steadily increasing every year until 2009 (see Figure 7.1). In 2006 they had 840.000 travellers, 2008 just over one million, 2009 there were 970.086 foreign travellers in Ecuador. The numbers for 2010 are slightly increasing again.

Proportionally most of the travellers come from the United States of America (21,16%), Columbia (20,49%) and Peru (16,03%). Germany ranks at number nine with 2,39% of visitors to Ecuador.

Ecuador is one of seven countries with the highest diversity on the planet. These countries are the richest in biodiversity (species of animals, plants and microorganisms) and endemism (species that only exist in one place). With just 256.370 km², only 0.17% of Earth's land surface, Ecuador has more than 11% of all terrestrial vertebrate species (mammals, birds, amphibians and reptiles), 16.087 species of vascular plants (plants more evolved) and about 600 species of marine fish.

In the Ecuadorian Amazon, which is composed mostly of lowland tropical rainforest, there are eight indigenous groups living including the Achuar, Zaparo, Cofan, Siona, Siecoya, Huaorani and the more numerous Sacha Runa (lowland Quichua) and Shuar.

Ecotourism in the Ecuadorian Amazon basin

Since its initial boom in the 1980s, tourism in Ecuador, particularly in the natural areas, has been increasing, and Ecuador is considered one of the world's leading

*Deutsche Gesellschaft für Internationale Zusammenarbeit (GIZ) Ecuador, Quito, Ecuador

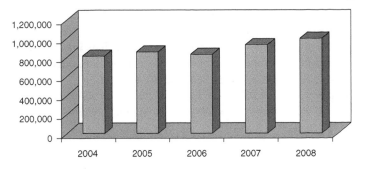

Figure 7.1 Entry of Foreigners to Ecuador, 2004–2008
Source: Ministerio de Turismo del Ecuador

ecotourism destinations both for its natural and cultural attractions and for its dynamic ecotourism projects involving indigenous communities.

There is a wide range of ecotourism possibilities in the region from high-end lodges with private reserves, to rustic cabanas and river adventure trips, to national parks and indigenous territories. In the region of the Ecuadorian Amazon Rainforest are located a number of lodges and eco-lodges, which are competing with each other. Some lodges offer an easy, fast and cheap access (e.g. by public transport) and some can only be approached by long and complicated travelling (Airplane, Motorboat, Canoe, Walk).

The high-end tour operators often combine trips to the Ecuadorian Amazon, which may cost as much as $200 per day, with cruises around the Galapagos Islands – one of the world's most popular nature tourism destinations. Most high level luxury Ecolodges offer trips which can only be booked in packages, for instance 'four days / three nights' per person between 720 and 799 US-$ plus airfare.

Still a vast number of travellers, who come to Ecuador and want to explore the Amazon region, are backpackers. The market for these independent travellers with limited economic resources offers all inclusive multi-day 'jungle adventure' trips between $35 and $50 per day. These jungle lodges also offer visits to 'indigenous villages' or 'places of interest' in national parks, but rarely with specific permission or with any financial participation for the local community members. There are also so-called 'middle class lodges' which offer a stay per day and per person of between 100 and 200 US-$.

The Huaorani Ecolodge offers a '4 days/3 nights' trip per person in a shared cabin for 600 US-$. Transportation costs are not included in this rate. Flight and road transportation is covered with about 250 US-$.

The Ecuadorian government is very interested in developing tourism in their country especially in high-profile areas such as the Amazon. In early 2010, a special law for tourism (*'Ley Orgánica de Turismo'*) was accomplished which should be seen as a priority state policy of high national interest. The Counsel for the Ministry of Tourism, Maria Teresa Lara, said that this law is a dynamic tool that will facilitate the development of tourism. It also includes the protection of the rights of a 'good life', respect for nature and the possibility of generating more employment opportunities and income for Ecuador.

This project also includes new forms of tourism such as internationally recognized ecotourism i.e. ethno-tourism, metropolitan tourism, adventure tourism, social tourism, cultural tourism and community tourism.

Unfortunately, in addition to recent external problems, the economic domination of the petroleum industry in the region prevents effective market expansion.

The people

The Huaorani (or Waorani) are an ethnic group who only live in the Ecuadorian provinces Napo and Pastaza in the headwaters of the Amazon. Approximately 2.400 individuals are considered as Huaorani. Before, their territory extended from the Napo River in the north to the Curaray River in the south, about 50 miles (80 km) south of the oil city of El Coca. According to their folklore, they migrated to this area a long time ago to escape from cannibals. Nowadays, their territory - some 6.800km^2 (1.7 million acres)- is only about one third the size of their traditional land.

They had been living as nomadic hunters and gatherers with no outside contact until 1956, when a group of American missionaries arrived in their territory. The Huaorani subdivided themselves into six groups. There are five communities (including the Tagaeri and Taromenane), with about 250 members, who decided to live in isolation with no contact to the outside world until the present day.

Most of the Huaorani maintain a largely traditional lifestyle living directly in and off the rainforest. They practice a sustainable economy, which means they do not overuse natural resources. As semi-nomads they usually grow manioc, corn, peanuts, sweet potatoes and fruit in their gardens and normally leave the settlement after ten years.

They speak a language unrelated to any other, and only a few community members speak Spanish; their name means 'the people'.

The average age of the community members around the lodge is 21 (men) and 20 (women). Maximum age is 75 (men) and 72 (women). The number of people of working age (between 18 and 65) is relatively limited in this area. Out of the 80 people living here (41 men and 39 women) only 16 men and 14 women were seen to be counted.

The needs of a sustainable income for the Huaorani

The Huaorani live on top of one of Ecuador's largest oil deposits, and since its discovery in the late 1960s they have been forced to deal with the presence of oil companies (foreign and Ecuadorian) and other outsiders. Special armed forces, lawyers, anthropologists and missionaries have tried to take advantage of their property. For example, the Huaorani have had excessive threats made on them from evangelical missionaries and because of development projects they had left their ancestral property to inhabit a western part of their territory. This immigration made it possible for oil-companies (in this case Texaco) to build a 90km long road from Coca deep into Huaorani-land.

The oil is transported in pipes all along these roads to the west coast of Ecuador. Some of these pipes burst from time to time, because of falling trees for example, which causes momentous contamination.

In addition settlers took over some of their land totalling about four kilometers along these roads to the left and right hand side. The former Ecuadorian government encouraged them to do so for free with the proposal that they should cultivate coffee or breed cattle. Both choices are not a sustainable way of using the land because there is a very thin layer of soil in the tropical rainforest. When it is no longer fertile they cut more wood and either sell or burn it.

The first official Huaorani protectorate was created in 1983, and the current much larger Huaorani Ethnic Reserve was established in 1990, at which time they formed the 'Organización de Nacionalidad Huaorani de la Amazonía Ecuatoriana' (ONHAE) to defend their interests, and in 2007 changed the name to 'Nacionalidad Waorani del Ecuador' (NAWE).

First tourist project with the Huaorani

The US American company 'Maxus' bought in 1993 privileges from the Ecuadorian government to exploit the so-called block 16 and 22, which are located on Huaorani-land. The ecologist and founder of TROPIC Ecological Adventures (TROPIC), Andy Drumm, wanted to help the Huaorani to resist against the impacts of the oil industry. A camera team from NBC joined him when he was about to meet Moi Enomenga, the former vice-president of ONHAE, at the Shiripuno bridge to inform him about the following possible actions. They agreed that it was and is very important for the Huaorani to find a sustainable and secure way of income. Tourism was seen as one of these possibilities.

TROPIC – the agency

The Welsh-born ecologist Andy Drumm founded TROPIC in 1993. While pioneering ecotourism in Ecuador, he also worked as Senior Ecotourism Specialist for The Nature Conservancy (TNC), leading to the implementation of sustainable tourism strategies that mobilized millions of dollars for the conservation of some of the world's most important protected areas from China to Bolivia.

Andy Drumm was a charter member and former Advisory Board member of The International Ecotourism Society and has been a Fellow of the Royal Geographical Society since 1990. He was a founding member of the Galapagos Guides Association (AGIPA) and a past president of the Amazon Commission of the Ecuadorian Ecotourism Association. He also led the Cuyabeno Defense Committee - an alliance of indigenous communities, conservation groups and tour operators, which successfully halted oil exploration and reinforced the protection of the highly sensitive Imuya flooded rainforest. TROPIC states that its main commitment is environmental and cultural conservation and support for local communities. To maintain this aspect of the work and still operate as a for-profit company, in 1998 Drumm together with other interested parties created 'Acción Amazonía', a separate non-profit organization. 'Acción Amazonía' is dedicated to working with indigenous communities and organizations to protect their environment and cultural integrity and to develop small-scale, sustainable, development projects including ecotourism.

The idea presented in Tropic's marketing material is that respectful and financially beneficial tourism will bring income needed at local level to encourage Amazonian indigenous communities to protect both their culture and environment.

Tropic's tourism initiatives are diverse and include: co-developing community based ecotourism operations with indigenous communities, promoting and marketing independent community-based ecotourism operations, creating business alliances with other responsible private companies in areas where Tropic and communities have no activity, playing an active role in industry associations to promote policy change, providing financial support for 'Acción Amazonía', and assisting with research in related areas. Currently he is working with the United Nations Development Program (UNDP) as a consultant on sustainable tourism around Latin America and the Caribbean.

Developing the Huaorani Lodge-Project

First meetings

After the meeting on the bridge TROPIC, Moi Enomenga and members of 16 Huaorani communities gathered for several months in workshops to develop a sustainable tourism project.

Very soon all of them agreed on bringing in more groups of tourists who were interested in getting to know the tribe, their life and culture. They decided to install a camp on the territory of the Quehueri'ono-community, a small settlement, where about 100 people live. In the early years Tropic had built some basic cabins which allowed clients and visitors to camp on the site. In these workshops they also agreed on following points:

- Most of the profit, gained by the project, stays in the participating Huaorani–communities and will not go to travel agencies.
- The Project should not have any negative impact on their socio-cultural tradition or the environment.
- The Huaorani are in charge of controlling who is visiting the lodge.
- They will define the prices.
- They are in charge of the infrastructure.
- Only members of the community work as cooks, staff, jungle or boat guides.
- No strangers are allowed to work on their property.

- Tropic attracts potential clients.
- Members of the community are the owners of the program; they participate in the planning and running of the program.
- Five US-dollars per person has to be paid to the indigenous organization ONHAE to strengthen them.

Description of the project

These first years were quite successful. In the early 2000s the Huaorani and Tropic decided that in order to start a professional business they needed more money, which meant they also needed more institutions to get involved in the project.

Therefore the 'Quehueri'ono Association' was founded. It consists of five Huaorani-communities, in which about 30 families with 250 people live in addition to the Ecuadorian tour operator 'Tropic Journeys in Nature'. The 'Quehueri'ono Association' is the owner of the project. To co-finance the Project, TROPIC applied to CORPEI (Corporation of Promotion for Export and Investment), GIZ (Deutsche Gesellschaft für Internationale Zusammenarbeit) and others.

The goal of the project was to provide sustainable development for the Huaorani and to provide high quality experiences for visitors to educate them about the environment of the rainforest and Huaorani culture. The goal was:

- To find friends and ambassadors for the Huaorani through tourists from different countries of origin.
- To finance the medical treatment of serious diseases in external hospitals.
- To find a secure and sustainable alternative means of income for the Huaorani instead of working for the petrol or timber industies.
- To assure that the Huaorani could maintain their own homeland.
- To prepare the Huaorani for getting in contact with the outside world through introducing them to sensitive small groups of tourists.
- To provide help in terms of lawyers and support them in keeping their property, heritage and culture.

Components of the project were to develop a product strategy, to construct the necessary infrastructure, to train members of the Huaorani in tourism service provision and management of the ecolodge, and to work with a travel agency which is specialized in sustainable tourism.

All this was provided to ensure a rewarding experience for the visitor as well as their welfare, health and safety in addition to maintaining a constant awareness of the impacts of these facilities on the environment.

The ecotourism project contributes to improving the wellbeing of the five Huaorani communities involved and to the conservation of their rainforest environment.

The Huaorani trust TROPIC and they are willing to see more tourism in their region. They can see that small groups of tourists, who pay more than in other

Other actors (funding):
NAWE Nacionalidad Waorani del Ecuador
Ministerio de Turismo
ASOCIACIÓN QUEHUERI'ONO

Proyecto Caiman – USAID
ECORAE
Private contributors

lodges, do not destroy their lifestyle. They have realized that TROPIC does not want to exploit their wildlife and they only cater to people who show respect for the environment and the culture of the Huaorani.

Since its opening in early 2008, the Huaorani Ecolodge has already received more than 340 guests (2008: 109; 2009: 102; 2010: so far 130).

The Huaorani Ecolodge won the award of the 'Best Sustainable Tourism Project' 2008 & 2009 from the Latin American Travel Association (LATA). In addition they won in 1997 the TO DO!-award for socially responsible tourism (Wettbewerb Sozialverantwortlicher Tourismus)

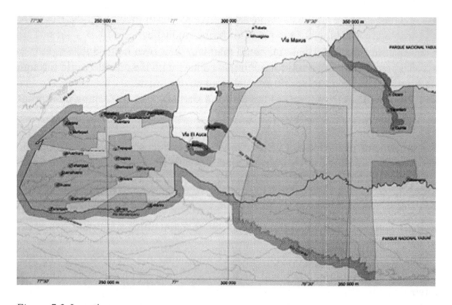

Figure 7.2 Location
   Source: TROPIC Journeys in Nature - www.tropiceco.com

The Huaorani Ecolodge complex has about three hectares and is located in eastern Ecuador in the middle of the Amazon Basin (see Figure 7.2). It is in the province of Pastaza near to the Quehueri'ono community, an Huaorani settlement with 13 families.

The region can be described as tropical humid rainforest with annual average temperatures between 23° and 25°C. The relative humidity lies between 70 and 90%.

The landscape is relatively plain with some rolling hills and a river called Shiripuno. The altitude varies between 300 and 350 meters above sea level. It is a highly diverse area with heterogeneous plants and trees which reach an altitude up to 40 meters.

Finding tourist attractions

Due to the lack of specific information and sufficiently scaled maps it was necessary to create one which emphasized the points of tourist interest with the help of Quehueri-ono community members (see Figure 7.3). Two maps were drawn, one by the women and another one by the men. The map which was drawn by the women was very precise in terms of the geographic area of the community itself, but was imperfect about remote areas of the community. The map drawn by the men was instead much more accurate in reflecting areas which were far away,

Figure 7.3 Quehueri-ono community member demonstrating native skills

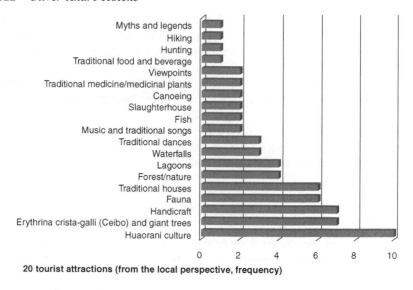

Figure 7.4 Tourist attractions
            (For leopard image) Source: Santiago Espinoza (ocelot)

including the Wentado and Nenkepade communities. The second step of the process was to identify potential attractions, which could be included as part of the product in terms of their accessibility, uniqueness and importance. The participating families were asked which were the most important things (culture, handicrafts, traditional houses etc.) a tourist should see or should know about the Huaorani (see Figure 7.4).

The Huaorani still use certain plants out of the rainforest for medical use. The consultant recommended including a program for the visitors to learn more about these plants. Because of its originality he also recommended serving typical Huaorani food, especially the traditional drink *chicha*.

The consultant recommended not including indigenous parties, ceremonies, dances, traditional music and songs in the list of attractions. He was afraid these cultural events could lose their original meaning and character. He also recommended not allowing the visitors to swim in the Shiripuno river, because of the dangerous devilfish.

Another important attraction for the tourists is a system of trails around the ecolodge. While hiking, visitors have the opportunity to watch wildlife. Around the lodge one can find self trails with easy access that can be walked in 45 minutes.

The consultant also suggested adding handicrafts as an attraction within the ecotourism-product, because it represents the cultural heritage of the Huaorani of the region, under the following conditions:

1.   Every household could participate in producing them.
2.   They are produced by men and women.

3. The crafts should not include parts of animals, even if they are leftovers of hunted animals, because this can encourage them to hunt.
4. They can be purchased by visitors in the ecolodge shop.
5. Prices for the same product should not vary in different places.
6. Incorporating crafts in the ecolodge's design and decoration.
7. Developing programs where visitors can learn the process of producing handicrafts.
8. Developing a small museum on the site with the most important examples.
9. Adding the Huaorani museum (in Puyo) as an activity within the itinerary.

An additional attraction is the installation of 25 heat and motion sensitive cameras. The purpose of the cameras is to survey the large mammals and birds in a range of habitats and to monitor their patterns of activity.

The information collected will be used for scientific studies of populations, animal density, behavior and use of specific habitats. The monitoring programmers have found the presence of many rare mammal species including jaguar, puma, ocelot, margay, jaguarundi, short-eared dog, giant armadillo, tapir and others.

The ecolodge also offers lectures on tropical forest ecology and ornithology.

Facilities

The lodge provides accommodation for a maximum of ten people housed in five comfortable, traditionally built cabins each with a private toilet, shower and a wooden patio.

The accommodation was built with used wood, which was found around the villages. The architectural style of the cabins is consistent with the philosophy and goals of ecotourism. The architects used Huaorani houses as a model to provide thermal insulation, protect against the elements (the roof was made out of synthetic material) and provide a cultural reflection.

Other facilities include:

- A lobby which contains a bar, a tiny shop for handicraft, restrooms and a restaurant (five tables and 20 chairs).
- A kitchen, which is divided in two sections for cold and warm food. It also includes the storage of dried products.
- Five dormitories (with a roof made out of Ethernit), each for four persons (employees), with a private bathroom, shower and electricity.
- A volleyball field.
- A dormitory for the administrator.
- A garage for repairing engines, motors etc. with a spare parts inventory.
- Five rooms for storage.
- A laundry.
- A reception located at the airstrip.
- A facility for trash. The lodge placed five different types of trashcans to collect the waste.

Food

The restaurant provides nutritionally balanced meals, prepared by Huaorani chefs trained for the project. Locally grown products are used wherever possible and purchased from the local communities.

In the beginning of the project, Bilingual Naturalist Guides from TROPIC took a cook and an assistant from Quito with them to the ecolodge to cook for the tourists. In addition they hired Huaorani to work with them. Later professional cooks were hired from the University of Tourism in Quito to train the Huaorani how to cook for tourists, prepare meals and work in the kitchen. The Huaorani still hunt but the wild food is not offered to the clients.

TROPIC buys as much local food as they can in the community (bananas, yuca, pineapple etc.). Some food, for instance chicken, salt, sugar, rice or green vegetables, comes in through Coca or Quito.

Water

There are two streams with clear water flowing through the site: a water management system ensures quality water for human consumption and use in the kitchen or bathrooms. A manual on how to use and maintain the water management system has been handed out to the participants.

The water in the lodge is obtained directly from a well and is filtered (in all cases) and purified (for some points in the lodge) by means of a system of sand, ceramic and carbon filters. The water used in the showers and washbasins of the visitor accommodation is not to be drunk. The only drinking water is to be found in the kitchen. Bottles of drinking water are located in each room and are refilled daily.

The following material has been acquired and installed:

- A sanitary water system for the lodge
  - 4 solar panels
  - 1 solar pump
  - 1 filter
  - Material for the installation
- A sanitary water system for the community
  - 3 solar panels
  - 1 pump
  - Material for the installation
  - A filter system
  - A tank to collect the water
  - Laundry
  - Water reprocessing plant
  - Construction of a well

Electricity

TROPIC and the Huaorani always had the vision to be sustainable. That's why it was important for them to raise a fund for solar panels. International organizations like GIZ helped to buy and install these. There are no fossil fuels at the lodge, only solar panels. That means, if it is cloudy for a long time, the solar panels cannot work and there is no energy to pump the water in the tanks for the showers. TROPIC is thinking of installing a fossil fuel back-up.

The following material has been acquired and installed for the solar panels:

- A light system for the restaurant and technical equipment
    - 2 solar panels
    - 1 control unit
    - 6 illuminants
    - 2 batteries
- A lighting system for the accommodation (5 rooms for the clients, 1 for the administrator)
    - 6 solar panels
    - 6 control units
    - 6 batteries
    - 6 illuminants

To run the lodge in an environmentally and client friendly manner it had to be rigged with a solar freezer and refrigerator. Manuals for the technical equipment were handed out to the Huaorani.

Transport

To reach the Huaorani Ecolodge is on the one hand very complicated and time-consuming, but on the other hand offers a lot of additional experiences regarding wildlife and understanding the region.

Contract with non-Huaorani transport providers had to be made to assure the arrival of tourists. The visitors are transported by a minibus from Quito through the valley of the volcanoes to Shell, a small town located in the eastern foothills of the Ecuadorian Andes, about 151 km from Quito. Its name comes from the Royal Dutch Shell Company. A small airstrip, which is 850 meters long and near the Huaorani-village, has been built so that a local air-company can transport the guests via light aircraft to the jungle.

On their way back to Quito the visitors paddle in traditional Huaorani canoes on a small waterway to the Shiripuno River Bridge near the Quehueri'ono settlement.

During the dry season from August to October the river level is particularly low and the use of an outboard-motor can be difficult or impossible. Paddling the waterway to the bridge takes between 8 and 12 hours with a combination of engine and paddle. The times vary depending on the river flow.

Administration

There are two administrators working in situ and they manage, together with the operational staff, all questions regarding the visitors. They register the number of tourists coming to the lodge, who has paid and what needs are being requested.

According to TROPICthere has not been any profit as yet. In the first year private contributors lost 15.000 $. They hope that in Year 3 the business is going to make a profit. TROPIC has to explain the dynamics of the market to the Indians and for this 'you need patience, understanding, flexibility and creativity to work with an indigenous community', says Andy Drumm.

Housekeeping and maintenance

Technical consultants were hired to teach the Huaorani how to run the ecolodge correctly. Ten Huaorani community members were trained during a 24-month education program. A report with images and protocols was accomplished at the end of the program. The staff of the Lodge had to undergo a biannual training, which was based on the education of multifunctional employees with a basic knowledge of tourism management in the areas of guiding, housekeeping and cooking. Training focused on: customer service, image, handling complaints and basic techniques of table service. (Implementation of training through appropriate techniques including class exercises, field exercises, oral presentations and assessments.)

Together with the Huaorani the consultants developed the following code of ethics:

- Alcohol or drugs are prohibited for tourists and employees.
- Drinking '*chicha*' during visits is not allowed.
- Tourists should avoid taking pictures. It is not forbidden, but only allowed with permission. Tourists should never give money for taking pictures.
- No gifts to be given in general.
- Visitors are not allowed to participate in the hunting activities of the Huaorani.
- Fishing is allowed.
- Tourists are allowed to visit Huaorani homes under the condition that a guide accompanies them.
- Tourists are allowed to change personal lanterns, knives, etc. for handicrafts. Tips are also allowed.

- Tourists with an illness like a potential contagious flu should not visit the Huaorani.
- Tourists should not show themselves naked in front of the Huaorani.

Accountancy

It was obvious that they had to implement an easy accountancy-system, so that the Huaorani could follow and control all financial transactions. A workshop was held, to explain to them the importance of managing funds in a transparent manner.

The treasurer manages the incomes and expenditures and reviews the budget together with the president of the community.

Marketing

TROPIC participates in two major trade fairs every year. The Ecotourism company organises appointments with outbound operators in the US and UK to get the lodge into their brochures: 'It's not enough to put a brochure or a handout on the stand and wait. You need to talk to the people who are going to sell your product. You need to put your heart behind it', says Andy Drumm. Tropic wants to work more with 'searchengine optimization' to make their site more visible for potential visitors.

Main Obstacles

Invaders

Oil-companies, illegal loggers, and settlers are mainly trying to invade Huaorani land.

The Huaoroni-Territory has been legally owned by the community-members since 1990. There is no fence or control system around their property, only a line drawn by the Huaorani and some signs. Non-Huaorani community members had tried to reach the territory, like illegal loggers, animal hunters, other tour operators, settlers, and even oil-companies. They had to be repelled physically with machetes or other weapons.

Medical Treatment

Two people from the community received basic training in health care. They are the only people within more than a five-hour ride who have received medical training. The community does not provide health care facilities. In case of emergencies, it is important for them to leave by plane for the nearest hospital, which is in Coca or Shell.

This accordingly applies to tourists as well. TROPIC hands out a list to the visitors on how to prepare for the visit and how to be prepared for the jungle. In cases of small injuries or some diseases the Lodge provides a first-aid kit.

Environmental impact

The Lodge and its program do not harm the environment significantly.

A conservation area of 60,000 hectares has been established on Huaorani community land with the ecolodge at the heart of it. It is designated and mapped for conservation purposes with no-hunting zones.

TROPIC utilizes local resources to lower impacts. They use traditional boats or canoes made out of wood: the engine of the boat is just used in exceptional cases. Jungle tracks for tourists are made by animals or ancient forefathers. TROPIC does not build new ones. Tourists can use the river to take a bath or the sandbanks for camping. The number of tourists is limited to eight persons per tour. Trash and waste which are not decomposable have to be carried out of the jungle back to Quito.

Social impact

The Huaorani and other indigenous groups have very limited opportunities to earn money. They could work for oil-companies for handouts (usually food, clothes, chainsaws, or outboard motors) or do jobs as manual laborers. They could also work in logging sites and clearing land for cattle. In addition, they could go in the jungle hunting endangered animals or selling timber to illegal timber merchants.

Unlike other indigenous groups in the Ecuadorian Amazon (e.g. the Shuar and Achuar), the Huaorani do not seem to have taboos on hunting wild animals. However, they recognize the importance of animals as part of the attraction for ecotourism and their protection as a basic precondition for sustainable ecotourism.

The Huaorani also recognize that certain species should be preserved. The reasons for conservation in their opinion are shown in Figure 7.5.

The indigenous people who are torn away from their traditional lives are faced with resource degradation, barefaced capitalism, alcohol and prostitution, western school curricula, hierarchical thinking and action, and ridicule of their forest life. Their way of living has been denigrated as live communism and denounced as devil-inspired barbarism.

Leaving their families also exposes them to diseases which oil workers, tourists and the first colonists introduced.

As indigenous groups become increasingly aware of the negative socio-cultural and environmental impacts of oil exploitation and other environmentally destructive practices, many indigenous communities see the development of tourism as one of their only economic alternatives, and one capable of promising economic benefits, environmental protection, and cultural pride and empowerment.

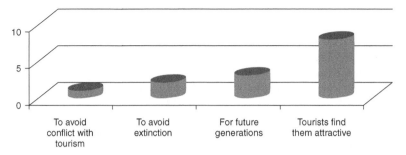

Figure 7.5 Reasons for animal conservation

Financial Income

Money is not an important factor for a 'good life' in the Huaorani community. Nevertheless they need money to afford clothing, health care and education. A monthly average income is 31,35 $. Although obviously their income is very low, they affirm having a 'good life': 17 out of 17 Huaorani, who were asked about their life conditions, said they were having a 100% good life.

Tourism simply makes a financial contribution: the presence of tourism is nearly irrelevant for them because it just gives them an irregular income and they are aware of the negative impact it could have. Negative aspects of tourism in the community are for instance alcohol, cigarettes, tourist nudity, parties, garbage, lies and deceit.

It is crucial that the communities understand ecotourism is an economic activity. A common mistake occurs when the operator acts as an NGO and the roles are mixed up.

This program helps the locals to continue their way of life.

Conclusion

TROPIC is about to organize several funds for projects which will develop certain aspects of their life. One of their ideas is to develop a better tourist infrastructure, a place for a community laundry, and different small, agricultural projects which will allow the Huaorani to cultivate more food to sell to the lodge.

TROPIC has spent a lot of money in building a radio tower for communication, but under bad weather conditions this is not reliable.

References

Braman, Scott and Fundación Acción Amazonia (2001); Practical strategies for pro-poor tourism TROPIC Ecological Adventures – Ecuador; PPT Working Paper No. 6.

CIA – The World Factbook (2010); https://www.cia.gov/library/publications/the-world factbook/geos/ec.html. [Accessed the 24th of May 2010,10:44]

Ministerio de Turismo Ecuador (2010); Ley Orgánica de Turismo; http://www.turismo-austro.gov.ec/index.php/es/descargas/67-noticias-anteriores/757-nueva-ley-organica-de-turismo. [Accessed the 8th of June 2010,15:28]

Rodríguez, Arnaldo (2004); *Huao Lodge - Establecimiento de Condiciones para una Operación Ecoturística de Base Comunitaria en la Comunidad Huaorani de Quehueri-ono.* Quito.

Rodríguez, Arnaldo (2006); Manual de Procedimientos Huao Lodge; Conservación en áreas indígenas manejadas; Biodiversity & Sustainable Forestry (BIOFOR) IQC. *Task Order No. 817*

Warth, Dr. Hermann (1997). TO DO! 1997 Wettbewerb Sozialverantwortlicher Tourismus. Begründung für die Preisverleihung.

Additional Information

http://www.huaorani.com

http://www.giz.de

Perfil de Proyecto: Proyecto ecoturístico con enfoque de género - Huao Lodge, (2007). GTZ – PPP Corpei

Source: Tropic Journeys in Nature, Director: Andy Drumm

Photos: www.huaorani.com (3)

8 Tourism in the Peruvian Amazon

Experiences of a private-communal partnership

Kurt Holle * *and Amanda Stronza* **

Introduction

Rainforest Expeditions is a private tourism company that operates three award-winning lodges in the Tambopata region of the southeastern Peruvian Amazon. The company manages or co-manages three lodges: Posada Amazonas (30 rooms), Refugio Amazonas (32 rooms), and Tambopata Research Center (18 rooms). All three have earned awards and international press coverage for combining high-quality tourism in the rainforest with achievements in conservation and community development. The lodges host 13,500 guests per year, and each caters to clients with different intensities and types of interest in the Amazon.

This region of Amazonia comprises lowland rainforest with high levels of biodiversity and social diversity, including indigenous peoples, long-established forest extractivists, and more recent migrant ranchers, farmers, and miners. All three of Rainforest Expeditions' lodges lie within or near the Tambopata National Reserve and Bahuaja Sonene National Park. Combined these represent a critical conservation unit of over one million hectares.

The region is currently threatened by the fact that it lies in the heart of the Brazil-Bolivia-Peru 'axis of integration' in South America. The centerpiece for the integration plan is building the Inter-Oceanic Highway, which by 2012 will link Atlantic ports in Brazil with Pacific ports in Peru and generate waves of migration and new industries in palm oil, soybean, and cattle ranching. The social and ecological impacts of the road will be tremendous. Some predict that without conservation intervention, 40 kilometers on both sides of the road will be completely deforested in ten years. The new road lies just 10 kilometers from the national reserve, and from several rural communities.

Ecotourism represents a potential buffer to land use change. In fact, many local leaders are currently seeking partnerships with NGOs and private investors to build a network of community-based conservation and development initiatives, with a particular focus on ecotourism and micro-enterprises.

*Founder, Rainforest Expeditions, Peru
**Associate Professor, Applied Biodiversity Science, Texas A & M

For nearly 20 years, Rainforest Expeditions has used tourism to connect economic benefits from clients who value standing forest to land tenants who also value standing forest, and generate a commitment to conservation. In simple terms, tourists value large old trees with monkeys in them. Land tenants often need an 'excuse' to maintain their forest standing: they want to do so, but often they cannot because they need to pay for education, housing or health. Rainforest Expeditions produces the 'excuse': profit-driven mechanisms by which revenues are shared locally through dividends, rental or entry fees, and employment and supplier contracts.

The Posada Amazonas Lodge

Posada Amazonas is a rustic lodge that features creature comforts for tourists, including full service, buffet meals, and airy, spacious rooms with full bathrooms (see Figure 8.1). It is owned by the Native Community of Infierno and managed with Rainforest Expeditions. The lodge was established in 1996 as a joint venture between business and the local community. As one of the first partnerships of its kind, the tourism lodge combines community empowerment, environmental conservation, and sound business practice. For Rainforest Expeditions, the joint venture was an important expansion project that allowed the company to move into the more commercial two and three day tour market from the four and five day tour market it was operating at Tambopata Research Center, located in a much more remote location.

Infierno is a 10,000-hectare community established in 1976 as a titled 'Native Community,' meaning all land is owned communally. In 2010, it had 179 families

Figure 8.1 Posada Amazonas Lodge
Source: Morgan Stetler

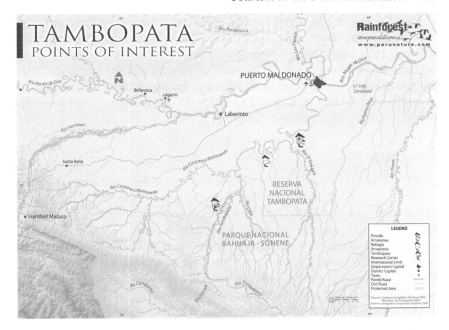

Figure 8.2 Map of the Tambopata region
Source: Rainforest Expeditions

and 558 people of Ese'eja, Andean and ribereño origins (see Figure 8.2). The Ese'eja are the indigenous peoples of the region; the ribereños are second or third generation settlers from other parts of the Amazon; and, the Andean residents are relatively recent colonists from the highlands. People's livelihoods in Infierno are based on farming, hunting, fishing, some timber extraction, and brazil nut collection. Since 1996, tourism and related services have become a more significant part of the community's economy.

People live along either side of the Tambopata River, and each family is allocated usufruct rights to approximately 30-hectare of forest and farmland. A 19-kilometer road connecting to the city of Puerto Maldonado ends in the communal center and two river ports. The communal center includes the school, medical facility, soccer field, two small stores, community office, and meeting grounds. One port serves tourists and tour operators primarily while the other serves farmers and the transport of agricultural produce. Finally, the community manages 3,000 hectares of forest as a reserve. On this land, only tourism is allowed, and all hunting, farming, and forest extraction is prohibited. Posada Amazonas is located within the reserve.

From its inception, Posada Amazonas has been a participatory project. Central to the project is a 20-year contract signed in 1996 by both the company and the community. This contract defines each participant's share in the profit. The lodge is owned by the community and co-managed with Rainforest Expeditions. For its ownership, the community receives 60% of the profits. Decision-making is by consensus. The community is represented by a five to ten member Ecotourism

Control Committee (the actual number of delegates depends on the community board's decision). Other fundamental concepts include the training of community members to occupy all lodge positions, the development and purchase of products and services from community suppliers if they are of equal quality and price to those available elsewhere in the market, and the gradual integration of cultural resources into the tour programs. Eventually the full management of the lodge will pass to the local community in 2016.

Lodge Activities

In 1997, one year after the joint venture was established, the partners gained financing for the lodge from the Peru Canada Fund. This technical cooperation agency provided a US$250,000 donation to the community and a US$100,000 loan to the joint venture to build the lodge. Additionally, the MacArthur Foundation produced a US$15,000 donation for capacity building. The lodge opened its doors in early 1998.

It was built using traditional architecture and implemented with hotel industry equipment. Only enough timber to fit the lodge was cut, resulting in fewer than 1.5 hectares of clearing. Rooms were limited to three walls, with the fourth non-existing one effectively serving as a balcony over the forest. Roofs were made from thatched palm leaves.

Three night tours were developed with a total of seven activities in the vicinity. Five of these are based on natural resources: a visit to a lake with giant otters, a visit to a canopy tower, a visit to a macaw clay lick, a hike along a rainforest trail and a night walk. Two of them are based on cultural resources contracted out to the community: visits to an ethno-botanical center and visits to a farm. Cultural activities have purposefully been limited because of the potential for their exploitation.

Training takes place in four spaces. Firstly, annual workshops have been conducted to train staff for all lodge positions (see Figure 8.3). These take place in-house via workshops in housekeeping, waiting, cooking, and driving. Secondly, annual guides courses have been conducted to train guides from all walks of life, including community members. Community members are trained in two stages: a month long workshop to explain the basic principles of biology and ecology and a semester long English course. Thirdly, managers have been trained recently using a shadowing approach, where community members substitute for managers for short periods of time or where they work as assistants to full time managers. Finally, the Control Committee meets with Rainforest Expeditions in monthly board meetings to discuss finances, operations and personnel issues. These meetings are effective training mechanisms in which management skills are transferred from RFE managers to community leaders, and vice versa. The board meetings, where decisions are taken by company-community consensus, touch on subjects such as budgets, financial results, personnel incorporations, process redesigns, new product development and infrastructure maintenance.

Figure 8.3 Posada Amazonas Staff
Source: Morgan Stettler

Posada Amazonas also funds a small community projects office. This has been a key element in the relationship, acting as a liaison between the community as a whole and RFE. The projects office is composed of a project coordinator and an assistant, in charge of facilitating the community infrastructure, territory integrity, education & health, supplier development and other projects. There is also a communicator, whose job it is to sit in at meetings and communicate decisions to the individuals involved. All these positions are covered by community members. Finally, there is also a community advisor, from an indigenous rights background, who helps community leaders navigate a way through the lodge's accounts books and administration.

As a result, overt the years, suppliers have emerged with different levels of integration and support from the lodge. An ecotourism port, ethno-botanical tour, and ecotourism concession have been implemented in close collaboration with the lodge. A fish farm and restaurant, an agricultural port and a home stay have also been designed and developed independently.

Local Impacts of the Partnership

We evaluated the economic, environmental, and social results of Posada Amazonas. Economically the lodge has been successful. Total economic impact in the community since the lodge's inception is of 2.3 million US dollars. In 2009 alone, overall economic impact was close to US$600,000. This included US$257,000 in dividends for the community, US$91,000 in payroll wages to community members, US$58,000 in community guide wages, US$51,000 in payments to community service suppliers, US$34,000 to community wage laborers, US$9,000 to community produce suppliers and US$6,000 to community artisans. Additionally US$77,000 was reinvested in the community lodge. Average annual growth of the economic impact of the lodge in the community has been 17%. Although that growth rate cannot be expected for the future, the absolute value for 2009 is a conservative estimate of future annual impact.

Tourism is an activity that supplements the farm economy in Infierno. As most community members have not abandoned farming, the opportunity cost of working in Posada Amazonas has been relatively small. Except for the guides, who do often abandon farming practices, community members at the lodge will either delegate farming to someone else in the family, or rent out their farm, or hire wage laborers to farm for them. In this manner, the income for families in the community has increased in the past 12 years. In 1998, the mean annual household income among 58 households from tourism alone was US$735 (Stronza, 2007). This compared with a mean annual income of US$2,082 from a combination of other activities outside of tourism, including farming, timber, and other sources. In 2010, just one household's annual share of tourism dividends of $800-1,000 was nearly half an average household's income for an entire year. In 2006, the mean annual income among 14 households was US$6,621 (Stronza, 2010). Several households in that sample included guides whose incomes have increased substantially over the years, partly because they have gained skills that enable them to earn tips, sometimes approaching $1,000 in one month. These numbers have been corroborated by an unpublished study conducted by Javier Gordillo among 63 families in 2008.

These new funds have led to various changes in the community infrastructure. A few of these include a high school, funded in great part through the Canadian embassy, a community office, a port for agricultural produce, co-funded by the government, a handicraft workshop, financed by the World Bank, and an after-school center for kids, also partly funded by the Canadian embassy. The community also used their tourism earnings to establish emergency medical loans and a program that covers funeral expenses for local families. A scholarship program has also worked on and off, helping to finance a university education for several students.

Most social and economic impacts have affected households. In 2008, Javier Gordillo surveyed 63 heads of household and found the following: 53% invested their dividends in farm equipment or home improvements; 16% purchased basic needs like clothes and food; 7% reported paying off debts or putting their earnings into savings; 5% noted health expenses; and 1% invested in a business venture. The remaining 8% reported spending on 'Other.' The number of consumer durables has increased with the new income. In 2008, about half of the families reported owning a TV set, and a quarter owned expensive items like chainsaws, 15hp outboard motors, motorcycles, generators, and cell phones (Gordillo, unpublished). Another social and demographic trend associated with this new income is the maintenance of two homes, one in the town of Puerto

Maldonado and one in the community. In 2008, 34% of 63 surveyed heads of household reported owning or renting a home in Puerto Maldonado (Gordillo, unpublished).

Socially, the project has had mixed effects. Over 80% of the community dividends have been distributed equally among family shares. This equitable division has helped ensure relative social stability, despite large infusions of new income. Nevertheless, community members are increasingly voicing concerns about how to function as a 'community,' one that shares communal tenure over land and resources while also gaining new skills and rewards associated with individual entrepreneurship (Stronza, 2010). The community's co-management of tourism with Rainforest Expeditions has also sparked a series of new organizations and small enterprises. These include five new family businesses, at least two new committees, and more monthly meetings to discuss the company management and other community matters. Most community members (95% of the 63 people surveyed) believe tourism has brought good things: money (41%), work (18%), conservation (12%), new capacities (8%), as well as miscellaneous aspects. Only 6% thought it had brought nothing good.

Environmentally, the effects of Posada Amazonas have been positive for conservation and the community management of forests and other resources. In addition to the 2,000-hectare reserve they already manage, the community has requested and obtained a 1,100-hectare ecotourism concession from the state. Altogether, about 3000 hectares are reserved for tourism, meaning that all farming, hunting, and extractive activities are either prohibited or restricted and monitored. These lands include a lake and a clay lick for macaws, parrots, and parakeets. People who break the rules have their weapons confiscated and their dividends withheld for that year. However, in the rest of the community, life goes on as usual, except now people have more money with which to purchase chainsaws or increase agricultural production.

Next Steps

Next steps for both partners are clear and already underway. For the community, these steps involve, first and foremost, capacity building for the transition from partnering with Rainforest Expeditions to managing the lodge on their own. Individual community members are already in training, or on the job, so that they can eventually assume top management positions. Within the community, people are also focused on building institutional strength. The challenge is to separate community life from business and technical matters. As a community that also now functions as a business, people are concerned about maintaining social and economic distinctions between the two. Local leaders are also focused on beginning to use tourism profits to reinvest in communal projects rather than for family dividends.

For Rainforest Expeditions, the next steps involve expansion, which will enable the company to withstand the loss of an important management contract in 2016. Also the company is looking for ways in which to capitalize on its know-how about community work and business associations, possibly expanding its operations into other community territories in the region. The focus is on strengthening the forest management around the reserve, so as to create a buffer zone where tourism provides an economic incentive to maintain forest standing.

Lessons Learned

- *Markets create tension*. Gaps are created: some families have prospered where others have stagnated. These groups have different agendas. Both are sources of tension.
- *Be prepared for the inheritor syndrome*. Many community members piggy-back on the most entrepreneurial. While some work and innovate, others are content to wait for the dividend check. Often, the latter will reduce their work calendar and farmed area. The former then tire of working for the rest.
- *Conservationists aren't produced, protected areas are*. Three thousand hectares around the lodge and ecotourism concession are well protected with experienced community guardians and sanctions. Family plots, however, which constitute another three thousand hectares, are now exploited more intensively and expansively. Families have more money, and this is used for small motors, chainsaws, guns, etc. So, a bird's eye view would tell us this: where the forest is being put to use through tourism, it is well protected. Where it isn't, it is being put to use extractively in a more intense fashion. In some ways, this approach to conservation mirrors the national park approach used in other parts of the world.
- *Trust is not in the manuals.* If one word were to describe the principal bottlenecks in a private company-community partnership, it would be trust. Why is it so difficult? Most reasons encompass deep-seated cultural differences, which manifest themselves in the individual or the organizational structures. For example, in a private company one usually negotiates with the most outspoken people. In communities, often silence carries equal importance. In a private company a majority is defined as 51%. In a community it could be defined as close to 90%, or can even come down to what the elders think. Listening is not part of business school, but it is an art well-mastered by traditional societies.
- *The market rewards but it doesn't sacrifice*. Operations must exceed their value proposition to the customer. This includes not only service quality and price, but also often overlooked product properties such as accessibility (time!) and ease-of-purchase.
- *The knowledge is difficult to capitalize*. Know-how in community enterprises is an important competitive advantage in that it is increasingly valued by societies, but monetizing this and scaling it up is extremely difficult. Too many stars must align for a company to replicate community partnerships of this intensity.

References

Gordillo, J. 2008. Socio-economic survey of households in the Native Community of Infierno. Unpublished report.

Stronza, A. 2010. Commons Management and Ecotourism: Ethnographic Evidence from the Amazon, *International Journal of the Commons* 4(1): 56–77.

Stronza, A. 2008. Through a New Mirror: Reflections on Tourism and Identity in the Amazon. *Human Organization* 67(3):244–257.

Stronza, A. 2007. The Economic Promise of Ecotourism for Conservation, *Journal of Ecotourism* 6(3):170–190.

9 Key issues and challenges to the development of community-based ecotourism in Guatemala

*Hanna Sophia Theile**

Introduction

In today's literature many authors agree that Community-based Ecotourism [CBET] seems to be the most promising method in tourism, one which combines the conservation of the environment as well as cultural heritage and at the same time improves the quality of life of the communites involved. Therefore, it is not surprising that especially within developing countries CBET has gained in popularity (Kiss 2004, p. 232). In 2001, the World Wildlife Fund for Nature (WWF) stated that the major goal of CBET is to protect the quality of the natural and cultural heritage of an area while trying to enhance it by tourism (2001, p. 14). Three years later, Kiss completed what had been said previously when claiming that CBET is not only concerned with maintaining attractive natural landscapes and a rich flora and fauna but also helps the involved communities to earn money, which provides both an incentive for conservation and an economic alternative to destructive actions. Thus development organizations often consider CBET as being a potential source of economic development and poverty alleviation, particularly in marginal rural areas with limited agricultural potential (Kiss 2004, p. 234).

Nonetheless, the WWF (2001) also revealed the downsides of CBET and claimed that often a major challenge is that projects are small in scale, but a sufficient number of inhabitants still have to benefit within the community to make a difference (WWF 2001, pp. 4-16). Therefore, the main reasons why projects fail are an insufficient number of visitors and too poor a quality of execution (WWF 2001, p.18). Another problem has been well stated by Shoka (2001, pp. 3-4) who maintained that it is unclear why people reinvest in biodiversity conservation or in other activities that are destructive of nature.

In order to overcome such negative obstacles financial support is required and communication with visitors, but tour operators also have to be improved (Shoka 2001, p. 22). Kiss (2004, p. 234) likewise upholds the idea that communities often need outside assistance when turning to tourism as a development option for their destination).

*University graduate in the field of International Hospitality Management at the InternationalUniversity of Applied Sciences Bad Honnef Bonn

Guatemala – geographical and rural states

Guatemala is a small republic located in Central America. It is bordered by Mexico in the north and northwest, Belize in the northeast, and El Salvador and Honduras in the southeast. It possesses two coastlines, namely on the Caribbean Sea and the Pacific Ocean which in sum cover up to 400km (Rosenberg 2005).

CBET in Guatemala

In 2005, representatives of several communities came together and founded the *Federacion Nacional de Turismo Comunitario de Guatemala* (FENATUCGUA). The organization was set up to represent, support and organize CBET within the country. It is nowadays strongly supported by the government but also by a range of Non-Governmental Organizations [NGOs]. Its mission statement points out that it strongly focuses on tourist projects that are managed by the local communities themselves, always having the focus on gender justness, respect and a valorization of the cultures and the environment involved (FENATUCGUA, 2008). These key values already reflect important aspects that must go alongside Community-based Ecotourism. Contributing to this, the FENATUCGUA's vision statement clarifies 'rural development, the protection and conservation of the biodiversity, the natural, cultural resources and coexistence in of the associate destinations, to contribute to the quality of their population's life' (FENATUCGUA 2008). At the present time, the organization is in charge of maintaining and supervising 29 communities.

Proyecto Ecológico Quetzal (PEQ)

Description

For further research, one of the numerous CBET projects had been singled out, namely the PEQ, which was created when a group of German students completed their social service in Guatemala in 1988. As recorded by Zeppel (2006, p. 99), these students came to Guatemala with the purpose of monitoring the rare Quetzal birds in the forests of Alta Verapaz, with 145 birds per km^2.

As Jacqueline Sarti, the reference person from the PEQ, states, there had been a need to accommodate and cater for the group of German students during their visit. For that reason, the group decided to risk getting in touch with the indigenous people. At the beginning, the local inhabitants, especially the women and children, were afraid and hid themselves from the foreigners. They were not familiar with seeing white people who were taller than themselves. However, after the German students explained their reasons for coming one family decided to cooperate and welcome them. After having heard that the family was being paid for their cooperation and hospitality, more and more families became more willing to get involved. At the present time, 54 Mayan Q'eqchi' families are involved in the program.

The PEQ has now become a Non-Governmental and Not-for-profit Organization itself, located in Cobán, A.V., and dedicated to the conservation and protection of the forests in the department of Alta Verapaz. It promotes the sustainable use of the natural resources found in the area. In 1997, the PEQ officially introduced the ecotourism project and with the families involved, the project team identifies alternative sources of work. This includes programs dealing with sustainable agriculture (with over 1,000 rural farmers), eco-tourism, bio-monitoring the vast bird populations, and providing environmental education to strengthen awareness and respect for the forests (PEQ, 2002a). Furthermore, the PEQ helps and supports the Mayan population to sell local products such as aromatic candles to tourists (Zeppel2006, p. 99). When doing so, the project obtains economic support from various international NGOs.

Objectives

The project aims at protecting the habitat of numerous species of wildlife in the forests of the department of Alta Verapaz including the Guatemalan National bird Quetzal (see Figure 9.1). Moreover, by providing its inhabitants with viable alternatives and promoting the rational and sustainable use of renewable natural resources, it tries to improve the quality of life for the region's impoverished rural inhabitants (PEQ, 2002a). In so doing, the project tries to avoid detrimental actions such as deforestation and excessive hunting.

Location

The project encompasses the mountain highlands of Yalijux, Guaxac Caquipec, and Chamúas, as well as three communities surrounding the Laguna Lachuá National Park. The eco-tourism communities are located in the high-altitude cloud forest and the sub-tropical rainforest (PEQ, 2010b) (see Figure 9.2). PEQ is working to provide low impact or ecotourism within the communities of San Lucas Sequilá, Caserío Nuevo Chicanab and Rocjá Pomtilá.

Case Study Main Section

Research Methods

In order to evaluate the design and management of the PEQ, the implementation of several sustainability principles provided by the UNWTO will be examined. Since the early 1990s UNWTO has pioneered the development and application of such sustainability principles and indicators to tourism in general and to destinations in particular (UNWTO 2004, Preface). All such principles refer to environmental, economic or socio-cultural aspects of tourism development and have been set up to guarantee long-term sustainability within a region or destination.

As laid down in the conceptual definition provided by the UNWTO in 2004, the sustainable development of tourism should:

Figure 9.1 The national bird the Quetzal
    Source: Jacqueline Sarti, PEQ

Figure 9.2 Cloud forest
    Source: Jacqueline Sarti, PEQ

1) Make optimal use of environmental resources that constitute a key element in tourism development, maintaining essential ecological processes and helping to conserve natural heritage and biodiversity
2) Respect the socio-cultural authenticity of host communities, conserve their built and living cultural heritage and traditional values, and contribute to inter-cultural understanding and tolerance
3) Ensure viable, long-term economic operations, providing socio-economic benefits to all stakeholders that are fairly distributed, including stable employment and income earning opportunities and social services to host communities, and contributing to poverty alleviation

Sustainable tourism development requires the informed participation of all relevant stakeholders, as well as strong political leadership to ensure wide participation and consensus building.

Achieving sustainable tourism is seen as an ongoing process, which requires a constant observation of possible impacts. Whenever necessary, preventive actions have to be taken to overcome the challenges and obstacles that occur. According to UNWTO (2004, p. 7), sustainable tourism should also 'maintain a high level of tourist satisfaction and ensure a meaningful experience to the tourists, raising their awareness about sustainability issues and promoting sustainable tourism practices amongst them'.

For the further analysis, seven principles were formulated out of this complex definition, whose implementation will later on be analyzed with regard to the PEQ. These principles are summarized and succinctly described as the following:

1. Conservation of natural heritage and biodiversity
2. Conservation of cultural heritage and traditional values
3. Participation/community involvement
4. Socio-economic benefits/education
5. Viability/long-term economic operation
6. Provision of employment and income/poverty alleviation
7. Raising tourists' environmental awareness

Research Findings

An extensive interview had been conducted with Jacqueline Sarti, a staff member of the PEQ, who is the person in the department responsible for dealing with the conservation of the environment. Right at the beginning she revealed that in the first place the PEQ had been interested in protecting the environment, followed by encouraging the local people to be productive and to work towards the development of their region as well as towards receiving the highest possible profits out of the CBET. However, for further investigations, the interview had been analyzed according to the seven principles of sustainable tourism development that had been described above.

1. Conservation of natural heritage and biodiversity

The conservation of the environment and biodiversity had always been a priority for the PEQ, especially the protection of the national bird species the Quetzal. In both the communities that are involved in the project, the team tried to make the inhabitants aware of the importance of conservation and sustainability through various educational sessions on environmental awareness. Even though the majority of the inhabitants are willing to cooperate, there still remains a number of people who refuse to take part in the project. These people prefer their ordered way of life and therefore they could not be convinced by the PEQ undertakings. This fact still poses a challenge to the project, since these people continue to perform destructive actions such as illegal hunting or corn growing whereby they continue to take a great deal out of the environment. Consequently, the PEQ did not succeed in completely fostering sustainability throughout the entire destination as they had desired.

2. Conservation of cultural heritage and traditional values

With regard to the second principle, Jacqueline Sarti emphasized in the course of the interview that it was important not to overlook the communities of the Mayan people during the process of sustainable tourism development. In quite the opposite direction the PEQ embarked on a strategy to support these communities through tourism while also providing them with gainful alternatives to continuing with harmful actions. The project is thus looking for a progression that allows the community to develop by learning and cultivating itself instead of being forced to adjust to its poor circumstances. Unfortunately, Jacqueline Sarti also indicated that additional problems had been brought about via tourism. As a result her main concern was about the indigenous population adopting the new and often exogenous culture of the tourists who visit. Instead of preserving the community heritage, this would entail a loss of the Mayan culture. This sure risk remains one of the biggest challenges within a successful tourism development process.

3. Viability/Long-term economic operation

Ever since the beginning of the project, the PEQ has strongly relied on a number of mostly Non-Governmental Organizations; however, recently the leadership decided to start working on its own assistance programs as well. With these programs, as explained by Jaccqueline Sarti, the PEQ wants to assure that it will be viable without the support of any NGOs in the future. She continued to underline the fact that one day the community will have to be able to carry on all such practices on their own. The indigenous population has to perceive that environmental awareness is the most important issue within the region and that through tourism the whole community is able to benefit on a long-term basis; they also have to realize that through tourism they will earn far more money than they would as day laborers in places that were miles away from home. Furthermore, the PEQ has tried to keep the project economically sustainable, however, she also admitted that this has not been possible. The reasons for this failure can be seen in a variety of external factors such as little tourism growth within the region of Alta Verapaz. The PEQ is almost being forced to attract a sufficient number of tourists, not only to be viable but also to differentiate itself from other communities on a long-term basis. At the moment, Jacqueline Sarti declares this purpose as considerably difficult when taking into account the overall economic situation.

4.   Socio-economic benefits/Education
Unfortunately, the PEQ reveals that the level of education within both communities remains fairly low compared to that in larger cities. This can be referred back to the low quality and financial assets of the rural schools wherever any of these exist. To keep up the quality of skills and knowledge of all inhabitants, all families are persistently taught and educated. There are special PEQ programs where only inhabitants that possess forested areas are allowed to enter. However, since this is not applicable for each and every community member, the PEQ has also established other programs dealing with sustainable agriculture. Furthermore, Jacqueline Sarti stated that there had been training sessions which educated the locals about tourism as a culture and how to suitably host CBET. The sessions had been introduced by the Technical Institution for Capacity and Production and they alternated with two seminars convened by the INGUAT. All the costs of these seminars were taken over and shared by the PEQ itself as well as the International Labor Organization [ILO] and INGUAT. In order to ensure the progress and success of every educational session, the participants have to pass a practical as well as an oral exam after each education period. In addition to the programs, the NGOs in cooperation with the communities have started to build a school with higher standards since the closest one is about two hours away from the communities. Therefore, as mentioned above, the local inhabitants are trained to be guides who will provide all the necessary information to tourists in order to reduce their impact on the environment and culture as far as possible. Moreover, to prevent the degradation of natural resources as well as the trash and pollution brought in by tourist traffic, the local inhabitants receive ongoing environmental education. Contributing to this, the PEQ equips them with the most suitable materials that they need for such work. Added to all this, everyone receives an education about how to handle trash and deal with liquids. Jacqueline Sarti claims that this is the most difficult part, since not everybody, be they locals or tourists, is aware of the urgent need for environmental protection.

5.   Provision of employment and income/Poverty alleviation
One requirement that led to the initiation of the ecotourism project was that the people participated while having the knowledge that they would receive economic growth and reduce their poor status within the country. Jacqueline Sarti stated that many of the indigenous people worked as guides and hosts. They not only welcome and teach all incoming tourists they also provide accommodation and integrate tourists in their daily lives. The objective here is to allow the tourists to experience a different culture and lifestyle in a rather rural and untouched surrounding.

The money that is gained through the project is afterwards equally distributed and mostly used for the development of the community. At the present time, the community tries to save money to build new educational facilities and continue to educate future generations, as well as increase the overall educational level within the community with the purpose of raising its standard of living.

6. Participation/Community involvement

Without the support and agreement of the community members to participate in the project, the PEQ would never have been as successful as it is today. Therefore, a further principle provided by the UNWTO fosters the involvement of all community members in order to keep up this sustainable development in tourism. As already mentioned, men usually work as guides and also make meals for incoming tourists and provide accommodations in their houses. Women are supported instead by participating in the monetary market producing and selling traditional handicrafts to tourists. This concept has paid off and at the moment 54 families are involved with and supported by the PEQ.

7. Raising tourists' environmental awareness

For the PEQ it is important to continuously educate not only the locals, this also encompasses teaching all incoming tourists. Jacqueline Sarti stated that most of the tourists already arrive with a certain attitude towards the environment and culture. The majority come from the United States and Europe. Their expectation is to experience living within a Mayan Q'qechi' family and they are usually highly interested in bird watching or nature in general. Nevertheless, continuously educating peopleabout environmental awareness is seen by the PEQ as necessary to maintain the image of sustainable development in tourism and to constantly bring to mind the necessity and objectives of the project.

Discussion/Recommendation/Conclusion

After extensive research and analysis, it became clear that the PEQ still finds itself in the earliest phase of an efficient sustainable development with regard to tourism. All of the seven principles that were set up by the UNWTO have to be fulfilled within the project in order to meet successful tourism development within a region. Certainly, the PEQ makes enormous efforts to follow these principles; however, there remains a shortfall in sufficient capabilities during the implementation. The most serious aspect certainly involves the financial capabilities. The communities remain incapable of funding such a project on their own and to provide the same education and training opportunities as they exist today. Not having a lot of financial assets, the project relies on outside help that most often comes from Non-Governmental Organizations. This dependency is considered harmful on a long-term basis when it comes to successful sustainable development. A second challenge is seen in the number of indigenous people who still refuse to cooperate with the project leadership. These people instead prefer living their ordered lives and are dedicated to cutting trees and hunting, which in turn poses a huge challenge to the PEQ. In addition, Jacqueline Sarti explained that sometimes the project led to false expectations with regard to profit making. It was feared that the indigenous people held that through tourism the community would easily make a profit in a short space of time. Furthermore, doubts were expressed about the adoption of the new exogenous culture brought innot only by tourists but also by members of the project team or NGOs. Up to then, the regions around the communities had been calm and free from danger. That was why it had been chosen for ecotourism to be realized. However, after a while, concerns arose that dealt with the various problems that arose through ecotourism, such as violence, the new infrastructure, and few promotion possibilities, leading to the subsequent frustration of the population. In terms of economical sustainability, the most serious problem has been that the PEQ at the current time has failed to achieve this goal since other activities became the priority and were seen as being more important to the overall project. Moreover, Jacqueline Sarti considered the fact that other competing regions in Guatemala such as Semuc Champey had received an enormous increase in tourist arrivals had negatively impacted on the PEQ. To overcome these challenges and obstacles in the future, the PEQ contin-ues to increase and improve the educational level of all people involved in the project to assure a certain degree of qualitative service that will be delivered to all tourists and is necessary to differentiate the project from others. Furthermore, the PEQ is exploring further how to expand its working areas and support other regions that have a high potential to become ecotourism destinations. In doing so, the PEQ in particularl plans to establish new alliances with further outside organ-izations. Referring to this, the PEQ finds itself in the act of expanding the coop-eration with a Guatemalan organization called Misterio Verde S.A.

In conclusion, it will be necessary to repeat this research again in the near future in order to work out exactly what progress has been made within the project. At the present time, no comparable data exist and therefore the study does not have the ability to measure exactly the PEQ's contribution to sustainable development. Nonetheless, it is hoped that this chapter has contributed to provid-ing information on the key issues and challenges to the development of Community-based Ecotourism in Guatemala.

Acknowledgement

The interview mentioned above was conducted with Jacqueline Sarti, a staff member in the conservation department of the PEQ. For the last seven years she has been involved in the project. Due to the fact that the PEQ is involved in different communities, she mostly works in its head office in the city of Cobán. According to her, this is the best place to work, since Cobán is in the centre of all the communities involved, thus giving the PEQ the opportunity to serve all of them equally. She is now planning to stay involved in the project and to support it by establishing new alliances that may help the PEQ's involvement overall.

References

Federación Nacional de Turismo Comunitario de Guatemala [FENATUCGUA]. (2008). About us. Retrieved September 6, 2010, from http://www.fenatucgua.org/en/index-1. html

Kiss, A. (2004). Is community-based ecotourism a good use of biodiversity conservation funds?. *Trends in Ecology and Evolution, 19*(5), 232–237.

Proyecto Ecológico Quetzal [PEQ]. (2002a). Who are we?. Retrieved September 3, 2010, from http://www.ecoquetzal.org/who.php

Proyecto Ecológico Quetzal [PEQ]. (2002b). Where do we work?. Retrieved September 3, 2010, from http://www.ecoquetzal.org/where.php

Rosenberg, M. (2005). *Guatemala*. Retrieved September 6, 2010, from http://geography. about.com/library/cia/blcguatemala.htm

Shoka, D. (2006). An analysis of tourist preferences for the development of ecotourism in Uaxactún, Guatemala, using choice experiments (Master of Science dissertation, University of Michigan, 2006). *Dissertation Section 1.1.2*, pp. 3-4.

United Nations World Tourism Organization. (2004). *Indicators of sustainable development for tourism destinations: a guidebook*. Madrid: UN.

United Nations World Tourism Organization. (2007). *Indicators of sustainable development: guidelines and methodologies*. New York: UN.

World Wide Fund for Nature [WWF]. (2001).*Guidelines for community-based ecotourism development*. Ledbury, UK: WWF International.

Zeppel, H. (2006). *Indigenous ecotourism: sustainable development and management*. Wallingford, Oxfordshire: CAB International.

10 Tourism cluster among livestock

The case of Bonito (MS), Brazil

Raul Suhett de Morais[*], *Gemma Cànoves*[**] *and Lluís Garay*[***]

Introduction

In Portuguese, '*bonito*' means 'beautiful' and there is no better word to describe the town that bears this word as its name. Located in the Central-West region of Brazil, the town of Bonito is one of the most remarkable tourism cases in the country. Its fame as a well-managed destination has spread all over Brazil, being studied by all tourism students. But Bonito is also famous amongst tourists, not only for its natural beauty but also for the marketing of its sustainable tourism model, and this makes it widely known and explored by travel agencies.

Bonito's population is around 17,000 people (IBGE, 2010) and it was not until the late 1980s that the balance of living patterns shifted from being primarily rural to becoming an urban majority (Barbosa & Zamboni, 2000). Although the totality of Brazil's coast (where most of the population lives) was already mostly urban by the end of the 1960s (IBGE, 2010), the interior remained rural for a couple of decades longer. The main reason for this were the intensive and well-developed farming and mining activities carried out in the three states which are part of the so-called Brazilian Central-West: Goiás, Mato Grosso and Mato Grosso do Sul (where Bonito lies). Since the construction of the city of Brasília (in 1960, inside a federal district in the center of the state of Goiás), the region has experienced an increase in the number of urban inhabitants.

The Central-West of Brazil is characterized by the meeting of three of the biggest ecosystems in the world: the Cerrado, the Pantanal and the Amazon Rainforest, forging a wide variety of landscapes and fauna/flora. Bonito is on the border between the Pantanal and the Cerrado, in one of the many valleys of the Bodoquena mountain range. Different authors have tried to define the extension of the Brazilian Pantanal, but there has never been an agreement on an exact number: Alvarenga et al. (1984) affirmed that it covered an area of a little more

[*]Tudistar Research Group, Department of Geography, Universitat Autònoma de Barcelona, Barcelona, Spain
[**]Tudistar Research Group, Department of Geography, Universitat Autònoma de Barcelona, Barcelona, Spain
[***]Tudistar Research Group, Business & Economics Studies, Universitat Oberta de Catalunya, Barcelona, Spain

than 130,000 km²; at the other extreme, the defunct Brazilian Ministry of the Interior (Brasil, 1974) delineated an area of almost 170,000 km². The Cerrado, on the other hand, is much bigger and covers an area of more than 8.5 million km² (Coutinho, 2000). Both of them have great differences (Cerrado being much drier, for example), but such diversity creates a splendid area filled with paradisiacal landscapes.

The town of Bonito and its related tourist attractions are located in southwest of the Mato Grosso do Sul state (Figure 10.1). Tourists keep coming, mainly by road, due to its proximity to the state of São Paulo (East) and the great distance from the nearest airport (Barbosa & Zamboni, 2000), situated at Campo Grande, the capital of Mato Grosso do Sul, 278km away. São Paulo[1], in Paraguay (West), and the Southern states of Brazil (South) are the origins for most of the tourists who visit Bonito.

Until the late 1980s Bonito was a calm village where farming was the main—and almost only—activity. At that time the current tourist attractions were visited only

Figure 10.1 Location of Bonito, other neighbouring Brazilian states and neighbouring countries.
Source: Adapted from IBGE (2010).

by the few inhabitants there, and the only outsiders that used to come were researchers (Mariani, 2002; Lobo & Moretti, 2008) and a few tourists on their way to or
from the Pantanal. The only attractive aspect of the town was fishing in its rivers,
but this did not represent the tourist trade and there was no intention to develop it.

Around that time the most prestigious monographic TV show in the country
presented the town of Bonito to the rest of Brazil. Great attention was given to its
natural beauty, mainly the *Gruta do Lago Azul* (Blue Lake Cave), which has since
then become Bonito's defining image (see Figure 10.2). People discovered that
the Brazilian countryside consisted of more than just wide-open spaces to farm
and raise livestock. This was first understood by people from outside the state of
Mato Grosso do Sul, mainly from the state of São Paulo where most of the potential tourists lived. A little later on, people from the Bonito area also realized that
they could earn their living by hosting and guiding the tourists that came. This
was when tourism started to take over the territory and the farming business
began to lose its solitary position in the economy of that region.

However, it was only in 1996 that tourism researchers started to take Bonito
more seriously (Labegalini, 1996). All of the socioeconomic dynamics in Bonito
are quite new, as is its tourism phenomenon. The conflicts between the primary
sector and tourism over territory are just beginning and this chapter will try to
delineate the boundaries that separate each side of the problem. By revising the
available literature on the theme, we will understand the state of the art of tourism
studies in Bonito and we will research the conflicts between the local inhabitants

Figure 10.2 Gruta do Lago Azul (Blue Lake Cave)
       Source: Raul Suhett de Morais, 2004

and outsiders, while at the same time attempting to include the former in the tourism phenomenon.

From Farming and Mining to Tourism

Brazil's countryside has always been primarily used for farming and, in specific areas, mining too. Due to its lack of big cities and its fertility, those areas in the western part of the country were traditionally used to plant soy, corn, and an extensive list of grain crops. They are also widely used to breed livestock, the main animal being cows. Never-ending landscapes of plantations and innumerable cattle are therefore the typical images of the Brazilian Central-West (see Figure 10.3). Because of its difficult access, it was only during the 20th century that villages were founded, when migrants from elsewhere in the country (mainly from the South) started to develop the agriculture and animal husbandry in the region. The farms are generally monocultures and they can easily encompass hundreds of thousands of hectares.

The three states, including the Federal District, which form the Brazilian Central-West occupy approximately 20% of Brazil's territory but contain less than 7% of its population (IBGE, 2010). The area around Bonito is even more sparsely population than it seems, due to the fact that the major urban centres are

Figure 10.3 Man herding livestock in Bonito
Source: Raul Suhett de Morais, 2004.

in Goias, about 1,000km away. As of 2006, the state of Mato Grosso do Sul, where Bonito is, had more than 60 million animals as livestock, of which more than 20 million were cows, while the current human population was only 2.5 million (IBGE, 2001). The low population coupled with the strength of the farming and mining industries help explain the lack of interest in tourism in the area. Another reason why tourism took so much time to arrive has been the poor transport connections with the main centres in Brazil, such as Sao Paulo, Brasilia (which is inside the state of Goias) and Rio de Janeiro. These cities, besides the fact that they receive the biggest share of international tourists, are also the ones with a bigger capacity to send tourists elsewhere in Brazil.

The arrival of the tourism phenomenon in Bonito must not be understood as a substitute for farming or mining. Those economic activities are as healthy now as they were during the late 1980s and early 1990s when mass tourism first started to appear in the area. The areas where tourists go today were not in danger and one cannot say that they are being protected because of tourism, for they were already protected by law before the 1990s and they had little interest in agriculture, farming or mining. Lobo & Moretti (2008) go further and believe that some of the places of interest in the region have been protected because of their value as products and not because of their value as human heritage. The tourism phenomenon started because tourists had started to come by themselves and the business community felt that it was time to build some structure, that is to say tourism did not begin in Bonito because the population was losing jobs or the dominant economic activity was decreasing. The arrival of tourists was due to Bonito's fantastic scenery and the desire of urban dwellers to revisit nature, as one can understand from Mariani's (2002) research.

The first step in providing the tourists with basic infrastructure was providing guided tours through the caves and rivers and accommodation. That was sufficient for adventure tourists (Plog, 2001) but not for the dependable ones who were beginning to arrive by the mid-1990s. This new kind of tourist arriving in Bonito was made clear by research from Santos et al. (2007) and also that of Lobo and Cunha (2009), when they confirmed that the average tourist in the town was highly educated, had a high income (five times the minimum wage) and was also young (16 to 50 years old). They demanded more services and comfort and the town (the inhabitants, public administration, together with both local and outside entrepreneurs) saw an opportunity to start new economic activity in the area. This was when tourism began to exist in Bonito as a definite economic activity.

The Consolidation of Tourism Activity and Controlled Tourism

Tourism activity in Bonito grew rapidly during the mid-1990s and the town was able to respond accordingly. Investments were made both in infrastructure and services, for the new tourists that had started to come were much more demanding. They needed more than just a space for their tent and a guided tour through the woods. By that time, the improvements in accommodation and the availability of guided tours were significant, with many hotels being built and numerous people undergoing training to become certified tourist guides. Tourism then became a significant economic activity, and thus it was given more attention. As is typical in all economic activities, the private sector was the first to see the potential of Bonito's beautiful sights. The owners of the farms where the most popular places of interest were located started to charge for entrance, and the town centre also saw a boom in the accommodation supply. In addition, people who used to work on the farms before the publicity given to Bonito started to find jobs as tour guides for the many visitors the town was receiving. As Sampaio (2005a, p. 76) stated, Bonito 'initially was an agriculture-related town, focused mainly in farming, [but] today is able to create a dynamic economy through tourism'.

Nevertheless, the public administration took a step towards the sustainability of the natural resources in the area and created a program to monitor the tourism trade and the flow of tourists. The goal to control tourism was never so well achieved in Brazil as it was in Bonito. The development of a unique voucher for every tourist was the key factor in this, as has been proven in recent decades. The whole idea behind the unique voucher policy is to know exactly what the tourist is doing and thus prevent the saturation of a specific attraction. The need for control is so strong that it could generate some controversy concerning the free-dom of the tourist when it comes to choosing the attractions he or she wants to visit, but the public administration believes that a *laissez-faire* system for tourists would not be the best for Bonito's treasures.

The public administration in Bonito started to work on controlling the tourist flow just when the National Program for Municipalization of Tourism (*Programa Nacional de Muncipalizacao do Turismo*, PNMT) was launched, around the end of the 1990s. Bonito was one of the key models for the implementation of the program. As Vieira (2003) concluded, the creation of the unique voucher guided the organization of the tourism activities in the town. The authors carried out interviews with many of the key stakeholders in Bonito and all of them agreed on the importance and benefits of the unique voucher.

Tourism in restricted areas is a research area that has been studied by many authors (Baker & Genty, 1998; Cifuentes, 1992; Pulido-Bosch et al., 1997; Alho, Sabino & Andrade, 2007; Takahashi, 1997; Mitraud, 2001; Lobo et al., 2008) and in Bonito many methodologies have been used to determinate the number of people allowed in a certain place of interest. The most well-known tourist attrac-tion in the town is the Gruta do Lago Azul, and this specific cave is the most studied because it is protected by the National Institute of the Artistic and Historic Heritage (IPHAN) (Boggiani et al., 2008). As Boggiani et al. (2007, p. 339) Hve stated, the visits happen 'during the day, always accompanied by certified tour guides, in groups of 15 people and there is no artificial lighting. Each group is in the cave for about 90 minutes and, at most, 3 groups can be in the cave at the same time.' The number of visitors has increased remarkably (see Table 10.1) and the number is currently very close to the cave's maximum capacity (now 305 visitors per day): Boggiani et al. (ibid, p. 340) calculate that during 27% of the open days the cave receives around 300 people per day.

Table 10.1 Total number of tourists in the Gruta do
Lago Azul / year

Year	Number of tourists
1996	32,937
1997	34,027
1998	36,248
1999	43,289
2000	43,785
2001	45,996
2002	48,136
2003	44,786
2004	43,869

Source: Secretaria Municipal de Turismo de Bonito (Bonito's
Municipal Tourism Secretary). Adapted from Boggiani, 2007

The concept of the unique voucher is being implemented by Bonito's town council and it covers all of the town's tourist attractions. Any tourist willing to visit any attraction, be it the caves, the rivers or trekking, needs to go to a travel agency to purchase his or her voucher. The travel agency then tries to match the tourist's desires with the site availability as allowed for by the public administration. Every step is processed in an integrated system and the tourist leaves the travel agency with his or her unique voucher that allows entrance only to the attractions he or she has been authorized to go to, at the date and time he or she has been given. Every tourist attraction has a certain quantity of slots that can be filled with a specific number of tourists and this is controlled by the public administration. It is important to note that despite the public administration controlling the whole process, all the payments and services are done directly with the travel agencies. The tourist leaves the agency with their unique voucher and is guided through the attractions.

Although the main utility of the unique voucher is to provide accurate figures on how many people are visiting each tourist attraction, it has another very important function: a fairer distribution of the profits from this tourism activity. As Sampaio et al. (2005a, p. 86) stated,

> there is an agreement between property owners of tourism sites, local guides and agencies, to control the flow of visitors and ensure egalitarian distribution of the profits obtained from the activity. Although the property owners are the ones to receive a higher percentage of the entry price, it is known that these also have higher costs. At least the profits are not concentrated only in their hands.

It is also because of the vouchers that the town council can control the taxes that should be deducted from each stakeholder.

Another important point about tourist control is that the unique voucher allows each tourist to access that specific tourist attraction, but only for a limited time and for a very specific purpose. If he or she buys a rafting package, it is impossible to go fishing or diving without going back to the travel agency. During the activity the tourist is always accompanied by a guide who explains and takes part in the activity, making sure that it is an environmentally conscious tour and that the tourist has an optimum experience within the timeframe he or she has been given. The guide is never away from the groups, which are usually very restricted in terms of attendance, because preserving the environment is the first priority for guides.

That decision was very well received not only by the institutions involved in environment protection, but also by the tourism trade, for they can easily predict how many employees and materials they will need on any given day due to the integrated system that assures them how many people they will be receiving. From the tourists' point of view, they are very satisfied with these policies for they do not have to queue and neither do they have a chance of being turned away from an overbooked attraction. There are, however, some adventure tourists who do not agree with the unique voucher system, complaining that it takes away their freedom to use the attractions as they like. But the ones who clearly lose out are the local inhabitants: before the tourism phenomenon had arrived in Bonito, they freely used those places for their leisure and now they are forbidden access if they do not pay for it.

Outsiders' Exclusivity on The Tourism Phenomenon

Because of the extreme control and high demand for the tourist attractions in Bonito, many of them became too expensive. This only allowed a small part of the public to have access to them, and the local inhabitants were practically excluded from their previously cherished leisure areas. Before the arrival of mass tourism and the necessity of the public administration's control, all of what now have become tourist attractions were free to be used and they were frequently visited by the citizens of Bonito, mainly during the weekends. Although many of them were on private land, people freely used the caves and the rivers without the need to ask for permission to enter these properties; nevertheless, with the new strict control on all the tourist attractions—mainly due to entrance capacity (Bogiani, 2007)—the local inhabitants were denied the privilege to use the places they always used to go to. They were now treated like tourists if they wanted to enjoy the same spots they used to go before the arrival of the tourists. As Mariani (2002, p. 42) has found interviewing locals in Bonito, they feel that the experiences of their childhood cannot be passed on to their children: 'my school friends and I used to leave home early. We used to skip school and head to Mimoso [river]. It was great fun ... Nowadays you have to be rich to do that. My kids don't have the same opportunity.' The author goes on to explain the increasing distance between locals and the new 'places of interest' when another inhabitant says that

'[...] I don't even know the excursions that the tourists go to, and I've lived here as long as I am aware of myself as a person. At the farms that receive tourists, my brothers and I used to swim every day. Today if I want to go in, I need to pay and it is very expensive. That is absurd!' (ibid., p. 43).

Trying to break the myth that tourism is good in all aspects, Araujo et al. (2005) affirm that tourism in Bonito also has bad elements, such as an increase of 300% in rent from 1995 to 2005 and that violence, drug consumption and prostitution have also grown or even become new issues in some areas. The testimony from another inhabitant exemplifies the existence of negative effects by comparing the state of the Formoso river before the arrival of tourists to that of nowadays: 'Anyone who saw this bathing spot before and comes here to remember the old days would be saddened to see how the old-time children's play area has turned into a place full of crowds and litter' (Mariani, 2002, p. 42). Another local says '[h]ere they just live off the tourists and forget the lives of the people here. Those who don't live in Pilad Rebua [town centre] suffer, because everything is done for the benefit of the tourists and the tourism companies' (ibid).

Being excluded from their one-time places of leisure is not the only area where outsiders took the local inhabitants' place. Entrepreneurs from other Brazilian states took the lead and were the first ones to start tourism-related businesses in Bonito. This situation was due to the fact that the greater part of tourists in the town came from other states, plus the market was created elsewhere, not in Bonito. Travel agencies were created as a response to the tourist demand to visit the previously 'discovered' Gruta do Lago Azul and other places of interest. They hired locally since once they arrived to Bonito they would be accompanied by a local guide. Also, the accommodation was owned and managed by outsiders because the small population of Bonito did not have the capital to start this kind of business, and around that time there was no available credit. The idea of converting homes into hostels—a practice very common in European countries (Garcia-Ramon, Canoves & Valdovinos, 1995; Canoves et al., 2004; Canoves, Herrera & Villarino, 2005; Canoves & Morais, 2011)—was unheard of, for the kind of tourist that arrived in Bonito was very demanding and wealthy, preferring to be hosted by resorts and luxurious hotels.

However, some inhabitants do see the bright side of tourism, as one local said that 'the hotels benefit, businessmen increase their profits and new jobs are created for the population'; another says that 'tourists bring new things to the town and the town becomes busy and lively. Thirty years ago, I would go out in January or February and not see anybody in the streets. Nowadays there are crowds of people' (Mariani, 2002, p. 42). The satisfaction of some part of the population with the tourism phenomenon can be explained by all of the improvements it has brought to the town and its inhabitants. From 1991 to 2001, Bonito has jumped from the 30th to the 18th position on the Human Development Index ranking in the state, as mentioned by Alho, Sabino & Andrade (2007). The owners of the farms have been adopting the best practices developed by the Ministry of Tourism in the last five years through the Tourism Development Program (*Prodetur*).

Recently, the local inhabitants of Bonito have found a new way to profit from the tourism phenomenon that took over the town. Many small communities nearby were completely excluded from the benefits of tourism, for they had neither accommodation to offer nor any tourist attractions. In the past two decades the town has tried to convince its inhabitants of the advantages of the tourism phenomenon (Barbosa & Zamboni, 2000), for some 22% of the entire population now works in a tourism-related job (IVT, 2004).

Many projects have been carried out in Bonito to help small communities develop ways to profit from the arrival of the tourists. The Fundacao Neotropica do Brasil has done training and consultancy with two communities in the Serra da Bodoquena, on the periphery of Bonito (Larceda et al., 2007). Together with the local inhabitants they developed a series of products made from surplus agriculture, such as fruits and vegetables commonly cultivated in the region, to be sold in supermarkets, trade fairs, handicraft shops and hotels. As has been said by many authors, creating new forms of working the countryside is the best way to avoid the need to move to the city in search of jobs and a better quality of life (Brasil, 2010; Sampaio, 2005b).

Conclusions and Future Questions

The tourism phenomenon can be tough on the places where it exists. Many places have experienced negative effects from the arrival of mass tourism (Divino & McAleer, 2010; Butler, 1991; McLeroy & Potter, 2006). Bonito has been receiving tourists for a relatively short time; nevertheless the numbers have grown consistently from the 1990s until now. The great affluence of visitors was key to beginning such strict controls on the part of Bonito's public administration, both to preserve the fundamental draw for tourists, the natural heritage of the area, and to create a better distribution of profits from the tourism phenomenon. The advent of the unique voucher in Bonito was the way the public administration found to control the tourism phenomenon in the town, by knowing exactly where the tourists were going and how many of them were visiting each specific place of interest. The unique voucher has also allowed the public administration to collect taxes properly and to arrange the social network in a way that all the people involved— travel agencies, tour guides, owners of the farms, hoteliers, etc. —could benefit from it.

However, it is important to note that even though this strict control is practiced in Bonito, not everything is perfect. The local inhabitants who are not involved with the tourism sector see the disadvantages of receiving so many people from elsewhere. They complain about the noise made by visitors as well as their litter, but the main objection is made regarding the matter of the privation of access to what have been made into tourist attractions. The local inhabitants who have lived their whole lives in the Bonito region traditionally used these very areas for leisure, places they used to go to in order to relax and meet friends. Currently, these are now tourist attractions and the control over the number of people allowed in plus the entrance fees make it impossible for them to be visited by Bonito's population. This is no small inconvenience, for the locals should be granted their right to leisure. This is a matter that shall be attended to in future discussions.

Small communities that never thought about entering the trade can also explore the tourism phenomenon. This was made a reality by programs carried out in small villages on the outskirts of Bonito that were recently incorporated into the tourism trade by producing products from fruits and vegetables. These villages are made up of families that have been working in agriculture for generations, and with the help of training and consultancy they are able to sell the surplus of their production to tourists. It is always positive to incorporate new local stakeholders into the tourism sector, for they attempt to maintain the countryside population where they currently are, thereby avoiding the depopulation of the area.

In today's world where telecommunications, traffic, pollution and the insanity of big cities are consuming (post-)modern man, places like Bonito need to be considered as more than just spas. They are the gateway through which people can better understand themselves, where they can reconnect with nature and maybe understand that life is more than work and consuming material goods. As has been said by many authors, Bonito with all its places of interest is an important part of Brazilian natural heritage and it must be preserved because of its unique beauty. Although Lobo and Moretti (2008) correctly asserted that the protection of tourist attractions has developed because of their value as goods that can be sold, the beauty of Bonito should be preserved not because of its mercantile value, but because of its unique place as a regional and Brazilian natural heritage. If this chapter helps to develop that feeling not only in Bonito, but also in other places like it, we believe we have reached our objective.

Note

1 São Paulo is actual the main origin for all national tourists in Brazil, for it is the biggest and most populated city in the country, with about 20 million people living in its metropolitan area.

References

Alho, C. J. R., Sabino, J., Andrade, L. P. (2007) O Papel do Turismo para a Conservação de Recursos Hídricos: O Caso de Bonito, em Mato Grosso do Sul. XVII Simpósio Brasileiro de Recursos Hídricos. http://www.acquacon.com.br/xviisbrh/ Retrieved on July, 27th, 2010.

Alvarenga, S. M., Brasil, A. E., Pinheiro, R., Kux, H. J. H. (1984) *Estudo geomorfológico aplicado à Bacia do Alto Paraguai e Pantanais Mato-grossenses*. Salvador: *Projeto RADAMBRASIL*, pp. 89–183.

Baker, A., Genty, A. (1998) Environmental pressures on conserving cave speleothems: Effects of changing surface land use and increase cave tourism. *Journal of Environmental Management, v 5, n 92*, pp 165–175.

Barbosa, M. A., Zamboni, R. (2000) *Formação de um 'Cluster' em torno do Turismo de Natureza Sustentável em Bonito – MS*. Brasília: IPEA.

Boggiani, P. C. et al. (2007) Definição de Capacidade de Carga Turística das Cavernas do Monumento Natural Gruta do Lago Azul (Bonito, MS). *Geociencias, v 26, n 4*, pp. 333–348.

Boggiani, P. C. et al. (2008) Gruta do Lago Azul, Bonito, MS: Onde a Luz do Sol se Torna Azul. In: Winge, M. et al. (eds). *Sítios Geológicos e Paleontologicos do brasil.* http://www.unb.br/ig/sigep/sitio107/sitio107.pdf Retrieved on July, 27th, 2010.

Brasil. Ministério do Interior. (1974) *Estudos hidrológicos da Bacia do Alto Paraguai.* Rio de Janeiro: DNOS. v.1, p. 284.

Brasil. Ministério do Desenvolvimento Agrário. (2010) Programa de Turismo Rural na Agricultura Familiar. www.pronaf.gov.br/turismo/programadeturismorural.pdf. Retrieved on July, 27th, 2010.

Butler, R. W. (1991). Tourism, Environment, and Sustainable Development. *Environmental Conservation, 18*, pp 201–209.

Canoves, G. et al. (2004) Rural tourism in Spain: an analysis of recent evolution. *Geoforum, v 35, issue 6*, pp. 755–769.

Canoves, G., Herrera, L., Villarino, M. (2005) Turismo Rural en España: Paisajes y Usuarios, Nuevos Usos y Nuevas Visiones. *Cuadernos de Turismo, n 15*, pp. 63–76.

Canoves, G., Morais, R. S. (2011) New Forms of Tourism in Spain: Wine, Gastronomic and Rural Tourism. In: Torres, R., Momsen, J. (eds) *Tourism and Agriculture New Geographies of Consumption, Production and Rural Restructuring.* London: Routledge.

Cifuentes, M. (1992) *Determinacion de Capacidad de Carga Turística en Areas Protegidas.* Centro Agronomico Tropical de Investigacion y Ensenanza – CATIE. Informer Tecnico, n 194.

Coutinho, L. M. (2000) O Bioma Cerrado. In: Klein, A., L. Eugen (eds) *Warming e o Cerrado brasileiro: Um século depois.* São Paulo: Editora da Unesp.

Divino, J. A., McAleer, M. (2010) Modelling and forecasting daily international mass tourism to Peru. *Tourism Management, v 31*, issue 6, pp. 846–854.

Garcia-Ramon, M. D., Canoves, G., Valdovinos, N. (1995) Farm tourism, gender and the environment in Spain. *Annals of Tourism Research, v 22, issue 2*, pp. 267–282.

IBGE – Instituto Brasileiro de Geografia e Estatística. (2010) www.ibge.gov.br Retrieved on July, 27th, 2010.

IVT – Instituto Virtual do Turismo. (2004) Sudeste: Bonito Integra Seus Habitantes ao Turismo Sustentavel. www.ivt-rj.net/clipping04.cfm?clip_id=738 Retrieved on July, 27th, 2010.

Lacerda, L. et al. (2007) Agroindustrialização de Alimentos nos Assentamentos Rurais do Entorno do Parque Nacional da Serra da Bodoquena e sua Inserção no Mercado Turístico, Bonito/MS. Interações – *Revista Internacional de Desenvolvimento Local, v 8, n 1*, pp. 55–64.

Labegalini, J. A. (1996) *Levantamento dos Impactos das atividades antrópicas em regiões cársticas – Estudo de caso: Proposta de minimo impacto para a implantacao de infra-estrutura turistica na gruta do Lago Azul, serra da Bodoquena (Bonito – MS).* Sao Carlos: Escola de Engenharia de Sao Carlos / Universidade Federal de Sao Carlos.

Lobo, A. S. L. et al. (2008) Espeleoturismo no Brasil: Panorama Geral e Perspectivas de Sustentabilidade. *Revista Brasileira de Ecoturismo, v 1, n 1*, pp. 62–83.

Lobo, H. A. S., Moretti, E. C. (2008) Ecoturismo: As práticas na natureza e a natureza das práticas em Bonito, MS. In: *Revista Brasileira de Pesquisa em Turismo, v. 2, n.1,* pp. 43–71.

Lobo, H. A. S., Cunha, F. M. (2009) Perfil dos Turistas e Percepção de Impactos Ambientais na Gruta do Lago Azul, Bonito-MS. *Revista Hospitalidade, ano VI, n 1*, pp. 34–49.

Mariani, M. A. (2002) Perception of tourists and inhabitants of the town of Bonito: the place, subjects and tourism. In: *Turismo: Visão e Ação, ano 5, n. 11*, pp. 27–40.

McLeroy, J. L., Potter, B. (2005) Sustainability Issues. In Baldacchino, G. (ed.) *Extreme Tourism: Lessons from the World's Cold Water Islands.* Oxford: Elsevier, pp. 31–40.

Mitraud, S. F. (2001) *Uso Recreativo do Parque Nacional Marinho de Fernando de Noronha: Um Exemplo de Planejamento e Implementacao.* Brasilia: WWF, 100p.

Plog, S. (2001). Why destination areas rise and fall in popularity: An update of a Cornell Quarterly Classic. *Cornell Quarterly Classic (42)*, 13–24.

Pulido-Bosch, A. et al. (1997) Human Impact in a Tourist Karstic Cave (Aracena, Spain*). Environmental Geology, v 31, n 3*, pp 142–149.

Sampaio, C. A. C. et al. (2005a) Arranjo Produtivo Local Como Estrategia Que Promove o Ecodesenvolvimento: Analises das Experiências de Bonito (MS), Lagoa de Ibiquera (Garopaba e Imbituba) (SC) e Santa Rosa de Lima (SC). *Turismo – Visão e Acao, v 7, n 1*, pp 69–91.

Sampaio, C. A. C. et al. (2005b) Arranjo Socioprodutivo de Base Comunitária: Analise Comparativa de Experiências de Turismo Comunitário no Brasil e no Chile. *Revistas de Negocios, v 10, n4*, pp. 288–301.

Santos, L. F. F. (2007) Turismo de Minimo Impacto no Balneário Municipal de Bonito, Mato Grosso do Sul: Diagnóstico e Propostas de Implatacao. *Ensaios e Ci, v 11, n 2*, pp. 87–98.

Takahashi, L. Y. (1997) Limite Aceitavel de Cambio (LAC): Manejando e monitorando visitants. In: *Anais do I Congresso Brasileiro de Unidades de Conservação, v I*, pp. 445–464.

Vieira, J. F. L. (2003). *Voucher Unico – Um Modelo de Gestão da Atividade Turística em Bonito-MS.* Master's Thesis. Universidade Católica Dom Bosco. Campo Grande.

11 Diversified nature tourism on St. Vincent

*Velvet Nelson**

Introduction

The Caribbean is a geographic region that has come to be characterized by tourism. As these islands experienced a long decline in their agricultural industries, they often looked to tourism as a means of new economic development. The region as a whole saw particularly strong growth in the period between the 1970s and the 1990s, when tourist arrivals quadrupled (Thomas, Pigozzi and Sambrook, 2005). Much of this growth took place in the form of conventional mass tourism that centered on the islands' beach resources. As such, the Caribbean has come to be identified as one of the world's leading tourism destinations (Duval, 2004), and, in particular, one of the world's leading sun, sea and sand (3S) destinations (Momsen, 2005). Yet, Caribbean tourism should not be seen as a one-dimensional tourism product. Sun, sea and sand may be the primary draw for the majority of the Caribbean's tourists, but these tourists also often have a range of secondary interests away from the beach and seek to participate in other types of activities (Nelson and Torres, forthcoming). In addition, not all of the islands possess the white sand beaches that are a fundamental component of the Caribbean 3S tourism product and have looked to their other environmental resources to build an industry based on nature tourism.

Nature tourism in the Caribbean has typically utilized conceptions of nature that date back to the nineteenth century and highlight scenes of 'wild' nature. Many islands have packaged this type of experience in the form of a rainforest hike. This development has been an important means of diversifying the traditional 3S tourism product, and the rainforest hike holds distinct appeal for many of the region's tourists. However, the reliance on the rainforest hike has created a somewhat one-dimensional nature tourism product in the region (with the exception of destinations such as Dominica, where nature tourism is their primary product). A single product cannot meet the interests and demands of a disparate set of tourists. Moreover, it contributes to the perceived homogenization of the

*Sam Houston State University, Huntsville, Texas, USA

islands, where tourists think that, if they have had the experience of one Caribbean island, the experience would be the same if they visited another.

St. Vincent and the Grenadines is a small island nation in the Caribbean Sea. The economic shift from agriculture to tourism has taken place slowly here, and, for the most part, St. Vincent and the Grenadines has been less developed as a tourism destination than many of its Caribbean neighbors, with smaller numbers of tourist arrivals and receipts. However, this is not necessarily considered to be a disadvantage. Minister of Tourism Glen Beache states, 'Visitors discover a friendly, quieter and more authentic Caribbean experience, quite different to other more developed Caribbean islands. We want it to stay that way' (Responsible Travel, 2009). Much of the nation's tourism has been concentrated on the smaller islands of the archipelago, but the 'mainland' of St. Vincent also has numerous attractions. There are a small number of golden beaches as well as black volcanic sand beaches, the cultural heritage of the Black Caribs, and film sites from the popular 2003 movie *Pirates of the Caribbean*. Like the other rugged volcanic islands in the region, St. Vincent has especially utilized its natural attractions; however, unlike many other islands, it has maintained several options for nature tourism experiences that provide for different interests and physical abilities, ranging from a relaxing stroll through the National Botanical Garden to the challenging climb up the La Soufriere volcano.

This chapter is based on a series of research projects designed to understand the relationships between tourists and the environment in the Caribbean. It has its origins in archival research on historic patterns of tourism in the region, fieldwork at nature tourism sites on various Caribbean islands including interviews with both tour guides and tourists, and a survey of potential Caribbean tourists to assess their perceived preferences and expectations of nature tourism – in other words, what they thought they wanted from a nature tourism experience in the Caribbean. This was followed up with the field research for this case study at four of St. Vincent's most popular nature tourism sites: the National Botanical Garden, Montreal Gardens, the Vermont Nature Trail, and the La Soufriere volcano. The following section first establishes the basis for traditional nature tourism experiences in the Caribbean and the shortcomings of such experiences. Then, it discusses the case study of St. Vincent's diversified nature tourism offerings.

Case Study

Nature tourism in the Caribbean

Nature tourism has become one of the most important and fastest growing subsectors of tourism, with a rate of growth that is three times faster than the industry as a whole (Donohoe and Needham, 2008; Wearing and Neil, 2009). Typical nature tourism experiences in the Caribbean have their origins in the concepts of the past and early patterns of tourism in the region. According to Sheller (2003), the rise of Romanticism in the nineteenth century created a preference for 'wild' natural scenery. Thompson (2006) argues that this was less about the geography of places located in the tropics than about the exotic, strange, and fantastic ideas of tropical nature that Europeans imagined. As travelers to the Caribbean wrote in travel narratives and other early tourism representations about their preference for seeing wild landscapes, subsequent travelers and tourists also sought to experience these and other such scenes for themselves. When they, too, represented these landscapes, they perpetuated patterns of tourism in a 'cycle of expectation' (Nelson, 2007).

Yet, it is worth noting that a contradiction has long existed between preferences for different types of natural landscape scenery in the Caribbean and attitudes towards the actual experience of those landscapes. For example, in Anthony Trollope's *The West Indies and the Spanish Main* (1858), the well known nineteenth century novelist frequently professed his preference for the picturesque natural landscapes that he saw in the course of his visit to the Caribbean. However, he had a very different opinion when he found himself within those same landscapes. In one instance, he decided to climb Jamaica's Blue Mountain Peak to witness the sunrise in all its glory but ultimately concluded of the experience, 'as for the true ascent the nasty, damp, dirty, slippery, boot-destroying, shin-breaking, veritable mountain! Let me recommend my friends to let it alone' (Trollope, 1968 [1858]: 50).

As tourism continued to develop in the region, there was a recognized need for improvements that would facilitate the experience and increase the comfort of tourists, but it was also recognized that such features should not compromise or destroy the expected tropical image or character of the landscape (Thompson, 2006). However, in the more than 150 years since Trollope's visit, the Caribbean has seen considerable growth and development in which the region became associated with mass 3S tourism. This continues to be the main attraction for most of the region's tourists, but modern tourists have increasingly diversified interests and tastes. As with travelers in earlier eras, modern tourists, typically from Europe and North America, have an interest in the exotic tropical nature that presents a dramatic contrast to the environments with which they are most familiar. As a result, the popular 'rainforest hike' has become a secondary activity for many of the region's mass tourists.

Yet, this type of nature tourism experience may be no less difficult for these tourists than it was for Trollope. The rainforest hike requires a measure of physical exertion under humid tropical conditions with which these tourists from predominantly northern climates are unaccustomed, and for which they are generally unprepared. Caribbean tourists travel without the equipment that would be used in other mountainous environments, such as hiking boots or trekking poles. Hiking trails are not always adequately marked, and trail maps are not always available; therefore, guidebooks and tourism websites typically recommend tourists hire a guide or join a tour. However, unless the size of the party is large enough to make special arrangements with a tour company, tourists are channeled into pre-packaged tours with other couples or families. These groups, ranging in size from four to 40 people, are comprised of tourists of different ages and physical abilities, as well as interests in environmental goals or landscape scenery.

Tourists are often encouraged through regional and destination promotional literature to participate in this type of nature tourism experiences as a means of generating interest in the region and a desire to explore more of what the islands have to offer 'beyond the beach.' Nevertheless, the rainforest need not be considered the only setting, or the rainforest hike the only activity, to accomplish these goals. The one-size-fits-all approach to nature tourism in the Caribbean is limited in its potential to create a real sense of satisfaction across varied participants. While many do, in fact, find that the experience exceeds their expectations, there is also often a sense of ambivalence. Some tourists will indicate that the rainforest hike was simply something to do other than spend another day of their holiday on the beach at their resort or that it did not really matter what they did, as long as they were not at home (tourist interviews, 2002). In some cases, dissatisfaction can result, for example, if the tourists are not adequately prepared for the duration or difficulty of the experience, if the pace of the hike is too fast or too slow, or if the group size is so large that they do not have meaningful interaction with their guide (tour guide interviews, 2006).

When explicitly asked, 70 percent of 206 survey participants indicated their perceived preference for participating in a rainforest hike over other nature tourism experiences, while 21 percent selected visiting a botanical garden. The remaining 9 percent was not interested in nature tourism. With a p value of less than .005, this result is statistically significant. As this result indicates that the rainforest hike is the desired nature tourism experience, it is not surprising that the rainforest hike is the most commonly offered nature tourism experience in the Caribbean. However, when these respondents were asked to evaluate the aesthetic appeal and their desire to visit different types of nature tourism sites, the results were not nearly so clear-cut. For example, participants were shown high-quality digital photographs of forest paths (from the La Soufriere path and the Vermont Nature Trail, Figure 11.1), mixed forest/garden scenes (from Montreal Gardens, Figure 11.2), and more traditional botanical gardens (from the National Botanical Garden, Figure 11.3). The location of the scene – forest versus botanical garden – was not identified. Results were widely varied, and only one scene – a forested scene from Montreal Gardens – received a statistically significant response. As such, respondents who indicated their preference for participating in a rainforest hike often gave the conflicting response of indicating their preference for visiting scenes from one of the two gardens (survey, 2008).

In qualitative responses typical rainforest hike trails and traditional botanical garden scenes were described in positive terms, and adjectives such as attractive, lush, and peaceful were used for both. However, each was also subject to criticisms. Scenes depicting the rainforest trails were described as chaotic, impenetrable, challenging, dangerous, and scary. Some respondents expressed concerns about whether or not there was a path or complained that there did not seem to be enough room on the path. Some indicated that they would 'feel lost,' while others cited fears that would prevent them from wanting to explore these areas, including

Figures 11.1 and 11.2 Vermont Nature Trail and Montreal Gardens (Photos by author)

Figure 11.3 The National Botanical Garden (Photo by author)

wild animals and 'critters,' reptiles (specifically snakes), and, most commonly, insects and 'bugs.' At the same time, scenes depicting traditional botanical gardens were described as too tame, sterile, artificial, or even 'touristy'. The hybrid scenes from Montreal Gardens received the fewest criticisms. These scenes often had the 'wild' appearance of rainforest vegetation along with the infrastructure of the botanical garden (e.g. sufficient clearings, paths, bridges, etc.). Such findings suggest that there is a demand for tropical nature experiences in the Caribbean but also that there is a need for a diverse range of options for such experiences (survey, 2008).

Nature tourism on St. Vincent

St. Vincent and the Grenadines is an independent commonwealth nation made up of an archipelago of small islands in the southeastern Caribbean Sea. According to World Bank figures for 2008, St. Vincent and the Grenadines ranked 100th in the world with a gross national income per capita in purchasing power parity of 8,770 international dollars. This was slightly below the mean for the Caribbean islands with reported incomes (11,044) but above the mode (World Bank, 2009). As a whole, the nation had been experiencing moderate economic growth with new developments primarily in construction and services; however, as with many tourism destinations, this growth was stalled by the global economic crisis (International Monetary Fund, 2009a). Nonetheless, early in 2010, the country's prime minister, Dr. Ralph Gonsalves, reported that he expected to see positive economic growth in the coming year (St. Vincent, 2010).

The island of St. Vincent is a mountainous volcanic island that comprises the northernmost extent of this archipelago. It is the largest island with 344 square kilometers of land area (Government of St. Vincent and the Grenadines, 2009) and approximately 91 percent of the nation's estimated 111,000 people (Pan American Health Organization, 2010). Much of the nation's economic activities are concentrated on St. Vincent as well. Although agriculture is frequently reported to be the most important economic activity (Government of St. Vincent and the Grenadines, 2009), International Monetary Fund (2009b) data indicate that, as of 2006, the tertiary sector was the largest sector in terms of income.

Tourism has become an important economic contributor. Although the island of St. Vincent accounts for the largest proportion of tourist arrivals with 151,235 of the 249,868 combined air and sea arrivals in 2008 (SVG Tourism Authority, 2009), the greatest concentration of tourism infrastructure and activities has been in the Grenadines (Caribbean Community, 2009). Indeed, Momsen (2004) finds that, as a whole, St. Vincent and the Grenadines has been mostly known for yacht tourism among the smaller islands. However, various authors have indicated a strong potential for greater eco and nature based tourism activities on the island of St. Vincent, particularly with the La Soufriere volcano and the Vermont Nature Trail (Weaver, 2004; Powell and Henderson, 2007).

Both of these areas meet traditional concepts of nature tourism in the region and interests in rainforest hike experiences; however, these sites provide tourists with options based on accessibility, duration, and difficulty. The Vermont Nature Trail is located approximately nine miles outside of the capital city, Kingstown, and the driving time is estimated at one-half hour. The St. Vincent and the Grenadines Tourism Authority recommends two hours to complete this trail. Although it is identified as 'medium' difficulty, the SVG Tourism Authority notes that it is appropriate for varied ages and abilities (SVG Tourism Authority, 2009). The trail is well maintained and well marked with both directional and informational signs; as such, the hike could be completed with or without a local guide accompaniment.

The La Soufriere volcano offers a nature tourism experience that is unique and cannot be obtained on other islands in the region. The main trail head is approximately 25 miles from Kingstown and over an hour in driving time. Most tour companies recommend a minimum of two and a half hours to reach the summit of the volcano at over 1,200 meters above sea level. An additional two hours is required if participants choose to descend inside the crater. The SVG Tourism Authority (2009) describes the experience as breathtaking and world class but also challenging and gives this hike a 'hard' difficulty level. Tour companies note that participants must be in good health. It is generally not recommended to do this hike without a guide.

The National Botanical Garden and Montreal Gardens further round out the tourist's choices for nature tourism. Botanical gardens clearly have the potential to serve as an attraction for international tourists, as such sites around the world are already estimated to receive 250 million visits a year (Ballantyne, Packer and Hughes, 2008). Although studies have shown that one of the most common reasons for visiting botanical gardens is to appreciate being in nature (Ballantyne, Packer and Hughes, 2008), these areas have not typically been packaged or represented as nature tourism. Again, this is a legacy of Romanticism's dichotomization of 'wild' and 'cultivated' categories. However, geographers have shown that the concept of nature is complicated and cannot easily be broken down into such simplified categories (e.g. Demeritt, 1994; Whatmore, 2002; Castree, 2005).

Thompson (2006) finds that botanical gardens have, in fact, long been recognized as a place in which Caribbean tourists might experience tropical nature. In contrast with the sites of the rainforest hikes, botanical gardens in the Caribbean have paths that are typically well maintained and clearly marked. Site maps are often provided, and tourists can easily explore the sites independently or pay a nominal fee for interpretation by a guide. These sites are designed to be aesthetically pleasing and range from neat ornamental gardens, examples of agricultural produce, and even natural ecosystems such as the rainforest.

The National Botanical Garden provides tourists with the experience of a more traditional, formal botanical garden. It is easily accessible from Kingstown, located on the northern perimeter of the city, and it is steeped in history. The Government of St. Vincent and the Grenadines (2009) puts forth the claim that, founded in 1765, these gardens are the oldest in the Western Hemisphere. The site is also in possession of a breadfruit tree that can be traced back to the produce that Captain William Bligh brought to the island on his second journey in 1793, following the infamous incident of mutiny on *HMS Bounty*. The National Botanical Garden has also preserved the Soufriere Tree that is indigenous to the island but disappeared from the wild in the early twentieth century and maintains an aviary for the St. Vincent parrot that is now rare in the wild. In addition, the site of the botanical garden also houses the National Museum. The National Botanical Garden has a paved road that encircles the property and grassy prom-enades through it, and plant species are identified with informational signs. There is also a gazebo in the center of the garden that is often used for picnicking. This garden can be visited with a tour company or independently, and local guides are available on site for interpretation.

Montreal Gardens provides tourists with a different type of botanical garden experience. It is located in the lush Mesopotamia Valley to the northeast of Kingstown. Driving time is approximately one hour. This site is less formalized than the National Garden with less emphasis on information and interpretation. With a specialization in tropical flowers that are grown in profusion and its immer-sion in the forest of the Mesopotamia Valley and adjacent hills, the experience is designed to appeal to the senses. It has a 'wilder' appearance than the National Garden with the density of lush vegetation, and the variety and color of the vegetation gives it a more interesting appearance than the rainforest which is often described as monotonous. Yet, it is also well maintained with good infrastructure, including paved or stone paths and steps that lead visitors through the garden.

Results from the survey of potential Caribbean tourists found that this type of infrastructure was particularly important. Tourists come to the islands of the region with the expectation of experiencing the tropical rainforest vegetation; however, many also appreciate, if not demand, features that would allow them to comfortably enjoy these experiences. While such infrastructure should not be so obtrusive that it seems artificial and out of place, features like well maintained paths and bridges are important. This not only ensures good footing for tourists but also provides a sense of security. A well maintained path gives tourists confidence they will not get 'lost in the woods' and creates a sense of boundary between them and the possibly scary or dangerous wildlife that could be encountered in the 'jungle'. Montreal Gardens is able to maintain this balance (Figure 11.4).

The range of nature tourism choices – from the challenging climb of the La Soufriere volcano to the relaxing stroll through the National Botanical Garden – provide all kinds of Caribbean tourists (mass and niche) the opportunity to expe-rience tropical nature in the setting and manner of their choosing. Moreover, it gives tourists interested in nature the option to participate in multiple excursions during the course of their holiday. This type of diversification has important implications for the sustainability of tourism on the island.

Discussion and Conclusion

St. Vincent's nature tourism sites generate little income from entrance fees. In particular, only Montreal Gardens charges a nominal entrance fee of 3USD. However, visits to these sites generate additional tourism revenues. Transportation

Figure 11.4 Forest and infrastructure in Montreal Gardens
(Photo by author)

is a key expenditure. Tourists must either: rent a car from one of the local companies, hire a taxi driver at an hourly rate to take them to the site, wait or accompany
them, and then return them to their original location, or sign up for a tour with
one of the local operators. A guide may be provided with the transportation as a
combined fee, but if one is not, guides can usually be obtained at the site for
a negotiated fee. Tour companies will often offer a lunch service contracted with
a local restaurant, and taxi drivers may suggest such an option. All types of nature
tourism sites require maintenance personnel, especially the botanical gardens that
are more labor-intensive. Also, the botanical gardens offer more skilled employment opportunities for site administrators and horticulturalists. Moreover, sites
like Montreal Gardens have additional income generation potential through the
sale of flowers grown on the property to hotels and other local businesses.

Beyond these direct economic impacts, nature tourism forms an integral part
of tourism generation for the island. The tourism industry is highly competitive,
and the Caribbean is a highly competitive destination region. Individual destinations must create a sense of distinctiveness that will distinguish them from other,
similar destinations in the minds of potential tourists. In particular, the island of
St. Vincent strongly promotes these nature tourism sites as the characteristics
that make it unique among the Caribbean destinations, specifically the active
La Soufriere volcano and the oldest botanical garden in the hemisphere.

Additionally, maintaining a diversified nature tourism product is important in generating tourist satisfaction that will contribute to positive word of mouth promotion and return visits. Because many of the Caribbean's typical mass tourists may only take one such tour as a diversionary activity during their sun, sea and sand holiday, the experience can have a significant influence on the tourists' perception of the destination. When tourists are channeled into an experience that does not match their interests, expectations or ability level, it can lead to ambivalence. These tourists are not engaged with the destination and are unlikely to develop an interest in further exploration, returning to the destination, or perhaps even returning to the region as a whole. If the dissatisfaction is great enough, they may even discourage friends or family from making a similar visit. As the most tourism dependent region in the world (Jayawardena, 2007), the economic implications of such dissatisfaction could be significant.

At the same time, the environmental damage caused by channeling large numbers of mass tourists into the interior forests on a typical rainforest hike could also be significant. These natural ecosystems have long faced threats from the region's important agricultural industries and the needs of growing local populations. While tourism has often been proposed as an opportunity to promote conservation of the forests in lieu of more intensive or extractive economic activities, tourism activities may also contribute to environmental degradation, especially if the carrying capacity of tourist sites is exceeded. This can be a problem at many Caribbean tourism destinations, especially during the high season. Yet, channeling all tourists into the same sites based on preconceived ideas of nature tourism would indicate that these sites are at risk of overuse and degradation unnecessarily.

A diversified nature tourism product not only provides options for tourists to experience tropical nature on the island in the manner that is most likely to generate satisfaction for them, but it also helps to distribute the tourist population. As visitors are less concentrated in the few available nature tourism sites, it eases the pressure placed on those natural environments. For example, a small number of ecologically-oriented stayover visitors are likely to undertake the journey through the primary forest of La Soufriere, while a larger number of tourists have the option to visit the secondary forest of the Vermont Nature Trail or the cultivated Montreal Gardens. Finally, the most easily accessible site, the National Botanical Garden, is well suited to the short visits made by the many cruise ship tourists.

There are still many logistical and conceptual obstacles to the continued development of a diversified nature tourism product on St. Vincent. One of the greatest logistical obstacles is access. The National Botanical Garden can be easily reached by taxi from Kingstown with a short trip and a relatively small fare. Although it is within walking distance of the city center, the way is uphill, and the entrance can be somewhat difficult to find on foot. The remaining sites are much more difficult to reach and can only be done with a personal car, hired taxi, or packaged tour provided by one of the local operators. As over half of St. Vincent's tourists are cruise ships passengers arriving in Kingstown

(SVG Tourism Authority, 2009), such visitors may not have the time to be able to commit to reaching these sites. Also, singles or couples may find that the cost per person of hiring a taxi or arranging a tour for one of these experiences is prohibitively high, particularly during the low season.

The conceptual obstacles are also significant. As discussed above, the conceptual division between 'wild' and 'cultivated' nature is longstanding and deeply embedded. Consequently, tourists have been culturally conditioned to assume that the rainforest hike would be the more interesting, more authentic, more natural experience. Evidence of the emphasis on the 'rainforest' as an integral characteristic of the Caribbean can be seen in modern tourism promotions, in which forested mountain slopes feature prominently into panoramic island scenes or as a picturesque backdrop in images of hotels or resorts. Yet, many tourists nonetheless have justifiable concerns about the attendant difficulties that the rainforest hike often entails. Similarly, the formal botanical garden scenes were subject to traditional biases that this would be the more boring, more artificial experience.

There is clearly a need for a diversified nature tourism product that gives tourists the ability to choose the experience that is right for them. However, there is also a need for greater information about different nature tourism options so that they can make an informed choice and not one that is made on the basis of preconceptions. For example, the information that is provided on the SVG Tourism Authority website (http://discoversvg.com) regarding the duration and difficulty of the hikes is valuable in helping potential tourists understand what is involved in each of these two experiences. At the same time, though, the website perpetuates the division between 'wild' and 'cultivated' nature by creating separate sections for 'hiking' and 'tropical gardens'. In addition to greater logistical information, more photographic representations and comparisons of the nature tourism sites may help potential tourists to see that such distinctions are not so clear-cut and to get a better sense of what the actual experience would be like.

Although still a developing tourism destination in the region, St. Vincent has a strong foundation with a varied set of nature tourism experiences that will appeal to a wide range of Caribbean tourists. This diversified nature tourism product can serve as an example for other destinations in the Caribbean that have also looked to nature tourism in recent years. Many islands may already have the polar experiences of a rainforest hike and a formal botanical garden; however, it is worth considering intermediate options. In particular, St. Vincent's Montreal Gardens provide an exceptional model for an alternative that balances Caribbean mass tourists' demands for a 'wild' rainforest setting and their need for a comfortable experience.

Acknowledgements

This project was made possible by funding from a Sam Houston State University Enhancement Grant for Professional Development. In addition, I would like to thank Dr. Rebecca Torres for her comments on an earlier draft of this chapter.

References

Ballantyne, R., Packer, J. and Hughes, K. (2008). Environmental awareness, interests and motives of botanic garden visitors: implications for interpretative practice. *Tourism Management, 29*: 439–444.

Caribbean Community. (2009) *St. Vincent and the Grenadines.* http://www.caricom.org/jsp/community/st_vincent_grenadines.jsp?menu=community. [Accessed 19th of April 2010].

Castree, N. (2005). *Nature.* London: Routledge.

Demeritt, D. (1994). The nature of metaphors in cultural geography and environmental history. *Progress in Human Geography, 18(2)*: 163–185.

Donohoe, H.M. and Needham, R.D. (2008). Internet-based ecotourism marketing: evaluating Canadian sensitivity to ecotourism tenets. *Journal of Ecotourism, 7(1)*: 15–43.

Duval, D.T. (2004). Trends and circumstances in Caribbean tourism. In D.T. Duval (Ed.), *Tourism in the Caribbean: trends, development, prospects (pp. 3-22).* London: Routledge.

Government of St. Vincent and the Grenadines. (2009). http://www.gov.vc. [Accessed the 14th of April 2010].

International Monetary Fund. 2009a. IMF country report no. 09/181. http://www.imf.org/external/pubs/ft/scr/2009/cr09181.pdf. [Accessed the 20th of April 2010].

International Monetary Fun. 2009b. IMF country report no 09/119: statistical appendix. http://www.imf.org/external/pubs/ft/scr/2009/cr09119.pdf. [Accessed the 20th of April 2010].

Jayawardena, C. (2007). Caribbean tourism for today and tomorrow. In C. Jayawardena (Ed.), Caribbean tourism: more than sun, sand and sea (pp. 3–22). London: Ian Randle Publishers.

Momsen, J.H. (2004). Post-colonial markets: new geographical spaces for tourism. In D.T. Duval (Ed.), *Tourism in the Caribbean: trends, development, prospects* (pp. 273–286). London: Routledge.

——. (2005). Tourism development and seascapes of the Caribbean. In C. Cartier and A. Lew (Eds.), *Seductions of Place: geographical perspectives on globalization and touristed landscapes* (pp. 209–221). London: Routledge.

N.A. (2010). St. Vincent Prime Minister optimistic about economic growth. *Caribbean Daily News.* http://www.caribbeandailynews.com/?p=3778. [Accessed 19 April 2010].

Nelson, V. (2007). Traces of the past: the cycle of expectation in Caribbean tourism representations. *Journal of Tourism and Cultural Change, 5(1)*: 1–16.

Nelson, V. and Torres, R. (forthcoming). Conceptualizing Caribbean tourism through hybridity: the Grenadian tour product. ARA [Caribbean] *Journal of Tourism Research.*

Pan American Health Organization. (2010). St. Vincent and the Grenadines. http://www.paho.org/english/dd/ais/cp_670.htm. [Accessed 19th of April 2010].

Powell, R. and Henderson, R.W. (2007). The St. Vincent (Lesser Antilles) herpetofauna: conservation concerns. *Applied Herpetology,* 4(4), 295–312.

Responsible Travel. (2009). *Responsible travel in St. Vincent and the Grenadines.* http://www.responsibletravel.com/svg/responsible-travel.htm. [Accessed 14th of April 2010].

Sheller, M. (2003). *Consuming the Caribbean: from Arawaks to zombies.* London: Routledge.

SVG Tourism Authority. (2009). *Tourism statistics.* http://discoversvg.com/index.php/en/about-svg/tourism-statistics. [Accessed 14th of April 2010].

Thomas, R.N., Pigozzi, B.W. and Sambrook, R.A. (2005) Tourist carrying capacity measures: crowding syndrome in the Caribbean. *Professional Geographer, 57(1)*, 13–20.

Thompson, K.A. (2006). *An Eye for the Tropics: tourism, photography, and framing the Caribbean picturesque*. Durham: Duke University Press.

Trollope, A. 1968. *The West Indies and the Spanish Main. 4th edition*. London: Dawsons of Pall Mall.

Wearing, S. and Neil, J. (2009). *Ecotourism: impacts, potentials and possibilities. 2nd edition. Amsterdam: Butterworth-Heinemann.*

Weaver, D.B. (2004). Manifestations of ecotourism in the Caribbean. In D.T. Duval (Ed.), Tourism *in the Caribbean: trends, development, prospects* (pp. 172–186). London: Routledge.

Whatmore, S. (2002*). Hybrid geographies*. London: Sage Publications.

World Bank. (2009). World development indicators: gross national income per capita, Atlas method and PPP. http://siteresources.worldbank.org/DATASTATISTICS/ Resources/GNIPC.pdf. [Accessed 19th of April 2010].

12 Can ecotourism support coral reef conservation? Experiences of Chumbe Island Coral Park Ltd in Zanzibar/Tanzania

*Sibylle Riedmiller**

CORAL REEFS: Among the World's most threatened ecosystems

Oceans cover over 70% of the surface of planet Earth. Especially in the tropics, coral reefs are a vital part of the ocean ecosystem, and often referred to as 'rainforests of the sea' for their immensely rich biodiversity. Coral reefs buffer coasts against erosion, provide habitats for over a quarter of all marine species and generate income for an estimated 200 million people. According to the UN's Millennium Ecosystem Assessment, coral reefs are worth about $30bn annually to the global economy through tourism, fisheries and coastal protection.

Coral reefs are also among the most threatened ecosystems. A fifth of the world's coral reefs have already died over the last few decades, and the surviving reefs could be lost by 2030 due to climate change, pollution and over-exploitation. Their loss would be catastrophic for hundreds of millions of people. The urgent measures required include global action against climate change, and locally, the creation of Marine Protected Areas (MPAs) (World Bank, 2006).

Though over the last decades, MPAs were established in many countries around the world, only 9% were found to have effective management, and thus only a very small fraction of the oceans' 361 million km2 surface is under some form of protection (McClanahan, 1999).

Traditionally MPAs, like all parks, were thought to be the exclusive domain of governments. However, the much quoted 'tragedy of the commons' that is even more pronounced in the open-access sea areas, pervasive governance problems especially in developing countries, declining budgets and the worsening economic situation in many countries has led to new thinking in conservation that seeks to involve other players, such as NGOs and the private sector, in marine conservation and the creation and management of MPAs (Francis et al., 2002).

*Chumbe Island Coral Park Ltd., Zanzibar/Tanzania

Chumbe Eco-lodge (Photo: Manolo Yllera)
Source: www.chumbeisland.com (2011)

Chumbe Reef Sanctuary (Photo: Oskar Henriksson)
Source: www.chumbeisland.com

ZANZIBAR in 1991: A window-of-opportunity for private investment in conservation

Tanzania and Zanzibar are no exception to the worldwide trend of rapid coral reef degradation and forest depletion. Since the early nineties, two basic dynamic forces increasingly threaten the once relatively healthy Tanzanian marine and terrestrial environment: the rapid population growth of close to 3% per year, and the economic development brought by liberalization and globalization. These forces have increased pressure on natural resources and lead to rapid depletion of the terrestrial and marine environment. The once breathtakingly beautiful coral reefs now suffer from over-fishing, destructive fishing techniques, such as dynamite fishing, and water pollution from sedimentation and urban sewage.

Forests are disappearing at a fast rate, to provide land for settlement and agriculture, and are cleared for firewood and charcoal; still the most important sources of domestic fuel in rural and urban areas. Endangered and protected species, such as sea turtles, duikers, large mammals and a myriad of unexplored indigenous flora and fauna lose their habitat or are hunted or collected for food. Formerly unexploited marine organisms, such as sea cucumbers and seahorses, are now harvested and exported to distant Asian markets.

The liberalization of the Tanzanian economy has over the last two decades opened up coasts and beaches to investment in tourism. This also contributes to the deterioration of coral reefs and coastal forests. Beach resorts are being constructed too close to the shoreline and sometimes pollute the sea with untreated sewage. For their constructions, large areas of indigenous shore vegetation that is needed to prevent beach erosion are removed. In the absence of garbage disposal systems, plastic bags, containers and packing materials litter streets and beaches.

Environmental awareness of the general public and government action lag far behind the pace of environmental deterioration. This is particularly the case concerning coral reefs that are important for biodiversity conservation, tourism, sustainable fisheries and protection from beach erosion. Traditionally, the national language Kiswahili had no word for corals (referred to as '*mawe na miamba*', stones and rocks). Moreover, formal education does not yet provide environmental knowledge on coral reefs, as they are insufficiently covered in the syllabi of primary and secondary education. As a result, decades of destructive fishing methods (dynamiting, smashing corals and beach-seining) have been met with little governmental and public concern.

On the conservation side, Tanzania traditionally has a well-established system of world-renowned terrestrial protected areas, while the several marine parks designated along the coast in the early seventies remained on paper only at least until the mid-nineties (Jameson et al., 1995).

How it all began

In 1990, after concluding a consultancy on environmental education in Zanzibar, the project initiator (a former aid worker with extensive experience in project development and management in Latin America and Tanzania) produced an investment proposal for a small marine park that would help conserve a pristine coral reef, offer environmental education for both foreign visitors and the local population, and generate management funds through genuine ecotourism. Disillusioned with the poor marine governance and the failure of most aid projects implemented through government institutions in the country, she felt that the future of marine conservation in Tanzania was in the hands of the private sector forming alliances with local resource users.

When searching the sea around Zanzibar for a suitable coral reef for a small privately managed Marine Park, she 'discovered' Chumbe Island, eight miles southwest of Zanzibar Town. An uninhabited fossil coral island of approximately 20 ha, covered by coral rag forest and bordered on its western shore by a fringing coral reef of exceptional biodiversity and beauty, Chumbe seemed to face little immediate threat. Similar to other historic sites in Zanzibar it appeared to be an abandoned place with signs of a passed glory, such as an old lighthouse built during colonial rule in 1904, and other ruined historical buildings. A lighthouse keeper was still on the payroll of the Harbours Authority but had not been residing on the island for decades.

Fishing was traditionally not allowed on its western side, as small boats would have obstructed vessels plying the shipping channel to Dar es Salaam, the capital of mainland Tanzania. Traditionally, the sea surrounding the island was a military area where the army routinely conducted shooting range exercises from the adjacent coast. In addition, few boatmen could then afford an outboard engine to go to this most distant of the islets surrounding Zanzibar town. As no traditional users were to be displaced, conditions appeared ideal for the creation of a marine park that depended on co-operation with local fishermen, not government enforcement.

Therefore, in 1991 she started campaigning for the protection of the island, and presented a business plan that would establish Chumbe Island as a privately managed marine park financed through ecotourism. When the Government of Zanzibar approved this in 1993, she registered Chumbe Island Coral Park Ltd. (CHICOP) Ltd in Zanzibar for the management of the reserve. After further two years of lengthy negotiations with several Government departments, CHICOP leased a small plot on the island for development and signed management agreements for the Chumbe Reef Sanctuary and the Chumbe Forest Reserve, after both had been declared protected areas in 1994 and 1995 respectively. The forest reserve covers the whole of Chumbe Island and has become a rare example of a still pristine coral island ecosystem in an otherwise heavily over-exploited area.

From the very beginning, CHICOP employed and trained former fishermen from adjacent villages as park rangers, and stationed them on the island. Up to the present, their main tasks are to patrol the reef and the island, educate fishers on the nature of coral reefs and park rules, keep daily monitoring records on any observations, assist researchers, and guide visitors over the marine and terrestrial nature trails. Between 1992 and 2004, altogether more than 50 volunteer marine biologists, zoologists, botanists and educators from several countries joined CHICOP for periods between one month and three years. They conducted baseline surveys on the ecology of Chumbe Island, trained the rangers on the different aspects of their work and helped manage the increasingly complex and challenging project.

CHUMBE ISLAND CORAL PARK – established for sustainable park management

The company objective of CHICOP, according to its constitution, is: 'To manage for conservation purposes, the Chumbe Island Reef Sanctuary and the Chumbe Island Forest Reserve. This includes educational and commercial activities related to the non-consumptive use of the above mentioned natural resources and the doing of all such other things as are incidental or conducive to the attainment of the above object.'

Thereby, the objectives of CHICOP are non-commercial, while operations follow commercial principles. In fact, the overall aim of CHICOP is nothing less but to create a model of sustainable conservation area management, where ecotourism supports conservation and education. Profits from the tourism operations are to be re-invested in conservation area management and free island excursions for local schoolchildren and their teachers as part of a comprehensive Environmental Education program.

The Chumbe Island Management Plans 1995-2016

To translate this commitment into practice, a ten-year Management Plan was commissioned in 1995, for a team of ecologists to be contracted for three months by CHICOP (with support of the British volunteer organization BESO) and who had previous experience in managing a tropical island nature reserve (Aride Island, Seychelles). They held extensive meetings with a wide variety of stakeholders including CHICOP staff, all concerned Government departments, representatives of other environmental projects, local fishermen and private diving companies.

The comprehensive document includes ecological data collected by the baseline surveys, on the physical, biological and historical features of Chumbe Island and the Reef Sanctuary, and specifies the aims and objectives, while also prescribing detailed management actions based on these. It outlines the management policy for sustainable development, eco-lodge management, research policy, safety and health regulations for staff and visitors, guidelines for visitors as well as responsibilities of essential personnel. In summary, the Management Plan specifies that only non-consumptive and non-exploitative activities are permitted in the Sanctuary area.

Permitted uses of the marine park include recreation (swimming, snorkelling, underwater photography), education and research. Extractive and destructive activities, such as fishing, anchorage, collection of specimens (even for research) are not allowed. Research is co-ordinated with the Institute of Marine Sciences of the University of Dar es Salaam.

The Government responsibilities outlined in the Plan (and based on the previously signed Management Agreements) are mainly the public announcement of all legal and regulatory measures concerning the reserve and their enforcement through the relevant organs if needed (Fisheries department, Navy, Marine police, Courts of Law). CHICOP has full managerial and financial responsibility for Chumbe Island. The Management Plan was endorsed by the Advisory Committee in 1995 and has since then been the basis for project operations. In early 2006, the Management Plan was revised and updated for another 10 years, again based on consultations with the relevant stakeholders.

From Plan to Action

Project activities from 1991-2009 are summarized below. The sequence of activities is listed in the following, and includes support by some sponsors:

- The gazetting of the Western reef and the whole island as a protected area was negotiated from 1991 to 1994 by the project initiator.
- Park rangers were employed and trained by expatriate volunteers from 1993, mostly in basic coral reef ecology, interaction with fishers, monitoring techniques and tourist guidance skills. Patrol boats and outboard engines were sponsored by GIZ-Small projects, the International School Schloss Buchhof/ Munich and EC-Microprojects in Tanzania.
- Also with the help of volunteers and some donor funds from the GIZ-Small projects fund, baseline surveys and species lists on the island's flora and fauna were conducted from 1993.
- An Advisory Committee was established in 1995, with representatives of the Departments of Fisheries, Forestry and Environment, the Institute of Marine Sciences of the University of Dar es Salaam and village leaders of neighbouring fishing villages.
- A Management Plan 1995-2005 was produced in 1995 and guided the project operations since then. The Management Plan was updated in 2006, with new developments for another ten years up to 2016.
- Forest and marine nature trails were developed from 1993 with information materials in English and Kiswahili, sponsored by the Netherlands embassy in Kenya and the Special Tropical Forest Stamp program of the German Post.
- Rats (*Rattus rattus*) were eradicated in 1997, with the help of an expert from Cork University, Ireland, supported by the Irish volunteer organization APSO and by ZENECA, the company producing the rodenticide used (Brodifacoum).
- A sanctuary for the highly endangered Ader's duiker (*Cephalophus adersi*) was established from 1997, in co-operation with the Commission of Natural Resources of Zanzibar, the Zoo Munich-Hellabrunn, Flora and Fauna International (UK), the WWF-Tanzania and the Chicago Zoological Society.

- The ruined lighthouse keeper's house was rehabilitated as a Park HQ and Visitors' Centre in 1997-98 with support from GIZ-CIM and the Netherlands Embassy in Tanzania.
- Seven visitors' bungalows ('eco-bungalows') and the Visitors' Centre were constructed in 1994-1998 according to state-of-the-art eco-architecture (rainwater catchment, grey water recycling, composting toilets, photo-voltaic power generation), based on designs of Prof. Per Krusche of the Braunschweig Technical University/Germany and his colleagues.
- From 1994, the Chumbe Environmental Education (EE) Program offers free guided island excursions for local schoolchildren, combined with in-service teacher training seminars from 2003. This was in its early phases supported by the US-National Fish and Wildlife Foundation, the Southern African Development Community Environmental Education Program, the International Coral Reef Action Network and others. Until end of 2009, around 4500 schoolchildren and 850 teachers hadalready visited the island under this program.
- Tourism operations (day excursions and overnight stay) commenced fully in 1998, with occupancy rates ranging from 13% to a peak of 86% between 2006-2009.

Social and cultural aspects

Essential to closing off the reef to fishing was the relationship with the local fishing communities to gain their understanding and support for the Chumbe reef sanctuary. Due to the committed work of the park rangers, there are now no major problems with infringements from fishers or other users, and the project was well accepted by the local communities after few years of operations (Carter et al., 1997).

Support from local communities was also gained due to the fact that CHICOP prefers the employment of local - even untrained - staff, in spite of the high on-the-job training needs. This was the case with employing local fishermen as rangers, for example.

Last but not least, in the local Islamic culture, women do not learn how to swim. Therefore, as is done on Chumbe, teaching schoolgirls how to swim and snorkel in coral reefs provides an environmental education. This also serves as an eye-opener that is necessary for developing feelings of ownership and more political support for marine conservation.

Preservation of historical monuments

Chumbe Island was uninhabited for many decades, but had historical buildings that had either been left untouched or carefully restored by CHICOP:

- A historic lighthouse, built by the British in 1904, is kept functioning with the AGA gas system installed in 1926. The Chumbe Park Rangers now

Chumbe Visitors' Centre (Photo: Jimmy Livefjord)
Source: www.chumbeisland.com (2011)

make sure that the lights are working for the traditional dhows that have no modern means of navigation. The lighthouse also facilitates monitoring of the reserve and provides spectacular views of the Chumbe Sanctuary and Zanzibar.

• A protected historic mosque on the island was renovated using traditional techniques and is visited daily by Chumbe staff. This is one of the few mosques of Indian architecture in Zanzibar, built for the Indian lighthouse keepers by their community at the turn of the 19th century.

• The former lighthouse keeper's house has been carefully restored and converted into a Visitors' Centre that harbours the restaurant and exhibits environmental information about the island reserve for all guests, including a classroom for local schoolchildren.

Eco-architecture and eco-technology

With the help of architects at the Technical University Braunschweig (Germany) and other specialists, the Visitors' Centre and seven 'eco-bungalows' were built with state-of-the-art eco-architecture and eco-technology that have close to zero impact on the environment. All buildings are designed to catch sea breezes for natural ventilation, that can be controlled with a movable panel made of woven local mats, and thus do not require air-conditioning. Small solar-powered fans provide a breeze over beds and sitting areas when needed.

Rainwater catchment and sustainable zero-emission energy

Technologies for water and energy supply on Chumbe Island are also of the highest environmental standards. As there is no freshwater source on the island, rainwater is collected using the large expanse of the palm-thatched roofs of all buildings during the rainy season. This water passes through, and is cleaned, by a natural gravel and sand filter located at each side of the bungalows, and is then stored in large cisterns underneath the living rooms. From there, the water is hand-pumped up through a solar-powered heating system into hot and cold water containers for the shower. Shower heads are equipped with a mechanical switch to reduce water consumption. Chumbe is the only known project using traditional palm-thatched roofs for harvesting rainwater, commonly thought impossible.

Solar energy, both direct and photovoltaic, provides decentralised, renewable and zero-emission power for water heating and light in each bungalow. The Visitors' Centre is also equipped with its own solar system for lights, communications, a freezer and a few electrical kitchen appliances, and has an area where guests and staff can recharge batteries for cameras, phones, computers or other electronic equipment.

Sewage avoidance and waste management

Waste and sewage disposal is particularly important in sensitive coral areas where nutrients and sedimentation from sewage and beach erosion suffocate corals and encourage algal growth. On Chumbe, the installation of composting toilets instead of flush toilets not only drastically reduces water consumption, but also avoids any sewage (so-called 'black' water). Less polluted 'grey' water from the showers and kitchen is recycled by vegetative filtration through garden irrigation and a small 'artificial wetland' plant bed adjacent to the restaurant kitchen, which is planted with fruiting species that are efficient at taking up the phosphates and nitrates in the used water.

Organic kitchen refuse is either composted and then used in the composting toilets, or removed from the island. As around 90% of all kitchen supplies are bought fresh from local market and transported in large baskets, hardly any tins or plastic containers reach the island. Therefore, as non-biodegradable materials are minimized and removed and others fully recycled, it can be said that Chumbe Island Coral Park generates close to zero pollution, both liquid and solid.

Restricting visitor numbers

Seven two- to three-bed Eco-bungalows offer accommodation for up to 16 guests. In addition, day trips are offered for up to a total of 16 visitors. Groups of schoolchildren are invited for day excursions during the low season, their numbers do not exceed 15 including teachers. Overnight capacity does not exceed around 4500 bed-nights per year and no further construction of overnight facilities is planned.

Traditional organic cuisine

As a pre-industrial country, Tanzania has no major food processing industry. Thus, foodstuffs are commonly produced and sold at local markets by small-scale farmers, who constitute over 80% of the population. The great majority still use traditional tools, farming and livestock production systems, such as the hand hoe and the free ranching of local breeds of chicken, goats and cattle. Given the very low productivity and limited income of such small-scale food production, farmers cannot afford expensive agro-chemicals, such as fertilizers and pesticides. Therefore, the farm produce sold at local markets can be generally considered as 'organically produced' by default.

Over the last two decades, the changing nutritional habits of the growing urban elites and population, as well as the demand of the emerging tourism industry have encouraged imports of processed food of sometimes doubtful quality that is sold in supermarkets and a myriad of small shops mostly found in urban areas.

In this context, CHICOP has deliberately opted for a restaurant cuisine that is based on traditional Zanzibari cooking, using with preference unprocessed fresh food that local markets can supply, mostly seafood, indigenous tropical staples, vegetables and fruits, spices and sweets. This is not only cost-effective, but also benefits local primary producers, small farmers and fishers, and at the same time satisfies the most stringent demands for healthy, tasty, safe and organic food. Fortunately, Zanzibar's history up to Independence, as a wealthy and thriving trade economy supported by an Arabic dynasty and enterprising migrants from Asia and Europe, has produced a rather sophisticated local cuisine that is a blend of Asian, Arabic, African and European traditions. The decision to 'go local' with the Chumbe cuisine also allowed for the employment of local women as cooks who had no formal training, but routinely produce culinary delights that they would otherwise serve at important social functions, such as weddings.

Another important aspect is that buying fresh food on local markets and transporting this in baskets to the island minimizes packaging materials and thus solid waste and environmental pollution. Plastic waste from bottled water is also avoided, by filtering drinking water and providing it in recycled wine bottles that are covered with coconut fibre ropes.

Search for zero-emission and appropriate kitchen energy

Against a backdrop of climate change, rapid deforestation and high energy costs in the country, the search for zero-emission and renewable cooking energy remains a challenge for Chumbe. To be manageable, a restaurant has to offer a variety of dishes that are prepared and served hot according to a strict time schedule for breakfast, lunch and dinner time, irrespective of the number of guests and of weather patterns and sunshine hours. While foodstuffs and drinks are cooled in a solar-powered freezer and cool-boxes, CHICOP has so far experimented with two models of solar cookers (solar box and parabola solar-cooker), a low-pressure gas cooker, kerosene cookers and traditional charcoal stoves. Of the several options examined, a flexible combination of charcoal stoves, kerosene and gas cookers has been found to be the most appropriate and cost-effective so far, though environmentally not yet entirely satisfactory.

As charcoal for cooking contributes to forest depletion, CHICOP tries to keep its consumption low by using improved traditional charcoal stoves that are insulated with a thick layer of clay around the fire chamber. These are manufactured manually and cost only around US$5 per unit, again creating a market for local produce. It also turned out that local women are far more skilful in the economical use of charcoal for cooking and baking, than people from industrial countries with their barbeques, for example. Zanzibari women constantly shift small quantities of glowing charcoal between several small stoves, under and on top of large clay pots that also have clay covers.

As a consequence, as traditional meal preparation and cooking technologies are very labour-intensive, and the photovoltaic system on Chumbe can also not cost-effectively produce sufficient energy for electrical kitchen appliances, CHICOP employs more staff in the kitchen than would be the case in most tourist restaurants of a similar size, thus generating additional employment for local people.

Environmental communication and marketing

While coastal communities depend on fishing for their survival in Tanzania and Zanzibar, there is little evidence of traditional reef management or awareness about the limitations of the resource (Scheinman et al., 1996). Government priorities, policies, legislation and management capacity are insufficient to meet the challenges of rapid environmental deterioration. As the international mass tourism and export market still favours environmentally destructive products and practices, investment continues to be directed into unsustainable development.

To contribute to improving this situation, and in line with the company mission, CHICOP has provided environmental information, education and training to the following groups:

- **The park rangers**. The employment of former fishermen, and the hands-on approach to capacity building and monitoring through inexpensive on-the-job-training by volunteers, have produced very competent and committed park rangers. They manage the Reef Sanctuary with no other means of enforcement than the persuasion of their fellow fishermen.
- **Fishermen**. The rangers 'educate' fishermen by stressing the role of coral reefs and the protected area as a breeding and feeding ground for fish. This has proven very successful. Village fishermen now generally respect the park boundaries and also report that catches outside the boundaries have increased since the establishment of the sanctuary. Regular yearly meetings between local village communities, CHICOP management and government officials encourage open communication between all parties.

- **Government officials**. The project has also helped to raise conservation awareness and understanding of the legal and institutional requirements among government officials. Seven government departments were involved in negotiating the project in the initial phase, followed (among other issues) by intense discussions on the Management Plans in the Advisory Committee. This has improved political support and prepared the ground for improvements in the legal framework. Environmental legislation, which has provisions for the private management of protected areas, was passed in 1996.

- **Schoolchildren**. All secondary schools in Zanzibar participate in a full Environmental Education program that includes school excursions to Chumbe Island and teacher training seminars regularly when the tides are safe for non-swimmers. This is organized in co-operation with Ministry of Education. Many of these children come from schools within fishing communities where the children benefit from learning about the resources upon which many of their families' livelihoods depend, and upon which they may be likely to depend upon themselves in later life.

- **Eco-tourists**. Last but not least, visitors to the island are offered a wide range of nature experiences, such as guided snorkelling in the reef sanctuary, guided walks in the intertidal zone around the island, into a mangrove cave and along forest trails. All this is accompanied by environmental exhibits and information in the Visitors' Centre, including project documentation, relevant literature and nature trail booklets. The so-called 'eco-bungalows' demonstrate state-of-the-art technologies of water and waste management and energy provision. From 1998, marketing through the Internet stressed the conservation orientation of the Chumbe Island project, with a comprehensive website that offers detailed information on the project activities in the Reef Sanctuary, the Forest Reserve, and Education programs. The website was created to target and attract the 'right' clientele in the nature and ecotourism market.

- **The international conservation community**. From the beginning, and as part of marketing efforts, CHICOP has sought support and recognition from the international conservation community. Chumbe Island is registered with the World Conservation Monitoring Center (WCMC) from 1995, and was chosen for presentation at the EXPO2000 World Exhibition in Hannover (Germany) for its achievements in private park management and the innovative eco-architecture of all buildings. One of the Chumbe eco-bungalows was exhibited in the Tanzanian pavilion in Hanover. The many prestigious international awards won for nature conservation and socially responsible tourism has also helped increase local political recognition.

Ecological results

As a result of successful management the coral reef has become one of the most pristine in the region, with 423 species of fish and over 200 species of scleractinian coral, at least 90% of all those recorded in East Africa (Veron, pers.com., 1997).

The coral communities in the sanctuary have survived the worldwide 1998 bleaching event better than most other reefs in the region (McClanahan et.al. 2007b). The Chumbe Reef Sanctuary has also become refuge for several resident hawksbill turtles.

Recent research has established that the Chumbe MPA is among the most resilient reefs in the Western Indian Ocean region and likely to be less affected by environmental stress, temperature changes and other causes of coral mortality linked to climate change (Mainia et al. 2008). Based on these findings, a related study concludes that the management status of MPAs in the region needs to be reprioritized based on areas that are both likely to survive climate change related thermal stress and have biodiversity. Chumbe ranks among the highest performers in all these categories (McClanahan, 2007b).

The forest covering the island is one of the last pristine semi-arid 'coral rag' forests in Zanzibar (Beentje, 1990) and has now become a sanctuary for the highly endangered Ader's duiker (*Cephalophus adersi*), the rarest antelope in the world, now probably facing imminent extinction from poaching and habitat destruction (Kingdon, 1997). These can later be re-introduced to the Jozani forest or other conservation areas, once these are established and fully managed with the support of neighbouring communities.

Furthermore, the island has probably the world's largest population of the rare Coconut crab (*Birgus latro*) recorded as 'data deficient' in the IUCN Red data book (Richard Hartnoll, pers. comm., Drew, M.M. et al., forthcoming, 2010). Attracted by the abundant fish in the reef sanctuary, the rare Roseate terns (*Sterna dougalli*) bred on Chumbe Island in 1994 (Iles, 1995) and 2007. Particularly after the successful eradication of rats (*Rattus rattus*) in 1997, Chumbe Island is also a safe haven for yet unknown flora and fauna typical of inter tidal reef flats and coral rag forests that are little researched and rapidly diminishing elsewhere in Zanzibar and Tanzania.

Community and social benefits

As a professionally managed conservation area, Chumbe Island Coral Park provides important community benefits and social services for the population of Zanzibar, particularly fishermen, schoolchildren and the population in general. In detail, the project:

- *Contributes to biodiversity conservation and ecological restoration*, by effectively protecting a pristine coral island for future generations, and in the absence of government agencies to do so. When CHICOP started in the early nineties, Zanzibar had neither conservation policies and marine protected areas, nor the institutions to establish and manage them.
- *Helps the restocking of locally depleted fisheries and promotes the recovery of degraded coral reef ecosystems*: Chumbe Island is located upstream of the most important fishing grounds opposite Zanzibar town. Thus the sanctuary provides a protected breeding ground for fish, corals and other species, which

are expected to spread out to re-colonize nearby over-fished and degraded areas. As the predominant sea current in the Zanzibar channel is northerly, the larvae of corals and other sea organisms and juvenile and adult fish are likely to migrate to the northern, heavily fished reefs (a 'spill-over effect') (McClanahan, 2010, forthcoming).

- *Provides a training ground for local people in conservation area management.* Since 1992 former fishermen have been made Park rangers and trained in Marine Park management and monitoring techniques for the reef and the forest. They have also learned English and gained the knowledge needed to guide both local and foreign visitors on the island. CHICOP also offers ranger training services to other marine parks in the region.
- *Helps create environmental awareness among the fishermen* in adjacent villages. As the Chumbe rangers have no policing powers, they have been trained to educate fishermen about coral reefs and the importance of no-take-areas as breeding ground for fish. They stress upon fishermen that they should respect the boundaries of the Reef Sanctuary and in exchange enjoy increased fish harvests in the vicinity. The rangers have been particularly successful in this, and over the last few years infringements of the park regulations have decreased considerably.
- *Gives permanent help to local fishermen in distress.* As there is no maritime rescue service available in Tanzania, the assistance given by the Chumbe rangers to fishermen during rough weather, and when boats, engines and sails need fixing, is crucial. They also provide radio communication from the island to anyone in need, and have even been involved in salvage operations for a sunken yacht. Over the many years of project operations there have been hundreds of cases where such help was given, and probably many lives saved.
- *Provides employment and career opportunities for local people.* As a fully managed nature reserve, and also due to the particular eco-technologies chosen, CHICOP is very labour-intensive. A third of the staff of 43 employees are directly involved in conservation management and education. With only seven rooms, CHICOP has probably the highest employee/room ratio of any tourism business in Tanzania, and, according to a recent study of the International Finance Corporation, three times the international average for ecolodges (IFC, 2004).
- *Provides a direct source of income to local fishermen and farmers.* Local fishermen and farmers also benefit directly by selling fish, other seafood and farm products to the island restaurant through local markets. Palm-thatched roofs in particular need regular fixing and thus also provide a ready market for the owners of palm trees and village producers of '*makuti*' thatching material that is woven from palm leaves.
- *Contributes to capacity building of government staff* from different departments who have been involved in initial negotiations or in the Advisory Committee. Over the years, the Committee dealt with important issues concerning the establishment and management of the reserve, particularly

through the discussions about the Management Plans. Another example of capacity building was the rat eradication campaign in 1997. Staff from the Plant Protection Division and a trainee supported by an EC-funded conservation project in Zanzibar were trained on the technicalities of rodent control in nature reserves, and could then conduct a similar operation on other Tanzanian islands later on.

- *Has created unique facilities for Environmental Education* for schoolchildren and other visitors. Nature trails and educational materials (in Kiswahili and English) have been developed for the reef and forest. From 2003, full-time Conservation and Environmental education coordinators were employed to manage conservation and education programs.

- *Co-operates with the Harbours Authority to keep the lighthouse functioning.* In the absence of Port staff on the island, the rangers act as lighthouse keepers and light the old AGA-gas-powered system when this has been extinguished for some reason. The Port Authority regularly calls the island to ask the rangers for assistance in such cases. Before this happened, the lighthouse rarely functioned. This service is particularly important for the traditional Indian Ocean shipping traffic made up of *dhows* that have no access to modern navigational aids, such as GPS.

- *Offers valuable research opportunities for Tanzanian and foreign research institutions.* The Institute of Marine Sciences of the University of Dar es Salaam, and foreign academic institutions linked with their co-operation program, conduct regular long-term research that is only possible in effectively protected areas. For the academic community this is of extreme value, as research plots and equipment are safe from theft and tampering in the Chumbe Reef Sanctuary and Forest Reserve, and conditions are ideal to compare protected areas with unprotected areas.

- *Provides valuable experience in the financially sustainable management of protected areas.* CHICOP provides many insights useful for solving the problem of financial sustainability in the management of protected areas in Zanzibar and elsewhere. It is hoped that lessons learned may contribute to sustainable management of protected areas system in Zanzibar and the region, once donor funding becomes scarcer. This is particular true for experiences with enforcement, environmental education and marketing in the ecotourism market.

Enforcement and Monitoring

The Park rangers patrol the island to ensure that the laws prohibiting fishing and anchoring on the protected reef and guarding of the closed coral-rag forest habitat are met. They monitor any event or infringement, and their reports provide daily data from 1992, on the type, number and names of vessels involved, nature of the intended activity and the fishers' reaction to the rangers' intervention. They also record observations on any major change in the coral reef, such as storm damage or coral bleaching. The coral reef, fish population and sea grass beds are systematically monitored based on a Monitoring manual specially designed for Chumbe.

The data gathered from these reports are unique as they give a daily account of the hands-on management of a small island environment and provide detailed information on methods used to deal with external pressures on the protected area. It has been possible to calculate accurately the number of incidents of fishermen breaching the boundaries of the protected zone from the very beginning of the project. With these data, trends in seasonal fishing pressures could be assessed, as well as trends in the origin of the fishermen, their vessel types and their target catches over time. In addition, the fishermen's reactions to the rangers doing their job have also been meticulously recorded.

Data extracted from the rangers' daily monitoring reports and continuous information thereafter demonstrate a clear decline in the total number of incidents over time particularly from 1995, suggesting the overall success of the rangers' methods in deterring activity within the protected area. However, the decline was not gradual. Confirming our prior assessment that Chumbe has not been a preferred fishing area, incidents were few throughout 1993, the first year of patrolling, with not more than between two and ten incidents per month. However, these incidents increased drastically between November 1993 and March 1994 (with a peak of 43 in March 1994) and again between July 1994 and February 1995 (with a peak of 19 in October 1994). After that, and up to present, the number of monthly incidents has been low (Carter et al., 1997).

Good relationships have developed over the years between the rangers and some of the local fishermen, and in some cases personal respect for the rangers has contributed to deterring attempts to fish in the protected zone. As a matter of fact, fishermen requiring assistance are never turned away, which has also contributed to the success of the park management.

After the successful rat eradication campaign in 1997, the island is regularly checked for any recurrence of these pests, with monitoring 'chew sticks' placed in once rat-infested areas. Another species monitored regularly is the highly endangered Aders duiker, after six animals had been translocated to Chumbe Island in 1998 and 2000.

Research cooperation contributes to the monitoring of the island environment, and is regulated by the Chumbe Island Management Plans 1995-2016. Past research programs with the Institute of Marine Sciences and others dealt with coral recruitment, coral transplantation, spill-over of the fish population from the sanctuary to adjacent fishing grounds, temperature and tidal current measurements, coral reef monitoring, fish population dynamics, and other topics.

Environmental impacts from tourism operations are also controlled and monitored. In order to minimize any environmental impact, all buildings on the island (seven visitors' bungalows, a Visitors' Centre and staff quarters) were constructed according to state-of-the-art eco-architecture. Most systems have worked well, others have needed adjustments. For example, as visitor numbers increased, the grey water vegetative filtration system could not cope with the nutrient-rich kitchen water anymore. With the professional help of specialists recruited by the volunteer agencies BESO and SES, the system was modified several times over three years and now works well.

A study calculating the phosphorus budget of the ecotourism operations on Chumbe Island recommended that compost from the composting toilets and wood ash of the staff kitchen have reached a saturation point and should be removed from the island in order to avoid nutrient leakage into the coral reef. (Lindstroem 2007) These management measures were then implemented.

Reporting and Publications

Research reports and quarterly reports on project progress are circulated among government departments and other institutions concerned. CHICOP is also an active participant in events organized by the International Coral Reef Initiative (ICRI), a leading world body campaigning for coral reef conservation. Papers on the management experiences of the Chumbe Island Coral Park as a private marine park and genuine ecotourism destination were presented to international conferences and workshops conducted by ICRI, IUCN, WWF, TNC, the Katoomba Group, in Tanzania, Australia, Mozambique, Saudi Arabia, Egypt, Philippines, the USA, also the World Parks Congress 2003 in Durban/SA, as well as international conferences on responsible tourism in Barcelona (2004) and Rio de Janeiro (2006) among other events. Most papers were published in conference proceedings, readers, scientific magazines and on the Internet. In a UNESCO sponsored Internet discussion forum on coastal zone management, www.csiwisepractices.org, the Chumbe case sparked off a lively debate on the merits of and benefits provided by the private sector management of conservation areas.

Awards versus Certification

International environmental and responsible tourism awards became a powerful marketing tool. In 1999, CHICOP was selected as the 'Worldwide project' for the EXPO2000 and exhibited in the Tanzanian pavilion in Hanover/Germany. The project also won the 1999 British Airways Tourism for Tomorrow Southern Global Award, the 2000 UNEP Global500 Award, and the 2001 Environmental Award of the International Hotel and Restaurant Association (IH&RA) dedicated to the theme 'Energy'. Further awards include the Environmental award of the Government of Zanzibar (2004), the Best Website Award For Responsible Tourism of the German Ministry for Economic Cooperation (2005), the TO.DO! Award of the Studienkreis Tourismus und Entwicklung (2005) and the Geotourism Award of National Geographic Traveller in 2008. CHICOP also became finalist of the World Legacy Award and twice of the Aga Khan Award for Architecture.

CHICOP did not apply for environmental certification offered by various international schemes, as they turned out to be costly and beyond the reach of small conservation projects and eco-lodges. They normally require the payment of high consultancy fees and international travel for surveyors. In addition, evaluations of the most common certification schemes have revealed that they have limited marketing value and are thus not very attractive to the tourism industry (Font, 2006). One recent promising exception has been the comprehensive and demanding Certification scheme for Global Ecosystem Reserves – The Long Run Destinations that is now being created by the Jochen Zeitz Foundation, which CHICOP has joined as a founding member.

Sustainable Conservation Area Management

In summary, Chumbe Island Coral Park combines sustainable tourism with sustainable conservation area management:

- Around 1.2 Million US$ were invested to develop the park (50% from the project initiator, 25% small donor grants for non-commercial project components, 25% professional work contributed by more than 50 volunteers over several years).
- The revenue generated from small-scale but high value ecotourism fully funds the Park management and conservation and education programs since the year 2000. About one third of the operational budget of Chumbe is spent on conservation management staff, e.g. marine biologists, park rangers, educators, and research and education programs.
- Due to extremely cost-effective operations and the continued assistance of volunteers, even a slump in tourist arrivals would not threaten the survival of the park, as an occupancy rate of around 40% is sufficient to cover basic operations.

Lessons Learned

As with many ambitious projects, the challenges for CHICOP turned out to be much bigger than envisaged. The advent of liberalization from the early 1990s brought rapid changes to Zanzibar. The booming tourism industry took possession of the most attractive sites (some apparently for speculative reasons) and also created an affluent market for marine products, leading to the overexploitation of lobsters, kingfish and other upmarket seafood. High prices made fishing an attractive occupation for urban youths who had little respect for traditional fishing grounds and the environmentally less damaging traditional fishing practices, and could also afford modern propulsion and fishing gear.

Therefore, challenges to the management of the protected area increased during project implementation, particularly for a private initiative that could not count on enforcement by government. Though the Government of Zanzibar had gazetted the Reef sanctuary in 1994 and agreed to assist with enforcement, this was in the formative years mostly left to the CHICOP park rangers. Cooperation with government enforcement agents improved considerably when two police officers were stationed on the island for security reasons.

However, the protection of the park on site turned out to be a minor challenge the project management had to face compared with the demands and bureaucratic requirements posed by the different Zanzibar Government departments. Even after approval of the project by the government, the innovative design of CHICOP has complicated project implementation to an extent that purely commercially oriented investment would not have accepted. The negotiation of the preparatory steps, such as land lease, building permits, gazettement, management agreements of the conservation area and research permits for scientists and project staff took several years to conclude. Unforeseen bureaucratic delays, red tape and obstructions, mostly caused by CHICOP's refusal to pay bribes, more than tripled the planned implementation time and costs.

The conservation activities and achievements of CHICOP are only beginning to receive official support and recognition within the country. Despite the fact that much of the investment funds and time were spent in the establishment of the protected area, CHICOP enjoys no favoured status or exemption from the substantial and ever increasing costs of land rent, licenses, permits, fees and taxation.

More challenges resulted from the very innovative architectural designs of the Visitor Centre and the eco-bungalows, as well as from the difficult logistics of operating on an island. All building materials had to be transported during high tides, as Chumbe is surrounded by reefs and has no natural harbour. The environmentally friendly technologies used were not only unknown to local builders and craftsmen, but there is also little experience available on their functioning under tropical island conditions. In addition, Tanzania and Zanzibar suffered from a severe energy crisis in 1994 to 1997 that created shortages of fuel and cement on the local market. All these factors complicated the building process and contributed to enormous delays. Building operations lasted over four years altogether instead of the one year originally planned for by the architects. As a consequence, the investment costs soared and the price structure had to be adjusted to aim at a more upmarket clientele.

Conclusion

Nearly two decades of effective park management have proven that private coral reef conservation can work on the ground and be sustained by ecotourism. The Chumbe experience suggests that private management of marine protected areas is technically and commercially feasible and efficient, even when State enforcement is not available or ineffective. This is probably the case for reefs that are not yet heavily exploited. To avoid user conflicts, it is easier to preserve an area that is not being used to a major extent for subsistence or other economic endeavours by local communities.

Effectively managed, a privately protected area such as Chumbe can also provide important community benefits on the ground, probably more so than government-run parks. Chumbe has benefited local communities by generating income, employment, and a market for local produce, as well as developing new work skills, demonstrating sustainable resource management, and restocking commercial fish species in adjacent areas (spill-over). Extensive work with government agencies in establishing the park has also enhanced the understanding of environmental issues among local and national authorities.

With an overall investment of approximately 1.2 million US$ over eight years, the cost of private park development and management is considerably lower than would have been the case with donor-funded parks through government agencies. And, most importantly, there are better prospects for sustainability. Incentives to struggle for commercial survival are much stronger, as private parks need to demonstrate tangible conservation successes on the ground, co-operate with local resource users, generate sufficient income for running the park, be cost-effective and keep overheads down.

Important risks remain, though, for such private investment in conservation, in particular, the higher investment and operational costs, as well as security of tenure, that is part of contracts and leases with the government. CHICOP used a window of opportunity in the early nineties, when Zanzibar started opening up to the outside world, and policies, legislation and institutions for both foreign investment and conservation were still being developed. While these are in place now, nearly two decades later, the challenge may come from a limited political will, mainly due to a massive increase in investment in the tourism sector and the higher income expected from large-scale corporate and mass tourism (Lange 2009).

Private investments in conservation and environmentally sound technologies, as well as the employment of additional staff for park management and environmental education programs, raises costs considerably, making it difficult to compete with purely commercial tourist enterprises. Favourable tax treatment would such encourage non-commercial investment components, but this is not granted in Tanzania.

Another political threat is the generous but unsustainable donor support given to government for marine conservation, which effectively crowds out private initiatives. The long-term prospects of CHICOP, like any private investment, depend on political stability in Zanzibar. They also require favourable government decisions on the extension of management agreements and land leases, which would acknowledge the conservation success on the ground, and the convincing contribution of CHICOP to both community benefits and sustainable park management.

References

Beentje, H.J. (1990). *A Reconnaissance Survey of Zanzibar Forests and Coastal Thicket.* FINNIDA-COLE, Zanzibar.

Carter, E. et al. (1997). 'Management Experiences of the Chumbe Reef Sanctuary 1992-1996'. Paper presented at the National Coral Reef Conference, 2-4 December, Zanzibar.

Carter, E. et al. (2008). Private protected areas: Management regimes, tenure arrangements and protected area categorization in East Africa. *Oryx, 42(2)*, 177–186.

Chumbe Island Coral Park (2006). *Management Plans 1995-2005, 2006-2016.* CHICOP, Zanzibar/Tanzania.

Font, X. (2006). Tourism Certification as a Sustainability Tool: Assessment and Prospects. *United Nations Environment Programme*. January 06.

Drew, M.M., et al. (2010). A Review of the Biology and Ecology of the Robber Crab, Birgus latro (Linnaeus, 1767) (Anomura: Coenobitidae). *Zoologischer Anzeiger (2010)*. doi:10.1016/j.jcz.2010.03.001. Elsevier.

Francis, J. et al. (2002). Marine Protected Areas in the Eastern African Region: How Successful Are They? *AMBIO: A Journal of the Human Environment*, Volume 31, Issue 7 (December 2002) pp. 503–511. http://ambio.allenpress.com/perlserv/?request=get-document&issn=0044-7447&volume=031&issue=07&page=0503&ct=1 (Accessed the 15th June 2010 14:00).

Iles, D.B. (1995). Roseate Terns. *Miombo, No.13*, July. Wildlife Conservation Society of Tanzania. Dar es Salaam.

International Finance Corporation (2004). *Ecolodges: Exploring Opportunities for Sustainable Business*. Washington DC: IFC.

Jameson, S.C. et al. (1995). State of the Reefs, Regional and Global Perspectives. An International Coral Reef Initiative Executive Secretariat Background Paper.

Lange, G.M. (2009). Marine conservation: How economic valuation of ecosystems' services can help. A case study of Zanzibar. in: *The Valuation of Marine Ecosystems' Services: A Gap Analysis*, New York: World Bank.

Langholz, J. & Krug, W. (2004). New forms of biodiversity governance: non-state actors and the private protected area plan. *Journal of International Wildlife Law & Policy*, 7, 1–21.

Lindstroem, B. (2007). *A phosphorus budget for the eco-tourist resort of Chumbe Island Coral Park, Zanzibar*. MSc Thesis 2007, No. 153, Swedish University of Agricultural Sciences, Dept of Soil Sciences.

Kingdon, J. (1997). The Kingdon Field Guide to African Mammals. *Academic Press*, 372-373.

Maina, J. et al. (2008). Modelling susceptibility of coral reefs to environmental stress using remote sending data and GIS models. *Ecological Modelling 212* 180-199. www.sciencedirect.com

McClanahan, T. (1999). Is there a future for coral reef parks in poor tropical countries? *Coral Reefs* 18: 321-325

McClanahan et al. (2007b). Effects of climate and seawater temperature variation on coral bleaching and mortality. Ecol. Monogr. 77, 503-525.

McClanahan, T. (2010 forthcoming). Effects of Fisheries Closures and Gear Restrictions on Fishing Income in a Kenyan Coral Reef, *Conservation Biology*, Society for Conservation Biology.

Riedmiller, S. (1991). *Environmental Education in Zanzibar: Proposals for Action*. Unpublished consultancy report for FINNIDA / Dept. of Environment. Zanzibar.

Riedmiller, S. (2000). Private Sector Management of Marine Protected Areas: The Chumbe Island Case. In: Cesar H.S.J. (ed.). *Collected Essays on the Economics of Coral Reefs*. CORDIO, SIDA.

Riedmiller, S. et al. (2001). Creating Self-Financing Mechanisms for MPAs: Three Cases. *MPA News, International News and Analysis on Marine Protected Areas*. Washington University, Vol. 2, No.8. March.

Riedmiller, S. et al. (2002). Stretching Your MPA Budget: How To Do More with less Funding, *MPA News. International News and Analysis on Marine Protected Areas*. Washington University, Vol. 3, No.9, April.

Riedmiller, S. (2008). Chumbe Island Coral Park: Helping save the coral reefs of Tanzania. Presentation to Workshop Using Marine Agreements for Marine Protection, The Nature Conservancy, Bainbridge Island, Seattle, USA, June. http://www.mcatoolkit. org/Field_Projects/Field_Projects_Tanzania.html (Accessed 15th of June 2010, 14:31)

Riedmiller, S. (2009). *Chumbe Island Coral Park: MPA Governance Analysis.* Paper presented to UNEP-IUCN International Workshop on Governing Marine Protected Areas. October, 2009. Veli Lošinj, Croatia. Publication forthcoming.

Riedmiller, S. (2010). *Private Marine Parks - The case of Chumbe Island, Zanzibar/ Tanzania.* Case study presented to Katoomba Group Meeting XVI, February 9-11, Palo Alto, CA. http://www.ecosystemmarketplace.com/documents/acrobat/k16_d1/ Riedmiller_Day%201.pdf (Accessed the 15th June 2010 15:00)

Scheinman, D. et al. (1996). *The Traditional Management of Coastal Resources, IUCN-Tanga Coastal Zone Conservation and Development Program.* Tanga/Tanzania, June.

Udelhoven, J., Carter, E. & Gilmer, B. (2010). *MCA Feasibility Analysis: Coral Triangle, Indonesia - Final interim findings & recommendatio*ns. Technical Report, The Nature Conservancy.

Wells, S. (2009). Dynamite fishing in northern Tanzania – pervasive, problematic and yet preventable. *Marine Pollution Bulletin* 58, 20–23. Elsevier, UK.

World Bank (2006). *Scaling up Marine Management: The Role of Marine Protected Areas.* Report no. 36635-GLB. Environment Department/Sustainable Development Network. Washington DC, World Bank, p. 100.

WPC (2003). World Parks Congress, Recommendation 5.19 IUCN Protected Area Management Categories. http://www.iucn.org/themes/wcpa/wpc2003/pdfs/outputs/ recommendations/approved/english/html/r19.htm (Accessed 14th June 2010, 20:15)

13 Blossoms & Butterflies, Waterfalls & Dragonflies

Integrating insects in the hospitality and tourism industries through Swarm supposition

R. Harvey Lemelin [*] *and Greg Williams* [**]

Introduction

Insects (butterflies, dragonflies) and arachnids (spiders, scorpions), members of the arthropod family of the animal kingdom, are for all intents and purposes the 'most abundant terrrestrial life-form' (Moris, 1998, p. 1). Indeed, the sheer multitude and adaptability of these animals has led Naskrecki (2005) to label them as the tiny majority. While most of the focus in this chapter is on insects some arachnids are discussed, therefore, the term insect will be used to denote both animal designations.

Building on the concept of 'blossoms and waterfalls' which refers to a type of ecotourism aimed at integrating cultural and spiritual dimensions with ecological aspects of tourism (Weaver, 2002), blossoms and butterflies, and waterfalls and dragonflies, seek to expand this type of tourism by emphasizing human interactions with insects in various environments and through various forms. Some of these activities may include learning about bees and apiaries at B&B's and hotels in Canada or Kenya, visiting a butterfly ranch in Kenya or Papua New Guinea, or walking through an insect exhibit in Thailand or England.

At first glance, the title of this chapter may appear somewhat absurd, as after all most visitors actually go out of their way to avoid insects (see the Bedbug Registry at bedbugregistry.com). Indeed, the notion of interacting with insects during our leisure time, whether they be 'pests' (cockroaches, flies), 'biting creatures' (mosquitoes, horse flies), or parasites (lice, ticks, bed-bugs), is usually not a high priority on most visitors' to-do list. In fact, the 'pest' label is often used to incorporate all of the creatures mentioned above, as well as insects including

[*]School of Outdoor Recreation, Parks and Tourism, Lakehead University, Thunder Bay, Canada
[**]Cree Village Ecolodge, Moose Factory, Canada

the agricultural, silvicultural, structural, household, and vectors of human diseases. The irony is that 'pests' represent approximately 1% of all insects, but it is this tiny minority that are responsible for significant economic losses as a result of their feeding activities on timber, stored products, pastures, and crops. Blood feeding insects, such as mosquitoes and other flies, are also responsible for spreading numerous pathogens, resulting in many human illnesses and millions of death annually (Evans et al., 2000, p. 74).

As a report produced for the U.S. Environmental Protection Agency indicates, international expenditures for pesticide (defined here as herbicides, insecticides and fungicides) use 'totalled more than $32.5 billion in 2000 and nearly $32.0 billion in 2001' (Kiely et al. 2004, p.4), and significant amounts of financing and marketing efforts are directed at 'controlling' this 'terrible minority'. In a study of public perceptions of pests and subsequent use of pesticides in American homes, Baldwin et al. (2008) suggest that the role of the pesticides industry is quite pervasive and influential. The power of this industry in fuelling the various fears and phobias associated with insects in leisure and tourism cannot be under-estimated.

Pest labelling aside, insects also provide numerous benefits including apicul-ture (bee keeping), sericulture (commercial silk), pollination and biocontrol agriculture (the deliberate introduction of predatory insects). In fact, the various socio-environmental and political values of insects were estimated at $57 billion annually (Losey and Vaughan, 2006). These figures do not, however, include contributions by insects to forensic entomology (a form of investigative science popularized by Gil Grissom in *CSI*), medical purposes, and entertainment (insect exhibitions) (Evans et al., 2004; Gullan & Cranston, 2004; Lemelin, 2009). Considering insects' numerous benefits, this is precisely why insect interpretation strategies should be included in tourism strategies. These strategies which are described below can best be described as various on-site strategies where interac-tion may be encouraged, like butterfly gardens, dragon-fly ponds, apiaries, and petting zoos, as well as non-interactive strategies like display cases (ant farms, terrariums), videos, crafts, books and guides, or story-telling. Indirect strategies include off-site visits to protected areas (Ramsar wetlands site), museums, insect exhibits like insectariums, butterfly conservatories and butterfly farms, and festi-vals or special events celebrating insects.

Through a conversation-narrative, the two authors (one a researcher, the other the director of an ecolodge operated by a Cree Indigenous community located in Northern Ontario) discuss how unique and authentic learning opportunities can be created through insect tourism strategies. The goals of this chapter are to (i) critique the pest label and various other concepts like anthromorphism and ento-mophobia; (ii) provide an international overview of the challenges and opportuni-ties associated with insect tourism activities; and, (iii) to develop a viable insect-tourism strategy for the ecolodge in particular. Suggestions regarding the value of insects in tourism and interpretation strategies in this particular context and other sites are provided in the discussion, recommendations, and conclusion sections.

Case Study: Main Section

The concepts of pests, as well as entomorphobia and anthropomorphism, are social constructions which help to encapsulate how insects are perceived. Since these concepts are central to our perceptions of insects and will, in all likelihood, influence how clients perceive and participate in these activities, we will now take the following opportunity to describe and criticize these concepts.

Preferred animals, according to Arluke and Sanders (1996) and Woods (2000), are those that are perceived to be most human-like. This concept, also known as anthropomorphism, suggests that our affinity with certain animals like bears and monkeys is due to our likeliness with these creatures. While anthropomorphism may make some sense when we are discussing some types of mammals, it fails to address the popularity of birds and birding worldwide (birding is believed to be to the biggest wildlife tourism industry), the attraction of certain reptiles as in visiting turtle nesting sites, and of course, the allure of fishing in all its various forms. Furthermore, it overlooks the aesthetic appeal of such insects like lady-bugs and butterflies (Knegtering et al., 2002; New, 1997). In fact, endangered or threatened butterflies are 'among the few insects to garner substantial public support for their protection' (Kellert, 1996, 125-126). Due to their role in controlling plant feeding pest insects in many agricultural and horticultural settings, lady-bugs or lady beetles enjoy a superb reputation (Cormier et al. 2000). As a result of this popularity, there have been numerous attempts to introduce various species of lady-bugs into North America (Cormier et al. 2000).

Kellert (1996) and Hardy (1988) argue that interest in insects is rather unusual, and that in most instances our relationship to insects can be best defined as one of apathy and anxiety or 'entomophobia,' (the unreasonable fear of insects) (Gurung, 2003). Other possible factors contributing to 'entomophobic' tendencies include social mores, research and management biases (Kerley et al., 2003; Lemelin, 2009; Woods, 2000), and a general tendency to lump all insects in the same 'pest' category (Samways, 2005). As stated in the introduction, 99% of insects are disproportionately represented by a very powerful pesticides industry aimed at controlling or eliminating 'pests' (Baldwin et al., 2008). Lost in these definitions of 'anthropomorphism' 'entomophobia' and 'pest' are the utilitarian roles (apiaries, butterfly farms, dragonflies as alternatives to the use of insecticides) and the roles of insects in various dimensions of leisure and tourism strategies. These are discussed next.

Utilitarian Uses for Insects

The utilitarian value of bees in the production of honey (Mitchell & Lasswell, 2005), silkworms in the production of silk, pollinators inr crop productions, or aquatic insects and upper-level predators such as dragonflies and damselflies as bio-indicators for wetland quality in Europe, Japan, the USA, and Australia (Clausnitzer and Jödicke, 2004), suggests that insects and their benefits are numerous and varied (see Table 13.1).

Table 13.1 Beneficial uses for insects

Beneficial Uses for Insects	Description/Examples
Arts	Inspiration
Apiculture	Beekeeping
Bio-control	Biological control
	Deliberate augmentation of predatory insects
Bio-indicators	Water, soil
Cultural entomology	Myth and lore
Educational	Experiential education
Engineering & Science	Bio-inspired engineering of exploration systems (BEES)
Entomophagy	Insects as food
Forensic Entomology	Investigative use of insects
Gardening	Ecological landscaping
Insect farming	Insects raised in captivity for commerical research, or biocontrol purposes
Medicinal insects	Immunenalogy, traditional medicines
Pets	Tarantulas, praying mantis, stick insects
Poetry	Inspiration (Haiku poetry)
Pollinators	Economic and ecological contributions
Sericulture	The production of silk

As Table 13.1 illustrates, insects 'are pervasive in fine arts and popular culture, they have been throughout history' (Laufer 2009, 183). Indeed, insects have long inspired writers and poets (Bogan, 1968; Kiauta, 1986, Tennyson, 2004), musicians (listen to Nikolai Rimsky-Korsakov,s *'Flight of the Bumblebee'* and Joseph Straus' s *'Dragonfly'*), and artists (van Gogh and Picasso) (Laufer, 2009). In contemporary times, artists and craftsmen still use insects as fabric motifs, models in painting, sculpture, jewellery, furniture, household items, toys and tattoos (Evans *et al.* 2003; Meher-Rochow, 2009; Samways, 2009). In the sciences and engineering, flying insects such as dragonflies have inspired 'ornithopters' while spider silk has also inspired bio-engineering projects (Thomas et al., 2004).

In ancient Egypt and Rome, scarab beetles were revered (Berenbaum, 1995), while butterflies adorn the palaces and burial chambers of kings and pharaohs (Laufer,2009). Spiders, according to the Cree and Hopi people, created North America, while elsewhere in North America, Hogue (1987) explains how butterflies, spiders, and moths were observed, studied and worshiped by the Choctaw, Navaho, and Cree, as well as the ancient Mexicans (Toltec, Mayan, Aztec) (Capinera, 1993; Cherry, 2006; Morris, 1979). Indeed, one entire temple (that of the Butterfly in Teotihuacan, Mexico) was solely dedicated to butterflies (Hogue, 1987).

Jiigiwiginabee (the Anishabee term for dragonflies) have also fascinated North Americans where their likeness is found on many petroglyphs in the southern USA and northern Canada (Feder, 1972; Lemelin, 2007), on Zuni altars, and in Navaho sandpaintings (Wyman & Bailey, 1964). *Odonata* were also a source of inspiration), in folklore (Hillerman, 1986), and in mythology (e.g., Ix Chel, the Mayan Goddess and the dragonflies). Much as in Japan, dragonfly designs have also influenced countless stone carvers (e.g., Teton Sioux stone pipes and pipe stems (Feder, 1972), Navaho jewellery and Zuni pottery (Cushing-Hamilton & Wright, 1992).

Through urbanization and technology, contemporary society, whether it be western, eastern, Indigenous, or otherwise, is increasingly becoming disconnected from the natural environment. Also lost in this transition is our understanding of, and reverence for, insects. Tourism, however, provides a tremendous opportunity for engaging tourists with insects, since many of the sights sought after by visitors are in natural areas. Since few places offer such opportunities, potential tourism developments involving insects are what follows next.

Insect Tourism

Despite the popularity of such movies as *'Bee Movie'* and *'Antz'* and such documentaries as *'Life in* the Undergrowth' and *'Beetle Queen Invades Tokyo'*, the role of insects in leisure and recreational activities has been largely ignored. As presented earlier, the omission of the largest contingent of the animal kingdom is somewhat surprising considering that insects have a long history of being involved in leisure and tourism activities. Some of these activities include insect exhibitions (i.e., butterfly houses, insectariums, museums, zoos); fairs and festivals (e.g., 12th annual Tarantula Awareness Festival, Coarsegold, CA, and the Cricket Festival, *Festa del Grillo,* in Florence, Italy); crickets trained to fight in competitive bouts in China (Raffles, 2010; Suga, 2006), the annual cockroach races held at Purdue University's Bug Bowl, educational traveling exhibits (see Project InSECT and the Pestival, a mobile arts festival examining insect-human interactivity through various mediums in England that attracted 10,000 people in 2006), citizen science, gardening, and insect and arachnid collecting and rearing (e.g., pets) (Laufer, 2009; Marshall, 2001; Schulz & Schultz, 2009).

Specialized tourism opportunities aimed exclusively at insects include the 40,000 tourists who visit the Waitomo Cave in New Zealand's North Island to view the large aggregation of glow worms (Buckley 2003), the *hotaru-matsuri* firefly festival in Japan (Kawahara, 2007) and the Firefly Park Resort in Kampung Kuantan, Malaysia (Othman and Othman, 1998 cited in Buckley, 2003), as well as invertebrate tourism in South Africa (Huntly *et al.* 2005; Kerley *et al.* 2003).

The charismatic micro-fauna of the insect, that is butterflies, dragonflies, tiger beetles, and bees, are celebrated in weddings and funerals (e.g., butterfly releases), and conservation strategies (i.e., the establishment of specialized sanctuaries such as pollinator parks) (Lemelin, 2009), population counts (i.e. 'bug counts'), dragon-hunting (seeking, collecting, transforming landscapes into ponds and otherwise interacting with *Odonata*) and butterflying (viewing, collecting, raising, releasing, creating butterfly gardens and otherwise interacting with *Leptidora*) (Lemelin, 2009). These are discussed next.

Beetles

While interest in beetles has been growing in North America through monitoring and conservation programs (Pearson & Shetterly, 2006) and beetle exhibits (i.e., insectariums, insect exhibits, the 'Bug House' at the London Zoo), as the *Beetle Queen Invades Tokyo* documentary illustrates, Japan's fascination with beetles is unsurpassed.

In modern Japan, the cicadas and other signing insects of old (Laurent, 2001), have been replaced by stag and rhinoceros beetles. Here, children interact with scarab beetles at the 'beetle petting zoo' in Shizuoka, while hundreds of participants attend the annual Rhinoceros Beetle Sumo Championships (Kawahara, 2007). According to New (2005), 'beetle wrestling is just one aspect of the fascination for beetles sweeping Japan, and which has spawned massive interest in collecting, rearing, and selling these insects' (p. 147). There are at least 300,000 beetle breeding fans (Kawahara, 2007), spending millions of dollars on insects, while the market for the stag beetle alone has been estimated at one hundred million US dollars, in special events, and entomological accessories (Goka et al. 2004).

Some of the impacts of these activities are minimized through national and regional conservation strategies like beetle conservation programs aimed at stag beetles (Hiatt and Shapiro, 1988, Kawaharta, 2007). Similar conservation and monitoring programs involving lady-bugs have also been initiated in North America (Pearson & Shetterly, 2006). While, the popularity of beetles outside of Japan may never surpass the interest in butterflies and dragonflies, one should not underestimate the potential interest in these animals, because media interest in the study (stating that dung beetles are strongest insects in the world) by Knell and Simmons (2010) indicates, there is a fascination with these particular insects. It is this interest in insects that Kerley et al. (2003) noted in their own study of African safari enthusiasts. In this they (2003) noted the tourism potential of insects, while also highlighting biased management perspectives, which despite the evidence from the research, did not recognize that visitors could have any interest in insects.

Dragonflies

Seeking out, collecting, transforming landscapes into ponds for, and otherwise interacting with dragonflies have been somewhat delayed compared to butterfly viewing and collecting (Kaufman, 2003; New, 1997), but dragonfly gatherings (e.g., counts, educational outings) have been increasing in popularity (Dunkle, 2004). Dragonfly preserves are now found in Britain, Japan, and even New York City's Central Park (Conniff, 1996). Dragonfly symposiums include the 'Dragonflies in Our Wetlands' hosted by the West Eugene Wetlands Education in Oregon; the Valley Nature Centre's 6thAnnual Dragonfly Days, in Weslaco, Texas; and annual *Odonata* counts (e.g., the Great Lakes Odonata Meeting).

La Maison des Insectes in France
Source: authors' own

Many parks worldwide feature dragonfly trails and interpretation strategies to increase awareness of these animals (Lemelin, 20078; Niba & Samways 2006). The most notable tourism dragonfly attractions are possibly the Dragonfly Centre that can be found at Wicken Fen in Cambridgeshire, England, the dragonfly awareness trails at the National Botanical Gardens in Pietermarizburdg, South Africa (Suh & Samways, 2001), and the Taomi Ecological Village in Taiwan. In the latter instance, a devastating earthquake in 1999 prompted the community and other stakeholders to develop an ecotourism strategy based upon the unique cultural and natural heritage (i.e., dragonflies, frogs, birds) of the area (Lemelin, 2008).

In contemporary Japan, dragonfly enthusiasts, much like birders elsewhere, pride themselves on recognizing many different types of Odonata. In fact, symposiums and festivals such as the *Dragonfly Citizen Summit*, and numerous sanctuaries including the Honmoku Citizens Park (Yokohama), the Dragonfly Kingdom at Nakamura (the world's first dragonfly nature preserve and museum), and the Conservation Area at Okegaya-numa, provide dragonfly enthusiasts with the opportunity to practice and perfect their skills (Kadoya *et al.,* 2004; Primack *et al.,* 2000). There are now 500 to 1000 artificial ponds for dragonflies in Japan (Kawahara, 2007).

Butterflies

As the painting of '*la chasse aux papillon*' by Manet depicts, viewing and collecting butterflies is a well established leisure activity, practiced by numerous cultures across the world (Russell, 2003). These activities are still practiced today and continue to be the biggest attraction in insect-related leisure and tourism activities (Samways, 2005). In fact many tourists now wish to see butterflies in the wild and increased leisure and wealth in the 'affluent world' may engender tropical butterfly-watching safaris in addition to the more widespread bird-watching and 'wildlife' vacations which have proliferated in recent years (New, 1997, p. 207).

Butterfly tourism opportunities offered in Costa Rica and in Taiwan attract nearly 500,000 butterfly tourists per year (Samways, 2005), while the Sierra Madre Biosphere Reserve in Mexico, home of the monarch butterfly (*Danaus plexippus*) aggregations, is visited by 250,000 people per season (Barkin, 2003). A more specific example of a micro-fauna being used as flagship species for tourism strategies includes the rare and threatened Karkloof blue (*Orachrysops ariadne*) found in southern Africa. A reserve, complete with a Karkloof blue logo, was created especially for this particular flagship species (Samways, 2005).

Butterflies feeding
Source: Lemelin 2010

Elsewhere, butterfly festivals such as the 9th Annual Texas Butterfly Festival of Mission, Texas and the El Cieolo Butterfly Festival in Cd. Mante, Tamaulipas, Mexico, attest to the popularity of these animals in recreation and tourism activities (Lemelin, 2009). There are over 100 butterfly exhibits in operation worldwide (Berenbaum 1995):, some like the butterfly exhibit at the Oakland Mall, USA, the butterfly garden at the Changi Airport in Signapore, the Penang Butterfly Farm (the world's '1st tropical live butterfly and insect sanctuary), the Butterfly Park and Insect Kingdom Museum in Sentosa, Signapore, the Museum of World Insects and Natural Wonders in Chiang Mai, Thailand, and the insect exhibition featuring a butterfly garden and farm and insectaruim in Phuket, Tailand, are multi-purpose facilities showcasing butterflies and other insects. Most of these exhibits consist of 100-1,000 m2 greenhouses, with hundreds or even thousands of butterflies flying freely amongst tropical plants and flowers (Brewster & Otis, 2009).

According to Parsons (2002) and Slone et al. (1997), the worldwide retail sales of butterflies may be as high as 100 million USD per annum, with some species like a pair of birdwing butterflies selling in Germany for 3,00 USD (Small, 2007). In order to contain the growth in collecting, butterfly exhibits, and more recently butterfly releases, several butterfly farms or insect ranches have been established to cater to these demands throughout the world. Butterfly farming is often promoted since it 'requires little investment, uses simple equipment and materials that are usually locally available [...] and the basic skills are easily learned' (Gordon, 2003, p. 85). While butterfly farming is now truly an international phenemon with sites in the USA, Central America, African and Asia, we shall discuss some of the early pioneers in butterfly farming below.

Butterfly farming has been practiced in Costa Rica since the early 1980s, and exports from this industry are estimated at around $1 million worth of live butterflies a year (Gordon, 2003). Butterfly ranching was established in Papua New Guinea in the mid-nineties, and since then over 4,691 ranchers located in 100 villages have sold insects to the Insect Farming and Trading Agency (IFTA). The Kipepeo Project is a community-based butterfly farming project next to the Arabuko-Sokoke Forest on the north coast of Kenya. According to Gordon (2003), there were 700 butterfly farmers in 2002 with earnings exceeding $130,000. The project has been financially self-sustainable since 1999 and future developments strategies aimed at capturing other tourists are examining the development of a tourist butterfly exhibit in Mombasa (Gordon, 2003).

Table 13.2 Butterfly ranching – the benefits

Direct use value of butterfly farming	
Salaries	Legal uses-royalties paid
Tourism and recreation	Entry fee, books, souvenirs, specimens
Collector sales	Export sales
Collectors	Export sales
Education	Healing

One of the most remarkable initiatives involving butterflies from a non-tourism perspective, yet deserving of mention here, is the butterfly gardens in Sri Lanka. Chase (2000) describes how butterfly gardens have also been incorporated in healing and reconciliation strategies for war-affected children and communities in Batticaloa, Sri Lanka. The program, which began in 1994, offers children various opportunities to interact and learn about butterflies through play and art activities (claywork, drama, storytelling, music arts and crafts).

Despite requiring foreign support, butterfly ranching has been described as a 'near perfect model of sustainable development initiative for local people' (Small, 2007, p. 387). In Papua New Guinea alone 'butterfly ranchers make as much as 60 times that nation's per capita income' (Small, 2007, p. 387). Examples like Kipepeo and Costa Rica, albeit on small scale, have demonstrated that 'integrating conservation and development can be a practical and effective strategy for natural resource management' (Gordon, 2003, p 85).

Pollinators

While some apiaries like the Galil Apiary in Israel have visitor centres, one of the most unique approaches to involving bees and tourism has been the Fairmont Hotels and Resorts' strategy. Since 2008 six of the Fairmont Hotels and Resorts, including the The Fairmont Algonquin in St. Andrews by-the-Sea, New Brunswick, the Fairmont Le Chateau Frontenac in Quebec, the Royal York in Toronto, the Fairmont Waterfront in Vancouver, the Fairmont Washington D.C., and the Fairmont Mount Kenya Safari Club, have established bee hives on their rooftops and in the onsite gardens of these properties. The hives are featured in lecture tours (over 3,000, 00 visited the Honeymoon Suite at the Royal York alone last year), while the honey is sold, and featured in speciality dishes, tea, and cocktails (Fairmont Hotels & Resorst, 2010). Recent attempts at increasing the visibility of pollinators (i.e., bees, butterflies) include the construction of pollinator parks in urban or semi-urban areas across North America (i.e., Guelph and Ottawa Ontario, Vancouver, B.C.; Milwaukee, Wisconsin; Berkeley, California) (Simaika and Samways, 2009; Spears, 2008).

As these examples above suggest, large, conspicuous, colourful, diurnal, and aerial insects such as beetles, dragonflies butterflies, and bees are excellent subjects for nature interpretation programmes and public education (Cannings, 2001). In fact, 'what butterflies do as flagships for the terrestrial environment dragonflies can do for the aquatic environment' (Moore, 1997, 5). By focusing on the more 'appealing' features of insects (aesthetics, colours, flight abilities, and mystery) we may be able to translate these findings into practical tools that will enhance our recognition of the interpretation and awareness that are essential cornerstones of conservation strategies.

Discussion and Recommendation

Featuring insects in tourism and interpretation strategies, whether it be through direct or indirect strategies, will require much more than the proverbial 'thinking outside the box', for such strategies are in some cases so unique, or so unconventional, that they might be best inspired from the swarm intelligence provided by such superorganisms as ant and bee colonies (Moffett, 2010). Events like the Dragonfly and Butterfly Symposiums in Thunder Bay Canada, the Pestival in London, England, or the Insect Fear Festival in Illinois, have demonstrated that 'unconventional' approaches to learning and educational approaches using insects, when properly developed and marketed, do generate interest and revenues. In England alone, 30 of these butterfly houses generated nearly five million pounds in the late 1980s (Berenbaum, 1995). As Table 13.3 below illustrates, tourism with its diversifying and specializing clientele, provides numerous opportunities to expand and cater for these groups.

On-site insect tourism featuring apiaries includes the Springmead B&B and Organic Farm in Ontario, Canada, Beatty's Miller Canyon Apiary & Orchard in the USA, and the Fairmont Hotelsand Resorts in Canada, the USA, and Kenya. Other examples of on-site strategies include the dragonfly ponds of the Hobo's Pond B&B in British Columbia, B.C., and the butterfly gardens of La Luna Azul and Montezuma Garden B&Bs in Costa Rica, as well as the Butterfly Fields and Antons on the Lake Country Inn and Marina of the eastern continental USA. While these developments were not specifically geared towards increasing the blossoms and butterfly and/or waterfalls and dragonflies clientele, the success of these initiatives nevertheless indicates that there is an interest in such ventures. No examples could be found of accommodation providing traveling exhibits, story-telling or crafts, but we did note that local honey produced in some of the establishments above was used for culinary purposes and could also be purchased. Other examples of popular items produced by insects are 'Bert's Bees' products and other arts and crafts. Many of these are sold worldwide.

A number of the off-site examples provided above required significant investment, can be quite competitive, and can also depend on a high number of visitations (both local and non): that said, establishments can benefit from these offerings by networking with these off-side providers, whether they are protected areas agencies, festivals, insect, exhibits, or zoos and museums, through various promotion means such as websites and links, pamphlets, video displays, staff training, souvenirs, and guides. As the co-author suggested, discussing how some

Table 13.3 On- and off-site insect tourism

On-site	Off-site
Traveling animal exhibits	Protected areas
Pollinator parks	Zoos
Dragonfly ponds	Museums
Butterfly garden	Butterfly conservatories
Terrarium	Butterfly farms
Story-telling	Self-guided walks
Crafts	Insectariums
Souvenir purchases	Symposiums & festivals

golf courses are now certified through Audubon International (see Audubon International at http://acspgolf.auduboninternational.org/ for further information), this is one ideal example where providing off-site information on new environmental approaches to leisure activities and sports can hopefully better inform visitors and perhaps transform their behaviours when they go home. The benefit of off-site activities is they require little investment while also promoting local or regional approaches to leisure and tourism strategies (i.e., the establishment can be linked to the insect tourism's website). However for some establishments located in rural and/or remote settings, such partnerships may not always be possible.

From small, specimen specific symposiums (Great Lakes Odonata Meeting) to large, multiple-events like the Hampyeong Butterfly Festival and Dragonfly Citizen Summit in Japan, examples of festivals celebrating insects worldwide do exist, and while these events are worthwhile considerations, it is important to note that they require a tremendous amount of planning, coordination, and collaboration. Sponsorship is a likely consideration as is becoming the host location for an event (providing room and board).

Recommendations for the CREE VILLAGE ECOLODGE

Coming back to our discussion, we now provide a number of low-cost venture opportunities that could be provided through insect tourism opportunities at the Cree Village Ecolodge. Considering that very little is currently known about insects in Northern Canada, the best way to increase the understanding of these animals is through research partnerships. An upcoming study by an entomological research team this summer (see the Northern Biodiversity Program http://insectecology.mcgill.ca/NBP/index.html) will provide a baseline study for the kinds of insects that are currently found in the area. The CVE is planning to partner with the research team to foster this partnership. The findings and potential outreach from this study in the community may provide inter-disciplinary approaches to entomology and cultural entomology in Northern Canada and perhaps very well result in the integration of insects in the school curriculum and

Table 13.4 Insect tourism strategies and capital investments

Capital	Strategy
Low	Story-telling & legends
	Crafts
	Information sessions
	Souvenirs
Mid	Exhibits
	Terrariums
High	Landscape modifications
	Learning vacations
	Apiaries

learning opportunities for tourists visiting the CVE. How the information acquired from this project can be best incorporated in the short term in learning opportunities for tourists is perhaps via tours (self and guided) around the island and story-telling at the CVE.

The information sheets, guidebooks, or guides could provide visitors with information highlighting specific insect species with their natural and cultural descriptions. The *Big Boreal Adventure*, a recent initiative celebrating natural and cultural heritage sites around Thunder Bay, Ontario, Canada, provides an ideal example of how insects can be incorporated into ecological learning opportunities (see the Big Boreal Adventure). In the longer term, local interpreters could be trained and hired to expand upon the information provided in the guidebook while also discussing how new species are also being found in the region. In the future, the possibility of establishing a butterfly garden or pollinator park will also be considered.

For isolated establishments like the Cree Village Ecolodge partnerships with off-site events, whether they be insect exhibits (the nearest butterfly conservatory in Cambridge Ontario), zoos (The Toronto Zoo) or festivals (Carden Nature Festivals), all of which are over 1,000km away, promoting or networking with off-site insect establishments is very limited. What can be done is providing information to visitors through the website, videos and books.

Conclusion

Enhanced public recognition of insects is an essential ingredient in the creation of an effective and meaningful insect conservation strategy (Kellert, 1993), and examples of such strategies already exist in protected areas in Canada and the USA including various interpretation programs in protected areas (e.g., the Bruce Peninsula and Point Pelee National Parks in Canada; the Rondeau and Sleeping Giant Provincial Parks in Ontario); experiential approaches promoted by such organizations as the Xerces Society and Invertebrate Conservation Trust (also known as Buglife), and insect exhibits, symposiums, and festivals (i.e., the Pestival, the Insect project) (Lemelin, 2009). As Samways (2009) explains, by providing unique opportunities to engage and interact with these animals, these experiences and events are raising public, professional, and conservationists' awareness of the diversity of insects, as well as their functions and conservation needs.

References

Baldwin, R.W., Koehler, P.G., Pereira, R.M., and Oi, F.M. (2008). Public perceptions of pest problems. *American Entomologist, 54(2)*: 73–79.

Brewster, A.L.E., & Otis, G. (2009). A protocol for evaluating cost-effectiveness of butterflies in live exhibits. *Journal of Economic Entomology, 102(1)*, 105–114.

Chase, R. (2000). *The Butterfly Garden, Batticaloa, Sri Lanka: Final report of a program development and research project (1998-2000).* Sarvodaya Vishva Lehka Printers, Ratmalana, Sri Lanka.

Corley, T. (2002). *Let's Go Buggy! The ultimate family guide to insect zoos and butterfly houses*. Corley Publications, Los Angeles, CA.

Cormier, C.M., Forbres, T.A., Jones, R.D., Moririson, R.D., & McCorquodale, D.B. (2000). Alien Invasion: The Status of Non-Native Lady Beetles (Coleoptera: Coccinellidae) in Industrial Cape Breton. *Nova Scotia, 7(3)*, 241–249.

Goka, K., Kojima, H., & Okabe, K. (2004). Biological invasion caused by commercialization of stag beetles in Japan. *Global Environmental Research, 8(1)*, 67–74.

Gordon, I. (2003). Harnessing butterfly biodiversity for improving livelihoods and forest conservation: the Kipepeo project. *Journal of Environment & Development, 12(1)*, 82–98.

Kawahara, A.Y. 2007. Thirty-foot telescopic nets, bug-collecting videogames, and beetle pets: entomology in modern Japan. *American Entomologist,53(3)*, 160–172.

Kerley, G. I. H., Geach, B. G. S., and Vial, C. 2003. Jumbo or bust: do tourists' perceptions lead to an under-appreciation of biodiversity? *South African Journal of Wildlife Research, 33(1)*, 13–21.

Kiely, T., Donaldson, D., & Grube, A. (2004). Pesticides Industry Sales and Usage 2000 and 2001 Market Estimates. Biological and Economic Analysis Division Office of Pesticide Programs Office of Prevention, Pesticides, and Toxic Substances U.S. Environmental Protection Agency Washington, DC 20460. On-line report available at http://www.epa.gov/oppbead1/pestsales/01pestsales/market_estimates2001.pdf. Retrieved, May 17, 2010.

Knell, K.L., & Simmon, L.W. (2010). Mating tactics determine patterns of condition dependence in a dimorphic horned beetle. Proc. R. Soc. B, published online before print March 24, 2010, doi:10.1098/rspb.2010.0257

Meher-Rochow, V.B. (2009). Insect and their uses in a cold country: Finland. *Entomological Research, 38*, S28–S37.

Morris, B. (1998). *The Power of Animals*. Oxford: Berg.

Myriithi, S., and Kenyon, W. (2002). Conservation of biodiversity in the Arabuko Sokoke Forest, Kenya. *Biodiversity and Conservation, 11*, 1437–1450.

New, T.R. (2005). 'Inordinate fondness': a threat to beetles in south east Asia? *Journal of Insect Conservation, 9*, 147–150.

Small, R.D.S. (2007) Becoming unsustainable? Recent trends in the formal sector of insect trading in Papua New Guinea. *Oryx, 41(3)*, 386–389.

Additional information: additional links and additional readings

Books:

- Berenbaum, M.R. (1995). *Bugs in the System*. New York: Helix Books.
- Halter, R. (2010). *The Incomparable Honeybee & the Economics of Pollination*. Surrey, B.C.: Rocky Mountain Books.
- Kritsky, G., & Cherry, R. (2000). *Insect Mythology*. San Jose: Writers Club Press:
- Laufer, P. (2009). *The Dangerous World of Butterflies*. Guilford, CN: The Lyons Press.
- Moffett, M.W. (2010). *Adventures among Ants*. Berkeley: University of California Press.
- Raffles, H. (2010). *Insect-opedia*. New York: Pantheon Books.

Websites:

- Big Boreal Adventure:
- The Northern Biodiversity Program: www.northernbiodiversity.com
- Pestival: http://pestival.org/
- Project Insect: http://www.projectinsect.com

14 Sustainable tourism development in the Masai Mara National Reserve Kenya

Stakeholder perspectives

*Joseph Onchwati** and Hazel Sommerville***

Introduction

Kenya

Kenya is bordered by the Indian Ocean, Somalia, Ethiopia, Sudan, Uganda and Tanzania. According to the *World Factbook* (2010), it is the forty-eighth largest country in the world in terms of its land mass (approximately 580,000 square kilometres) and the thirty-fourth most populous country, with a population of approximately 39 million people. According to the United Nations Human Development Index, Kenya ranks one hundred and forty-seventh (EconomyWatch, 2010).

Although Kenya straddles the equator, it has considerable topographical diversity, ranging from low-lying, fertile coastal regions fringed with coral reefs and islands, through a dry coastal plain, to a high mountainous plateau bisected from north to south by the Great Rift Valley.

Most of the population and the majority of economic activities are concentrated in the plateau area. Unemployment runs at 40% and almost 50% of people live below the poverty line (EconomyWatch, 2010). Approximately 75% of the labour force works in agriculture (tea, coffee, corn, wheat, sugarcane, fruit, vegetables, dairy products, beef, pork, poultry, eggs). The remaining 25% work in industry (the production of small-scale consumer goods, oil refining, aluminum, steel, lead, cement, commercial ship repair) and the service sector (primarily tourism). However, an over reliance on agricultural production and an increasing reliance on tourism make Kenya's economy vulnerable to international market highs and lows. In addition, the country suffers from a high population

*Top Chefs Culinary Institute Kenya
**Hotel and Tourism Management Institute Switzerland

growth rate and widespread corruption, which further hampers its development and holds back its economic growth.

Kenya's GDP has varied widely since it gained independence in 1963. Initially, the country achieved high economic growth (6%) but over the following few decades its GDP plummeted. When it sank to 0.2%, in 2000, the International Monetary Fund and the World Bank intervened and offered loans to prevent a severe economic crisis (EconomyWatch, 2010). Inflation remains a serious concern. It has remained above 9% since 2004, and reached a staggering 26.3% in 2009. Political instability, corruption and budget deficits lie at the root of Kenya's economic problems.

Declining fortunes in agriculture, mining and manufacturing have led many developing countries to look to other sources of revenue with tourism being widely seen as one potential avenue for development. Kenya provides a good example of an African country which has embraced tourism as an important tool for socio-economic development (Akama, undated). Tourism is viewed as a rapid and reliable source of foreign exchange, job creation and economic growth. In the longer term it is generally anticipated that tourism development will contribute to economic diversification and therefore reduce the excessive over-reliance on conventional occupations and exports. Indeed, in Kenya, since 1990 tourism has generated more foreign exchange per year than the traditional exports of coffee and tea combined (CBS, 2007).

The tourism industry in Kenya

Kenya is one of the most popular tourism destinations in Africa. Its emphasis has been on the development of wildlife tourism. Kenya rates as one of the top five bird-watching destinations in the world, is home to many unique species, and offers protection to a number of endangered species. Its annual wildebeest migration is claimed to be one of the world's most amazing natural sights. However the development of wildlife tourism has been erratic, and at times, uncontrolled.

Since independence in 1963, tourism development in Kenya has been made the responsibility of a number of different government departments including the Ministry of Tourism and Wildlife, the Ministry of Wildlife and Natural Resources, the Ministry of Trade, Tourism and Industry and, currently, the Ministry of Tourism (Karethithi, 2003). This constant ministerial restructuring has in itself hampered tourism development. There are presently 31 Ministries in the Kenyan Government, eight of which, including the Ministry of Agriculture, the Ministry of Forestry and Wildlife and the Ministry of Lands and Livestock Development, could arguably be linked to tourism development.

This *laissez-faire* policy approach has led to the growth of tourism facilities with little consideration of the long-term social, economic and environmental impacts. Consequently, rapid, unplanned and haphazard development has resulted in resource degradation, a reduction in the quality of the tourism product and an inequitable distribution of tourism revenue among different stakeholder groups.

The perceived benefits of tourism development are based on two assumptions. First, that the consumption of tourism products occurs at the place of production (the destination), and second, that via links and associations with other industries (including transport, construction and souvenir production) together with increased and enhanced labour market opportunities, there will be the benefits of multiplier effects on the local, regional and national economies.

However, tourism is not benign (Walpole *et al.*, 2003). An evaluation of tourism development in many developing countries indicates that there are extremely high leakage rates from tourism revenues to external sources such as foreign owned tour operators and airlines; and further leakages due to the import of commodities for tourists and the tourism industry (Sinclair, 1990, 1998). Consequently, only a small proportion of the overall tourism revenue reaches local communities. Further, in general those locals who are employed in the tourism industry have low-level jobs and low incomes.

Thus local people see few of the positive benefits of tourism development, yet bear most of the negative social and environmental impacts. This is true in Kenya with regard to the development both of its wildlife resources in its game reserves and its beach resorts along the Indian Ocean coast.

The Masai Mara National Reserve

The Masai Mara National Reserve, widely considered to be Africa's greatest wildlife reserve, comprises approximately 1500 square kilometres of open plains, woodlands and forest alongside the Mara River in South Western Kenya. It is home to an amazing array of wildlife, some of which are unique, and many of which including the African elephant and the black rhino are endangered species. Each year the Masai Mara plays host to the Great Wildebeest Migration from the Serengeti.

South western Kenya is also home to the Masai tribespeople. Historically the Masai are a strongly independent people who hold onto and value tradition and ritual as an integral part of their daily lives. They regard themselves as an essential part of the life of the land just as the land is an essential part of their lives.

The Masai Mara people have traditionally lived off the land alongside and in harmony with the wildlife that are both a source of livelihood and an integral part of their cultural beliefs (Walpole *et al.*, 2003). The development of tourism has, of course, impacted not only on the wildlife but also on the people of the Masai Mara. The loss of grazing pastures, the dedication of large areas to safari businesses and the building of hotels and lodges throughout the Reserve have all served to undermine the livestock economy and pastoral lifestyle of thesei people. Such developments must therefore be held in check to ensure that tourism is sustainable in this beautiful and unique part of Africa.

Sustainable development

Sustainable development is a much-used phrase in international circles, but it is a concept that has no clear definition, nor a clear time-frame in terms of what constitutes a sustainable period. In broad terms, sustainable development presents an attempt to combine growing concerns about a range of environmental issues with associated socio-economic issues. Sustainable development therefore has the potential to address fundamental challenges for humanity, both now and in the future (Hopwood *et al.*, 2005).

In 1987, the report of the Brundtland Commission offered the definition of sustainable development as *'development that meets the needs of the present without compromising the ability of future generations to meet their own needs'* (Brundtland, 1987a: 3). This definition can be directly applied to the situation in the Masai Mara where current economic, social, environmental and cultural factors are closely dependent on one another and will remain so even if the needs of its various stakeholders change. Thus, sustainable development requires achieving a balance between current stakeholder needs, while at the same time anticipating the needs of future stakeholders, otherwise resources may be irretrievably depleted.

When Bundtland presented her Report to the United Nations Environmental Programme Governing Council in Kenya, two key messages were emphasized. First *'the present pattern of development cannot continue and must be changed'* (Bruntland, 1987b: 2) and second, *'change is not only necessary, it is also possible'* (1987b:3). In other words, action is needed but it is not yet too late to take action.

From a disaster management perspective, Tol *et al.* (1996) argue that sustainable development policies must be implemented and evaluated with respect to economic viability, environmental sustainability, public acceptability and behavioural flexibility, thus emphasizing the importance of all stakeholder views in policy decisions and implementations.

The key issue in balancing stakeholder needs lies in managing the inevitable tensions between these and addressing issues before irreparable damage is done. Tensions between stakeholders may be economic, social, environmental or cultural and could arise between different stakeholders or between different individuals within stakeholder groups. Some stakeholders may think sustainability is not an issue, others may think it is one particular stakeholder's function to ensure sustainability, while yet others may even think sustainability is impossible to achieve. Thus while the stakeholders may be segmented by groups, they may also be segmented internally by attitudes and beliefs (Slater, 1990).

The challenge now being faced by the Masai Mara is how to create a sustainable situation that protects the interests of the tourists, the wildlife, the Masai people and the natural environment while also continuing to provide the revenue stream which is so essential to the country's economy.

The Research Undertaken

Introduction

A stakeholder approach (Freeman, 2010) was adopted to the research which was designed to explore the issues facing the Masai Mara Game Reserve. An extended period of observation was combined with a series of one-to-one interviews carried out with ten individuals chosen to represent the key stakeholder groups:

(1) the wildlife;
(2) the Masai Mara people;
(3) the tourism operators; and
(4) the Kenyan Government.

It could be argued that the wildlife of the Masai Mara constitute the major stakeholder group. It has long been acknowledged that *'wildlife is a peculiarly fragile resource, too much human handling and it can be gone forever'* (Mackillop, 1973: 3).

(1) *The wildlife*: in the present research, this fragile resource was represented by local and international wildlife and environment conservationists including a senior officer fromthe Kenya Wildlife Service; a senior warden from the Masai Mara National Reserve; and a regional representative from the Ecotourism Society of Kenya.
(2) *The Masai Mara people*: these were represented by members of the local Masai group ranches and people living within the surroundings of the Masai Mara Reserve. The interviewees included a Masai administrative officer for the Mara Conservancy who was also a member of the local community; a Masai village elder; and a community officer. The village elder was present at all interviews involving Masai people to ensure cooperation and to act as an interpreter where needed.
(3) *The representatives of local tourism operators*: these included the owner of a lodge in the Reserve who also runs a safari company; and the owner of a local tourism company.
(4) *The Kenyan Government representatives:* these included an executive officer within the Ministry of the Environment and National Resources.

Stakeholders were asked for their views on three main issues. First, what they perceived to be their needs and wants from tourism in the Masai Mara. Second, whether or not they believed these needs and wants were currently being met, and if not, why not. And third, each stakeholder was asked for suggestions and ideas for improving things in the Masai Mara, both in the short- and the long-term. The questions did not explicitly address the issue of sustainability, however when interviewees introduced this term in their discussions, the topic was examined.

The information gathered in the interviews was supplemented by an extensive period of observation in the Reserve both prior to conducting the interviews and subsequently on field tours with some of the interviewees.

Findings

There was a consensus among stakeholders that the future of the Masai Mara and its wildlife was under threat and that urgent action was required to address issues surrounding their preservation. The threats were perceived to stem from a wide variety of sources including historical approaches to land ownership; recent government decisions on the sub-division of land traditionally used by the Masai people for cattle grazing; deforestation to make way for an ever-expanding human population; the encroachment of people into areas previously given over to animals; the pollution and waste generated from human activity; and the potentially *'disastrous surge in tourism'*.

Issues arising from changing land usage across the Masai Mara Reserve and, indeed, the creation of the Reserve itself, were recurrent themes leading to dissatisfaction among stakeholders.

In order to designate land for wildlife and enable the development of tourism, the government had taken action by subdividing the land where *'Masais have grazed their cattle for generations'* and implementing a policy that:

> [The Government] would then hand out the individual plot to every registered adult Masai tribesman, and the rest would then be sold on to developers. By making this move, their motive was to protect wildlife, prevent mass tourism and generate a fair income for the Masai communities who own the land.

In effect, the desired outcomes were not fully achieved. Two consequences were significant. First, in order to be viable, many Masai joined their individual pieces of land into communal ranches, however:

> Setting aside several pieces of land to form group ranches which were to be communally owned by a group of people caused a situation whereby it led to the restriction of livestock movement within their group ranches as well as non-members being forbidden to bring in and graze their animals. Since there was essentially no planning to be preceded over the Masai land designation into group ranches or individual parcels, many of these ranches were left vulnerable to being co-opted by a few powerful Masai, who were then able to channel all infrastructure development funds to their personal benefit just because many of these group ranches forced together incompatible family groupings.

Second, without sufficient controls being put in place after the land was subdivided, there was a danger of further exploitation, as explained by one stakeholder:

> I can see a picture of several greedy investors eyeing closely to buying up these plots directly from the Masai tribesmen and come up with new hotels and other new infrastructural developments thus affecting the ecosystem inside the reserve.

For centuries, the Masai Mara people have lived in harmony with wildlife and nature. It is only relatively recently that they have been asked to *'share this space'* with tourists. New relationships must therefore be formed. These relationships must respect the Masai traditions and culture and result in them being an integral part of the overall situation. Stakeholder views reflected both the positive and negative impacts of tourism on the local people. Among the positive benefits at the micro level were opportunities for employment in the tourism industry; for learning foreign languages to facilitate interactions with tourists; and for preserving traditional music, dance and handicrafts by performing for and selling to tourists. It was also suggested that tourism activities had helped raise the level of environmental awareness among the communities living near the Reserve. At the macro level, the benefits included improved transport; improved health care; the building and staffing of schools and hospitals for local people; and improved security patrols.

However, while the positive benefits accrued, the development of tourism has also had negative impacts, most notably resulting in a fundamental change in the way of life of the Masai people:

> Tourism has caused an undesirable impact on the Masai through them losing massive lands for the sake of creating considerable space and investment of the parks and reserves ... also [they] have had to exchange their lifestyle from pastoralism to subsistence and commercial farming.

This change has had considerable financial implications for how the Masai can now earn a living, how they are compensated for the loss of previous sources of income, and how they can share in the new sources of wealth. Without exception, stakeholders agreed that the distribution of tourism revenues is neither equal nor perceived to be equal and that the government is guilty of a number of *'policy failures'* in this regard. Policies have not been implemented, in particular the policy that states that 19% of the revenue from tourism will be reinvested in the local community:

> There has been inconsistency when it comes to payments to the Masais and at times they ceased altogether from making the payments. If at all the local government really functioned, the best they could do is give money or services to the Masai who lost land to the reserves and parks.

In addition to the lack of even a minimal reinvestment, there is a lack of transparency accounting for the park revenue. This has led to resentment, suspicion and speculation:

> All I know and can tell is that most of this money goes directly to the private business sectors such as the tour operators, luxury lodges, transporters and the rest goes straight to the central government treasuries. This is a sensitive issue ... and there remains to be some inconsistencies and irregularities on how the money circulates and its distribution ... because there is no accounting transparency which leads to the money set aside purposely for development projects that concern the rural Masai being funnelled to projects benefiting especially the politically powerful class. Indeed there is a massive imbalance in tourism incomes in favour of a certain small elite.

It was felt that if the Masai did receive their fair share of the tourism income, this would not only help them financially but couldalso have other spin-off benefits as suggested by one stakeholder:

> By helping out these pastoralists in having a direct share of the hundreds of millions of dollars from tourism-related revenues, they will come to find that wildlife is more valuable than crops or cattle, and they will eventually start protecting the wildlife themselves.

Stakeholders agreed that the fundamental problem facing the Masai people is that they have lost much of their traditional grazing land without adequate compensation and that they are victims of circumstances over which they had no control. The resentment was deeply felt, as is evident in this comment from the Masai elder interviewed:

> We did not fault in any way for us to be robbed of our land.

The Masai people feel strongly that they are not receiving their due revenue and they do not perceive that they derive any benefit from the development of the tourism industry. Two issues were raised in this context. First, as mentioned above, the benefits from tourism revenue are perceived to be diverted internally into the hands of *'a small elite'* and diverted externally to the international *'tourism cartels'* which have rapidly moved into Kenya. In other words:

> You will also note that many of these investors are foreigners and that means whatever profits they plough won't get back to the local economy.

Further, the promised job opportunities for local people have failed to materialize:

> When it comes to employment opportunities, you will find out that most of the employees are of a better-education background and also come from other parts of the country or other countries.

Such leakage of income is a further source of resentment as locals feel that they have not had the chance to move into the new labour markets created and take advantage of the new kinds of employment which would enable them to compensate for their loss of traditional sources of income. In order for tourism to become sustainable, it is important to take account of these *'longstanding inequalities'* and ensure that the benefits of tourism are shared. The need for *'community involvement'* was seen as critical. There was a consensus that the way forward is for stakeholders to work together for the mutual benefit of the environment, the wildlife and the local community:

> Continuously working closely with the local community through informing and consulting and engaging them with not only financial benefits but also

with local development projects where the local people can help themselves and their families.

There was much sympathy for the plight of the Masai Mara people whose traditional ways of life have been dramatically changed without prior consultation and agreement that the time had come to ensure that their views were taken into account:

> I suggest that they should also be consulted on tourism development, and rather than being ignored, they must be made to feel that they are partners in decision-making. I think this kind of gesture plays a big role of empowering them.

It was felt that an important consequence of the greater involvement of local people in decision-making would be:

> To enable the communities to benefit from their presence at discussions where they get actual experience and knowledge, which contributes to them having a sense of the importance of their own actions to protect and be responsible.

There was also a consensus among stakeholders about the urgent need for action to be taken to preserve Kenya's unique game reserve. This action should include putting an infrastructure in place to manage the development of tourism; dispersing the tourism revenue in an equitable fashion and in line with government policy; putting procedures in place to manage energy conservation and waste management; and looking beyond the tourist market to ensure the sustainability not only of tourism, but also of the vital asset which is the Masai Mara:

> Despite tourism being the key economic activity in the Mara region, my piece of advice is that let us not rely too much on what tourism benefits us in this area. Otherwise over reliance might lead to the Mara region being susceptible to seasonal, economic fluctuations and also changes in tourist tastes. My thinking is let tourism be one of the several activities in the region that fit in with the traditional activities for example complementing it with agriculture rather than competing with it or causing its decline.

Fundamentally, action is required by all stakeholders and the need for this is both *'urgent'* and *'very important'*. Very real fears were expressed that if there were delays in seeking to protect what the Masai Mara had to offer *'it will be too late for us to save the diminishing wildlife that make up the park'*.

It is important that the Masai people do not develop negative attitudes towards the wildlife and do not target the animals directly in order to make their voices heard. In the past, there have been reported instances of the Masai taking action into their own hands and becoming involved in poaching and the black market in *'unplanned trading centres dealing in the bush meat trade'*. The impact of such activities on the development of tourism could be catastrophic.

Many stakeholders agreed that the rapid rise in tourism and the failure to address issues of sustainability lie at the heart of the problems experienced. In addition to the damage done to the grasslands of the Masai Mara by safari traffic, wildlife is also under threat from the pollution which has followed in the wake of increasing population and tourist numbers:

> I would mention about pollution which is caused by human refuse, both from the local communities and the tourists. There is also the issue of dumping especially plastic bags, leaking camera batteries, glass and metal litter in the bushes or thrown in open pits which not only causes a danger to scavenging of wildlife but also pollutes the environment. Also for example there is the dumping of the sewage material away from the tourist accommodation which is allowed to flow onto neighbouring grazing grounds and Masai settlements areas, or simply throwing the sewage materials from these camp-sites into the river from which wildlife, livestock and local communities draw their drinking water.

Overpopulation and a lack of government control are working against the interests of the conservationists and, in turn, sustainability is threatened. Conservationists view population growth as a *'depressing issue which must be addressed with seriousness and a sense of urgency'*. An expanding human population places pressure on available land which in turn leads to shrinking areas where wildlife can thrive, with the inevitable consequence of declining numbers and threats to entire species.

Further pressure is placed on the land by the construction of lodges and hotels to accommodate tourists and the development of trading centres and markets for the sale of local goods. Ultimately, all arguments return to the theme of balancing stakeholder needs to achieve a conservation of the natural environment, the wildlife and the Masai people, along with the development of the tourist trade. Concerns are also expressed by those involved in the tourism industry about the challenges they face in ensuring that they survive as business enterprises given that they are dependent on the presence of wildlife, natural resources and local communities. One way to help conservation would be to limit tourist numbers. However, the Kenyan government appears to be reluctant to follow this strategy.

Across the world, there is much government rhetoric in favour of sustainable tourism development. However, making this a reality requires governments to build local infrastructure to protect both the economy and, in this instance, the wildlife, and to retain the attractiveness of the tourist destination. The challenge for the Kenyan government is to plan development so as to deliver net benefits to present and future generations and fulfill Agenda 21 (UN, 1992), which expresses the imperative to achieve sustainable tourism and balance stakeholder needs.

From the stakeholder interviews, it was evident that the government was perceived to have failed to play its role effectively to ensure an appropriate balance among the stakeholders in the park. Stakeholders laid most of the blame for the current conflict-ridden situation at the feet of the government and its lack of capacity to govern the reserve with any interdisciplinary cohesion; its lack of reinvestment; its mismanagement of land usage; its reluctance to limit the growth of tourism; and its lack of transparency in dispersing park revenue.

The overall view was that from the government *'there are ineffective controls and concern for sustainability'* and stakeholders were somewhat pessimistic about the future prospects for the wildlife of the Masai Mara:

> [If we] go head to head with baboons, zebra, gazelles and elephants eventually, I bet with you, it's a contest the animals will lose.

Summary of findings

In summary, according to the Brundtland report (1987), sustainable development requires meeting the basic needs of all, to achieve a balance of stakeholders needs for the long term. In the case of the Masai Mara the wildlife need safety, no poaching, and an unspoiled ecological environment; the Masai people need to be satisfied that tourism benefits them and that the revenue due to them is paid; the tourists need an unspoiled harmonious and peaceful atmosphere to relax and enjoy nature and high quality accommodation; tourism operators need a high level and sustainable tourism revenue; and the Kenyan government needs to sustain the revenue from tourism to boost the country's economy. Thus, many stakeholders have a vested interest in maintaining the Masai Mara as an attractive tourist destination.

Discussion

For Kenya's tourism industry to ensure long-term sustainable development, the government has a major role to play in developing an integrated tourism strategy which addresses the social, cultural, economic and environmental challenges that seriously confront the industry. The success of tourism development must not be measured in terms of increased gross tourism revenue statistics which, while important, are only one measure of success.

In addition, how the development of tourism fits with local, regional and national economies and how it delivers benefits to local communities are equally important. The research undertaken has fully illustrated the need for local communities to support tourism development and to explicitly see the individual and collective benefits from doing so; and, on the other hand, the benefits of making use of the wisdom of the indigenous people. They have much to contribute from their long history of living in and making a living from the local environment.

For long-term sustainable tourism development, this involvement by local communities is critical. It must be embedded in policy decisions at the highest level and occur at all stages in the developmental process, from the initial design to its final implementation and beyond to management of the provision put in place. The local Masai Mara tribespeople are central and critical to successful and sustainable development.

Thus, the main objectives of any new tourism strategy should include a procedure for the transparent and equitable distribution of tourism revenues; local participation in decision-making processes; reduced leakage so that more benefits directly accrue to local individuals and communities; increased multipliers so that more employment opportunities arise for local people; and minimization of the negative impacts of tourism development on the natural environment and its wildlife on which they and the industry so critically depend. Without the wildlife there would be no tourism industry in this area.

Conclusion

It is inevitable that the social, economic and cultural impacts of tourism will be both positive and negative in the longer term. In order to minimize the negative impacts of tourism development in the Masai Mara and to enhance its effectiveness in promoting long-term sustainable development, a number of suggestions are put forward here:

- First, tourism activities in the Masai Mara Reserve should be appropriately planned, implemented, monitored and managed to ensure that they do not conflict with conservation of the local populations and indigenous wildlife or overstretch the sustainable use of available resources. One strategy could be to closely monitor the Masai Mara visitor carrying capacity and ensure that the number of tourists is regulated to avoid putting undue pressure on the available facilities through overcrowding and the degradation of the natural environment.
- Second, visitors should be educated on conservation and sustainability issues so that their attitudes and behaviours do not cause physical, psychological or social damage at the local level. Similarly, local people need to be made aware of the importance of these issues for their future.
- Third, environmental impact reports should be required ahead of all new construction. There should also be an integrated approach to infrastructure developments and the construction of new tourist facilities to avoid an overlap of provision and undue pressure on the physical environment. New developments should not conflict with the principles of wildlife conservation and the sustainable use of available resources, hence those involved in construction also need to be educated about conservation and sustainability issues. The sites of tourism facilities must respect Masai history, culture and traditions and also be sensitive to critical wildlife habitats, such as breeding grounds, feeding areas and watering holes.
- Fourth, the government should re-evaluate the role of multinational corporations within Kenya's tourism industry. While the involvement of multinationals has perhaps been beneficial in kick-starting the industry, it is time to reconsider their role. The beneficial outcomes of reducing multinational involvement

could be widespread, including a reduction in the leakage of tourism revenue out of the country; an increase in the multiplier effects of employment by providing jobs for locals in the hospitality and tourism industries and, for example, selling locally made souvenirs and handicrafts rather than imported goods. Such actions would help build a skills base within the Kenyan tourism industry to secure its future and minimize the risks that external factors could intervene and lead to its rapid decline if the multinationals pull out of the country.

- Fifth, policies and institutional mechanisms should be put in place to encourage local participation at all stages in the design, implementation, monitoring and management of the development of tourism. Local people should have an input into the tourism developments which impact on their local communities in order that there is a consensus on the developments which take place, leading to communities taking ownership of what happens to them and their environment.
- Sixth, there must be transparency in determining how the costs and benefits of tourism revenue are dispersed between stakeholders, in particular between the government and local communities.

In essence, such suggestions may ensure that tourism in the Masai Mara National Reserve is sustainable and that all stakeholders learn to '*share this space*'.

References

Akama, J.S. (undated). The efficacy of tourism as a tool for economic development in Kenya, http://unpan1.un.org/intradoc/groups/public/documents/IDEP/UNPAN002584. pdf, [Accessed 11th of September 2010].

Brundtland, G. (1987a). *Our Common Future: The World Commission on Environment and Development.* Oxford: Oxford University Press.

Brundtland, G. (1987b). Presentation of the Report of The World Commission on Environment and Development to UNEP's 14th Governing Council Session, Nairobi, Kenya.http://www.regjeringen.no/upload/SMK/Vedlegg/Taler%20og%20artikler%20 av%20tidligere%20statsministre/Gro%20Harlem%20Brundtland/1987/Presentation_ of_Our_Common_Future_to_UNEP.pdf, [Accessed 27th October 2010].

CBS (Central Bureau of Statistics) (2007). *Crop Product Statistics*, http://www.knbs. or.ke, [Accessed 11th of September 2010].

EconomyWatch (2010). *Kenya Economy*, http://www.economywatch.com/world_economy/kenya/, [Accessed 11th of September 2010].

Freeman, R.E. (2010). *Strategic Management: A Stakeholder Approach.* Cambridge: Cambridge University Press.

Hopwood, B. Mellor, M. and O'Brien, G. (2005). Sustainable development: mapping different approaches, *Sustainable Development, 13(1),* 38–52.

Karethithi, S. (2003). Coping with Declining Tourism, Examples from Communities in Kenya, PPT Working Paper No. 13, Economic and Social Research Unit, UK Department for International Development.

Mackillop, A. (1973) *Talking About the Environment*, London: Wayland.

Sinclair, T. (1990). *Tourism Development in Kenya*, World Bank, Nairobi.

Sinclair, T. (1998). Tourism and economic development: a survey. *Journal of Development Studies*, *34*(5), 1–51.

Slater, F. (1990). Editor. *Societies, Choices and Environments: Issues and Enquiries*, London: Harper Collins.

UN (United Nations), (1992) *Agenda 21*, United Nations Department of Economic and Social Affairs, Division for Sustainable Development, http://www.un.org/esa/sustdev/documents/agenda21/index.htm, [Accessed 11th of September 2010].

Walpole, M. Karanja, G. Sitati, N. and Leader-Williams, N. (2003). Wildlife and people: conflict and conversation in Masai Mara, Kenya, *Wildlife and Development Series Number 14*, London: International Institute for Education and Development.

World Factbook (2010). Africa: Kenya, http://www.cia.gov/library/publications/the-world-factbook/geos/ke.html, [Accessed 9th of September 2010].

15 Ecotourism in vulnerable regions

Opportunities and obstacles to development – The case of Cantanhez, Guiné-Bissau

Fernanda Oliveira[*,**] and
Filipe Silva[*,***]

Ecotourism – Dynamics and Limitations

In the current setting, where there is a need for more sustainable ways to develop tourism, the demand for tourism has been changing, revealing preferences for new destinations (other than the traditional) and new forms of tourism, and expressing a new attitude towards the places already visited. In relation to new destinations, '… tourism has been growing and increasing particularly in biodiversity hotspots …' (Christ *et al.*, 2003: 4).

In fact, the sites essentially characterized by their natural resources, protected areas, forests, islands, mountains, lakes, environmental reserves are increasingly attractive for a tourism experience. The facilities created for these natural areas which stimulate the simple motivation to travel for pleasure incorporate a tourism typology called ecotourism. This is a responsible way to develop leisure activities in natural settings, concerned mainly with environmental conservation (ensuring biological diversity and the maintenance of ecological systems) and the well-being of local people (TIES, 2006).

As highlighted by the Quebec Declaration on Ecotourism (WES, 2002), some forms of tourism, particularly ecotourism, may contribute to the balanced and sustainable use of natural, cultural and human resources of certain sites, mainly by:

- Contributing to the creation of economic benefits within the native communities;
- Guaranteeing the conservation of natural resources and cultural integrity of the communities;
- Encouraging community involvement and their interest in conservation issues;

[*]School of Tourism and Maritime Technology, IPL-Polytechnic Institute of Leiria, Portugal
[**]Research Center for Identity(ies) and Diversity (ies), IPL
[***]Tourism Research Group (GITUR), IPL

• Promoting tourists' awareness regarding the importance of the natural and human inheritance.

Moreover, it is a fact that these sites combine natural wealth with a unique cultural diversity that allows for the promotion and appreciation of all this heritage – legends, history (and stories), traditional activities, *know-how*, crafts, customs and sustainable practices. On the other hand, many times these sites are inhabited by very poor rural populations who have serious problems in terms of health, education, and accessibility (road and communication), as well as other infra-structures that are needed for an adequate development. In these cases, and as a priority, the development of any (eco) tourism activity should begin with efforts to solve these problems.

From the standpoint of the direct involvement of the local communities in providing some tourism services, many limitations may arise. On the one hand, local communities may have difficulty in knowing and understanding the demands of the tourism activity and, on the other hand, there may be restraints in the communication and collaboration between the tourism companies and local communities. To this end, it is necessary to encourage collaboration between the residents, private operators, NGOs and governmental agencies or local authorities which will allow the identification of each of the actors' roles, thus ensuring that the commitments made by each of the involved parties are accomplished and will fundamentally help the process of communication in many cases.

Generally, one of the priorities of community-based ecotourism is to allow the generated flows to contribute to the environmental, economic, and human balance of these sites. Although this is generally small-scale tourism, there are some delicate issues that should be carefully addressed. The challenges are not only based on the possible sensitivity and need to conserve natural resources but also on the socio-economic reality of the local communities. As such, it is fundamental for the different stakeholders - government, NGOs, tour operators and local communities - to make a joint effort.

In the case study presented here we present a brief characterization of the ecotourism infrastructure and services yielded in Cantanhez Forest, in southern Guinea-Bissau, and identify the main positive and negative effects of the emergence of this project for the local communities. Moreover, we focus on the challenges and obstacles that lie ahead in the future development of this tourism product, both in the local context and taking into account the structural constraints concerning the region and the country in general.

Guinea-Bissau – Some Key Aspects of The Country

Guinea-Bissau is located on the western coast of Africa, bordering Senegal in the north, the Republic of Guinea in the south east, and the Atlantic Ocean in the west. Aside from the continental territory, this country also has a group of 40 islands that make up the archipelago of Bijagos (data available in www.republica-da-guine-bissau.org) (see Figure 15.1).

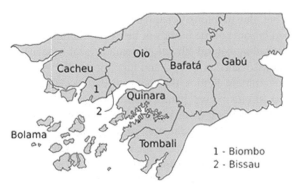

Figure 15.1 Map of Guinea-Bissau, by regions
Source: www.republica-da-guine-bissau.org

It has a population of approximately a million and a half inhabitants spread throughout eight regions (Bolama, Cacheu, Gabu, Bafata, Quinara, Oio, Biombo and Tombali) and Bissau as an independent sector and capital of the country, in a total area of 36 500km2 (see Figure 15.1). The country's climate is tropical with an average temperature of 20 degrees centigrade.

Although rich in natural resources, the country has a high poverty rate, since 75% of the population is rural and is therefore the primary sector of the economy, with a base weight of 50% in the Gross Domestic Product (GDP), 82% in employment, and 93% in exportation (data obtained from www.imvf.org). With this, the GDP *per capita* (GDP) is 477 dollars with an average annual growth rate of 2.61% (UNDP, 2009). The main imports are food, transport equipment and machinery and fuel, at an estimated annual total of 58 million dollars. The main exports are cashew-nuts, shrimp and timber, totalling 23.9 million dollars annually.

It is important to note that the most common social indicators such as the average life expectancy, basic sanitary conditions and access to basic education are significantly below the African continent's average.

From a socio-cultural perspective, Guinea-Bissau is characterized by extensive ethnic diversity, namely the Balanta, Fula, Manjaco, Mandinga, Papel, Felupe, Mancanha, Bijagó, Nalu and Beafada groups. Each of these presents specific cultural particularities that are reflected in their way of being and living, in terms of spatial planning, construction methods and materials used, religious beliefs and rituals, gastronomy, craftwork and all other productive activities with economic value. Regarding communication, there are also differences among the referred ethnic groups. Although the official language of the country is Portuguese, the most spoken language is the Creole from Guinea-Bissau, and in some ethnic groups, their own dialects prevail which is the case with the Balanta, Fula, Mandinga, Manjaco, and Papel.

With regard to the tourism activity in Guinea-Bissau, this is still very limited. The existence of a variety of hotels as well as some occasional tourism accommodation units in natural spaces is highlighted in the capital Bissau. Possibly the ones that stand out, due to international recognition, are the small tourism investments developed in some of the islands of the Bijagós,archipelago resulting from the diversity of existing natural attractions (paradisiacal beaches, calmness, ecotourism activities associated with bird and hippopotamus watching, and fishing). According to government entities, the country has important features for tourism development, its strong points being gastronomy, the landscape, the natural surroundings and the cultural diversity resulting from the great number of different ethnic groups. The tropical climate, with a relatively short period of rain coinciding with winter in Europe, is an important factor for success. These features adapt perfectly to the various tourism typologies such as ecotourism, rural tourism, nature tourism and adventure tourism.

Brito (2007) cites a publication from the World Tourism Organization (UNWTO) and the United Nations Development Programme (UNDP) entitled 'Strategy and Plan of Action for the Development of Tourism in Guinea-Bissau' *(Estratégia e Plano de Acções para o Desenvolvimento do Turismo na Guiné-Bissau)*,where some statistical data are presented referring to the tourism activity in Guinea-Bissau. These data show that between 2001 and 2006 there was an increase in the number of tourists from 7,754 to 12,549, with most of these coming from Portugal, the United Kingdom, France, Italy and Spain, mentioned here in order of importance.

The Ecotourism Project in Cantanhez

Ecotourism in Cantanhez emerges from the implementation of the U'Anan Project – Building the Sustainable Community Development in the region of Tombali: Ecotourism and Citizenship. This project was created by the Guinean NGO Action for Development (AD) and was implemented through a partnership set up with the Instituto Marquês de Valle Flôr (IMVF, a Portuguese NGO), with the support obtained from the Portuguese Institute for Development Support (IPAD) and co-financing from the European Commission. Some time later, the Polytechnic Institute of Leiria (IPL) became another element of cooperation in the area of training in ecotourism and hotel management. The period of development took place between 2005 and the first trimester of 2010.

The main objective of this project is to improve living conditions for the entire population of the region of Tombali through the focus on sustainable human, social, cultural and economic development (IMVF, 2004).

On a socio-cultural level, it is intended to implement measures that promote access to drinkable water which include its management and supply, as well as to improve health conditions, give greater access to education, and encourage sociability and solidarity networks by promoting communication and development channels, thus reinforcing community self-esteem and citizenship. Economically, the production regularity in the primary sector is encouraged as a stimulus for the development of sustainable marketing channels in order to ensure the increase of household incomes (Brito, 2007).

It is still within the economic and environmental field that the Ecotourism Project arises as one of the major points of U'Anan, aiming at greater economic growth and the preservation of forests and the conservation of endangered species in the area of the project implementation. With these objectives, a set of essential measures are in progress:

- Construction of accommodation facilities and support infrastructures such as a restaurant and a bar;
- Creation of a museum near the ruins of the old fort at Guiledje;
- Community awareness of a demanding culture in terms of hygiene and waste treatment and also the harmonization between environmental resources and the prominent needs of the population.

Fundamentally, the aim of this project is to use a number of tools that allow greater communication and 'decrease distances' for the region of Tombali, seeking to create the necessary conditions for a sustainable community development of the population.

This way, the AD defined a number of 'golden rules' to increase the community involvement:

- As many *tabancas* as possible should be involved in the project;
- There should be a big effort to involve all social and age groups;
- The communities are a priority, so measures of implementation should not be imposed but rather exposed for a better understanding and acceptance;
- The preservation and proper management of the natural resources must go hand in hand with the improvement of the real living and working conditions of the communities.

The Ecotourism project in Cantanhez is situated in the region of Tombali which is located in the south of Guinea-Bissau, bordering the North of Guinea Conacri, being approximately 250 kilometres from the country's capital – Bissau. It is an area with approximately 86,850 inhabitants spread over five areas: Bedanda, Catio, Komo, Quebo and Cacine and 13 *tabancas*. The Ecotourism project is developed in Bedanda and Cacine where the Cantanhez forest is situated.

This forest is a very rich area in fauna and flora that have been preserved due to their isolation from the main urban centres. It is composed of 14 big forest areas considered the last primary forests because of their state of preservation and ecosystem maintenance (Brito, 2004). Regarding the fauna, it is a safe haven for different species where you can particularly find chimpanzees, elephants, buffalos and a vast number of different species of birds that are included in the list of endangered species. The diversity of fauna and flora, the cultural values associated to the existing communities in this forest and the initiatives of community development and the preservation and conservation of nature that had been implemented since the end of the Seventies, led to its classification as the National Park of Cantanhez in 2008.

Besides the ecological value, the region of Tombali also has historical value since it was once considered the 'cradle of the Guinean nationality'. In the Sixties and Seventies, the Fort of Guiledjie, one of the main determinant forts in the fight for the national liberation operated in this region. Given the territorial dimension of this fort, its military importance and diversity of infra-structures and military equipment, the museum at Guiledje was inaugurated in January 2010, embodying the historical-cultural tourism that also aims to enhance this region.

The strongly marked ethnicity has a great cultural diversity in the form of music, lifestyles, and social organization in the form of the *tabancas* (the name given to the villages existing inland, in rural or natural spaces). As an integral part of the Guinean culture we also have gastronomy, with recipes that are rich in nutrients and which favour the use of local products.

In the region of Cantanhez, agriculture and the gathering of forest or marine products are the basis of subsistence for the local populations. The extraction of palm products, more specifically the palm oil and the Cibi wine, is important, as well as the rice crop which is cultivated by most households. The rice produced is used solely for consumption by the population and is not commercialized.

In addition, the cultivation of cashew nuts and peanuts is crucial not only because of the agricultural area occupied but also because they are key to house-hold incomes and the country's trade balance. Fishing activity is also common in Cantanhez and although it was initially seen as a means of subsistence, new techniques have been acquired with the presence of foreign fishermen, allowing some fishermen to increase their household income.

The creation of tourism accommodation, nature activities and complementary services has arisen with the objective of promoting income. The first accommo-dation facility was built in the village of Iemberém, followed by Faru Sadjuma, but the third, which was initially planned for the Riparian village of Canamine, ended up not being built. As shown in Table 15.1, the accommodation available in Iemberém and Faru Sadjuma totals 24 beds. There are two types of bungalows: one with two beds and the other with four beds and all of these have private bathrooms, mosquito nets and fans. There is also another type of accommodation in Iemberém resulting from the remodelling of one of the park guard shelters. This house is composed of five bedrooms (also with mosquito nets and fans) and has two common bathrooms.

Table 15.1 Summary of the accommodation in Cantanhez
(number of beds)

	Bungalows	*Park shelters*	*Number of beds*
Iemberém	3	5	18
Faru Sadjuma	3	0	8
Total	6	5	24

Source: authors' own

Figure 15.2 Iemberém bungalows and park shelter view.
       Source: Sílvia Barata

The architecture project, developed by the Portuguese architect Rodrigo Nero, followed local architectural characteristics in terms of shape, structure and dimension, thus contributing to the perfect integration of the bungalows within the group of houses in the village (see Figure 15.2). Although the intial intention was to use traditional construction materials, in reality, imported materials were chosen in order to ensure longer durability and weather resistance and also a better quality of living conditions. Traditionally, the bungalows for housing are built with loam bricks. However, this was an excluded option because it is not a resistant material. In terms of roofing, all the bungalows for ecotourism have the traditional thatched roof held up by a metallic structure or by traditional funnel-shaped structures made of bamboo.

In terms of the interior spatial organization of the bungalow, there was a need to improve this by taking into account the traditional constructions, namely by creating a bathroom with minimal equipment (a shower, toilet, basin, mirror and clothes hook). Generally, the houses in the forest villages do not have these commodities given that people wash themselves by using a washbowl and usually go into the brushwood to relieve themselves.

The construction phase was initially undertaken by a civil construction technician from Bissau and a local group of construction workers. The technician coordinated the construction of the first bungalows in Iemberém and provided the local construction workers with guidelines and training, allowing them to later carry out this task alone (which subsequently happened with the construction of bungalows in Faru Sadjuma). As for carpentry, painting, electricity, plumbing, and the like, these were all done by local workers.

The bungalow clusters have tap water. In the case of Iemberém, water was taken initially from a well that already served the community. However, with the Ecotourism Project this resource was improved and sealed by placing a cover on it. The objective was to avoid debris falling into the water, and to ensure the safety of the well's users, mainly women, children, and young people. Recently, as part of the Ecotourism project, a loan was undertaken to make a water borehole and a water tank with a capacity of ten thousand litres was purchased to ensure the availability of water for both tourism infrastructures and the community. This investment was particularly vital in order to guarantee a water reserve at times of the year when there was more drought.

In relation to Faru Sadjuma water is pumped from a well. It is extracted with a submersive pump that is powered by electricity produced by solar panels. The water is pumped daily, until the tank holding four thousand litres has been filled. In this village, solar panels produce electricity for the necessary equipment (fans, freezers, lighting in the bungalows). In comparison to Iemberém, this is a differentiating factor given that the existing electricity for this village's needs comes from two electric generators that represent an environmentally less-sustainable option (in terms of the noise produced and the fact that these need fuel to work). Usually, when there are tourists visiting there is electricity during the evening period (from 18h/19h to 23h/24h).

The bungalow clusters have a septic tank and a sump well, but the main sewer does not receive any treatment. Also, in terms of solid waste, there is no specific place for its deposit and subsequent treatment. This is obviously one of the areas where action is needed. In terms of culture, rural communities living in the forest have never felt the need to have sanitation. The brushwood has always served this need. To change this reality, some health education initiatives have been developed for the younger population. The aim is to try to teach the students (particularly the younger population) the importance of using latrines and the negative effects of the traditions practiced by older people.

Furthermore, with regard to waste, the communities are in close proximity to the household waste produced. Aside from the adverse effects this has on public health, the tourists' visual impact may affect the image they receive of the destination. In fact, this is one of those issues that, in the case of Cantanhez, can condition the practice of ecotourism. The intention is for each (eco)tourist to get involved in the host community, visit the areas of craft production, and participate in some traditional activities and cultural events. For this this to happen (eco) tourists must not only stay in the bungalows, it is a necessity that they go around the village, interact with those who are working and with the children playing in the streets, watch the football games taking place in the late afternoon, and visit schools, markets, and other points of interest.

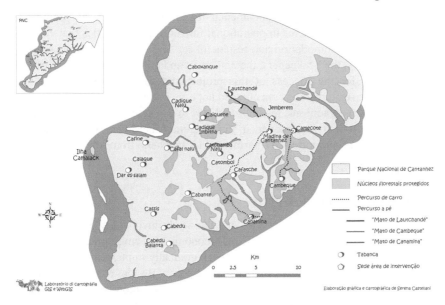

Figure 15.3 Example of itineraries
     Source: Provided by IMVF

Iemberém provides tourists with several walking trails accompanied by a guide, catering services (breakfast, lunch and dinner) and a housekeeping service. All of these are provided and controlled by members of the community. In Faru Sadjuma there is food, beverage and housekeeping services provided by only one family.

There are 14 routes planned and plotted using GPS and maps, developed in conjunction with the guides and the community park guards. The itineraries offer the opportunity to experience the different environments in the park, from the forests to the islands, from the mangroves to the traditional farming fields. These routes can be followed on foot, by canoe or by bike. Four groups of itineraries are planned: in the forest, on the islands, by land and sea, and also visiting the traditional culture.

This ecotourism offering does not have a defined marketing strategy yet. For those who are abroad, the only way to access and book services including accommodation, restaurants and nature walks is through the AD website. At the moment, a project is being carried out which aims to create organized tour packages that will include transport (return flights to Bissau, accommodation and food in Bissau and Cantanhez, AT transport from Bissau to Cantanhez, ecotourism itineraries and a guide-interpreter). The aim is to develop, in coordination with other agents and tour operators, a product that can be competitive, given the vast range of ecotourism offers in other African destinations.

Despite the AD having a fundamental role in coordinating the project the community is the main actor in operational functions and activities that complement tourism, accommodation and restaurant services. For instance, we referred to jam producers, the beekeepers, the craftsman and other actors whose activities are important for the success of this project and for their own subsistence. Therefore this participation is encouraged not only in this sense, but also as a way of showing off the traditions, festivals and, day to day activities, as well as socializing with the tourists. Moreover, in the restaurant the diversity and quality of meals offered is supported by farmers and ranchers from the villages and surrounding areas.

Positive and Negative Aspects

Given the characteristics of the sites and the actors involved, the ecotourism in Cantanhez has been developing its social, economic and environmental dynamics in an integrating way. Key aspects have been gradually implemented to apply the concept of ecotourism using a sustainable perspective. Besides relating the benefits of this project's development, it is still important to mention those points where there are more difficulties and where the results have been zero or even negative.

Thus one of the main positive aspects is related to the fact that, since the beginning, the project has been developed with the support of the various communities and their willingness to participate actively. The direct involvement of some of the indigenous members of the community, by ensuring the provision of all tourism services, is undoubtedly an significant factor. Consequently, this involvement allows an increase in incomes for the community (not only for those who ensure the functioning of the bungalows and restaurants, but also for nature guides, farmers, craftspeople and all others in the villages who produce goods which directly or indirectly complement the tourism product) and creates more jobs.

The fact that the visitor appreciates and values local products has been boosting some traditional activities. The wood carvings and the basketry production, which until recently was very irregular, has now become more dynamic. On the other hand, the respect and recognition that tourists give to the different social and cultural activities has increased the pride of the local population in their values and traditions.

As a result, additional tourist flows to the area have been growing positively. Indeed, one of the main attractions of this area is associated with the conservation effort, as it allows people to find species of wild fauna and a well preserved landscape setting. In contrast, tourism development is a source of income that in part supports conservation. As a result, the local communities show their greater dedication to ensuring environmental balance.

With respect to energy, it was through the project of Ecotourism that solar panels were introduced in villages in the region of Cantanhez and this action allowed people to realize the benefits of this form of electricity. Until then, diesel powered generators were the only means used. Therefore, the solar panels implemented in Faru Sadjuma served as a reference to cultivate their appreciation and adoption by the communities. This was later verified when the AD, with the support of some European NGOs, undertook an initiative aimed at providing financial support to whoever wanted to buy small solar panels for domestic use. Panels measuring 20/20 cm that power solar lightbulbs, providing 6-7 hours of lighting autonomy, are now in place. Moreover, this equipment has improved communication in Cantanhez by enabling people to charge mobile phones (an essential piece of equipment for communicating between villages and the outside world).

However, there are also some less positive aspects. With the development of the project the nature guides have a heavier workload (Ghiurghi, 2008). This happens because although there are a total of 14 trained guides, some of the individuals are more active and therefore carry out various functions. Due to the irregularity of tourist arrivals some problems occur in terms of maintaining jobs and remuneration. This has been noticeable particularly in the restaurant business which requires people with certain skills, but who in the low-season end up being dismissed or kept in precarious situations. This factor ultimately encourages increased staff turnover, penalizing their learning process and destabilizing relationships between those who are responsible for tourism services and some parts of the population.

Another problem has arisen in regard to the observation of chimpanzees. Sometimes this takes place at the primates' feeding points, which most of the time end up being in the orange groves belonging to local farmers. Some of the guides and farmers have started demanding the payment of an entrance fee due to the damage caused by these animals.

In projects of this nature a strong attempt is made to share the returns among the community, whether in the provision of services or the supply of various products. However, it has been a slow process to encourage some local producers to increase production and make it more regular, namely in the production of wooden carvings (for decoration) and other household utensils. And although ecotourists are not very demanding in terms of luxury, they are demanding in aspects related to hygiene and cleanliness which require, in this case, a change in the population's attitude towards waste production and management.

Main Obstacles

This project has some characteristics that can lead to success. In the current setting of the tourism sector development, tourism demand itself has been changing, revealing preferences for new destinations and new forms of tourism, and expressing a new attitude towards the places already visited. The ecotourist's trip motivations are to have contact with wildlife and go trekking where their main objectives are to explore nature, visit new places and have new experiences. This kind of tourist does not seek luxurious accommodation, beaches and nightlife, rather they live according to local conditions and foodstuffs while also experiencing different lifestyles. In relation to new destinations, Christ et al. (2003: 4) refer to the fact that: '… tourism has been growing and increasing particularly in biodiversity hotspots…'. Compared to the general growth of tourism demand, in 2004 the global demand for ecotourism and nature tourism offerings grew three times faster (WTO, 2004).

Although the current setting of the tourism sector indicates a trend for destinations that privilege direct contact with natural resources and local communities and supply the products of green tourism, nature tourism and ecotourism, the truth is that the success of the tourism development depends largely on other factors and not only on the existence of unique attractions. For example, in the case of Guinea-Bissau, the country's political and socio-economic context is consequently reflected in many aspects of the project, revealing some weaknesses and limitations that are hard to overcome.

Some of the obstacles encountered in the development of ecotourism in Cantanhez resulted from existing structural problems within the country. Firstly, there were the issues associated with a road network that is limited and of poor quality. The trip to the accommodation clusters in Cantanhez takes 6-7 hours, in part using dirt roads with a very irregular surface (due to the fact that they become streams during the rainy season). For a successful trip it is necessary to use all-terrain vehicles, but even so a few hours' worth of bumps and potholes are inevitable. From another perspective, there is no room for boredom or to take a nap and the tourist may take advantage of the landscape and cultural diversity of the places they pass through (the luxuriant vegetation, farmlands, daily or weekly roadside markets, crafts selling points, rivers and streams, etc.).

Nevertheless, this limitation oin the transport of goods and people becomes a concern when medical emergency situations arise. The alternative waterway and maritime transport, which could be used in some parts of the region of Cantanhez, in general, does not meet the minimum requirements in terms of transport and safety.

Other issues related to the health system and medical services are, in general, a cause for great concern and include limitations in relation to medical facilities and equipment, specialized staff and medication availability. Also, there is the problem of dealing with highly serious health problems that will need the fast and safe transportation of patients.

The quality of water for domestic consumption is also a problem that can directly affect the tourist experience. In this case, the fact that water is not treated is a factor that threatens the well-being both of communities and visitors.

The political instability that exists in Guinea-Bissau is another problem. The constant changes in political power, and the aggressive way in which some have occurred, are a factor in determining the country's image. The impression which goes out to the international community is not very positive, as it is one of instability and insecurity.

Leadership skills in tourism management are lacking as well. This is particularly true in Iemberém where various services (cleaning the bungalows, the cleaning and maintenance of outdoor spaces including gardens, cooking meals and managing the restaurant) are performed by numerous people. Receiving tourists is something completely new in these communities and there is therefore a need, at least at this early stage, to have someone who is aware of all the features of the tourism services and can coordinate the different actors.

In Cantanhez the mobile network has a very weak signal and there is no Internet access point, all of which complicates the booking process. At the moment bookings are made through the AD who subsequently communicates them to Cantanhez. The problem is that there are also walk-in tourists who go on expeditions in the south and then stay overnight in the tourism facilities: this can then lead to overbooking.

As already mentioned, Guinea-Bissau has political, economic and social problems. Therefore it is extremely important to create a joint and targeted strategy for tourism promotion and marketing that is specifically designed to appeal to international markets.

Challenges for The Future

Using the perspective of continuous and permanent improvement, one of the challenges for the future of ecotourism in Cantanhez is to improve tourist satisfaction. In this context, a questionnaire was drawn up to evaluate guests' satisfaction regarding the various services making up the ecotourism product. Although the use of bungalows for tourism purposes is still quite low, some opinions have been obtained. Between February 2009 and January 2010, 35 questionnaires were filled in by 23 men and 12 women. These questionnaires referred only to Iemberém.

Most respondents (78%) were aged between 26 and 55. In terms of nationalities the majority (58%) were visitors from Portugal, followed by Guineans with 19%. The remaining 23% were distributed between Belgian, Dutch, Italian and Norwegian tourists.

Among other issues, they were asked to give suggestions for the improvement of the available services and sites. The most common comment referred to issues of cleanliness, particularly the cleanliness of the bathrooms and also of the accommodation units. Some of the visitors indicated that they would like to have more interaction with the community and others actually suggested possible activities to be developed. In terms of information, they indicated the need for some means of publicity for the existing natural resources and other attractions. They stated that this information should be available in the rooms and in the public spaces such as museums and restaurants.

In the food and beverage sector, several suggestions were made, with the most common one relating to the diversity of meals, and the food that could be served at breakfast (more fruit and jams). In general, the visitors complimented the experience and the site and others specifically praised the food.

Regarding the creation of tourism packages, this is the biggest challenge since it depends on the coordination of a set of actors including not only the members of the community but also tourism agents, transportation companies, hotel facilities in Bissau and the guides-interpreters.

Concerning the training of nature guides and of people involved in the functional activities connected to reception, accommodation and food and beverage - we consider this to be a strategic aspect in the success of the tourism service provided, which should be considered as a continuous and constantly updated process. The biggest challenge is to identify the tools and modes of transmission of knowledge that allow effective learning, given the specific needs of the communities. These are individuals who have never had contact with the demands of the tourism activity.

A future objective is to try to solve these issues and prevent their recurrence, for example, the optimization of the interior space of the bungalows, more main-tenance and protection of their roofs and an improvement in terms of furniture and decoration following local traditions. Environmental sustainability (and even economic) action is essential as far as renewable energy is concerned. However, to extend the use of solar energy in a more consistent way, by creating infrastruc-tures and acquiring equipment that guarantees more autonomy and greater terri-torial coverage it is essential for this to become an objective in terms of governmental policy. The country has a huge need for energy and so far the strat-egy has almost exclusively been to use generators that are not powered by envi-ronmentally-friendly fuels. The challenge in this case is to convince political decision makers of the importance of investing in a renewable resource that exists in abundance in Guinea-Bissau, namely sunlight. However, demanding a very large investment with economic returns that will only become visible in the medium or long term is considered a difficult challenge to overcome.

Another project to be developed has to do with the use of rainwater, namely channelling it into tanks where it would be properly treated and thus these would then function as a reservoir. Once again the implementation of this system can only be achieved by establishing partnerships with organizations that have some experience in this field. There is a site already developed in neighbouring Senegal that has rainwater reserves with the capacity to meet the needs of some popula-tions for about six months. This project is particularly important because it could solve some of the problems surrounding groundwater depletion.

Conclusion

Guinea, and particularly the region of Cantanhez, has natural, human and cultural resources that are rich and increasingly valuable in terms of environmental tour-ism. Projects such as the ecotourism in Cantanhez may represent an opportunity to economically boost local communities and promote and advertise their natural and cultural values in a responsible way.

The mere fact that it is a country with numerous development problems places many obstacles in front of the implementation of a project like this one. Reflecting on the entire development process from the outset there has been a desire to gather contributions from different entities, establishing partnerships and learning from the experiences and know-how of different authorities and experts. With this aid, and always bearing in mind the features of the region, the objective is to find the best solutions in terms of planning, construction, decoration, environmental education and training. The assumptions, at each stage of the project and in every decision taken, are always the same: to protect, involve and make dynamic the local environment. We refer to the human, natural, cultural, socioeconomic and administrative environment that characterizes and distinguishes this reality and which should be, above all, highly respected.

We would like to thank the AD Guiné-Bissau Director, Mr Carlos Schwarz, for the information provided about the U'Anan Project.

References

Brito, B. (2007). *Estudo das Potencialidades e dos Constrangimentos do Ecoturismo na Região de Tombali.* Desenvolvido no âmbito do Projecto U'Anan – Construir o Desenvolvimento Comunitário Sustentável na Região de Tombali: Ecoturismo e Cidadania. Intituto Marquês de Valle Flor/Acção para o Desenvolvimento.

Christ, C., Hillel, O., Matus, S. e Sweeting, J. (2003). *Tourism and Biodiversity – Mapping Tourism's Global Footprint.* Washington, DC: CI-Conservation International /UNEP.

Ghiurghi, A. (2008). *Volet formation des écoguides et sélection des itinéraires - Rapport de Mission. (Version Preliminiere).* Guiné-Bissau: AD - Projet EcoGuiné. [Document non publié].

TIES, *TIES Global Ecotourism Fact Sheet:* Washington DC, 2006. URL: www.ecotourism.org.

UNDP (2009). *Human Development Report 2009 - Overcoming barriers: Human mobility and development.* NY: UNDP. http://hdr.undp.org/en/media/HDR_2009_EN_Complete.pdf. [Accessed 16th of August 2010, 11:00]

WES-World Ecotourism Summit (2002). *Québec Declaration on Ecotourism.* http://www.gdrc.org/uem/eco-tour/quebec-declaration.pdf [Accessed 16th of August 2010,11:03]

WTO (2004). WTO press release, June.

Website

http://www.adbissau.org/adbissau/temasnaordemdodia/Ecoturismo.pdf

16 Minimission-Tourism in Ethiopia

A new subspecies of sustainable volunteer tourism?

*Claudia Hensel**

Introduction

Volunteer tourism represents a relatively new concept in tourism combining volunteering and travelling. People travel to other places, mainly developing countries, to work in projects to alleviate the deficiencies of local communities or the environment (Wearing, 2001). Along with an enormous increase in the number of organizations and projects offered, volunteer tourism recently became the focus for many researchers.

Whilst the existing literature has looked mainly into the benefits for the volunteer or critically discussed the impact and challenges of volunteer tourism, only a little academic research has focused on a more general examination of the benefits for all involved stakeholders (Raymond, 2008).

Developing countries often suffer from economic underdevelopment and a negative image which do not act as motivators for the usual traveler who will have to decide on a destination for their yearly holiday. So there must be a different motivation to choose volunteer travel over 'usual holiday trips'. Within the area of volunteer travelling, which is not necessarily linked to destinations in underdeveloped countries, the idea of Minimissions will only concentrate on short-term journeys to the 'bottom of the pyramid'. Here altruistic reasons as the main motivation for the trip will serve as indicators to differentiate travelers from minimissionaries.

The indeterminate number of helping organizations which offer volunteer work, and not only in underdeveloped countries, will often concentrate on projects which will last from 1-3 months at minimum and perhaps up to one year, with fewer opportunities for working people to join in. This kind of volunteer work will be mostly targeted at younger people like students who will have the chance for a longer break without this having a negative impact on their careers. In particular the Baby Boomers often cannot afford to leave their profession and take a sabbatical. Therefore Minimissions may provide an opportunity for them to experience volunteering within their given job boundaries.

*FH Mainz, University of Applied Sciences, Mainz, Germany

The east African country of Ethiopia distinguishes itself by its diverse natural conditions which have created a unique existence of flora and fauna. The country offers many natural and cultural attractions (Gish et al., 2007). And even while today's Ethiopia still faces a trade deficit, it has recorded strong economic growth over the last few years. Furthermore, tourism arrivals have constantly risen over these years (UNWTO, 2010) though these still remain low at 0,7% of all African tourist arrivals when compared to other African countries.

How far and with what benefits to the local communities can volunteer tourism help Ethiopia to ease its living conditions and become a self-supporting part of the global community? And what benefit to the country and the involved stakeholders can the idea of Minimissions provide?

Volunteer Tourism

The notoriety of changing values in society, the growing importance of sustainability, and a reluctance to spend favors the growth of service-based tourism in the mainstream leisure travel market (Cohan, 2010). Wearing (2002, p. 240) identifies volunteer tourists as those 'who, for various reasons, volunteer in an organized way to undertake holidays that might involve aiding or alleviating the material poverty of some groups in a society, the restoration of certain environments or research into aspects of society or environment'.

In this definition, Wearing makes clear that it is the combination of vacationing and providing help that characterizes this type of tourism. 'For various reasons' highlights the fact that the motivation behind this can be manifold. Additionally, it shows that even though the projects can be very diverse, they always focus on some kind of alleviation of deficiencies.

Holmes and Smith (2009) structure volunteer tourism and differentiate between:

- VolunTourism, where the main purpose of the trip is having a holiday with only a small proportion of this dedicated to voluntary service
- Volunteer vacation/service trips/working holidays/conservation holidays, where the main motivator for the journey is the will to serve people and nature. Recreation will only be a side-effect if at all planned.
- Gap year volunteering, bridging from 3 to 24 months, mainly working on a set long-term project.

Brown and Morrison (2003) introduced 'the mini mission or so-called "mission light"'. These 'Missions' describe excursions that take place during vacationing and include some kind of voluntary task. Concerning time, voluntary tasks can only be limited to one afternoon during the entire vacation trip and will consequently include only a small portion of volunteering activities. However, these kinds of travellers still account for volunteer vacationers even though they look for a 'lighter' version of volunteering. Later research by Brown (2005) provides further information on these two types of volunteer tourists. She describes tourists with a focus on volunteering as 'volunteer-minded' and consequently labels this type of tourism volunteerism. By contrast she identifies the type of tourism that attracts the 'vacation-minded', such as the mission light travellers, as 'volunTourism'. Consequently, 'volunTourism' represents the product sold by tour operators.

The proposed concept of Minimissions will be developed based upon these findings. Minimissions will not interfere with the travelers' employment and therefore can be undertaken during yearly holiday breaks and has a target group which goes beyond younger people. The main motivator is altruistic, being part of a project to help people who are at the bottom of the pyramid.

As Ruhanen et al. (2008) discuss knowledge transfers can serve as a major factor in generating benefits to the volunteer and can contribute 'to the broader economic and social goals of society'. The World Tourism Organization has launched a Volunteer Programme, which trains young professionals in tourism to enable them to handover knowledge to people in underserved countries and help them establish sustainable initiatives (UNWTO, 2010). Although this initiative is limited to tourism development itself it shows the importance of knowledge as a key factor in alleviating poverty. Therefore this knowledge transfer will be one of the three pillars of Minimissions.

Stakeholder Benefits

To understand the motivation of all stakeholders in Minimission there is a need to look at the benefits each part will get out of participating in the mission. Here we have to differentiate between organizational involvement and individual involvement (see Figure 16.1).

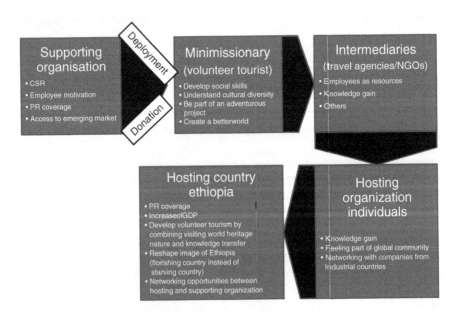

Figure 16.1 Stakeholder benefits

Therefore the volunteer traveler can either travel as part of the company's CSR programme or as an individual traveler. The success of a mission will be determined by the hosting organization matching the demand with traveler offers to be sent out by a supporting organization or as individual. Overall a successful project will serve the host country not only by generating additional income. In the following we will look in more detail at the motivators and benefits for different stakeholders.

The supporting organization – employee volunteerism

For-profit companies can contribute by donating either money or donations in kind and/or involving their own employees in initiatives. Austin et al. (2006) stated that companies worldwide are faced with push and pull factors to engage in social entrepreneurship. Whilst push factors (changing the expectations of major stakeholder groups) lead to reactive engagement, an active engagement will lead to consumer rewards and therefore create business value (pull factor).

Without doubt Corporate Social Responsibility will increase in importance. Therefore Corporate Societal Marketing (CSM), where non-economic objectives are met (Drumwright and Murphy, 2001), will influence the future brand equity (Hoeffler and Keller, 2002). Drumwright and Murphy include not only strategic philanthropy but also volunteerism as part of CSM.

This vast increase in understanding the importance of showing social responsibility has led to much CSR research with resulting programmes and the birth of social business. Muhammad Yunus (2010) defined social business as a business that sustains itself but whose purpose is to create social benefits rather than generate a profit.

The German firm, Adidas, announced its willingness to produce its first 1€-shoes in cooperation with Grameen and Mohammed Yunus in Bangladesh for the local market. To maximize the social benefits the shoes will be produced locally. These will protect the poor against infections (*Social Business News*, December 2010). Some other larger companies such as DHL in Germany have organized own volunteer groups like the Disaster Response Team (DRT). This network of employees, short-term yet ready-for-action, is sent voluntarily on humanitarian missions in areas of natural catastrophes (DHL, 2008).

But how far are companies willing to help, not only by donating money but also by sending out 'troops' (an organized group of volunteer travelers) with a specific mission using their core competencies to serve the poor? The latest survey showed that 30% of the companies offered employees 25-39 hours paid time annually and 24% offered 40 hours and more: 69% of the companies offered paid time off as part of their volunteer programme (Deloitte Volunteer Impact Survey, 2010). A new trend in the industry is therefore 'Micro-Volunteering', which is the 'new term for web-based volunteer tasks that can be accomplished in small increments of time', as stated in a blog on the internet platform Volunteermatch.org (Kelly, 2010).

Besides a positive impact on brand awareness, a volunteer initiative would enhance a company's reputation as well as improve employee loyalty and retention. These corporate-nonprofit alliances can thus have a positive influence on brand preference and future business success (Kotler, 2009).

The Missionary Traveler

The Corporate Minimissionary

New research in the United States shows that companies that are engaged in employee volunteerism are more admired by the younger generation. Nearly two-thirds of the respondents (62%) in the 2007 Volunteer IMPACT survey by Deloitte & Touche USA said they would prefer to work for companies that give them opportunities to contribute their talents to nonprofit organizations: 97% percent of Gen Y volunteers believed companies should provide opportunities for their employees to volunteer. VolunteerMatch, the largest online network for volunteering, offers corporations employee engagement solutions and describes the benefits to the employee as follows (VolunteerMatch, 2010):

- Improves performance
- Increases job satisfaction, attitude and morale
- Encourages teamwork
- Promotes leadership and skill development
- Improves communication between employees and their supervisors, and across departments.

The Private Minimissionary

In general, there are projects available for volunteers of all ages between 18 and 75 (Lonely Planet Publications, 2007). Nevertheless, some age groups dominate this type of tourism. Students and younger people in general perhaps dominate the volunteer tourism market due to their flexibility. They are usually not in a full-time career, or married, or parents yet (Holmes & Smith, 2009). Furthermore, there is an increase in the number of retirees who participate in volunteer vacations (TRAM, 2008). Retirees might again be more flexible due to their independence from jobs and children.

Understanding the motives of volunteers can be quite complex. In past research, this field has been approached using different perspectives. The most cited concept describing motivation is Maslow's 'hierarchy of needs' as was also used by Brown (2005) to compare travel motives in general with those of volunteer tourists. With regard to Wearing (2004), traditional vacationers are situated more in the lower levels of need (physiological, safety, social and esteem needs), while volunteer tourists are rather more concerned with the higher levels such as self-actualization.

The target market for volunteer tourism has been the focus for much research. Wymer et al. (2010) looked into the dependence of sensation seeking and volunteering to define a target market. The overlap between backpacker tourism and volunteer tourism was also researched by Ooi and Laing (2010).

The main motives of volunteer tourists have been divided into two categories: altruistic and egocentric. Altruism describes the behaviour of people that focuses on satisfying and delighting others (Hornby, 2000). Experienced volunteers had stated in Wearing (2001) that they wanted 'to do something for another country,' by working with the people 'and trying to improve their lives'. Consequently, altruistic motives describe volunteers' desire to contribute with their own efforts aimed at enhancing the life of others. Egocentrism represents the other side to altruism and therefore exemplifies having a focus on oneself instead of caring for others (Hornby, 2000).

To get a better understanding of the topic an online questionnaire was created, collecting data by distributing this via email and using social platforms such as *Facebook*, *StudiVZ*, and *Wer-kennt-Wen*. After a sample size of 620 was reached (Enderle, 2010) the outcome clearly indicated that a combination of altruistic and egocentric motives existed. Surprisingly the adventure aspect of the experience is mentioned by only half of the respondents. The choice of distribution via the internet had also led to a younger sample, with 88% of respondents below the age of 30.

Benefits for the minimissionary

It is only if the motivation to volunteer is matched by the experience that a sustainable impact with travelers will be reached. McGehee and Santos (2005) researched the impact of volunteering on social change. Results showed that expeditions improve ''global citizenship'' and participants became more involved

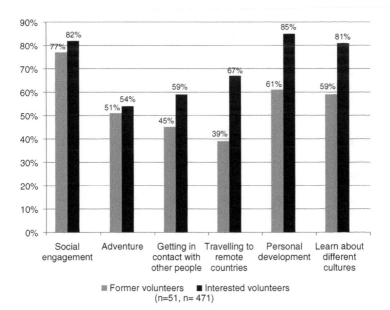

Figure 16.2 Motivation to participate in volunteer projects

in 'changing the world'. The survey undertaken in 2010 with only a small number of respondents (n=51) revealed that with 73% of participants their expectations were met and 16% were disappointed: 70% agreed or agreed strongly with the statement that their contribution made a difference to the community (Enderle, 2010) (see Figure 16.2).

The hosting organization

The hosting organization is the immediate receiver of the knowledge brought into the company by the missionary. It is of utmost importance to first evaluate the organization's knowledge requirements. Different ways to categorize these needs will be discussed. The hosting organization can be either a local NGO or a private company.

Possible benefits for the hosting organization

- Provides skilled and talented volunteer pool, as employees devote their personal and professional skills to community needs and provide knowledge transfers
- Offers direct cost savings for community service organizations in saved recruiting and labor costs
- Generates social impact
- Helps to bring community needs into focus

These possible benefits have to be critically analyzed. Talking to NGOs and searching the web, some negative comments have to be taken seriously: '... a volunteer is someone that is more of an annoyance because the job at hand does not really match with the hours and the limited time commitment ... what it really costs to screen, place and train a volunteer is ignored ...' (Minges, 2011). The same voice can be heard talking to NGO representatives: 'We don't need people planting trees for us'. This highlights the importance of a need evaluation when undertaking beneficial volunteering.

Intermediaries

The volunteer travel agent

The market for volunteering has dramatically increased and many different channels and providers of volunteering opportunities have emerged, making it very difficult to structure and provide an overview. The two organizations *i-to-i*, a subsidy of *TUI* and originally a British organization, and *Experience e.V.*, will represent two different types of volunteer travel intermediaries in the German market (Enderle, 2010). Unfortunately neither of these companies offers projects in Ethiopia.

Can for-profit tour operators offer 'real' volunteering? Is this a form of Social Business or does this carry the idea of volunteering ad absurdum?

Table 16.1 Volunteer travel intermediaries

Company	Experiment e.V. (NPO)	i-to-i (PO)
Project	Health project in Athlone, South Africa	Health project in Capetown, South Africa
Activity	Between five and 33 weeks, volunteers take care of paraplegic people and give them their attention. Additionally, they participate in carpenter workshops and sell wood work to support the community.	Between four and twelve weeks, volunteers take care of and work with mentally and physically handicapped children
Length of the Project for product example	Nine weeks	Nine weeks
Working hours per day	Not stated	4,5 h/day
Price	1,880 Euro	2,859 Euro
Included in the fee	Airport pick-up, six-day orientation in destination incl. accommodation and five daytrips, accommodation and food provided by a host family, free internet, overnight stay in Cape Town before going back, 24h telephone support, visa support, pre- and post-preparation workshops	Airport pick-up, in-country orientation, accommodation in a shared dormitory room, local in-country team providing 24h support
Not included in the fee	Flights, pocket money, insurance, airport transport, costs for visas	Food, flights, insurance, visas, return airport transfer
Source	www.experiment-ev.de	www.i-to-i.com

International NGOs

"Capacity and capabilities of NGOs vary enormously. Some NGOs are well known and have strong symbolic, cognitive, social, and monitoring power. Such power resources clearly relate to material strength, as financial resources are significant for investing in the other types of power. Most NGOs, however, are small, unknown, and local." (Bostrom and Tamm, 2010)

Weltwärts, the volunteering organization of the German Federal Ministry for Economic Cooperation and Development, lists on their homepage more than 1500 volunteer projects, though only 19 are based in Ethiopia (www.weltwärts.de).

The 'Deutsche Gesellschaft für Internationale Zusammenarbeit' (GIZ), newly formed on 1 January 2011 incorporating the expertise of the former organizations DED, GTZ and Inwent (www.giz.de), is the biggest organization in

Germany, working on 1.189 projects with seven based in Ethiopia. In Germany alone more than 200 nonprofit organizations can be noted as working on the African continent. The number of organizations doing so world-wide are impossible to calculate.

Internet platforms

VolunteerMatch (http://www.volunteermatch.org) serves as example of online platforms where corporations can align their volunteering strategies to allow employees to find volunteer opportunities that will meet their passions, skills, and schedules. A variety of online services are offered to support a community of nonprofits, volunteers and businesses committed to civic engagement, with over 50,000 nonprofit organizations participating.

Local NGOs

In Ethiopia 3.522 NGOs were registered before the new civil society law of Ethiopia was introduced in 2009. Under the new law, criticized by many international organizations, only 1.655 NGOs have now been able to re-register, leaving the rest out in the cold (Africa News, 2010). Among the various articles of the new law are that NGOs should not spend more than 30 percent on administrative expenses, reporting requirements and mandatory license renewals.

African NGOs meanwhile suffer from tight fiscal controls on international donors. On the 'International Symposium to Build the Capacity and Resources of African NGOs' held in Addis Ababa in 2005, two main financial needs were clearly to the fore. First of all, African NGOs would need to cover operational overheads and contribute to the core costs that are involved in growing organizations, such as training for employees. Secondly, financial coverage is required to fight humanitarian crisis situations (Cater, 2005).

African NGOs have difficulties in raising funds in domestic markets, but international funding is not only hard to get but also involves tight controls limiting the coverage of core costs. Empowering local NGOs will be one of the most important success factors for reducing poverty in Africa and empowering the African community. In Ethiopia therefore most NGOs mainly employ local people. Working with international volunteer travelers is regarded as difficult, time-consuming and less beneficial. Furthermore the Ethiopian Government is very restrictive in giving work permits to foreigners, unless it can be proven that no Ethiopian has the capabilities to do the job.

The hosting country

There are positive and negative economic impacts in tourism which are, according to Mason (2003), highly dependent on the scale of tourism that takes place at the destination,the time when the tourism takes place, and factors such as the development of infrastructure. Furthermore, Mason lists the following positive economic impacts of tourism:

- Contribution to foreign exchange earnings;
- Contribution to government revenues;
- Generation of employment;
- Contribution to regional development (p. 35).

In volunteer tourism, furthermore, people make contributions to local communities as well.

TRAM (2008) analyzed the study of the WYSE Travel Confederation and found that volunteer tourists spend money on accommodation, food and beverage, activities and entertainment, transportation within the destination, and communication. Additionally, volunteers might help to bring funding for certain projects or direct donations for the community. Considering the scale of volunteer tourism, the economical impacts are smaller than those from conventional forms of tourism. The implementation of projects can also be an opportunity for the creation of new jobs which was also recognized by Tomazos and Butler (2009, pp. 207-208). There might be a need for 'local drivers, cooks' or 'guards'.

Figure 16.3 Mojo Catholic clinic, maternal and child health services (Photo by author)

The projects themselves offer opportunities for locals to become trained by volunteers and adopt new skills which might benefit them for further jobs afterwards. This will be dependent on the degree of skills of the volunteers (see Figure 16.3).

The Minimission

The idea

To develop sustainable volunteering impact Minimissions need to be based on three pillars:

1.   Knowledge share

One reason the volunteer tourism sector has expanded so rapidly is that many volunteer tourism projects have minimal or non-existent requirements regarding the skill set someone needs to participate. Not surprisingly, however, some authors have questioned the benefits that can be provided by volunteer tourists who potentially do not have useful skills, are not familiar with the local culture, and only stay for a very short period of time (Guttentag, 2009).

Financial support

New OECD figures show continuing growth in development aid in 2009, despite the financial crisis (OECD, 2011). But the scandal of UNICEF (2009) has led to a noticeable drop in donations for them from private donors, which might be related to a loss of trust. With task-related Minimissions private donors will actually know what has been achieved by their donations and tangible evidence can be given. A higher degree of transparency can be granted (see Figure 16.4).

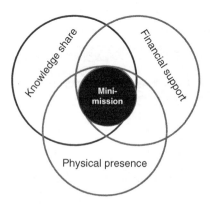

Figure 16.4 The three pillars of sustainable Minimissions

Physical presence

Volunteer Tourism by definition is travelling to areas of the world where benefits can be achieved and serve as a powerful force for change, both for those who *volunteer* and for the wider community. The above mentioned and widely researched motives and expectations of volunteer travelers can only be met if their actual physical presence is a given.

The Process of sustainable Minimissions

The need to establish a blueprint to achieve sustainable task-related Missions is presented below (see Figure 16.5).

Need Evaluation

To gain maximum impact from volunteering it is important to understand the needs of the underserved countries. Different ways to structure needs have been established. Bill Clinton's 'Global Initiative' structures put these into the following modules (clintonglobalinitiative, 2010):

- Empowering girls and women by investing in female education
- Strengthening market-based solutions produced by companies, NGOs and governments researching and developing win-win situations at the bottom of the pyramid
- Enhancing access to modern technology to enable the world's poor to participate in global developments
- Harnessing human potential by the creation of new job opportunities.

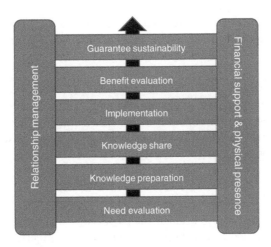

Figure 16.5 Steps for sustainable missions

The difficulty in structuring the support needs lies in its overlapping: a more tangible approach is chosen by the African Development Bank. The structure of the strategy paper produced by the African Development Bank listed below establishes a structure for need evaluation (African Development Bank, 2006):

- Agriculture
- Manufacturing
- Transport
- Water and Sanitation
- Power
- Education
- Health
- Environment

The needs have to be clearly evaluated and the objectives defined. These will serve as segmenting criteria to find a suitable volunteering partner. Need evaluation can only be done successfully with input from the receiving partners.

Knowledge Preparation

Intensive exchanges are needed involving all stakeholders in the process and training based upon the findings must be provided. This will not only include skills to provide the service but also an understanding of cultural diversity to avoid negative vibrancies in the process. Training needs have been identified and structured by Raymond (2007, 2008), Power (2007) and Callanan and Thomas (2005).

Knowledge Share

Knowledge management tools are needed to establish a long-term communication between the stakeholders. There will be a further need to develop and establish tools.

Implementation

Not only in the implementation phase will a physical presence be beneficial, this would be the best time for volunteer travel. Based upon the first steps on mutual knowledge creation a Minimission can profit most from personal exchanges while implementing projects.

Benefit Evaluation

Further blueprints in how to evaluate the achievements of the missions will have to be set up based upon the identified objectives of the project.

Guarantee Sustainability

It is of utmost importance to see the missions not as single experiences but as accompanying the project further and serving as mentor for future issues. Most NGOs have a goal of handing over projects to local people, often because the planned and budgeted time-frames of projects will come to an end. To guarantee their ongoing success, tools have to be put in place not only to monitor but also to accompany projects for longer periods and therefore make sure that the missions will create a sustainable impact.

Ethiopia

Basic facts

'Ethiopia is sometimes called the roof of Africa' (Gish et al., 2007, p.8) because of its mountainous landscape and the highlands reaching a height of up to 12,000 feet above sea level (see Figure 16.6). According to the World Factbook provided by the Central Intelligence Agency (CIA) (n.d.), about 88 million people live in Ethiopia (2009). This represents the second largest population after Nigeria in

Figure 16.6 Gilgal Gibe (Photo by author)

Africa (Auswertiges Amt, n.d.). The country reports a population growth rate of 3.21 percent per year (2009) and therefore belongs to one of the eight fastest growing populations worldwide (CIA, n.d.). There are eight Ethiopian sites published on the list of World Heritage sites by *UNESCO*. Overall, this list includes 890 natural and cultural sites of 'outstanding universal value' worldwide and has the goal of protecting and conserving them (UNESCO, n.d.). Two of these sites in Ethiopia are the cave churches of Lalibela which date back to the 13th century and the ruins at Aksum which remained from the Kingdom of Aksum (UNESCO, n.d).

The country strategy paper 2006-2009 of the Country Operations Department North, East & South of the African Development Bank stated the following main issues in June 2006:

> "Ethiopia's human development indicators are amongst the lowest in the world (p. ii)... Currently, 36 percent of Ethiopians live below the poverty line of 1 US Dollar per day. Food insecurity at the household level is a defining characteristic of poverty in Ethiopia (p. 2) ... Ethiopia's budget is heavily dependent on aid flows which finances close to 40 percent of expenditure... (p. 4)
>
> The share of manufacturing in GDP is only 6 percent. The manufacturing sector .... is characterized by low productivity and weak competitiveness resulting from low skills, shortage of capital and lack of modern technology." (p. 8)

(African Development Bank 2006)

Tourism in Ethiopia

Tourism in Ethiopia has been growing continuously over the last few years. However, compared to other East African countries such as Tanzania and Kenya

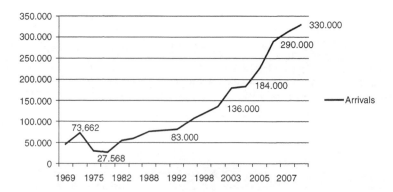

Figure 16.7 Development of international tourist arrivals in Ethiopia over four decades (Enderle, adopted from Schumann, 1994, p. 67; Díaz Benavides & Pérez-Ducy, 2001, p. 42; UNWTO, 2007, p. 142)

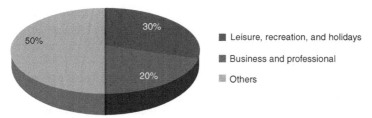

Figure 16.8 Arrivals by purpose of visit in percentages in 2008 Enderle (according to the statistics provided by the UNWTO, 2009)

which both registered more than 1.5 million international tourist arrivals, Ethiopia's arrivals remain relatively low. Consequently, it can be said that the numbers do not represent the potential that the country has concerning natural and cultural attractions (see Figures 16.7 and 16.8).

The development of arrival numbers simultaneously resulted in the development of air travel. Air travel has become 'the second largest sector of the economy' in Ethiopia 'in terms of export receipts' (Díaz Benavides & Pérez-Ducy, 2001, p. 47). The east African country is one of the countries demonstrating rapid developments in air travel over the last years. A reason for this is that the country's airport serves as a regional hub. Hence, this development of air travel is more due to the development of neighboring regions than the development of its own tourism industry (Diaz Benavides & Perez-Ducy, 2001).

Others could be regarded as part of volunteering tourism, but this needs to be researched further.

Current Support

Besides the support of the World Bank, AfdB, USAID, EU DFID and UNDP, some European countries have already established support in areas of governance such as Italy (strengthening planning capacity in Tigray/Promia and Bene, Shangul), Germany (GIZ/KFW: support for urban management), Sweden (support for civil service reform and gender rights) and Norway (the training of judges and prosecutors) (Country Governance Profile, African Development Bank, Democratic Republic of Ethiopia, March 2009).

Needed Support

1. *Agriculture:* environmental degradation and diminishing soil fertility due to inappropriate land management practices, fragmented size of land, low use of modern agricultural technology, lack of clear and effective land tenure system to support agriculture development, weak access to markets due to poor transport and marketing infrastructure.
2. *Manufacturing*: The share of manufacturing in GDP is only 6 per cent. The manufacturing sector is dominated by light manufacturing, such as food

processing, textiles, and leather which account for nearly 70 per cent of manufacturing value added. It is characterized by low productivity and weak competitiveness resulting from low skills, a shortage of capital and a lack of modern technology.

3.   *Transport*: Road transport is critical for Ethiopia's development, given its geography and the remoteness of large parts of the country.

4.   *Water and sanitation:* Water and sanitation coverage in Ethiopia is estimated at 42 *per cent and 18 per cen*t respectively, which is amongst the lowest in the world. In rural areas, the rate for water borne diseases is extremely high.

5.   *Power*: Ethiopia possesses vast hydro potential, variously estimated from 15,000 to 30,000 Megawatts. However, less than 5 per cent of this potential is exploited and only 16 per cent of the population has access to modern sources of energy.

6.   *Education*: One major challenge is the low quality of education. The quality of education has suffered due to limited resources to support the phenomenal expansion in gross primary school enrolment. In 2004/05, the average pupil-teacher ratio in Ethiopia was 70:1, amongst the highest in Sub-Sahara Africa.

7.   *Health*: The expansion of health services to ensure sustainability in service delivery would require substantial financial resources. Ethiopia will also need to address the shortage of health workers to ensure effective delivery of basic health services to strengthen the provision of preventative and primary health care services with a focus on diseases that afflict the poor such as malaria and Tuberculosis.

8.   *Environment*: Ethiopia faces major environmental problems, some of which stem from *rapid popul*ation growth, inappropriate land management practices, and unplanned urban growth. The environmental problems in Ethiopia include soil erosion, deforestation, and water resource depletion, the threat to biodiversity and fisheries resources, human habitat degradation and pollution.
     (African Development Bank: Country Strategy Paper 2006-2009 by the Country Operations Department North, East & South, June 2006)

Negative impacts of Minimissions

With the rapid expansion of the volunteer tourism sector, much research has been undertaken to better understand the positive impacts on the hosting country and volunteers, but negative impacts have also been researched, looking at the following aspects:

*   Dependency creation in host communities (McGehee and Andereck, 2008)
*   Questioning the experience and personal growth of volunteer tourists (Simpson, 2004)
*   Researching the value of crosscultural interactions (Raymond and Hall, 2008)

- Questioning project benefits and personal gains (Callanan and Thomas, 2005)

Wearing (2001) recognized early on that increased commercialization could endanger environments and communities. While discussing Minimissions with different audiences one of the most common statements received by the author of this chapter was that volunteer travelers would 'take away locals' jobs and therefore disrupt the labour market and create dependency'. This statement was underpinned by Guttenberg's assertion (2009): '*In fact, the presence of volunteer laborers may have the opposite effect and may actually negatively impact labor demand or promote dependency. The presence of free volunteer labor may also disrupt local economies in a broader sense by promoting a cycle of dependency.*' Palacios (2010) also argues that there is a danger of creating a new form of neocolonialism when sending out especially young people from Western countries to underdeveloped areas.

By sending volunteers with high qualifications and skills who will follow the steps of sustainable Minimissions by evaluating needs and building a relationship with the receiving partners before travelling to destinations at the bottom of the pyramid, some of the negative impacts raised can be avoided. Good training based upon a skills-segmentation of the volunteer market could be the first step in establishing a new era of volunteer tourism.

Conclusion and Call for Action

From the research it could be illustrated that volunteer tourism is a broad field, which needs further in-depth evaluation. The received insights into stakeholder motivation to participate and the different kinds of volunteer tourism thus far can only be a starting point for further research and to develop concepts and frameworks that will integrate findings from different faculties and serve as helpful means by which to examine the mutual objectives of volunteer tourism.

The idea of Minimissions bases volunteer tourism on three pillars which in the eyes of the author are necessary to make sustainable changes: with knowledge transfers as the most important mission task, and a presence in the country to deliver the knowledge and financial support necessary to turn ideas into real help. Further steps should include a more strategic view on the topic of volunteering and embedding the ideas into more general approaches that will merge different academic views and provide some practical use. Ethiopia has been chosen as the example here to show how volunteer tourism could well blend together visiting world heritage sites and helping one of the poorest countries in the world, which would be a good starting point for further initiatives and one that is desperately needed by the Ethiopian people. By following the six steps for sustainable missions only some of the possible negative impacts discussed can be avoided. More research and concept development in this area will be needed and Ethiopa would be a good beginning.

References

African Development Bank (2006) Country Strategy Paper 2006-2009 by the Country Operations Department North, East & South, June, http://www.afdb.org/fileadmin/uploads/afdb/Documents/Project-and-Operations/Ethiopia_Eng.pdf (accessed 12th of December 2010).

Africa News (2010) http://www.africanews.com/site/1867_NGOs_vanish_from_Ethiopia/list_messages/33257 (posted on 6th of July 2010, accessed 12th of December 2010).

Austin, J. et al. (2006) Social Entrepreneurship: It is for corporations, too, in A. Nicholls (ed.), *Social Entrepreneurship: New models of sustainable social change*, Oxford, OUP, pp. 169-180.

Austrian Development Cooperation (2008) http://www.entwicklung.at/uploads/media/Ethiopia_Country_Strategy_2008-2012_02.pdf (accessed 12th of June 2010).

Bloom,P.N. & Gedlach,G.T. (eds) (2000) *Handbook of Marketing and Society*, Thousand Oaks, Sage.

Bostrom, M. &Tamm, K. (2010) NGO Power in Global Social and Environmental Standard-Setting, *Global Environmental Politics*, November, Research Articles, p. 36.

Brown, S. & Morrison, A.M. (2003). Expanding Volunteer Vacation Participation:An Exploratory Study on the Mini-Mission Concept. Journal of Tourism Recreation Research, 28 (3), pp. 73-82.

Brown, S. (2005). Travelling with a purpose: understanding the motives and benefits of volunteer vacationers. Current Issues in Tourism, 8 (6), pp. 479-496.

Callanan, M. & Thomas, S. (2005). Volunteer tourism: deconstructing volunteer activities within a dynamic environment, in *Niche Tourism: Contemporary Issues and Trends*, Novelli, M. (ed.), Elsevier, New York, pp. 183–200.

Cater, N. (2005)Empowering NGOs, *New African*, February, pp. 44-47.

Central Intelligence Agency (n.d.). Ethiopia, https://www.cia.gov/library/publications/the-world-factbook/geos/et.html (accessed 5th of May 2010).

Chen, J. S., Legrand, W., Sloan, P. & Zhou, J. (2005) Evaluating environmental initiatives of German hotels: tourism, Review International, 9(1), pp. 61-68.

Clinton Global Initiative, http://www.clintonglobalinitiative.org/ (accessed 10th of December 2010).

Cohan, A. (2010). Voluntourism: The human side of sustainable tourism, in *HVS Global Hospitality Services*, http://www.hvs.com/staticcontent/library/nyu2010/Journal/Articles/Voluntourism.pdf (accessed 1.12.2010).

Deloitte Volunteer IMPACT Survey 2010, http://www.deloitte.com/view/en_US/About/Community-Involvement/50eed830bee48210VgnVCM200000bb42f00aRCRD.htm (accessed 6th of January 2011)

Deutsche Post, http://www.dp-dhl.com/de/presse/pressemitteilungen/2008/finalist_in_einem_csr_programm.html (accessed 7th of December 2010).

Drumwright, M. & Murphy, P. (2001). Corporate Societal Marketing, in Elkington, J. (ed.), *Cannibals with forks: the Triple Bottom Line of 21st century business*. Oxford: Capstone.

Enderle, F. (2009) Evaluating the Opportunities of Volunteer Tourism in Developing Countries. Bachelor Thesis, Bad Honnef.

Federal Ministry for European and International Affairs, Austrian Development Cooperation and Cooperation with Eastern Europe, Ethiopia Country Strategy 2008-2012, http://www.entwicklung.at/uploads/media/Ethiopia_Country_Strategy_2008-2012_02.pdf (accessed 6th January 2011).

Gish, S., Thay, W., & Latif, Z. A. (2007) *Ethiopia.* New York: Marshall Cavendish Benchmark.

Governance, Economic & Financial Reforms Department (OSGE) (2009) Country regional department East (OREB): Country Governance Profile African Development Bank, Democratic Republic of Ethiopia, March.

Guttentag, D. A. (2009). The Possible Negative Impacts of Volunteer Tourism, in *International Journal of Tourism Research*, 11, pp. 537–551.

Hoeffler, S. & Keller, K.L. (2002). Building Brand Equity through Corporate Societal Marketing, *Journal of Public Policy & Marketing*, 21 (1), Spring, pp. 78-89.

Holmes, K. & Smith, K. A. (2009) *Managing Volunteers in Tourism: Attractions, destinations and events.* Oxford: Butterworth-Heinemann.

Hornby, A. M. (2000) *Oxford Advanced Learner's Dictionary of Current English.* Oxford: Oxford University Press.

Kelly, M. (2010). Micro-Volunteering is a New Trend in the Industry and it's no Small Matter, in *Volunteering in the News*, http.//blogs.volunteermatch.org/volunteeringiscsr/ (accessed 19th December 2010).

Kotler, P. & Andreasen, A. (2009) *Strategic Marketing for Nonprofit Organizations*, 7th edition, London: Pearson.

Lonely Planet Publications (2007) *Volunteer: A traveller's guide to making a difference around the world.* Footscray, Vic: Lonely Planet.

Mason, P. (2003). *Tourism Impacts, Planning and Management.* Amsterdam: Butterworth Heinemann.

McGehee, N. & Andereck, K. (2008). 'Pettin' the critters': exploring the complex relationship between volunteers and the voluntoured in McDowell County, West Virginia, USA, and Tijuana, Mexico, in *Journeys of Discovery in Volunteer Tourism*, Lyon K. and Wearing, S. (eds), Cambridge MA: CABI Publishing, pp. 12–24.

McGehee, N. G. & Santos, C. A (2005). Social Change, Discourse and Volunteer Tourism, *Annals of Tourism Research*, 32 (3), pp. 760–779.

Minges, J., http://nonprofitexpert.com/volunteers.htm (accessed 9.1.2011).

OECD: Development aid rose in 2009 and most donors will meet 2010 aid targets #http://www.oecd.org/document/11/0,3343,en_2649_34487_44981579_1_1_1_1,00.html (accessed 8.1.2011)

Ooi, Natalie,Laing, Jennifer (2010). Backpacker tourism: sustainable and purposeful? Investigating the overlap between backpacker tourism and volunteer tourism motivations, *Journal of Sustainable Tourism*, 18 (2) March, pp. 191–206

Palacios, C. M. (2010) Volunteer tourism, development and education in a postcolonial world: conceiving global connections beyond aid, *Journal of Sustainable Tourism*, 18 (7) September, pp. 861–878.

Power, S. (2007) Gaps in development: An analysis of the UK international volunteering sector. *Tourism Concern.*

Raymond, E. & Hall, C. (2008) The development of cross-cultural (mis)understanding through volunteer tourism, *Journal of Sustainable Tourism*, 16 (5), pp. 530–543.

Raymond, E. (2008) "Make a Difference!": the Role of Sending Organizations in Volunteer Tourism, in Lyons, K.D. &Wearing, S (eds), *Journeys of Discovery in Volunteer Tourism*, Cambridge MA: CABI, pp. 48-60.

Ruhanen, L. et al. (2008) Volunteering Tourism Knowledge: a Case from the United Nations World Tourism Organization, in Lyons, K. &Wearing, S. (eds), *Journeys of Discovery in Volunteer Tourism.International Case Study Perspectives*, Cambridge: CABI, pp. 25-35.

Simpson K. (2004) 'Doing development': the gap year, volunteer-tourists and a popular practice of development, *Journal of International Development*, 16, pp. 681–692.

Social Business News (2010) www.social-business-news.com, http://www.social-business-news.com/news/projects/social-business/53-adidas-project.html?ad10ccba3380d 463c5217bee4453e8ac=542c7fed25b916cd9aee2b9e7f298cdc (accessed 7th December 2010).

Spiegel (2011) #http://www.spiegel.de/international/germany/0,1518,536587,00.html

Tomazos, K. and Butler R. (2009) Volunteer tourism: The new ecotourism?, Journal of *Tourism and Hospitality Research*, 20 (1), pp. 196-211.

Tourism Research and Marketing & European Association for Tourism and Leisure Education. (2008) *Volunteer tourism: A global analysis*. Arnhem: ATLAS.

UNICEF (2009) *Report on Regular Resources 2009*, http://www.unicef.org/publications/files/UNICEF_RR_Report2009_091410.pdf (accessed 13th December 2010)

UNWTO (2010) *Tourism Highlights* (accessed 6th January 2011) http://www.unwto.org/facts/menu.html.

UNWTO, Volunteers Programme, #http://unwto-themis.org/en/programmes/volunteers.

Volunteer Match, http://volunteermatch.org.

Wearing, S. (2001) *Volunteer Tourism: Experiences that Make a Difference*. Wallingford,Oxon: CABI.

Wearing, S. (2002). Re-centering the self in volunteer tourism. In Dann, G.S. (ed.), *The Tourist as a Metaphor of the Social World*. Wallingford: CABI, pp.237-262

Wearing, S. (2004). Examining best practice in volunteer tourism, in Stebbins, R.A. and Graham. M. (eds), *Volunteering as Leisure, Leisure as Volunteering: An International Assessment*. Wallingford: CABI, pp. 209-224.

Wymer Jr., W. W., Self, D. R. and Findley, C.S. (2010) 'Sensation Seekers as a Target Market for Volunteer Tourism', *Services Marketing Quarterly*, 31: pp. 3, 348-362.

Yunus, M. (2010) *Building Social Business: The New Kind of Capitalism that Serves Humanity's Most Pressing Needs*. NY: Public Affairs.

17 Botswana

The Selinda Reserve

*Dorian Hoy**

Introduction

Tourism in Botswana is as challenging as it is in any country across the globe. We all in southern Africa are competing for travelers wanting to experience a wildlife safari, whether it be for the first time or as a repeat visitor. Botswana is a country that has a reputation for offering high quality safari destinations – less guests paying more.

Botswana

The Botswana economy has gone through a series of changes and improvements that have seen it develop rapidly from independence in 1966. At this stage Botswana was one of the World's poorest countries, with a GDP of P36 million, but with the discovery of diamonds it was transformed into having the fastest growing economy in the world up until the mid 1990s, with a mean annual growth rate of 10%.

At independence the country was mainly dominated by agriculture with most of the able bodied men employed in the South African mines. The discovery of diamonds after independence, transformed the economy, with the mining sector rapidly overtaking cattle exports as the country's most important foreign exchange earner. While there has been a lot of turbulence within the mining sector it is still the most important sector in the country's economy, contributing 33.4% of GDP in 2001, while agriculture has steadily declined from 39% in 1969 to just 2% in 2005 although it is still one of the most important socio-economic factors in rural communities, providing a livelihood for more than 80% of the population.

The relative importance of mining reached a peak of 47% of GDP in 1986 before starting to decline to its current share of 38% of GDP (2005/06). The economic strength of the country is also under-pinned by one of the highest foreign reserves in Africa, while the economy continues to grow at an average rate of 5%. Botswana's GDP now stands at P57,134 million.

*Regional Managing Director for the Botswana arm of Great Plains

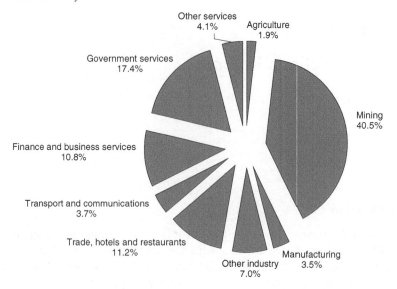

Figure 17.1 Botswana GDP by sector, 2005/06
   Source. Review of the National Map of Botswana

Despite Botswana having recorded impressive rates of growth over the past four decades, unemployment remains one of the major challenges faced by the country. This is mainly because mining contributes very little to employment at around only about 3%. To ensure the country has a stable and positive future in an uncertain global market greater diversification and internal value added development is required.

Botswana has an unemployment rate of 17.6%, which while high has been seen to decline over the past 10 years; down from 21% in 1998. This may be related to the continued growth of the non-mining sectors, spurred on by the economic stability of the country. The principal non-mining sectors which have seen significant growth rates are transport, communication and tourism (including hotels and restaurants) (16%). These sectors play an important role in employment throughout the country, and while tourism only constitutes 11% of total GDP at present, it remains one of the most important avenues for achieving the diversification goals of Botswana and most importantly to be able to provide employment in remote rural areas (see Figure 17.1).

Tourism

One of the key benefits of tourism is the high rates of employment it generates, providing almost 40% of the country's employment. Continued growth within the tourism industry must therefore be encouraged. The Tourism Master Plan (2000) states '*Tourism has been identified as one of the economic sectors with a considerable potential to contribute to the process of diversification*', while '*the infancy state of the tourism sector with its under-utilised potential, creates opportunities for a market-oriented product diversification both in terms of segments and regions'* (Tourism Master Plan, 2000).

There was a 60% increase in the number of visitors entering the country between 2001 and 2006, with the majority of travelers coming from other African countries, most notably South Africa. However the majority of tourists visiting the world renowned natural destinations of northern Botswana are from America, Europe, UK and Australasia where a significant increase in numbers has been recorded.

A 15% increase in the tourism sector is expected over the period to 2014 if the economies of the world can get back to where they were, with an 11% increase in employment. The core of this tourism market is centred on the fragile ecosystem of the Okavango, Linyanti and Chobe region. The tourism market within Ngamiland alone is currently worth approximately P1, 115 million, making a direct contribution towards real GDP of P401 million.

These figures outline the importance of tourism to the national economy and the local business environment within Botswana. The increased demand for growth within the tourism market must however be matched with an increased environmental awareness, ensuring lodge and camp development occurs within the countries environmental policy and especially within the framework of environmental sustainability.

Botswana is a leading nation, when the commitment to conservation is analysed according to the percentage of land dedicated towards wildlife and conservation. Botswana has protected 17% of its land through National Parks and Game Reserves, while a further 20% has been conserved as Wildlife Management Areas (WMAs). NG16 falls within part of this latter 20%. Conservation within these areas is supported through a well balanced legislative environment, that encourages development, but in a sustainable manner. Of key importance is the Wildlife and Conservation Policy (1986) that acts as an umbrella policy '*encouraging the development of a commercial wildlife industry that is viable on a long term basis*' and '*serving to create economic opportunities, jobs and incomes for the rural population in particular and the national economy in general*'. Development within wilderness areas such as NG16 is regulated by the Environmental Impact Assessment (EIA) Act (2005) that through adjudication by the Department of Environmental Affairs that determines whether such development is appropriate, or requires mitigation via an EIA or an EMP. Further acts support the sustainable development of tourism operations such as the Waste Management Act (1998), the Atmospheric Pollution Act (1978), the Water Act and the Monuments and Relics Act (2001). These Acts combined ensure that there is no pollution of the water, soil or air from development activities, and that no relics of national importance are disturbed during construction and operation. While NG16 is not within a National Park the National Parks and Game Reserves Regulations (2000) provide further guidance on sustainable operations within a wilderness environment, while the Tourism Regulations (1996) ensure that the staff and guests are accommodated within a safe and healthy environment.

As tourism becomes an increasingly significant contributor to economic growth, it helps to diversify the national economy. The need for diversification is ever more apparent with the recent global economic downturn, which had severe impacts on Botswana's mining sector. Apart from the need to maintain high rates of economic growth, the economy is also facing a number of economic challenges. One of the most pressing problems are HIV/AIDS which has major budgetary and human resource implications.

The Selinda Reserve

The Selinda Reserve is situated in the northern reaches of Botswana extending from the north eastern parts of Okavango Delta through to the Kwando / Linyanti systems in the north west. The extent of the area covers 320,000 hectares on which we operate 3 separate camps. The names of the camps are Selinda (16 beds), Zarafa (8 beds) and Motswiri (10 beds). Each of these camps cater for a certain level of expectations from our guests, Zarafa being a premier camp, Selinda is known as a classic camp and Motswiri Camp has a horse safari operation operating out of it.

The Selinda Reserve is part of a company called Great Plains Safaris. Great Plains is a company formed by 5 like-minded partners who have belief in the expansion and conservation of natural habitats. The company has interests in Botswana, Tanzania, Kenya, Seychelles, Rwanda and India. The main criterion of getting involved in a project is that it must have a conservation angle to the project. More on these projects can be found on www.greatplainsconservation.com.

Great Plains Conservation

The Selinda Reserve is associated for marketing purposes with the Great Plains Conservation portfolio. The founding members of Great Plains have been successfully building, managing and marketing small luxury lodges for nearly 30 years. Their experience has been focused on running lodges and safaris in remote, pristine parks and reserves, initially within Botswana and then expanding into Rwanda, Kenya, Tanzania and the Seychelles. The aim of Great Plains is to take the lessons learnt over nearly thirty years and apply them to similar developments throughout Africa, the Indian Ocean and in India.

The company's experience in low volume / high revenue tourism, attracting discerning customers who can afford to pay US$1200 to US$1500 per person per night, is unrivalled, and this experience is at the core of its proposal to create good business sense for all stakeholders while also helping to nurture and protect the land.

Great Plains is managed by Colin Bell, who started his career in tourism in Botswana in 1977. Colin created many successful and sustainable partnerships during his 23 years tenure as CEO of Wilderness Safaris. He has now moved on to create Great Plains Safari Company with Dereck and Beverly Joubert. His projects have successfully linked conservation, wildlife, communities and tourism, and have won many prestigious conservation tourism awards, including The World Tourism Council's 'Tourism for Tomorrow' award for sustainable conservation tourism.

The philosophy of Great Plains Conservation is based on a few principles:

- doing everything right and in the best possible way;
- doing what's best for the communities, parks and governments – as well as for our guests and partners;
- helping these countries and regions gain international prestige through superb marketing and PR programmes
- building in the very best possible way and to the greenest possible international standards to attract the very top end of the international traveller;
- adhering to the philosophy of high revenue; low volumes; low impacts
- being an observer but not a spectator, of leaning forward in life and embracing or engaging, not letting the richness of the moment fly past – and travelling with a soft touch that helps to preserve the integrity of the parks and the countries.
- being open to the fact that we don't know everything and enjoying that; the constant pursuit of knowledge and experience is what drives us forward. We are amazed at the world. As a twin motivation we feel a burning desire to use what we know to secure the Great Plains and wildernesses and the animals and birds that roam them, by being proactive about preserving these areas.
- Making choices by location first, in combination with iconic and threatened species. We have identified only the very best places in and around Africa which harbour some of the most threatened wildlife. We go to places because of the wildlife or nature experience, places that are off the beaten track and are often unknown.
- We are based on wholesome values of touching the earth softly and using the opportunity to spread that philosophy to our guests.
- We believe in striving to fit into the environment. Wewill build with the environment. We spend what it takes to design around trees, over sensitive streams and outcrops, to build with natural products that are sustainably harvested by communities that are not forced into labour. Where it's appropriate we use canvas.
- We will not be in conservation-tourism without creating great eco-lodges and eco-camps ensuring that conservation efforts are sustainable.
- We also like our expert guides to say when they don't know. They will try to find out the answers to difficult questions.
- We live by an ethic that says that we are polite and ethical, welcoming and gentle. We subscribe to the involvement of communities and conservation in our commercial ventures.

The Selinda Reserve basically forms a corridor between the Okavango Delta and the Kwando / Linyanti areas. An important feature on the reserve is the

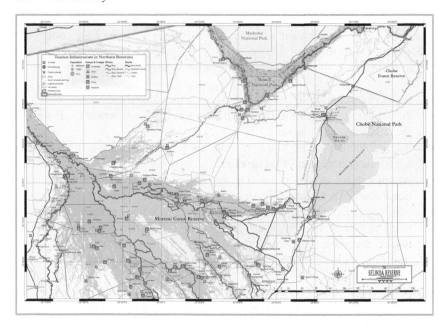

Figure 17.2 The Seinda Reserve is located in the center of the above map marked NG16

Selinda Spillway that forms an overflow from the Okavango Delta in the west and an overflow from the Kwando and Linyanti systems in the east (see Figure 17.2). On August 17ᵗʰ 2009, the two bodies of waters met for the first time in 30 years along the Selinda Spillway. The area plays an important role for wildlife, as it is a natural migratory route for animals and in particular elephants. This was probably the main reason for acquiring the concession back in 2005. The first decision made when taking over the concession was to stop all forms of hunting on the concession. Since that date, the neighboring concession areas continued to hunt up until the end of 2009. We are not in favour of any form of hunting and do not support any arguments that try to justify this activity.

One of our first projects when taking over the concession was to build a camp that that would offer extreme luxury in a remote area run off renewable energy. Of course there were the skeptics who said that it just would not work and the only way to operate in such a remote area was with massive generators emitting carbon deposits into the atmosphere. The camp was completed in July of 2008 and since that date has made a big impact regionally as well as globally in the industry.

All of the power requirements for Zarafa camp (lighting, refrigeration, pumps, etc.) are supplied from a solar farm located at the back of camp. There are 170 solar panels providing 120m² of light capture area. A separate system of solar water heaters provides hot water to the rooms.

The Zarafa Solar Farm

The 170 panels are set up in six rows of twenty-four 24V solar panels (each row is called an array) (see Figure 17.3). We also have one set of 26 panels which are an older generation panel and not as efficient. The panels are paired to give a 48V system. Each array feeds into its own regulator, which regulates the amperage to the batteries. Each array can push a max of 72A at 48V, but the amperage varies depending on the state of charge of the batteries and the ambient light. When the batteries are low (around 50%-65%), the regulators allow more power to be supplied into the batteries. The seventh array (of older generation panels) supplies about half of what the other arrays do. A total of around 450A can be supplied into the batteries from the solar panels alone. On a normal day, when the batteries are not too low (say around 75-85%) and sunshine is good, each regulator supplies between 50A and 60A, producing a total of around 350A which is supplied into the batteries.

The batteries have a capacity of 5200Ah. Between 800Ah and 1600Ah (around 15% to 30% of capacity) is used through the night, which can easily be replaced the following day.

The camp runs on 48V-240V inverters, which draw 48V from the batteries and supply 240V to the camp. There are 3 x 3000VA inverters (totaling 9KVA) for the front of house (with another 2 on standby) and 2 x 3000VA inverters (totaling 6KVA) for the back of house, so together there is 15KVA available to run the camp. Daily running of camp draws around 7-10KVA.

Figure 17.3 Solar panels (Photo by author)

Figure 17.4 Power generating unit (Photo by author)

The daily running of camp draws between 100A and 150A from the batteries before it gets inverted. So, there is around 350A being supplied from the solar panels and 150A being drawn by the camp, resulting in a net current of 200A being supplied to the batteries to replace the power used the previous night.

There is a 40KVA generator on standby to ensure there is always power available in camp. During the rainy season (November to April), when there may not be enough sunlight for the solar system, the generator can also be used to top-up the batteries. During November it was necessary to run the generator around once a week to top-up the batteries (see Figure 17.4).

The solar system was commissioned at the beginning of November 2008 and during its first month the generator was only needed for 30 hours (reduced from an average of 200 hours per month since it was installed). Diesel use in camp dropped from an average of 1500l per month to only 250l in November.

Recent calculations have given us the following information:

Zarafa Camp's carbon emissions

Zarafa power usage: 3000Ah in 24 hours
1200Ah overnight from18h00 – 07h00 and
1800Ah from 07h00 – 18h00

- Therefore the generator would need to replace 3000Ah in a day
- Generator (charging) output: 350A to charge batteries

- To replace 3000Ah generator needs to run for 8.5 hours (3000Ah/350A = 8.5h)
- The generator uses around 10litres of diesel per hour
- It would thus use 85 litres of diesel to run for 8.5 hours
- **Carbon output: 713 g C per litre of diesel (or 2.664kg CO_2)**
- Over a day it would produce 60.6kg carbon (713g C/litre x 85litres = 60.6kg)

In a month we would produce 1900kg carbon (almost 2 tonnes of carbon) and over 7 tonnes of CO^2

Over a year we would produce over 22000kg (or over 22 tonnes of carbon) and over 82 tonnes of CO_2

- Since November 2008, we've used 2800 litres of diesel, which when combusted produces 2000kg carbon (7540kg CO_2)
- Without the solar, we would have used 23000 litres of diesel, equating to emissions of 16500kg carbon (61200kg CO_2)
- So we have reduced our carbon emissions from the generator by 14500kg carbon (almost 15 tonnes) and CO_2 emissions by 53 tonnes which represents a reduction of over 85%.

Game Drives and Protocol

Guides operating within the concession are expected to adhere to several in-house guidelines whilst conducting open vehicle safaris, some of these are as follows, and their obvious emphasis is on minimal environmental impacts:

- Game drives can be comfortably conducted at between 20-30km/h if the road/terrain allows and must be conducted in High-range 4x4. This will ensure that there is as little damage to roads as possible and will reduce the amount of inputs needed to maintain, divert or reconstruct them.
- Off-road driving must be considered the exception rather than the norm – any off-road driving must be conducted in such a way that the impact to the environment is at the absolute minimum, with every consideration possible taken into account.
- No driving on sodic soils - these areas are ecologically sensitive and highly susceptible to erosion and degradation
- Move branches off the road, do not drive around them – this will ensure that any unavoidable impacts resulting in the creation of a road remain 'once-off' and are contained within the road itself. By removing obstacles we will avoid the situation whereby there may be adverse effects caused to the environment from creating alternative paths and roads around movable objects.
- Switch vehicle off when viewing game.
- Don't race to any sighting anytime, anywhere.
- When viewing animals at night, do not shine directly in an animal's eyes, rather shine the light on the body or bounce the light off the ground.

- Do not shine the spotlight on any diurnal species – the tapetum of these animals is extremely sensitive and may render them temporarily disorientated and thus vulnerable.
- When animals are hunting, do not shine the light on predator or prey.
- Do not intentionally influence the behavior of any animal or cause a reaction.
- No standing in the vehicle at any time or unnecessary noise by staff or guests that may disrupt or impact the wildlife you are viewing.

Ecological monitoring

As per the concession lease agreements the company has maintained environmental and ecological monitoring programs since 1995. Where ecological monitoring of large areas is concerned one of the most obvious and common hindrances is the cost involved in obtaining thorough and reputable data suitable for statistical analysis over time. NG16 as occupied by Linyanti Explorations has faced exactly these challenges, however, where many other occupants may have opted for cheaper and basic data collections methods, we have maintained that over the last fifteen years the ecological monitoring program implemented for NG16 adheres to a strict set of parameters to ensure reputability, with this as the emphasis and not necessarily the cost of such a program. The objectives for this are to have a continuously running data set that will cater not only for estimates of change in population sizes of various large mammals, but more holistically to allow identification of trends regarding animal population dynamics; animal diversity and composition; vegetation / habitat condition; seasonal influences and variation; the importance of water availability and how it relates to both seasonal and population dynamics. This ultimately ensures that there is always sufficient data and knowledge to encourage sound and sustainable environmental management by the company. In order to achieve this we have created an ecological monitoring program that has been improved and perfected over the last fifteen years to include fields that offer reputable data for:

- Waterhole levels (as a percentage of potential capacity)
- Flood levels and water movements from the Okavango delta system
- Flood levels and water movements from the Kwando River system
- Tstetse fly distribution and densities within NG16
- Rainfall distribution and variation within NG16
- Temperature ranges within NG16
- Extent and damages of bushfires in NG16
- Unusual species observations in NG16
- Mortalities and predation trends in NG16
- Status of Red Lechwe in NG16
- Relationships between biomass and population estimates in NG16
- Species diversity within NG16 through aerial and full-moon ground counts
- Vegetation structure, distribution and relation to population densities

In order to achieve precise records regarding animal populations and their movements we have been implementing aerial game counting techniques. Any employed counting technique is susceptible to various forms of error, which may taint data analysis. As an attempt to overcome these potential variables the method of aerial counting has been based on the well-known and respected technique of strip counting from a light fixed wing aircraft. Aerial counts, although the most expensive method per time unit, are without question the most reliable in observing game population trends for large areas as is the case with NG16 and hence have been employed for the last fifteen years. The general technique regarding aerial counts in this form take into consideration flying time, height above ground and allow for the removal of variables such as counter variances in eye-height and positioning, likewise strip width and sample sets are pre-defined over the entire concession and repeatedly counted annually. All though a single aerial count conducted at the driest time of the year where visibility, due to low vegetation, is at its highest, would possibly be considered sufficient, within NG16 the company decision has been to allow for a more comprehensive data set to be collected and thus the aerial counts are conducted no less than three times per annum. The selection of these counting times caters for the various shifts in water availability, temperature and rainfall and how they may affect animal movements and population dynamics. As a result Mid-summer (peak wet season); Autumn (start of the cold and dry) and the Spring count (start of the hot and dry) have been identified and used as most likely to illustrate the largest variances in game movements across the concession.

In addition to these aerial counts the collection of the various data fields, as mentioned previously, are simultaneously recorded form the air. The remaining contributions for the data analysis of animal populations throughout NG16 are conducted throughout the year by various members of staff that have direct contact with 'on the ground' sightings. This includes full-moon game counts, records of known mortalities; casual ground counts; ongoing bird records and sightings lists and more specifically vegetation surveys.

The broad spectrum of variables that are monitored by the company in NG16 each year accompanied by the thoroughness and longevity of data collection has meant that several valuable insights pertaining to the seasonal shifts and movements within the concession can be realized. The method in which this data is manipulated and analyzed is as important as the methods of its collection. In order to ensure minimal precision error and correct data analysis is present the company has been using the techniques described by G.M. Jolly (1969) as published by the Journal for East African Agriculture. These techniques have been widely used in the counting of large mammal populations in the Serengeti complex.

Overall, the largest inference that has been made possible pertains to the dependability of most of the game species present on the concession to both permanent water availability, seasonal shifts in this availability and the location of such water within various habitats. As a means of being able to further understand this, the company has identified different vegetation zones and their extent of cover over the concession. This has been mapped and described in the annual monitoring data document. Overlaid on this is soil variations and bio-resource groups and furthermore the movement trends of various animals species within each major vegetation unit. The more obvious conclusions pertaining from the data gathered over the past fifteen years is the seasonal movement of large mammal species, in particular elephant, and their preference for different vegetation units seasonally. Likewise the diversity and density of game is heavily influenced by vegetation structure, type and availability of surface water. As a result vegetation health and condition is proportionately influenced by such factors as seasonal movement of game. Because of the design of the data set and the methods of recording, what is also evident is the movement holistically into and out of the entire concession with regards to both animal numbers and biomass estimates. This is considered in relation to the changes in land-use from controlled off-take to entirely photographic policies. Over the years several rare and unexpected species have been counted and noted through the casual, 'on the ground' counts and are valuable in both distribution and occurrence amendments for some rarer species of mammal.

Overall the ecological management, observation and analysis within NG16 with the current lessees have been both thorough and well maintained over the past fifteen years. This emphasizes the heavy weighting put on sound environmental policies and an ultimate desire to ensure sustainability of the safari operation currently operating within the concession. To entertain any thoughts of changing or lowering the standard of ecological monitoring within the concession will only have adverse effects and ultimately render much of the meticulously recorded data and research as obsolete.

Waste Management

This has become a huge challenge for camps operating in remote areas. The reason it becomes a challenge is because there is a cost associated to the removal or processing of solid or liquid waste either by reduction of waste, reuse of waste, recycling of waste and final disposal of waste. NG16 is a designated RAMSAR site and is therefore seen as an ecologically sensitive and needs to adhere to specific requirements.

We do not believe in burning any waste materials that has been bought into the concession. We have had to then implement a system whereby we can firstly reduce the amount of waste produced. We have achieved this through a number of ways. All three of our camps have a reverse osmosis filtration plant for drinking water. Guests and staff are able to drink this safe water instead of making use of bottled water. The disposal of plastic water bottles is a global problem that we certainly do not want to add to. Guests are given a stainless steel bottles to make use of during their stay at the camps and these are refilled from the filtration plant. Previously our camps were going through up to 200 bottles per day which adds up to a huge amount of waste.

As is required of our camps, we are separating waste materials into wet waste, plastic, glass, paper and tins. We have started a pilot project with worm farms to reduce the amount of wet waste that has to be removed from the concession. This is a process whereby we collect certain wet waste into a container with a local worm species where they break down the waste and produce a fertilizer. We will then remove this fertilizer from the concession in bags.

I believe that one of our limiting factors for us to become even more environmentally friendly is the limited facilities for re-cycling the country has to offer. Our operation is located in the remote region of northern Botswana and the closest town of reasonable size is Maun. Our head office is based out of an even smaller town called Kasane in the north eastern corner of Botswana and this town has even less facilities than Maun, which is just about non existent. We are exploring options to open a re-cycling facility in Kasane as part of our business that initially will act as a depot where tins and glass can be collected and sent to a city for recycling. The only way for this project to be cost effective would be for us to negotiate a subsidized transport rate.

Cost is one of the biggest obstacles for every business to reduce their carbon foot-print. Another example of this is the maintenance of our solar plant at Zarafa. Of course the capital expense was very high, but added to that the suppliers are based in Cape Town so as this technology is new to us and under warranty, we are obliged to get the technicians up from Cape Town to repair the system. The flights alone to get one technician into camp from Cape Town are $1000 per person. The up side though is that there are other lodges in the area who have seen that having solar power in the bush can work and our system has been copied by other lodges. This, we are delighted with as not only are we always encourage others to reduce their carbon foot-print, but it means that we can all share the costs of getting technicians in.

Demands of travelers can be an obstacle in our whole philosophy of environmental awareness. As mentioned before, we have put in a big drive to eliminate all plastic water bottles that we bring into the concession. A major global problem these plastic water bottles have become. Even though we have reverse osmosis filtration plants in the camps, some guests still insist on having commercially produced water in plastic bottles.

Conclusion

We may never get it completely right and we will always have guests who visit our lodges who do not share the same beliefs as we do. There will always be the critics sitting on the side not agreeing with our methods. We are a committed company and will continue to explore new ways to conserve the natural habitats, conserve the wildlife that exists around us, reduce our carbon foot-print as far as possible and empower our surrounding communities.

18 Sustainable development of a remote tourist destination

The case of Soomaa National Park, Estonia

Heli Tooman* and Aivar Ruukel**

Introduction

Estonia is the smallest and northernmost of the three Baltic states bordering on Russia, Latvia, and Finland (Figure 18.1). The Republic of Estonia was proclaimed on 24 February 1918. Although Estonia lost its independence during the Second World War, independence was re-established on 20 August 1991. On 1 May 2004 Estonia became an EU member state and joined the Schengen visa space in December 2007. In 2011 Estonia will probably join the euro zone. Estonia has a population of 1.34 million, of which Estonians (68.7%) make up the majority while 25.6% are Russians. The average population density is 30.9 inhabitants per sq km. Tallinn is the largest city with a population of almost 404,500 while the other major centres include Tartu (98,500), Narva (65,800), and Pärnu (43,000). The official language is Estonian (Estonian Ministry of Foreign Affairs, 2010).

Despite its small size Estonia's geography and culture are surprisingly varied. About 40% of the country is covered with natural forests; there are numerous lakes, wetlands, and swamps, and the 3,794 km coastline are strongly indented. There are about 1500 coastal islands. Historical traditions, culture, and buildings are well preserved, and the medieval old town of the capital Tallinn is a UNESCO World Heritage site. The status of a UNESCO Masterpiece of the Oral and Intangible Heritage of Humanity has been awarded to the Kihnu Cultural Space (2008), the Baltic Song and Dance Celebrations (2008), and the Seto Leelo, Seto polyphonic singing tradition (2009) (The Intangible Heritage List, 2010).

Volumes of international tourism are relatively low (1.38 million foreign tourists in 2009) whereas its intensity is high – one foreign tourist per resident a year. According to a survey by the World Economic Forum, Estonia won the 28th place for tourism competitiveness among 124 countries (World Economic Forum, 2009). Although the statistical indicators of Estonia's tourism appear good, there

*Pärnu College, University of Tartu, Estonia
**Estonian University of Life Sciences

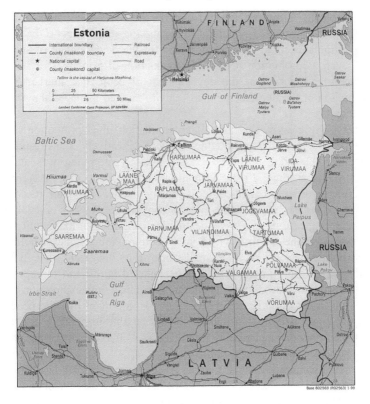

Figure 18.1 Map of Estonia
   Source: University of Texas Libraries

are a number of bottlenecks that may potentially endanger competitiveness and sustainable development.

The Ministry of Economic Affairs and Communications prepares and develops tourism policy as a component of the overall economic policy with the aim of ensuring people's economic and social welfare through stable economic growth, increased international competitiveness, and secure sustainable development. It is also responsible for the preparation of draft legislation, implementation of regulations, coordinating tourism policy and activities, sourcing state funds, inclusion of EU funding, and communication with international organizations (Eesti turismipoliitika, 2003; Majandus- ja kommunikatsiooniministeerium, 2010). The Enterprise Estonia Foundation (EAS) absorbed the Tourist Board in 2000, established the Tourism Development Centre, and assumed responsibility for the implementation of the national tourism policy. Its tasks include domestic and international marketing, target market research, coordination of the network of national Tourist Information Centre (TIC), and international cooperation (Enterprise Estonia, 2010).

In November 2006, the Estonian Parliament adopted the National Development Plan for Tourism for 2007–2013 (Eesti riiklik, 2006). The plan costs ca 206 million euros and is mostly financed through the Enterprise Estonia / Estonian Tourist Board from the EU structural funds and the state budget (OECD, 2010). The plan stipulates some specific measures for the development of sustainable tourism, such as promotion of the implementation of principles of sustainable development; promotion of the development of ecological tourism products and promotion of the implementation of environmental managerial systems and certification.

Estonia is little known as a tourism destination, thus promotion is highly prioritized. The Estonian marketing concept 'Positively transforming' was launched in 2002, and its updated version 'Positively surprising' was launched in 2009 (Introduce Estonia, 2009). A small country needs to make a significantly bigger effort in order to become internationally visible. Above all, its communication has to be clear and distinctive since a big picture consists of small details. Thus, presenting Estonia as a travel destination includes four main topics that are most important to the country – city holiday, cultural holiday, nature holiday, and wellness holiday. Each topic is a small world in its own right, though in some cases they are closely intertwined. For example, it is difficult to approach the topic of city holiday without paying attention to culture, and exploration of nature certainly promotes good health. Therefore, it is important that the people who present the topics of Estonian tourism should be able to perceive the fine line between a city holiday and a cultural holiday, as well as the differences between a nature holiday and a wellness holiday.

There is no common regional tourism policy on the regional level as yet, but regional organizations have a clear understanding of their development visions and objectives. Regional development plans also provide for obligations and responsibilities of the private and public sectors in the development of sustainable tourism. Thus, tourism is better integrated cross-sector-wise, which reduces leakage through imported tourism services and regulates the efficient and sustainable use of limited resources available. The development activities of the tourism organizations depend on various aid programmes, and regional development is largely project-based, which may become a critical issue in terms of long-term and sustainable development. On the positive side, regions are active stakeholders, whose aim is to put all the resources to good use, thereby stimulating the interest of both domestic and incoming tourists.

Sustainable Development In Estonia

The idea of sustainable use of resources in the travel and tourism industry is not new in Estonia. Already in 1938 the Institute of Nature Preservation and Tourism was established, under the Ministry of Social affairs, in order to address these issues. Since regaining independence in 1991, Estonia has been developing rapidly. Harmonization of Estonian legislation with the requirements of EU legislation has been an integral part of Estonia's transition to market economy. Estonia was one of the first countries in the world to adopt its Sustainable Development Act in 1995. Environmental legislation has often been changed after Estonia regained its independence. Therefore, it is not easy to bring oneself up to date with all the pertinent information. There is a separate Tourism Law (Turismiseadus, 2000), which directly addresses sustainable development in tourism.

The legal basis for sustainable development in Estonia is provided by the Constitution of the Republic of Estonia, which entered into force in 1992. The Act on Sustainable Development was approved in 1995. According to the amendment to this act in 1997, long-term plans with regard to sustainable development are elaborated in energy, transport, agriculture, forestry, tourism, chemical industry, building materials, and food industry. Estonia's active partnership in sustainable processes on the global level started at the UN Conference on Environment and Development (Rio Conference) in 1992, and the implementation of the Agenda 21 and Millennium Development Goals were renewed at the UN Summit on Sustainable Development in Johannesburg in 2002 (Sustainable Development in Estonia). Estonia was among the eleven countries that launched the regional sustainable cooperation process Baltic Agenda in 1996. The main document of the Agenda 21 for the Baltic Sea Region was adopted in 1998. The overall aim of the process is to constantly improve the living and working conditions of all the inhabitants of the Baltic Sea region within the framework of sustainable development, the sustainable management of the natural resources, and environmental protection.

The Estonian Commission on Sustainable Development was founded in 1996 as an advisory body to the government on the issues of sustainable development. The task of the commission is to analyse the policy of the state on sustainable development and to make proposals to the government and to the state and local government institutions in order to ensure synergy among developments in the economy, social affairs, and the environment. The commission also has the right to propose draft legislation, to organize research on the subject, and to supervise the development of the Estonian National Strategy on Sustainable Development – Sustainable Estonia 21, which was approved by the Estonian Parliament in September 2005 (Sustainable Estonia, 2005). Sustainable Estonia 21 (SE21) is an integral conception, which is clearly focused on the sustainability of long-term development of the Estonian state and society until the year 2030. The general development goal of the country is to integrate the requirement to be successful in global competition with a sustainable development model and preservation of the traditional values of Estonia.

According to the strategy, the long-term goals of the development of the society are as follows:

- **Viability of the Estonian cultural space**. According to the Constitution of the Republic of Estonia, the state of Estonia shall ensure the preservation of Estonian nature and culture through the ages. Sustainability of the Estonian nation and culture constitutes the cornerstone of sustainable development of Estonia.
- **Growth of welfare.** Welfare is defined as the satisfaction of material, social, and cultural needs of individuals, accompanied by opportunities for individual self-realization and for realizing one's aspirations and goals;

- **Coherent society**. Achievement of the first two goals will be possible only if the benefits from these goals can be used by the majority of the population, and the price for achieving these goals is not destructive for the society as an integral organism;
- **Ecological balance**. Maintenance of ecological balance in Estonian nature is a precondition for sustainability. It is also Estonia's contribution to global development, following the principle that requires a balance both in matter cycles and energy flows at all levels of the living environment.

The first report on the state of the implementation of the Estonian National Strategy on Sustainable Development was compiled and submitted to the government in 2007. It included a review of the principal activities necessary for the implementation of the strategy and an analysis of the attainment of the objectives set by the strategy. The Estonian Environmental Strategy 2030 builds upon the principles of 'Sustainable Estonia 21' and serves as the basis for the preparation and revision of all sector-specific development plans within the sphere of the environment. The strategy was approved by the Estonian Parliament in 2007, and it defines long-term development trends for maintaining a good status of the natural environment while keeping in mind the links between the environment, economic and social spheres, and the overall impact on the natural environment and people. The National Environmental Action Plan for Estonia for 2007–2013 serves as the implementation plan of the Strategy.

According to the EC eco-label regulation, after EU accession in 2004 Estonia had to develop a system enabling enterprises to apply for and use the EC ecolabel – the flower. According to the environmental impact assessment and the environment management system act, the competent institution for issuing the ecolabel in Estonia is the Information and Technical Centre of the Ministry of Environment. In 2009 the EC ecolabel was issued to only two Estonian enterprises. In fact, several labels similar to the ecolabel (FSC, Fair Trade, etc.), organic farming labels, and various self-declared labels (Green Energy, etc.) are much more common than the EU ecolabel. The introduction of environment management systems is on the increase. As of 22 October 2009, there were 278 enterprises in Estonia certified according to the ISO 14001:2004 standard and one according to the EMAS standard (UN CSD18, 2010).

One of the key challenges of sustainable development is the introduction of the combined conception of nature as a value and as a central development resource of society in the context of the overall development of Estonia. The overall aim of the maintenance of ecological balance in Estonian nature is to integrate the considerations of the self-regeneration capacity of nature into the use of nature. The main function of environmental protection is to achieve harmonious and balanced management of resources and the natural environment in the interests of the Estonian society.

Governance in the field of environmental is based on adequate information, and for this purpose generalized data on Estonian nature, the state of the environ-ment, and different impact factors are provided by the Estonian Environment Information Centre (Estonian Environment Information Centre). An additional objective information service with regard to the economic, demographic, social, and environmental situation, as well as the present trends in Estonia, is provided by Statistics Estonia (Statistics Estonia). Inter-linkages and the core set of sustainability indicators on maps for European countries, regions, and Estonian counties, as well as the performance evaluation of countries, regions, and counties can be found at Dashboard of Sustainability (Statistics Estonia).

Estonia's own experience proves that economic growth and the environmentally sustainable path of development can be achieved if the relevant measures are applied both at the national and the local levels. There are many instances of best practices and cooperation in rural areas in the field of sustainable development all over Estonia, which the authors of the present study would like to share (Sustainable development in Estonia).

The case study of Soomaa National Park

Soomaa tourism development region

In 1957 in a small part of the present national park – Halliste wooded meadow – was established as botanical restriction area. Later in 1981 large raised bogs – Valgeraba, Ördi, Kuresoo, and Kikepera – were selected among the valuable wetlands of bog conservation areas. Soomaa 'bog land' National Park (SNP), which was established in 1993, is the youngest national park in Estonia. Its area is 390 km², which makes it the second largest park after the Lahemaa National Park (see Figure 18.2). The first area-based protection rules were adopted in 1995.

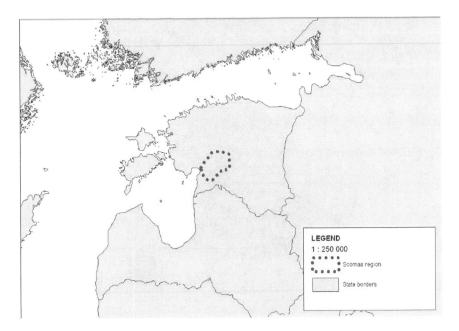

Figure 18.2 Map of Estonia, Soomaa tourism development region (Sustainable tourism development strategy for Soomaa NP 2009-2013, 2008)

However, because of changes in Estonian nature conservation legislation in 2004, the protection rules were revised, and the new protection rules were adopted in 2005. The national park lies in south-western Estonia in a forest-rich zone (Figure 18.3), and the purpose of its establishment was to protect large raised bogs, flood plain grasslands, swampy forests, and meandering rivers (Soomaa National Park, 2010).

Throughout its history, SNP has been used for agriculture, logging, and forestry, which has made an impact on the area. In 1997 SNP was awarded the status of a CORINE biotope area and was included in the list of Europe's most important nature protection areas. It also became a Ramsar site and was put on the Ramsar List of Wetlands. A year later, in 1998, SNP was proposed to become a UNESCO World Natural Heritage site. In 2004 SNP joined the Natura 2000 network. The visitor centre of SNP was also established that year, and it is located in the middle of the park. The visitor centre is situated at an ancient crossroads that lead from Pärnu to Viljandi and was used for transporting goods in the early 20th century (Soomaa National Park, 2010).

The territory of the national park is mostly covered with large mires, separated from each other by the rivers of the Pärnu river basin. Among the raised bogs the most noteworthy one is Kuresoo, whose steep southern slope, which falls into the Lemmjõgi river, rises by 8 metres over a distance of 100 m. On the eastern edge of the national park lie the highest dunes on the Estonian mainland, situated some 50 kilometres off the contemporary coastline. The most characteristic coastal

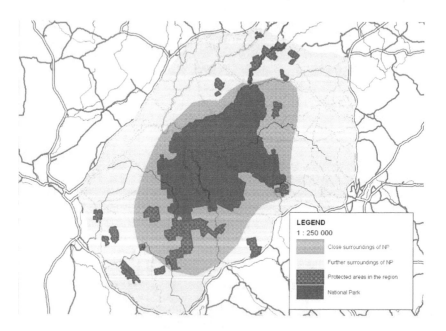

Figure 18.3 General zoning of the Soomaa tourism region (Sustainable Tourism Development Strategy for Soomaa NP 2009-2013, 2008)

formations of the predecessor of the present Baltic Sea, the Baltic Ice Lake (11,200–10,600 years ago), which marks the one-time water level, are situated on the north-western and western edges of the Sakala Upland. The Ruunaraipe Dunes are the highest in the area. The dune ridge, winding from the north-west to the south-east is a 1.2 km long sand ridge with a maximum height of 12 metres.

Soomaa tourism development region is an area where sustainable tourism (especially nature tourism) is strongly related to Soomaa National Park, and the tourist visiting the area will get the 'Soomaa experience'. The area does not follow any former geographical divisions but resulted from an agreement of the stakeholders of Soomaa tourism. The boundary of the region is not absolute, which means that, in principle, one can get the Soomaa experience outside the fixed boundary. Nevertheless, the area shown is the region agreed by all the stakeholders in Soomaa tourism and corresponds to the present state of the Soomaa tourism environment.

The boundary of the Soomaa tourism region was fixed with the following considerations:

- Soomaa NP and its landscape scale management unit (Large Soomaa);
- Tourism development influence area (products and services of sustainable tourism related to Soomaa NP);
- Soomaa landscape region;
- Staying in Pärnu and Viljandi counties and reaching both towns;
- Keeping the boundaries flexible; the border is not absolute and it is possible to find common ground outside the boundaries as well.

The main value of Soomaa is its wilderness. Also, the local settlement, which has evolved in the course of millennia, is unique and invaluable. People in Soomaa have become adapted to the natural conditions. In the land of mires and rivers, the local people have developed their own lifestyle and traditions. This sparsely populated and almost natural area is a magnificent example of people living together with wilderness.

Soomaa NP is designated to preserve both of these values. Tourism (in and around the national park) requires understanding the values of Soomaa and respect for the principles of local livelihood. The tourism products must take into account nature and local cultural heritage in marketing, service provision, expansion of business and other related activities.

Strategy of sustainable tourism development for Soomaa National Park

In 2009 Soomaa National Park, the largest intact peat bog system in Europe preserved as wilderness joined the PAN Parks network of wilderness areas as it proved excellence in combining wilderness protection and sustainable tourism development (PAN Parks). The sustainable Tourism Development Strategy for Soomaa National Park (STDS) was initiated when Soomaa NP applied for membership of the PAN Parks network of best-managed wilderness protected areas in Europe. At present the PAN Parks network consists of eleven national parks all over Europe; the concept of PAN Parks combines conservation with sustainable tourism. The Sustainable Tourism Development Strategy of Soomaa National Park is the first regional tourism strategy that has been developed in cooperation with different tourism stakeholders related to Soomaa NP (Sustainable Tourism Development Strategy for of Soomaa NP 2009-2013, 2008).

The strategy, though, was not the first document of its kind. The management plan of Soomaa NP management plan, which was drawn up in 1999, deals with visitor management in the national park. From a broader perpective, tourism in the region has been planned in accordance with the development plan of recreation and tourism management of Pärnu county, the strategy of Viljandi county, the development plans of local municipalities, the management plan of the Sakala recreation area of the State Forest Management Service, and the tourism and recreation development plan and strategy of the Green Riverland.

While all the previously mentioned documents cover tourism and its development in and around Soomaa NP, then none of them covers the entire Soomaa NP region, and most of them do not focus on Soomaa NP. The strategy was worked out in cooperation with the regional nature conservation office (State Nature Conservation Centre / Environmental Board), the county governments of Viljandi and Pärnu, local municipalities, several NGOs, and tourism entrepreneurs. In the present document the tourism stakeholders have agreed on shared vision and development goals and have planned joint steps to achieve the aforementioned goals.

There are four strategic aims of tourism development in Soomaa:

- **Ecological aim** – Soomaa tourism supports the objectives of nature conservation in Soomaa NP and does not harm the natural environment of the Soomaa tourism region;
- **Economic aim** – tourism supports local livelihood with job creation and entrepreneurship and supports the sustainability of traditional businesses;
- **Social aim** – tourism supports the welfare of the local community and preservation of local way of life and does not harm the social environment of the area;
- **Tourism development aim** – Soomaa tourism products and services have an outstanding quality, and the tourism entrepreneurs are competitive and sustainable.

The aim of the strategy is also to support the development of sustainable tourism in Soomaa NP and thus to support the nature conservation goals of the national park. The strategy:

- sets the principles for sustainable tourism in the area and provides operational guidelines for the next five years;
- sets priorities for making funding decisions and the implementation of the action plan;

- provides guidelines to tourism stakeholders how to develop future tourism products;
- serves as a base document for funding the development of sustainable tourism in the area.

STDS is a strategy that is developed and implemented in cooperation with the Protected Area Authority and important stakeholders in the region of the PAN Park. Together these bodies aim at creating a synergy between the conservation of natural values and sustainable tourism.

The tourism stakeholders of Soomaa include different individuals and organizations, who have a special interest or who are affected by tourism in Soomaa. These stakeholders are as follows.

- The local community – people who live in the national park as well as people in the wider region that are involved with Soomaa and interested in it. This interest has to be manifested in the planning of tourism in the area and in creating a situation where tourism would not affect their life significantly.
- Local municipality governments – five from Pärnu county and three from Viljandi county. Their interest is to preserve their municipalities as the enjoyable living environment and to develop it as an attractive tourist destination. Tourism is an important area of life in all the municipalities in that it creates job opportunities.
- The county governments of Pärnu and Viljandi are interested in creating an attractive tourist destination, which links the interests of different municipalities.
- The Environmental Board, the administrator of the protected areas, is responsible for the favourable conservation status of the protected values and for raising the awareness of conservation issues.
- The State Forest Management Service is interested in sustaining the management of state forests and creating recreation possibilities. Among other things this institution is responsible for providing information to visitors of the protected areas and for maintaining tourism infrastructure.
- Green Riverland, a cooperation initiative, is an organization that develops local initiatives in the area under the Leader programme. It includes local municipalities, NGOs, and entrepreneurs. The entire Soomaa tourism region lied within Green Riverland, and many of the activities listed in the action plan could be funded through the funds available from the Leader programme of Green Riverland. Its interest is to increase welfare in the region.
- NGO Soomaa Tourism is a network of entrepreneurs and other stakeholders with the purpose of supporting the development of tourism in the Soomaa region. Its interests include the development of the tourism sector in the Soomaa region, larger visitor numbers, the image of Soomaa, and, better marketing.
- NGO Viljandimaa tourism – its interest is the development of the tourism sector in Viljandi county.

- Foundation Pärnumaa Turism – its interest lies in the development of the tourism sector in Pärnu county.
- Tipu Nature School is a NGO with the aim of developing a nature school from the former Tipu schoolhouse. Interest – the development of Tipu village.
- Village societies. More than ten villages. Interested in the development of the area.
- Estonian Logboat Society. Interest – promotion of logboats.
- Friends of Soomaa. Interest – support of the management of Soomaa NP.
- Landowners, who live outside the site. Interest – not connected with tourism development.
- Tourism entrepreneurs. Interest – development of their businesses, growth of tourist numbers.
- Researchers. Interests – special fields of research in the Soomaa region and development of sustainable tourism.
- Hunting societies with hunting land in the Soomaa tourism region. Interest – tourism should not affect significantly hunting and population control activities.
- Fishermen. Interest in fishing.
- Visitors' interest – unique experience, quality, and diversity of services.
- Soomaa Cooperation Panel – Commission of different organizations that affect or are affected by Soomaa NP. The panel acts as a local PAN park group. Interest – improvement of information exchange, development of the region, cooperation between organizations.

The Soomaa Cooperation Panel as a coordinating unit, a network of different stakeholders related to the Soomaa tourism area. The role of the Soomaa Cooperation Panel is to coordinate the activities of state organizations as well as NGOs and entrepreneurs and supervise sustainable development in the Soomaa area. A prerequisite for cooperation is dissemination of information and under-standing the other parties. The cooperation panel meets four times a year on a regular basis and if necessary also more often. It makes suggestions on how to solve problems and face challenges. It also acts as a local PAN park group and is responsible for the development of sustainable tourism in the area.

According to the strategy of sustainable development, the Soomaa region is divided into four tourism zones (Figure 18.3). The aim of zoning in the Soomaa tourism area is to avoid or minimize the negative impacts of tourism and increase its positive impacts. Zoning takes into account the rules of the protected areas, the present tourism corridors (roads and rivers) and the trail system. It also takes into consideration the municipal plans and the existing land use, the wishes of the local community, and the development potential. Zoning serves as a basis for the following activities:

- Organization of different types of tourism (avoiding contacts between non-sustainable tourism and sustainable tourism, etc).

- Setting of priorities for land use (tourism vs. habitat management, etc).
- Planning and management of tourism intensity.
- Guiding of independent tourists and estimation of the need for guiding.
- Development of new tourism infrastructure or expansion of the existing facilities.

General zoning is divided into four zones (Figure 18.3):

- **National park territory** (39,640 ha) – the most sensitive area as well as the most attractive part of the region. All the activities are regulated by the protection rules. Unsustainable varieties of tourism are prohibited. The area exposes wilderness, nature-friendly lifestyle, and sustainable businesses.
- **Other protected areas in the region** (10,770 ha) – small protected areas that depend on the well-being of the national park and the surrounding region. All the activities are regulated by the protection rules. In most cases tourism is minimized.
- **The immediate surroundings of Soomaa NP** (~52,240 ha) – the NP depends greatly on its immediate surroundings and the other way round. Usually the Soomaa experience starts in this zone. Settlements and businesses are favoured; the village should provide the necessary supporting services. The local municipalities set general limitations on business. The tourism businesses use Soomaa NP as an attraction for marketing, and therefore are willing to follow the principles of sustainability.
- **The further surroundings of Soomaa NP** (~118,300). This area is more loosely related to Soomaa. It connects the Soomaa area with larger towns (Pärnu and Viljandi), major roads (Via Baltica, Tallinn-Valga). There are also many tourism entrepreneurs who use Soomaa NP as an attraction, but at the same time there are also opportunities for less sustainable businesses (off-road driving, hunting, etc). It is important that undesirable businesses should not be developed in this area.

In matters of services and specialized activities the immediate surroundings of NP are zoned in greater detail, and for this reason additional zones are designed:

- **The taboo areas of local community** – private areas of local people, where rules set by the owners apply.
- **The impact zones of tourism objects** – the surroundings of the existing facilities where the tourism has an impact on nature. In these zones it is recommended to improve the existing facilities and to develop new attractions.
- **The impact zones of waterways** – the immediate surroundings of the rivers. In these zones new facilities can be developed only in designated places.
- **Areas that should be visited with a guide** – inaccessible areas with sensitive values.

- **Areas with a limited number of visits** – areas that are sensitive to disturbance; protection rules regulate moving restrictions.
- **Restricted areas** – protection rules prohibit entry in these areas.

Zoning is an important means of planning sustainable tourism; it is an agreement that serves as a basis on which the present and the future enterprises draw
up their business plans Also, zoning provides guidelines with regard to guided
and independent visits as well as tourism activities.

Local people and tourism

There are three villages – Tipu, Riisa, and Sandra – within the boundaries of
Soomaa National Park; altogether there are 70 permanent residents. In the
Soomaa Tourism Region the number of local residents is ca 1,500. Tourism has
not been a traditional activity in the area, and most tourism businesses are less
than five years old. It is estimated that about 10% of the people in the Soomaa
region are directly or indirectly engaged with tourism, and ca 20% of people live
within the boundaries of the national park. Most of them have no full-time jobs
in tourism; rather, they have part-time and seasonal jobs.

Two most popular varieties of tourism businesses in the area are accommodation providers and canoe rental operators. There are 14 guesthouses and other
types of lodging, which altogether provide ca 300 beds. Seven rivers flow through
Soomaa National Park and connect the area. Paddling on the rivers is one of the
best ways to experience the wilderness of the area; canoeing became popular
about ten years ago (Figure 18.4). There are eleven canoe rental companies,
which can provide ca 220 canoes. Other tourism activities are less popular and
include fishing, rambling on nature trails, snowshoeing in bogs (all year round),
horse riding, skiing in bogs, kick sledging on ice, and educational trips
(Figure 18.5 and Figure 18.6).

Other tourism services are less developed, the weakest being food service.
There are no permanent restaurants within the boundaries of the national park;
pubs are few and can be found only in the village centres of the region. The
second weakest area in tourism service is guide service in foreign languages. As
a peripheral area Soomaa is faced with typical challenges. Unemployment is a
serious problem on the local level. It is the main reason why many people leave
for towns apart from the younger generations who also moving to towns. The
income of many people who live in the national park comes from forestry, furniture production, service industry, and metal industry. Furthermore, agriculture
plays an important role, and some locals produce local food products as well as
handicrafts. However, many locals also go to work in towns outside of the
national park.

The study of the socio-cultural and economic impacts of the PAN Parks
membership of Soomaa by Christina Timmermann (2009) claims that 'the most
apparent issues, which the field work findings revealed can be concluded of being

Figure 18.4 Dugout canoe: the traditional vehicle in Soomaa (photo by author)

the following: Insufficient income and employment from tourism particularly during the low season, the main reason being a lack of tourism demand for a local business to sustain themselves in the long run. In addition, missing entrepreneurial spirit and know-how of many local people hinders them to find income opportunities in tourism. Furthermore lacking infrastructure, especially concerning the access to the park and insufficient stakeholder cooperation are stated of being insufficient at different levels. Furthermore, some of the current tourists visiting the National Park are considered being a threat for the area, disturbing local people and therefore local satisfaction levels towards tourism' (Timmermann, 2009).

The attitude of the village people towards tourism is positive. It is perceived that many village people see good business opportunities in tourism, but they tend to forget that tourism is a seasonal activity, and it takes years to attract tourists and make tourism economically viable. Another problem is that tourism is often approached from the solely economic perspective and in terms of making money. The protection of nature is tends to be forgotten. Tourism can be regarded as a relatively underdeveloped industry in SNP. Concerning the perceptions of members of the municipalities and counties, it has potential for growth in terms of its great amount of resources. While the attitude of the local population

Figure 18.5 The floating sauna called Pühamüristus 'holy thunder' is immensely popular
with tourists (Photo by author)

towards tourism is rather positive, the lack of expertise in the field and the seasonality of the industry make tourism problematic (Többe, 2009).

Forestry and agriculture are the main industries in the Soomaa region. Plant
cultivation and animal production, as well as food production, are crucial from
the perspective of tourism. Most tourists wish to eat local food and appreciate it

Figure 18.6 Building a dugout canoe and Aivar Ruukel on the doorstep of his home during
the fifth season (Photo by author)

as a component of visiting experience. Thus, food production and service play an important role from the perspective of revenue growth.

What makes Soomaa National Park unique?

What makes Soomaa unique is the so-called 'fifth season' – the spring flood, which can raise the water level five metres above the low-water level! The flood is everywhere – it covers meadows, fields, forests, roads, and sometimes even houses. At the maximum flood level the water-covered area can be 7–8 km across and in some extreme years the flood area has covered 150 km². Roads are impassable during the fifth season. Canoeing is the best way to explore the watery wilderness of Soomaa, and several canoe tour companies operate in the area.

There is a local saying that the people who live in the area have five seasons: spring, summer, autumn, winter, and flood. The local people have adapted their lifestyle well to these circumstances, and therefore many historical and traditional values are associated with the periodically rising water levels of the area. Specific means of transport, called dugout canoes or log boats, are used during the floods in order to get from point A to point B. The dugout canoes are made by hollowing out a 'smooth-barked and sound trunk of aspen tree' and tarring it so that it does not rot. While standing, a person steers the dugout with a paddle. Most of the time these log boats were only paddled from one side using long sweeps. The largest dugout canoe could carry as many as thirteen people, but usually the log boats were used by fewer people (Többe 2009).

Tourism has played an important role in the renaissance of dugout canoes in Soomaa. This culture had become almost extinct in the 1960s–1990s. In 1996 the first summer camp for dugout canoe building was organized at Saarisoo by local tourism stakeholders. It has become hugely popular and has also enjoyed a lot of media interest. Since then dugout canoe building workshops have been organized, and exclusive and authentic canoe trips are available as an alternative to plastic canoes.

For wildlife enthusiasts, the region is home to over 185 bird species, such as cranes and the Ural owl. In addition, carnivorous animals, such as lynxes, wolves, beavers, and brown bears roam the lands.

The unique selling points of the Soomaa region that attract the potential market to visit Soomaa and not any other area include the flooding season (fifth season), the unspoiled wilderness areas and mires, the wildlife – carnivores, raptors, etc., the sparse population, space, silence, darkness, natural light – no light pollution, cultural heritage (suspension bridges, other bridges, traditional farming, etc), log boats – boats dug out from large aspen trunks, etc. Soomas is one of Estonia's five national parks, and it represents large wetlands. Kuresoo is the largest and best-preserved bog in Estonia, and the highest bog slope in Europe.

The uniqueness of the Soomaa area was pointed out in 2009 when it was awarded the EDEN Award (European Destination of Excellence) by the European

Commission as a special place 'off the beaten path' where economic, environmental, and social sustainability is valued.

Potential Markets for Soomaa

Soomaa National Park has great potential for the development of sustainable tourism. It is a relatively unspoiled and vulnerable destination that is highly conscious of the importance of its conservation. Its stakeholders strive for sustainable development and are willing to cooperate in order to achieve conservational objectives.

The main visitor groups for the Soomaa tourism region as counted by tourism entrepreneurs are as follows: students (and organized groups), hunters, fishermen, Estonian companies – corporate events, seminars, etc., friends and families travelling in groups, backpackers (mostly foreigners), nature observers (birders, etc.), adventurers (canoeing, ATV, etc), culture-interested tourists, caravan travellers, and disabled tourists.

The impacts of these visitor segments are different. It makes a huge difference whether the tourists are informed and whether they are guided. It especially concerns student groups and adventure tourists, whose behaviour can be very much influenced. It is better not to allow company trips and adventure tourists to visit local people, who are usually not interested in their visits. Also, awareness of restrictions in protected areas and the code of conduct influence the behaviour considerably. Hunting tourists and corporate clients are always valuable customers. The members of organized hunting parties are always well informed and managed. Fishermen constitute a problematic group because of littering. They do not sometimes respect the privacy of locals and are most problematic regarding this matter. Adventure tourism canoeing is neutral, but off-road vehicles make a negative impact (even if kept in specially designated areas). Student groups lower the impacts of seasonality. Backpackers are less valuable economically because they usually come alone. Individual tourists who hire cars are relatively valuable customers. Special interest tourists make a beneficial impact because they raise the awareness of others. Nature observers have not discovered Soomaa as yet; therefore there are no products for them. Caravaners need a specialized infrastructure. There is great potential for developing services for disabled tourists. Timing and special planning for tourists are very important.

The stakeholders generally agree as to the types of products that are missing in SNP and the kind of tourists who itwould be most 'ideal' to attract to SNP. In order to support its objectives, SNP applied for membership of the PAN Parks Network, which will support it in working towards STD and developing tourism in harmony with conservational objectives. Working on the prerequisites for becoming a member of this network has already enhanced cooperation between the stakeholders and has made them more active.

Tourism businesses have high expectations with regard to the PAN Parks membership. They expect to increase the number of international tourists as the network promises that a member will become a primary international destination.

However, some disadvantages may not enable SNP to become a primary international destination. Soomaa is situated in the Baltics, which is a less-known area and provides a limited destination mix and therefore lacks competitiveness. Nevertheless, if the facilities are improved, SNP might have a chance to become a primary destination for domestic tourists (Többe, 2009).

The main strength of the Soomaa area is its pure and rich nature and the wilderness in Soomaa NP. Also, the sparse population is a strength that allows the visitor as well as the person living in the area to feel comfortable and enjoy silence and solitude. The strength is related to important trends in tourism development – the wish of town people to leave the populous urban environment for nature.

At present the Soomaa brand is known mostly in Estonia, but its status as a national park and its potential to join the PAN Parks network provide the area a good opportunity to find its place in foreign markets as well. The cultural heritage resources of the area give additional value to the natural assets and give the opportunity to make the tourism products more special and interesting. An important challenge to the area is the cooperation level between the tourism stakeholders. At present this cooperation is coordinated by the Soomaa cooperation panel. The Green Riverland initiative also supports the increase in the variety and quality of tourism products, and the NGO Soomaa tourism brings together all the tourism entrepreneurs.

Conclusion

Tourism development is by no means the only possible future scenario for villages in the hinterland and their inhabitants. However, if one is dealing at the same time with a national park, then it is likely that the values that were decisive in awarding the status of a national park could be interesting and attract also nature-interested visitors. At this it is important that the residents of the region should be responsible for the management and shaping the tourism pattern in their home area. The residents and tourism stakeholders of Soomaa have selected this path. They have already achieved some success and recognition, such as the certificate of a PAN Park and the EDEN award. However, there is much work ahead; the developments need constant monitoring, and the plans have to be renewed on a regular basis. Life is dynamic and offers new challenges all the time.

The overall vision of Soomaa NPis this: by the year 2030 Soomaa NP would be a wilderness area with a healthy environment, natural processes, and a strong self-acting local community that is valued by informed visitors. The vision for sustainable tourism as regards Soomaa NP, which belongs to the network of European wilderness areas, as well its impact region, is as the most popular wilderness tourism destination of the Baltic countries. Its tourism products are based on the wilderness experience, the park's uniqueness, its cultural heritage, and the quality service that is offered by the local tourism entrepreneurs and stakeholders. Tourism is not the only aim but it serves as a tool to guarantee sustainable development of the area.

References

Act on Sustainable Development. (1995) Riigikogu. http://www.envir.ee [Accessed on the 3rd June, 2010]

Baltic 21. An Agenda 21 for the Baltic Sea Region. http://www.baltic21.org [Accessed on the 1st June, 2010]

Eesti Pank. Estonia's Economic Indicators. http://www.eestipank.info [Accessed on the 3rd March, 2010]

Eesti riiklik turismiarengkava 2007-2013. Majandus- ja Kommunikatsiooniministeerium. [The National Tourism Development Plan for 2007-201. Ministry of Economic Affairs and Communications]. (2006). Appendix to the State Gazette, 53, 400.

Eesti turismipoliitika põhimõtted [Principles of Tourism Policy. Ministry of Economic Affairs and Communications] (2003). http://www.mkm.ee [Accessed on the 5th of February, 2010]

Eesti säästva arengu riiklik strateegia "Säästev Eesti 21". http.www.riigikantselei.ee [Accessed on the 3rd June, 2010]

Enterprise Estonia. http://www.eas.ee [Accessed on the 5th of February, 2010]

Estonian Environmental Strategy 2030. Ministry of Environment. http://envir.ee [Accessed on the 5th of May, 2010]

Estonian Environment Information Centre. http://keskkonnainfo.ee

Estonian Ministry of Foreign Affairs. http://www.vm.ee [Accessed on the 15th of February, 2010]

Introduce Estonia Brand Manual (2009). Estonian Enterprise. http://tutvustaeestit.eas.ee [Accessed on the 16th of February, 2010]

Keskkonnaamet. http://www.keskkonnaamet.ee [Accessed on the 3rd of June, 2010]

Majandus- ja kommunikatsiooniministeerium [Ministry of Economic Affairs and Communications]. http://www.mkm.ee [Accessed on the 26th of February, 2010]

Pertel, J. (2006). Ecotourism Impact on Nature and Local Community in Soomaa National Park. Tallinn University. http://www.docstoc.com/docs/42249395/Ecotourism-Impact-on-Nature-and-Local-Community-in-Soomaa-National-Park [Accessed on the 5th of June, 2010]

Rebassoo, K. (2005). Visitor Satisfaction Survey of Soomaa National Park. Pilot project. Tartu University Pärnu College. http://www.docstoc.com/docs/42248968/Visitor-Satisfaction-Survey-of-Soomaa-National-Park [Accessed on the 5th of June, 2010]

Ruukel, A. (2008). (Compiled by) Sustainable Tourism Strategy of Soomaa NP region 2009-2013 http://www.docstoc.com/docs/42244416/Sustainable-Tourism-Strategy-of-Soomaa-NP-region-2009-2013 [Accessed on the 5th of June, 2010]

Soomaa National Park. http:// www.soomaa.ee [Accessed on the 18th of March, 2010]

Statistics Estonia. http://www.stat.ee [Accessed on the 3rd of June, 2010]

Sustainable Estonia. (2005). Riigikogu. http://www.riigikogu.ee [Accessed on the 1st of June, 2010]

Sustainable development of Estonia. Ministry of the Environment. http://envir.ee [Accessed on the 3rd of June, 2010]

Sustainable Tourism Strategy of Soomaa NP 2009-2013. (2008). http://www.docstoc.com/docs/42244416/Sustainable-Tourism-of-Soomaa-NP-region-2009-2013 [Accessed on the 3rd of June, 2010]

The Intangible Heritage List. http://unesco.org [Accessed on the 3rd of June, 2010]

The National Environmental Action Plan of Estonia 2007-2013. (2006) http://www.envir.ee [Accessed on the 3rd of June, 2010]

The Republic of Estonia Land Reform Act. RT 1991, 34, 426.

The Travel & Tourism Competitiveness Report. World Economic Forum (2009). http://www.weforum.org [Accessed on the 28th of March, 2010]

Timmerman, C. (2009). How to measure socio-cultural and economic impacts of PAN Parks sustainable tourism concept? http://www.docstoc.com/docs/42247630/How-to-measure-socio--cultural-and-economic-impacts-of-PAN-Parks-sustainable-tourism-concept [Accessed on the 5th of June, 2010]

Tourism trends and policies. (2009). OECD Publications. http://www.oecd.org/statistics [Accessed on the 15th of February, 2010]

Turismiseadus. (2000) Riigikogu. https://www.riigiteataja.ee [Accessed on the 15th of January, 2010]

Többe, A. (2009). Assessment of the sustainable tourism potential of the Soomaa National Park - A research study on potential markets and marketing strategies as part of the STDS that is required for becoming a member of PAN Parks http://www.docstoc.com/docs/42246169/Assessment-of-the-sustainable-tourism-potential-of-the-Soomaa-National-Park [Accessed on the 5th of June, 2010]

UN CSD18: National Reporting on 10 year Framework of Programmes on Sustainable Consumption and Production. http://www.un.org/esa [Accessed on the 5th June, 2010]

University of Texas Libraries. Estonia maps. #http://www.lib.utexas.edu/maps/estonia.html [Accessed on the 15th of April, 2010]

19 Challenges in rural ethnic tourism development

A case study from Yunnan, China

Li Yang and Xueqin Qiu***

Introduction

Ethnic tourism is a unique form of travel motivated by visitors' search for exotic cultural experiences through interaction with distinctive ethnic groups (Yang, Wall & Smith, 2008). Such tourism typically includes visiting minority villages, ethnic theme parks and homes, being involved in ethnic events and festivals, watching dances or ceremonies, or merely shopping for ethnic handicrafts and souvenirs. It provides tourists with opportunities to experience a unique place, landscape, and ways of life that are different from their own. In recent years, ethnic tourism has developed at a considerable pace worldwide. It has been promoted and widely adopted as a strategy for economic development and cultural preservation in many countries. Such tourism development has significant impacts on rural ethnic communities where the opportunity for development is limited (Yang & Wall, 2009). It has the potential to bring economic and social benefits to host communities (Adams, 1997; Boissevain, 1996; Grunewald, 2002; Smith, 1989, 2001; Wall & Xie, 2005). However, it can also adversely impact the culture, way of life and sense of identity of ethnic groups (Cohen, 1987; Greenwood, 1989; Oakes, 1998; Selwyn, 1996; Wood, 1997).

China is a multi-ethnic country with a large number of ethnic and linguistic groups. There are 56 ethnic groups identified by the central government. The Han Chinese make up 92% of the population, while 55 minority groups (many of which include sub-groups) comprise 8% which total about 104.49 million people scattered across two-thirds of China's total area (IOSC, 2005). Substantial cultural, regional and developmental differences exist among the various groups. The minority groups occupy a vast territory, although much of it is in the poorest western regions of the country. These regions have the lowest levels of industrial development, urbanization, provisions for health care and education, literacy, communication and transportation infrastructure, and standard of living

*Western Michigan University, Michigan, USA
**Yunnan University, Yunnan, China

(Lee, 2001; Shih, 2002). Minority people engage primarily in traditional farming and animal husbandry, with low productivity, resulting in underdeveloped local economies (Mackerras, 2003). Because of their isolation in mountainous areas, many minorities have been able to preserve their culture and heritage, which often appeal to Han Chinese and international visitors (Morais, Dong & Yang 2007).

Since the 1980s, the Chinese government has taken initiatives to develop western regions to reduce disparities in economic development between eastern and western China, and between rural and urban areas (Jackson, 2006). They have encouraged the use of minority regions' natural and cultural richness for the development of tourism and the stimulation of the regional economy to alleviate poverty (Morais *et al.*, 2007). State policies and regulations are designed to guide development through the complexities of investment, production and consumption (Swain, 1990). Many western provincial governments have increasingly taken advantage of their cultural diversity by formulating policies to advance ethnic tourism with diverse tactics. Ethnic tourism, thus, has emerged as an important regional development strategy to foster the economic independence of ethnic minorities.

This study examines the impact of ethnic tourism development on a host minority community and discusses the challenges faced by minorities who are attempting to improve their living standards through tourism. Minority perceptions of the impacts of tourism and government intervention in tourism development in an ethnic village are examined. Implications for the development and planning of community-based rural ethnic tourism are discussed.

Case study main section

Study Methods

A case study was conducted in a rural ethnic tourist village – Damuyu in Yunnan, China. Fieldwork took place in the summer of 2009. Multiple research methods, including in-depth interviews, informal discussions, on-site observations and secondary data review were employed. During the field research, the authors spent substantial time in the village to observe local life and tourism events and to acquire insights into tourism issues through direct participation and observation. Tourism plans, official documents, newspapers, and journal articles were examined to identify issues in ethnic tourism and to understand the impacts of tourism on local people.

In-depth interviews were conducted with 35 key informants, including village heads, elderly and young villagers, and government officials. Semi-structured, open-ended questions were used to gather informants' perceptions of tourism impacts, their roles, objectives and involvement in tourism, and their concerns and suggestions for future development. Village tourism business operation situations, opportunities and constraints were examined. Each interview took 30 to 60 minutes to complete. Some informants were interviewed more than once to clarify responses and to seek more insights. Informal conversations were also carried out with residents both individually and in groups to learn their perspectives on village tourism business.

Study Site

Damuyu village is located in Mosha Town, Xinping Yi and Dai Autonomous County, Yuxi Municipality, Yunnan Province (Figures 19.1 and 19.2). It is well-known for its subtropical scenery, rich animal and botanical resources, and unique ethnic culture. It is home to the Huayao Dai, a sub-group of the Dai people. The Dai has three subgroups including the Han Dai (Dry Dai), Shui Dai (Water Dai) and Huayao Dai (Colorful-waist Dai). The Dai has 1.159 million people in total and it is ranked 19th largest of 56 ethnic groups, comprising 0.09 percent of the total Chinese population, according to the fifth national China census in 2000 (NBSC, 2005). The Huayao Dai usually live in adobe houses with flat roofs and the women wear a long and colorful waistband. Damuyu village consists of 104 households with a population of 439 (225 men and 214 women). The Huayao Dai constitutes 99% of the total population of the village. Three Yi people and two Han Chinese live in the village as a result of intermarriages.

Damuyu village covers an area of 5.383 square kilometers. The village is geographically isolated and the villagers mainly depend on small-scale paddy rice agriculture resulting in a meager income. The annual average income per person in the village in 2008 was only 2,474 RMB (US $362) (interview with a village head, 2009). Within this impoverished village, tourism has become virtually its only industry outside of agriculture. The village is a newcomer to the tourism market. Village tours started as a trickle in the early 1990s and a small number of tourists visited the village for sightseeing and recreation. Local villagers initiated small-scale tourism businesses by selling food, fruits and crafts to visitors and providing homestays for tourists. The Huayao Dai's traditional Flower Street Festivals have drawn many scholars and visitors to the region after a journalist from Hong Kong reported about the Festival in the newspapers in the early 1990s. An increasing number of Han Chinese tourists, mainly from urban areas such as Kunming (capital of Yunnan), Yuxi and Xinping, drive their own vehicles to the village during the ethnic festivals, long weekends or national holidays. The village entertains tourists with local foods, handicrafts, and ethnic dances and songs. Villagers have entered the tourism business by opening restaurants and family inns. The first village inn owned by a resident was opened in 2007, consisting of 8 standard guest rooms and a large restaurant for 200 people.

Impacts of Tourism Development

The interviewed residents generally welcome tourism development in their village and they appreciate economic opportunities brought by tourists. They agree that tourism has provided more jobs, has brought more investment to the community's economy, and has improved community recreation and their

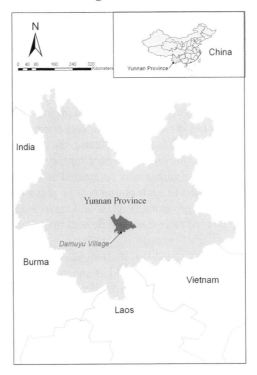

Figure 19.1 Yunnan and Xinping County (Map by Yang and Qiu)

Figure 19.2 Location of study site (Photo Yang and Qiu)

living standards. The community has better roads and landscape due to tourism. The income of households engaged in tourism has increased rapidly. Provision of food and lodging is very popular during the long holidays and ethnic festivals. The average living standard of the village has become higher than that of neighboring villages in terms of disposable income, and quality of housing and roads. Many villagers wish more tourists would visit the village and those not involved in tourism also express a desire for tourism jobs. Several interviewees commented that tourism has contributed to the conservation of the local natural environment and the protection of the ecosystem in the community. For instance, areca trees create beautiful sub-tropical scenery for the village. These trees have been well preserved since the village was designated as a main ethnic attraction. The trees have been assigned to each household for preservation. The villagers have cooperated with the government plan and have stopped cutting down trees. They have also planted more trees and flowers in their yards to improve the village scenery.

A number of interviewees stated that tourism has contributed to the preservation of traditional Huayao Dai culture and has enhanced their cultural pride and ethnic identity. They had little overt knowledge of their cultural heritage and knew little about their history and traditional music before they began their work as dancers or tour guides. They have not only learned about their own history, customs and music through job training, they have also learned about the outside world and other cultures through their interaction with tourists. They appreciate the knowledge and skills learned at work. Several women indicated that they are proud of their culture when tourists said that they like unique local dances and gorgeous ethnic dresses. An interviewee thought that the Cultural Exhibition Center was an excellent showcase of Huayao Dai culture as it provided an authentic exhibition of their heritage.

While most residents like tourism-induced economic development, some are concerned about associated negative impacts. Since the village was turned into a tourist attraction, the traditional way of life of local people has been changing due to economic growth and the entry of outside commercial influences. Several village elders pointed out that tourism has caused the disruption of traditional cultural behavior patterns in local residents and it has negatively impacted simple and hospitable folk customs. The community elders have been the backbone of the local community culturally. They have helped preserve and transmit the secular and sacred traditions from one generation to another. They were highly respected by the community, but today their comments have little influence on community affairs. The original friendly neighborhood relationships have been undermined by tourism business competition. Villagers used to help each other generously, but now each household has put high priority on making their own money. Close relatives and good neighbors have become strangers due to business competition. The money-oriented life has a significant impact on young villagers who consider farming as a tedious and poorly-paid job. Working in towns or cities ranks high on young peoples' wish lists. A growing number of young people leave home and move to cities to seek better job opportunities.

Cultural change and assimilation is a major concern in the village. Acculturation can be seen in the adoption of Han dress, architecture and lifestyles. The young generation of the Huayao Dai generally receives elementary or high school education in Han schools and they can speak Mandarin and write Chinese fluently. However, most of them cannot write their native language. Since the arrival of tourism in the village, Dai women who were never part of the public domain are becoming the centre of the tourist gaze. They have become a symbol of Huayao Dai culture and the face of hospitability in the community. Local men, on the other hand, are less visible due to the different gender roles within the community. While many women are working on the street selling goods to tourists, most men are farming.

One of the Huayao Dai's most famous ethnic symbols is their traditional costumes. A village head said that except for the old villagers, few young people wear traditional ethnic clothes today. It is partly because of the impact of past government policy that required minority people to wear Han clothes in the 1950s-70s. Young villagers indicated that they prefer to buy Han clothes from shops because they are more simple and convenient than ethnic clothes. Traditional Huayao Dai's costumes use lots of shining silver decorations, which look fancy and pretty, but they are very costly and heavy because a set of silver decorations for a dress weighs 4 to 5 kilograms. Women used to wear several long and colorful waistbands to show their slim figures. Most people only wear traditional dress for their wedding or important events. It is not common to see residents wearing ethnic clothes nowadays. As a result, the local government has to pay residents to wear their traditional costumes during ethnic festivals to create a more 'authentic' setting. In the past, some artists paid local women for modeling in a traditional ethnic outfit. It caused jealousy among village women and some approached tourists for money when they were photographed. A villager said sadly that 'our friendly and hospitable folk customs are ruined by craving for money.'

With the increase of disposable income, demand for the accoutrements of modern life is growing. Several families abandoned traditional adobe houses and built modern Han-style cement or brick houses in the village. The adobe house is made of clay and wood. It usually has two floors with a flat roof. People live on the second floor with a big balcony attached. The balcony is used for resting or making farm tools or pottery. The first floor consists of a kitchen, a living room and a store room. The adobe house is cool in the hot summer, but it does not last long (a maximum of 10-20 years). It requires frequent repairs to extend its life. With the increase in the price of timber, it is very costly to build and maintain an adobe house (see Figure 19.3). Therefore, villagers prefer to build cement or brick houses if they have enough money. These modern houses are symbols of wealth and modernity but reduce the appearance of exoticism for visitors. The villagers' attitudes towards new houses are divided. While some villagers want to keep traditional houses to attract tourists, others prefer modern houses. Some suggest maintaining the style of the adobe house, but using cement for the roof and door posts.

The increased tourism has also changed the lifestyle of villagers. The first KTV (karaoke) and tea house was open in the village in 2006 and the first bar and

Figure 19.3 Adobe house (Photo Yang and Qiu)

barbecue restaurant was opened in 2007. As Damuyu has become the center of nightlife for neighboring villages, loud karaoke music often breaks the tranquility of evenings in the village. People used to play cards at home in the evening, but today a lottery that was set up by an outsider has become a highlight of village nightlife. Both local villagers and tourists participate in lottery gambling. Because the lottery owner pays a fee to the village, most people do not oppose the lottery. However, several interviewees are concerned about its negative impacts on the young generation. They commented that 'nowadays young people dream about making a fortune from gambling instead of working hard on the farm.'

Challenges in Tourism Development

An official stated that the development and promotion of village tourism has been planned and controlled by the local government. In an attempt to draw international attention to Huayao Dai Culture, the Xinping County government planned and hosted the first International Huayao Dai Culture Conference in 2001. Subsequently, a tourism development plan was formulated by the government. Its main goals are to promote the rich folk culture of the Huayao Dai and to develop Xinping County into a distinctive ecological and ethnic tourist destination. Information on Xinping and Huayao Dai culture has been broadly circulated in the mass media. Damuyu and Dabinlangyuan villages in Xinping have been

Figure 19.4 Huayao Dai dance (Photo Yang and Qiu)

aggressively promoted as authentic showcases of the culture and life of the Huayao Dai. Damuyu was selected by the Yuxi Municipal Tourism Bureau as a key village for rural tourism development after it was designated by the Xinping County Government as a main tourist attraction. The village was renamed Damuyu Ethnic Cultural and Ecological Village.

In 2004, the Haoyao Dai Flower Street Tourism Festival, jointly sponsored by the Yuxi Municipal Tourism Bureau and the Xinping County Government, was held in Xinping (see Figure 19.4). The County Government invested 300,000 RMB (US $43,941) for the festival and built parking lots, tourist facilities, public washrooms, roads and sidewalks. Experts from Yunnan University were hired to create a tourism development plan for Damuyu in 2004. Supported by the government, a research center was built in the village to promote the study and preservation of the traditional Huayao Dai culture. The government invested 2,000,000 RMB (US $292,938) to build tour paths, a culture exhibition center and performance arenas in the village for the Huayao Dai International Costume Festival, which was held in Damuyu in 2007. During the festival, a variety of activities were presented to visitors, including staged dance performances, visits to Dai houses, and local food tasting. The Cultural Exhibition Center displays agricultural tools, music instruments, costumes, and the history and religion of the Huayao Dai. A performance team consisting of 13 local people has been created by the government to showcase Huayao Dai dances and songs to visitors.

Young pretty women and men from the villages are hired as dancers. New dance programs and costumes have been invented for the tourist shows.

The interviewees generally agreed that the government plays a vital role in providing incentive policies and financial support for initial village tourism development. They have assisted the village in planning and hosting a variety of ethnic festivals and events as well as marketing village tours. Especially, the County Government has actively searched for and secured funds from upper level government agencies to facilitate local development. The funds have been used for building roads, bridges and tourist facilities, planting trees and beautifying the village environment, and bringing new cash crops to famers. The natural and cultural environment of the village has been dramatically improved due to the governmental projects. However, the villagers were dissatisfied with the current government in terms of tourism policies, allocation of funds, compensation for expropriated land, and the festival entrance fee.

Many villagers that were interviewed thought that the government policies were unstable and inconsistent towards tourism development. They stated that government policies and regulations have dramatic impacts on village tourism businesses. The former county government officials were very passionate about and supportive of tourism projects. They helped the village build roads and encouraged people to open restaurants and lodges for visitors. However, the current officials show little interests in village tourism and they promote tourism projects mainly in the town. There were many more tourists when the village was actively promoted and marketed by the government. However, in recent years, it has become rare to see tourists wandering around the village except during the long holidays and Flower Street Festivals. The villagers are disappointed with the limited support of the current government officials towards their businesses. The future of village tourism seems dim. An interviewee cited an example of an investor as follows:

> The former government officials provided substantial help for initial tourism investors. Encouraged by the officials, a business man sold his nightclub in the town and opened the first bar and barbecue in Damuyu. The officials often arranged their meals at his bar to support his business. However, the current officials never pay a visit to his bar. When he was building a pool house near the tour path, the officials charged that the house affected the village view and required him to tear it down. After a difficult negotiation, he was allowed to build the pool house with hollow walls. He lost interests in tourism business (interview with a villager 2009).

Another villager said,

> The bureaucrats have screwed up our business. The restaurants in the village have few customers and family inns are close to bankruptcy. Newly-built tourist facilities become playgrounds for young kids. We have very limited business experiences and do not know how to increase tourism business.

We are hoping that the government can create a sound development plan for our village and provide more effective policies to help our businesses.

Other villagers hold the same opinion that the current government is indifferent to village tourism. They have done little in terms of the village promotion and planning of tourism events. The allocation of tourism funds is a critical issue to the villagers who complained that the County Government did not give the village adequate funds, which were granted from the upper level governments. The officials only held a single meeting with villagers in 2006. Since then, the villagers have not been informed how these funds have been used. A villager said that there are rumors that the officials spent more funds on governmental receptions and meals than tourism projects. Many villagers suspect that tourism funds were used for other purposes rather than tourism. The land use compensation is a major concern for the villagers. The government promised to compensate households whose lands were taken for building roads, bridges, tour paths, parking lots and other facilities. However, the compensation was limited and only a few families received compensation. Many landowners have not received their compensation since their lands were taken. The villagers complain that losing those lands makes their lives difficult because their livelihood mainly depends on farming. Governmental compensation was too little to cover their losses. A number of villagers strongly disagree with the building of roads on their land, but they had to give up the land eventually under the strong government pressures. The villagers held the village head, who was in charge of the road project, accountable for these important land issues. Encouraged by the government, some villagers built restaurants or guesthouses to accommodate tourists, but they now see less business. Farmland in the village has shrunk substantially due to the increase in tourism-related land uses. However, the visitation to the village has declined rapidly in recent years. It has become a big challenge for famers who lost considerable lands to make a living.

The unbalanced development of the village has also caused complaints among residents. Several interviewees indicated that the roads and other facilities were built only in a certain area of the village. The water supply does not cover the entire village and some households still do not have running water. The environment of the tourist area in the village looks much nicer than that of other areas. Thus, it is easier for the households near the tour paths to do business than their counterparts in other areas. Some villagers felt that the tourism benefits were not distributed equally in the village and that they have been left out of development. The government is the main decision maker in tourism planning and local residents have little say in the development of village tourism. The residents neither know about local tourism plans nor participate in the planning process. Although there are a few community consultation meetings, the villagers feel that such consultation is merely a symbolic procedure, but not real democracy. The purpose of the meetings is to inform residents about governmental decisions rather than to listen to the villagers' opinions. The meeting participants have not had an influence on governmental plans. An interviewee complained that villagers' suggestions are never respected by the officials. When cobblestones were used to pave village tour roads in a governmental project, a village head warned not to place cobblestones close to the roots of areca trees. However, the officials ignored his suggestion. As a result, cobblestones suppressed the growth of the areca trees.

Social connections make a big difference in tourism business. Several interviewees indicated that, in general, the villagers who have connections with the officials receive more benefits from tourism than others. The households who received land compensation usually had family members working for the government. An interviewee gave an example:

> In 2008, a tour group made a dinner reservation of 10 tables first at a restaurant run by a villager, but later this group switched to a small restaurant owned by the village head. This restaurant is not large enough to host all guests, thus some tables were set in the yard. These two restaurants are located next to each other. However, the village head's restaurant has good business all year round, whilst the other villager's restaurant has no customers except during festivals. It is simply because the village head has good connections with officials and business people (interview with a villager in 2009).

In attempt to encourage the development of tourist facilities, the government offers subsidies to villagers who build family inns or guesthouses. Therefore, two households were provided with 20,000 RMB (US $2,929) cash plus land subsidies. Other villagers feel that such subsidies were unfair because they only help rich people become richer. The government built a recreation center along the river in the village aimed at enriching local people's nightlife. However, the recreation center is not leased to the local villagers. Instead, it is run by a relative of a government official who is from another village. The government does not charge him any fee. The villagers complain that the center should be run by the members of the community instead of an outsider.

The festival entrance fee is a major concern in the village. The government started to plan ethnic festivals and charge entrance fees a few years ago. However, the majority of fees were kept by the government and the village shared few benefits. When the Huayao Dai International Costume Festival was held in Damuyu in 2007, all visitors were required to pay a 10 RMB (US $1.5) fee to enter the village. Tourists from a distance accept the fees, but the visitors from other nearby villages were upset about the entrance fees. A villager said that '10 RMB may not mean a lot to city people, but it is not a small amount of money for farmers who make meager income. It is ridiculous for local visitors to pay the fees because they are relatives or friends of the families in Damuyu.' Another villager said that 'when my sister's family of five people came to Damuyu, they were charged 50 RMB (US $7.3), which was half the amount of money that they brought. After paying the fee, they could not afford to eat a hot pot. They also needed money to travel back to home.' Many people from other villages cancelled their plan to visit when they knew that they had to pay an entrance fee. Consequently, the visitor numbers dropped dramatically on the second day of the festival. The villagers thought that it was unreasonable to make profits from their relatives and friends. They might have benefited more from the festival if the fees were lower. A few people pointed out that the festival was not planned and managed well, which reduced the attractiveness of the festival. Many tourists did not enjoy the festival and few of them revisit it.

The government decided to relocate the Flower Street Festival to Mosa town in 2009. The majority of villagers disagree with the relocation of the festival, although a small number of people think that it was a good idea because the village is small and lacks convenient transportation. The villagers can enjoy a tranquil environment and they are no longer disturbed by tourists. Mosa town can accommodate more visitors. It is cheaper to eat and buy things in the town. However, many villagers do not like the change to tradition. Damuyu is well known locally because the traditional Flower Street Festival was held there. Fewer tourists frequent the village since the festival was moved. Consequently, the tourism revenue of the village has declined significantly. Additionally, the festival fund that was given to the village has been reassigned to the town, which has weakened the economy of the village.

While tourism has played a crucial role in the survival of the community's economy, tourism development has brought complicated outcomes to the village. Although physical infrastructure in the village has been improved, other support-ing services, such as health care, internet access and visitor centers, are not available. The remote location of the village, combined with inconvenient trans-portation, is detrimental to visitation. Visitors without a car have a two-hour bus ride from the city of Yuxi and an over four-hour bus ride from Kunming, the provincial capital. The promotion of village tourism is limited in the province and tourists from other regions have little access to village information. The village does not have adequate tourism services and returning visitation is very low. There is low capacity to host larger tour groups and tourist activities are limited to sightseeing, food sampling and dance shows. The residents generally lack higher education and business management skills. They rely on the government investment and assistance. The training and education of tourism workers and the provision of quality services is crucial for sustaining village tourism.

The local County Government is the main authority to plan and direct village tourism. The residents have mixed feelings towards the government actions. On the one hand, the villagers support government leadership and regulation of the tourist market. On the other hand, they are dissatisfied with inconsistent tourism policies and inadequate land use compensation. They want more government support and assistance for village business. Tensions and conflicts arise when tourism benefits are not equally distributed in the community. The government intrusion into community affairs has created tensions between residents and the officials.

Discussion and Conclusions

With the opening up of the Chinese economy in the 1980s, tourism has emerged as a sector of strategic importance for local development. Inspired by government policies, ethnic tourism has developed rapidly in rural China since the 1990s. It provides host communities with opportunities to improve their livelihoods and also to showcase their rich culture and heritage, and to revive their traditions, languages and cultural pride (Chow, 2005; Wall & Xie, 2005). However, such tourism has brought both opportunities and challenges to the host populations (Oakes, 1998; Swain, 1989, 1990). Based upon an empirical study in a rural village in Yunnan, China, this study examined the impacts of ethnic tourism development on a host minority community and discussed the challenges faced by minorities who are attempting to improve their living standards through tourism.

This case study provides insights into residents' perceptions of tourism-related impacts and complicated outcomes experienced by ethnic minorities in China who have - under ethnic tourism - attempted to pursue wealth and modernity. The government's role in tourism development and the empirical evidence of the results of intervention have been discussed. The government is commonly an important determinant of the context in which development occurs and, in a top-down system such as that which exists in China, it has multiple roles: as a developer, marketer, arbiter and protector of the public interest among these (Yang, Wall & Smith, 2008). However, government intervention in community development often results in complicated outcomes. This case study furthers the understanding of the impacts of government policies and intervention in village tourism, and raises awareness of the community conflicts and fragmentation that arises due to conflicting development priorities and the commodification of ethnic culture. While specific to Yunnan, this study has implications for communities in other destinations whose landscape and cultural traditions are being used as the catalyst for ethnic tourism development.

The study findings indicate that, since the 1990s, tourism has contributed to the economic growth of the village. Minority people generally support village tourism and they appreciate more jobs, increased economic opportunities, the improved community environment, recreation and livelihoods that tourism development has brought. While local residents like tourism-induced economic development, they are concerned about the associated negative impacts such as cultural change and assimilation. Since the village was turned into a tourist attraction, the traditional way of life of local people has changed due to economic growth and the entry of outside commercial influences. Acculturation can be seen in the adoption of Han dress, architecture and lifestyle. The arrival of affluent tourists, usually from cities, has not only created hopes in this impoverished community but also resentment among the residents when the money does not trickle down to them. This has resulted in some residents asking for money in exchange for photographs or villagers fighting for more guests - situations that had not occurred before in the community.

Economic advantages have been a driving force for local people to engage in tourism. The improvement of livelihood and pursuit of a modern lifestyle are of high interest to minority people. However, with dramatic changes to the architecture and lifestyles of minority communities, ethnic villages are losing their attractiveness to metropolitan tourists. Culture is not static but dynamic; it is not possible to 'freeze' minority culture in a rapidly changing world but policymakers and developers need to find an appropriate balance between economic development and cultural preservation (Yang & Wall, 2009). The maintenance of cultural integrity should receive serious consideration when making investments, developing amenities and improving infrastructure. The preservation of ethnic traditions and heritage is critical for the survival of minority cultures in tourist villages.

As revealed by this study, the local government plays a vital role in providing incentive policies and financial support for initial village tourism development. The government has assisted the minority village in planning and hosting a variety of ethnic festivals and events as well as marketing village tours. However, local people have little say in tourism planning and development, and tensions rise when the government seeks to transform local culture into marketable products. The villagers are concerned about inconsistent tourism policies, inadequate allocation of funds, insufficient compensation for lost land and unequal distribution of festival entrance fees. Minority people and their lands and culture constitute an important resource on which ethnic tourism is based, but their views on tourism are seldom incorporated into the development decisions that ultimately affect their lives. Current tourism practice does not appear to be a viable alternative to traditional farming in Damuyu. Farmland in the village has shrunk substantially due to tourism-related land use. Meanwhile, the visitation to the village has declined rapidly in recent years. The villagers who lost their land are worried about their livelihoods.

Capitalizing on their rich cultural heritage, minority people see ethnic tourism as a potential catalyst for economic development and cultural sustainability. Unplanned and poorly planned tourism development, however, can have adverse impacts on the community and its fragile culture (Yang & Wall, 2009). Community support is crucial for sustainable tourism development (Walsh & Swain, 2004). Government officials need to listen to the local voice and develop more effective policies and plans in order to mitigate issues and reinforce the benefits of development. In particular, attention is needed to the issues of ethnic control of tourism resources, cultural preservation, and public participation in decision-making processes. Grass-root resident participation is essential for the success of community tourism. It is important to retain tourism benefits in the community and to keep entrepreneurs from outside to a minimum.

Governmental financial support and investment are needed as the community does not have the financial or human capital to develop tourism on its own. More training and education programs for entrepreneurial development need to be provided for minority people for them to acquire the necessary skills to develop and manage tourism on their own. The community should be encouraged to participate in the designing, planning, and managing of ethnic festivals and tourism programs. Fair economic returns to local residents need to be ensured. Community concerns should be addressed and the government decision-making process needs to be more transparent. Governmental tourism plans should be tailored to local needs, with optimal participation of ethnic community residents in the development process and with tourism benefits accruing, to the greatest extent possible, to local residents. Effective communication and cooperation between the government and local residents needs to be enhanced. Collaborations and partnerships with other relevant stakeholders such as tour operators, tourism associations and ethnic organizations should be explored in order to borrow expertise and resources. If ethnic tourism is to contribute to the development of minority groups as conceived, it will be necessary to create a supportive environment for the involvement of village businesses through incentive policies, enhanced access to capital, increased education and training, and facilitation of ethnic entrepreneurship.

References

Adams, K. M. (1997). Touting touristic "primadonas": Tourism, ethnicity and national integration in Sulawesi, Indonesia. In M. Picard & R. Wood (Eds.), *Tourism, ethnicity, and the state in Asian and Pacific Societies* (pp. 155–180). Honolulu, HI: University of Hawaii Press.

Boissevain, J. (1996). Ritual, tourism and cultural commoditization in Malta: Culture by the pound? In T. Selwyn (Ed.), *The tourist image: Myth and myth making in tourism* (pp.105-120). Chichester, United Kingdom: John Wiley.

Chow, C. (2005). Cultural diversity and tourism development in Yunnan Province, China. *Geography, 90*(3), 294–303.

Cohen, E. (1987). Tourism: A critique. *Tourism Recreation Research, 12*(2), 13–18.

Grunewald, R. (2002). Tourism and cultural revival. *Annals of Tourism Research, 29*(4), 1004–1021.

Information Office of the State Council of the PRC (IOSC) (2005) *Regional Autonomy for Ethnic Minorities in China*. Online documents at URL http://english.gov.cn/official/2005-07/28/content_18127.htm (Accessed on October 10, 2009).

Jackson, J. (2006) Developing regional tourism in China: The potential for activating business clusters in a socialist market economy. *Tourism Management* 27(4), 695–706.

Lee, M.B. (2001) *Ethnicity, Education and Empowerment: How Minority Students in Southwest China Construct Identities*. Aldershot, England: Ashgate Publishing Limited.

Mackerras, C. (2003) *China's Ethnic Minorities and Globalisation*. London: Routledge-Curzon.

Morais, D.B., Dong, E., and Yang, G. (2006) The ethnic tourism expansion cycle: The case of Yunnan Province, China. *Asia Pacific Journal of Tourism Research* 11(2), 189–204.

Oakes, T. (1992). Cultural geography and Chinese ethnic tourism. *Journal of Cultural Geography, 12*(2), 2–17.

Oakes, T. (1997). Ethnic tourism in rural Guizhou: Sense of place and the commerce of authenticity. In M. Picard & R. Wood (Eds.), *Tourism, ethnicity, and the state in Asian and Pacific Societies* (pp. 35–70). Honolulu, HI: University of Hawaii Press.

Oakes, T. (1998). *Tourism and modernity in China*. London: Routledge.

Selwyn, T. (1996). *The tourist image: Myths and myth making in tourism*. Chichester, United Kingdom: Wiley.

Shih, C. (2002) *Negotiating Ethnicity in China: Citizenship as a Response to the State.* London: Routledge.

Smith, V. (1989). *Hosts and guests: The anthropology of tourism* (2nd ed.). Philadelphia: University of Pennsylvania Press.

Smith, V. (2001). Power and ethnicity in "Paradise": Boracay, Philippines. In V. Smith & M. Brent (Eds.), *Hosts and guests revisited: Tourism issues of the 21ˢᵗ century* (pp. 141-152). New York: Cognizant Communication Corp.

Swain, M. (1989). Developing ethnic tourism in Yunnan, China: Shilin Sani. *Tourism Recreation* Research, *14*(1), 33–39.

Swain, M. (1990). Commoditizing ethnicity in southwest China. *Cultural survival quarterly, 14*(1), 26–29.

Wall, G., & Xie, P. F. (2005). Authenticating ethnic tourism: Li dancers' perspectives. *Asia Pacific Journal of Tourism Research, 10*(1), 1–21.

Walsh, E., & Swain, M. (2004). Creating modernity by touring paradise: Domestic ethnic tourism in Yunnan, China. *Tourism Recreation Research, 29*(2), 59–68.

Wood, R. (1997). Tourism and the state. In M. Picard & R. Wood (Eds.), *Tourism, ethnicity, and the state in Asian and Pacific Societies* (pp. 1-34). Honolulu, HI: University of Hawaii Press.

Yang, L., Wall, G. & Smith, S. (2008). Ethnic tourism development: Chinese government perspectives. *Annals of Tourism Research, 35*(3), 751–771.

Yang, L., & Wall, G. (2009). Minorities and tourism: Community perspectives from Yunnan, China. *Journal of Tourism and Cultural Change, 7*(2), 77–98.

20 Hotel Management education in Bhutan

Teaching sustainable principles

*Paul Strickland**

Current challenges of Hotel Management education in Bhutan

The Kingdom of Bhutan is a very unique country in a number of ways. Firstly, it is one of the last countries to open its borders to Western influence, and this includes international standards of hospitality and tourism practices. Secondly, the Royal Government of Bhutan (RGoB) regulates the number of international tourists that visit through strict visa control, and has introduced a tariff system that requires a daily minimum spend, but also controls tourist movements through systematic check points. Thirdly, as a developing economy limited tourism infrastructure and the inability to deliver international hotel service standards directly impacts tourist perceptions of their overall experience in a negative way. Finally, and most importantly for this case study, there has been no formal tertiary education for the middle to senior management in Bhutan hotels, therefore international service standards and sustainable environmental hotel practices have been overlooked. In the past, to try and bridge this gap, foreign hotel managers with tertiary qualifications were acquired from countries such as New Zealand, Australia, Singapore, Switzerland and India, but this has always been a temporary solution and does not form part of the RGoB future plans.

The RGoB implements five-year plans in which all government policies are built on. Currently in its 9th plan cycle, tourism is high on the agenda. The main reason for this is that tourism is the second biggest Gross Domestic Product (GDP) generator, second only to hydro-electricity (of which India is the main purchaser). It also means that the RGoB strongly influences hotel and tourism policies, and can therefore guide future direction with relative ease (Ritchie, 2008). To capitalize on the tourism sector, international visitors are set to increase from 27,000 per year in 2008 to 100,000 per year by 2012. All hotels that are accredited to host international visitors must reach a minimum 3 star rating and adopt guidelines for sustainable and responsible hotel practices by the end of 2010. Other RGoB declarations include an increase in aircraft and helicopter

*La Trobe University, Bundoora, Australia

capacity, an increase in nature based tourist attractions and implementation of worldwide banking practices allowing tourists greater flexibility to access their finances therefore spend more (Thinley, Prime Minister of Bhutan, 2009).

Currently relying on foreign aid for many projects, Bhutan has a desire to become self sufficient and not be considered a developing economy. As a consequence, the RGoB is equipping the country with educational facilities and programs to help achieve this goal. One such area identified is further education in hotel management. Since the first official tourists were accepted into the country for the fourth king's coronation in 1974, (274 people), hotels have been allowed to be built and operated by the Bhutanese people, however many have no further education than a high school certificate. This lack of hotel knowledge meant many hotels were not operating to the satisfaction of tourists. Conducting exit polls on departing international tourists, the biggest complaints were that hotel and service standards were not consistent. Tourists paying the daily tariff of US$200 daily (which includes visa, internal transport, accommodation, meals and a guide) may have had a totally different experience as other tourists for the same price (Dorji, 2007). For example, a hotel in the country's capital Thimphu may have all the modern conveniences of a four star hotel including running water, flushing toilets and electricity. However, tourists travelling outside this city, even a day's drive through the mountains along the windy roads may find themselves paying the same tariff with no electricity or heating. It also became apparent from customer feedback that service standards in hotels were not consistent. The Bhutanese staff often did not understand the 'demands' of western tourists such as ice in their drink or requesting fresh meat as these are not always available. International guests did not understand that they are paying a high tariff and not receiving basic services that are typically available in western countries. These differing perceptions have lead to negative experiences from both sides. It is only through education of both parties that these perceptions can be understood.

In 1964, The RGoB built the Royal Institute of Management (RIM) as a tertiary training institution. RIM offered management programs, but nothing specifically for hotels until recently. With the help of foreign investment and taking almost 5-years to set up, 2009 saw the first intake of 30 students in to the inaugural Bhutan Hotel Middle Management Program (BHMMP). The program is designed to educate middle to senior managers in a variety of hotel management topics. These topics include service expectations of western visitors, health the hygiene principles, sustainability of services and staff during off peak times, adopting eco-friendly hotel business practices, developing hotel waste management programs whilst maintaining unique cultural and architecture, concept of Gross National Happiness, national dress codes, religion, language, food and the natural environment. These topics closely follow RGoB policy. As a result, a new facility including a training hotel will be commencing in August 2010 to continue the hotel management program with students graduating with a Diploma in Hotel Management (Planning Commission, 1999).

During the two year program, the hotel management students' learn the advantages of adopting sustainable business practices that can attract tourism into the country. For example, Bhutan is known as a wilderness region, as 60% of the country must remain forested (Wangchuk, 2005). Nevertheless, the country is developing at an extraordinary rate and the natural environment that attracts visitors to begin with may be in danger. The BHMMP highlights case studies from other countries avoid the mistakes that other tourist destinations have made in the past. Even as a developing economy, Bhutan is extremely rare in trying to balance its cultural, spiritual, environmental and tourism demands. This case study investigates some of the many challenges hotel management education needs to address in order to achieve each stakeholders' agendas, namely; Bhutan's Royal Family, RGoB, Bhutanese spiritual leaders, foreign aid programs, international governments, the Bhutanese people, environmental and conservation groups plus the demands of international tourists.

Brief history of modern Bhutan

The Kingdom of Bhutan is situated in the Himalayas bordering India and the Tibet region of China. Bhutan is a mountainous land locked country with a population estimated at less than 800,000 people, however records have only been kept for the last 15 or so years so this figure is only an approximation. Most Bhutanese have no record of when they were born and consequently do not celebrate birthdays. Bhutan is one of the last developing countries to open its borders and to embrace 'select' western customs. This is to ensure that most traditional customs will remain, and not be over shadowed by western culture.

The fourth Druk (known as the Dragon King) Gyalpo Jogme Singye Wangchuck has abdicated his throne to his young (now thirty year old) son and created a new constitution which allows the monarchy to remain but which gives power to government ministers to operate the country's affairs (in affect introducing democracy) (Pek-Dorji, 2007). Both the fourth and fifth Druk's have seen the introduction of television, the internet, and mobile phones, and have created new roads and invested heavily in public health, tourism and education. Consequently, they highly regarded by the Bhutanese citizens (Planning Commission, 1999).

The Kingdom of Bhutan known by the locals as Druk Yul (Land of the Dragon) was created in 1907 with Ugyen Wangchuck being elected as the first hereditary monarch of Bhutan and first Druk. This family monarchy has continued with the 5th King (Jigme Khesar Namgyel Wangchuck) currently on the throne, however much of the power has been given to the government with democratic elections to choose the Prime Minister and other government officials, however the Druk still wields huge influence. Another unique attribute of Bhutan is the power sharing arrangements in developing the five year plan cycles. Although official policy is made by the RGoB, most Dzongs (original fortresses) house a seat for the King, Prime Minister and the spiritual leader of Bhutan, as they are all considered equal.

The concept of Gross National Happiness

Bhutan has a philosophy of Gross National Happiness (GNH) which was implemented by the fourth ruler in the year 2000 to increase the happiness and satisfaction of the people, rather than just focus on monetary value or gain (Bauer Brunet, De Lacy and Tshering, c1999; Ritchie, 2008). The idea is that if the people are happy, the flow on effects will help stimulate economic development, environmental conservation, promote culture and meet the spiritual and emotional needs of the people (Ministry of Finance, 2000). This has meant the introduction of educational programs such as the BHMMP to teach current middle to senior managers' effective hotel operations, internationally recognised service standards, minimising potential environmental impacts and waste management whilst maintaining cultural integrity and the concept of GNH. It is envisaged that this will create employment for the Bhutanese people, and gradually allow them to become less reliant on foreign aid, foreign managers and foreign teachers (Du, 2003). GNH principles are reinforced via the hotel management education being incorporated into the BHMMP.

National dress code

Traditional dress is worn by the locals (*Drukpa*) and is extremely important to their culture. So much so that the king has declared that it must be worn by all local inhabitants while working. This is particularly true for the hotel and tourism sector due to their high exposure with international visitors. The *Kira* is worn by the females, and consists' of a full length dress secured by a chain at the shoulder and a belt at the waist. A blouse is worn underneath and a cropped jacket over the top. The *Gho* is worn by the males, and is a long robe hoisted to the knee and held in place by a belt. The large pouch at the front is used as a carrying aid. Ceremonial *Kiros* and *Ghos* are hand woven in traditional patterns and are highly prized. Additional scarves must be added when entering *Dzongs* (and monasteries) out of respect (Ritchie, 2008). Although to some, the national dress may appear impracticable and perhaps uncomfortable (especially in the hospitality industry), the insistence that it is worn helps Bhutan retain its cultural identity and adds to the overall perception of the tourists' experience and national pride. Consequently, all hotel workers must where the *Kiro* or *Gho* at all times.

Religion

Religion dominates every part of the Bhutanese way of life. Bhutan is a country where Buddhism is very strong (75% of the population), with the balance Hindi (25% of the population), due to the close proximity to India. Dubbed the only remaining Lamaist Kingdom, Buddhism is evident from the *Dzongs*, monasteries, *stupas*, prayer flags, and prayer wheels that punctuate the Bhutanese landscape. Although many of the tourists that visit Bhutan may not be Buddhist, Hindi or

Figure 20.1 Takshang Monastery, known as the 'Tiger's Nest' (Takshang)

even religious, the religious aspect is still a major draw card. Some of the most famous images of Bhutan are of its monasteries with the most famous being Tiger's Nest, expertly built on the side of a cliff (see Figure 20.1).

Simply walking down the main street of Thimphu, tourists will hear the chime of ritual bells, sound of gongs, see people circling temples and *stupas* and the fluttering of prayer flags, witness red robed monks conducting rituals among many others which are all examples that Buddhism is an essential part of Bhutanese life. The impact on the hospitality industry is great. For example, as Buddhists' cannot slaughter animals (including fish), meat, fish and poultry is either unavailable or purchased from neighbouring India and trucked in by road. This can take days often on unrefrigerated transport vehicles. Hotel guests therefore may not receive quality food or fresh food items. Although this is slowly being rectified, food is not in abundance during off peak tourist times and a vegetarian meal is often the only option. On the other hand, this can also add to the overall experience and appreciation of the country. However, exit polls suggest that the majority of tourists will adhere to religious beliefs, although many would prefer greater options in hotels.

Language

Education starts in primary school and continues for the next eleven years all fully subsidized by the Bhutanese government (Worden, 1993). This means all children have the opportunity to attend school however some people live in such remote parts of the mountains that attending school daily is impractical. The only other option is attending boarding school.

To move forward into the 21st century and also to protect the Bhutanese culture, the schools teach in the national language Dzongkha and English. However, there are at least another twenty four Bhutanese dialects spoken, (depending on the province) and Nepali is spoken in the north (van Driem, 1994; SAARC Tourism, 2010). All tertiary qualifications are taught in English allowing qualified teachers from all over the world to contribute however, as mentioned earlier, Bhutan would like to be self sufficient and eventually it will the Bhutanese that will take over tertiary teaching roles. Currently, most tertiary educated Bhutanese studied abroad however, programs such as the BHMMP are slowly being introduced with funding being the main constraint for any new program.

It is essential that all 'front of house' staff in hotels speak and understand English. This is the language that most international visitors are able to communicate in. The BHMMP strongly encourages improvements in English therefore many tasks the students must complete are essays and oral presentations. Some Bhutanese guides specialize in other languages therefore translating into Korean, Japanese or German for example. As international visitors must apply for a visa, translators can easily be arranged. Although the official languages are Dzongkha and English, other Bhutanese dialects are not discouraged, as once again these promote traditional customs and culture.

Food

The Bhutanese food is quite unique, despite adopting strongly influences from China, India and Nepal, and now a small 'western' selection for the benefit of international tourists. Although Bhutan may not have a strong reputation for its cuisine, it is surprisingly tasty, especially with its prized ingredient added to almost every dish; chilli. Cheese and egg dishes are also in abundance. Arguably only eccentric tourists visit Bhutan, however they may not be as adventurous when it comes to the food. This is mainly due to the impression of poor sanitation conditions in food transport, preparation, and perhaps service. The BHMMP aims to teach the importance of sanitation in all aspects of the hotel. From the kitchen, to the dining room, the laundry to the guests' room, cleaning and sanitation are becoming paramount. The theory is once the guests feel comfortable that sanitation standards have risen, they will venture outside their hotel into other local restaurants therefore spreading the tourist dollar to other establishments. This is accomplished through HACCP principles that are being slowly introduced into the hotel especially the kitchens. HACCP stands for Hazard Analysis Critical Control Point and 'is a proactive process of consecutive actions to ensure food safety to the highest degree' (Payne-Palacio and Theis, 2009, p.105).

HACCP principles also occur outside the hospitality industry. Newly introduced government initiatives have seen the rebuilding of the fresh produce market in the capital. All food products must be kept off the ground, washed and stored correctly. The surrounding environment must be clean and well sanitized. Government-appointed inspectors constantly monitor any violation. Relatively large fines occur if a violation is determined. This is an attempt to increase food hygiene practices, and includes home kitchens benefiting locals and tourists alike.

Natural environment

As previous mentioned, the Kingdom of Bhutan is land locked in the Himalayas bordered by India and China (Tibet Autonomous Region). It is only 300 km long and 150 km wide, however the windy roads make it a minimum three days journey from one side to another. Depending on what part of the country is visited, distinct landmarks are present: from glacial regions to temperate pine forests. The RGoB has strong beliefs that Bhutan's biggest asset is its natural environment. Hydro-electricity is the largest GDP earner therefore should be protected. But this is also in line with other aspects such as their way of life, religion, architecture etc. It is all part of the overall strategy to increase the standard of living for the people while protecting their delicate history and culture. As a result, 60% of the country must be kept under forest, roads will only be built in certain areas, sustainable harvesting of trees occurs through replanting of forests, and constraints on new housing developments assist in population control. The purchase of land is highly regulated and expansion of family property is often denied to achieve this goal.

Birds and rare animals can also be found in Bhutan and has been identified by the World Widelife Fund for Nature (WWF) 'as a global biodiversity hotspot and counted among the 234 globally outstanding eco-regions of the world' (WWF Website, 2010, para., 5). As a consequence, the RGoB has responded by creating wild life areas, wetlands and non-inhabitable areas to try and conserve animal populations and eco-systems. These areas are now constantly monitored by locals to assess any changes. The BHMMP teaches the importance of the natural environment and that all environmental concerns should be identified before the commencement of any new hotels.

Mainaining unique cultural architecture

Bhutan has very distinctive architecture from the traditional Dzongs (built as fortresses and places of worship in the 1600s) to the modern day apartments built in the traditional style (see Figures 20.2 and 20.3). The creation of new towns and cities is government driven and aims at sustainable living. For example, if more people relocate to the cities, who will harvest the crops? The government is striving to strike a balance between modernization, and continuing traditional occupations. Although this may be difficult to achieve, only allowing traditional external architecture helps achieve this aim. Other customary links with architecture include religion and superstition. Much of the artwork adorning buildings, cornices and building entrances are for this purpose, not just decoration. A fine

Figure 20.2 Traditional Dzong (Punakha)

Figure 20.3 Modern Taj Tashi Hotel (Thimphu)

example would be the phallic symbols of the male anatomy that are prevalent everywhere. Although uncustomary to the average tourist, this unique artwork serves to offer a welcoming invitation, to ward of demons and to give good fortune. Hotel management education reinforces these traditions and all hotels must adhere this policy even if is an additional cost to the hotel owner.

Service expectations of international visitors

With the introduction of the BHMMP, actively teaching Western customs regarding hotel management has proven truly valuable for the hotel industry. Although considered students in the classroom, many of these managers have the authority to pass on their learned knowledge and actually implement some of the ideas that were presented in the classroom. This offers a unique opportunity to apply the knowledge that has been acquired immediately. Currently enrolled students believe that they understand much more about Western expectations and would truly like to deliver to their standard. This has been passed on to other hotel staff members. Rather than dismissing international visitors as 'demanding' (as they previously would have), hotel staff have more of an understanding about the standard of living many international visitors enjoy. They now offer an explanation why some of the expectations cannot be fully met. For example, a hotel outside a large city may not enjoy the benefit of electricity. As a compromise, the program has taught to offer alternatives such as a generator being used for four hours per day. This gives the guest electricity, hot water and heating during this time. The hotel staff advises showering, reading or any other activities that require light should be undertaken during these times. Although this may seem obvious to the guests, the surrounding houses must undertake these same activities without the aid of electricity.

With the introduction of a training hotel to be opened in 2010, future service standards with the hotel industry in Bhutan will be directly affected. Students will be taught both 'front of house' and 'back of house' procedures from international hotels perspective. This includes setting a table, to cleaning a room, to checking a guest in; the students will learn a uniformed approach to handling international visitors. The aim of the new training hotel is to introduce uniformity to the industry and reduce inconsistencies between untrained hotel staff country wide.

Health and hygience principles

One aspect of the BHMMP is to concentrate on increasing health and hygiene practices in the hospitality industry. Although the country has an abundance of natural water and diverse river systems, unfortunately it is not always of a consumable standard or quality. This is due to pollution mainly from local industry and other cultural practices of littering and exploitation of the natural environment. The RGoB has identified Bhutan's biggest asset for tourism is its last 'Shangri la' reputation, meaning that it is naturally pristine and relatively unaffected by other cultures.

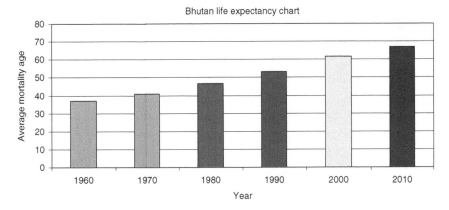

Figure 20.4 Average life expectancy of Bhutanese people over the last fifty years
Source: World Bank, World Development Indicators – March 2, 2010

Although this is not completely true, the government wishes to hold this reputation and also increase the life expectancy of its people (see Figure 20.4).

In the BHMM program, occupational health and safety issues are being taught. This is to give an internationally recognized benchmark of the quality and safety of the products offered to tourists. For example, flushing toilets are being introduced to the majority of hotels and main tourist destinations, replacing the squat toilet. Although considered costly, the benefits are great, such as allowing international tourists to feel more comfortable in and out of the hotel. They will more likely give a positive response of their experience rather than a negative one if they feel more comfortable (Ciddor, 1997).

The internationally recognized HACCP principles are being applied in hotel kitchens and restaurants. Teaching cleaning and sanitizing procedures in food preparation areas not only helps individuals introduce these into their own homes, but allows guests to feel more comfortable in consuming food products. Students are taught the purpose of boiling water and why international guests often will not risk consuming food products that could potentially make them ill. Food transport and storage is also an important factor therefore the BHMMP focuses heavily on these topics.

Sustainability of services and staff at off peak times

A major dilemma for the Tourism Council of Bhutan (TCB) is attracting tourists all year round. Being located in the Himalayas automatically conjures an image of cold temperatures mainly due to the highest peaked mountains being snow capped all year round (Acharya, 1999). This is not necessary the case. Although temperatures may vary throughout the year, the climate also varies within the country. For example, winter in the main cities of Paro and Thimphu falls below

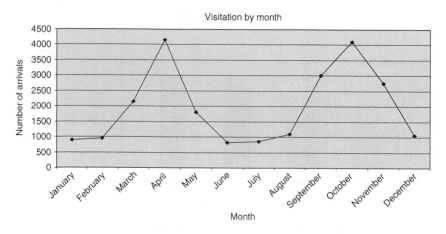

Figure 20.5 International visitation by month
    Source: Bhutan Tourism Monitor Annual Report - 2009

freezing overnight but is a comfortable 16-20 degrees Celsius during the day. In the south, the weather may be consistently above 10 degrees Celsius during the same time period throughout the night. The BHMMP has identified factors such as this to incorporate in their marketing campaigns.

Another draw card for tourists during peak times is the festivals that take place during the warmer months. These festivals are colorful and appeal to tourists as they truly reflect lifestyle, culture and heritage, and the warmer months are considered the 'peak season' for Bhutan. The challenge for hotel operators and the TCB is to attract international visitors during off peak times (see Figure 20.5). One suggestion has been to abolish the tariff system altogether and attract other markets such as backpackers. This would allow companies to market their own business through competition. This has worked in many other countries, however the decision has been made to increase the daily tariff from US$200 per day to US$250 per day (M. Ritchie, 2010, pers. comm. 9 April). The theory is that the international visitation has been steadily increasing each year and shows no signs of slowing and obtaining a higher yield per visitor and encouraging greater visitation will generate greater wealth for the government and the Bhutanese people. The BHMMP obviously has to incorporate the RGoB policy therefore teaching opportunities to increase tourist spending is encouraged.

Adopting eco-friendly hotel practices

The hotels planned on being built in Bhutan are in a position to incorporate eco-friendly hotel practices. This is seen as essential to the future design and development of the industry. With a desire to preserve the environment, many hotels are being constructed with locally harvested sustainable wood products. Having the advantage of advertising the re-establishment of forests also adds to the overall experience of the tourist. Although electricity advancement continues to be developed, hotels should only purchase wood for their fires from a renewable source. New hotels should only use the rocks and stones that are removed from mountain sides when building new roads. Not only are these items recycled, the hotels exterior appearance often blends into the backdrop allowing the mountains and terrain to dominate. This fits well with the overall sustainable and eco-tourism philosophy.

Most large hotels have already adopted water saving measures such as washing sheets every second day, providing towels on request, and turning off electrical items such as heating (if available), lighting and clocks if the room is not occupied. Other options are to pre order meals in restaurants (therefore being more precise with food quantities thus reducing waste). This idea has been operational in many hotels for years where meals are included in the tariff. As there are constant improvements in hotel environmental practices, the BHMMP program not only highlights environmental concerns, it also constantly re-enforces conservation principles even if some practices cannot be easily implemented.

Developing hotel waste mangement practices

The hotel industry in Bhutan needs to improve its waste management programs. It faces the same problems and issues as all other countries worldwide. But that is not to say that these trends cannot be altered. Currently, water, although abundant, could be used more efficiently. Reducing shower flow nozzles on guests' showers for example is an option that has not been explored. Food waste could be composted, garbage can be collected and disposed of correctly and recycling programs could be introduced. Roaming dogs are common and scavenge for food in garbage piles that litter the streets. Removing these piles may also reduce the over-populated dog problem that is a major concern to authorities. These simple but effective ideas would make the industry less wasteful and more desirable. Waste management is relatively new in Bhutan however recommendations have been put forward to implement waste management practices for the hotel industry through formal government policy. Current waste management practices are also taught in the BHMMP, but implementation is hard to achieve without RGoB support and funding.

Recommendations

The BHMMP can introduce many topics into the program to address some of these issues especially in the design of new hotels, and the retro-fitting of existing hotels. These include maintaining the concept of Gross National Happiness, national dress code, religious beliefs, languages and cultural architecture, as these all help define Bhutan. Other practices should include improving health and hygiene practices of all Bhutanese people as well as the hotel staff. This can only be achieved through education and re-enforcement. The RGoB already has employees that travel all over the country, village to village introducing sanitation

programs such as boiling water when required for human consumption and introducing septic tanks or pits for toilets. This must be maintained (or even introduced) to all hotels. Health and hygiene campaigns can be re-enforced in the main
cities through television and radio advertising (as the country now has two channels dedicated to Bhutanese programs). These practices should continue in the
BHMMP, as managers can then share this knowledge with all their employees
who, in turn will introduce them into their homes and communities.

The new training hotel will certainly impact the service standards of the hotel
employees. For the first time students will be taught international Western service
standards in all areas of the hotel. Employees will then be shown these techniques
and eventually will become the standard. This will directly address the main
complaints by tourists highlighted in the exit surveys.

A major challenge for hotel operators and the Tourism Council of Bhutan
(TCB) is encouraging tourism during the off peak season. Figure 20.6 illustrated
the huge discrepancy between tourist visits on a monthly basis. An increase in
tariffs may not address this issue. More aggressive advertising, marketing to
travel agents and greater exposure via the internet maybe required. As most of the
tourists arrive to view the cultural festivals, perhaps the introduction of a few
more during the off peak season may be a solution.

A major concern is also protecting the natural environment. As Bhutan's reputation has been built on natural pristine, nature conservation is imperative and
needs to be upheld as much as possible. Bhutanese hotels and businesses in
general can assist in this goal introducing mandated environment hotel guidelines. These may include:

- Using solar energy for water heating, lighting and other electrical energy
  consumption utilities
- Installation of wind generators and turbines for similar applications
- Using energy efficient devices such as globes, lighting sensors and natural
  ventilation
- Installing heat pumps to reduce energy consumption
- Have a alternative power source (such as a generator) in case of power failures
- Introduce reserve water storage containers in case of power failures (pumps
  operate on electricity)
- Reduce high polluting fuels such as burning bucaris to reduce black smoke
- Introduce recycling programs for glass, aluminium, cardboard and paper
- Introduce a food waste recycle program for composting
- Introduce an animal feeding program reusing vegetarian food waste
- Using hotel food waste to help feed people that are extremely poor

If it is not possible to mandate these issues, the BHMMP and training hotel
could certainly raise these issues for future managers to discuss and perhaps
incorporate into their individual hotel practices. The RGoB has a strong influence
over the hospitality industry therefore these concerns should become government
policy.

Conclusion

Since international tourism started in Bhutan the industry has evolved and grown exponentially. Having 274 visitors in 1974 compared to over 23,500 in 2009, many hotels were built to meet this expanding demand. Consequently, many hotel managers were employed with little to no tertiary training. Not surprisingly, complaints about service standards and facilities were received, and as a result, qualified hotel managers were sourced from other countries to try and improve hotel standards, and the image of the industry. However, this was never meant to be a long term solution.

To aid the overall developing economy (as tourism is the second largest contributor to the country's GDP) hotel management programs need to be implemented. The RGoB has responded by employing Bhutanese nationals in hotels, increasing education standards and overhauling the hospitality industry to improve facilities and standards with the first hotel management program (BHMMP) being introduced in 2009. The BHMMP aims are to assist future hotel management business practices in many ways. Being able to train managers (i.e. students) directly may be the best option for the future of the hotel industry. These managers will impart their learned knowledge to other hotel staff and into their own homes.

It is envisaged that through tertiary education and the introduction of a hotel training school, the aims of the government and the industry will be met. Hotel ratings will be a minimum of three stars, staff will be trained at internationally recognized standards, local heritage and culture will be maintained through national dress codes, language and architecture. Greater health and hygiene practices will lead to better food preparation practices and sanitation. As a result these will install greater confidence in the overall tourist experience. The hope is that the flow on effect will help increase the life expectancy and standard of living of locals by adopting better health and hygiene practices.

Lastly, environmental concerns of the industry can be reduced by teaching waste management practices, energy and water conservation, and the promotion of alternative energy sources. This will help protect the natural environment of Bhutan and aid in giving international visitors a positive experience and protecting the heritage, culture and natural diversity of this unique country in the Himalayas. Although many of these principles are not new to the hotel industry, this is the first time formal hotel management education has been available in Bhutan.

References

Acharya, S. (1999). *Bhutan: Kingdom in the Himalaya.* New Delhi: Roli Books.

Bauer, J., Brunet, S., De Lacy, T., Tshering, K. (c1999). *Milk and Cheese Always: Proposal for collaboration in education, training and research for conservation and sustainable tourism in Bhutan,* CRC Tourism.

Ciddor, A. (1997). *Unplugged! The Bare Facts on Toilets through the Ages.* St Leonards, N.S.W: Allen & Unwin.

Dorji, P. (2007). *International Tourism Monitor Bhutan 2006*. D.o. Tourism. Thimphu: Royal Government of Bhutan.

Du, J. (2003). "Reforms and Development of Higher Tourism Education in China", *Journal of Teaching in Travel & Tourism 3(1)*: 103–113.

Ministry of Finance, R. G. o. B. (2000). *Development towards Gross National Happiness*. D. o. A. a. D. Management. Thimpu: Ministry of Finance, Royal Government of Bhutan.

Payne-Palacio, J., Theis, M. (2009) *Introduction to Food Service*. 11th Edn. New Jersey: Pearson/Prentice Hall,.

Pek-Dorji, S. S., Ed. (2007). *The Legacy of a King: The Fourth Druk Gyalpo Jogme Singye Wangchuck*. Thimpu, Bhutan:, Department of Tourism. Royal Government of Bhutan.

Planning Commission, R. G. o. B. (1999). *Bhutan 2020: A vision for peace, prosperity and happiness*. Thimpu, Bhutan: R. G. o. B. Planning Commission

Ritchie, M. (2008). *Tourism in the Kingdom of Bhutan: A Unique Approach. Asian Tourism. Growth and Change*. J. Cochrane. Oxford: Elsevier.

SAARC, T. (2010). "*The South Asian Association for Regional Cooperation*." Retrieved 05/04/10, 2010, from http://bhutan.saarctourism.org/bhutan-language.html.

Thinley, J. Y. (2009). *Prime Minister of Bhutan*. R. G. o. Bhutan. Thimphu, Royal Government of Bhutan.

Van Driem, G. (1994). *Language policy in Bhutan. Bhutan: Aspects of Culture and Development*. M. Aris and M. Hutt (eds), Gartmore, Scotland: Paul Strachan - Kiscadale Ltd.

Wangchuck, S. (2005). Biodiversity at its best. in: *Bhutan: Land of the Thunder Dragon*. D. o. Tourism. Thimphu, Bhutan. pp. 52–56.

Worden, R. L. (1993). *Bhutan. Nepal and Bhutan country studies*. A. M. Savada. Washington: Library of Congress.

WWF (2010). "*WWF Bhutan*." Retrieved 12th April, 2010, from http://www.wwfbhutan.org.bt/aboutwwfbhutan.php.

21 Investigating potential benefits of proposed eco-retrofits to an existing tourist lodge in The Sundarbans, India

*Suchandra Bardhan**

Introduction

Tourism involves first-hand knowledge and cultural exchanges between different communities at different scales of interaction in different parts of the world. These exchanges and interactions take place in diverse domains like Nature, wild-life, adventure, the built heritage, and pilgrimage and leisure sectors amongst many others. With its close connections to the environment and climate itself, tourism is considered to be a highly climate-sensitive economic sector similar to agriculture, insurance, energy, and transportation (Simpson *et al.*, 2008). This demands that the sector adapts to climate change, and, more importantly, lessens its contribution to climate change through reduced emissions of greenhouse gasses, and brings down the overall environmental footprint of the industry (Simpson *et al.*, 2008).

Hospitality services being integral to tourism, it is important that these buildings conform to the sustainable development goals and are conscious of biodiversity and ecosystems, water consumption, land usage and physical impact, protection of the atmosphere, waste disposal, noise levels and visual impact (Blangy *et al.*, 2006).

India is a country rich in natural resources and bio-diversity as well as having an invaluable cultural and archaeological heritage. With a multi-lingual and multi-cultural population and widely varying landscapes across its length and breadth, it has always been a major attraction in the global arena. At present, India Tourism is already a well-established brand name in the country. The Government of India recognizes that tourism can play a dual role in economic development and employment generation and has a potential for high rate of growth and infrastructure development. India's performance in the tourism sector has been quite satisfactory with more than a 100% increase in the Foreign Tourist Arrivals from 2002 to 2009 and the growth rate in Foreign Exchange Earnings in 2009 has been reported to be 8.3 % compared to 2008 (Ministry of Tourism, 2010). Its contribution to India's Gross Domestic Product has increased from

*Dept. of Architecture, Jadavpur University, Kolkata, India

Figure 21.1 Tidal creek
 Source: author's own

5.83% to 6.11% during the period 2002-2003 to 2007-2008 (Bagga *et al.*, 2010). The Ministry of Tourism is now in the process of evolving Sustainable Tourism Criteria for India, which is considered to be at a very nascent stage. It is believed that environmental and cultural degradation is the result of unimaginative and unregulated tourism activities and an assessment of carrying capacity and Environment Impact Assessment studies is essential while developing tourism in ecologically fragile areas to guide all developmental activities. Providing a legal framework via appropriate legislation for ensuring the social, cultural and environmental sustainability of tourism development is also underway. In addition to these steps, initiatives by hospitality providers to promote recycling, energy efficiency, water reuse, and the creation of economic opportunities for local communities are also considered to be an integral part of sustainable tourism (MoT-I, 2010).

In the above context, this paper examines the environmental footprint of an existing tourist lodge located in the Sundarbans region of coastal Bengal in Eastern India. The Indian Sundarbans forests are a World Heritage Site constituting a complex and unique tiger inhabited tidal mangrove eco-system and saltwater swamp making up the lower part of the Gangetic delta. It is located between 21°31' to 22°53'N latitude and 88°37' to 89°09'E longitude in the State of West Bengal and is about 100 km southeast of the Calcutta (now Kolkata) metropolis.

With an intricate network of tidal creeks, the Sundarbans comprises of 100 islands, out of which 52 are inhabited and the rest 48 islands constitute the

Figure 21.2 The Bakkhali sea beach at sunset
Source: author's own

Reserve Forests (see Figure 21.1). Agriculture, pisciculture, aquaculture and animal husbandry are some of the main occupations of the local people. Over the last decade, the population of this region has increased from 3.2 million as per the 1991 census to around 4.0-4.5 million at present. Majority of the people are living below poverty line (BPL), an income group with a family income of not more than US$ 130 per year or less than one US $ per day. Since eco-tourism has the potential to generate economic opportunities through non-destructive use of natural resources, it was important to find out the role played by the present system of tourism activities and possibilities for bringing them to the 'non-destructive' path, in case these are not found to be in compliance with it.

Case study main section

The area chosen for carrying out this study is one of the most popular tourist locales - the *Bakkhali* Island (21°33'50" N, 88°16'28"E) of *Namkhana* Block (see Figure 21.2). The easy accessibility and the expansive sea beaches with excellent natural qualities have made *Bakkhali* an all season get-away destination, especially for city people. Located about 140 km from Calcutta (now Kolkata), it is well connected through State Transport buses and vessels that ferry private vehicles too. The choice of public and private transport has also contributed into its high tourism growth, which has been largely organic in nature. At present *Bakkhali* alone has about 25 kinds of major and minor hotels and lodges

Figure 21.3 Part view of the lodge
   Source: author's own

to suit all budgets, which are comprised of a regular design and construction style similar to typical urban aesthetics. Coupled with a conventional system of providing artificially conditioned spaces for the comfort-seeking high-end tourists, these also depend heavily on the local natural resources ending up loading the environment on a recurrent basis (Bardhan, 2008). Hence, assessing a typical long-functioning tourist lodge in terms of its recurring impact on ecology and environment and examining the retrofit possibilities to improve its environmental performance was considered to be imperative.

The tourist facility chosen as a case study is a three-storied budget accommodation of about 387 sq m (4164.12 sq ft) plinth area and a capacity of 60 beds (see Figure 21.3). Energy and water were considered as the major environmental indices for this assessment and the average annual energy consumption, referred to as the energy footprint as well as the average annual water consumption, or water foot-print, were calculated in detail on the basis of field survey results (Bardhan *et al.*, 2010a). The operational energy footprint of the Tourist Lodge was found to be about 212 kWh/Sq m/year while the water footprint was found to be 11.3 Cum/Sq m/year. It must be mentioned here that ground water is the only source of potable water in the region, which is extracted from a depth of nearly 400 metres. The energy expended in pumping this water in the overhead tank with a 1.5 H.P. pump was found to be an additional 13.5 kWh/Sq m/year. Hence, the total energy footprint of the said lodge worked out to be about 225 kWh/sq m/year. This value was converted into an equivalent quantity of carbon emission and referred as carbon footprint, calculated on the basis of Carbon emission per unit of oil based electricity produced (IEEE, 2008). It was found that the lodge's average carbon foot-print was 74.01 tonC/year, which is very high and detrimental to the region when considered in extended spatial and temporal terms. The present paper discusses the results of the proposed integration of the retrofits with respect to energy and water resources and their cost-benefit analyses, and also assesses the potential environmental and socio-economic benefits derivable from this integration.

The lodge, like many others in the area, is equipped with its own captive power generation system in the form of diesel generator as a back-up power for using during frequent power interruptions, which is very common in the region. The emissions from these diesel generators cause negative impacts on the environment since pollution norms are not followed strictly. It was estimated that about 821 litres of diesel and 810 kg of bio-mass are consumed annually by the lodge. In order to achieve sustainability, it was crucial for the lodge to meet its annual energy demand from clean and renewable sources instead of fossil fuels and forest bio-mass. In Indian solar radiation condition, the availability of solar power in that region is about 800 W/m^2 for five hours duration i.e. 4000 Wh/m^2/day (School of Energy Studies, 2004). With this abundant solar energy, retrofitting potential with renewable energy systems like the solar Photovoltaic (PV) and solar thermal was considered to be highly viable, since these would allow an easy integration with the existing building fabric, especially the roof. The electricity generated from photovoltaic-s would also reduce the diesel consumption and production of hot water through a and solar thermal route would lessen the load on the bio-mass consumption, optimize energy-efficiency and therefore reduce the energy footprint considerably. Similarly, water sustainability was considered to be achievable through water recycling measures and other available technologies. Apart from these building retrofits, landscape measures were considered to be of very high potential in terms of carbon sequestration, environmental amelioration and ecological restoration. These techniques and measures have been matched with the actual conditions and demands of the said tourist lodge to address the case-specific needs and adjudge the corresponding environmental benefits achieved through the suggested retrofits.

Retrofit Potential with solar PV

Since the solar photovoltaic (PV) applications generate power without any noise pollution or emission, these can be installed over the Lodge's roof facing the south–east direction and at an inclination of 22.5° to obtain maximum efficiency in electricity generation. With a nominal voltage of 24 V, these can cover the entire roof area of 387 Sq m and can generate about 220 kWh per day, which is found to be slightly lower than the daily energy demand. The reduction in Carbon emission was estimated at 68.25 tonC/year amounting to an equivalent savings of 25756 Litres of diesel fuel per year. After accounting for the captive emission component of the multi-crystalline silicon based PV modules, this figure comes down to 65.28 tonC/year (Bardhan *et al.*, 2010b). Thus, the net annual negation potential in CO^2 emission is nearly 89% of the measured carbon footprint or the annual CO^2 generated by the Lodge.

Retrofit Potential for solar thermal

Hot water demand in hospitality buildings is very high and hence, a lot of energy is used in providing heated water for the guests. With a predominance of hot and humid weather in the region, it was considered that hot water would only be required for bathing and the total volume of this was estimated at 54 litres per capita per day (Bardhan *et al.*, 2010b). Considering a total of 64 people including guests and staff, this comes to (64 x 54) = 3456 litres/day. In order to estimate the energy required to heat this volume of water, the following assumptions were made:

i.   Since hot water requirement is mostly required during the winter i.e. October to February, the average number of days requiring the heating of water is 150.
ii.   Temperature of the water in winter is 20 °C.
iii. Temperature of this hot water at a comfortable level is 26 °C.

Detailed calculations (Bardhan *et al.,* 2010b) indicated that 24 kWh of energy would be required per day to heat the said volume of water to the stated temperature and 5.4 Kg per day of bio-mass is required to supply this energy. The corresponding CO^2 emission from this burning was estimated to be 162 KgC/year. Incomplete burning of bio-mass is also known to be contributing to air pollution through toxic pollutants like the particulates including all its sub-types i.e. Respirable Particulate Matter (PM^{10}), Fine Respirable Particulate Matter ($PM^{2.5}$), Non Respirable Particulate Matter (NRPM), Total Suspended Particulate Matter (TSPM), Sulphur Dioxide (SO^2), Nitrogen Dioxide (NO^2), Carbon Monoxide (CO) and Ozone (O^3), which are detrimental to man and biosphere alike (Mukherjee et al., 2010). Hence, the benefits of solar thermal retrofits are both 'direct', i.e. avoiding bio-mass based energy consumption along-with its subsequent CO^2 emission and air pollution, as well as 'indirect', i.e. preventing bio-mass burning and thus saving the bio-mass itself. This implies saving the vital Carbon sink, thereby multiplying its positive effects. In this particular study, the retrofit possibilities of Building Integrated Solar Thermal (BIST) were found to apply either to the roof or the balcony parapet having a high solar exposure. Calculations showed that six nos. of 2.0 M x 2.0 M solar thermal panels are sufficient to yield the required water, implying a 12 RM (running meter) length of roof parapet, which is easily possible for the lodge.

Assessment of indirect environmental benefits involved estimating the annual quantity of bio-mass required from the above findings, followed by translating this bio-mass quantity into the actual number of trees being felled annually and finally, quantification of the CO^2 fixed by such trees, if retained, and their collective contribution as the Carbon sink. The annual consumption of biomass (i.e. for

150 days of the winter-time) for this Lodge was calculated to be (5.4 x 150) = 810 Kg/yr. Since the mangrove tree Avicennia spp. is dominant in the region, a reasonable height and girth of the species was assumed to calculate the volume of a matured Avicennia tree to provide usable bio-mass and it worked out to be about five to six numbers per year. It has been reported (Karmakar, 2006) that the Carbon assimilation efficiency of Avicennia dominated mangrove eco-system is 54.75 tonnes of Carbon/hectare/year (or 5.47 $KgC/m^2/year$). Further estimations on the basis of a reasonable Avicennia cover in the forest showed a sequestration potential of 246.15 KgC/year (Bardhan et al., 2010b). Thus, the cumulative benefit in terms of total CO^2 offsetting achieved by retrofitting solar thermal technology for providing hot bath water to the tourists is the sum of the direct and indirect emission reduction, which works out to be (162 KgC/year + 246.15 KgC/year) 408.15 KgC/year.

Retrofit Potential for Rain Water Harvesting systems

In the context of its coastal location, Rain Water Harvesting (RWH) was considered to be one of the most significant water retrofit tools for the Lodge as it would not only reduce its water footprint, it would also reduce the extraction of precious ground water, thereby preventing salt water intrusion into the ground water.

The total annual RWH endowment of the lodge was assessed considering average annual rainfall in the region and a reasonable run-off coefficient for the roof. The annual RWH potential has been considered to be 60% of this endowment, accounting for losses due to first flushing requirements, evaporation and others. As per State Pollution Control Board recommendations, 40% and 60% of annual RWH potential should be used for storage and ground water recharge respectively (WBPCB, 2008). However, it was found after detailed calculations that the annual RWH potential is a meager 8% of the total annual water demand of the lodge.

Recognizing that being water use-wise is not prevalent among the guests, and being a beach destination, a large quantity of water is used by the guests for bathing and washing clothes after a dip in the sea, it is essential to ensure 'use efficiency' through water-efficient fittings and fixtures. Most of the toilets surveyed in this facility (and other lodges, too) had the conventional 13.5 litre flushing closets. Detailed estimates have revealed that replacing these by the dual flush toilet with a 9-litre capacity, a larger amount of water could be saved and the annual savings worked out to be 1156.32 Cum/year (Bardhan *et al.,* 2010b).

Retrofit Potential for Grey Water recycling systems

The per capita waste water generated in this lodge per day was estimated on the basis of Urban Development Plans Formulation and Implementation Guidelines in India (Ministry of Urban Affairs and Employment, 1996) and was thought to be 144 litres per capita per day. This consists of both grey water and black water. Considering grey water to be 60% of the waste water and limited open space in the lodge's premises, the retrofit potential with available techniques like grey water gardens/pressure leaching chambers etc. seemed to be only 10-5 % maximum, which comes to about 210.2 Cum/year.

Retrofit potential with Vegetation

Vegetation and other natural components are known to be excellent Carbon sinks. Considering an available open space of 200 Sq m, local species of Avicennia spp. plantation was considered along-with indigenous plant species. Researches (Wackernagel *et al.,* 1996; Post *et al.,* 2000) have reported carbon accumulation figures for different forests as well as soil under natural vegetation cover. Using these assessments, the total CO^2 sequestration possibility through landscaping measures was estimated to be 325.39 KgC/year.

Post-retrofit Environmental Audit and Sustainability Status

With the above discussions on the proposed retrofit measures for the Lodge, it was important to look into the collective impact of these on its resource utilization status as well as its modified Carbon foot-print. Since the study had begun with its current energy and water foot-prints, the post-retrofit resource audit was carried out with respect to these two natural resources, with the former expressed in terms of CO^2 - a direct outcome of energy consumption and are presented in Tables 21.1 and 21.2.

It is interesting to note that while considerable savings in fresh water usage could be made possible, the water balance still remains substantially debited. On the other hand, the carbon balance sheet has yielded high positive results. Overall, the encouraging results of the post-retrofit reduced footprint of this lodge establishes the potentiality of using sustainable retrofit measures for an existing tourist facility to be a strong possibility. However, with improved efficiency in energy consumption like adopting energy efficient lamps and gadgets, and

Table 21.1 Water resource balance sheet

Water Debit	Water Credit				Balance
A	B	C	D	E=(B+C+D)	A-E
Annual Water consumption	Total Harvested Rain Water	Recycled Grey water	Water saved by dual-flush toilets	Total water saved	Net reduction in Annual Water consumption
Cum/yr	Cum/yr	Cum/yr	Cum/yr	Cum/yr	Cum/yr
4380	352.94	210.2	1156.32	1719.46 [39.25%]	2660.54 [60.75%]

Table 21.2 CO_2 emission balance sheet

CO$_2$ Debit	CO$_2$ Credit				Balance
A	B	C	D	E = (B+C+D)	A-E
Annual CO$_2$ Emission	CO$_2$ Negation through solar PV	Total CO$_2$ Negation by solar thermal	CO$_2$ fixation by Landscape components	Total CO$_2$ sequestered	Net reduction in Annual CO$_2$ Emission
KgC/year	KgC/year	KgC/year	KgC/year	KgC/year	KgC/year
74.01 x 10³	65.28 x 10³	408.15	325.39	66.01 x 10³ [89%]	8 x 10³ [11%]

avoiding the use of woody bio-mass as fuel, the post-retrofit annual emission is expected to be further lowered.

Extending the above results to some directly related and inter-dependent environmental parameters of bio-mass and fossil-fuel consumptions, a comparative enumeration of the annual resource consumption by the Lodge in pre-retrofit and proposed post-retrofit situations is presented in Table 21.3. Energy consumption has been expressed in Giga Joules (GJ) per year. With renewable energy retrofits, the lodge's dependence on bio-mass and fossil fuel will be minimized, though not completely eliminated. These have not been quantified in this chapter.

When expressed graphically in the form an eco-profile, the post-retrofit resource footprint of the lodge is clearly found to be substantially reduced as shown in Figure 21.4. Although the water retrofit's achievement was much less compared to the energy retrofits, it can be stated that the overall performance of the eco-retrofits have proved to be potential enough to bring the lodge closer to sustainability.

With improved eco-compatibility thus reached, the question of economic pay-back period will come to the fore. The next section attempts to take up a cost-benefit analysis of these measures through their financial assessment.

Table 21.3 Comparative annual resource consumption pattern before and after retrofitting

Sl. No.	Environmental Parameters	Pre-retrofit Annual Resource Consumption: As Existing	Post-retrofit Annual Resource Consumption: As Estimated
1.	Water	4380 cum/year	2660.54 cum/year
2.	CO$_2$ emission	74.01 tonC/year	8 tonC/year
3.	Energy	313.2 GJ/year	24.35 GJ/year
4.	Bio-mass consumption	810 Kg/year	Minimized (not estimated)
5.	Fossil-fuel consumption	821.25 Lt/year	Minimized (not estimated)

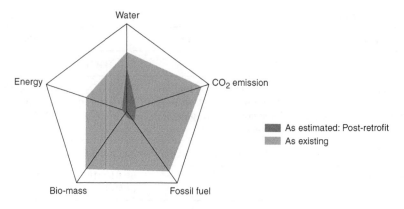

Figure 21.4 Comparative annual eco-profile of the Lodge

Cost Benefit Analysis of the proposed retrofits

Although *Bakkhali* is supplied with grid electricity, power disruption is very common, as mentioned before. Therefore, hospitality providers are considerably dependent on decentralized systems to ensure twenty-four hour comfort conditions for their guests. Even a budget accommodation like the lodge detailed here has six of the rooms (20% of capacity) fitted with air-conditioners. The decentralized power system of the Lodge operates as a conventional power generation system using diesel, as also mentioned before. This has a recurring cost aspect, not only in terms of the fuel itself, but also in transporting these materials to the site of power generation. In this case, these have to be carried from the urban areas resulting in substantial additional transportation cost and ultimately a high generation cost(Ghosh, 2004). Moreover, combustion of these fuels emits toxic gases, thereby affecting the surrounding environment. In case of Renewable Solar Power, the initial investment in PV involves cost of the modules and Balance of System (BoS) including battery, storage and infrastructure and was about 350 INR per watt at the time of the study. The total expenditure on solar power at the said rate after taking the battery replacement costs into account worked out to be INR18.6 millions or US\$ 3.72×10^5 (at one US \$ = INR 50). A battery back-up system made up of solar panels needs to be provided for this power component, while the surplus power generated from the photo-voltaic modules can be fed to the grid directly and off-set the cost. Carbon Credit at available contemporary financial rates was also considered for cost recovery and based on these, the cost pay-back period for the solar PV was found to be 22 years. This was considered positive and economically viable when seen against the solar PV's average service life of 25 years. If conventional electricity was not subsidized or if the entire power had to be generated through a diesel generator, the payback period would have drastically come down in both cases. The payback period would also be considerably lowered had the additional cost of conventional roof construction been considered for the additional storey thus available with PV roof.

A similar Cost-Benefit Analysis was carried out for the solar thermal flat plate collector system, though unlike the solar PV-s, the payback period in this case did not yield economically viable results, especially because it counters the use of naturally available resources like bio-mass and vegetation. As per the present practice, these resources are readily available and therefore, almost 'free commodities'. As per the contemporary rates, the cost of flat plate collector suitable to meet the hot water requirement of the Lodge and with 15 years of service life was estimated at INR75,000 or US$ 1500. Pitted against 'cheap' and readily available bio-mass coupled with seasonality of the hot water demand, the analysis generated a skewed result against the solar thermal retrofit for this case-study. Since one kg of wood is available locally at a cost of INR2.00, it was found that by using bio-mass as an energy source, the user pays only INR0.45 per kWh against INR4.00 per unit of electrical energy, almost nine times that of the former (Bardhan, 2008). This shows that such under-valuation of natural resources always come in the way of the cost effectiveness of sustainable technological practices.

Similar here is the situation with the water resource. The financial assessment of rain water harvesting scheme was not conducted here for the same reasons cited above. The eco-system goods and services of air, water and vegetation have traditionally been obtained free of cost, hence the likelihood of many eco-technologies to be financially justifiable stand remote in such backdrop.

Discussion

With the environmental compatibility as well as the financial viability of solar PV, the main eco-retrofit, thus broadly established, and an investigation into its possible effect on the two other dimensions of sustainability i.e. social and economic aspects were thought to be relevant and important. The following section briefly discusses the envisaged effects in beneficiaries' as well as temporal scales. From the lodge owner's viewpoint, the architectural integration of the solar PV modules at a height with enough headroom from the existing roof top is virtually adding another storey, and with the covered space so formed, it can also be utilized for tourism-related activities and help in additional revenue generation. Further, shading from the solar PV will substantially reduce the heat gain of the building from the roof and keep the interiors cooler. Thus direct and immediate benefits through this solar PV installation can somewhat offset the initial investment. The direct commercial gains of the lodge owner come from cost savings on fossil fuel purchase as well as from the option of selling the excess power to the grid supply. It is expected that once successful, this example would also be followed by fellow service providers, which would multiply the positive environmental benefits. Better ambience translates into better business and the collective contribution of these good practices would create an improved tourist perception, boosting the number of tourist arrivals and the corresponding revenue generation. For the local people, a reduction in air and noise pollution as well as reduced hazards from waste oil disposal would lead to better community health, and therefore, better working capabilities. In the long-term, energy security, reduced pollution and Carbon emission, conservation of bio-mass and bio-diversity, and growth in Foreign Tourist Traffic (FTT) and Foreign Exchange Earnings (FEE) are envisaged to be the major contribution of the suggested eco-retrofits. Most importantly, planned initiatives for keeping a back-up stock of solar power for use during natural disasters like cyclones, which are very common in the region, can be used for recharging cell phones and keeping communication active during these crisis periods, thus reducing risk and the vulnerability of the local population.

A survey carried out in Bakkhali revealed that the average age for tourists is between 26-55 years and most are service holders or belong to the professional class. Together they contribute to about 60% of total tourist numbers. A study of the economic profile of these tourists indicated that 40% belonged to the income group of more than INR20, 000 or US$ 400 per month family income and 70% belonged to the category of more than INR15,000 or US$ 300 per month. Thus the pay capacities of these tourists are also expected to be high. However, the FTT in West Bengal was found to be only 4% of total tourist volume (WEBCON, 2002) and local survey results pointed out that only 1% foreign tourists visit Bakkhali. According to the hotel owners, this is due to lack of promotion and marketing in Sundarbans Tourism. However, it was felt during the study that the current state of affairs in the Bakkhali tourism belt with its comfortable but non-innovative hospitality facilities fails to attract foreign tourists, who are more keen on experiencing the forests and wildlife of the Sundarban Reserve forests. A typical tourist looks for the quality of accommodation in the region and novelty in the place they stay in among other aspects like the uniqueness and attractions of a region, accessibility, the support infrastructure and the volume of tourist traffic in that region. Since the hospitality sector in Bakkhali is already functioning on the strength of regional tourists, the discussed eco-retrofits to these existing buildings can help them expand their business by attracting a larger section of domestic tourists as well as international guests. Favourable feedback on the 'good and sustainable practices' adopted by this sector can help promote and market them to the global community and encourage more visits. 'Sustainable Architecture' can easily convince the global base of responsible eco-tourists about its quality and novelty, and ensure repeat visits by them.

The exact contribution of tourism in terms of income to the State and employment generation is difficult to estimate because of the involvement of a large number of establishments and agencies in the tourism industry. With tourism, some core and peripheral sectors will be energized by activities and economic regeneration. While the core sectors are transport, food supply and general service, the peripheral sectors are secondary beneficiaries like small time vendors, local fishermen, local handicraft-makers and the entire village community. As such the expenditures by tourists are spread over a wide variety of businesses, big and small. It is estimated that excluding air transport, for every 100 units spent in the country, the breakdown for respective sectors is as follows: Lodging 30–35%,

Food / beverages 20–25%, Handicrafts 10–15%, Local Transport 10%, and Shopping guides / Entertainment etc. 20–25% (WEBCON, 2002). Apart from the above, direct employment generated as per World Travel & Tourism Council (WTTC) is 1 in 9 i.e. 11.11% (of total population). In socio-cultural terms, tourism initiates an interaction between the tourists coming from different corners of the world and the locals resulting in a two-way impact that acts mutually in exchange of cultural ethos and exposure to ways of life. While the host community acquires additional job skills, education / training and empowerment, the guest community gains in terms of knowing about the traditional ways of life, ethnicity and cultural practices. The two dimensions of social development - horizontal (health and education) and vertical (income) can ensure all-round progress for a particular region (Ghosh, 2007). This effect is mostly positive. Detailed calculation indicated that implementation of PV power in that locality may enhance the HDI up to 16-18% from its initial value (Ghosh *et al.*, 2009). All these arguments and envisioned benefits have been presented in Table 21.4.

Table 21.4 Potential three-dimensional benefits of eco-retrofits as envisaged

	Individuals	*Local Community*	*Society*
Environmental			
a. Short term	Minimize dependence on fossil fuel supplies	Conservation of local bio-mass	Reduced air pollution, energy security
b. Long term	Lower per capita Carbon emission	Conservation of bio-diversity	Contribution to climate change mitigation
Social			
a. Short term	Social recognition, sense of pride and leadership	Good practice application will attract world attention and boost 'eco-tourism'	Respiratory ailments due to air pollution reduced
b. Long term	Inspire fellow service providers to adopt similar practices	Better health and income due to fossil fuel omission	Better communication, reduced risk and vulnerability
Economic			
a. Short term	Sell excess power, use additional floor for rentals, save on fossil fuel cost		Energy security
b. Long term	Can increase tariff by publicising and generate better revenue	Better image of tourism would result in growth and job opportunities	Sustainable tourism would attract FTT and generate FEE

Conclusion

Any anthropogenic activity is bound to have some impact on the environment. The main aim of sustainable tourism is to develop an eco-friendly environment and mitigate its negative ecological impacts by adopting certain principles and techniques. The effect of tourism activity on energy, waste and water during its operational stage has been found to be negative in most cases, especially in the developing countries. The case study documented here shows similar results. Considerable use of biomass for both household and agricultural purposes, increasing use of diesel, kerosene and petrol as fuel in generators and use of kerosene in households are all collectively contributing to pollution, since combustion of these fuels lead to substantial emission of the well-defined criteria air pollutants (Particulates, Sulphur Dioxide, Nitrogen Dioxide, Tropospheric Ozone, Carbon Monoxide). All these pollutants have proven records of deteriorating an environment, destroying the ecological balance and also negatively affecting human health. A degenerated and degraded environment in the long-run affects tourism prospects negatively, especially if these include nature-based tourism, and finally undergoes an economic collapse as it becomes robbed of its main values.

The retrofit possibilities against the three major resources of energy, water and landscape elements were explored in this chapter and the environmental benefit derivable from this integration was assessed in quantitative terms. These were presented as environmental audit and expressed in terms of water and Carbon emission. About 89% of the total annual CO^2 emission was found to be compensated by the energy retrofits, though the water retrofit situation still has a lot of scope to improve. However, with improved efficiency in energy consumption like adopting energy efficient lamps and gadgets, and avoiding use of woody bio-mass as fuel, the post-retrofit annual emission would further come down. Related additional benefits like reduction in environmentally damaging fossil fuel and woody bio-mass use were also discussed and all these found reflections in the changed eco-profile of the studied Lodge. The post-retrofit reduced foot-print of the Lodge establishes the potentiality of sustainable retrofit measures into a strong possibility. It can, therefore, be stated that the building will become sustainable in the long run if the retrofits discussed here are adopted and adapted. Since a more environmentally compatible hospitality building has the potential to generate economic opportunities through non-destructive use of natural resources, it would have a positive contribution towards development of eco-tourism in the region. The possible socio-economic contribution of a more environmentally compatible hospitality sector in the short and long term that can percolate down to the different hierarchy of beneficiaries right from the individual lodge owner/s to the local community and finally to the society at large was also discussed simultaneously. This showed the three-dimensional cascading effect of one small step towards the 'non-destructive' and 'low carbon' path in creating a major difference in the global sustainability efforts and the climate-change-mitigation-and-adaptation drive.

Acknowledgement

The author wishes to thank the All India Council for Technical Education (AICTE) for their support in carrying out this study.

References

Bagga, S. and Kothari, S. (2010). World Class Tourism Infrastructure: The Key to Enhancing Tourism Opportunities, *Architecture- Time, Space & People*, *10(5)*, 18–25.

Bardhan, S. (2008), *Carbon Foot-Print Studies and Sustainable Architectural Concepts for Coastal Eco-Tourism*, unpublished Doctoral thesis, Jadavpur University.

Bardhan, S., Chattopadhyay, M. and Hazra, S. (2010a), Quantifying Environmental Sustainability of Buildings through its Carbon Foot-Print: An Analytical Approach, *Journal of Civil Engineering and Architecture*, *4(1)*, 20–34.

Bardhan, S., Ghosh, B., Hazra, S. and Chatterjee, M. (2010). Retrofitting Potential of an Existing Tourist Lodge for Improved Environmental Performance: An Investigation, *Proceedings of New Sustainable Cities 2010*–WIT.

Blangy, S. and Mehta, H. (2006). Ecotourism and Ecological Restoration, *Journal for Nature Conservation*, *14(3-4)*, 233–236.

Ghosh, B. (2004). *Towards Modernized Bio-Energy*, Ministry of New and Renewable Energy, Govt. of India.

Ghosh, B. (2007). *Plugging into a New Life*, TEQIP Report of Jadavpur University, West Bengal, India.

Ghosh, B. and Bardhan, S. (2009). Analysis on the Integration of PV Power at Eco-Tourism Site, Proceedings of 24th European Photo Voltaic and Solar Energy Conference, 21–25 September '09, Hamburg, Germany. *IEEE Spectrum*, *(2008)*, *45(2)*, 56.

Karmakar, S. (2006). *Study of Mangrove Biomass, Net Primary Production & Species Distribution using Optical and Microwave Remote Sensing Data*, unpublished M. Tech. Thesis, Andhra University, India, 36–40.

Ministry of Tourism, Government of India (2010), Annual report, (2009-2010) http://www.tourism.gov.in [Accessed the 30th of July 2010, 14:40].

Ministry of Tourism, Government of India (2007).http://www.incredibleindia.org [Accessed the 1st of August 2010, 15:28].

Ministry of Urban Affairs & Employment (1996). Urban Development Plans Formulation and Implementation [UDPFI] Guidelines, Govt. of India, 151–152.

Mukherjee, I., Chakraborty, N. and Bardhan, S. (2010b). Synergies between Energy, Environment and Sustainable Development in the mangrove eco-system of the Sundarbans, *Proceedings of 17th National Symposium on Environment*, Centre for Environmental Science & Engineering, IIT Kanpur, 410–414.

Post, W. M. and Kwon, K.C. (2000). Soil Carbon Sequestration and Land-Use Change: Processes and Potential, *Global Change Biology*, *6*, 317–328.

School of Energy Studies (2004*). Field Station Data*, Jadavpur University.

Simpson, M.C., Gössling, S., Scott, D., Hall, C.M. and Gladin, E. (2008). *Climate Change Adaptation and Mitigation in the Tourism Sector: Frameworks, Tools and Practices*, UNEP, University of Oxford, UNWTO, WMO: Paris, France.

Wackernagel, M. and Rees, W. (1996) Our Ecological Footprint, New Society Publishers.

WBPCB (2008). West Bengal Pollution Control Board. http://www.wbpcb.gov.in/html/RWH.pdf [Accessed the 24th of March 2008, 18:35].

West Bengal Consultancy Organization Limited (WEBCON) Report (2002). 20 year Perspective Plan for West Bengal Tourism, Kolkata. http://www.wikimapia.org [Accessed the 9th of August 2010, 19:20].

WTTC (2008). World Travel and Tourism Council http://wttc.org [Accessed the 27th of March 2008, 18:35].

22 Urban green parks

Sustainable tourism, biodiversity and quality of life: A case study

*Corazon Catibog-Sinha**

Introduction

Cities are known not only for the high densities of people and man-made structures but also for the diverse and high level of socio-cultural and economic activities (Pearce, 2001). Comprising almost half of the world's entire population, the world's urban population is about 3.3 billion, and it is expected to double in 2050 (United Nations, 2007). In the Philippines more than 50% of the country's total population live in urban areas. In Metro Manila alone, at least 14 million people have been recorded (Philippine Information Agency, 2008).

The importance of urban green parks in promoting sustainable tourism is increasingly being recognized worldwide. Sustainable tourism takes into account the environmental, economic, and social elements for the management of both the visitors and the tourist destination. Sustainable tourism has been expounded in the literature (e.g., Catibog-Sinha, 2007; Harris et al., 2002; McCool & Watson, 1995; Swarbrooke, 1999). Given that the social and natural environments are inextricably connected, the success of tourism development depends on the quality and sustainability of the natural system. The loss or deterioration of the natural system will lead to the decline of economic wealth and the deterioration of the quality of life (Burr, 1995; Costanza et al., 1997).

Providing green open space in highly populated urban areas can help improve the quality of life of city residents (Burgess et al., 1988; Kaplan, 1984; Madanipour, 1999). The notion of quality of life includes 'opportunities for contact with nature, satisfactory human relationships, creative expression, and making a positive contribution to human society' (Furnass, 1996, cited in Senior & Townsend, 2005, p. 114). Several studies have shown the positive effects of green parks on human health especially among the elderly, homemakers, and persons with low socio-economic status (e.g. De Vries et al., 2003; Nielsen & Hansen, 2007). Visiting green parks on a regular basis can facilitate recovery from physical and psychological ailments (Ulrich et al., 1991) and prevent

*Senior Lecturer in Environmental Management & Tourism, School of Social Sciences, University of Western Sydney, Kingswood Campus, PG.21, Locked Bag 1797 Penrith South DC, NSW 1797 Australia

lifestyle-related diseases (e.g., hypertension, obesity, depression) (Nielsen & Hansen, 2007; Milligan & Bingley, 2007). Visiting urban green parks can also minimize the stress of urban living (Munoz, 2003; Pares-Franzi & Sauri-Pujol, 2006; Ulrich, 2006). For example, Grahn and Stigsdotter (2003) found that the frequency of visits to green open space is indirectly correlated with the occurrence of stress among city residents. A society with less stress tends to have fewer incidence of crime and social unrest (Ferris et al., 2001; Kuo, 2001).

Because cities are always crowded and busy, many city dwellers tend to be alienated from nature (McNeely, 2005). McDonnell (2007, p. 83) states that urban parks can play an important role in biodiversity conservation when city dwellers are given the opportunity to interact with nature even within an urban setting. Several authors have recommended visiting urban green spaces to help address the weak human-nature linkage in cities (e.g. Alvey, 2006; Dimoudi & Nikolopoulou, 2003; Madanipour, 1999; McDonnell, 2007).

The World Conservation Union-IUCN recognizes the benefits of nature to cities and urban residents. During the Third IUCN World Conservation Congress, a resolution (WCC 3.063) linking nature conservation to human settlements in urban areas, was overwhelmingly approved (IUCN, 2004). Consequently, an IUCN Task Force on Parks and Cities was created to mainstream biodiversity issues in cities. According to Trzyna (2005, p. 9), the Chair of the Task Force, 'protecting nature and improving city life are interdependent goals.' One way to implement the goals of this Task Force is to incorporate the principles of sustainable development such as promoting sustainable tourism in open green spaces. Although the application of sustainable tourism principles in an urban setting is a new concept, it is a challenging idea being embraced by many green urban planners (Gibson et al., 2003).

Case study: The Philippines

The case study was conducted at the Ninoy Aquino Park and Wildlife Center (henceforth Ninoy Park or the Park), a 22.7-hectare open green area and a major nature-based tourism destination in Metro Manila. The study aimed to determine the contribution of urban parks to nature/biodiversity conservation and sustainable tourism. The study also aimed to gather some preliminary data on the interactions of city dwellers with nature in urban parks. Knowing the experience of tourists during their visits and transforming this experience into a better understanding of nature conservation and improvement of the quality of city life are important elements of sustainable tourism. This preliminary study, using a combination of research methods (i.e. visitor questionnaire survey, structured interview of visitors, field observation, and literature review), was conducted within the Park precinct in various occasions from 2006 to 2009. A review of pertinent government records and interviews with key staff of the Park was also conducted.

Features of Ninoy Park

This section discusses the attributes of Ninoy Park and analyses these attributes in the context of sustainable tourism, quality of life, and biodiversity conservation. The attractiveness and availability of park facilities are important determinants of the level of use of urban green parks for leisure and recreation. The discussion is divided into bio-physical setting, managerial setting, and social setting. If properly managed, these tourism settings can improve the sustainability of urban parks.

Bio-physical setting

Unlike the usual formal parks found in many major cities, Ninoy Park has 'reconstructed' landscape features that simulate the attributes of a natural park. The Park falls under Class 5 based on the ROS (Recreational Opportunity Spectrum) framework of analysis (Clark & Stankey, 1979), indicating that it is heavily modified, intensively managed, and very accessible.

Biodiversity

There are no available written records on the past ecology of the Park; but anecdotal data reveal that the Park's location was once a forested area. After the Second World War, the site was heavily deforested, transforming it into an open grassland area predominantly covered with cogon grass (*Imperata cylindrica*) and interspersed with some woody trees and shrubs (P. Calimag, personal communication, February 5, 2008). The Park is now a rehabilitated urban forest, where few surviving century-old trees (e.g. *Ficus*) are being protected and considered important tourist attractions. Although not all urban green parks such as Ninoy Park have high biodiversity value, they can be developed by using naturalistic landscape style to foster greater conservation awareness and to enhance ecotourism experience (Özguner et al., 2007).

As a result of urbanization, the diversity and abundance of native species have declined over time; this trend becomes more apparent as one approaches the city core (McKinney 2002; 2006). As in many urban parks worldwide, the native species found in the Park have been displaced/replaced by more resilient and adaptable exotic species. For example, the present vegetation cover consists of a mixture of 80 species of trees and shrubs, the majority of which are exotic (M. Eduarte, personal communication, February 1, 2008). As a result of the homogenization of the vegetation and predominance of exotic plants in many city parks, the diversity of native birds is low although exotic and more resilient ones are abundant (Beissinger & Osborne, 1982; Cam et al., 2000; Chace & Walsh, 2006). In Ninoy Park, only 9-12 native bird species have been recorded (M. de la Cruz, personal communication, March 11, 2009), representing a miniscule fraction of the country's avian diversity of about 200 endemic species (Catibog-Sinha &

View of the lagoon

Heaney, 2006). Despite the scarcity of indigenous biota in urban green parks, they nevertheless provide a pleasant atmosphere for recreation and leisure.

Wetland ecosystem – Lagoon

One of the focal attractions in many urban parks is a 'water body', whether it is man-made or natural. A 4-hectare man-made lagoon, which was originally a mineral (adobe stone) excavation and was later re-constructed to catch stormwater run-off, is located at the centre of the Park. Although no form of water-based recreation is permitted due to potential safety and health hazard issues, the lagoon has remained one of the most popular attractions in the Park.

Studies have shown that birds tend to aggregate in waterways within the busy metropolis of Tapei (Jim & Chen, 2009), Melbourne (White et al., 2009), and Metro Manila (Vallejo et al., 2009). Riparian vegetation is likely to attract native bird species, providing opportunities for visitors to enhance appreciation of nature and tourist experience. The native birds that frequent the Park's lagoon include herons, egrets, and kingfishers (M. dela Cruz, personal communication, March 11, 2008).

Architectural design and natural ambience

A safe open space with interesting outdoor recreational setting and architectural design offers visitors a range of opportunities to relax, enjoy, and learn. Urban green space can have a 'designed or planned character as well as a more natural character' (Schipperijn et al., 2010, p. 26). Urban green parks that simulate natural settings can reduce the visual effects of concrete buildings, congested traffic, and smoggy atmosphere (Fang & Ling, 2003). Some parks are also designed to reflect the natural vegetative characteristics of a particular region (Tzoulas et al., 2007). Studies have shown that adult visitors prefer to visit urban parks that have some degree of man-made amenities (Baur & Tynon, 2010) and those with moderately dense vegetation cover (Bjerke et al., 2006).

Law (2002, p.39) states that 'architecture has always been symbolic as well as…functional… image of a destination.' Balancing the naturalistic and formal styles in landscaping can attract a broad range of visitors (Özguner et al., 2007). The 'natural' backdrop of the Ninoy Park and the native architectural design of many buildings contribute to the Park's local appeal and popularity. The *salokot* (sunhat)-shaped roof of the main building and the native architectural and landscape designs of various facilities (e.g. Fishing Village and Craft Village) give the Park a national iconic identity and provide an aura of nostalgia of the simple rural Filipino lifestyle.

Mini zoo

Visiting zoos is a popular family-oriented recreation, usually involving a one-day visit (Ryan & Saward, 2004; Turley, 2001). The mini zoo in the Park is the most popular attraction, especially among school children. The mini zoo keeps around 1,000 animals (excluding the arthropods) belonging to approximately 100 taxonomic groups (PAWB, 2007). Some studies reveal that adults who visited zoological parks often as children tend to value the educational benefits from their interactions with nature and have greater commitment to wildlife conservation (Holzer et al., 1998; Ryan & Saward, 2004).

The World Association of Zoos and Aquariums states that a zoo is a 'venue for researchers and visitors to meet, thus assisting with the public understanding of science and offering opportunities to raise awareness about research and its conservation implications… and has a 'powerful part in achieving global sustainability … and should inspire people who visit zoos to become part of the same movement' (WAZA, 2005, p. 6). Thus, zoo tourism can be a tool in promoting biodiversity conservation especially through education and interpretation (Catibog-Sinha, 2008). The zoo also serves as a platform for various collaborative research initiatives in *ex-situ* conservation and animal care. Although the zoo currently lacks the technical capacity to maintain the genetic diversity of the captive wild animals, it provides numerous opportunities for basic wildlife research and learning (J. de Leon, personal communication, February 11, 2009).

Managerial setting

The Park is currently managed as a component of the Philippine Protected Area System in accordance with the National Integrated Protected Areas System (NIPAS) Act of 1992. It is administered by the central government within the auspices of the Protected Areas and Wildlife Bureau of the Department of Environment and Natural Resources. The management of the Park is heavily dependent on the income of the Park.

Ninoy Park has been receiving an annual average of about 4 million visitors (PAWB, 2010). For the last 10 years, the Park's annual average revenue has been 3-4 million pesos (US$ 74,000 to 99,000). The main sources of tourism income are various user fees (e.g. entrance fees. parking fees, concession fees for special events). The collection of the user fee is authorized by DENR Administrative Order (DAO No. 47/1993). As provided for in the NIPAS Act, 75% of the Park's total revenue shall be allocated exclusively for site management, while 25% shall be used to subsidize the management of other NIPAS sites in the country. However, to defray the Park's additional maintenance costs and capital outlays, it is often necessary to secure new and additional funds from the national treasury; this has at times problematic.

The financial ability of urban residents to visit urban green parks is an essential issue in sustaining urban tourism and quality of life in the city. Pigram & Jenkins (2006) point out the need to address equity in the provision of recreational opportunities. Willis (2003) suggests that discriminatory pricing, based on differential user charges, is more equitable and will likely increase revenue than single user fee charges. Reasonable user fees, especially for low income groups, can help reduce the socio-economic imbalances among those who would like to participate in nature-based recreation (Dahmann et al., 2010). This is relevant to many developing countries like the Philippines, where nature-based recreation is considered by many city dwellers as a luxury rather than as a necessity.

When the visitors of the Park were asked if they would support a user fee increase, 68% (n=54) of the respondents declined. However, 81% (n = 65) said that the increase is justifiable only when the recreation facilities and zoo animal care were improved. The study of Ulep (2000) also reveals that the visitors were willing to pay higher user fees subject to the improvement of the facilities and services. The willingness of the visitors to pay suggests their desire for more rewarding tourist experience and strong support for the recreational, educational, and conservation values of the Park. However, when the idea of privatization of the Park was raised during the interview, several visitors and staff members expressed apprehension because of the perceived consequences of such initiative, namely the imposition of unaffordable user fees especially to low-income city residents, commoditisation of the leisure experience, and inequitable access to some privileges and benefits from the use of the Park. It is apparent that the perceived capitalist control of the management of the Park, which is considered as a public domain by the majority of the respondents, could lead to socio-economic and environmental conflicts (Hjalager, 2007).

Social setting

Urban park visitors are generally classified as psychocentric because they tend to travel for only short distances and with people they know (Plog, 1987 cited in

Weaver & Oppermann, 2000). This pattern is consistent with the results of this survey at Ninoy Park. Restricted by the day-use function of the Park, the visitors may be classified as 'day-trippers'. Law (2002, p. 60) defines leisure day-trip as one that 'lasts for at least 3 hours, by people travelling outside their usual environment and not one taken on a regular basis.'

The city residents, especially those living at nearby residential districts, constitute the majority of the Park's visitors. Schoolchildren on class excursions and other young kids who are accompanied by their parents or adult relatives represent the greater part of visitor number. The literature states that the 'direct experience of nature early in life is essential for healthy, intellectual, emotional and even moral development' (Kahn & Kellert, 2002 cited in Tryzna, 2005, p. 9). Loukaitou-Sideris and Sideris (2010, p. 89) state that 'parks and open spaces allow children to burn off surplus energy, improve their motor skills, and interact with other children in environments that are usually less restrictive than those of home and school.'

Table 22.1 shows the sex and age distributions of the adult visitors surveyed. Females (65%) comprised the majority of adult visitors. Regardless of gender, the majority of the visitors surveyed belonged to the 18-28 age brackets (82%). All the visitors surveyed are literate, with the majority pursuing tertiary education and postgraduate studies (54%). A study in Norway (Bjerke et al., 2006) reveals that visitors in their mid-40s, who have strong pro-ecological value orientation, high level of educational attainments, and high interest in wildlife, are frequent visitors of urban green parks.

In addition to students and family groups, some of the visitors surveyed at Ninoy Park used the Park for 'spiritual enlightenment'. Visitors interviewed in this study mentioned the peaceful and natural ambiance of the Park during their 'prayer-meeting' sessions. Traditional open spaces in urban areas such as those in Thailand (called *kuang* or 'religions land') are being promoted in that country to improve the spiritual and socio-cultural well-being of city dwellers (Samadhi & Tantayanusorn, 2006).

Table 22.1 Sex and age structures and level of educational attainment of visitors.

Variables		n	%
Sex (n= 80)	Male	28	35
	Female	52	65
Age (n= 80)	18-28 years old	66	82
	29-38 years old	8	10
	39-48 years old	3	4
	> 48 years old	3	4
Educational attainment (n=80)	High-school	21	26
	Undergraduate	40	50
	Masters	3	4
	No reply	16	20

Visitation pattern

Visitation pattern is a useful management indicator of the level of use of urban green parks as well as the attractiveness of tourism sites (Weaver & Opermann, 2000). The participation in recreation and leisure activities in urban green parks varies depending on environmental, socio-cultural, and economic factors.

Visitation pattern is influenced by the distance or proximity of urban green parks to where people live. The occurrence of a distance-decay phenomenon in the use of urban green spaces within the Danish city of Odense was reported as a barrier to the frequency of park use (Schipperijn et al., 2010). The majority of the visitors surveyed at Ninoy Park stated that they use either private or public transport conveyances to access the Park. More than 80% of the respondents do not have private cars and are dependent on public transportation system. The spatial distribution of urban parks is therefore a concern in urban planning and city development.

Individual preferences and idiosyncrasies as well as the positive attitude of visitors towards the environment influence park visitation (e.g. Del Saz Salazar & Menendez, 2007; Tzoulas & James, 2010; Schipperijn et al., 2010). The visitation pattern at Ninoy Park changes within a day. Majority of the visitors, especially parents with young children, preferred to stay in the morning until mid-afternoon. On the other hand, young couples chose to come later during the day. About 56% of the visitors, who did not have any other leisure plans for the rest of the day, stayed for 5-7 hours. The rest of the visitors (44%), who stayed only for less than four hours, indicated that they came primarily to see the zoo animals. About 76% of the respondents had previously visited the Park primarily because of a range of positive effects of urban green parks on them.

Visitation motives

Understanding the visitors' motives for visiting parks provides some insights into tourist expectations. Table 22.2 shows the primary reasons for visiting the Ninoy Park in three different temporal scenarios: their visits in 2005 (a year prior to this study), their visit in 2006-2007 (the period covered by the field survey/visitor interviews), and their planned visits in 2008. The study revealed that the Park's semi-natural environment and zoo animal collection have provided a range of opportunities for city dwellers to interact with nature.

In summary, the primary motives for visiting the Park are recreation and leisure (N= 111, 46%) learning and nature conservation (N=78, 33%), and developing social relationships (N=51, 21%). More extensive studies on visitor motivation are needed to determine tourism trends, visitation patterns, and recreation preferences.

Recreation and leisure

Urban green parks offer a range of recreation opportunities, which include both passive (e.g. relaxation, meditation) and active (e.g. walking, jogging, cycling)

Table 22.2 The primary reasons for visiting the Ninoy Park in three temporal scenarios (2005, 2006–2007, and 2008)

Reasons	2005		2006 to 2007		2008		Total	
	N	%	N	%	N	%	N	%
A. Recreation & Leisure								
A.1 Relaxation	21	62	24	63	23	59	68	61
A.2 Picnicking & other leisure activities	10	29	9	24	10	26	29	26
A.3 Jogging, leisure walking	3	9	5	13	6	15	14	13
A. Total	34		38		39		111	
B. Leaning & nature conservation								
B.1 Informal learning	10	32	12	48	10	45	32	41
B.2 Study/review for exam	15	48	10	40	9	41	34	44
B.3 Research project	6	20	3	12	3	14	12	15
B. Total	31		25		22		78	
C. Social relationship								
C.1 Meeting with friends	15		17		19		51	

N = multiple responses (240) from 80 participants

recreation activities. In this study, participating in various recreation and leisure activities was the most popular reason (46%) for visiting Ninoy Park for the period 2005-2008. Among these activities, relaxation (61%) was the most widely held reason for visiting the Park in all three temporal scenarios. One of the respondent's statements, i.e., 'I just like to relax and temporally get away from my daily toil,' embodies the majority's main purpose for visiting the Park. Kaplan (1984, p. 196) states that 'even very small parks... provide patterns that humans attend to effortlessly and, in the process, they permit moments of recovery from the strains of the day.'

The other respondents stated that the semi-natural features of the Park stimulate mental relaxation and provides a peaceful place to 'think', 'contemplate', 'concentrate', and 'temporarily escape from personal problems.' The respondents, who were mostly from crowded and less affluent urban residential areas in Metro Manila, stated that the Park gives then an aura of being 'back in their rustic home provinces'. Many respondents felt that the 'wildernesses' atmosphere of the Park triggers a nostalgic sense of place and belonging. Picnicking and other leisure activities (e.g. story telling, singing, playing cards/games, reading) ranked second to relaxation (26%), while more active recreational pursuits such as walking and jogging were ranked lowest (13 %) (Table 22.2).

All the respondents commented on the pleasant microclimate of the Park ('it is refreshing here' or *ang presko dito*), which is attributed to the presence of big shade trees. These trees reduce solar radiation and air temperature, contributing to visitors' feeling of comfort especially in summer months. Several studies have shown that trees can reduce the hot radiation from concrete surfaces and buildings, help cool the air by evapotranspiration, reduce wind velocity (Georgi & Zafiriadis, 2006), and trap air pollutants (Sheng et al., 2000). The natural 'airconditioning' effect of urban trees was also mentioned in other studies (e.g. Chang et al., 2007; Dimoudi & Nikolopoulou, 2003; Kjelgren & Clark, 1992; Kuchelmeister, 2000; Wong et al., 2007).

Public awareness and nature conservation

Developing educational interpretation programs is essential in promoting public awareness about the value of biodiversity. This study found that a number of respondents have had limited knowledge of Philippine biodiversity. For instance, many of them could not differentiate the native plants from non-native ones. Even if they knew a plant was exotic, they still would consider it more valuable than a native plant because of the former's aesthetic appeal or economic importance. The low level of understanding of the concept of biodiversity was also observed in other studies (Gyllin & Grahn, 2005; McKinney, 2002, 2006). According to Hinds and Sparks (2008), the busy and modern lifestyle of city residents is producing a generation of children with weak affective connection with nature, Furthermore, McKinney (2006, p. 248) states that 'since so many people live in cities... and so many urban flora an fauna are not indigenous to the local environment... the human species is becoming increasingly unfamiliar, some would say disconnected, from their native biological environment.'

Through well-planned educational/tourism interpretation programs, urban green parks can offer opportunities for the city residents to learn and appreciate nature. Despite the limited interpretation facilities at Ninoy Park, many visitors visit the park to learn. This study showed that the second most popular reason for visiting Ninoy Park in all three temporal scenarios was learning (33%). The modes of learning, however, differed among the respondents. For instance, some of the responses (41%) indicated that the self- guided tour and watching zoo animals enabled them to learn something about nature and wildlife. Collecting data for their natural science projects in school (15%) and 'studying or reviewing for the exams' (44%) were identified as the other forms of learning. The respondents, who stated that they came 'to review for their exams,' affirmed that the Park's relaxing and quiet ambience can help improve memory retention. The positive effects of green parks to attention were also reported in the literature (Kuo, 2001; Tennessen & Cimprich, 1995). The majority of the respondents claimed that visiting the mini zoo at the Ninoy Park gave them a great opportunity to become acquainted with native animals and instil a deeper understanding of the conservation issues in the country. In a separate study of the Park (Catibog-Sinha, 2008), 65% (n=25) of the zoo visitors interviewed stated that viewing the animals at close range had enabled them to learn more about Philippine wildlife and appreciate their conservation value.

To improve public awareness about biodiversity values, the educational interpretation programs should include topics about biodiversity as well as pragmatic ways on how to conserve nature and protect the environment in day-to-day existence (Catibog-Sinha, 2007; Hill et al., 2007; Lindström et al., 2006). The symbolic power of rare and endemic species to arouse conservation awareness cannot be underestimated (Catibog-Sinha & Heanery, 2006). Appreciation of biodiversity in urban parks can serve as a 'social bridge' even in a poor and congested city (Davies, 2005). Such bridge could create civic pride and cohesion, which are the prerequisites to the promotion of social responsibility and quality of human life.

Promotion of social relationships and quality of city life

In a crowded urban setting, where commercialization and personal isolation tend to dominate, visiting green parks serves as an opportunity to develop or even strengthen social relationships. According to Senior & Townsend (2005, p. 112), urban parks can 'improve the ability of people to establish networks, norms, social trust and facilitate coordination and cooperation for mutual benefits.'

The third most popular reason for visiting Ninoy Park during the period 2005-2008 suggests that respondents have inherent desire to develop social relationships and improve their quality of life (21%). Studies have shown that visiting urban green parks is a valuable occasion for social interactions especially among newly arrived city residents (Burgess et al. 1988). A significant push factor in visiting the Ninoy Park was social grouping, which indicates the importance of family members and/or friends. Nearly 80% of the visitors surveyed came with at least one family member and/or friend (average group size = 5). Some 9% of the respondents considered the Park as a convenient social 'meeting or rendez-vous point.' All the respondents stated that they enjoy just sitting out in the open shady green area, strolling, bonding with friends and relatives, and meeting new friends. The respondents indicated that their families/friends had helped in choosing the Park for the occasion. Some studies reveal that social and family groups can influence decisions in choosing recreational destinations and involvement in certain recreation activities (Crompton, 1981; Law, 2002).

Forming social relationship in urban parks may be affected by the volume of visitors in a park at a given time. There are numerous studies on the impacts of crowding on the quality of the destination and tourist experience (e.g. Catibog-Sinha, 2007; Catibog-Sinha & Wen, 2008; Weaver & Oppermann, 2000). In this study, about 74% of the respondents stated that moderate crowding in the Ninoy Park did not at all diminish their leisure experience interestingly, a few respondents stated that they actually enjoyed having other people around them because they could easily make new friends and even 'watch other visitors having fun themselves.' Nonetheless, the extreme crowding of the Park especially during peak periods should be addressed to ensure that the visitor experience and aesthetic integrity of the Park as a green open space are not compromised.

Conclusion

Achieving sustainable tourism involves a balanced approach aimed at attaining the environmental, social, and economic goals of urban park management. Achieving the goals of sustainable tourism through conservation, education, and recreation is a challenge that urban green parks should uphold in order to promote a healthy and liveable city.

Urban green parks, such as the Ninoy Aquino Parks and Wildlife Center can help promote sustainable tourism and nature/biodiversity conservation albeit semi-natural setting. The management of urban green parks should endeavour to make the public enjoy their contact with nature through biodiversity-focused interpretation program, participation in nature-based recreation, and provision of adequate and green open space to highlight the different levels of biodiversity and their values. Carefully managed tourism settings of urban green spaces can help in achieving sustainable tourism. Given that urban green parks play an important role in promoting public health and well-being, it is necessary to integrate social equity and accessibility of green parks in urban planning.

Acknowledgement

The author is thankful for the support and cooperation of the Protected Areas and Wildlife Bureau and its officers and staff, particularly Director Mundita Lim, Inocensio Castillo, Precy Calimag, Carlo Custodio, Josefina de Leon, Marlynn Mendoza, Jing Esmael, Myrna Ramos, and M. dela Cruz. Special gratitude goes to M. Eduarte, the Park Superintendent and to the field staff members who helped in the field survey.

References

Alvey, A. A. (2006). Promoting and preserving biodiversity in the urban forest. *Urban Forestry and Urban Greening, 5*, 195–201.

Baur, J., & Tynon, J. (2010). Small-scale urban nature parks: Why should we care? *Leisure Sciences, 32*, 195–200.

Beissinger, S. R., & Osborne D. R. (1982). Effects of urbanization on avian community organization. *Condor, 84*, 75–83.

Bjerke, T., Østdahl, T., Christer Thrane, C., & Strumse, E. (2006). Vegetation density of urban parks and perceived appropriateness for recreation. *Urban Forestry & Urban Greening, 5*, 35–44.

Burgess, J., Harrison, C. M., & Limb, M. (1988). People, parks and urban green: A study of popular meanings and values for open spaces in the city. *Urban Studies, 25*, 455–473.

Burr, S.W. (1995). Sustainable tourism development and use: Follies, foibles and practical approaches. In S.F. McCool, & A.E. Watson (Eds.). *Linking tourism, the environment and sustainability* (pp. 8–13). Annual Meeting of the National Recreation and Park Association, 12-14 October 1994; General Technical Report INT-GTR-323. Washington (DC): USDA Forest Service.

Cam, E., Nichols, J., Sauer, J., Hines, J., Flather, C. (2000). Relative species richness and community completeness: Birds and urbanization in the mid-Atlantic. *Ecological Applications, 10*, 1196–1210.

Catibog- Sinha, C. S. (2007). Monitoring visitor impact and biodiversity: A framework for protected areas in Southern Highlands, New South Wales, and Australia. In I. McDonnell, S. Grabowski, & March R. (Eds.), *Proceedings CAUTHE Tourism-Past Achievements, Future Challenges.*, Manly 11–14 February 2007.

Catibog-Sinha, C. S. (2008). Zootourism: Conservation through tourism. *Journal of Ecotourism, 7* (2 & 3), 155–173.

Catibog-Sinha, C., & Wen, J. (2008). Sustainable tourism and management model for protected natural areas: Xishuangbanna Bisophere Reserve, South China. *Asia Pacific Tourism and Research Journal, 13* (2), 145–162.

Catibog-Sinha, C., S., & Heaney, L. (2006). *Philippine biodiversity: Principles and practice.* Quezon City, Philippines: Haribon Foundation.

Chace, J. F., & Walsh, J. J. (2006). Urban effects on native avifauna: A review. *Landscape and Urban Planning, 74,* 46–69.

Chang, C. R., Li, M. H. & Chang, S. D. (2007). A preliminary study on the local cool-island intensity of Taipei parks. *Landscape and Urban Planning, 80,* 386–395.

Clark, R. N., & Stankey, G. H. (1979). *The Recreational Opportunity Spectrum: A framework for planning, management and research* (General Technical Report, PNW-98). US Department of Agriculture, Forest Service.

Costanza, R., dArge. R., de Groot, R., Farber, S., Grasso, M., Hannon, B., Limburg, K., Naeem, S., O'Neill, R.V., Paruelo, J., Raskin, R.G., Sutton, P., & vanden Belt, M. (1997). The value of the world's ecosystem services and natural capital. *Nature, 387,* 253–260.

Crompton, J. L. (1981). Dimensions of the social group role in pleasure vacations. *Annals of Tourism Research, 8* (4), 550–568.

Dahmann, N., Wolch, J. Joassart-Marcelli, P., Reynolds, K., & Jerrett, M. (2010). The active city? Disparities in provision of urban public recreation resources. *Health & Place, 16,* 431–445.

Davies, G. (2005). Biodiversity conservation as a social bridge in the urban context: Cape Town's sense of the urban imperative to protect its biodiversity and empower its people. In T. Tryzna (Ed.), *The urban imperative: Urban outreach strategies for protected areas* (pp. 96–104). Retrieved April 12, 2009, from http://www.interenvironment.org/pa/papers2.htm

Del Saz Salazar, S., & Menendez, L. G. (2007). Estimating the non-market benefits of an urban park: Does proximity matter? *Land Use Policy, 24,* 296–305.

De Vries, S. Verheij, R. A., Groenewegen, P. P., & Spreeuwenberg, P. (2003). Natural environments – healthy environments? An exploratory analysis of the relationship between green space and health. *Environment and Planning A, 35,* 1717–1731.

Dimoudi, A., & Nikolopoulou, M. (2003). Vegetation in urban environment: Microclimate analysis and benefits. *Energy and Buildings, 35,* 69–76.

Fang, C. F., & Ling, D. L. (2003). Investigation of the noise reduction provided by tree belts. *Landscape and Urban Planning, 63,* 187–195.

Ferris, J., Norman, C., & Sempik, J. (2001). People, land and sustainability: community gardens and the social dimension of sustainable development. *Social Policy and Administration, 35,* 559–568.

Georgi, N. J., & Zafiriadis, K. (2006). The impact of park trees on microclimate in urban areas. *Urban Ecosystem, 9,* 195–209.

Gibson, A., Dodds, R., Joppe, M., & Jamieson, B. (2003). Ecotoruism in the city? Toronto's Green Tourism Association (Special Issue). *International Journal of Contemporary Hospitality Management, 15* (6), 324–327.

Grahn, P., & Stigsdotter, U. (2003). Landscape planning and stress. *Urban Forestry and Urban Greening, 1* (2), 1–18.

Gyllin, M., & Grahn, P. (2005). A semantic model for assessing the experience of urban biodiversity. *Urban Forestry and Urban Greening, 3,* 149–161.

Harris, R., Griffin, T., & Williams, P. (Eds.). (2002). *Sustainable tourism: A global perspective.* Oxford, United Kingdom: Elsevier Science.

Hill, J., Woodland, W., & Gough, G. (2007). Research note: Can visitor satisfaction and knowledge about tropical rainforests be enhanced through biodiversity interpretation, and does this promote a positive attitude towards ecosystem conservation? *Journal of Ecotourism, 6* (1), 75–85.

Hinds, P., & Sparks, P. (2008). Engaging with the natural environment: The role of affective connection and identity. *Journal of Environmental Psychology, 28,* 109–120.

Hjalager, A. M. (2007). Stages in the economic globalization of tourism. *Annals of Tourism Research, 34* (2), 437–457.

Holzer, D., Scott, D., & Bixler, R. D. (1998). Socialization influences on adult zoo visitation. *Journal of Applied Recreation Research, 23* (1), 43–62.

International Union for the Conservation of Nature (IUCN). (2004).Cities and conservation: A resolution approved by the Third IUCN World Conservation Congress. Retrieved May 10, 2009, from http://www.interenvironment.org/pa/wccmotioncc.htm

Jim, C., & Chen, W. (2009). Diversity and distribution of landscape trees in the compact Asian city of Taipei. *Applied Geography, 29,* 577–587.

Kaplan, R. (1984). Impact of urban nature: A theoretical analysis. *Urban Ecology, 8,* 189–197.

Kjelgren, R. K., & Clark, J. (1992). Microclimate and tree growth in tree urban spaces. *Journal of Environmental Horticulture, 1* (3), 139–145.

Kuchelmeister, G. (2000). Trees for the urban millennium: Urban forestry update. *Unasylva 200, 51,* 49–55.

Kuo, F. E. (2001). Coping with poverty: Impacts of environment and attention in the inner city. *Environment and Behavior, 33,* 5–34.

Law, C. M. (2002). *Urban tourism: The visitor economy and the growth of large cities* (2nd ed.). London: Cromwell Press.

Lindström, M., Johansson, M., Herrmann, J., & Johnsson, O. (2006). Attitudes towards the conservation of biological diversity: A case study in Kristianstad Municipality, Sweden. *Journal of Environmental Planning and Management, 49* (4), 495–513.

Loukaitou-Sideris, A., & Sideris, A. (2010). What brings children to the park? Analysis and measurement of the variables affecting children's use of parks. *Journal of the American Planning Association, 76,* (1), 89–107.

Madanipour, A. (1999). Why are the design and development of public spaces significant for cities? *Environment and Planning B: Planning and Design, 26,* 879–891.

McCool, S. F., & Watson, A. E. (Eds.). (1995). *Linking tourism, the environment and sustainability:* Annual Meeting of the National Recreation and Park Association 12–14 October 1994 (General Technical Report INT-GTR-323). Washington,

McDonnell, M. J. (2007). Restoring and managing biodiversity in an urbanizing world filled with tensions. *Ecological Management & Restoration, 8* (2), 83–84.

McKinney, M. L. (2002). Urbanization, biodiversity, and conservation. *BioScience, 52,* 883–890.

McKinney, M. L. (2006). Urbanizatiion as a major cause of biotic homogenization. *Biological Conservation, 127,* 247–260.

McNeely, J. A. (2005). Foreword. In T. Tryzna (Ed.), *The urban imperative: Urban outreach strategies for protected areas* (p.5). Retrieved April 12, 2009, from http://www.interenvironment.org/pa/papers2.htm

Milligan, C., & Bingley, A. (2007). Restorative places or scary spaces? The impact of woodland on the mental well-being of young adults. *Health and Place, 13*, 799–811.

Munoz, F. (2003). Lock-living: Urban sprawl in Mediterranean cities. *Cities, 20*, 381–385.

Nielsen, T. S., & Hansen, K. B. (2007). Do green areas affect health? Results from a Danish survey on the use of green areas and health indicators. *Health and Place, 13*, 839–850.

Özguner, H., Kendle, A. D., & Bisgrove, R. J. (2007). Attitudes of landscape professionals towards naturalistic versus formal urban landscapes in the UK. *Landscape and Urban Planning, 8*, 34–45.

Pares-Franzi, M., & Sauri-Pujol, D. (2006). Evaluating the environmental performance of urban parks in Mediterranean cities: An example from the Barcelona metropolitan region. *Environmental Management, 38*, 750–759.

Pearce, D. G. (2001). An integrated framework for urban tourism research. *Annals of Tourism Research, 28* (40), 926–946.

Philippine Information Agency. (2008). National Capital Region. Retrieved June 10, 2010, from http://www.pia.gov.ph/mmio.asp?fi=about&su=NCR

Pigram, J., & Jenkins, J. (2006). *Outdoor recreation management* (2nd ed.) Lomdon: Routledge

Protected Areas and Wildlife Bureau (PAWB). (2010). Annual statistical report. In-house Accomplishment Report. Author.

Ryan, C., & Saward, J. (2004). The zoo as ecotourism attraction – Visitor reactions, perceptions and management implications: The case of Hamilton Zoo, New Zealand. *Journal of Sustainable Tourism, 12* (3), 245–266.

Samadhi, T. N., & Tantayanusorn, N. (2006). Reinventing religious land as urban open space: The case of *kuang* in Chiang Mai (Thailand). *Habitat International, 30*, 886–901.

Schipperijn, J., Stigsdotter, U., Randrup, T., & Troelsen, J. (2010). Influences on the use of urban green space – A case study in Odense, Denmark. *Urban Forestry & Urban Greening, 9*, 25–32.

Senior, J., & Townsend, M. (2005). Healthy parks, healthy people and the social capital initiatives of Parks Victoria, Australia. In T. Tryzna (Ed.), *The urban imperative: Urban outreach strategies for protected areas* (pp. 111–120). Retrieved April 12, 2009, from http://www.interenvironment.org/pa/papers2.htm

Sheng, G. D., Jian, D., & Lin, W. (2000). The impact of tourism and environmental pollution on plants and soil forests in urban parks of Guangzhou. *China Environmental Science, 20*, (3), 277–280.

Storksdieck, M. (2005). How to reach urban communities: Lessons learned from museum evaluation. In T. Tryzna (Ed.), *The urban imperative: Urban outreach strategies for protected areas* (pp.157–164). Retrieved April 12, 2009; from http://www.interenvironment.org/pa/papers2.htm

Swarbrooke, J. (1999). *Sustainable tourism management*. Oxford, United Kingdom: CABI Publishing.

Tennessen, C. M., & Cimprich, B. (1995). Views to nature: Effects on attention. *Journal of Environmental Psychology, 15*, 77–85.

Tryzna, T. (Ed.). (2005). The urban imperative urban outreach strategies for protected areas agencies. Retrieved April 12, 2009; from http://www.interenvironment.org/pa/papers2.htm

Turley, S. K. (2001). Children and the demand for recreational experiences: The case of the zoo. *Leisure Studies, 20*, 1–18.

Tzoulas, K., & James, P. (2010). Peoples' use of, and concerns about, green space networks: A case study of Birchwood, Warrington New Town, UK. *Urban Forestry & Urban Greening, 9*, 121–128.

Tzoulas, K., Korpela, K., Venn, S., Yli-Pelkonen, V., Kazmierczak, A., Niemel, J.,& James, P. (2007). Promoting ecosystem and human health in urban areas using green infrastructure: a literature review. *Landscape and Urban Planning, 81*, 167–178.

Ulep, C. B. (2000). *Visitor assessment of the recreational and environmental qualities of the Ninoy Aquino Park and their willingness to pay.* Unpublished masteral thesis, Miriam College, Quezon City, Philippines.

Ulrich, R.S. (2006). Evidence-based health-care architecture. *Lancet, 368*, S38–S39.

Ulrich, R. S., Simons, R. F., Losito, B. D., Fiorito, E., Miles, M.A., & Zelson, M. (1991). Stress recovery during exposure to natural and urban environments. *Journal of Environmental Psychology, 11*, 231–248.

United Nations. (2007). *World urbanization prospects: The 2007* Revision. Executive Summary. Department of Economic and Social Affairs of the United Nations. Retrieved April 28, 2009, from http://www.un.org/esa/population/publications/wup2007/2007WUP_ExecSum_web.pdf

Vallejo, B. Jr., Aloya, A., Ong, P., Tamino, A., & Villasper, J. (2008). Spatial patterns of bird diversity and abundance in an urban tropical landscape: The University of the Philippines (UP) Diliman Campus. *Science Diliman, 20*, 1, 1–10.

World Association of Zoos and Aquariums (WAZA). (2005). *Building a future for wildlife - The world zoo and aquarium strategy.* Bern, Switzerland: WAZA.

Weaver, D., & Oppermann, M. (2000). *Tourism management.* John Wiley and Sons Australia: Queensland.

White, J.G., Fitzsimons, J.A., Palmer, G.C.· & Antos, M.J. (2009). Surviving urbanisation: Maintaining bird species diversity in urban Melbourne. *Victorian Naturalist, 126 (3)*, 73–78.

Willis, K. G. (2003). Pricing public parks. *Journal of Environmental Planning and Management, 46* (1), 3–17.

Wong, N. H., Jusuf, S. K., Win, A. A., Thu, H. K., Negara, T. S., & Xuchao, W. (2007). Environmental study of the impact of greenery in an institutional campus in the tropics. *Building and Environment, 42*, 2949–2970.

23 Philippine sustainable tourism initiatives

Issues and challenges

*Corazon Catibog-Sinha**

Introduction

Sustainable tourism is a form of development that focuses on the linkages between/amongst environmental, economic and socio-cultural aspects in order to attain sustainability (UNEP, 2001). Sustainable tourism development is as a long-term strategy, which is carried out continuously over time without diminishing the cultural and environmental values of destinations for the present and future generations. On the other hand, short-term goals in tourism development are generally profit-oriented with very little or no consideration of the welfare of the host community and the environment (Choi & Sirakaya, 2006; Hall & Lew 1998; Holden, 2008).

Sustainable nature-based tourism is often referred to as 'ecotourism'. Despite the unclear definition of ecotourism, many authors consider it as a form of sustainable tourism (e.g. Clarke, 2002; Diamantis & Ladkin, 1999; Sharpley, 2006). Over the years, the definition of ecotourism has been broadened to include the notion of sustainability. The guiding principles of sustainability in the context of nature-based tourism are the conservation of the natural assets of a tourist destination, enrichment of the tourist experience through education and interpretation, and the sustainable management of visitors and destinations (Newsome et al., 2002). Sustaining tourism especially in destination areas with high biodiversity value involves the protection of these areas from adverse visitor impacts (Fennell & Weaver, 2005).

The simplest definition of biological diversity (or biodiversity) refers to the variety of plants and animals and their habitats. The conservation of biota as well as ecological complexes ensures the sustainability of all life support systems on earth. Several authors have recognized the mutual reliance between tourism and nature (e.g. Budowski, 1976; Catibog-Sinha & Bushell, 2002; Ceballos-Lacustrain 1996). Tourism, if properly managed, plays an important role in

*Senior Lecturer in Environmental Management & Tourism, School of Social Sciences, University of Western Sydney Kingswood Campus, Locked Bag 1797 Penrith South DC NSW 1797 Australia

Puerto Galera, Philippines (Photo taken by Corazon Catibog-Sinha)

biodiversity conservation and sustainable development (e.g. Catibog-Sinha, 2008; IUCN, 2003; Newsome et al., 2002).

This chapter, with a focus on nature-based destinations such as protected areas and natural heritage sites, presents the initiatives of the Philippines in promoting sustainable tourism. It also explores the issues and challenges in the development and implementation of these initiatives. In this chapter, the term 'sustainable tourism' is used interchangeably with the term 'ecotourism'. The study included is based on the review of relevant academic literature, government policies, and national reports. Face-to-face interviews with key tourism and natural resource management officials and field visits in the Philippines were conducted for several months from 2008-2010. The results of this will serve as a basis on how the Philippines, as well as other developing countries in a similar situation, will move forward in pursuing the notion of sustainability in tourism.

Sustainable tourism: Philippine style

The Philippines, an archipelago of more than 7,100 islands, lies in the tropical region – the centre of the world's biodiversity. On the mega-diversity country list, the Philippines is ranked in second place (after Indonesia) on global endemism for butterflies, fifth place for birds and mammals, eighth place for reptiles, and tenth place for freshwater fish (Mittermeier et al. 1999). At least 60% of island endemics (or oceanic island species that evolved in isolation) are considered 'globally rare'. This rich biodiversity is a major tourist attraction. However, the country is also one of the 'hottest' of the 34 terrestrial hotspots in the world in terms of the high vulnerability and irreplaceability of threatened species (Mittermeier et al., 2004). As in many archipelagic countries, the islands and coastal areas of the Philippines are the most popular tourist destinations; but the socio-economic and natural systems of islands are quite vulnerable to external risks from both human and natural activities (Conlin & Baum, 1995; D'Ayala, 1992).

In fact, the Philippines is top of the list of the 18 global marine hotspots (Roberts et al., 2002).

From 1970s to mid-1980s, tourism in the Philippines was used as a tool to advance the economic and political agenda of few individuals who were in position and power (Richter, 1999). The revival of democracy after the People's Revolution in 1986 paved the way to a broader view of tourism in which both the economic and non-economic goals of tourism were incorporated, although superficially, in national planning (Choy, 1991). After many years of suppressed democracy, the economic recovery of the country remained slow and difficult, and the tourism industry, among other developmental sectors, continued to suffer. For instance, tourism arrivals from 1996 to 2001 continued to decline largely because of home security issues, inadequate tourism product development, and weak marketing strategy. Nevertheless, the subsequent efforts of both the government and private sectors to improve the industry became evident when several travel nodes were added in strategic regions throughout the country concurrently with the enhancement of tourism products to promote both domestic and international tourism. Eventually, employment prospects in the tourism industry improved, although inbound tourism still lags behind from its neighbouring ASEAN countries (e.g. Singapore, Thailand, and Malaysia). From 2000 to 2007, tourism had contributed an average of 6.2% of the annual Gross Domestic Product. In 2007 alone, the direct employment in tourism totalled 3.25 M, representing 9.7% share to the country's total employment (DOT, 2009).

The Philippine initiatives in sustaining tourism began with the formulation of the working definition of ecotourism, which is considered as a form of sustainable tourism in natural and cultural heritage areas. It focuses on the protection and management of natural and cultural resources including indigenous knowledge and practices. It also involves community participation, promotion of environmental education and ethics, provision of local economic benefits, and enhancement of visitor satisfaction (DOT-DENR, 2002). Various international fora on ecotourism, such as those sponsored by the World Tourism Organization (WTO, 1992) and the International Union for the Conservation of Nature (IUCN, 1994) inspired the Philippine in pursuing sustainable tourism at the policy level. However, its operational application is complex and sometimes controversial. Since the notion and practice of ecotourism in the Philippines is still young, there is a considerable gap between policy development and field implementation.

After the Earth Summit of 1992, the Philippine government took serious steps in incorporating the notion of sustainable development in tourism policy and planning. For example, the Philippine Agenda 21 (Tourism sector) affirms that ecotourism can be implemented through sustainable use of natural and cultural resources while protecting the environment and providing employment opportunities. As a signatory to the Convention on Biological Diversity (UNEP, 1992) the Philippines has the legal obligation to develop measures to link biodiversity and tourism development. The Philippine Department of Tourism (DOT) in collaboration with the United Nations and Development Programme (UNDP) and the World Tourism Organization (WTO) also developed a comprehensive

Tourism Master Plan (1991-2010), which spells out the activities that are compatible with sustainable tourism and economic growth. However, the Plan has narrow strategic approach to nature tourism. Meanwhile, the Department of Environment and Natural Resources (DENR) pursued the enactment of the National Integrated Protected Areas Law [NIPAS] (RA Act 7586 of 1992), which recognizes the need to establish and manage protected areas in a holistic manner and underscores the value of tourism as a new source of funding for the management of protected areas in the country.

The following discussion focuses on sustainable tourism initiatives within nature-based destinations in the Philippines from 1991 to the present.

National Integrated Protected Areas Law [NIPAS] (RA Act 7586 of 1992)

The park system in the Philippines is known as the National Integrated Protected Areas System (NIPAS), which encompasses 'outstanding remarkable areas and biologically important public lands that are habitats of rare and endangered species of plants and animals, biogeographic zones and related ecosystems, whether terrestrial, wetland or marine...' (Section 2, NIPAS Act, 1992). Sustainable tourism is permitted in all categories of protected areas except in Strict Nature Reserve.

The major provisions of the NIPAS Act that are relevant to sustainable tourism are:

- permission for tourism to take place only in designated zones within a protected area system (i.e. buffer zone, recreational zone, multiple use zone)
- representation of the tourism sector in the Protected Area Management Board (a decision making-body at the local level) created for each protected area
- tourism income to accrue to the Integrated Protected Area Fund (a funding mechanism) to help support the management of protected areas
- tourism project proposals to comply with the national Environmental Impact Assessment system
- tourism to recognize and respect the rights and aspirations of the indigenous community residing in protected areas.

The Philippine National Ecotourism Strategy (PNES)

The Philippine policy initiative to officially integrate the notion of sustainability in tourism development began in 1991 during the National Tourism Congress, where participants from several government and non-government organizations resolved that 'the State shall develop and promote ecotourism as a tool for sustainable development to support the development, management, protection and conservation of the country's environment, natural resources and cultural heritage' (DOT-DENR, 2002 p. 49). This resolution serves as the basic tenet of the Philippine National Ecosystem Strategy (henceforth PNES), which is considered the fundamental national tourism policy framework by virtue of a Presidential Order (Executive Order No. 111 of 17 June 1999) that was signed after eight years worth of numerous consultative meetings and technical workshops.

The PNES consists of basic elements that serve as the theoretical foundation of ecotourism in the context of sustainable development. These elements are the management of the natural and cultural resources, environmental education and conservation awareness, empowerment of the local communities, and development of tourism products that satisfy visitor needs and promote the Philippines as a globally competitive destination (DOT-DENR, 2002, p. 3).

Philippine Ecotourism Program (PEP)

The Philippine Ecotourism Program (henceforth PEP) is the over-arching ecotourism plan in the country. It was framed within the PNES and covers the following more specific operational concerns: the identification of key ecotourism ('banner') sites, development and marketing of tourist products and destinations, public education and advocacy, provision of support to the tourism industry, development of national ecotourism fund, and assessment and monitoring of tourism activities (DOT-DENR, 2002). The New Zealand Agency for International Development (NZAID) served as a major facilitator that helped galvanized the national ecotourism strategy through the provision of technical and financial assistance at the policy and field operational levels.

The PEP consisted of two implementation phases, each with a 3-4 year operational period. The PEP-Phase I (mid-2001 to mid-2003) and PEP-Phase II (mid 2004 to mid- 2008) were led, respectively, by DOT and DENR. Both government bodies were tasked to collaborate in all aspects of the program. As part of the collaborative arrangement, DOT had the leading role in the management of the business and promotional aspects of ecotourism, while DENR was responsible for the environmental and social (community) aspects. PEP-Phase I paved the way to the implementation of PEP- Phase II. More specifically, Phase I identified 32 tourism banner sites, of which 12 key sites were selected for PEP-Phase II for the implementation of key tourism activities. Currently, the government is negotiating with foreign aid agencies for the implementation of PEP-III (P. Calimag, personal communication, 20, May 2009).

PEP-Phase II, which aimed to mainstream the notion of ecotourism and sustainability in field operations, focused on the development of community-based tourism in selected sites. These sites are all located in protected areas where local communities are dependent on the natural resource. Technical and financial support by NZAID Programme were provided to assist the local communities in shifting from exploitative use of resources (e.g. dynamite fishing, whale hunting, illegal logging and forest product gathering) to sustainable practices through ecotourism. The unemployed members of the community, especially the youth, were also targeted for socio-economic reform by engaging them in tourism development. Basically, not all site projects, especially those with strong internal

Table 23.1 Key initiatives and achievements of PEP-Phase II in selected tourism sites in the Philippines

Names of ecotourism sites	Initiatives and achievements
Luzon Island Region	
Hundred Islands National Park	Technical and financial assistance to out-of-school youth were provided through the creation of HIETA (Hundred Islands EcoTour Association); the Association is managed by talented young residents in the community.
	The capacity of HIETA members were developed through training in business planning, tour guiding, tourism management in seakayaking. NatureSpecs, a tourism organization and trainer in sea kayaking in the Philippines, was commissioned to undertake the field training.
	The local government unit and the Department of Tourism provided additional financial and technical support to HIETA in tourism marketing and management.
Mayon Volcano Natural Park	A master plan was developed and facilities built at Lidong campsite.
	The local government provided financial support. Technical and financial assistance was provided to develop and set up camping faculties.
Sapang-Bato	The Sapang-Bato trek guides (Aetas- tribal people) were given training in nature tour trekking.
	The Sapang-Bato Visitor Center was improved.
	A private sector investment (Korean) was mobilized.
Banaue (Ifugao Province) – UNESCO World Heritage Site	The members of the Banaue Travel Guides and Tour Organization were given training in mountain guiding, first aid, etc.
	A strong linkage was established with the Banaue Tourism Council of the local government unit.
Visayas Region	
Rajah Sikatuna Protected Landscape	DOT provided financial and technical assistance for the development of thecamping site.
Pamilacan Island Fish Sanctuary	The Pamilacan Island Dolphin and Whale Watching Organization (PIDWWO) was re-structured and strengthened.
	The members of PIDWWO were given in-depth training in tour guiding, marketing, and the management of wildlife tourism, first aid, and catering.
	The Pamilacan Island Marine Life Tour was set up to improve product development and marketing.
	A municipal ordinance on dolphin watching procedures and user fee policy was drafted and eventually passed by the local government.
	A national non-government organization (e.g. Ayala Foundation) was mobilized for additional financial and technical support.

Table 23.1 Key initiatives and achievements of PEP-Phase II in selected tourism sites in the Philippines (*Cont'd*)

Names of ecotourism sites	Initiatives and achievements
Mindanao Region	
Lake Sebu	The members of the Lake Sebu Kenhulung Federation received hands-on training in product development and the marketing of indigenous arts and crafts.
	Having developed confidence in their handicraft marketing skills, they were able to participate in local, regional, national travel fairs and exhibits, travel marts, festivals and events.
	The local government provided additional support.

social conflicts were successful (M. Lim, personal communication, 8 February 2010).

Tourism banner sites that exhibit great potential for successful tourism venture can serve as models for sustainable community-based tourism (Table 23.1). In the Philippine context, the factors considered crucial for the success of the pilot projects are (a) community organization – displaced and marginalized groups keen in tourism ventures are formally organized into the so-called 'people's organization' or 'community cooperatives' to ensure that members have common goals and expectations; (b) capacity building – the members of the local organizations are empowered through involvement in the planning process as well as providing informal training and hand-on-experience in tourism business planning, marketing, and operations; (c) networking – both private and government sectors cooperate/collaborate in promoting community-based tourism; and (d) social change – the capacity of the host community to develop self-sufficiency and become less dependent on external support is enhanced.

Other ecotourism initiatives

Even before the concept of ecotourism was official adopted as part of the Philippine policy agenda in the late 1990s, tourism had already been recognized as an economic incentive in some natural resource management programs However, during that time the notion of ecotourism as a form of sustainable development was hardly understood. One of these programs was the Integrated Coastal Management Program (ICMP) that evolved from various community-based marine protected areas established since the 1970s (e.g. Alcala, 1998; Balgos, 2005; White, Eisma-Osorio, & Green, 2005). Today, ICMP has been implementing various measures to balance sustainable use and the protection of coral reefs; marine-based tourism is the major alternative livelihood opportunities introduced in the program (C. Custodio, personal communication, 29 January 2010).

Another important initiative was the Debt for Nature Swap (DNS) program. This is a funding mechanism, which buys out the debts of poor countries with heavy foreign debt burden so that these countries do not over-exploit their natural capital merely to pay back their debts (Resor, 1993). In 1998, the World Wildlife Fund for Nature purchased at a discount price some of the Philippine debts; in return, the Philippines raised the equivalent amount in local currency to finance national conservation projects. The ecotourism-relevant projects that were implemented under this program were located in UNESCO's natural heritage sites (e.g. Tubbataha Marine Natural Park, Puerto Princesa Underground River National Park). Today, these parks are self-sustaining.

Sustainable tourism issues and challenges

This section focuses on the Philippine experience in developing and implementing its ecotourism initiatives and the inherent complexities involved in undertaking these initiatives. The issues that consistently emerged in this study are outlined and discussed below. Some measures are also suggested to address these issues.

Nature Conservation Issues

As in many emerging ecotourism programs worldwide, the Philippines faces many challenges in harmonizing tourism and nature conservation. Since none of the established protected areas in the country is free from human habitation, local involvement in tourism planning and implementation has remained a management challenge.

More than 400 protected areas (but only 105 of which are officially proclaimed as of 2007), covering about 12% of the country's total land area, have been established so far (Catibog-Sinha & Heaney, 2006). PEP-Phase I identified 32 banner tourism sites; more than 50% of which are inside protected areas. Although the PNES is a major improvement of the country's approach to tourism as it underscores livelihoods in achieving sustainable development, it has to also emphasize the role of tourism in promoting biodiversity conservation (a major principle of sustainable development) rather than merely focusing on what tourism can derive from biodiversity and culture. After all, maintaining the ecological and social integrity of destination sites ensures the sustainability of tourism and provision of long-term benefits to the host communities. The government officials (M. Lim, personal communication, 8 February 2010; A., Manila, personal communication, 10 February 2010) interviewed for this study stated that 'the proper management of natural areas is important because ecotourism cannot exist without biodiversity, but government resources are inadequate.' As a result, biodiversity conservation in protected areas is often compromised by the economic demands driven by the short-term benefits of tourism.

A paradigm shift from the utilitarian view of the environment to sustainable use is crucial in sustainable tourism. Environmental ethics in the context of tourism refers to the appropriate behaviour of tourists while interacting with the environment. Holden (2003, p. 97) states that 'environmental ethics is concerned with redefining the boundaries of the obligation to the environment and evaluating the human position towards it.' Public awareness, code of practice, and government regulations have all major influence in establishing these boundaries. The tourism industry should be made more aware of the tangible and intangible values of protected areas as destination sites and implement ways to encourage tourists to respect nature and people. The *Guidelines on biodiversity and tourism development* (CBD, 2004) provide recommendations on how this can be done.

Environmental Issues

The Philippines, being an archipelagic country, is highly vulnerable to the adverse impacts of tourism. The negative environmental impacts of tourism especially on small islands are long-term and irreversible (e.g. Catibog-Sinha, 1997; Ceballos-Lascurain, 1996; Conlin & Baum. 1995; DeAlbuquerque & McElroy, 1992; Eagles, McCool, & Haynes, 2002; Holden, 2008).

In the Philippines, the impacts of unsustainable tourism on natural ecosystems are widespread. Christie (2005) reported that the tourism growth of a marine-based destination area (i.e. Mabini, Batangas, southern Luzon) resulted in soil erosion because of unregulated infrastructure developments such as the construction of roads, hotels and houses along the coastal area. In addition, shellfish populations and seagrass beds on beaches fronting resorts have declined because of the construction of hotels and boats landing on certain sections of the beach. Because there are weak zoning or setback regulations, diving and boat anchoring are damaging the coral reefs. In another tourist attraction (i.e. White Beach of Boracay, central Philipines), mass tourism had compromised the integrity of the island due to unregulated tourism growth. In 1997, the beach was considered unfit for swimming because of high level of coliform bacteria from untreated organic waste; in addition, golf courses occupy about 10% of the island's land area. Carter (2004, p. 400) concludes that the underlying cause of the environmental and social disaster on this island was due to the 'lack of preparedness for rapid and sporadic growth' of tourism.

Decision makers should recognize the inherent complexity in assessing tourism impacts because most of the negative consequences of tourism on natural areas are not immediately manifested (Catibog-Sinha, 2007). The primary (direct) impacts can give rise to a series of secondary and tertiary effects, which are not readily detected or measured in the short-term. An inability to proactively address potential consequences of tourism could cause irreplaceable damage.

Economic Issues

Tourism in the Philippines is seen as a major industry that can enhance the standard of living through improved infrastructure and increased employment, income, and tax revenue. The government in partnership with the tourism industry should, however, recognize both the direct and indirect benefits from the diversity of nature-based attractions. In a valuation study of a coastal destination area in the

Central Philippines (Bohol Marine Triangle, Visayas), it was found that tourism accounts for 44% (5% more than municipal fisheries) of the total net benefits from the use of the coastal and marine sites where diving, snorkelling, dolphin-whale watching are among the favourite tourist activities (Samonte-Tan et al., 2007).

Other studies have shown that the direct economic value from tourism is less than the total economic value from biodiversity (Pearce & Moran, 1994; Tisdell, 1999). Samonte-Tan and Armedilla (2004) report that the non-economic value (e.g. shore like protection, carbon sequestration, and other option values) of coral reefs in the Philippines was three times greater than the direct market value (e.g. fisheries and mass tourism) of the resources. Sustainable tourism and traditional livelihood practices can co-exist to support local economies and conservation, as in the case of certain marine protected areas in the Philippines (e.g. Alcala, 1998; White, Eisma-Osorio, & Green, 2005). The local fishermen in these areas have realized that protecting the coral reefs has actually sustained fish production and harvesting in the adjacent 'take' zone of the marine park. Likewise, the pristine quality of the coral reefs has added a premium to the tourist experience. Maintaining the coral reefs through coastal protection and ecotourism provides much higher economic returns than from harvesting and destructive fishing (World Research Institute, 2005).

Clearly, ecotourism is an effective tool to improve both the local economies and heritage conservation efforts. As Goodwin (2002, p.340) states, 'ecotourism … contributes to the maintenance of species and habitats either directly through a contribution to conservation and/or indirectly by providing revenue to the local community sufficient for local people to value, and therefore protect, their wild-life heritage area as a source of income.' Generating and/or increasing the economic benefits from the use of protected areas is one way for local communities, especially those living inside or adjacent to these areas, to value the resources that support ecotourism. For instance, the user fee system developed for the Tubbataha Reef Natural Marine Park (group of atolls in south-western Philippines) has been effective in generating tourism revenue, enough to support 80% of the annual core cost needed to protect the Reef (Tongson & Dygico, 2004). The sale of hand-crafted materials (i.e. *tinalak* product made from *abaca* (hemp) plants from Lake Sebu in the southern Philippines) has been financially rewarding to the local tribe and the rest of the stakeholders who participate in the various stages of product development and marketing. These native crafts can also be used as a tool to educate the tourists about traditional culture and sustainable use of natural resources.

As in the many island tourism worldwide (Catibog-Sinha & Bushell, 2002; Conlin & Baum, 1995), the Philippines faces a negative economic backlash, such as the leakage of tourism revenue. In Boracay (located on the small island of Aklan, central Philippines), the majority of items for sale including food and labour are imported (Carter, 2004; DOT-DENR, 2002), whereas in Mabini (coastal shore of Batangas, southern Luzon) only 23% of the resorts are locally owned (Majanen, 2007). A similar situation was observed in Puerto Galera (on the island of eastern Mindoro, southern Luzon) during the author's visit in July 2009. It is apparent that the proper valuation of marine and coastal resources is necessary to provide policy guidance on how tourism income should be equitably allocated as well as on how user fees should be formulated to account for the social and environmental costs associated with tourism.

Legislative support to finance protected areas from tourism revenues is already in place. A funding mechanism, known as the Integrated Protected Areas Fund (IPAF), has been established by virtue of the NIPAS Act and its implementing rules and regulations. Accordingly, the IPAF has to be set up for each protected area, and the income generated from its use should accrue to site management (75%); the rest (25%) is used to support the management needs of other protected areas. Unfortunately, accessing the IPAF remains bureaucratic and complex (I. Castillo, personal communication, 21 January 2008). As a result, some tourism revenues are not remitted to the National Treasury in full or on time, which can lead to damaging social conflicts and inappropriate transactions.

Social and Poverty Issues

The local people with a more traditional simple life and material needs are vulnerable to western influence and exploitation (Catibog-Sinha & Wen, 2008). Since the resource base of small islands in the Philippines is limited, competition between the tourists and local residents is inevitable (Catibog-Sinha & Bushell, 2002). Land clearing to make way for tourism developments and the abandonment of traditional agriculture and fishing are the common and immediate effects of tourism. Traditional island farmers/fishermen (e.g. Boracay) have become dependent on tourism (Carter, 2004), which is detrimental to the sustainability of their livelihoods. In general, the social changes brought about by mass tourism can create difficulties in achieving sustainability (Tisdell & Xiang, 1996).

Nearly all developing countries have identified tourism as a developmental option to alleviate poverty (Hawkins & Mann, 2007). Poverty occurs not only because people lack income and assets but also because they do not have access to livelihood opportunities and are not equipped to voice their opinion on matters affecting them (Scherl et al., 2004). The benefits from tourism are also not always equitably shared. In one destination site (Mabini, Batangas), discontented fishermen claimed that they did not receive any benefits from tourism. They argued that work opportunities in the tourist resorts were limited because many of the resort owners, who were usually not local residents, preferred to hire staff from their home provinces or towns; and if work was available, the employment on offer is seasonal, short, and contractual (Majanen, 2007; Oracion et al., 2005).

The big gap in the distribution of tourism income between the poor and the rich could also exacerbate poverty (Blake, Arbache, Sinclair, & Teles, 2008). In some Philippine destination sites, the economic benefits from tourism, which are enjoyed by the local tourism sector (represented by boat operators, dive operators, and resort owners), have allegedly disadvantaged fishermen in terms of access to and control of the marine resources within marine protected areas

(Carter, 2004; Majanen, 2007). The fishermen claimed that the local regulatory measures favoured tourist divers by giving them preferential rights to access the coral reef and fish sanctuaries. As a result, fishermen consider marine protected areas and tourism as alienating factors that cause further economic and social disparities between them and the tourists.

Addressing poverty through the provision of alternative livelihoods, such as through tourism, will be a constant challenge because success is not always consistent and constant; often such success is not apparent in the early stages of tourism/community development. The government has yet to demonstrate that the tourism developmental projects can help improve the economic welfare of the local people and enhance biodiversity conservation. Addressing these concerns requires innovative and even simple community-driven measures. For instance, some of the tourism revenue may be used to subsidize the schooling of local children, a support measure that would have long-term benefits for the local community.

Governance and Community Participation Issues

In the implementation of the Philippine Ecotourism Program, an organizational structure consisting of government and non-government representatives, was set up pursuant to a presidential order (Executive Order No. 111). The combination of the top-bottom and bottom-up approaches to management is the functional framework being pursued under the Program. The main role of the central management body is to spearhead the development of policies based on the advice and experiences from the local and regional communities. The field administrators are tasked to enact these policies judiciously at the community level. The local governance consists of representatives from the provincial or regional government representatives, local government units, local community/ residents, and indigenous people. Likewise, the Philippine Local Government Code of 1991 directs the decentralization of certain government functions, one of which is tourism development.

The Philippines recognizes the need for relevant stakeholders (e.g. local residents, policy makers, park managers, tourism industry, and scientists) to be involved in its policy initiatives in ecotourism and biodiversity conservation, and to harness their support for the implementation of these initiatives. Catibog-Sinha and Heaney (2006, p. 17) state 'the importance of integrating facts, values and feelings of society as a way to attain sustainability ... including the maintenance of biodiversity.' Genuine participation fosters stewardship for environmental protection. For instance, Christie (2005) reports that the protection of a marine sanctuary (Twin and Cathedral Rocks in Mabini, Batangas in southern Luzon) would have not been possible without the vigilance of the resort owners and the local fishers. The strong leadership and dedication of local politicians, as in the case of the tourism management of two other sites—Puerto Princesa Subterranean River National Park (DNS project) and Lake Sebu (PEP Phase II)—are good examples.

The effective participation and empowerment of local residents, especially those in remote and often impoverished tourist destination areas, may require early external interventions in the form of technical and financial support, leadership training, community organizing, and environmental education. Goodwin (2002, p.344) argues that the 'level of education and capital possessed by local people restrict their involvement in the industry'… and opportunities for retraining appear to be sparse.' As in many community-based projects, local community participation becomes problematic when resources and expertise, including mutual trusts, are wanting. A strong political will is necessary to ensure that the governance at the national and field levels is firm and dependable.

Collaboration and Networking Issues

One of the ultimate goals of community participation in tourism is the development of a network of stakeholders who are bound together by a common goal. This tourism network, whether formal or informal, is meant 'to describe the dynamic social relationships which actors form in order to achieve tourism-related goals' (Saxena & Ilbery, 2008, p. 236). Networks can expand the tourism markets and increase the access of members to resources and technologies. They can also encourage the sharing of market information by linking attractions, events, and other goods and services. This will stimulate the country's destination competitiveness through cooperative branding, image building, and integrated tourism product development. Networks can also spread the notion of biodiversity conservation because natural destinations are ecologically inter-connected, especially those in marine and coastal areas.

Community networks in the Philippines can be encouraged by enhancing the existing community spirit of solidarity and cooperation. The existence of weak community networks in certain destination areas had occurred, and this could have been the result of miscommunication and mistrust (A. Meniado, personal communication, 8 February 2008). Ecotourism networks can only be successful if socially meaningful relationships are built on trust, transparency, and the sharing of both material and non-material benefits.

Since local capital is a major economic impediment for gainful tourism development in the Philippines, forming networks can encourage external investments. Hence local people should be given better opportunities to participate in the running and marketing of tourism destinations. Through collective efforts, members of the network can lobby for better support from government-sponsored programs and developing better ways to access modern technologies and effective marketing strategies. However, investor-driven projects can potentially limit the involvement of local stakeholders, which could result in the loss of local ownership, disempowerment, and economic leakage. Thus all forms of external interventions, at the local and national levels, should be transparent and democratic because a failure to do so could lead to the 'commoditization of people and artefacts by non-local actors effecting change and control from afar' (Saxena & Ilbery, 2008, p. 238).

Visitor/Tourist Experience Issues

Ecotourism involves attracting visitors to natural areas and making them appreciate the value of human-nature interrelationships. More and more tourists prefer to visit natural and authentic destinations. Catibog-Sinha and Heaney (2006, p. 383) state that 'maintaining the biodiversity assets of a natural destination enhances the recreational experience of tourists, which leads to repeat and longer visitation, high quality recreational experience, and better support for biodiversity conservation.' The host community should not hope for mass tourism and the expansion of tourism facilitie, rather they should aspire to optimize the quality of the tourist experience since many tourists are willing to pay a premium for unique natural products.

Further field research in the Philippines is needed to determine tourist motivations in taking pleasure vacations in natural areas. Research is also needed to assess tourist idiosyncrasies. The information about tourist motivations is used as basis for developing tourism products, assessing the extent and limits of recreational demands, and developing appropriate marketing strategies in promoting recreational activities (Crompton, 1981; Yoon Uysal, 2005).

Conclusion

The Philippines faces many issues and challenges in balancing ecotourism and biodiversity conservation in natural destination areas. A tourism venture that focuses on short-term goals can undermine the ecological integrity of nature-based destinations and deprive the local community from benefiting from tourism. Tourism products that are well-planned or conceived, but also strongly influenced by economic imperatives and other market forces, will be unsustainable and would weaken current efforts to conserve biodiversity. Relevant stakeholders should ensure that the benefits from ecotourism exceed the social and environmental costs both in the short- and long-term.

The role of protected areas is pivotal in promoting tourism in rural areas where many pristine and unique attraction areas remain unexplored. Any policy measure that would water down the NIPAS Law in order to accommodate liberal approaches to tourism practices in protected areas could jeopardize the biodiversity conservation initiatives in the country. Linking the agricultural and fishery sectors with tourism on islands and coastal areas is essential to ensure that local economies and host communities are benefited through an integrated tourism approach. Tourism management, therefore, should include not only the economic feasibility of the proposed tourism developmental projects but also the long-term sustainability of tourism and the natural attractions upon which the industry is dependent.

Long-term support for sustainable tourism can be implemented in various ways, such as through a voluntary code of conduct, the imposition of government regulations and penalties, and fostering environmental ethics among tourists and the tourism industry.

For tourism to be sustainable, management should ensure that efforts to meet the demands of tourists will not compromise the integrity of the natural and cultural heritage of a destination area. Equally important in tourism management is to recognize that the linkage between tourism and the needs of local people is binding and inseparable, and thus, the social and economic welfare of the host communities should be given a high priority in tourism planning and implementation. Furthermore, tourism benefits should be shared equitably among present and future generations. Precautionary measures should also be in place to minimize visitor impacts on the ecological, social and cultural environments of a destination.

Acknowledgement

The author benefited from interviews with key officials and staff from the Protected Areas Bureau (Philippines), particularly Director Mundita Lim, Marlynn Mendoza, Carlo Custodio, Angelita Meniado, Norma Molinyawe, Teresita Balstique, and Inocensio Castillo; Celestino Ulep and Precy Calimag of the National Ecotourism Strategy Philippine Program, and some members of Regional Ecotourism Committee representing the Department of Environment and Natural Resources and Department of Tourism.

References

Alcala, A.C. (1998). Community-based coastal resource management in the Philippines: A case study. *Ocean and Coastal Management*, 38, 179–186.

Balgos, M.C. (2005). Integrated coastal management and marine protected areas in the Philippines: Concurrent developments. *Ocean & Coastal Management*, 48, 972–995.

Blake, A., Arbache, J.S., Sinclair, M.T., & Teles, V. (2008). Tourism and poverty relief. *Annals of Tourism Research*, 35 (1), 107–126.

Budowski, G. (1976). Tourism and environmental conservation: Conflict, coexistence and symbiosis. *Environmental Conservation*, *3* (1), 27–31.

Carter, R.W. (2004). Implications of sporadic tourism growth: Extrapolation from the case of Boracay Island, the Philippines. *Asia Pacific Journal of Tourism Research*, *9* (4), 383–404.

Catibog-Sinha, C.S. (1997). Ecotourism in protected areas: Integration into conservation programs and policies in the Philippines. *Proceedings Australian Tourism and Hospitality Research Conference* (pp. 132–141); 6-9 July 1997; Sydney, Australia.

Catibog- Sinha, C. (2007). Visitor impact assessment and management in protected areas: Euroka Clearing, Glenbrook at the Greater Blue Mountains World Heritage Area, New South Wales, Australia. *Proceedings International Heritage Tourism*, Guangzhou, China, 12-15 July.

Catibog-Sinha, C. S. (2008). The role of urban green parks in promoting sustainable tourism and biodiversity conservation: Case study. In Y.H. Hwang (Ed.), *Proceedings 14th Asia Pacific Tourism Association Conference, Tourism and Hospitality in Asia Pacific* (pp. 245–255), Bangkok, Thailand.

Catibog-Sinha, C.S., & Bushell, R. (2002). Understanding the linkage between biodiversity and tourism: A study of ecotourism in a coastal village in Fiji. *Pacific Tourism Review*, 6, 35–50.

Catibog-Sinha, C.S., & Heaney, L. (2006). *Philippine biodiversity: Principles and practice.* Quezon City, Philippines: Haribon Foundation.

Catibog-Sinha, C. C., & Wen, J. (2008). Sustainable tourism and management model for protected natural areas: Xishuangbanna Bisophere Reserve, South China. *Asia Pacific Tourism and Research Journal, 13* (2), 145–162.

Ceballos-Lacustrain, H. (1996). *Tourism, ecotourism, and protected areas. The state of nature-based tourism around the world and guidelines for its development.* Gland, Switzerland, and Cambridge, UK: IUCN.

Choi, H., & Sirakaya, E. (2006). Sustainability indicators for managing community tourism. *Tourism Management 27,* 1274–1289.

Choy, D. (1991, September). National tourism planning in the Philippines [Report]. *Tourism Management,* pp. 245–252.

Christie, P. (2005). Observed and perceived environmental impacts of marine protected areas in two Southeast Asia sites. *Ocean & Coastal Management, 48,* 252–270.

Clarke, J. (2002). A synthesis of activity towards the implementation of sustainable tourism: Ecotourism in a different context. *International Journal of Sustainable Development 5 (3),* 232–250.

Conlin, M.V., & T. Baum. (1995). *Island tourism: Management principles and practice.* New York: John Wiley and Sons.

Convention on Biological Diversity. (2004). *Guidelines on biodiversity and tourism development.* Montreal: Secretariat of the Convention on Biological Diversity.

Crompton, J.L. (1981). Dimensions of the social group role in pleasure vacations. *Annals of Tourism Research, 8* (4), 550–568.

D'Ayala, P.G. (1992). Islands at a glance. *Environmental Management, 16(5):* 565–568.

De Albuquerque, A. & McElroy, J.L. (1995). Alternative tourism and sustainability In M.V. Conlin, & T. Baum (Eds.), *Island tourism: Management principles and practice* (pp. 23–32). New York: John Wiley and Sons.

Department of Tourism (DOT). (2009). *Philippine Tourism: Stable amidst a global tourism downturn* [Brochure]. Manila: Author.

Department of Tourism - Department of Environment of Natural Resources. [DOT-DENR]. (2002). *National Ecotourism Strategy.* Quezon City: DOT, DENR, New Zealand Agency for International Development.

Diamantis, D., & Ladkin, A. (1999). Sustainable tourism and ecotourism: A definitional and operational perspective. *Journal of Tourism Studies, 1(2),* 35–46.

Eagles, P., McCool, S. F., & Haynes, C. D. (2002). *Sustainable Tourism in Protected Aas: Guidelines for planning and management.* Gland, Switzerland and Cambridge, UK: IUCN.

Fennell, D., & Weaver, D. (2005). The ecotourism concept and tourism-conservation symbiosis. *Journal of Sustainable Tourism, 13* (4), 373–390.

Goodwin, H. (2002). Local community involvement in tourism around national parks: Opportunities and constraints. *Current Issues in Tourism, 5* (3 &4), 338–360.

Hall, C. M., & Lew, A.A. (1998). *Sustainable Tourism: A geographical perspective.* London: Prentice Hall.

Hawkins, D.E., & Mann, S. (2007). The World Bank's role in tourism development. *Annals of Tourism Research, 34* (2), 348–363.

Hjalager, A. M. (2007). Stages in the economic globalization of tourism. *Annals of Tourism Research, 34* (2), 437–457.

Holden, A. (2003). In need of new environmental ethics for tourism? *Annals of Tourism Research, 30* (1), 94–108.

Holden, A. (2008). *Environment and Tourism* (2nd edn). London: Routledge

International Union for the Conservation of Nature (IUCN). (1994). *Guidelines for protected area management categories*. Gland: IUCN.

International Union for the Conservation of Nature (IUCN). (2003). *Fifth World Park Congress,* World Commission on Protected Areas; 8-17 September 2003; Durban, South Africa.

Majanen, T. (2007). Resource use conflicts, in Mabini and Tingloy, the Philippines. *Marine Policy, 31,* 480–487.

Mittermeier, R.A., Myers, N., Robles, G.P, & Mittermeier, C.G. (Eds.). (1999). *Hotspots: Earth's biologically richest and most endangered terrestrial ecosystems.* Mexico City: CEMEX.

Mittermeier, R.A., Robles, G.P., Hoffmann, M., Pilgrim, J., Brooks, T., Mittermeier, C.G., Lamoreux, J., & da Fonseca, G.A.B. (2004). *Hotspots: revisited.* Mexico City: CEMEX.

Newsome, D., Moore, S. A., & Dowling, R. K. (2002). *Natural area tourism: Ecology, impacts and management.* Clevedon: Channel View Publications

Oracion, E., Miller, M. L., & Christie, P. (2005). Marine protected areas for whom? Fisheries, tourism, and solidarity in a Philippine community. *Ocean & Coastal Management, 48,* 393–410.

Pearce, D., & Moran, D. (1994). *The economic value of biodiversity.* Earthscan: London.

Resor, J.P. (1993). Debt-for-nature swaps: A decade of experience and new directions for the future. Retrieved on 1 May 2010, from http://www.fao.org/documents/show_cdr. asp?url_file=/docrep/.htm)

Richter, L.K. (1999). After political turmoil: The lessons of rebuilding tourism in three Asian countries. *Journal of Travel Research, 38*:41–45.

Roberts, C.M., McClean, C.J., Veron, J.E.N., Hawkins, J P., Allen, G.R., McAllister, D.E., Mittermeier, C.G., Schueler, F.W., Spalding, M., Wells, F., Vynne, C., & Werner, T.B. (2002). Marine biodiversity hotspots and conservation priorities for tropical reefs. *Science, 295* (5558): 1280–1284.

Samonte-Tan, G. & Armedilla. M. C. (2004). Sustaining Philippine reefs: National coral reef review, Series No.2 - Economic valuation of Philippine coral reefs in the South China Sea biogeographic region. *UNEP-GEF South China Sea Project.* Quezon City: Marine Science Institute, University of the Philippines.

Samonte-Tan, G., White, A. T., Tercero, M., Diviva, J., Tabara, E., & Caballes, C. (2007). Economic valuation of coastal and marine resources: Bohol Marine Triangle, Philippines. *Coastal Management, 35*: 319–338.

Saxena, G., & Ilbery, B. (2008). Integrated rural tourism: A border case study. *Annals of Tourism Research, 35* (1): 233–254.

Scherl, L., Wilson, A., Wild, R., Blockhus, J., Franks, P., McNeely, J., & McShane, T. (2004). *Can Protected Areas contribute to Poverty Alleviation: Opportunities and limitations.* Gland, Switzerland and Cambridge, UK: IUCN.

Sharpley, R. (2006). Ecotourism: A consumption perspective. *Journal of Ecotourism, 5* (1&2): 7–22.

Tisdell, C. (1999). *Biodiversity, Conservation and Sustainable Development: Principles and practices with Asian examples.* Massachusetts: Edward Elgar Publication.

Tisdell, C. & Xiang, Z. (1996). Reconciling economic development, nature conservation and local communites: Strategies for biodiversity conservation in Xishuangbanna, China. *The Environmentalists, 16*: 203–211.

Tongson E. & Dygico, M. (2004). User fee system for marine ecotourism: The Tubbataha Reef experience. *Ocean & Coastal Management, 32*: 17–23.

United Nations Environment Programme (UNEP). (1992). *Convention on Biological Diversity.* Nairobi: United Nations Environment Programme.

United Nations Environment Programme (UNEP) (2001). *Principles for Implementation of Sustainable Tourism.* Final version for Governing Council-21. (20 Sept 2002; www.unep.org)

White, A.T., Eisma-Osorio, R.L., & Green, S.J. (2005). Integrated coastal management and marine protected areas: Complementarity in the Philippines. *Ocean & Coastal Management, 48*: 948–971.

World Resources Institute (WRI) (2005). *Millennium Ecosystem Assessment. Ecosystems and Human Well-being: Biodiversity Synthesis.* Washington, DC: Author.

World Tourism Organization (WTO) (1992). *Guidelines: Development of national parks and protected areas for tourism.* WTO Report Series 13.

Yoon, Y. & Uysal, M. (2005). An examination of the effects of motivation and satisfaction on destination loyalty: a structural model. *Tourism Management, 26*: 45–56.

24 Turtle night watch nature tourism

Sharing benefits to sustain local community and Sea Turtles in Rekawa sanctuary, Sri Lanka

*Thushan Kapurusinghe**

Introduction

Sri Lanka is an island nation situated at the Southern point of India, separated from the mainland by the shallow seas of the Gulf of Mannar. It is located between the latitudes of 5°55N and 9°51N and the longitudes of 79°41E and 81°53E. The island has a 1,585 km coastline and is 353 km from north to south and 183 km at its widest point, covering a land area of 65,610 Km^2 (CCD,1997).

The Green turtle (*Chelonia mydas*), Leatherback turtle (*Dermochelys coriacea*), Olive ridley turtle (*Lepidochelys olivacea*), Loggerhead turtle (*Caretta caretta*) and the Hawksbill turtle (*Eretmochelys imbricata*) come ashore to nest on the beaches (Kapurusinghe, 2000b). All five species are listed by the World Conservation Union (IUCN) as either critically endangered or endangered (IUCN 2001). Despite this international legislation and the local protection of marine turtles by government legislation since 1972, marine turtles are still being extensively exploited in Sri Lanka for their eggs and meat. In addition, turtle nesting beaches (rookeries) are being disturbed by tourist industry development and feeding habitats, such as coral reefs and sea grass beds, are being destroyed by pollution and unsustainable harvesting. Many turtles are accidentally caught and drowned in fishing gear each year, while the critically endangered hawksbill turtle has been hunted to the brink of extinction for its carapace to provide raw materials for the illegal 'tortoiseshell' trade (Hewavisenthi, 1990; Fisher, 1995; Kapurusinghe, 2006 and 2008).

The Turtle Conservation Project (TCP) of Sri Lanka was established in 1993 by a group of young volunteers with the aim of conserving marine turtles in

*Turtle Conservation Project (TCP), No.11, Perera Mawatha, Madakumbura, Panadura, Sri Lanka (e-mail: Kjthushan@yahoo.co.uk).

Sri Lanka. Coastal communities in Rekawa exploited marine & coastal resources for their survival due to poverty. Turtle egg poaching, the slaughtering of turtles for meat consumption and coral mining were direct threats to marine turtles in Rekawa. After conducting a series of community meetings, TCP realized the chain connection between the coastal communities and coastal resources, which depend heavily on each other. As a solution, TCP implemented various community livelihood, community infrastructure development, environment restoration and awareness programmes including a 'Turtle Night Watch' nature tourism initiative in Rekawa village (Kapurusinghe, 2000a) to address the environmental problems and break out of the vicious cycle of poverty and resource destruction.

The sea turtle-based tourism in Sri Lanka was initially represented by the existence of the turtle hatcheries. However, all these hatcheries are operated illegally according to the Fauna and Flora Protection Ordinance of Sri Lanka (Hewavisenthi, 1993). The turtle hatchery owners purchase turtle eggs from the egg poachers and rebury them in the hatchery enclosure. After incubation, hatchlings are kept in tanks for several days prior to then release them into the water. In addition, juvenile sea turtles are also kept in captivity in these hatcheries as a tourist attraction (Amarasuriya, 1996). Tourism provides the major income for these hatcheries, enabling to them to maintain the facility. However, these hatcheries are in a doubtful situation as many of their practices are not properly contributing to the conservation of sea turtles in a scientific manner. The ex-situ conservation of sea turtles is represented by those turtle hatcheries initiated by various organizations, hotels and individuals along the south-west and southern coast of Sri Lanka (Kapurusinghe 2006). Poorly maintained hatcheries typically adopt procedures that disregard the sex ratio produced and/or have no regard for ensuring the hatchlings undergo their vital imprinting process (Mrosovsky, 1994 & Brand, 1999 in Richardson 1996). If hatchlings are kept in tanks for a few days, they will spend their first day constantly swimming around the tanks without feeding. On the second day the hatchlings' behaviour changes to feeding behaviour. Therefore, when the hatchlings are released on the third day, instead of swimming out to sea and away from the dangerous coastal waters, they will continue the feeding behaviour within the coastal waters and are therefore more vulnerable to predation. The retention of hatchling turtles in tanks could seriously reduces the probability of their survival after release and serves absolutely no conservation purpose. This view is shared by international turtle biologists world-wide (Richardson, 1996).

The Project Site - Rekawa

The TCP has selected Rekawa, a small fishing village on the south coast of Sri Lanka, approximately 10 kilometres eastwards along the coast from Tangalle in Hambantota District, for the community-based turtle conservation activities (see Figure 24.1). Rekawa is located on the border of the intermediate and dry climatic zones of Sri Lanka, and borders a large saline lagoon surrounded by extensive mangrove forests. Income-generating activities for the families in the Rekawa

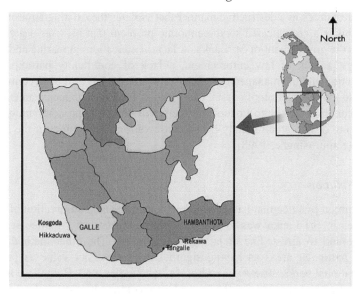

Figure 24.1 Map showing the Rekawa TCP project area

area back in 1993 included agriculture (47%), lagoon fishing (10%), sea fishing (18%), coral mining (9%) and others (17%) such as masonry, carpentry, government services and labour (Banda, 1994).

Rekawa's Biodiversity

As Rekawa is located between two climatic zones, the area is rich in biodiversity. In addition to the five species of sea turtles, there is a wide range of coastal fauna and flora such as coral reefs, marine algae, sea grasses, reef fish, crustaceans, echinodermates, molluscs, annelids, hydrozoans, holothurians and arthropods to be found in Rekawa. Furthermore, 160 species of birds, 28 species of mammals, 37species of reptiles, 35 species of butterflies and 17 species of mangrove plants have been reported from the Rekawa area (Kapurusinghe, 1995). However, further research must be carried out to identify the species' richness in the Rekawa area.

The Problem

When TCP first arrived in Rekawa in 1993, there were many environmentally destructive practices being undertaken by the local community members. The killing of sea turtles, turtle egg-gathering, mining corals, sand, and shells from the lagoon, cutting mangroves, and poaching wild animals such as black nape hares (*Lepus nigricolis*), mouse deers (*Tragulus meminna*) and jungle fowls (*Gallus laffeyetti*) were among the destructive practices. Although many of these natural resources are legally protected, coastal communities continue to use coastal resources in a destructive manner that violates the existing environmental laws. This is a complicated socio-economic problem that presents a great challenge to the government of Sri Lanka. A lack of education on marine and coastal resources, a lack of law enforcement, a lack of community participation in conservation and the management of coastal resources have all been contributory factors to the destruction of coastal ecosystems. TCP has conducted an extensive socio-economic survey to understand the environmental and community issues and then to design a community-based conservation programme for the Rekawa village (Kapurusinghe, 1998).

TCP's Solution

The common practice that had been implemented for the conservation of natural resources in Sri Lanka was to ban or prohibit the use of a particular natural resource and to arrest, fine or jail the perpetrators. The other method was to declare particular areas as having significant bio-diversity value as protected areas (national parks, strict nature reserves, sanctuaries etc.). Both these methods did not take into consideration the lives of local communities most of whom lived well below the poverty line. The members of these communities who are less educated, ignorant and struggling to feed their families depend on natural resources from the surrounding environment. Understanding community attitudes to conservation and its linkage with conservation behaviours needs a sound understanding of the variety of socio-economic and cultural factors involved (Holmes, 2003.)

When TCP identified the 'problem tree' with issues that needed to be addressed, the 'solution tree' clearly appeared as a wide angle community-based ecosystem conservation approach. TCP's aim was to develop a mechanism that would allow the community to utilize their natural resources in a sustainable manner and let them earn an income while also preserving and managing natural resources. TCP realized this chain connection between the coastal communities and coastal resources which heavily depend on each other. As a solution, TCP developed the concept which is referred to as the 'Community Based Ecosystem Conservation Approach' (CBECA) to address the problems described above. Campbell *et al.* (2007) described the durability and flexibility of the incentive, legal and administrative structures associated with a successful example of community-based conservation. When the TCP decided on a community-based approach, this meant the direct and indirect involvement of the community in the implementing process and in gaining benefits from it. In this case, the local community is benefited through various community livelihood development projects, infrastructure development projects, education and awareness programs, capacity and skills development programmes, etc. In ecosystem conservation, although the TCP's main focus is on protecting marine turtles, the link of this species as a flagship species with other species and habitats which are critical for the survival of marine turtles both in land and water has been taken into consideration. Therefore, the TCP has focused on protecting not only marine turtles, but also other habitats such as coral reefs, nesting beaches, beach vegetation, mangroves, sea grass beds and lagoons etc.

The TCP has taken a multi-pronged approach to the implementation of CBECA. There are seven main components to this approach.

1) Community livelihood development
2) Community infrastructure development
3) Environmental restoration and management
4) Education and awareness/capacity development
5) Partnership building/networking
6) Knowledge management and sharing lessons learned
7) Promotion and utilization of traditional knowledge and local culture

TCP's main aim is to use the symbol of the marine turtle as a charismatic or flagship species in the development process of the Rekawa community and its environment. The project aims to facilitate the implementation of sustainable marine turtle conservation strategies through education, research and community participation. It envisions attaining and maintaining sustainable levels of sea turtle populations in Sri Lanka. TCP conducts research and surveys to gain valuable knowledge about the status of marine turtles. The 'hands-on' conservation of marine turtles is achieved by community-based conservation and management programs. The educational and awareness programs and research opportunities provided by the TCP for both local and foreign nationals, coupled with nature tourism activities such as the 'Turtle Watch', enable TCP to act as a role model for responsible tourism. The successful implementation and execution of the above projects and training programs is embedded within the seven components of the CBECA. TCP's nature tourism programs are also conducted as part of the 'community livelihood development' component.

The Rekawa Nature Tourism Project: the 'Turtle Night Watch'

The 'Turtle Night Watch', the nature tourism program in Rekawa which involves ex-turtle egg poachers as nest protectors/tour guides, is one of the best examples of the alternative livelihood provisions for destructive natural resource practices. In 1998, TCP trained a select group of local people as 'Tourist Guides' with the assistance of the Sri Lanka Tourist Board (SLTB) and the Sri Lanka Hotel School, which resulted in them receiving their Guide Licenses. These guides were then employed on the beach and visitors paid a fee to experience the turtle watches in Rekawa (see Figure 24.2). Publicity for the program was generated through the TCP website, printed materials (such as brochures, leaflets and posters), electronic and print media, and promotional presentations at hotels and guest houses etc.

The profits from the 'Turtle Night Watch' nature tourism initiative has been shared by the stakeholders of the project with 10% of the tourism income being allocated for the Rekawa community Tourist Guides (TG), and another 35% for a 'Turtle Conservation Fund (TCF)' that covers the future salaries of the nest

Figure 24.2 A local guide explaining turtle biology (Photo by author)

protectors when funding gaps occur. In addition, 25% was allocated for the Nature Friends of Rekawa (NFR), 10% for the Community Welfare Fund (CWF), 10% for the Department of Wildlife Conservation (DWC), and lastly 10% for the TCP to continue their conservation and other community programs in Rekawa. During the tourism period fo 2002-2003 (during the cease fire period), a sum of Rs 1,050,000 was raised from the Rekawa Nature tourism programme.

TCP's 'turtle watch' program and other nature tourism initiatives are well organized using social and cultural sensitivity. People in the Rekawa village are well cultured and very friendly and hospitable towards the tourists who visit the site for the program. During the day the guides (former turtle egg porches) accompany the tourists to the beach and Rekawa lagoon for sightseeing and during the night they are dedicated to the tourism programme which they carry out discreetly. TCP motivated the villagers of Rekawa towards giving an enthusiastic response as regards the initiated programme. Therefore, they always focused on a positive response. TCP's initiative has never had negative impacts on the culture, instead it has always worked towards the betterment of the society. TCP's Rekawa nature tourism promotional brochures educate tourists about the social and cultural sensitivity. Well-trained TCP officials and wildlife officials also regulate the programme carefully.

In order to reduce the environmental impact of tourism, TCP conducts periodic beach cleaning programs to keep the beach clear with the assistance of schoolchildren and TCP's dedicated volunteers. In addition, garbage collection bins have been placed on the beach. Turtle Watch guidelines have been put in place at Rekawa beach and tourism promotional publications now include these guidelines which must be strictly adhered to by locals as well as tourists. A signboard displaying the guidelines is erected at TCP's beach hut in Rekawa. The guidelines include the prohibition of flash photography when watching turtles, no disturbance of the turtles, eggs or hatchlings, no beach fires, no trash on the beach etc. TCP's education and awareness programs conducted at tourist hotels also help to reduce the environmental impact. Strict beach regulations promoted by the TCP research officers and wildlife officers also reduce the environmental impact.

Benefits to the Rekawa community

The introduction and development of markets for alternative livelihoods (products) and services could play a significant role in reducing the over-exploitation of natural resources (Campbell, 2010). The impact of TCP's economic benefits to the local community can be measured by comparing the status of the Rekawa village in the early 90s and its present status. Earlier on there was not a single bus-stop in Rekawa and local people and schoolchildren had to shelter under a tree till the bus came. But today TCP has provided two bus-stops in Rekawa for local people. The road to the beach was also not in a good condition so TCP used the income gained from the 'turtle watch' tourism fund to renovate this. Today hundreds of visiting tourists and locals are benefiting from this renovated road. In addition, TCP has provided electricity, water and shelter for many community members in Rekawa. With the funds raised from tourism TCP has donated books for the Rekawa community library (established by TCP) and the library is used by many children in the village.

TCP has improved the socioeconomic conditions and wellbeing of the community through a 'Community Based Ecosystem Conservation Approach' (CBECA). In this case, TCP has implemented various community-based projects at the same time, through different CBOs. TCP has formed CBOs such as the Nature Friends of Rekawa (NFR), community Batik group, fish breeding group, sewing, coir matting, bee keeping, organic farming etc. and provided alternative livelihood development skills training for these CBO members. TCP also provided the equipment and initial stocks of material/raw material. Further, initial capital needs were met through the revolving fund scheme. Turtle egg poachers are now employed as turtle nest protectors and tourist guides through the in-situ turtle nest protection and research program. Furthermore, TCP has also implemented community skills development programs such as primary school programs, computer classes, free English language classes, swimming training and disaster preparation training. Children's clubs were established in order to involve them in the coastal eco-system conservation and management process, providing the necessary awareness through various educational programs. Further, TCP implemented community health programs such as medical clinics, free herbal drinks for schoolchildren, community welfare services and first aid training.

Figure 24.3 Local products (Photos by author)

TCP has formed a local performing arts group and art school in Rekawa in order to preserve the local culture (see Figure 24.3). Local children receive training from this school and tour groups are entertained by the local cultural dancing group and gain benefits from the TCP's tourism program. Part of the income received from the TCP's Turtle Night Watch initiative has been donated to this art school for purchase of the equipment required. It is a privilege for the schoolchildren to show their preserved local cultural talents. TCP's visitor center in Rekawa which is currently under construction will provide a stage for this local dancing group to perform and make an additional income while preserving the local culture. Through the TCP/US AID partnership program, this art performing school was provided with a shelter that allowed them to conduct training programs.

Furthermore, TCP ensures that both women and men play an integral part in the implementation of the activities and will thus gain some benefit from this. Activities such as coir mat production, sewing garments, Batik production, bee keeping and coastal vegetation replantating programs directly involve many local women who benefited. Women are also involved in progress evaluation meetings as well. All turtle nest protectors are male and TCP has kids clubs and youth clubs working on environmental conservation in Rekawa. In addition, swimming classes, English classes, first aid classes and computer training classes are provided to all sections of the community.

Benefits to the Rekawa environment

Prior to the implementation of the innovative concept 'Community Based Ecosystem Conservation Approach' (CBECA) all the turtle eggs were poached in Rakawa and hundreds of live turtles were transported to Jaffna (a northern part of Sri Lanka) for meat consumption. In addition, occasionally turtles were killed for meat locally. Howeve,r at present, all turtle nests are protected in-situ and hatchlings are produced and released immediately. No killing of turtles exists on the Rekawa beach. The TCP, through the Department of Wildlife Conservation, has been able to declare Rekawa beach as Sri Lanka's first marine turtle sanctuary. Therefore, not only the turtles but also the beach is legally protected.

Benefits to Sri Lanka's tourism and wildlife institutions

Institutions such as the Department of Wildlife Conservation and the Sri Lanka Tourist Board are benefited by this project with training specially provided for the wldlife officers on research and conservation techniques such as sea turtle biology, conservation and management. Students and researchers, both local and foreign, gain from the academic research facilities provided at Rekawa. These are especially beneficial for those who are involved in postgraduate studies. Genetic studies have been carried out in association with the University of Peredeniya, Sri Lanka. Satellite tracking programmes were also conducted in conjunction with the Marine Conservation Society, the University of Exeter and the Wildlife Institute of India. The tourism industry in Sri Lanka has benefited through the Rekawa turtle conservation project. After the project implementation, Rekawa was recognized as one of the top ten eco-friendly destinations named by the online travel community IgoUgo, which was owned by Travelocity in January 2008. The list is based on recommendations from IgoUgo editors who reviewed the journals of some of its 350,000 members with comments by the travelers listed. This recognition has promoted the Rekawa turtle watch and benefits tourism in Sri Lanka. Journalists from various media institutions also gain from using Rekawa as a model site for training environmental journalists. It has also benefited the NGOs involved in wildlife conservation as a training site for staff members. Donor agencies also get rewards from using the Rekawa project as a showcase for success in knowledge management aspects. Further, local and foreign volunteers benefit from working at the Rekawa project, gaining firsthand experience and knowledge of Sri Lanka's natural resources especially on community-based coastal eco-system management.

Traditional Knowledge Management and Sharing

TCP utilized the traditional knowledge and culture in implementing various aspects of the project. Fish breeding, an indigenous medicinal plant project, mangrove restoration, and turtle nest protection are some examples, and traditional knowledge has been extensively utilized. To strengthen the local culture and support local tourism a local performing arts group has been formed. This is a unique aspect of the project not seen in many other conservation projects prior to Rekawa. TCP organizes knowledge sharing workshops and also attends national, regional and international conferences in order to disseminate information. Further, the Rekawa project allows opportunities for local and foreign volunteers to gain experience on community-based natural resource management.

Awareness, attitudes and capacity building

The effects of tourism based conservation projects on conservation awareness, attitudes and conservation behaviours reveal its importance as a tool for conservation and management (Waylen et al., 2009). TCP took a leading role in developing the local community capacities in managing their own resources in a sustainable manner. TCP has provided training programmes for locals in nature tourism, supplied guidebooks for the Rekawa library on wildlife in Sri Lanka, conducted free English language classes, and provided training on vocational training to develop their capacity and take responsibility for their livelihoods. Aided by the English classes conducted by TCP, they are now able to communicate with tourists, while also showing a fair ability in reading and comprehension. Training given on nature tourism to the community by TCP and the Sri Lanka Tourist Board made them more aware about nature, people and responsible tourism. When TCP started conservation activities in the village of Rekawa, the people were dejected about their livelihoods and uncertain about the future. But when they were guided in learning about the importance of conserving ecosystems and the hazards of overexploitation, they were willing to change their lifestyles and as a result ex-turtle egg poachers were converted into turtle nest protectors, and ex-female coral pickers are now being engaged in environment friendly Batik production as their income generating activity.

With the tourism income the TCP has supported various people in Rekawa village with disabilities. In addition, politically abused local villagers and victims of the civil unrest that occurred in 1989/1990 have been immensely supported by the project and some of them are currently employed full-time at TCP. The turtle egg collectors were previously known as 'beach boys' who were a neglected part of the community. Today, this group is no longer called 'beach boys' but respectable 'turtle nest protectors' . Therefore, TCP was able to change the 'status' of the group in Rekawa. Likewise former women divers are presently converting to community-based organizations and engaged in batik production, sewing, fish breeding, coir production etc.

Partnerships

The TCP developed multiple partnerships in order to make the project a success. TCP facilitated the establishment of CBOs that are linked to relevant government institutions, local business organizations, and international organizations such as the Marine Conservation Society (MCS), UN Volunteer Program, SCOTIA-USAID, UNDP GEF SGP, Mercy Corps, etc. for necessary training, business links, marketing opportunities etc. For example, SCOTIA-USAID helped the community Batik Group, by financing a production facility in Rekawa. Mercy Corps helped both the Batik and Coir groups by financing kiosks at 10 large hotels in Tangalle, to display and sell community products. The Wildlife Conservation Department has been invited to these and involved in the project to enforce the law and also to declare the Rakawa beach as Sri Lanka's first Marine Turtle Sanctuary.

The project showcases how partnerships can be effectively used in the conservation of natural resources and poverty alleviation. Therefore, TCP thinks this is an ideal project which can be replicated anywhere else in the world. When TCP was severely affected by the 2004 tsunami even the giant waves could not stop the its community-based conservation efforts as TCP was able to recover strongly and efficiently.

The Future

The establishment of a new visitor centre in Rekawa is the next priority for TCP (currently under construction). This proposed visitor centre will include more facilities such as accommodation for tourists, parking, a lecture hall/display area, a sea turtle hospital, a research/study area, a restaurant and a sales outlet to sell community products. With this initiative, TCP wishes to provide more opportunities for local people to sell their local products to visiting tourists and TCP will also be able to educate tourists about the program more effectively and efficiently. TCP will then strengthen the community livelihood development program by purchasing local products such as ornamental fish, batik products, coconut coir products, fruits and vegetables, garment fabrics etc. from local community members and selling them in Colombo. The relationship between TCP, the Department of Wildlife Conservation and the Rekawa community members will be further strengthened by joint turtle conservation programme at Rekawa.

Potential negative or unintended consequences

The school of environmental activists who wish for the rigid application of law, without considering human aspects and the sustainable use of natural resources poses a problem to the implementation of this kind of community-based project in Sri Lanka. These people question the legality of allowing tourism in a designated sanctuary. TCP is currently working with the DWC, the Sri Lanka Tourist Board and the Ministry of Environment and Natural Resources to resolve this problem.

TCP's Global Recognition

This is against so much positive media attention such as being awarded the British Airways 'Tourism for Tomorrow' highly commended award in 1998 for its community based Turtle Night Watch nature tourism programme in 1996. In 2006, through TCP's involvement, the Rekawa beach was officially declared a wildlife sanctuary by the Department of Wildlife Conservation. In 2008, World Travel and Tourism Council (WTTC) awarded TCP the 'Conservation Award (finalist)'. In addition, TCP received another 'highly commended' award from the Virgin Holidays Responsible Tourism in 2008. Further, the Ministry of the Environment and Natural Resources awarded TCP the 'Green Employment award' in year 2009.

Sustainability

TCP is still in the process of becoming fully sustainable. Its sustainability plan includes the turtle watch nature tourism programme, organizing fee paying volunteers, merchandizing community products, using the fair trade concept, building partnerships, and showcasing and marketing all these concepts (e.g. the BBC's *Saving Planet Earth* documentary covered the TCP project costs for two years). It also successfully promotes social wellbeing and the spirit of volunteerism. Recognition of the Rekawa community-based ecosystem conservation approach allows other interested parties to study the CBECA concept and replicate the model in other areas as appropriate.

Conclusion

The community-based ecosystem conservation approach (CBECA) concept has well deserved the recognition it has gained in its conservation strategy in Sri Lanka that previously relied heavily on law enforcement and a non-participatory approach. In addition, the previous emphasis on a single species conservation approach was changed in Rekawa in order to adopt a wider ecosystem conservation approach. The use of sea turtles as a flagship species enables TCP to generate an income through ecotourism that plays a vital role in the futurity of project. As Kruger (2005) suggests, ecotourism projects with no flagship species are rarely classified as sustainable. Multidisciplinary components embedded in the CBECA provide the opportunity for all the stakeholders to act together and to share the benefits from nature tourism. Although Waylen et al. (2009) attempted to describe nature tourism as a tool that was only suitable for awareness and attitude changing and not the modification of conservation behaviours, the Rekawa case study showcases how nature tourism can positively affect these same behaviours.

References

Amarasooriya, D. (1996). Turtle Hatcheries. Is it additional disaster for the turtle fauna of Sri Lanka? Proceedings of the International conference on the biology and conservation of Amphibians and Reptiles of South Asia, Kandy, Sri Lanka,1996.

Banda, R. (1994). People, Resources and Development potentials in the Rekawa SAMP area (Unpublished report). Coast Conservation Department, Sri Lanka.

CCD (1997). Revised Coastal Zone Management Plan of Sri Lanka. *Coast Conservation Department Report*, 1997. 17.

Cambell, L.M., Haalboom, B.J. and Jennie, T. (2007). Sustainability of community community based conservation: sea turtle egg harvesting in Ostional (Costa Rica) ten years later. *Environmental Conservation, 34 (2)*: 122–131.

Cambell, L.M. (2010). Studying Sea Turtles and learning about the world: Insight from Social Science. *Conservation and Society, 8 (1)*: 1–4.

Fisher, S. (1995). Illegal turtle trade in Sri Lanka and the Maldives- An encouraging note of progress. *Marine turtle newsletter, No. 71*, October 1995.

Hewavisenthi, S. (1990). Exploitation of marine turtles in Sri Lanka: Historic background and the present status. *Marine Turtle Newsletter, No 48*, January 1990.

Hewavisenthi, S. (1993).Sri Lanka's hatcheries: boon or ban? *Marine Turtle Newsletter, No 49*, 1993.

Holmes, C.M. (2003). The influence of protected area outreach on conservation attitudes and resource use patterns: a case study from Western Tanzania. *Oryx, 37*: 305–315.

IUCN (2001). A marine turtle conservation strategy and action plan for the Northern Indian Ocean. *IUCN/SSC, Marine Turtle Specialist Group, publication No 3.*

Kapurusinghe,T. (1995). A checklist of the fauna composition in Rekawa. Unpublished TCP report. *Turtle Conservation Project, Sri Lanka, 11*, Madakumbura, Panadura, Sri Lanka.

Kapurusinghe,T. (1998). Destructive exploitation of natural resources and the decline of nesting marine turtle population in Rekawa, Sri Lanka. 1993-1996. Biology and Conservation of the Amphibians, Reptiles and their habitats in South Asia. *Proceedings of the international Conference on the Biology and Conservation of the Amphibians and Reptiles of South Asia*, Sri Lanka, August 1-5, 1996. 189–193.

Kapurusinghe,T. (2000a). Community Participation in Turtle Conservation in Sri Lanka: a Summary of Community-Based turtle Conservation Project's (TCPs) Activities in Sri Lanka.

Kalb,H.J. and T.Wibbels, compilers. *Proceedings of the Nineteenth Annual Symposium on Sea Turtle{Biology and Conservation*. U.S.Dept. Commerce. NOAA. Tech. Memo. NMFS-SEFSC-443. 57–58.

Kapurusinghe,T. (2000b). Community Participation in Turtle Conservation in Sri Lanka. In *Sea Turtles of the Indo-Pacific: Research, Management and Conservation*. Nicolas Pilcher and Ghazally Ismail Editors. *Proceedings of the Second ASEAN Symposium and Workshop on Sea Turtle Biology and Conservation*, Malaysia. 35–44.

Kapurusinghe. T. (2006). Status and Conservation of Marine Turtles in Sri Lanka. In Kartik Shanker and B C Choudhury editors. *Marine Turtles of the Indian Sub continent*. pp. 173–187.

Kapurusinghe, T., Ekanayake, L., Saman, M.M., and Rathnakumara, D.S. (2008). Community based marine turtle conservation in Kosgoda, Sri Lanka: nesting results from 2005 to 2007. *TESTUDO, 6 (5)*: 40–47.

Kruger O. (2005). The role of ecotourism in conservation: panacea or Pandora's box? *Biodiversity and Conservation 14*: 579–600 DOI 10.1007/s10531-004-3917-4

Richardson, P. (1996). The marine turtle hatcheries of Sri Lanka: A TCP review and assessment of current hatchery practices and recommendations for their improvements. Unpul. *TCP report*. Turtle Conservation Project, 11, Madakumbura, Panadura, Sri Lanka.

Waylen, K. A., McGowan, P.J.K., PAWI Study Group and Gulland, E.J.M. (2009). Ecotourism positively affects awareness and attitudes but not conservation behaviours: a case study at Grande Riviere, Trinidad. *Oryx, 43 (3)*: 343–351.

25 Six Senses Hideaway, Ninh Van Bay, Vietnam

Where luxury meets sustainable tourism

Pascal Languillon*, Simon Milne**and Bui Thi Tam***

Six Senses: A leading eco-luxury brand in the hospitality industry

Six Senses Resorts & Spas (SSRS) is a luxury hotel management and development company established in 1995 which currently operates 16 resorts and 32 spas worldwide, with a strong focus on Thailand (7 resorts in 2010), Vietnam (3 resorts in 2010 and 2 more planned for 2012) and the Maldives (3 resorts). With headquarters in Bangkok, Thailand, the company does not usually own the physical properties, instead it offers consultancy, development and management services for resorts and spas operated under its Six Senses brand. Six Senses branded resorts employ around 4,000 employees and accommodate around 400,000 guests per year. For the past 15 years the company has based its marketing on the idea of 'intelligent luxury', presenting the image of exclusive eco-resorts which attempt to integrate luxury and environmental responsibility.

The name of the company comes from the desire to craft 'an overall experience that is absorbed by all the human senses with consistency and harmony between what is seen, touched, heard and smelt' (Six Senses, 2010a). Furthermore, its core purpose is 'to create innovative and enlightening experiences that rejuvenate guests' love of SLOW LIFE (Sustainable-Local-Organic-Wholesome-Learning-Inspiring-Fun-Experiences)'. Ideally involved with a resort project from the start, the company guides the development and assures that the brand spirit and values influence all facets of the project (Six Senses, 2010c).

*Research Officer, New Zealand Tourism Research Institute, Auckland University of Technology, Auckland, New Zealand

**Professor of Tourism and Director, New Zealand Tourism Research Institute, Auckland University of Technology, Auckland, New Zealand

***Dean of Faculty of Hospitality and Tourism, Hue University, Hue, Vietnam

SSRS resorts are generally located in pristine and rather secluded locations where the main appeal is the natural setting. With room prices ranging from US$300 to US$10,000 a night, the brand attracts honeymooners as well as the rich and famous. SSRS is internationally acclaimed for the quality and beauty of its resorts and spas. For example the chain was ranked 'best in the world' by Conde Nast Traveller readers in 2000 and 2008, and the Evason Ana Mandara was voted Vietnam's leading resort in 2009 (World Travel Awards). The company is equally praised for its social and environmental ethos, claiming the Tourism for Tomorrow Awards in 2007 (World Travel & Tourism Council), among others.

The SSRS marketing strategy revolves around public relations with a focus on media exposure in which the group's environmental practices receive a lot of attention. For instance, the company declared that it wants to become the first in the world to be 'decarbonising' by 2020, through the implementation of programs that result in a net absorption of CO^2. Green living appears to be more than a slogan for Sonu and Eva Shivdasani, the founders of the company: 'The challenge we have at Six Senses is to take people luxuriously back to nature, to show that natural harmony with the environment and luxury can work hand in hand', says Sonu Shivdasani (Elite Traveler, 2010). Wong (2006, p. 2) notes that 'Six Senses has internalized its sustainability mission in virtually all aspects of the business from its organizational structure to its staff and programs'.

The corporate social responsibility team (called 'Social & Environmental Conscience' within the company) works to develop policies, strategies and procedures to assist the various resorts and spas to improve their social and environmental performance. At the property level, almost all resorts have an employee who is specifically dedicated to leading sustainability initiatives. At the corporate level, a team oversees all of the sustainability programs and initiatives. Six Senses take a holistic approach to sustainability and has identified ten key areas for its operations: Energy Management, Water Management, Waste Management, Biodiversity (Restoration and Preservation), Chemical Management, Air Quality, Responsible Purchasing, Mobility, Stakeholder Engagement, Health & Safety and Wellness. Each property has to endeavour to improve performance in these areas using indicators developed by EarthCheck Benchmarking, one of the leading eco-labels in the hospitality industry. Six Senses' environmental performance is constantly measured and evaluated, as daily monitoring (e.g. electricity metres, water metres, weighting of waste) are recorded. Monthly data from all properties are then sent to the head office and compared, and external audits make sure that resorts comply with EarthCheck benchmarking.

Six Senses has also established a Social and Environmental Responsibility Fund (SERF) that receives 0.5% of the total revenue of the company in order to fund various activities in and around the resorts. Currently, this program contributes about 500,000 US$ annually to various causes, with a substantial budget to support institutions and NGOs which develop best practice activities. Another significant initiative is the Six Senses Carbon Offset Program (2010b) which is designed to offset the carbon footprint of clients' flights as well as all emissions arising from resort operations and staff travel. The company calculates the CO^2 emissions by asking guests where they have travelled from, and then for certain resorts contributes approximately 2 per cent of its room revenue to carbon offset payments run by the Converging World, an NGO which funds wind turbines in the Indian Ocean in order to provide clean energy to local communities. In addition, a reforestation project, Six Senses Fragrant Forest, has been established in northern Thailand. Finally, Six Senses' clients are involved as much as possible in the sustainability process, as a 'Little Green Book' is provided in each room to educate guests on resort environmental practices and to help them become more responsible travellers.

The company provides a very interesting example of a hospitality brand that has managed to become both profitable and sustainable. The chapter now investigates the case study of the Six Senses Hideaway Ninh Van Bay resort in Vietnam to examine how these global approaches are implemented at a local level. The following discussion is based on a review of company documents and web content and is complemented by in-depth interviews and correspondence with the manager of Social and Environmental Conscience for Six Senses.

Case study: Six Senses Hideaway, Ninh Van Bay, Vietnam

Six Senses currently operates three resorts in Vietnam, with two other developments under way.

After introducing the opportunities and threats of tourism development in Vietnam, this section presents the case study of the Six Senses Hideaway Ninh Van bay resort, located just a short boat ride away from Nha Trang City.

Effects of tourism development in Vietnam

After decades of war, communism and trade embargos, Vietnam opened its doors to the world in 1994. It has therefore only recently emerged as a safe and attractive destination in the eyes of foreign tourists. The country is blessed with a wide array of natural and cultural sites of interest throughout the country and these have led to international tourism arrivals increasing rapidly from 2,355,000 in 2001 to 4,253,740 in 2008 (VNAT, 2010). The Vietnamese are also discovering their own country, with domestic tourism estimated to reach 25 million tourists in 2008, with annual increases of up to 15 to 20%.

Tourism revenues in Vietnam have quadrupled in 10 years, and they represented approximately 5% of the GDP in 2009 (VNAT, 2010). Consequently, it is not surprising that the number of hotel rooms has almost doubled in the last 5 years, from 122,144 hotel rooms in 2005 to 215,000 in 2009. The development of tourism in Vietnam has created a boom in newly built resorts across the country. According to the real estate advisory and management company CB Richard Ellis (2009), many tourism projects worth several hundred million dollars are currently being implemented in Vietnam. For instance a 4.2 billion-dollar resort and casino strip is currently being developed near southern Ho Chi Minh City (Ho Tram Strip, 2010).

Nha Trang in the province of Khanh Hoa is undoubtedly one of Vietnam's best known 'beach destinations'. With approximately 350,000 inhabitants (Nha Trang Travel, 2010), Nha Trang is a vibrant beach town that offers plenty to keep tourists occupied. The area is famous for its white sand beaches and unique rock formations (Figure 25.1). Its warm turquoise waters teem with life, making it a perfect place for snorkelling or scuba diving. The region is thought to have received 1.6 million international arrivals in 2008 (Khanh Hoa Provincial Committee, 2009). The rapid tourism development in Nha Trang and Vietnam has provoked some criticism from environmental organizations and academics as unmanaged development aggravates the danger of pollution and the destruction of natural resources (Bui, 2009).

As a local environmentalist notes (Vietnam Economic Times, 2007):

> *According to statistics from several sources, most tourism projects in Vietnam have not had positive effects on the local environment. The main reason is that the locals, who are the true owners of the tourism destination, have not been given the knowledge or skills needed to protect their environment when they take over as managers.*

Figure 25.1 The Nha Trang region is famous for its spectacular landscapes
Source: Kiattipong Panchee, sixsenses.com

The Vice Chairman of the Khanh Hoa People's Committee, Nguyen Chien Thang, adds (*Vietnam Economic Times*, 2007):

> *People encroach on the sea to build hotels and entertainment complexes and the increase in tourists has resulted in an increase in traffic that has also contributed to the pollution in the province. If effective measures are not put into place to manage these issues, the province's maritime environment will soon be destroyed.*

Following the 2003 designation of Nha Trang Bay as one of the 30 'Most Beautiful Bays in the World' (World Bays, 2003) awareness of environmental issues has played a more important role in the region. Nha Trang Bay retains some of the few intact coral reefs in south central Vietnam, with some of the highest biodiversity on Earth (over 350 species of hard coral from a total of 800 species in the world). In 2002, a Marine Protected Area was established in Nha Trang Bay with the support of the International Union for Conservation of Nature (IUCN) in order to protect this fragile and valuable environment. A local journalist notes that (Lew, 2010):

> *Green-minded initiatives, started by local government, local organizations or international NGOs, are becoming more commonplace in the tourism industry. There is definitely reason to hope that Vietnam's natural areas will become resources for the eco-tourism industry, not casualties of the country's astonishing economic development.*

The Six Senses Hideaway Ninh Van Bay Resort

The Six Senses Hideaway Ninh Van Bay resort sits on Ninh Van Bay, a peninsula north of Nha Trang with beautiful rock formations overlooking the South China Sea, a white sand beach and soaring mountains behind. The resort can only be reached by boat, some 20 minutes away from the hustle and bustle of Nha Trang City. It is composed of 58 private villas with luxurious amenities including outdoor plunge pools, floating terraces and wine cellars. With an average room rate of US$681 per night (TripAdvisor, 2010), the resort charges a premium price. Opened in November 2004, the resort is ranked best hotel in the Nha Trang region on Tripadvisor.com (2010). Client comments on this website include 'it really is perfection all round', 'this is the ultimate resort in eco luxury', and 'we have travelled around the world, but we have never been in this mixture of nature, luxury, elegance and simplicity'.

Six Senses manages the resort, but the property is owned by a Vietnamese company, Ninh Van Bay Travel Real Estate Joint Stock Company (NVT), which has recently been listed on the Ho Chi Minh Stock Exchange. This company is planning to develop other eco-luxury resorts in Vietnam (NVT, 2010). NVT announced that the company may reach pre-tax profit of 75 billion dong (approximately 4 million US dollars) in the first six months of 2010, mostly from selling villas in the upcoming Six Senses Saigon River resort complex and from selling tourism services in Six Senses Ninh Van Bay resort (*Vietnam Business News*, 2010).

Six Senses took a holistic approach to environmental sustainability when planning the resort in the early 2000s. As with every new Six Senses project, an environmental management plan was drawn up for both construction and ongoing operations. Responsible design was a priority early on. The architectural style embodies the traditions of Vietnam and takes full advantage of the setting. The reception and dining pavilions are classic Vietnamese structures which were transported across the water and assembled at the site. Wood and ylang ylang construction blends in with the native vegetation, where as the 'water villas' infinity pools are sculpted into the basalt boulders (Figure 25.2). Nature is integrated both functionally and inspirationally in the indoor and outdoor living spaces. Each unit features thatched roof, timber beams and dried palm leaves lining the ceiling. All building materials came from sustainably managed forests and where possible sourced locally.

The building process for the Ninh Van Bay resort was as eco-friendly as possible, with no plastic, chemicals, or paint used during its construction. All elements of the design were seriously reviewed with consideration for the impact on the environment both locally and globally. Local bamboo was used for fences and

Figure 25.2 Water villas are designed to blend into the rock formations
Source: Kiattipong Panchee, sixsenses.com

wall cladding. All the wood used in construction came from a sustainable renewable source, with the majority being recycled wood. Woven baskets, wooden pencils, as well as day beds and chairs covered with natural fibre set the interior atmosphere. Al fresco bathrooms and open-air living rooms add to the feeling of being one with nature, but also mean natural ventilation instead of air conditioning, and thus energy and cost savings for the resort (Figure 25.3). All three on-site restaurants are also naturally ventilated.

Other initiatives to reduce energy consumption include equipping guests with rechargeable torches to bring along when walking around the resort at night, thus minimizing the need for garden lighting. Additionally, all lights are turned off for one hour during the monthly 'Slow Life Hour' in order to raise awareness about climate change, enabling guests to dine by candlelight while the resort saves energy.

Water management is another priority at the resort. Water has to be secured and protected from contamination early on, particularly in this environment where the water supply is vulnerable. With an estimated 250 days of sunshine per year, the Nha Trang region is quite dry, and Ninh Van Bay, being isolated, does not have any public water supply. There was therefore a need to create a self-sufficient water supply, and the resort has its own rainwater collection reservoir and groundwater deep wells. Great care is taken to avoid any environmental concerns such as saline intrusions caused by over pumping groundwater.

Figure 25.3 Open air rooms mean no air-conditioning
Source: Kiattipong Panchee, sixsenses.com

The construction of a waste water treatment plant of very high standards was also of paramount importance. The treated water is recycled and used for garden irrigation. Water saving measures include the installation of water saving shower heads and taps and dual flush toilets. Unlike most luxury resorts in the world, bed linens and towels are not washed each day unless clients request it. The resort also built its own drinking water plant on the site, and has banned all water plastic bottles which would otherwise generate waste and carbon emissions created by their transport. Six Senses recognizes the value of waste from construction (for instance unused building materials, pieces of wood, etc.) and consequently recycles this as much as possible for furniture and building repair. Bathroom amenities such as soap, shampoo, conditioner and body-lotion are in ceramic dispensers instead of plastic containers. It also strives to minimize non-biodegradable waste by use of natural products.

Vegetation was left as much as possible untouched and only native plants were used for the few planted areas. Sonu Shivdasani, CEO of Six Senses, explained in a recent interview (Small, 2010):

> *We have ensured our guests are exposed to the environment they are in and that they also benefit from this environment. You don't really need to have tropical hardwoods. You can have plantation teak or bamboo. A lot of our restaurants have sand floors*

An additional company concern is to reduce the use of harmful chemicals as much as possible. Most of cleaning products used at the resort are biodegradable. Colourful day bed linens are made with natural dye instead of chemicals. The spa also only uses natural or organic products, with an emphasis on local treatments and products. In order to reduce carbon emissions, guests are given bicycles to get around the property. Electric-powered buggies are used by staff and clients when necessary. Fuel-efficient engines power the resort boats.

The environmental impact of industrial agriculture is now well documented (Horrigan, Lawrence, & Walker, 2002) and includes a loss of biodiversity and unsustainable water management as well as the consumption of large amounts of energy to grow and also transport produce, the so-called food miles (MacGregor & Vorley, 2006). In developing nations like Vietnam, it is also critical to generate positive economic outcomes for the poor by using local produces in hotel restaurants (Tam, Milne, & Tinh, 2010). To ensure sustainable practices, the three main principles of the Six Senses food policy are therefore to source organic produce, local food and to compost food waste. At Ninh Van Bay, a herb and vegetable garden provides fresh organic food for the guests. Not only does this reduce food miles, it also produces healthier and tastier food. The purchasing department also has a policy to avoid items that have unnecessary packaging, and to exclude food products from menus that are unsustainable such as shark, blue-fin tuna or caviar. Local suppliers are used as much as possible, and this responsible purchasing rule is argued to have a positive social and economic impact on the surrounding communities.

Stakeholder engagement is a cornerstone of the Six Senses' social responsibility policy. Nearly all (98 per cent) of the employees of the Ninh Van Bay resort are Vietnamese, thus considerably reducing the repatriation of wages and salaries often observed in luxury hotels located in the developing world (Chok, Macbeth, & Warren, 2007). The resort also collaborates with local academic institutes such as the Nha Trang University and the Khanh Hoa Culture and Art College and gives students the opportunity to gain work experience through internships. Some of these young people end up with a job at the resort after graduation. Staff facilities are of a good standard, and employees are served healthy food. Employee salaries are higher than the average salaries in Vietnam for equivalent positions, and the company provides additional benefits such as transportation, accommodation, meals, and training. The monthly mandatory beach and reef cleaning enables staff members to practice an eco-friendly activity. Guest activities include many water sports such as kayaking and scuba diving, but jet-skis were banned from the resorts as they are noisy and polluting. Guests are also encouraged to recycle their waste, to visit the herb garden, and to give feedback on the environmental policy of the resort.

Obstacles encountered

Implementing a responsibility policy is always a learning process and it is rare to 'get it right' without committing mistakes. Although already very comprehensive in comparison to other resorts in Vietnam, the green policy at Ninh Van Bay could go even further, but there are obstacles that prevent it from reaching its full potential. One major challenge identified by Six Senses at Ninh Van Bay is the management system under which the brand operates. The company operates the resort but reports to Vietnamese property owners who do not necessarily have the same priorities and values when it comes to sustainability. Whereas in almost all Six Senses resorts there is either a part-time or full-time employee dedicated specifically to sustainability issues, this is not the case at Six Senses Hideaway Ninh Van Bay simply because the owners do not want to pay for this position.

Another example of divergence between brand aspirations and resort reality is energy management. Being off the national electric grid, the resort has to produce its own electricity. It is usual for Six Senses resorts to use renewable energy sources such as wind power, solar panels, and biodiesel. Such installations do not however exist at Ninh Van Bay because the investors went with the short-term costs of this investment rather than their long-term benefits. This conflicting vision between property owners and property managers brought some environmental initiatives to a standstill as some trade-offs were inevitable. Six Senses believes that a sustainability-based business model is the right business model, as environmental responsibility also saves on resort operating costs. However despite the brand rationale and the associated marketing benefits, bringing its property investors onboard does not always prove easy.

Another obstacle to further implementing environmental practices is the difficult access to clean technology in a developing nation like Vietnam. The cost of installing efficient renewable energy devices is higher in Vietnam than for instance Europe and China where the major manufacturers are based. With the added bureaucracy inherent to post-communist countries, access to sustainable energy is still complicated in Vietnam (Clancy & Kooijman, 2006). The SSRS manager interviewed notes that 'it is also difficult to keep up with the constant technological advances, and a resort planned a few years ago already seems outdated in terms of energy management the day it opens to the public'.

Other threats that the company has recently faced include the concomitant global financial crisis and political turmoil in Thailand, a country where most Six Senses resorts and the company headquarters are located. These events have strongly impacted the company economically. The drop in business has resulted in fewer funds being available for social and environmental activities, in line with what has been observed for companies around the world during the financial crisis (Marcela, 2009).

Gaining competitive advantage through sustainability

Six Senses has learned many lessons from the development of the Six Senses Hideaway Ninh Van Bay resort. Environmentally friendly practices generally require capital expenditure which often results in some reluctance in undertaking these as they are seen as a potential source of decreased profits in the short term (Bohdanowicz, 2006). Some investors in the resorts managed by Six Senses do not necessarily share the view that eco-friendly development may be used to differentiate the resort and gain a competitive advantage. However the Six Senses corporate team strongly believes that 'eco-friendly practices will offset initial costs due to increased efficiency, additional guests and the possibility to charge a premium' (Oines & Assenov, 2005), and has decided to improve the resort development guidelines. SSRS has updated its management agreements to make sure that its brand ethos is preserved and not dependent on investors' desires and constraints. The company is moving toward a more proactive approach, and developing a more comprehensive social and environmental proposal for each new planned resort.

Six Senses has entered into an agreement with the Ninh Van Bay Travel Real Estate Joint Stock Company for the management of two new luxury resorts in Vietnam: Six Senses Saigon River, which is located in Dong Nai Province, and scheduled to commence operations by the fourth quarter of 2011, and Six Senses Phu Quoc, located in Kien Gang Province, which is envisaged to open at a later date. Due to the updated management agreements, these resorts will have stronger environmental practices than the Ninh Van Bay resort: 'We learnt a lot from building the other resorts, and we have developed a lot of green techniques, so we are taking all the best features of those and putting them in our new resorts', summarizes Sonu Shivdasani (Small, 2010). The Ninh Van Bay resort will also be greened further during a second phase of development due to start in late 2010 (NVT, 2010).

The long-term viability of a company correlates with its ability to adjust to the needs of the market. While hotels might hope to reduce the costs of their

environmental and social policies during a recession, the consumer demand for
eco-luxury experiences is rising (Languillon, Zei, & Kate, 2009). To gain a
competitive advantage over time, it is therefore important to maintain a sustainability focus. Arnfinn Oines (personal communication, May 31, 2010) concludes:
'The current global financial crisis has changed some of the mentalities in the
hospitality industry, and more investors turn to Six Senses because of its eco-
luxury stance than ever before. The road to sustainability is long but worth all the
hard work: Having a sustainable hospitality business is the best way to increase
profitability and guest satisfaction'. This view is in line with the findings that
companies focused on sustainability outperformed their peers by 15% during the
first year of the financial crisis (A.T. Kearney, 2009). Further research is needed
to evaluate how eco-luxury brands can gain a competitive advantage in a post-
crisis world.

References

A.T. Kearney. (2009). *Green Winners, the performance of sustainability-focused companies during the financial crisis.* Retrieved 22 April 2010, 2010, from http://www.
atkearney.com/images/global/pdf/Green_winners.pdf

Bohdanowicz, P. (2006). Environmental awareness and initiatives in the Swedish and
Polish hotel industries—survey results. *International Journal of Hospitality
Management, 25*(4), 662–682.

Bui, D. T. (2009). *Tourism industry responses to the rise of sustainable tourism and
related environmental policy initiatives: the case of Hue City, Vietnam* (PhD thesis).
Auckland University of Technology, Auckland.

Cb Richard Ellis. (2009). *Nha Trang Market View 2009.* Retrieved 25 May 2010, 2010,
from http://www.cbrevietnam.com/news/Nha%20Trang%20MarketView%202009
%20-%20W.pdf

Chok, S., Macbeth, J., & Warren, C. (2007). Tourism as a tool for poverty alleviation: a
critical analysis of 'pro-poor tourism'and implications for sustainability. *Current
Issues in Tourism, 10*(2), 144–165. doi:10.2167/cit303

Clancy, J., & Kooijman, A. (2006). Enabling Access to Sustainable Energy, a Synthesis of
Research Findings in Bolivia, Tanzania and Vietnam. *EASE Synthesis Report.*

Elite Traveler. (2010). *Leaders in Luxury.* Retrieved 15 April 2010, 2010, from http://
www.elitetraveler.com/leaders_detail.html?lid=56&p=8

Ho Tram Strip. (2010). Retrieved 14 June 2010, from http://www.hotramstrip.com/

Horrigan, L., Lawrence, R. S., & Walker, P. (2002). How sustainable agriculture can
address the environmental and human health harms of industrial agriculture.
Environmental Health Perspectives, 110(5), 445.

Languillon, P., Zei, T. M., & Kate, O. B. (2009). *Ecochic* (Editions Didier Millet ed.).
Singapour

Lew, J. (2010). Retrieved 28 May 2010, from http://www.good.is/post/how-vietnam-is-
going-green/

MacGregor, J., & Vorley, B. (2006). Fair Miles? The concept of "food miles" through a
sustainable development lens. *International Institute for Environment and Development
(IIED).*

Marcela, M. (2009). Corporate social responsibility in an economic crisis: An opportunity for renewal. *Global Business and Organizational Excellence*, *29*(1), 50–60. doi:10.1002/joe.20298

Nha Trang Travel. (2010). Retrieved 12 May 2010, from http://www.nhatrangtravelonline.com/

NVT. (2010). *Projects in our pipeline - Ninh Van Bay Travel Real Estate joint stock Company*. Retrieved 14 June 2010, from http://www.ninhvanbay.vn/projects/projects-in-our-pipeline/six-senses-hideaway-ninh-van-bay-%E2%80%93-the-second-stage.aspx

Oines, A., & Assenov, I. (2005). *Competite advantage through developing environmentally friendly hotel resorts*. Forum proceedings, The Fifth Asia Pacific Forum for Graduate Student Research in Tourism. Faculty of Service Industries, Prince of Songkla University. Phuket.

Six Senses. (2010a). *Management Style*. Retrieved 14 June 2010, from http://www.sixsenses.com/About-Six-Senses/Management-Style.php

Six Senses. (2010b). *Six Senses Resorts & Spas Carbon Offset Programme*. Retrieved 2 June 2010, 2010, from http://www.sixsenses.com/Environment/Downloads/PDF/Six_Senses_Resorts_and_Spas_Carbon_Offset_Programme.pdf

Six Senses. (2010c). *Social and Environmental Conscience*, Retrieved 1 June 2010, 2010, from http://www.sixsenses.com

Small, S. (2010). *Eco-chic*. Retrieved 3 June 2010, 2010, from http://www.property-report.com/thailand-property-magazine.php?id=1755&date=0811

Tam, B. T., Milne, S., & Tinh, B. D. (2010). *Local linkages and pro-poor tourism: Food value chains in Hue, Vietnam*. Hue, Vietnam. Retrieved from http://nztri.org/sites/default/files/Food%20value%20chains%20Hue.pdf

Trip Advisor. (2010). *Nha Trang Hotels*. Retrieved 2 June 2010, 2010, from http://www.tripadvisor.com/Hotels-g293928-Nha_Trang_Khanh_Hoa-Hotels.html

Vietnam Business News. (2010). Retrieved from http://vietnambusiness.asia/business-and-stock-briefs-may-28/

Vietnam Economic Times. (2007). *Coastlines under threat from tourism industry*. Retrieved 28 May 2010, 2010, from http://english.vietnamnet.vn/travel/2007/07/723292/

VNAT. (2010). *Tourist Statistics*. Retrieved 27 May 2010, 2010, from http://www.vietnamtourism.com/e_pages/news/index.asp?loai=1&chucnang=07

Wong, S. (2006). *Responsible luxury*: Harvard Business School. Retrieved from www.sixsenses.com/Environment/Downloads/PDF/Six-Senses-Paper.pdf

World Bays. (2003). Retrieved from http://www.world-bays.com

World Travel & Tourism Council. (2007). *Tourism for Tomorrow Awards*. Retrieved 1 June 2010, 2010, from http://www.tourismfortomorrow.com/Winners/Previous_Winners_and_Finalists/Global_Tourism_Business_Award_/Six_Senses_Resorts_and_Spas/index.php

World Travel Awards. (2009). Retrieved 14 June 2010, from http://www.worldtravelawards.com/winners2008-4

26 Tourist destinations with planned interventions

The success of Kumily in Kerala, India

*Leena Mary Sebastian** and*
*Prema Rajagopalan***

Introduction

Nature-based tourism is increasing dynamically and the growth is largely concentrated on destinations with a high ecological significance. Destinations with ecological significance offer immense tourism opportunities and challenges simultaneously, and hence their sustainability should be ensured. The sustainable tourism paradigm advocates planned interventions with community participation to enhance positive impacts and minimize the negative impacts of tourism. However, the literature shows that the reality could be contradictory. This chapter explores the socio-economic and socio-cultural aspects of linking biodiversity conservation with tourism development in Kumily, Kerala.

Biodiversity Conservation in India

India, a country in South Asia, is one of the fastest growing economies in the world. Identified as one of the 17 mega-diversities of the world (Mittermeier, Robles Gil, & Mittermeier, 1997), it has more than 500 Protected Areas (PAs) (Banerjee, 2010), covering approximately 5 percent of its land area. Similar to most other developing countries, the communities residing within and nearby the PAs in India were largely dependent on PA resources for their subsistence and livelihoods. In the past, the regulation of common pool resources through village-based institutions alongside traditional beliefs about certain flora and fauna as sacred resulted in sustainable practices (Gadgil and Rao, 1994). However, the 'fortress-style' conservation approach implemented in the country both during the colonial era and post-independence tried to eliminate the human use of forest resources (Guha, 1983). The alienation of forest dependent communities from the PAs led to frequent conflicts between the PA authorities and local communities. Being the second most populated country in the world, the anthropogenic and

*Department of Humanities and Social Sciences, Indian Institute of Technology Madras, Chennai, India
**Department of Humanities and Social Sciences, Indian Institute of Technology Madras, Chennai, India

development pressures made biodiversity conservation daunting at PAs. In this context, the Government of India attempted to link biodiversity conservation with community development through the India Ecodevelopment project at seven PAs, including the Periyar Tiger Reserve in Kerala, South India (see Figure 26.1).

Tourism Development in Kerala

Owing to its outstanding accomplishments in terms of the social development indicators Kerala's development experience has gained wide international acclaim. However, the dismal performance of the economic sphere has led many critics to question the sustainability of the *Kerala model of development* (Heller, 2000). The state has been confronted with several development issues that could be mainly attributed to the limited prospects of the industrial sector, the stagnated growth in agriculture and traditional sectors, and the uncertainties facing the employment of expatriates in the Gulf countries (Netto, 2004).

In an attempt to alleviate low industrial development and the high incidence of unemployment in the state, conscious efforts were made to develop the service sector. In this context, tourism gained a prominence that has never existed before

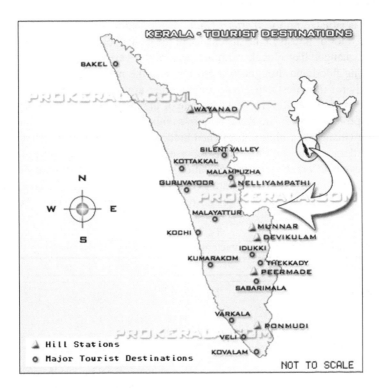

Figure 26.1 Kerala tourism map
Source: Prokerala.com.

and is now increasingly promoted as a strategy for the development of communities. The tenth Five-Year Plan (2002-2007) in India recognizes tourism as a leading economic sector in Kerala, and as having the potential with its natural resources to generate an income and employment through further tourism development.

With only 1.1 percent of the total geographical area of India, Kerala is justifiably known as *God's own country* since it sustains more than 24 percent of the plant species, 30 percent of animal species and 35 percent of freshwater species (Padmakumar, 2007). While nature forms the key tourist attraction in the state, environmental destruction and degradation are critical concerns in contemporary Kerala. The environmental issues apparent in Kerala are a consequence of deforestation in the past, ongoing paddy field conversions and the isruption of backwater ecosystems (Veron, 2001). In this changing scenario, the impact of tourism activities on the physical environment is worth exploring. The relevance accorded to tourism in the development of Kerala makes sustainable and responsible tourism practices unavoidable (Netto, 2004). However, regardless of the prominence accorded to tourism as a developmental strategy, key questions like tourism's contributions to local and regional development remain unexplored.

Ecological Significance of Kumily

Kumily is situated on the *Western Ghats* region and is famed for its forest. The multiple roles of forests in the sustenance of the gene pool, preventing undesirable climatic changes like global warming, performing various ecological functions, controlling flood and drought, soil erosion, and the maintenance of livelihoods, especially for the forest dependent communities, are well documented.

The Periyar Tiger Reserve (PTR) is one of the largest (777 sq. km) and most-visited protected areas in Kerala. It is a significant conservation unit in the Western Ghats and a highly threatened biodiversity hotspot. With its rich spectrum of flora and fauna, the PTR is representative of bio-geographic zone 5-B. It has seven different types of vegetation, with evergreen and semi evergreen forests constituting the major part (Vegetation Periyar Tiger Reserve, 2007). Kumily serves as the gateway to the reserve's tourism zone. The reserve has

Table 26.1 Socio-demographic characteristics of Kumily

Parameters	Kumily
Population	33,722
Sex ratio	952: 1000
Literacy rate (in %)	83.63
Households below poverty line (in %)	57.48
Scheduled caste population	7,539
Scheduled tribe population	1,787
Major occupations	Agriculture; animal husbandry; quarry; daily wage labour; Tourism

Source: Panchayat level statistics Kerala (Department of economics and statistics, Government of Kerala, 2006).

around 2000 recorded plant species, of which 26 percent are endemic to the region and 7.5 percent threatened. PTR has 62 species of mammals including a tiger population of 40, 320 species of birds, 45 species of reptiles, 27 species of amphibians, and 38 species of fishes. Tiger (*Panthera tigris*) is an umbrella species and the conservation of tiger population would naturally result in the conservation of a large number of plants and animals.

Tourism at Kumily and the India EcoDevelopment Project

Tourism activities at Kumily are centered on the Periyar Tiger Reserve (PTR). Kumily's emergence as a prominent international tourism destination is closely associated with a planned intervention at the PTR. Since its inception, PTR was confronting a series of conservation issues due to poaching, sandalwood smuggling, marijuana cultivation, illegal tree felling, bio-mass dependence, and littering associated with Sabarimala pilgrimage and mass tourism activities (Kutty and Nair, 2002). Besides, frequent conflicts occurred between the Forest Department and the resource dependent communities, due to the traditional top-down conservation approach. The majority of the PTR fringe area inhabitants are financially marginalized and to a certain extent forest exploitation could be associated with the high incidence of poverty.

A key factor that initiated community involvement in tourism at Kumily was the multi-state India Ecodevelopment Project (IEDP), funded by World Bank and Global Environment Facility. The PTR intervention spanned 1996-2001. The main objective of the intervention was biodiversity conservation by reducing negative human interactions on PTR through participatory conservation strategies and alternative livelihoods (Ohrling, 2001; Kutty and Nair, 2002; Thampy, 2005). Village Eco Development Component (VEC) has been the key strategy under the IEDP, and 55% of the total project cost was allocated to it (Gurukkal, 2003).

The target group of the intervention was financially marginalized fringe area inhabitants. To attain the project objectives at the village level, Ecodevelopment Committees (EDCs) with income generating and welfare functions were constituted. While the Ecodevelopment Committees were varied in their activities, the members of a particular EDC shared similar circumstances and interests. From each household, two adults (of which one would be a woman) were envisaged to become EDC members. The seed money was utilized for diverse purposes such as organize capacity building programmes, to initiate alternative livelihoods, repayment of EDC members' debts to moneylenders, and also to provide loan to EDC members. The EDC function through an elected seven-member executive committee. Though the project was over in 2001, and the *Periyar Foundation* was constituted to sustain and monitor the eco-development activities.

The Socio-Economic Impact of Tourism

Worldwide, tourism is a highly preferred development strategy owing to its socio-economic benefits. Its proponents cite various benefits such as foreign exchange earnings, employment generation, enhanced living standards, and regional development. Nonetheless, the economic benefits of tourism are not without their apprehensions. Scholars argue that tourism perpetuates the existing inequalities between the developed and developing countries, leads to economic leakages and dependency, and establishes new forms of colonialism. Studies also point to the seasonality, servile nature, and low remuneration associated with tourism employment. However, only a few have analyzed the socio-economic impacts of tourism in developing countries, which could be dissimilar from those of developed countries (Cukier, 1998).Mathieson and Wall, (1982) classify tourism employment within the following categories:

- **Direct employment**: Jobs that directly cater to the tourists or in the tourism industry
- **Indirect employment:** Generated in industries supplying to tourism
- **Induced employment**: Results when tourism income is spent in other sectors.

The following section explores the local community's opportunities to derive economic benefits from tourism activities in Kumily.

Community-Based Ecotourism at the Periyar Tiger Reserve

Community Based Ecotourism (CBET) ihas been one of the most effective and popular alternative livelihoods initiated during the PTR intervention. The prominent aspects of CBET are the involvement of marginalized sections like the Scheduled Caste (SC) and Scheduled Tribe (ST), the conversion of ex-poachers to nature protectors, habitat improvement in and around PTR, the eduction in ganja (*Cannabis sativa*) cultivation, and poverty reduction. The majority of the CBET programmes (around 14) are integrated within the reserve surveillance activities and therefore constitute a component of the conservation strategy. In accordance to the ecotourism ideology, CBET progammes are jointly run by the local community and Forest Department, and this contributes significantly to community welfare. Regardless of the demand, tourist participation in a particular programme is limited to minimize the impact on nature.

Generally, there is a trend towards adopting exorbitant pricing strategies for ecotourism activities as a measure to restrict the number of participants and thereby reduce negative impacts. However, such overpricing approaches will render ecotourism unaffordable and inaccessible for low-spending tourists. This in turn will give rise to concerns pertaining to the equity of access as suggested by Cohen (2002). Compared to ecotourism programmes offered elsewhere, CBET programmes at PTR are relatively low priced (Rs[1]. 50 to Rs. 5000 per person). These are affordable and accessible to larger number of tourists due to their low prices, thus minimizing equity of access concerns based on pricing.

A significant feature of CBET is the identification and development of tourism activities based on traditional knowledge and the capacity of the local community. The intervention was successful in transforming many forest offenders (e.g. poachers and smugglers) into nature protectors. The criminals joined the Forest Department subsequent to an agreement to withdraw the cases against them (Thampi, 2005). Based on their familiarity with the forest ecosystem, the ex-poachers now conduct the CBET program '*The Periyar Tiger Trial- Adventure trekking and camping*'. Drawing upon their indigenous knowledge, marginalized sections like ST and SC are also involved in a range of ecotourism activities.

The tribal people work under various capacities in Eco-lodges, the Tribal Heritage Museum and as guides, trackers and so on. Sustainable accommodation options such as ecolodges (bamboo grove), jungle inn and jungle camps are available within the tourism zone of the reserve (see Figure 26.2).

Bamboo Grove, for instance, is constructed using locally available natural materials like bamboo and grass, thus, making it eco-friendly. Built in the form of traditional tribal houses, this exemplifies the fact that nature and human beings can co-exist sustainably. In addition, it offers facilities for nature education. One major impact of such sustainable low-cost accommodation facilities is that it provides insights into the local community on how to engage in tourism activities.

The study revealed that the tribal people have a strong desire to be involved in tourism activities, particularly the CBET. Among the diverse livelihoods generated during the intervention, they consider CBET jobs as the most attractive. This preference has stemmed from a combination of factors like a better income, a greater social status, increased self-confidence, an opportunity to be in the forest

Figure 26.2 Bamboo Grove (Photo by author)

and the relative physical ease of the CBET jobs. The CBET jobs are innate to tribal people due to their link with the forests and hence are also enjoyable.

The tribal people believe that they are inseparable from the forest, the abode of their Gods and ancestors. On the other hand, they resettled in *Labbakkandam and* are not longing for a permanent return to the forest. At present, they are relatively well adapted to living outside the forest. They wish to reside in their present hamlet so that they will be 'civilized' and educated like the mainstream society. According to them, permission to use the forest for economic and cultural requirements while residing near Kumily town will enable them to achieve both progress and maintain forest links concurrently.

It has also emerged that the unemployment and poverty among tribals are steadily declining with tourism jobs. Those employed in CBET mentioned that they could obtain loans from the welfare fund. Such services assist them in coping with emergencies without depending on local money lenders. Tribal people also talked about how the intervention has rescued them from the exploitation of money lenders and foul bidders. Prior to the intervention, almost all the land adjoining the tribal hamlet was mortgaged to money lenders in Kumily. Nevertheless, the tribal guides face occasional delays in receiving their salary. The tips provided by tourists (particularly international tourists) are of huge economic significance to the tribal guides and *compensate for the delays in receiving their salary.*

Another key change brought about by the intervention is on gender specific roles. Respondents mentioned that, earlier, tribal women rarely came outside their hamlet or communicated with outsiders. The awareness and capacity building programmes, and also the training in small-scale enterprises conducted during the intervention, have initiated empowerment among women. Additionally, respondents identified that there is enhanced interest in educating tribal children for future tourism jobs.

Nevertheless, CBET is not without concerns. One of the drawbacks of CBET pertains to the limited number of jobs it may generate. With the improved socioeconomic status of tourism guides in the colony, almost every tribal youth aspires

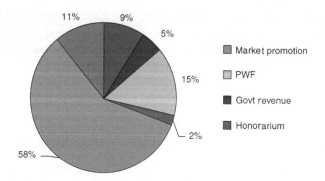

Figure 26.3 Benefit sharing of CBET financial assets
Data Source: Periyar Foundation

to a job within PTR. A few tribal respondents (3/30) mentioned their futile attempts and long waits for tourism jobs in PTR. Besides this, the *Paliyans* complained that the Forest Department (FD) showed favoritism towards the *Mannan*, as they get more jobs in PTR. However, most of the *Paliyans* perceive that this inequality in CBET jobs as due to their inferior education. Moreover, the *Paliyans,* who are introverts, refused CBET jobs initially. Elders observed that there was a decreasing influence on youngsters by traditional leaders within the tribal community. Earlier, the major decisions in the hamlet were taken by these tribal leaders. Now, such decisions are increasingly taken during Ecodevelopment Committee (EDC) meetings. Yet another issue emerging is regarding the power relations between Forest Department officials and the locals engaged in CBET. The tribals mentioned that a few officials (particularly those at lower level) consider them inferior and are authoritarian in their behaviour.

About 12% of the residents and local business entrepreneurs said that only the SC and ST communities were able to benefit from CBET. Apart from these concerns raised by a small section, stakeholders in general support CBET. The major success element according to the stakeholders is the involvement of tribal people in CBET programmes which provide for their socio-economic requirements through sustainable livelihoods (see Figure 26.3).

Socio-economic impact of the accommodation sector

Tourist accommodation in Kumily encompasses two major forms – hotels/resorts and homestays. First we will consider the economic impact of hotels/resorts on the local economy.

Hotels

Kumily has around 37 hotels/resorts, of which 16 are in the starred category. The destination has seven 4-star hotels. About 68% of the hotels are owned by non-locals, mainly from other parts of Kerala. Hotels are situated mostly around Thekkady and Kumily town, in close proximity to PTR. Besides, state-owned accommodation facilities are available within PTR. Accommodation services inside the reserve are provided by both Forest and Tourism Departments[2].

Sixty-nine of the residents pointed out that job openings accessible to the locals are typically temporary and on a daily wage basis. The residents' general lack of specific skills required by the hospitality sector is a major constrain from securing permanent jobs. Residents are employed as security guards, gardeners, waiters, house-keeping assistants and as traditional cooks (due to the demand for local cuisine): 61% of the residents and other local tourism businesses view hotel jobs as unattractive due to their low wage structure compared to other tourism jobs in Kumily. Residents mentioned that low-paid jobs are obtainable, but they are unenthusiastic about engaging in such jobs. This is reflected by the low rate (~15 %) of local employment in the hotel sector.

Table 26.2 Profile of Hotels/Resorts in Kumily

Total number of hotels/ resorts	37
No. of star hotels/ resorts	16 (43%)
Total number of employees	790
No. of male employees	621 (79%)
No. of female employees	169 (21%)
No. of skilled/ semiskilled employees	439 (56%)
No. of local employees	118 (15%)

Tribal respondents observed that hoteliers are keen on employing them. With a few exceptions, the tribals are not interested in the standard hotel jobs. The tribal women, who were employed in hotels, mostly left these jobs as they found the timings socially inappropriate.

An equally significant factor hindering the recruitment of the locals for permanent jobs is the trade union culture in Kerala: 27% of the residents perceive that the hoteliers are reluctant to employ locals as a precaution against issues such as employee strikes. Respondents cited that a leading hotel was forced to close down due to labour issues. The strike was triggered when the manager asked for an explanation from a local employee for being absent without taking formal permission for leave. It was also alleged that youngsters qualified in catering or hotel management do not get permanent jobs in the hotel sector, unless someone close to them is influential. Nonetheless, a few up-scale hotels employed qualified residents at their branches elsewhere. According to the residents such strategies will help prevent issues like employee strikes, as it would consume time for the employees to get involved with labour unions at a new place.

On the other hand, all the hoteliers (8/8) interviewed indicated their willingness to employ locals. Employee turnover is considered as a key challenge by (4/8) hoteliers as many quit shortly after the training period. Two out of the 8 hoteliers observed that local's take-up hotel jobs mainly for gaining experience. This will prepare them to start their own businesses such as homestays and small restaurants. The employee turnover could be associated with the opportunity to engage in other gainful tourism enterprises in Kumily; job insecurity due to the temporary nature of the employment; and fewer prospects for upward career mobility ensuing from the lack of hospitality skills. Further research is necessary to identify the specific causes and scale of employee turnover.

Conventions/business meetings are a major source of revenue for (3-4 star) hotels in Kumily, particularly during the off-season. Two out of the eight respondents pointed out that the earnings from convention tourists are often higher than those from regular tourists.

Homestay

'Homestay' is a general term that refers to a form of vacation that involves residing with a host family (Hamzah, 2008). The host is often recognized as an integral element of the homestay experience. The element of homeliness and intimacy of guest-host interaction distinguishes homestays from other forms of hospitality. Hamzah (2008) points out that homestays typically entail a guest's participation in the host's way of life. Many studies identify these as a significant part of small business firms. In these studies the emphasis is on the size of the property. Furthermore, these have also shown that, the smaller the size of the hospitality firm, the greater is its contribution to the local community (Andriotis, 2002).

In recent years, the Kerala government has conferred increasing prominence to the homestay sector. This took place under three main contexts. Firstly, to insti- tute the homestay sector as a strategy to bring tourism's benefits at the household level. The state has introduced several new schemes and incentives to encourage further local involvement in the homestay sector. Secondly, to overcome the shortages of tourist accommodation facilities in the state, following rapid tourism expansion. Whilst, Kerala has around 50,000 rooms providing accommodation, less than 10,000 rooms are of good quality. With the development of reasonably priced homestay accommodations the government anticipates resolving room shortages. Thirdly, homestays could play a central role in enhancing the tourist experience. Scholars have observed that contemporary tourism is gradually shift- ing towards experiential vacations rather than just consuming places and things. Under these circumstances, homestays are one of the most fascinating ways to experience Kerala.

Overall, the residents, Panchayat and Tourism Department officials opined that homestays are a highly preferred form of tourist accommodation in Kumily. Moreover, these are viewed as a primary income source, contributing significantly to the local econom: 77% of the residents perceive homestays as a much desirable and prestigious occupation. Residents from diverse socio-economic backgrounds (e.g. auto rickshaw drivers and architects) run homestays in Kumily.

All homestay respondents (7/7) in Kumily identified homestays as their primary occupation though they have other income sources such as agriculture. While economic benefits were stated as the major merit of homestays, social benefits (e.g. new relationships) were viewed as being equally significant. Both men and women were found as homestay operators in Kumily: 61% of residents mentioned that tourism enterprises like homestays and plantations assisted women with coming out of the traditional gender roles. Previously, women in Kumily seldom worked in the town, as it was perceived to be unsafe. But now,

Table 26.3 Homestays in Kumily

Category	Number of units
Diamond	2
Gold	13
Silver	23
Unclassified	35
Total	73

the residents pointed out, the town has become safer and women are progressively engaging in tourism jobs.

As indicated in Table 26.3, about 35 (47.9 %) of the homestays in Kumily are unclassified. Residents and Panchayat authorities observed that (poor) homestay operators often lack the capital to provide the required facilities for Government classification. Another concern was that though the tribals desire to run homestays, the Forest Department authorities do not permit them due to security concerns. The tribals stated that when other communities are capitalizing on tribal culture (by modeling homestays and restaurants as tribal huts) they are unable to gain from the opportunity.

Tourism–Agriculture Linkages

Kumily forms a part of the Idukki district, renowned as the *Spices District because of* its vast spice plantations. Agriculture is the primary occupation in Kumily. The majority of the residents are either marginal/small-scale farmers with landholdings below five hectares or landless agricultural laborers.

All stakeholders perceive positive linkages existing between tourism and agriculture. The nature of local produce might also be decisive in establishing tourism-agricultural linkages. To a certain extent, the opportunity to benefit from tourism has prevented the transformation of agricultural land for other purposes. The spices grown in Kumily are of high demand among the tourists. Accordingly, tourism generated new buyers for spices, particularly in a situation where its prices are unstable. Kumily has around 76 spice shops that are mostly dependent on tourists and Sabarimala pilgrims. The spice shops acquire produce (except for non-native spices like saffron) mostly from Kumily Grama Panchayat or nearby localities, thereby contributing to the local economy.

The tourism possibilities along with the low profitability of agriculture engendered innovative tourism products such as plantation tours and tea factory visits in Kumily. Plantations are visited by international and domestic tourists, and also students as part of their education. Typically,on a plantation tour, the tourists are taken around the plantation and the properties of various plants are explained by the family members or local tour guide. According to the plantation tour operators, tourists visit plantations mainly to experience traditional rural farming, unavailable in the places they come from. Besides, tourists are often curious to see the plants on which spices they use grow.

Nearly 18 families offer guided plantation tours: 77% of the residents perceive that plantation tours are more profitable than traditional agriculture. The majority (6/7) of the respondents initiated plantation tours as an endeavor to diversify their income. The plantation owners pointed out that agricultural diversification into tourism has noticeably increased their household income. In most (5/7 plantations) cases, income from tourism outweighs the returns from agriculture. In terms of job generation, good number plantation owners' (excluding small ones) has employed locals either permanently or temporarily. Similar to other tourism activities in Kumily, plantation tour is also seasonal. Consequently, the number of staff in a plantation varies. During tourist season, plantations hire locals fluent in foreign languages, thus, generating local employment. The land holdings in the plantations visited varied from 1.5 acres to 12 acres. To increase the attractiveness of plantations, the owners grow both endemic and exotic medicinal plants, vegetables and flowering plants along with spices. In all the plantations visited, agriculture was undertaken on a regular basis. Nonetheless, there is a probability that gradually these plantations might cease to be working farms demonstrating agriculture to the tourists.

Tourism-agriculture linkage in Kumily is not without its apprehensions. Conflicts occur between spice shops and plantation tour owners regarding the spice trade. Plantation tour operators mentioned that the tourists are keen to buy spices from plantations due to the belief that these are more *genuine* and *cheaper* than at spice shops. On the other hand, the spice shop owners (5/7) pointed out that the opportunistic behaviour of some plantation tour owners, such as selling fake ayurvedic[3] products, claiming false medicinal properties to sell spices, and the sale of inferior and overpriced spices, is having negative consequences on their business. In an attempt to safeguard their businesses, the spice shop owners distribute leaflets to tourists cautioning about plantation tours.

Given that a considerable fraction of tourists' spending is on food, the host communities could gain substantially by supplying local produce such as fruits and vegetables to the tourism sector (Torres, 2000). All the hotel respondents revealed that they procure food items from other places (mainly from Cumbum in Tamil Nadu) leading to economic leakages. Interestingly, the hoteliers indicated that they prefer to use locally-grown produce, if this is available. The present pattern of agricultural production in Kumily is dominated by cash crops, and consequently, crop diversification is essential in order to supply food items to the tourism sector. Local farmers (particularly small-scale farmers/women who are unable to benefit from opportunities like plantations tours or spices trade) have possibilities to benefit from tourism by growing and supplying agricultural produce to hotels, restaurants and other food outlets. The recent state intervention on *Responsible Tourism* is a move in this direction. Through this intervention, it is envisaged that all the hotels in Kumily will contribute to the local economy by purchasing locally produced organic vegetables, poultry and milk.

Whilst the India Ecodevelopment Project generally fostered pro-conservation attitudes among the residents, some respondents (13%) on the PTR fringes were concerned about increased crop raiding. The fringe area inhabitants associate the widespread crop-raiding to the increase in wildlife, following the intervention. For instance, the tribals are unable to grow cereals such as finger millet (*Eleusine coracana)* which supplied their children with the required nutrition. The tribals who practice organic farming perceive the inorganically grown produce they purchase from the market as inferior. According to respondents, the conservation measures restrict them from responding to crop raiding that has adverse consequences on household food security.

At present, the tribals cultivate cash crops like organic pepper that is less vulnerable to damage from wild animals. With the assistance of the Forest Department and a hotel in Kumily, the *Mannan* and *Paliyan* sell the organic pepper at a price higher than the market value. This initiative supports the livelihood of tribals who are unable to benefit from tourism (Franz and Hassler, 2010). These tribals will shortly join the *Oorali* (another tribal community residing in PTR) who export organically grown pepper to Germany.

Although the tribals recognize the organic pepper sale is beneficial, they (along with other fringe area inhabitants) pointed out that the authorities frequently disregard their complaints about crop raiding. However, the FD authorities maintain that the human-wildlife conflict mitigation strategies such as electric fencing, provided as part of the intervention, were not maintained by the community.

Additional Jobs Generated by Tourism

Apart from the above-mentioned jobs, tourism development also gave rise to informal and indirect jobs in Kumily. To illustrate this, the auto-rickshaw and taxi (car and jeep) drivers mentioned that they benefit significantly from tourism. Kumily has around 231 auto rickshaws, 55 car and 61 jeep drivers, who are largely dependent on tourism. Some drivers (2/5) offer guided tours in their auto-rickshaws.

Excluding the tribal guides in PTR, there are about 70 local tour guides, including three women. Moreover, residents observed a shift in traditional gender roles as women take up jobs in spice shops, homestays, and plantations.

Tour guiding is an occupation that is accorded high status among the locals; youngsters fluent in foreign languages aspire to working as guides. All stakeholders perceive that tour guiding offers employment prospects to local youth, regardless of their socio-economic backgrounds. The high regard towards guiding in Kumily is shaped by the recognition, admiration, and media coverage received by the tribal guides in PTR. The guides in Kumily work both independently and for travel agents. The seasonality of the ourism business is a challenge among the guides. To overcome seasonality issues, they are reliant on multiple income sources (e.g. agriculture). Guides mentioned that they save money during the peak season to meet their needs during the lean season.

In spite of the overall positive perception of the guides there were still a few concerns. For example, the spice shop owners pointed out that the majority of guides in Kumily adopted unhealthy business practices. According to these respondents, tour guides accepted excessive commissions from plantation owners, and assisted them in selling allegedly fake products. Other issues pertained to the lack of licenses and service professionalism. A guide training programme was organized recently by the Tourism Department addressing these issues.

The Socio-Cultural Impact of Tourism

First, we will consider tourism's influence on the dynamics of interactions among the residents, and then, between various stakeholders in Kumily.

Figure 26.4 Periyar Tiger Reserve: boat landing
    Source: own

Intra-community Interactions among permanent residents

In Kumily, 54% of the residents perceive that tourism has engendered significant changes in the interactions among the community members. The tribals, the *Mannan* and *Paliyan,* said that their involvement in tourism activities within Periyar Tiger Reserve (PTR) had enhanced their self-esteem, identity, and acceptability in mainstream society (see Figure 26.4). Besides this, the locals engaged in tourism felt that tourism fostered cooperation among the residents. In a few cases, business interactions among the locals had evolved into intimate relationships. Notably, the youngsters were said to have established new friendships across the social classes.

The tribals observed a change in the attitude among other residents towards them following the implementation of India Eco Development Project (IEDP). The two tribes, relocated from PTR to Kumily, are the descendants of aboriginals who came to Kumily from Madurai district in Tamil Nadu in the 17th century. Interaction between the tribals and other residents was minimal in the past. Previously, according to the tribals, the non-tribals considered them uncivilized, unclean, and as being easily fooled in their transactions. As they became associated with the Forest Department (FD) and obtained tourism jobs within PTR, the tribals gained respect from the locals. The tribals also acknowledged that, due to the better mathematical skills achieved through various capacity building programs during the intervention, they were not now cheated by the locals in transactions.

Nonetheless, the tribals mentioned that they disliked non-tribal residents visiting their colony. This was perhaps due to the history of exploitation by non-tribals or the tribals' desire to stay aloof from non-tribals. At the same time, they desired and encouraged more tourists to visit their colony for economic and social benefits. Therefore, the motive behind discouraging non-tribal residents in the colony may not be an attempt to stay isolated, but the fear of exploitation. Besides, as the tribal colonies are in the PTR fringes, the Forest Department has instructed them not to entertain non-tribals in the colony, to prevent illegal activities such as poaching.

Another concern was regarding the tensions between the long-term residents and the Kashmiri handicraft dealers. The opportunities and amenities from tourism attracted new residents into Kumily. The Kashmiri handicraft dealers, approximately 150 individuals, have settled here with their families for nearly a decade. Many have purchased their own houses and stay in Kumily for the greater part of the year. During off-season, the male members of the family visit their relatives in Kashmir. The native residents in Kumily consider Kashmiris as outsiders, as not belonging to the local community. However, the Kashmiri handicraft dealers live as a separate subpopulation within the community.

The conflict between Kashmiri handicraft dealers and the local community is caused by an amalgamation of social, economic and political factors. Most residents (72%) complained that the Kashmiris do not mingle with the locals to protect their business secrets. The Kashmiris and other residents have considerable cultural variations. For instance, language could be a possible impediment in establishing strong social relationships between the locals and Kashmiris.

In addition, the way the Kashmiris conduct business is also problematic in the eyes of the locals. When dealing with a potential client, the Kashmiri traders shut their door to minimize any possible distractions. According to the Kashmiris, this practice is part of their culture. This intensifies the widespread suspicion among the locals that the Kashmiris are involved with anti-national activities. An equally significant factor is Kashmiris' higher entrepreneurial proficiency in the tourism business. In Kumily, many stakeholders consider Kashmiris to be the most successful at tourism business.

Interactions among various stakeholders

In this section, we will look at the relationship among the various stakeholders. Following the intervention, the dynamics of social relations between the residents and Forest Department (FD) underwent significant transformations. The resolution of the longstanding conflict between the FD and fringe area inhabitants regarding forest usage was noteworthy. As part of conflict resolution, customary rights allowing the use of forest resources that are not detrimental to biodiversity conservation were recognized. Besides, the tribals are allowed to access to forest in order to perform ceremonies. This facilitates their nexus with the forest and also the continuity of tribal culture. Furthermore, the fringe area inhabitants were provided with alternative livelihoods which in turn reduced their forest dependence drastically.

Most (73%) of the tribal respondents stated that their relationship with the Forest Department has improved considerably. The tribals' perception of the new intimacy with Forest Department was reflected when they said '*we are like one family now*'. The Forest Department authorities also mentioned that they had a cordial relationship with the locals, particularly the tribals. All the Forest Department officials interviewed were content with the harmonious relationship they shared with the tribals. Nevertheless, some (2/5) tribal guides were concerned about a few recent undesirable changes occurring in the CBET. For instance, initially, the tribal guides, Forest Department staff and tourists used to have meals together during the trip. Now, the Forest staff are progressively avoiding the tribals sharing in meals, pointing out that the tribals would prefer to have their own cuisine. However, the tribal guides view this as a form of discrimination. A further concern was about the unequal power in the relationships between Forest Department staff and tribal staff. If ignored, these changes could have adverse implications on the group dynamics and the quality of the working relationships, jeopardizing the effectiveness of CBET.

The presence of dedicated Forest Department officials at PTR during the intervention was cited as a key factor which led to its success. However, the newly transferred officials lacked the sense of commitment towards IEDP and biodiversity conservation according to a few Forest Department staff. One Forest Official was annoyed about the frequent transfers of authorities in key positions. It is time consuming for the new officials to understand the field setting, local community and the staff in various programmes. Such time lag, according to him, might threaten the institutional continuity. Banerjee (2010) also argues that the enforced cyclic transfer of Forest Department Officials creates discontinuity and decreases the motivation for a long-term involvement.

Most stakeholders perceive that the *Periyar Foundation* is successfully continuing the networking among various stakeholders, even after the intervention period. The *Periyar Foundation* supports many local development projects technically and financially. For instance, the tribal houses were constructed through the Periyar Foundation, with financial assistance from the Panchayat. The tribals perceive that such an intervention has helped to avoid corruption at the Panchayat level, and has enabled the construction of better houses. However, the lack of coordination among the various Government Departments engaged with tourism development is a constraint. For instance, as noted by Hannam (2004), there are disagreements between Tourism and Forest Departments regarding control over tourism activities (e.g. boating in Periyar Lake) and benefits from tourism activities within PTR. According to a Tourism Department official, the Forest Department monopolizes tourism development in Kumily.

All the hoteliers opined that there was good cooperation among most stakeholders in Kumily. There are instances of collaborations between hoteliers and Forest Department leading to successful tourism ventures, benefiting the community. For example, a leading hotel in Kumily and FD jointly developed the

Bullock Cart Discoveries, a guided eco-friendly tour through the farmlands of Cumbum in Tamil Nadu. This rural tourism initiative is an attempt to rehabilitate ex-poachers from Tamil Nadu, who once posed a major threat to PTR.

In contrast, hoteliers pointed out that the Tourism Department is not undertaking any measures to further develop tourism. The views of Tourism Department about the hoteliers were dissimilar, as they consider the hoteliers to be supportive. There were also conflicts between unauthorized local tourist guides (who take tourists into the forest unlawfully) and FD authorities. The guides feel that the stringent conservational measures at PTR stand in the way of their livelihood.

Conclusion

This case study suggests that the India Ecodevelopment Project at Periyar Tiger Reserve (PTR) has instituted positive linkages between environmental conservation, tourism and community development. Rather than assuming that the fringe area inhabitants constitute an homogeneous entity, attempts were made to gain insights into community heterogeneity, intra-community dynamics, and divergent interests on the reserve. Another feature of the PTR intervention was the implementation of site-specific conservation measures based on the local socio-cultural and economic aspects, and the factors hindering conservation. For effective biodiversity conservation, mutual trust and cooperation among various stakeholders is inevitable. During the PTR intervention, substantial time and effort was devoted to eliminate mistrust, and attain genuine local support for conservation. The numerous environmental awareness campaigns conducted as part of the intervention raised knowledge about the significance of forest, encouraging pro-environmental behaviors among the residents.

The PTR experience emphasizes the need for institutional mechanisms such as the Eco-development Committees that can play a central role in promoting collective action towards eco-development. The monitory and non-monitory incentives fostered reciprocity and induced the fringe area inhabitants to act as a 'social fence' protecting the reserve. Though the intervention ended in 2001, interestingly, many of the conservation programs still continue. A major factor enabling the sustainability of eco-development activities is the Eco-development Committee involving forest dependent communities. Besides, the establishment of *Periyar Foundation* as a supporting institution is imperative to sustain desirable changes.

Most importantly, the intervention addressed the socio-economic concerns of marginalized social groups like the tribals by converting them into project beneficiaries. PTR held an advantageous position for Community Based Ecotourism (CBET) as the reserve was already popular among the tourists. Careful identification of alternative livelihoods such as CBET activities based on the tourism potential of the destination and also the skills of the local community is yet another merit of the intervention. CBET was successful in involving indigenous people and ex-forest offenders, resolving the long standing conflict between the locals and Forest Department (FD) authorities, creating financial mechanisms for community welfare and reserve protection, and enhancing biodiversity conservation within the reserve. The capacity building programs organized enhanced the capabilities and confidence of the residents to actively engage in tourism.

Given the vast range of locals benefiting from tourism, the local community has emerged as a key beneficiary of the tourism sector in Kumily. It is argued that the locals in Kumily were able to seize on the tourism opportunities as a result of the increased capacity and social capital following the intervention. The findings highlight the role of tourism in facilitating the diversification of Kumily's predominantly agrarian economy. All stakeholder groups recognize that the local community has achieved remarkable socio-economic benefits through tourism. Apart from CBET jobs, Kumily offers tourism opportunities such as homestays, spices shop, plantation tours and tour guiding. It is obvious that tourism has established strong linkages with other local economic sectors given that farmers, taxi and auto rickshaw drivers benefit considerably from tourism. Tourism has also enhanced social capital and effectuated upward social mobility of the locals, particularly the disadvantaged. Generally, all stakeholder groups perceive that tourism has enhanced local community wellbeing. The intervention was successful in instigating local participation, and thereby, allowed greater control of the tourism industry. This is evidenced by the number and the diversity of tourism jobs and locally-owned small-scale tourism enterprises.

While the improvement of relationships between the tribal residents and Forest Department is a remarkable achievement of the intervention, there are concerns regarding discrimination against tribal tourist guides. It is necessary to engage with the unequal power relations between the tribal guides and Forest Department staff (particularly those at lower level). The lack of coordination and collaboration between Forest and Tourism Departments is another issue that emerged from the study. Consequently, Kumily lacks a holistic tourism development approach. There is a need for strong policy links that would establish the conditions for an effective inter-department coordination to further advance tourism development sustainably.

Homestays are a much desirable tourism venture in Kumily. These have assisted in raising the local control and share from the tourism sector. On the other hand, local employment in hotels is largely confined to unskilled and semi-skilled jobs with relatively low wages. Nonetheless, hotels/resorts can contribute substantially to the local economy by improving the pay structure, employing more residents, and purchasing locally grown produce. Local communities in rural areas often have limited capacity to take advantage of the employment opportunities in the hotel sector. To enable the locals to benefit from such opportunities, it is imperative to enhance their generic employability by providing training in hospitality/tourism skills. Grama Panchayat authorities should take the initiative in forming effective partnerships between relevant government agencies, tourism businesses, academia, NGOs, and the local community itself, to mobilize resources and expertise, and organize vocational training programs in hospitality/tourism.

In addition, the demand for eco-friendly stationery products for convention tourism should be determined. Opportunities to supply stationery products (by agreement with hoteliers) would be a supplementary source of income for the local women. Adopting socially responsible measures to improve the residents' quality of life would also serve to create a more favourable position towards the hoteliers.

Spice trade and plantation tours offer immense potential for tourism-agricultural linkage in Kumily. However, the local self-government institution should play a stronger regulatory role to sustain this linkage. Standardizing the price of spices and plantation tours, and ensuring the quality of spices and plantation tour experiences (by providing scientific knowledge about plants) through monitoring schemes, could be a few suggestions in this regard. It is encouraging that Kumily Grama Panchayat has organized a few training programs on conducting plantation tours.

There is already an evident displeasure that the FD is ignoring crop raiding that has implications for the wellbeing of the poor. There is also an urgency to identify and resolve the factors which deterred the communities from maintaining mechanisms against wildlife damage. Based on the information and incorporating insights from various stakeholders (especially indigenous knowledge) the existing infrastructure should be modified and/or more efficient and acceptable mechanisms should be developed to mitigate human-wildlife conflicts.

Notes

1   Indian Rupees (INR); 1 INR = US$ 0.02)
2   As part of the Community Based Ecotourism, Forest Department runs *Bamboo Grove, Jungle Inn and Green Mansions* (Forest lodge at Gavi). Kerala Tourism Development Corporation operates *Lake Palace, Aranya Nivas and Periyar House.* As the name suggests, *Lake Place* is situated on an island in the Periyar Lake. Formerly, it served as a summer retreat to the King of Travancore.
3   Ayurveda is an ancient system of alternative medicine, originated in India. The treatment involves the use of various plants with medicinal properties. At present, Ayurveda is an inseparable aspect of wellness tourism in Kerala, and there is much demand for ayurvedic products among the tourists.

References

Andriotis, K. (2002). Scale of hospitality firms and local economic development-evidence from Crete. *Tourism Management, 23(4)*, 333–341.

Banerjee, A. (2010). Tourism in Protected Areas: Worsening prospects for tigers? *Economic & Political Weekly, 45(10)*, 27–29.

Cohen, E. (2002). Authenticity, Equity and Sustainability in Tourism. *Journal of Sustainable Tourism 10(4)*, 267–276.

Cukier, J. (1998). Tourism employment and shifts in the determination of social status in Bali. In G. Ringer (Ed.), *Destinations: Cultural Landscapes of Tourism* (pp.63–79). United Kingdom: Routledge Advances in Tourism.

Franz, M., & Hassler, M. (2010). The value of commodity biographies: integrating tribal farmers in India into a global organic agro-food network. *Area*, 42, 25–34.

Gadgil M ., & P. R. S. Rao (1994). A System of Positive Incentives to Conserve Biodiversity. *Economic & Political Weekly, 29(32)*, 2103–2107.

Guha, R. (1983). Forestry in British and post-British India: A historical analysis. *Economic & Political Weekly 18(44)*, 1882–1896.

Gurukkal, R. (2003). The eco development project and the socio-economics of the fringe area of the Periyar Tiger Reserve: A concurrent study. *Kerala Research Programme on Local Level Development*. Retrieved from http://www.krpcds.org/report/Rajangurukkal.pdf

Hamzah, A. (2008). Malaysian Homestays from the Perspective of Young Japanese Tourists: the Quest for Furusato. In J. Cochrane (Ed.), *Asian Tourism: Growth and Change* (pp.193–208). London: Elsevier.

Hannam, K. (2004). Tourism and Forest Management in India: The Role of the State in Limiting Tourism Development. *Tourism Geographies, 6(3)*, 331–351.

Heller, P. (2000). Social capital and the developmental state: Industrial workers in Kerala. In G. Parayil (Ed.), *Kerala: the Development Experience: Reflections on Sustainability and Replicability* (pp. 66–87.) New Delhi: Zed Books.

Mathieson, A., & Wall, G. (1982). *Tourism: economic, physical and social impacts.* New York: Longman.

Mittermeier R.A., Robles Gil P, Mittermeier C.G. (1997). *Megadiversity: Earth's biologically wealthiest nations*. Mexico City: CEMEX.

Mowforth , M. and I. Munt, (1998). *Tourism and Sustainability: A New Tourism in the Third World*, London: Routledge.

Netto, N. (2004). Tourism Development in Kerala. In B.A Prakash (Ed.), *Kerala's Economic Development: Performance and Problems in the Post-liberalization Period,* pp. 269–292. New Delhi: Sage Publications.

Ohrling H.S. (2001). From Environmental Exploiters to Enthusiastic Protectors? An insight to an award winning ecotourism programme in Kerala. *The International Ecotourism Society* URL: http://www.ecotourism.org

Padmakumar, K.G. (2007). Kerala the biodiversity hotspot. *Kerala Calling*, 27 (4), 40–42. URL: http://www.kerala.gov.in/kercalfeb07/pg40–42.pdf

Thampi, S.P. (2005). Ecotourism in Kerala, India: Lessons from the eco-development project in Periyar Tiger Reserve. *International Ecotourism Monthly*, 13. Retrieved from http://www.ecoclub.com/library/epapers/13.pdf

Torres, R. (2000). *Linkage between Tourism and Agriculture in Quintana Roo, Mexico.* (Unpublished doctoral dissertation), University of California, Davis.

'Vegetation', Periyar Tiger Reserve URL: http://www.periyartigerreserve.org/html/vegetation.htm

Véron, R. (2001). The "New" Kerala Model: Lessons for Sustainable Development. *World Development, 29(4)*, 601–617.

27 The development and promotion of guidelines for organic farms for sustainable tourism

*Nartsuda Chemnasiri**

Introduction

Thailand has recognized that the development of agriculture is a difficult process. As in many countries, unemployment and the number of landless laborers in Thailand have grown and real wage rates in agriculture have fallen. The government tried to solve this problem. Because Thailand has a great amount of income from tourism they have set up the idea of farms being agro-tourism tourist attractions. Many educators, researchers and specialists have advocated the idea. Agro-tourism is a kind of ecotourism, based on a philosophy of sustainable development. Tourists will learn about the way of life and culture of people living in communities through agro-tourism. Moreover, this is in accordance with the 8th and 9th national plans of economic and social development that emphasized the community strength for an adjustment and community participation in the development. (Aphirom Phomjanya & et al, 2003:1) The most important national strategy at present is to eliminate poverty, especially in rural areas.

Moreover, it needs community involvement in the development and operations of tourism. Another important feature is that a reasonable share of the revenues is enjoyed by the community. This type of tourism also maintains and respects the local culture, heritage and traditions. Often, community-based tourism actually reinforces and sometimes rescues these aspects. Community-based tourism also implies respect and concern for the natural heritage, particularly where the environment is one of the attractions.

Case study main section

Chiangmai Province is located some 700 km (435 mi) north of Bangkok, among some of the highest mountains in the country. The city stands on the Ping river, a major tributary of the Chao Phraya river. Prao is a district about 90 km far from Chiangmai city. There was a strong community involvement in organic farm

*Chandrakasem Rajabhat University, Bangkok, Thailand

development in Prao and there is also a strong support from government sectors in the community.

Objectives of the Study

This study has four main objectives:

1. Survey organic farms in Chiangmai for tourism
2. Study tourists' behaviors and the requirements of the agro-tourism area
3. Study the potential of organic farms for being agro-tourism tourist attractions
4. Propose development and promotion guidelines of organic farms for sustainable tourism.

Literature Review

Agro-tourism has two dimensions: one can be classified as a forward linkage, meaning that the agricultural sector is part of the destination's tourism appeal. In this context, it is of special interest to visitors and forms part of their itinerary. The other dimension involves a backward linkage whereby the agricultural sector provides the raw material for the food and beverage required by the hospitality industry. Certainly, before there can be any forward linkages we must develop the backward looking ones (Agricultural Information and Documentation System of the Americas, 2009). On the other hand, it is indicated that agro-tourism is an alternative activity in the rural development process. The concept of agro-tourism is a direct expansion of ecotourism, which encourages visitors to experience agricultural life at first hand. Agro-tourism is gathering strong support from small communities as rural people have realized the benefits of sustainable development brought about by similar forms of nature travel (Ecotourism directory, 2006).

Rural tourism, agrotourism and ecotourism have proved to be effective and efficient tools of sustainable development for economies in transition. The development of rural tourism, agrotourism, and ecotourism lead to sustainable economical development of the rural localities due to the multiplying effect of these activities. The positive influences on the environment, agriculture, transports, constructions, on the alimentation and processing industries and on the services from the most diverse fields are felt (GMO Project Concept, 2005).

Sustainable tourism is a tourism that is:

- long-lasting (economically viable in the long-term, planned and well managed, which implies avoidance of mass tourism and has low impact).
- environment friendly (adapted to the carrying capacity of the natural and cultural spaces, minimizing seasonal effects).
- diversified (in relation to the hinterland, adapted to the site's personality, based on local enterprises and avoiding total dedication to tourism).

- participatory (with the participation of the local towns and villages) (Mediterranean NGO Network for Ecology and Sustainable Development, 2007).

In Thailand, agro-tourism activities can be classified into six groups.

1. Product displays or demonstrations such as paddy seeds plots, agricultural steps of growing rice, and agricultural cultures in the past.
2. Agricultural activities with tourists' participation such as field ploughing, rice harvesting and fruit gathering.
3. Home stay: tourists stay overnight with farming families to learn more about their way of life.
4. Agricultural knowledge training: This training aims to provide both modern agricultural knowledge and the local wisdom of villagers, such as fruit preservation, making fruit and vegetable juice.
5. Agricultural products distribution such as flowers, fresh fruit, handicrafts, and preserved eggs.
6. Agricultural business offerings: Some tourists are business men and women who search for investing in new agricultural projects. Therefore, they may be interested in working together with local farmers to make money. For example, they could form a joint venture to process agricultural products.

Organic farming is a form of agriculture that relies on crop rotation, green manure, compost, biological pest control, and mechanical cultivation to maintain soil productivity and control pests, excluding or strictly limiting the use of synthetic fertilizers and synthetic pesticides, plant growth regulators, livestock feed additives, and genetically modified organisms (Wikipedia: The Free Encyclopedia, 2008).

The International Federation of Organic Agriculture Movements (IFOAM) is an international umbrella organization for organic organizations established in 1972. The primary goal of organic farming is defined as follows: 'Organic agriculture is a production system that sustains the health of soils, ecosystems and people. It relies on ecological processes, biodiversity and cycles adapted to local conditions, rather than the use of inputs with adverse effects. Organic agriculture combines tradition, innovation and science to benefit the shared environment and promote fair relationships and a good quality of life for all involved' (IFOAM, 2008).

Organic farming is labor- and knowledge-intensive whereas conventional farming is capital-intensive, requiring more energy and manufactured inputs (Strochlic and Sierra, 2007). Research studies are as follows.

The Organic Farming Research Foundation (2004) concluded that organic refers to agricultural production systems used to produce food and fiber. All kinds of agricultural products are produced organically, including produce grains, meat, dairy, eggs, fibers such as cotton, flowers, and processed food products. Organic farming management relies on developing biological diversity in the field to disrupt habitat for pest organisms, and the purposeful maintenance and replenish-ment of soil fertility. Organic farmers are not allowed to use synthetic pesticides or fertilizers. Some of the essential characteristics of organic systems include: design and implementation of an 'organic system plan' that describes the prac-tices used in producing crops and livestock products; a detailed recordkeeping system that tracks all products from the field to point of sale; and the maintenance of buffer zones to prevent inadvertent contamination from adjacent conventional fields.

Jamieson, Walter and Alix Noble (2000) indicated that 'Increasing evidence shows that an integrated approach to tourism planning and management is now required to achieve sustainable tourism. It is only recently that there has been a growing recognition of the importance of combining the needs of traditional urban management (transportation, land use planning, marketing, economic development, fire and safety etc.) with the need to plan for tourism.' They concluded that some of the most important principles of sustainable tourism development include:

- Tourism should be initiated with the help of broad-based community-inputs and the community should maintain control of tourism development.
- Tourism should provide quality employment to its community residents and a linkage between the local businesses and tourism should be established.
- A code of practice should be established for tourism at all levels – national, regional, and local - based on internationally accepted standards. Guidelines for tourism operations, impact assessment, monitoring of cumulative impacts, and limits to acceptable change should be established.
- Education and training programs to improve and manage heritage and natu-ral resources should be set up.

In earlier work, Pawinee Wachasitnirapai (2000) researched 'The potential and the problems of agro-tourism in Chiangmai Province', The results showed that the important factors for agro-tourism potential development were the availabil-ity of tourism specialists, tourism management, and community participation, respectively. Moreover, the government's tourism experimental projects lacked the necessary budget. Likewise, the royal projects which provided tourism activities for tourists encountered the following problems: lack of officers; diffi-culty in accessing tourist areas. Recommendations from this study were: 1) feasi-bility studies of the tourist areas should be done before tourisms development, 2) agro-tourism areas should be developed, 3) effective management and sustain-able tourism should be concerned, 4) a marketing index should be developed, 5) a comparison of the potential between Chiangmai province and the other prov-inces should be investigated, and 6) farmers' attitudes toward tourist management should be examined.

Ramate Promchat (2002) researched 'Participation of the Community in Agro-tourism Development: A Case Study of Ban Pong, Pa Phai Sub-district, San Sai District, Chiangmai Province.' The results of the study showed that the people in the community had a low degree of involvement in agro-tourism development in aspects of tourism resource management, services and marketing. Moreover, it was found that people with different ages and differences in the periods of living in the area, had significant differences in the involvement in agro-tourism development.

Nartsuda Chemnasiri (2007) looked at the 'Development guidelines of farms as agro-tourist attractions and an international learning center: A case Study in Chainat Province, Thailand.' Concerning the development guidelines of an agro-tourism area and tourists' attraction, the results showed that there should be: 1) a training activity and knowledge transfer regarding services and agro-tourism management for farmers or farmers' housewives; and 2) a master plan for general tourism management to be developed by tourism entrepreneurs in cooperation with all concerned groups. Concerning the development guidelines of an international learning center, the results of the study suggested that there should be: 1) a strong coordination for the cooperation of all concerned groups; 2) training provision on knowledge transferred and English conversation; 3) development of short course training curriculums including contents, tools, study periods, number of students, tuition fees, etc; and 4) publishing agro-tourism information, in both the off-line and on-line media.

Research Methodology

This study utilized quantitative and qualitative research methodology. It included the following :

1. Participants

1. Two farm leaders in Prao District and one farm leader in Doi saket District, Chiangmai Province
2. Groups of farmers' housewives, twenty-five in Prao District and five in Doi saket District, Chiangmai Province
3. Three hundred and fifty Thai tourists

4. Instruments

The instruments in this study were comprised of semi-structured interviews and a set of five-point Likert rating scale questionnaires ranging from strongly agreed, agreed, were uncertain, disagreed and strongly disagreed. Interviews were conducted with the owners of organic farms to elicit the attitudes of potential farms to be agro-tourism tourist attractions, whereas questionnaires aimed at obtaining tourists' opinions about their interests, behaviors and requirements in agro-tourism. The questionnaires consisted of two parts. The first parts asked about the respondents' personal information and the second part contained seven statements asking for the respondents' opinions.

5. Data Collection

Data collection was carried out between April and August 2008 with the following procedures.

1. Farms in Chiangmai were randomly selected from the list at the Agricultural Extension Department and Ministry of Agriculture and Cooperatives.
2. The selected farms were explored in search of their potential and qualification for being agro-tourism attractions such as the availability of attractions, basic facilities, environment and accessibility, etc.
3. Interviews with the owners of organic farms in Doi saket and Prao District were conducted.
4. Questionnaires were distributed to Thai tourists in Chiangmai who were asked to indicate their opinions about their interests, behaviors and requirements in agro-tourism.
5. A focus group discussion of two district officers, two local people, one specialist in tourism and researcher was conducted in order to develop guidelines of organic farms for sustainable tourism
6. A farm was selected as an experiment using the guidelines.

4. Data analysis

For the first objective, the qualitative data were explained.

A statistical package based on social science formula was then utilized to analyze the quantitative data to answer the second research objective.

Qualitative data were analyzed to answer the third research objective by grouping the information into the following headings.

1. Physical information about farms such as location, accessibility, environment, basic facilities, etc.
2. Tourism information such as attraction spots, agricultural way of life, etc.
3. Community participation.
4. Readiness on being agro-tourism tourist attractions.
5. Problems and limited factors on being agro-tourism tourist attractions.

Concerning the fourth objective, a focus group was conducted among two tourist entrepreneurs, three local people and a researcher to develop guidelines.

Results

1. Regarding the organic farm survey, it was found that there were not many successful organic farms in Chiangmai due to the fact that chemical fertilizers and pesticides could not be used in organic farms. This resulted in fewer products in organic farms than in conventional farms. The farmer sometimes

had to wait for many crop cycles until they could increase productivity and earn more money. There were five districts, Maerim District, Prao District, Doi-saket District, Samaeng District and Sankumpang District, where farmers were members of the Organic Farm Cooperation in Chiangmai. Among these, Prao and Doi-saket were well organized by the leaders of villages and there were many farmers who still planted organic crops because of a strong community involvement in development of organic farms. Prao received a strong support from government sectors in the community, whereas Doi-saket did not.

2. Concerning the tourists' behaviors and requirements of the agro-tourism areas, the characteristics of these tourists are presented in Table 27.1.

Table 27.1 reveals that the tourists were males and females almost equally (50.86 and 49.14%) within the age groups of 21-30 years (32.57%). Most of them were married (58.57%), the highest educational attainment was a Bachelor's degree (42.57%), and they were employees (30.28%).

Table 27.1 Tourist characteristics

Characteristics	N	%
1. Sex		
1.1 Male	178	50.86
1.2 Female	172	49.14
2. Age		
2.1 21-30 years	114	32.57
2.2 31-40 years	97	27.71
2.3 41-50 years	89	25.43
2.4 51-60 years	43	12.29
2.5 > 60 years	7	2.00
3. Marital Status		
3.1 Single	116	33.14
3.2 Married	205	58.57
3.3 Widowed	17	4.86
3.4 Divorced	12	3.43
4. Highest Educational Attainment		
4.1 <Secondary School	37	10.57
4.2 Secondary school	56	16.00
4.3 High school	92	26.29
4.4 Bachelor's Degree	149	42.57
4.5 >Bachelor's Degree	16	4.57
5. Experience in occupation		
5.1 Student	89	25.43
5.2 Government official/ state enterprise officer	54	15.43
5.3 Businessman	35	10.00
5.4 Employee	106	30.28
5.5 Retired official	66	18.86

Table 27.2 The opinions on agro-tourism

No	OPINIONS	mean	S.D.
1	Interested in agro-tourism	4.18	.95
2	There are many interesting agro-tourism tourist attractions in Chiangmai	3.85	.79
3	Your interest in visiting the following agricultural places :		
	3.1 Rice growing	3.14	.98
	3.2 Gardening	4.29	.85
	3.3 Field crops growing	3.91	.97
	3.4 Mushroom cultivation	3.17	.82
	3.5 Basketry	3.97	1.06
	3.6 Agricultural products processing	4.04	.84
	3.7 Organic farms	4.13	.91
4	During visiting, the following activities should provide for tourists		
	4.1 Farmers' explanation	4.14	.89
	4.2 Participating in agricultural activities	4.45	.98
	4.3 Cooking or Eating farm products	3.98	.91
	4.4 Selling farm products	4.04	.85
	4.5 Home stay	4.18	.97
5	Your expectation in visiting agricultural places		
	5.1 Convenience in traveling	4.12	.92
	5.2 Its scenic environment	4.38	.93
	5.3 Its environment	4.22	.91
	5.4 Friendship and good services	4.33	.95
	5.5 High quality but low price of farm products	4.28	.98
6	Type of traveling		
	6.1 Travel by yourself	3.98	.99
	6.2 Travel by tour agency	4.25	.86
7	The best media of tourism public relations		
	7.1 Papers / Brochure	3.92	.95
	7.2 Radio	3.25	.98
	7.3 Television	4.12	.87
	7.4 Newspaper	4.05	.95
	7.5 Internet	4.28	.87

The tourists' opinions on agro-tourism are presented in Table 27.2.

As seen in Table 27.2, the tourists showed their positive interest in agro-tourism (mean = 4.18). They were also aware that there were many interesting agro-tourism tourist attractions in Chiangmai (mean = 3.85). Besides these, they were interested in visiting gardens and organic farms (mean = 4.29 and 4.13, respectively). During their visit, they preferred to participate in agricultural activities, experience a homestay and listen to farmers' explanations (mean = 4.45,4.18,4.14, respectively). In addition, they expected to visit scenic places, and experience friendliness and good service (mean = 4.38 and 4.33, respectively) when visiting agricultural area. They preferred to travel using agencies (mean = 4.25). Moreover, they agreed that the best media for tourism public relations was the internet (mean = 4.28).

3. Concerning the potential and qualification of organic farms on being agro-tourism tourist attractions, it could be concluded that the villages in the Prao District and the Doi-saket District were qualified to be agro-tourism tourist attractions among the five districts mentioned above owing to their unique physical and biological values and agricultural way of life such as organic longan orchards, organic vegetable plantations, etc. In addition, it was found that easy accessibility and the safety of the attractions as well as a high degree of readiness in tourist services was important. However, an important factor for success in operations is the support from government officers. In the Prao district, the officers were willing to give support to the people in the villages in almost every activity, while in Doi-saket the officers were not so close to the people in the community except for the leader. The qualitative data are grouped and described as follows:

    • Physical information of farms: villages in Prao district were located in scenic areas and were easily accessible, while villages in Doi-saket district were more difficult to reach than in Prao.
    • Tourism information: there were many tourist attractions in Prao and Doi-saket but there were more in Prao.
    • Community participation: there was a stronger community participation in Prao, whereas, it seemed difficult for the leader in Doi-saket who tried to organize activities for the people in the community. These people realized that being an organic farm yielded low productivity without government support.
    • Readiness for being agro-tourism tourist attractions: the villages in Prao were ready to be agro- tourism tourist attractions. Moreover, the government officers of sub-districts in Prao always supported all the activities of the people in the villages (see Figure 27.1).
    • Problems and limiting factors with agro-tourism attractions: Although Prao District was easily accessible, it was a bit too far from Chiangmai city. Furthermore, the villages were still far removed from the main street. Thirdly, the people lacked knowledge about tourism management. However, they were ready to be developed as home stays.

4. Concerning the development and promotion guidelines of organic farms for sustainable tourism, the results from focus group discussions among two district officers, two local people, one specialist in tourism and the researcher produced the following guidelines:

    • Surveys and analysis of farm potential factors should be done.
    • Training for farmers or the owners of organic farms about tourism services and management and how to improve and manage heritage and natural resources should be provided.
    • Conduct a role-playing activity to experiment with agro-tourism management by selecting suitable candidates.

Figure 27.1 House readiness to be a home stay (Photo by author)

- Propose community agro-tourism projects to the government for budget allocation and other support provisions such as improving the infrastructure.
- Use the internet to advertise.

According to the guidelines the researcher conducted activities as follows:

1. A farm was selected according to the factors showing potential indicated in the above results from the focus group discussions. Firstly, the farmers in the villages in the sub-district of Prao owned organic farms growing green beans, longan, and vegetables. In addition, a group of farmers' wives remained strongly co-operative. There were many interesting places to visit in the village and nearby, such as a waterfall, a big pond with fresh water, beautiful temples with an interesting cave, and a hill tribe village.
2. A one-day training session on tourism services, management and how to improve heritage and natural resources was provided for members of the community by the researcher. An expert in tourism from Chandrakasem Rajabhat University was invited to be their trainer. The training focused on how to welcome tourists, activities, preparation and a community plan for tourism. The local people were trained to explain the details and history of the district.
3. A role playing activity was conducted by inviting twelve tourists, three from Chiangmai city, five from Prao, three from Bangkok and one from the

United States of America, to join in the activity (see Figures 27.2, 27.3, 27.4, 27.5 and 27.6). The tourists had a chance to participate in farm activities such as grinding and cleaning rice seed. Two tourists had a chance to stay overnight in a farmer's house as a homestay. The recommendations of this activity indicated by the tourists were:

- the owners should tell the tourists about the background of the community,
- the members of organic farms should have more practice on giving demonstrations on the necessary steps in organic farming; and
- the farmers and farmers' wives should know how to compute homestay management. Moreover, they should know how to organize a variety of activities to entertain the tourists during homestays.

Conclusions

From the guidelines proposed in this study, the farmers should be trained to be the owners of agro-tourism tourist attractions, especially in hosting homestays. This will result in an increase in tourism in the community as well as in farmers' incomes. At the same time, they will be able to sell their agricultural products to the tourists. In earning more income, they will become more self reliant and will not have to migrate to the big cities in search of work. The results of this study indicated several important issues that related to the development guidelines of farming, such as the concept of a sufficiency economy.

His Majesty King Bhumibol, the great king of Thailand, has developed the philosophy of a 'Sufficiency Economy' to guide Thai people towards a balanced way of life. This concept is considered the key to sustainable development. 'Sufficiency' means moderation, reasonableness, and having an adequate 'immune system' to protect each level against impacts caused by both external and internal changes. This concept is connected with His Majesty's 'New Theory' in agriculture, aimed at helping small landholders to increase farm income and food production through the appropriate division and utilization of land.

Regarding the problems and limiting factors on sustainable agro-tourism attractions, it was found that the farmers encountered a lack of knowledge of tourism. This result confirms the fact that education concerns everyone and is a lifelong process. Some farmers are not knowledgeable and do not even understand the benefits to them. Therefore, training programs on tourism management and service, and on how to improve and manage heritage and natural resources, should be offered.

Concerning the development and promotion guidelines of the organic farms and sustainable tourism indicated above, there should be: 1) a training activity and knowledge transfer regarding services and agro-tourism management, and the improvement and management of heritage and natural resources for farmers or farmers' wives, 2) a strong coordination of all concerned groups such as the chief of the district and community leaders or key persons in the community, 3) a master plan for general tourism management by all concerned groups

Figures 27.2 and 27.3 Implementing role playing and a Thai blessing ceremony (Photos by author)

Figure 27.4 Hill tribe dancing by children (Photo by author)

Figure 27.5 Preparing a food offering for Buddhist monks in the morning (Photo by author)

Figure 27.6 A local community (Photo by author)

cooperating, and 4) good public relations for marketing. It can be concluded that the most important factors which enabled sustainable agro-tourism were: 1) community participation, 2) support from government sectors in the community, 3) a fair distribution of profits to the people involved; and 4) the preservation of culture, heritage and environment.

References

Agricultural Information and Documentation System of the Americas.2009.*Agro-tourism.* http://www.orton.catie.ac.cr [Accessed the 20th of December 2009].

Aphirom Phomjanya and et al. (2003). *The Rural Tourism Development Project : A Case Study in Changwat Phuket.* Research Report.

Ecotourism directory, 2006. *Agrotourism-Definition.* http://www.ecotourdirectory.com/agrotourism.htm [Accessed the 15th of March 2006]

GMO Project Concept, 2005. *Capacity Building and Strengthening of Partnership of Public, Civil Organizations and Business in Biosafety Issue in Moldova.* http://www.rolnictwo.eko.org.pl/parts.php [Accessed the 4th of November 2008].

IFOAM.2008. *Organic Definition.* http://www.ifoam.org/growing_organic/definitions/doa/index.html [Accessed the 4 of November 2008].

Jamieson, Walter & Alix Noble.2000. *A Manual for Sustainable Tourism Destination Management.* Pathumthani: CUC UEM Project.

Mediterranean NGO Network for Ecology and Sustainable Development. 2007. *Sustainable Tourism.* http://www.medforum.org [Accessed the 10th of September 2007].

Nartsuda Chemnasiri. 2007. *Development Guidelines of Farm on Being Agro-Tourism Tourist Attractions and and International Learning Center: A case study in Chainat Province, Thailand.* Bangkok: Chandrakasem Rajabhat University.

Organic Thailand. 2004. *What is organic farming?* http:// www.organicthailand.com/ product-en-361260-Organic+Farming+Information.html [Accessed the 10th of September 2007].

Pawinee Wachasitnirapai (2000). *Potential and Problems of Agro-toursim in Chiang Mai Province.* Thesis for Agricultural Extension. Chiangmai: Chiang Mai University.

Ramate Promchat (2002). *Participation of the Community in Agro-tourism Development : a Case Study of Ban Pong, Pa Phai Sub-district, San Sai District, Chiang Mai Province* Independent Study for Tourism Industry Management. Chiangmai: Chiang Mai University.

Strochlic, R.; Sierra, L., 2007.*Conventional, Mixed, and "Deregistered" Organic Farmers: Entry Barriers and Reasons for Exiting Organic Production in California.* Los Angeles: California Institute for Rural Studies.

Wikipedia The Free Encyclopedia. 2008. *Directorate General for Agriculture and Rural Development of the European Commission.* http://www.wikipedia.org/wiki/Organic_ farming) [Accessed the 4th of November 2008].

Glossary

Accreditation A procedure to establish if a tourism business meets certain standards of management and operation.

Adventure tourism A form of tourism in natural areas that incorporates an element of risk, higher levels of physical exertion, and the need for specialised skills.

Agenda 21 Programme of action adopted by the 1992 United Nations Conference on Environment and Development

Agro-tourism A form of tourism which encourages travelers to experience rural and agricultural settings.

Air pollutants Particulates, Sulphur Dioxide, Nitrogen Dioxide, Tropospheric Ozone, Carbon Monoxide.

Alternative tourism In essence, tourism activities or development that are viewed as non-traditional. It is often defined in opposition to large-scale mass tourism to represent small-scale sustainable tourism developments. AT is also presented as an 'ideal type', that is, an improved model of tourism development that redresses the ills of traditional, mass tourism.

Amazon Cooperation Treaty Organization (ACTO) An international organization aimed at the promotion of sustainable development of the Amazon Basin.

Anthropogenic activity A term which designates an effect resulting from human activity.

ASEAN The Association of Southeast Asian Nations.

Assets Something of value that will provide future benefit or utility, can be used to generate revenue. Usually owned, so simply described as 'things we own'.

Auditing A process to measure and verify the practices of a business.

Benchmarking Process of comparing performance and activities among similar organizations either against an agreed standard or against those that are recognized as being among the best.

Benchmarks Points of reference or comparison, which may include standards, critical success factors, indicators, metrics.

Best Practice Operational standards considered the most effective and efficient means of achieving desired outcomes.

Biodiversity Shorthand for biological diversity.

Biomass   A renewable energy source from biological material such as wood or waste.

Biomes   A classification of ecosystems based on climatic and geographic conditions.

BRIC   Brazil, Russia, India And China.

Capacity building   Process through which individuals, organization and societies to develop certain skill or competence to meet development challenges.

Capacity management   A process that seeks to ensure that their organisations operate at optimum capacity whilst maintaining customer satisfaction levels.

Capital expenditure   The cost of long-term assets; such as computer equipment, vehicles and premises. Importantly these are bought to use over several years and not to resell.

Carbon footprint   A representation of the effect human activities have on the climate in terms of the total amount of greenhouse gases produced (measured in units of carbon dioxide).

Carbon dioxide (CO2)   A greenhouse gas produced through respiration and the decomposition of organic substances. Combustion of fossil fuels is primarily responsible for increased atmospheric concentrations of this gas.

CARICOM   Caribbean Community and Common Market.

Carrying Capacity   In tourism, the number of travelers who can be supported in a given area within natural resource limits, and without degrading the natural social, cultural and economic environment.

Code of conduct   Guidelines advising a tourism stakeholder, including tourists, on how to behave in an environmentally responsible manner.

Code of Ethics / Conduct / Practice   Recommended practices based on a system of self regulation intended to promote environmentally and/or socio-culturally sustainable behavior.

Commercial ventures   A business form where generated profits are redistributed to shareholders.

Community Based Ecotourism (CBET)   A tourism form used as a community development strategy with the aim to strengthen the ability of rural communities to manage its tourism resources with the participation of local people.

Composting   Biological process used to treat organic waste (green waste, fermentable fraction of municipal waste, sludge from urban treatment plants, etc.), by degrading them in an accelerated manner.

Conservation   A term broadly interpreted as action taken to protect and preserve the natural world from harmful features of tourism, including pollution and overexploitation of resources.

Conservation-tourism   A form of tourism in which travelers participate towards the conservation of biodiversity and contribute to local economic development.

Convention on Biological Diversity (CBD)   An international treaty to sustain the diversity of life on Earth.

Corruption perception index (CPI)   Measures how corruption is perceived by a panel of experts in a country and is conducted by Transparency International.

Cultural tourism   Travel for the purpose of learning about cultures or aspects of cultures.

CSR   Corporate Social Responsibility is a concept by which companies integrate the interests and needs of customers, employees, suppliers, shareholders, communities and the planet into corporate strategies.

Deforestation   The removal or permanent destruction of indigenous forest for other purposes.

Degradation   Any decline in the quality of natural or cultural resources, or the viability of ecosystems, that is caused directly or indirectly by humans.

Dependency theory   A theory based on how developing and developed nations intereact.

Direct employment   In tourism, direct employment comprises all jobs where workers are engaged in the production of direct tourism output (hotel employee, restaurant servers, airline pilots).

Direct impact   The immediate consequence of an activity (e.g. tourism) on the environment, the community or the economy where the cause and effect relationship is generally clear.

Direct spending   In the tourism,money that goes directly from a the tourist into the local economy of the destination.

Discrimination   Unequal treatment of persons on grounds which are not justifiable in law, e.g. in the UK, discrimination on the grounds of sex or race.

Division of Technology, Industry and Economics (DTIE)   A UNEP's division working environmental strategic priorities.

European Commission (EC)   The administration of the European Union.

Eco-architecture   Term, also referred to as 'Sustainable Architecture', describing environmentally conscious design and architectural techniques.

Eco-Label   Information (typically provided on a label attached to a product) informing a potential consumer of a product's characteristics, or of the production or processing method(s) used in its production.

Eco-technology   A term depicting engineering practices that seeks to help conserve and restore the environment through the integration of ecological principles.

Ecological Monitoring   The action of developing indicators and using those to monitor the condition of ecological resources.

Ecologically sustainable   Using, conserving and enhancing the community's resources so that ecological development is maintained, and the total quality of life can be sustained now and in the future.

Ecosystem   A dynamic system of plant, animal, fungal and micro-organism communities, and the associated non-living physical and chemical factors.

Ecotourism   Ecologically sustainable tourism with a primary focus on experiencing natural areas that foster environmental and cultural understanding, appreciation and conservation.

EMAS   The EU Eco-Management and Audit Scheme (EMAS) is a management tool for companies and other organisations to evaluate, report and improve their environmental performance.

Energy conservation   Positive initiatives to reduce the consumption of energy to the minimum level required.

Energy Management   In hospitality, energy management is the practice of controlling procedures, operations and equipment that contribute to the energy use in hotels.

Energy security   Access by countries or regions to sufficient and affordable energy sources.

Environment   The ecosystem in which an organisms or a species lives, including both the physical environment and the other organisms with which it comes in contact.

Environmental auditing   Inspection of a tourism organisation to assess the environmental impact of its activities.

Environmental communication   Communication by enterpresises or organisations about environmental affairs.

Environmental deterioration   The degradation of the environment through depletion of resources.

Environmental education   Formal and informal learning processes that are designed to raise awareness and teach new values, knowledge and skills, in order to encourage more sustainable behavior.

Environmental impact   The effects that a community has on the environment as a consequence of its activities.

Environmental impact assessment   A study undertaken to assess the effect of an action upon a specific environment or the social or cultural integrity of a community.

Environmental impact statement   The report resulting from an environmental impact assessment.

Environmental Management System (EMS)   System that a tourism organization can use to implement its environmental policy and achieve associated objectives to control environmental impacts significant of its activities and to respect regulatory requirements.

Environmental Management Programme   Also labelled as Environmental Management Plan is the activation of the Environmental Management System and policies into activities.

Environmental Stewardship   Long-term management aimed at preserving and enhancing the quality of an environment.

Environmental Tax   A tax that is of major relevance for the environment, regardless of its specific purpose or name.

Ethnic Tourism   A form of tourism where visitors and travelers have a desire to experience and interact with people of communities of different ethnic backgrounds.

EU   The European Union is an economic and political union of 27 member states.

Fauna   The animal characteristics and life of a region or particular environment.

Flora   The plant characteristics and life of a region or particular environment.

Footprint (ecological) A measure of the hectares of biologically productive area required to support a human population of given size.

Foreign Aid Also known as International Aid, is a voluntary transfer of resources in the forms of technical or financial development aid from one country to another.

Foreign Exchange Earnings (FEE) The proceeds from the export of goods and services and the returns from its foreign investments.

GDP The Gross Domestic Product is a measure of the total value of goods and services produced by the domestic economy during a given period, usually one year.

GIZ (GTZ) Deutsche Gesellschaft für Internationale Zusammenarbeit (German International Cooperation); Deutsche Gesellschaft für Technische Zusammenarbeit (German Technical Cooperation).

Global Reporting Initiative (GRI) A private initiative offering sustainability reporting guidelines that take into account environmental, social and economic performance.

Globalisation Generally defined as the network of connections of organisations and peoples are across national, geographic and cultural borders and boundaries. These global networks are creating a shrinking world where local differences and national boundaries are being subsumed into global identities. Within the field of tourism, globalisation is also viewed in terms of the revolutions in telecommunications, finance and transport that are key factors currently influencing the nature and pace of growth of tourism in developing nations.

Governance A term describing how a business or a non-profit organisation is directed and controlled.

Green Economy An economic development model based on sustainable development concepts.

Green Globe/Green Globe 21 A worldwide benchmarking and certification programme which facilitates sustainable travel and tourism for consumers, companies and communities. It is based on Agenda 21 and principles for Sustainable Development endorsed by 182 governments at the United Nations Rio de Janeiro Earth Summit in 1992.

Greenhouse effect The trapping of the sun's thermal radiation by gases and water vapour, keeping the surface of the earth warmer than it would be otherwise.

Greenhouse gas A gas such as carbon dioxide or methane that reflects infrared radiation emitted by the earth, thereby helping to retain heat in the atmosphere.

Green marketing Integrating business practices and products that are friendly to the environment while also meeting the needs of the consumers.

Greenwash The unjustified appropriation of environmental virtue by a company, an industry, a government, a politician or even a non-government organization to create a pro-environmental image, sell a product or a policy.

Gross Domestic Product (GDP) see GDP.

Gross National Happiness (GNH)   An Index conducted by the government of Bhutan which measures the happiness of the population.

Hazard Analysis Critical Control Point (HACCP)   A management system in which food safety is addressed through the analysis and control from of raw material procurement to the finished product.

Heritage   Things of value that are inherited which people want to keep. Heritage can be natural, cultural, tangible, intangible, personal or collective. Natural heritage is often conserved in places such as reserves and national parks. Cultural heritage practices are often conserved through ongoing traditions and practices.

Historical-cultural tourism   A form of tourism where visitors and travelers are concerned with the culture and heritage of a specific region or country.

HIV/AIDS   Human immunodeficiency virus/ Acquired immune deficiency syndrome.

Hospitality Industry   Industry made up of businesses that provide accommodation, provide food and beverages, provide entertainment.

Human Development Index (HDI)   An index developed and conducted by the UNDP (United Nations Development Program) composed from data on education, health, security, inequality and income.

ICC   The International Chamber of Commerce created a Business Charter for Sustainable Development comprising 16 principles for environmental management.

Indirect impact   The secondary effects of an activity (e.g. tourism) on the environment, the community, the economy but the relationships are often misunderstood and/or difficult to establish.

International Monetary Fund (IMF)   An organization assisting countries with balance of payment difficulties.

IH&RA   The International Hotel and Restaurant Association.

Impacts   Effects, which may be either positive or negative, felt as a result of tourism-associated activity.

Income per capita   Total income of a country divided by population.

Indicator   A summary measure that provides information on the state of, or change in, a system.

Indirect employment   In tourism, employment form where goods and services produced are used to create the final goods and services are sold to visitors and travelers.

Indirect impact   The secondary effects of activities (e.g. tourism) on the environment, the community or the economy.

Induced employment   In tourism, indirect employment comprises all jobs where the workers are engaged in indirect tourism-related output (employee of a hotel-supplies company, employees of a food and beverage distributor).

industrial agriculture   A form of agriculture where farming is industrialized to achieve economies of scale in production.

Institutional Economics   A model that looks at the formal rules (laws and regulations) and informal rules (norms, values) in the general behaviour of people.

International Coral Reef Initiative (ICRI) A partnership among governments, international organizations, and non-government organizations striving to preserve coral reefs and related ecosystems.

International Federation of Organic Agriculture Movements (IFOAM) The worldwide umbrella organization for the organic agriculture movement.

International Union for Conservation of Nature (IUCN) An international organization dedicated to natural resource conservation.

ISO International Organization for Standardization responsible for international management standards.

Kyoto protocol Protocol that came into force in 2005 in extension of the United Nations outline agreement on climate change. In particular, it fixes limiting values for greenhouse gas emissions in industrial countries.

Leakage In tourism, leakage occurs when revenues earned by the tourism industry does not remain within the host country.

Least developed countries (LLDC)/ Less developed countries (LDC) United Nations' ranking of countries with low indicators of development.

Lifecycle The particular pattern through which a destination evolves.

Life Cycle Assessment (LCA) LCA is the investigation and valuation of the environmental, economic and social impacts of a product or service. A product's life cycle starts when the raw materials are extracted from the earth through to processing, transport, use, reuse, recycling or disposal. For each of these stages, the impact is measured in terms of the resources used and environmental impacts caused.

Lifestyle A person's pattern of living as expressed in his or her activities, interests, and opinions.

Mass tourism Traditional, large scale tourism commonly, but loosely used to refer to popular forms of leisure tourism pioneered in southern Europe, the Caribbean, and North America in the 1960s and 1970s.

Mesoamerica A geographical and cultural region extending from central Mexico to Costa Rica.

Millennium Development Goals (MDGs) Initiatives adopted by the United Nations in year 2000 to tackle poverty and other related dimensions.

Minimal impact practices Deliberate human behaviour that reduces the negative impact of people or objects on the environment to a minimum.

Modernization theory A development theory used to explain the process of modernization within societies.

Monitoring The ongoing review and assessment of the natural or cultural integrity of a place in order to detect changes in its condition with reference to a baseline condition.

Nature Tourism (Nature-based tourism) Ecologically sustainable tourism with a primary focus on experiencing natural areas.

Neoliberal model One of the models that explains how economic development takes place.

NGO Non-governmental organization refers to a non-profit making, voluntary, service-oriented or development oriented organization, either for the benefit of members or of other members of the population.

Nonprofit organization (NPO)   A term to designate an organization that uses surpluses or profit to help pursue its goals (e.g. charities, cooperative, foundations).

Overseas development assistance (ODA)   A statistic compiled to measure the development aid paid by governments.

Organic Farming   A form of agriculture based on farming techniques aimed at maintaining soil productivity without the use (or limited use) of fertilizers, pesticides, herbicides and other non natural additives.

PDCA (plan–do–check–act)   Known as the Deming Cycle, it refers to a four-step problem-solving process.

Photovoltaic (Solar) Cell (PV)   Generally speaking, a device incorporating a semiconductor that generates electricity when exposed to (sun)light. The technology may be further sub-divided into crystalline, multi-crystalline, thin-film and concentrator variants.

Pollution   Harmful effects on the environment as a by-product of tourism activity. Types include air; noise; water; and aesthetic.

Population Density   Inhabitants per square meter.

Poverty   The inability to afford basic food and non-food items such as health care, education, clothing and shelter.

Precautionary Principle   An approach to risks that involves acting to avoid potential harm despite the lack of scientific certainty as to the likelihood or relative importance of that harm.

Protected areas (PAs)   A geographical space which is managed to achieve long term conservation of nature.

Public policy   A course of action or inaction taken by a government.

Public Relations   A set of activities with a goal to maintain a chosen public image for a business or organisation and enhancing its reputation.

Rain Water Harvesting (RWH)   Capturing and storing rain water for commercial, operational or personal use.

Recycling   The process by which discarded materials are collected, sorted, processed and converted in to raw materials which are then used in the production of new products.

Renewable resource   A resource that is capable of being replenished through natural processes or its own reproduction, generally within a time-span that does not exceed a few decades.

Renewable energy   Energy sources that are practically inexhaustible. For example solar, hydro and wind energy.

Responsible Purchasing   Procurement deemed socially responsible and environmentally sustainable.

Responsible tourism   Type of tourism which is practised by tourists who make responsible choices when choosing their holidays. These choices reflect reponsible attitudes to the limiting of the extent of the sociological and environmental impacts their holiday may cause.

Restoration   Returning existing habitats to a known past state.

Retrofit   The subsequent addition or implementation of new features to existing fixtures and facilities.

Rural tourism Similar to agro-tourism, a form of tourism which encourages travelers to experience rural lifestyle.

Scarcity The concept which stems from unlimited wants but limited resources

SME(s) Small and Medium Enterprises.

Social Relating to human society and interaction between its members.

Stakeholder Any person, group or organisation with an interest in, or who may be affected by, the activities of another organization.

Stakeholder Engagement A process linked to achieving corporate social responsibility goals by engaging stakeholders.

Subsistence economy An economic situation where people barely meet their everyday needs.

Sustainable Something which can be kept in the same or a better condition for the future.

Sustainable Design and construction A term describing environmentally and socially conscious design and construction techniques.

Sustainable development Development carried out in such a way as to meet the needs of the present without compromising the ability of future generations to meet their needs.

Sustainable tourism Tourism that can be sustained over the long term because it results in a net benefit for the social, economic, natural and cultural environments of the area in which it takes place.

Sustainability Sustainability is effectively the goal of sustainable development. It is the ideal end state which we must aspire.

The Nature Conservancy (TNC) A charitable environmental organization focused on natural habitat conservation.

Tourist Anyone who spends at least one night away from home, no matter what the purpose.

Triple bottom line An expanded baseline for measuring performance, adding social and environmental dimensions to the traditional monetary benchmark.

UNCED The United Nations Conference on Environment and Development promotes global cooperation between developing and industrialized countries in planning and managing environmentally responsible development.

UNDP The United Nation Development Programme is the United Nations global development programme.

UNEP The United Nations Environment Programme coordinates United Nations environmental activities.

UNESCO The United Nations Educational, Scientific and Cultural Organization promotes international collaboration through education, science, and culture.

UNWTO The United Nations World Tourism Organization is a United Nations agency dealing with questions relating to tourism.

Value added The additional value a product obtains through the different stages of production.

Waste Management The collection, transport, processing, recycling or disposal, and monitoring of waste.

Water Management The planning, developing, distributing and managing of water resources.

WBCSD   The World Business Council on Sustainable Development is a global association of some 200 international companies dealing exclusively with business and sustainable development.

World Bank (WB)   An international financial institution that assists developing countries.

World Commission on Environment and Development (WCED)   Also known as the Brundtland Commision, the WCED's report, 'Our Common Future' (1987) defined the modern notion of sustainable development.

World Conservation Monitoring Center (WCMC)   A cooperation between the UNEP and the UK-based charity organization WCMC 200 with the goal to foster knowledge gains for decision-making surrounding biodiversity issues.

World Economic Forum (WEF)   A non-profit and independent international organization creating a platform for leaders in various fields to discuss the current challenges facing the world.

World Travel & Tourism Council (WTTC)   An international organization dedicated in promoting travel and tourism.

WWF   The World Wide Fund For Nature aims to conserve nature and ecological processes by preserving biodiversity, ensuring sustainable use of natural resources and promoting the reduction of pollution and wasteful use of resources and energy.

Zoning   A plan of land usage designed and used by local governments.

Index

eBooks – at www.eBookstore.tandf.co.uk

A library at your fingertips!

eBooks are electronic versions of printed books. You can store them on your PC/laptop or browse them online.

They have advantages for anyone needing rapid access to a wide variety of published, copyright information.

eBooks can help your research by enabling you to bookmark chapters, annotate text and use instant searches to find specific words or phrases. Several eBook files would fit on even a small laptop or PDA.

NEW: Save money by eSubscribing: cheap, online access to any eBook for as long as you need it.

Annual subscription packages

We now offer special low-cost bulk subscriptions to packages of eBooks in certain subject areas. These are available to libraries or to individuals.

For more information please contact webmaster.ebooks@tandf.co.uk

We're continually developing the eBook concept, so keep up to date by visiting the website.

www.eBookstore.tandf.co.uk

eupdates

Taylor & Francis Group

Want to stay one step ahead of your colleagues?

Sign up today to receive free up-to-date information on books, journals, conferences and other news within your chosen subject areas.

Visit
www.tandf.co.uk/eupdates
and register your email address, indicating your subject areas of interest.

You will be able to amend your details or unsubscribe at any time. We respect your privacy and will not disclose, sell or rent your email address to any outside company. If you have questions or concerns with any aspect of the eUpdates service, please email eupdates@tandf.co.uk or write to: eUpdates, Routledge, 2/4 Park Square, Milton Park, Abingdon, Oxfordshire OX14 4RN, UK.

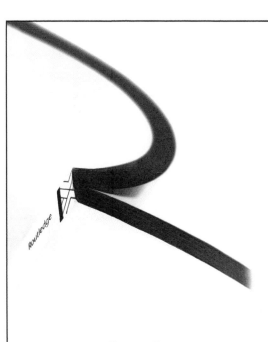

Routledge
Paperbacks Direct

Bringing you the cream of our hardback publishing at paperback prices

This exciting new initiative makes the best of our hardback publishing available in paperback format for authors and individual customers.

Routledge Paperbacks Direct is an ever-evolving programme with new titles being added regularly.

To take a look at the titles available, visit our website.

www.routledgepaperbacksdirect.com

Routledge
Taylor & Francis Group

ROUTLEDGE PAPERBACKS DIRECT

ROUTLEDGE Revivals

Are there some elusive titles you've been searching for but thought you'd never be able to find?

Well this may be the end of your quest. We now offer a fantastic opportunity to discover past brilliance and purchase previously out of print and unavailable titles by some of the greatest academic scholars of the last 120 years.

Routledge Revivals is an exciting new programme whereby key titles from the distinguished and extensive backlists of the many acclaimed imprints associated with Routledge are re-issued.

The programme draws upon the backlists of Kegan Paul, Trench & Trubner, Routledge & Kegan Paul, Methuen, Allen & Unwin and Routledge itself.

Routledge Revivals spans the whole of the Humanities and Social Sciences, and includes works by scholars such as Emile Durkheim, Max Weber, Simone Weil and Martin Buber.

FOR MORE INFORMATION

Please email us at **reference@routledge.com** or visit:
www.routledge.com/books/series/Routledge_Revivals

www.routledge.com